FLASH™ 5 MAGIC

WITH ACTIONSCRIPT

By J. Scott Hamlin and David J. Emberton

Contributions by Matthew David, Jennifer S. Hall, John Lenker, and Samuel Wan

201 West 103rd Street, Indianapolis, Indiana 46290

Flash 5 Magic

International Standard Book Number: 0-7357-1023-6

Library of Congress Catalog Card Number: 00-103157

Printed in the United States of America

First Printing: January 2001

05 04 03 02 01 7 6 5 4 3 2

Interpretation of the printing code: The rightmost double-digit number is the year of the book's printing; the rightmost single-digit number is the number of the book's printing. For example, the printing code 01-1 shows that the first printing of the book occurred in 2001.

Trademarks

Warning and Disclaimer

Publisher
David Dwyer

Associate Publisher
Al Valvano

Executive Editor
Steve Weiss

Product Marketing Manager
Kathy Malmloff

Managing Editor
Sarah Kearns

Senior Development Editor
Jennifer Eberhardt

Development Editor
Barb Terry

Senior Editor
Kristy Knoop

Copy Editor
Audra McFarland

Technical Editors
Scott Balay
Jennifer S. Hall
Suzanne Pettypiece

Cover Designer
Aren Howell

Interior Designers
Wil Cruz
Steve Gifford

Compositor
Kim Scott, kim@bumpy.com

Indexer
Lisa Stumpf

Software Development Specialist
Jay Payne

1 Navy Bay Entertainment

2 FishStik Educational Software

APPENDICES

About the Authors

J. Scott Hamlin

J. Scott Hamlin is the director of Eyeland Studio (www.eyeland.com), a company that specializes in intertainment design mostly in Flash. Eyeland Studio's clients include Nickelodeon, Procter and Gamble, and Nabisco. Hamlin is the author of several books, including *Flash 4 Magic* (New Riders Publishing) and *Effective Web Animation* (Addison Wesley Longman). Scott is also the director of NavWorks, whose products (which include Flash-based products) are now sold at Eyewire (www.eyewire.com).

David Emberton

David Emberton is an internationally acclaimed author, programmer, and columnist. Based on extensive experience in Flash application development, David has isolated tried-and-true techniques for building high-impact Flash content that works. His educational works share a unique focus on simplicity, planning, and thoughtful execution, making life easier whether you operate solo or as part of a team.

Matthew David

Matthew David has more than ten years of multimedia experience, as a theater and video producer and director and, over the last six years, as an Internet Technologist. Matthew contributed to the *Macromedia Dreamweaver Bible* (IDG WorldWide) and *Flash 5: Visual Insight* (The Coriolis Group). He has also written three courses for Ziff-Davis and four courses for SmartPlanet.com, and he is currently working on new courses for eHandsOn.com. He is Allen Interactions's lead instructor for Macromedia Flash, Fireworks, and Dreamweaver.

Jennifer S. Hall

Jennifer S. Hall changed careers after managing and programming in a scientific research environment. For the past four years, Jennifer has worked with leading multimedia companies including Top Drawer/Human Code, Thought Interactive, and Eyeland Studios. Much of her work has focused on the development of educational materials for kids and adults. Some of her clients include Disney; Holt, Rinehart and Winston; NavWorks; Deal of Day; Jugamos; and the Austin's Children's Museum. In her spare time, Jennifer eats, reads, runs, sits, rock climbs, and, most recently, windsurfs.

John Lenker

John Lenker is a Creative Supervisor and User Experience Specialist for Martin/Williams, a national advertising agency located in Minneapolis. Prior to joining Martin/Williams, John was the executive in charge of the eBusiness Group at Allen Interactions. John has been featured in industry trade journals for his work as a digital/photo illustrator, has won state Addy awards for Illustration and Poster of the Year, and is a photographer for Uniphoto/Pictor International.

Samuel Wan

Samuel Wan recites ActionScript in his sleep and dreams vividly in vector format. During the day, he builds advanced game engines and interactive features for various studios as an independent developer. When he's not writing or talking about Flash, he enjoys pushing the creative possibilities of this technology alongside fellow dreamers in the community. Samuel currently pursues graduate studies in Human Computer Interaction at the University of Michigan's School of Information. He would like to take this opportunity to thank his music mentors, teachers, professors, friends at were-here.com, colleagues, and most of all, his parents for their generosity, insight, and foresight.

Acknowledgments

J. Scott Hamlin

As usual, I must acknowledge the source. It is only by the grace of God that I have come to be capable of directing, writing, and illustrating this book. For my part, it is He who should be given all credit—not me.

I'm grateful for such a great team of individuals who I worked with on this book. It was an honor and privilege to work with professionals like David Emberton, Samuel Wan, John Mathew, John Lenker, Martin Thomas, and Scott Balay. I'd particularly like to thank Jennifer S. Hall and Barbara Terry for their extraordinary efforts. Their outstanding work truly made this a substantially better book.

I'd also like to thank New Riders for giving me the freedom to take a unique approach to this book. By allowing to me to take more of a director-like role in the book, we were able to hone the book to a higher standard, despite the fast turnaround time typically associated with books like this one that are tied to a particular version of software. This book was easily one of the most challenging I've ever worked on, and I'm grateful for all the support that New Riders gave to me and the rest of the *Flash 5 Magic* authoring team.

I am among the richest of men for my wife and children. Thank you, Aidan and Audrey, for again keeping things in joyful and playful perspective. Your crazy sense of humor never fails to melt away the real nonsense. To my wife, Staci, I am—as ever—uncommonly blessed by your support and friendship, for which I will be eternally grateful.

David Emberton

I'd like to start by acknowledging the extraordinary individuals who have worked to make this project a reality, even under trying circumstances. To Scott Hamlin, my eternal gratitude: We've never met face-to-face, yet you're the reason why I have the opportunity to be writing this sentence.

To Barb, Sam, Jennifer, John, Matthew, and everyone at New Riders who I've only encountered briefly: Thanks for all your effort and professionalism.

Thanks to all the people that have allowed me to indulge my love of teaching, because you are the reason that this book exists at all. The best way to learn is to teach, and so my appreciation goes out to anyone who has ever taken time to email me a question or feedback about my work. It all makes a difference.

Finally, and most important of all, I'd like to acknowledge my parents, family, and friends for providing the mold into which I have been so carefully poured. Thanks everyone!

Matthew David

I would like to thank the person who inspires me, my wife. And to my three children, Jake, Emma, and Liam, I love you loads!

Jennifer S. Hall

I'd like to thank my parents for allowing and encouraging me to be whatever kind of girl I wanted to be; I could be good at math and science if I wanted to. My sister for always seeing me as a god—well, usually. Finally, I'd like to thank all my friends (past and present) and family for the continual support in all my endeavors. Thank you, thank you, thank you.

John Lenker

My chapters would not have been written without the valuable contributions from the following:

Jobe Makar (www.ultimatearcade.com) for creating the project files and writing the steps. Brett Michlitsch for developing the database, as well as the middleware for the project. Jennifer Jesse for designing the look and feel of the project. Mike Teller for contributing the artwork. Allen Interactions Inc., the company we all worked for when the book was written (www.alleninteractions.com).

Samuel Wan

There are more people than I have space to list, people who gave their time, knowledge, and wisdom to help me reach the point of joining the *Flash 5 Magic* team. I'd like to thank David Emberton for opening doors and for his insight and perspective. My thanks to Scott Hamlin, the guy who puts it all together, for his remarkable generosity and experience and for demonstrating how to be a true professional while having fun. I'd like to thank Eric Wittman at Macromedia for introducing me to the next level of this industry and for his vision of things to come. My deep gratitude to the Were-Here.com community for the opportunity to share and learn among friends. Most of all, I'd like to thank my parents for their support and understanding.

A Message from New Riders

As the reader of this book, you are our most important critic and commentator. We value your opinion and want to know what we're doing right, what we could do better, in what areas you'd like to see us publish, and any other words of wisdom you're willing to pass our way.

As Executive Editor at New Riders, I welcome your comments. You can fax, email, or write me directly to let me know what you did or didn't like about this book—as well as what we can do to make our books better. When you write, please be sure to include this book's title, ISBN, and author, as well as your name and phone or fax number. I will carefully review your comments and share them with the authors and editors who worked on the book.

Please note that I cannot help you with technical problems related to the topic of this book, and that due to the high volume of email I receive, I might not be able to reply to every message. Thanks.

Email: steve.weiss@newriders.com

Mail: Steve Weiss
Executive Editor
New Riders Publishing
201 West 103rd Street
Indianapolis, IN 46290 USA

Visit Our Web Site: www.newriders.com

On our Web site, you'll find information about our other books, the authors we partner with, book updates and file downloads, promotions, discussion boards for online interaction with other users and with technology experts, and a calendar of trade shows and other professional events with which we'll be involved. We hope to see you around.

Email Us from Our Web Site

Go to **www.newriders.com** and click on the Contact link if you

- Have comments or questions about this book.
- Want to report errors that you have found in this book.
- Have a book proposal or are interested in writing for New Riders.
- Would like us to send you one of our author kits.
- Are an expert in a computer topic or technology and are interested in being a reviewer or technical editor.
- Want to find a distributor for our titles in your area.
- Are an educator/instructor who wants to preview New Riders books for classroom use. In the body/comments area, include your name, school, department, address, phone number, office days/hours, text currently in use, and enrollment in your department, along with your request for either desk/examination copies or additional information.

Call Us or Fax Us

You can reach us toll-free at (800) 571-5840 + 9 + 3567 (ask for New Riders). If outside the U.S., please call 1-317-581-3500 and ask for New Riders. If you prefer, you can fax us at 1-317-581-4663, Attention: New Riders.

Technical Support for This Book Although we encourage entry-level users to get as much as they can out of our books, keep in mind that our books are written assuming a non-beginner level of user-knowledge of the technology. This assumption is reflected in the brevity and shorthand nature of some of the tutorials.

New Riders will continually work to create clearly written, thoroughly tested and reviewed technology books of the highest educational caliber and creative design. We value our customers more than anything—that's why we're in this business—but we cannot guarantee to each of the thousands of you who buy and use our books that we will be able to work individually with you through tutorials or content with which you may have questions. We urge readers who need help working through exercises or other material in our books—and who need this assistance immediately—to use as many of the resources our technology and technical communities can provide, especially the many online user groups and list servers available.

FOREWORD

A movement is underway in which pioneers are leveraging a technology affecting every communication medium we know. The movement involves everyone from elementary school students to Hollywood animation legends who are developing compelling Web content to enhance hundreds of millions of individuals' lives worldwide. For the first time, artists are able to express themselves like never before, businesses can effectively convey their brand identity, and integrators are able to deploy dynamic Web applications previously seen only on the desktop. The vehicle for all these people is Macromedia Flash.

Macromedia Flash community members are unlike any seen before. They are extremely passionate, vocal, innovative, and supportive, making up an ecosystem that fosters progress. Centers for knowledge, such as flashkit.com and were-here.com, bustle with thousands of developers who seek the latest tips, techniques, and examples to assist with the creation of content within Macromedia Flash. This energy inspired the Macromedia Flash Team throughout the product's evolution.

Since FutureSplash Animator (Macromedia Flash 1), the Flash development process has been centered on developer community needs. Feedback and problems reported are massaged through a process involving an advisory board, customer visits, surveys, phone interviews, usability testing, and scenario testing—all contributing to the final product. Your feedback solidifies Macromedia's commitment to you and how we construct initiatives such as:

- Making a smoother production process for Flash content by evolving design, workflow, and automation tools, such as Macromedia FreeHand and Macromedia Generator.
- Assuring a consistent medium for delivering content through the bundling of Macromedia Flash Player with every major browser, platform, and device.
- Supporting the broadest range of delivery options possible by adopting new technologies and device platforms.

The same spirit displayed in our development process and throughout the Macromedia Flash community is encapsulated within this book. *Flash 5 Magic* delivers a series of essential real-world techniques for developing content with Macromedia Flash. This book has a special place on my bookshelf, as it should yours.

Eric J. Wittman
Director of Product Management, Flash Products
eman@macromedia.com

INTRODUCTION

It's been said that the more things change, the more they stay the same. In the case of this book, that's definitely *not* true. In addition to creating completely new projects for *Flash 5 Magic*, we made several changes in response to feedback we received from *Flash 4 Magic*. For instance, the projects in *Flash 5 Magic* are geared more toward professional application to real world requirements. Also, we have expanded the amount and detail for the code explanations. Finally, we removed unnecessary busy work in the projects so that we could cover more techniques in more detail. As a result, *Flash 5 Magic* covers far more ground in more detail than *Flash 4 Magic* did.

We made every attempt to respond to popular requests from the *Flash 4 Magic* book, such as requests for techniques covering work with external files, such as .asp and .xml and techniques covering work with form elements.

Who We Are

Flash 5 Magic is the result of the creative vision of its lead authors: David Emberton and J. Scott Hamlin. Part technologist and part writer, David works to make Internet technologies more accessible to busy professionals and hobbyists alike. Scott is a seasoned author with a background in industrial-strength graphics and animation and is the director of Eyeland Studio (eyeland.com), whose products are now being sold at Eyewire (eyewire.com).

Also lending their inspiration, talent, and effort to the book were Matthew David, Jennifer S. Hall, John Lenker, and Samuel Wan. Each of these exceptional people is a professional Web developer, specializing in the creation of Flash content.

If you want to learn how to set up volume control in Flash 5, there's no reason why you can't jump straight to Chapter 18.

Who You Are

Whether you've been using Flash since before it was a Macromedia product, or whether you just picked it up yesterday, there's something for everyone in *Flash 5 Magic*. Primarily though, we've targeted the book at Web developers who want to leverage Flash more effectively in the production process.

This book does not cover the basics of the Flash authoring environment or the .swf file format. What it does cover are basic to advanced examples of object-oriented scripting, Flash application development, client/server interaction, rich media content development, and of course, animation.

You can be either a linear or a non-linear reader and get equal enjoyment from *Flash 5 Magic*. It is built around projects and integrated techniques, rather than individual features of Flash, so don't feel as though you need to start at the beginning.

What's in This Book

We took a look at the great Flash work being published on the Web today and divided it into a number of core categories. Then we created a Web site concept to match each of those categories and broke it down into a set of individual projects and techniques you can use in your day-to-day operation.

Section 1: Navy Bay Entertainment
Online entertainment and streaming video

Section 2: FishStik Educational Software
Education, games, and simulations

Section 3: Splendos
Product promotion and brand marketing

Section 4: Penny Davis Online Retailing LLC
Web retailing and XML integration

Section 5: Piyk's Webfolio
Freelance portfolio and rich media/animation

Section 6: Dynamik Action News
External database integration

> **Note:** Note that the project files included with this book are for learning purposes. You will need to obtain permission from the authors if you wish to use them in any other manner, for example, as a commercial project or public display. Also, look for free samples from Eyeland Studio, including Flash-based interfaces, buttons, animations, and more.

The CD

The CD that comes with this book contains source files for each of the projects and techniques covered throughout. Each file comes in two versions—a final completed version and a working version you can use to follow along with the book's instructions. The final copies are especially useful for comparison, so you can double-check your progress.

> **Warning:** If you encounter problems with files not opening, please install the latest Internet browser of your choice (Internet Explorer and Communicator are included on the CD). If you continue to have problems with some of the .fla files or .swf files and you have not installed Flash 5, install the Flash 5 demo.

Our Assumptions As We Wrote the Book

It helps if you know where we were coming from in writing this book—in order for you to appreciate why we did what we did. We made every effort to come up with 22 projects that would be of real and substantial value to you, the reader. We've made the following assumptions in an attempt to maximize the impact of the content in the techniques.

It's Gotta Be Real

Ever found yourself searching the Web for instructional material on a particular technology and turned up plenty of hypothetical how's and why's but not a lot that's specific and useful? The truth is that professional developers get paid to come up with innovative techniques and rarely (if ever) want to give those techniques away. So there's a great deal of general or vague material out there. We believe that effective training material has to be real and relevant. So everything in this book is immediately transferable to real-life situations—and that's true value.

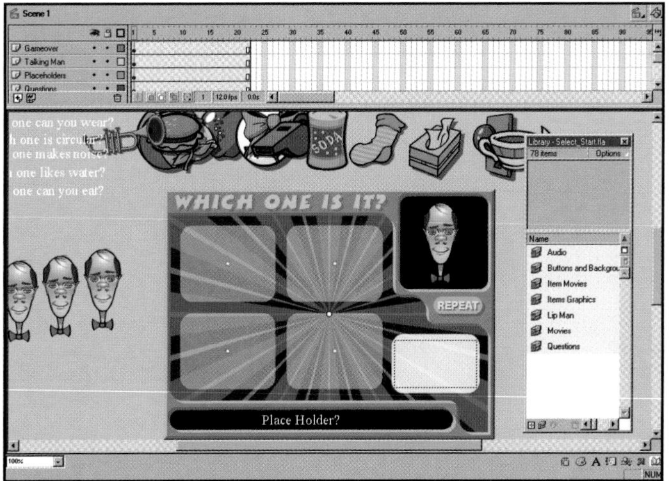

All the techniques come with prebuilt Start files with prepositioned art so that you can jump right into learning valuable techniques rather than wasting time positioning art.

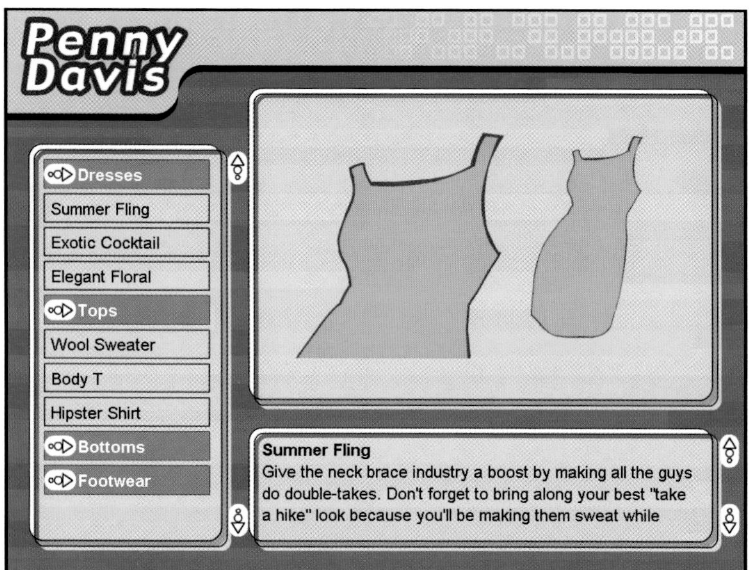

The techniques covered in this book are designed to be applicable to real-world requirements, such as techniques geared toward e-commerce design and educational design.

Everyone Learns Differently

It's a given. Part of the premise of *Flash 5 Magic* is that the joy of learning Flash for many people is the thrill of independent discovery. For others, it's simply getting step-by-step guidance through a complicated technique. So we kept the source files and instruction sequences, and added even more theory and explanatory material to bolster the learning process.

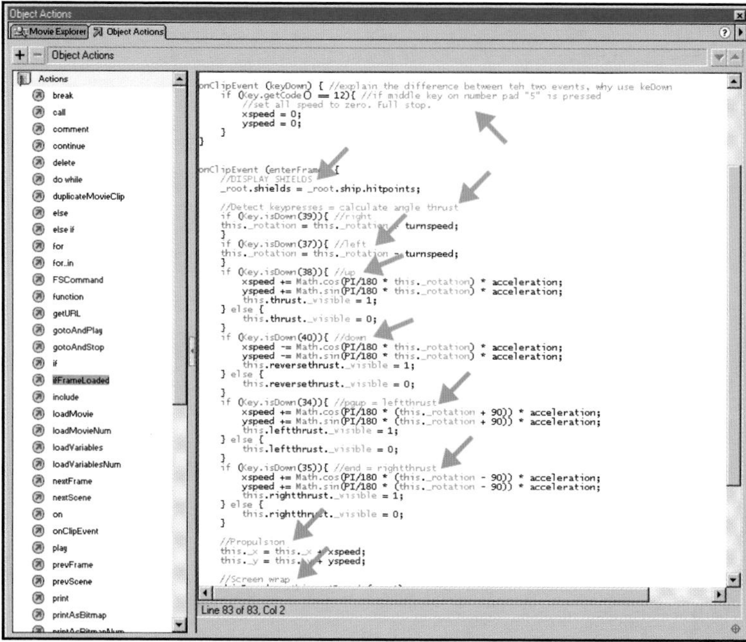

Most of the code featured in the book includes multiple code comments to help you keep track of what each section of code does.

Conventions Used in This Book

Most of the techniques in this book direct you to enter code or ActionScript into the Start files or the Flash files that go along with each technique. This code is set apart from the first column of text into the second column (where most of the figures are). The code that you will be asked to enter will be set on a colored box.

Some of the lines of code featured in the following techniques are too long to fit on one line. The lines will be wrapped around. Whenever you see the ➥ symbol, this indicates that the line of code has been wrapped around. In other words, when you enter a line of code with the wrap-around symbol, enter it as one line without the wrap-around symbol included.

For information on troubleshooting techniques and a list of common programming terms in Flash, see the appendixes.

Introduction to ActionScript

Flash 5's ActionScript is used extensively throughout this book to create richly interactive movies once considered impossible with anything other than Director or Java. The creators of Flash have managed to create an accessible, powerful authoring environment—but it is not without idiosyncracies. In this short introduction, we'll try to prepare you for the possible pitfalls, whilst giving a general overview of the ActionScript language in its latest incarnation.

If You're New to Flash

While the examples and techniques used in this book are explained as thoroughly as possible within the scope of the *Magic* series, it will definitely help to have at least some familiarity with basic programming principles—if you are to fully understand the ActionScript code you are inputting.

ActionScript can be characterized as intelligent glue, allowing you to combine various elements of a project programmatically, and to create movies that go far beyond simple linear animation. ActionScript, based on JavaScript's standardized parent language ECMAScript, exposes a lot of the raw power of the computer to you so you can use Flash as a simplified Visual Basic or other program development tool. The advantage is that Flash has a media engine already built-in, so all you have to do is create the various elements (graphics, animations, audio) and then use ActionScript coding to control them.

If You're Already a Flash User

If you have used previous versions of Flash, you're probably already fairly familiar with what ActionScript is all about. Flash 5 incorporates a vastly superior—and therefore more challenging—version of ActionScript that comes close to matching the power and flexibility of JavaScript used in conjunction with a Web browser. Along with a strong "object oriented" focus, ActionScript includes standard flow control mechanisms, math functions, operators, and even XML support.

Flash 5 ActionScript supports all previous Flash 4 actions. However, it comes complete with a new JavaScript-like syntax, or way or writing things, and seasoned Flash 4 users might need time to come to grips with it. Also, a number of operators and actions that were commonly used in the past are now *deprecated*, which essentially means that although they're still supported, it is recommended that you start migrating to their newer replacements just in case they are dropped in the future.

The ActionScript Reference

To familiarize yourself with ActionScript, we recommend that you read at least the introductory sections of the ActionScript Reference that comes bundled with Flash 5. It explains the basics of the language and introduces the Actions panel—the new interface for editing ActionScript code.

Assigning Scripts in Flash 5

Flash 5 allows for two basic types of scripts: Object and Frame. The former can be applied to buttons and movie clips, whereas the latter is limited to—you guessed it—key frames. When you are editing your Flash document and using the Actions panel to create scripts, it is important to keep track of what object or frame is currently selected. Sometimes the task of opening the Actions panel will cause Flash to deselect the object to which you wanted to assign a script, so Flash starts applying the code to the currently selected frame instead. As a quick check, always take note of whether the Actions panel is labeled Frame Actions or Object Actions; that will give you a rough guide to what you're actually editing.

For previous users of Flash, the thing you'll notice almost immediately is that the Actions editing environment is no longer *modal*. In other words, instead of a dialog box that you activate in relation to a particular object (complete with an OK and a Cancel button), there is now a floating Actions panel that stays open constantly, and its contents change depending on what is selected. If you're used to the old way, this new *non-modal* method of working will take some time to adjust to, but eventually it starts to feel just as natural as the original.

Working with Expert and Normal Modes

To complete the exercises in *Flash 5 Magic*, we recommend that you switch your preferences so that the Actions panel remains in Expert Mode instead of Normal Mode. What's the difference? Normal Mode borrows from the original method of assembling ActionScript that is associated with previous versions of Flash. Although Normal Mode is useful in some instances where you are unsure of how to write a particular action and need hints, Expert Mode's text editor interface is faster to use and actually helps you learn the language faster.

Checking Syntax and Diagnosing Errors

The downside to inputting script in Expert Mode *and* Normal Mode is that we are all prone to making copying errors. Human languages are designed with a lot of built-in redundancy, so you can still understand what someone is saying even if you pick up only pieces of the conversation. Computer languages however, are nowhere near as flexible or error-tolerant. The simplest of typing mistakes can, and does, prevent Flash movies from working as expected. Even the tiniest detail makes a difference. Consider the following example:

```
MyName = "David";
```

In ActionScript, anything that is to be treated as a piece of text must be enclosed in quotation marks. Otherwise, it will be interpreted differently. So if you copied the previous line of code as

```
MyName = David;
```

it would not have the same effect as the original, even though in English the two statements would appear to be saying the same thing. As you can see, ActionScript is a lot more sensitive to details than the languages we are familiar with in day-to-day living, so it's especially important that you take care in transferring code from the printed page to the screen.

One of the tools at your disposal when using Expert Mode is the Check Syntax command, available from the Actions panel triangle menu. It attempts to read all the code currently displayed in the panel, and if it finds any errors, it will identify them and their likely causes.

Another invaluable option in the Actions panel is Show Colored Syntax. This color codes various elements of your script, making it easier for you to skim through a script and pick up simple errors.

Finally, there is the source code on the book's CD. The first step to take if your projects don't work as expected is to try to track down copying errors you may have made along the way. Often, however, if you've been working on something for a long while, or if the script used in the example isn't very familiar to you, those errors can be easily overlooked. In these cases, it's more than okay to open up the final version of the project you're working on from the CD and cut and paste code from there. Once you've satisfied yourself that the project really does work, it will be easier to go back and track down the cause of the problem.

Dazed and Confused

Learning ActionScript is akin to learning any other new language: At first it seems totally alien, but after a time, you can make out a few words here and there. Eventually though, you'll stop having to consciously translate the code; it will just seem to make sense to you (if it's written well of course!).

The best strategy is to just surrender to the fact that things might be confusing at first but to realize that with patience and help from the explanations included in this book, it will start to make sense along the way. Even JavaScript experts will have a small learning curve because ActionScript is still quite different in many ways. Just remember to relax, take it easy, and enjoy the ride!

Conclusion

If you're new to programming, learning ActionScript in Flash 5 can be a daunting task. We hope this book will make that task much easier and more rewarding. Furthermore, we hope you will find the techniques in this book more applicable to your everyday job requirements. Although the art resources in this book are not freely available, you're certainly welcome to use the code featured in this book for your own projects (as if we could stop you). Soldier through it, have fun, and Happy Flashing!!!

NAVY BAY ENTERTAINMENT

"Of all the diversions of life, there is none so proper to fill up its empty spaces as the reading of useful and entertaining authors."

—JOSEPH ADDISON

Increased bandwidth on the Web and advances in streaming video and audio technology have allowed developers to expand entertainment or "intertainment" models into areas previously associated only with broadcast television. Navy Bay Entertainment is somewhat like an online soap opera sans the silly melodrama. Visitors can keep tags on their favorite characters via short video clips and daily journal entries. Online drama sites entice visitors to return, often by leveraging a slightly voyeuristic appeal and regular content updates.

The Navy Bay Entertainment section of this book explores valuable techniques such as using QuickTime Video with Flash, using Smart Clips, parsing XML data, working with external data streams, as well as several other techniques that are useful for online entertainment sites.

QuickTime video is one of the most powerful and flexible systems available for Web-based media. It can integrate more than 135 different file formats, but one of the more potent combinations is QuickTime Video and Flash. The Flash Player is built right into the QuickTime Player, and it's possible to create interactive QuickTime presentations right in the Flash authoring environment.

There are thousands of possibilities for combining Flash and QuickTime. This chapter will demonstrate how to add play controls to a video and how to include English subtitles that can be toggled on or off. The video is an episode of Navy Bay, the fictional drama series.

1

INTEGRATING FLASH AND QUICKTIME VIDEO

by David Emberton

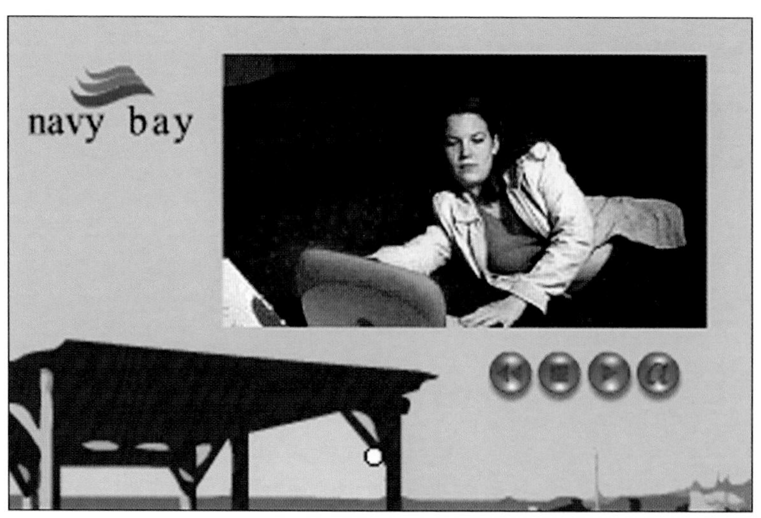

Importing QuickTime into Flash

In this chapter, the final file created will be a QuickTime file instead of a Flash movie, and the Flash elements will be displayed in conjunction with the video as a Flash track in QuickTime Player. The first step toward creating this Flash track is to import the video file for use as a reference.

1 Open the Episode7_start.fla file from the Chapter 01 folder on the accompanying CD and save a copy of it to your hard disk. (Episode7_final.fla is the finished file.)

A layer for placing the video file has already been created; it's called QuickTime Video.

2 Click to select the first frame of the QuickTime Video layer, and then choose File > Import.

3 In the Import dialog box, locate the file Episode7.mov in the Chapter 01 folder, click the Add button, and then click Import.

In the center of the stage, there should be a 200×110 pixel bitmap image, representing the first frame of the video file.

4 Use the Info panel to position the video at X: 92.5 and Y: 15.9.

For the file to work, a frame has to be inserted on the Flash timeline for each frame in the video file. To do that accurately, the frame rate of the Flash movie needs to match that of the QuickTime movie, which in this case is 10fps (frames per second).

5 Click the Modify menu, choose Movie, set the Frame Rate to 10, and then click OK.

The frame rate is now correct, but there is only one frame.

Import the Episode7.mov file to the QuickTime Video layer and reposition it using the Info panel.

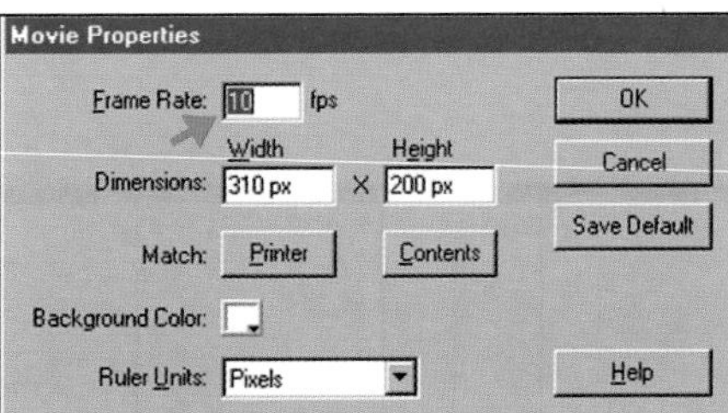

Change the movie's frame rate to 10 fps.

6 Click the red playback head selector above the Timeline to deselect all frames and layers, and then press F5 to insert new frames on each layer. Keep inserting frames until the QuickTime movie changes to a green or blue box with a cross through it, signifying that there are no more frames in the video.

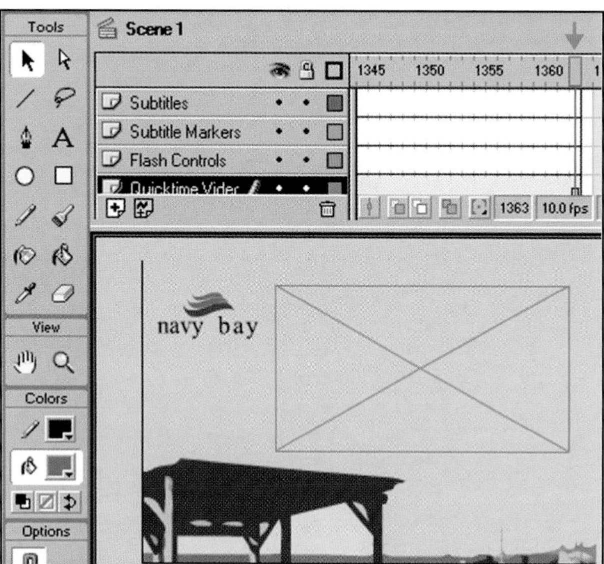

Add enough frames to every layer to accommodate the video.

Adding Flash Playback Controls

One of the more compelling aspects of this technique is that a Flash track can be used to control playback in the QuickTime Player. Although QuickTime 4 is equipped only with Flash 3 Player, this still creates exciting possibilities for interactive Flash and video combinations, not the least of which is the ability to supplant the standard QuickTime controls with custom versions.

1 To add the Play button, select the first frame of the Flash Controls layer. Open the Library, select the Play symbol from the Buttons folder, and then drag an instance of it onto the Stage.

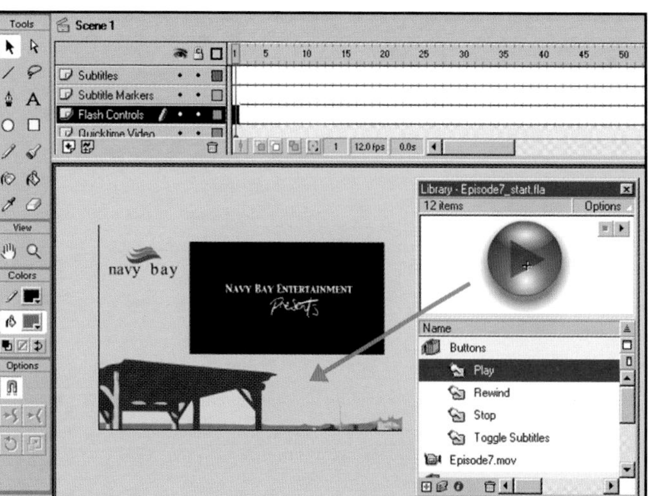

Drag the Play button onto the stage on the Flash Controls layer.

2 Use the Info panel to reposition the Play button at the coordinates X: 241.7, Y: 135.

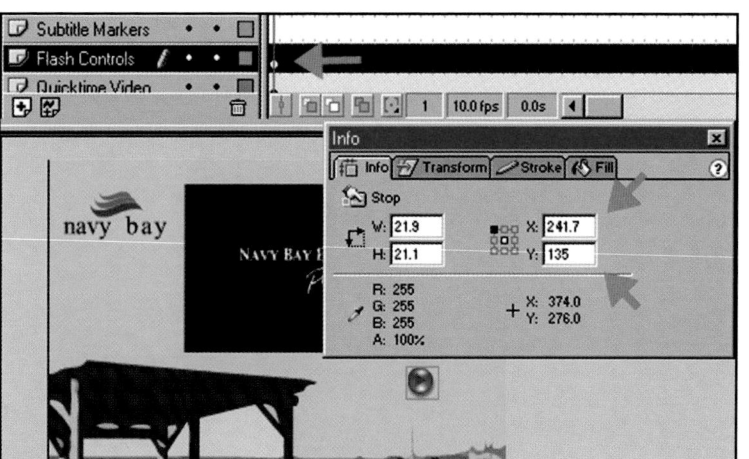

Use the Info panel to position the Play button.

3 With the Play button still selected, open the Actions panel and assign the code.

This is a fairly simple script. The **on(release)** handler captures any clicks on the Play button; and when it does, **play()** causes the Timeline to move forward, starting the video.

```
on (release) {
   play ();
}
```

Use the **play()** action to control the QuickTime video.

4 From the Library, drag an instance of the Stop symbol onto the Flash Controls layer. Then use the Info panel to position it alongside Play at the coordinates X: 221.3, Y: 135.

5 Open the Actions panel and insert the code.

```
on (release) {
   stop ();
}
```

Assign the **stop()** action to the Stop button.

The QuickTime Player responds to Flash actions that are applied to the main Timeline, so whenever the Stop button is clicked, playback ceases.

For viewers to return to the beginning of the video presentation and watch it again, they need a Rewind button. Let's set up that button next.

6 Drag an instance of Rewind from the Library to the Flash Controls layer, reposition it to X: 201, Y: 135, and use the Actions panel to apply the actions.

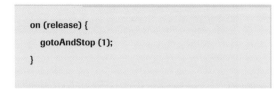

```
on (release) {
   gotoAndStop (1);
}
```

Use **gotoAndStop()** to rewind the video presentation.

The **gotoAndStop()** action is executed whenever the user clicks Rewind. **gotoAndStop()** causes the main Timeline to return to frame 1, the number one specified as its argument.

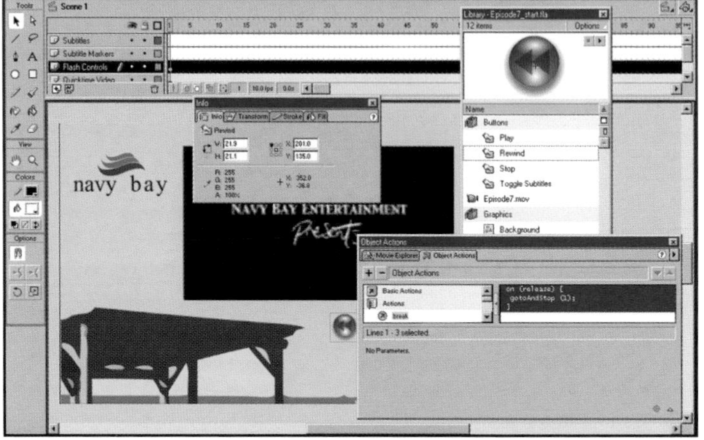

Position the Rewind button on the stage and apply the code to it.

> **Note:** In ActionScript, an argument refers to just about anything enclosed in parentheses. Arguments can be composed of text, numbers, or variable or object names, and they are used to influence the operation of a function or action.

Finally, you must create the Toggle Subtitles button. Subtitles are traditionally limited to the world of cinema or television, but using Flash and QuickTime, adding them to Web-based video is a straightforward job as well. This button will toggle the subtitle display on and off by controlling a movie clip that's to be added in the next section.

Notice the Subtitles button that toggles captions on and off.

7 From the Library, drag an instance of Toggle Subtitles onto the Stage, reposition it to X: 262.1, Y: 135, and use the Actions panel to assign the actions to the button.

When a visitor clicks the Toggle Subtitles button, the **tellTarget()** action is used to control the Subtitles Movie Clip instance.

If you're new to Flash, you may not have encountered **tellTarget()** before. It's actually an older action that must be used in this situation because QuickTime 4 supports Flash 3 or lower. Flash 3's range of actions was much more limited than Flash 5's, so get ready for some vintage coding.

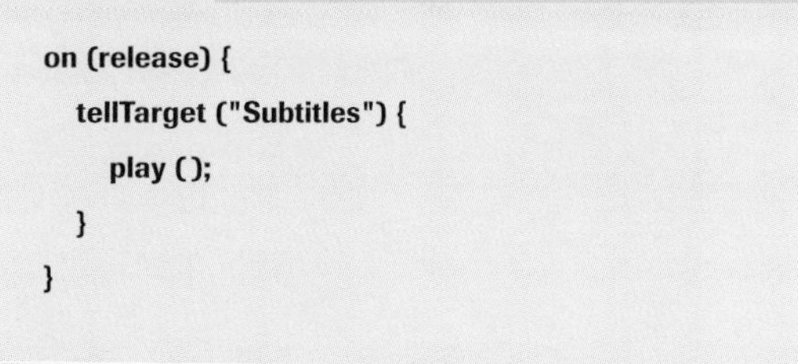

```
on (release) {
    tellTarget ("Subtitles") {
        play ();
    }
}
```

Add **tellTarget** to control the subtitles, as QuickTime 4 is limited to Flash 3 functionality.

The Toggle Subtitles button is on the Stage and has the specified code.

Incorporating Subtitles

Because almost half of all Web users speak a language other than English, knowing how to add a simple subtitling system to video presentations is a valuable skill. It can be done with the help of a few Movie Clip symbols and, of course, the text itself. In this section, you use a prefabricated movie clip. The subtitle text has been laid out previously and is stored in a Movie Clip symbol named Subtitle Text, which is located in the Library's Subtitles Movie Clips folder.

1 Select the Subtitles layer, drag an instance of Subtitle Text onto the Stage, and position it at X: 0, Y: 168.9.

2 Open the Instance panel and assign the Subtitle Text clip the instance name **Text**.

Naming the instance allows for the currently displayed frame, and therefore the currently displayed subtitle, to be controlled from the main Timeline using **tellTarget** actions.

The Subtitle Text movie shouldn't always be visible, because the subtitles should be turned off by default and be able to be toggled on and off by the user.

Position an instance of the Subtitle Text movie clip on the Subtitles layer.

3 To achieve this, wrap Subtitle Text in another Movie Clip symbol by selecting it, clicking the Insert menu, and selecting Convert to Symbol:Movie Clip. Name the new movie clip **Subtitles**, and when it appears in the Library, drag it into the Subtitles Movie Clip folder.

4 Double-click Subtitles in the Library to edit it.

Another way to allow the subtitle text to toggle is to add a blank keyframe in front of the one containing the text and add a **stop()** action to both. That way, whenever the user clicks the Subtitles Toggle button, Subtitles plays to the next frame. That next frame will either be the one that does show the text, or the one that doesn't.

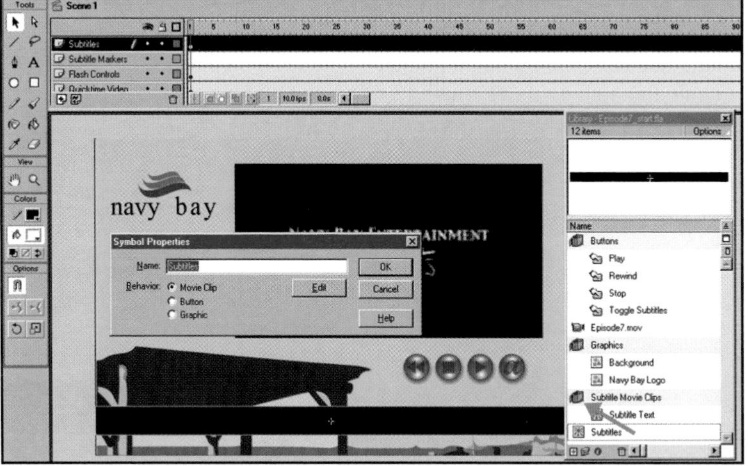

Convert the Subtitle Text Symbol into a movie clip named Subtitles, and then drag it into the Subtitle Movie Clips folder in the Library.

5 To begin, select the first keyframe and drag it to the second frame position. This automatically creates a blank keyframe in position 1; that frame will show by default.

6 Select each of the two frames, open the Frame Actions panel, and insert the code.

It's important to add a **stop()** action to both frames, so that each one will "stick" when it is the currently displayed frame.

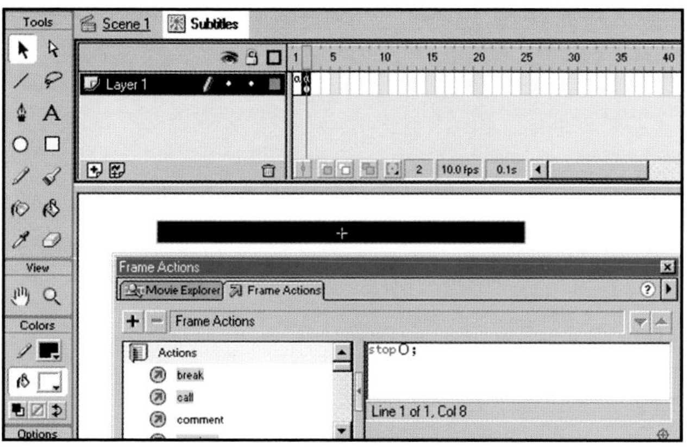

Add **Stop** actions to both frames.

```
stop();
```

Use the **stop()** action to prevent the Timeline from playing, allowing the subtitles to remain on or off.

7 Return to the main Timeline, select the Subtitles movie clip, and use the Instance panel to name it Subtitles.

The Subtitles are now set up and can be toggled on or off. But how will the right text be displayed at the right time? This is where the Subtitles Markers layer comes in.

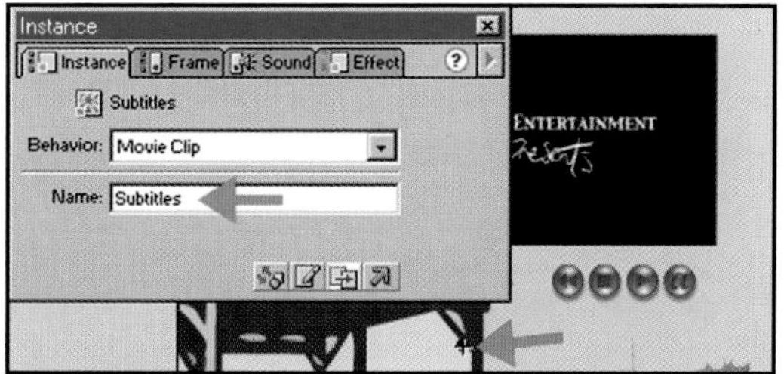

Give the Subtitles movie clip the instance name **Subtitles**.

8 Select the Subtitles Markers layer. Add a blank keyframe to frame 1, and then assign this code to the new keyframe on frame 1 of the Subtitles Markers layer.

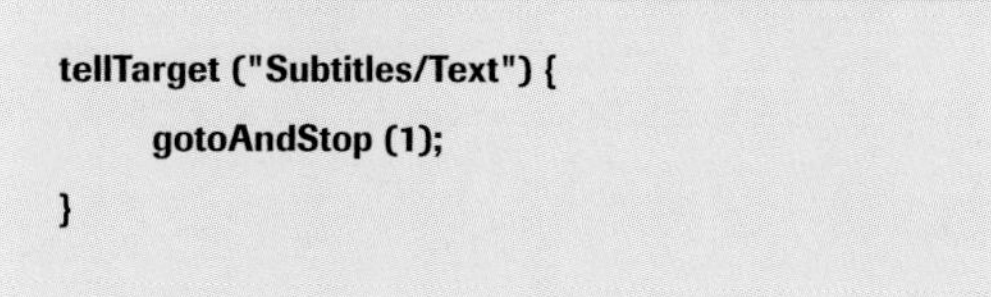

```
tellTarget ("Subtitles/Text") {
    gotoAndStop (1);
}
```

Use **tellTarget()** to send the Subtitles/Text movie clip to the first frame.

9 Repeat step 8 for each of the following Subtitle entries shown in the table. For example, for the next entry, go to frame 290 on the Subtitles Markers layer, add a blank keyframe, and assign the following code:

```
tellTarget ("Subtitles/Text") {
    gotoAndStop (2);
}
```

Insert this code on frame 290 on the Subtitles Markers layer.

For the entry after that, go to frame 360 on the Subtitles layer, add a blank keyframe, and assign the following code:

```
tellTarget ("Subtitles/Text") {
    gotoAndStop (3);
}
```

Insert this code on frame 360 on the Subtitle Markers layer.

Frame to select on the Subtitles Markers Layer:	Number to assign the GotoAndStop line:
290	2
360	3
460	4
520	5
590	6
700	7
790	8
850	9
880	10
920	11
980	12
1040	13
1090	14
1200	15
1360	1

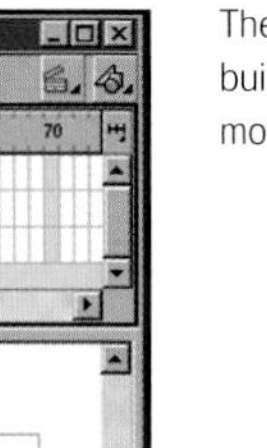

The subtitles are already built into the Subtitle Text movie clip.

Assign the **tellTarget** commands to each of the indicated frames.

Publishing the Movie

As was mentioned earlier in this chapter, QuickTime/Flash combinations must be exported as QuickTime files instead of Flash Player movies in order to work. This is because the QuickTime Player incorporates Flash, not the other way around. Flash Player is too small a plug-in to be able to display full-blown video, so part of getting the project to work properly is specifying the Publish settings from the File menu.

1 Choose File > Publish Settings.

2 On the Formats tab, deselect the Flash and HTML options and select QuickTime. By default, Flash will attempt to export the movie as a file named Episode7.mov. But as you'll remember, that's the name of the source video file imported earlier. Trying to export with this default filename will cause an error.

3 Deselect the Use default names option and change the QuickTime filename to **Episode7_Flash.mov**.

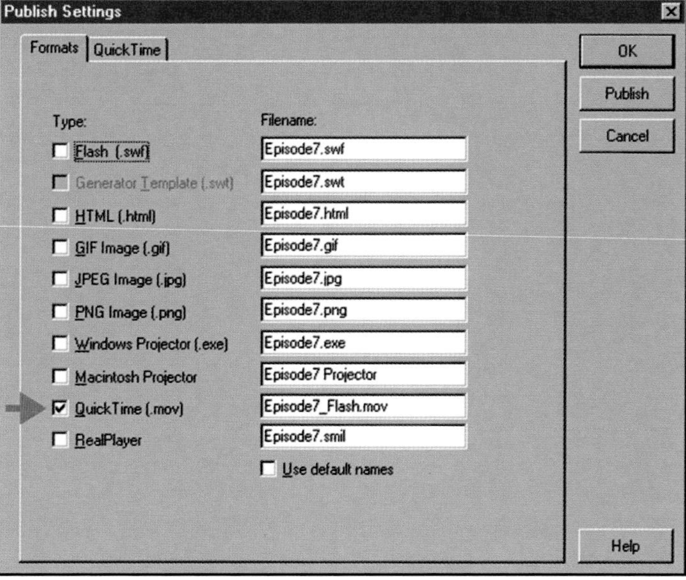

Select QuickTime as the format for this movie.

4 To make sure the movie doesn't begin playing right away, click the QuickTime tab, select the Paused At Start option, and then click Publish.

5 To test the movie, run QuickTime Player, and then open Episode7_Flash.mov. The Navy Bay video will appear, and the Flash controls will appear as expected.

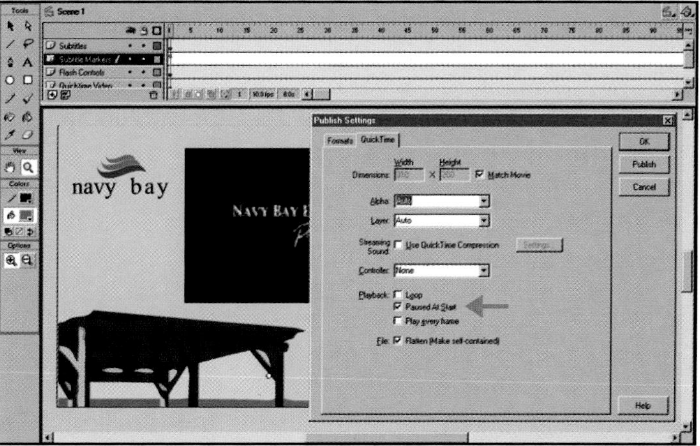

Make sure that the QuickTime movie will not immediately start playing when it is opened.

How It Works

QuickTime is a robust media platform that is able to play and integrate a huge number of formats, along with its own built-in formats QuickTime Video and QuickTime VR. Thanks to cooperation between Macromedia and Apple Computer, the QuickTime Player has a version of Flash Player built right into it, which makes it possible to overlay Flash artwork and animation right on top of QuickTime video—as well as control playback using ActionScript.

Flash-based controls and subtitles have been built into the QuickTime movie.

Because of this cooperation, Flash can be used as a basic QuickTime authoring application for adding Flash tracks to other QuickTime media. In this case, only a few simple Flash buttons were added, but the level of integration is not limited to just that. In fact, a Web-based video presentation like this could use Flash animation for all its titles and credits to improve readability.

The Flash elements and ActionScript code are combined with the video for playback in QuickTime Player. In this project, movie clips are used to allow for the display of subtitle text. However, a similar technique could be applied to display information about the actors featured in a scene, including links to Web pages or character biographies.

When a QuickTime video is imported into Flash, it is essentially for reference only. Flash isn't capable of actually editing the video file, so regardless of the frame rate you set for the Flash movie, the duration of the video representation will be stretched or shrunk to compensate, as its frame rate is already fixed. Because the video will determine the frame rate in QuickTime Player, it makes sense to set the frame rate of the Flash track to match so that precise synchronization is a no-brainer. The synchronization makes it possible to predict that jumping to a certain frame on the Flash track will jump to the same frame on the video track, like the Rewind button does in this chapter.

2

PRINTING WITH FLASH

by David Emberton

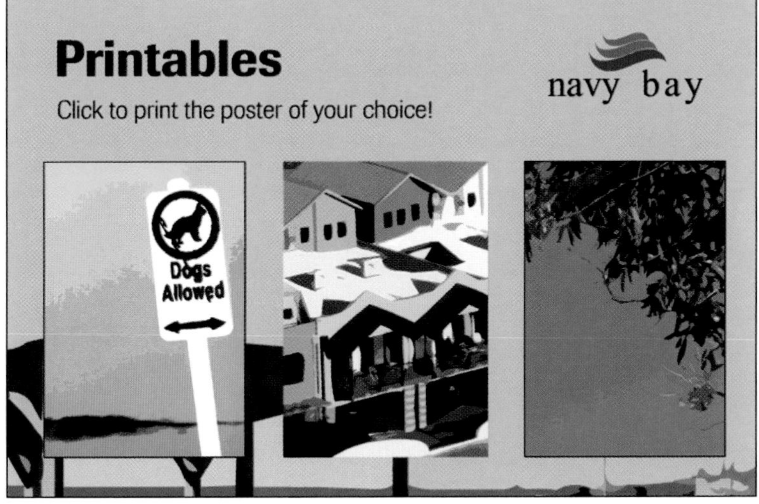

Anyone not paying close attention will have missed the addition of printing capabilities into Macromedia Flash 5. In actuality, printing was added late in the life of Flash 4, and it is (unfortunately) one of the best kept secrets about the Flash Player format.

The limitations of printing from a Web browser are many: inconsistent rendering of content between browsers, no vector graphics support, limited ability to print frames... and the list goes on. Flash printing overcomes these problems by providing a standardized Player that has full vector and bitmapped graphics support plus, of course, full-color rendering. What's most compelling however, is that Flash can print content that is both not visible to the user *and* of a different size than the current movie. So, it's easy to format your Web movie to suit a browser, yet simultaneously offer material formatted for the printed page.

This chapter covers the preparation of a series of Navy Bay posters and the scripting of buttons that allow the user to print each one. Flash Player supports two primary methods of printing: the less precise option of right-clicking the Player and choosing the Print command, and the laser-beam accurate method of using scripted buttons and the **print** action.

PREPARING FRAMES FOR PRINTING

In this section, the Navy Bay posters will be prepared for printing. By default, all Flash frames are printable, but it is also possible to disable printing of some parts of a movie and not others.

1 Open the Printables_start.fla file from the Chapter 02 folder and save a copy of it to your local hard disk.

2 To disable printing of the main Timeline, select the first key frame of any layer. Open the Frame panel, and type **!#p** in the Label field.

On the Stage, you'll see that an instance of each poster symbol has been resized for display and placed in a row. These three symbols contain the content that will be printed by the user.

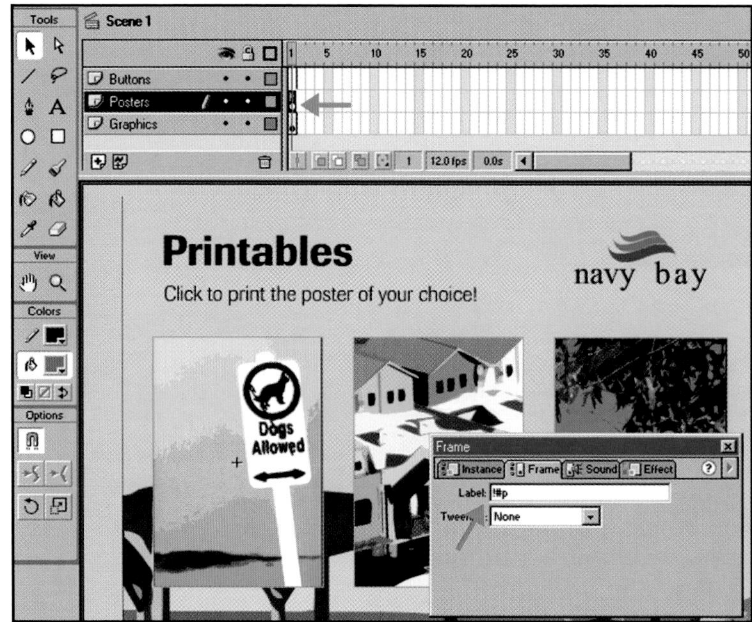

Type **!#p** as the frame label for the first frame of any layer on the main Timeline.

Note: In programming circles, the exclamation mark is usually interpreted as "don't" or "isn't." For example, if you wanted to show that 1 is not equal to 2 in ActionScript, you could use the expression 1 != 2, where != means "isn't equal to." In this case, the exclamation precedes #p, which is the label used to allow the printing of a particular frame.

3 To enable printing of the first poster, open the Library and locate Poster One in the Posters folder. Double-click to edit it.

4 Select the first key frame of the Poster layer and open the Frame panel. Type **#p** into the Label field.

This will explicitly allow this frame to be printed by the **print** action. The **print** action can be assigned to buttons so that users can click and choose which object to print.

5 Repeat steps 3 and 4 for both Poster Two and Poster Three.

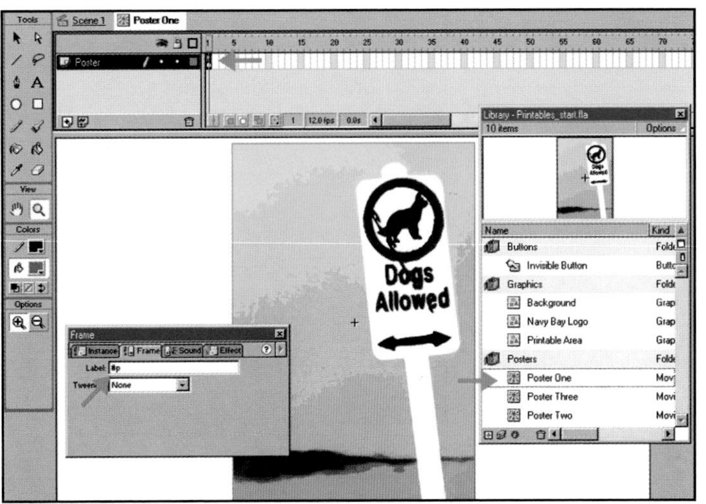

Type **#p** as the frame label for the first frame of the Poster One layer to make the Poster One movie clip printable.

DETERMINING THE PRINT AREA

Whereas Poster One and Poster Three both have a fairly obvious outline and print area, Poster Two consists of a few graphics clustered towards the middle. By default, Flash would stretch these graphics to fill the entire page, using the overall dimensions of the Poster Two Timeline as the print area. In this section, you force Flash to use a full-page print area of the same dimensions as the other two posters, making them print out with the same proportions.

1 Double-click Poster Two from the Library once again to edit it.

2 Select the first key frame of the Poster layer, and open the Actions panel. Add a **stop()** action to prevent the symbol from looping upon playback (another frame will be added in step 3 that should not be visible).

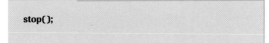

```
stop();
```

Use the **stop()** action to prevent the movie clip from looping.

3 Insert a blank key frame at position 2 on the Poster Timeline. Select it, open the Frame panel, and type **#b** in the Label field.

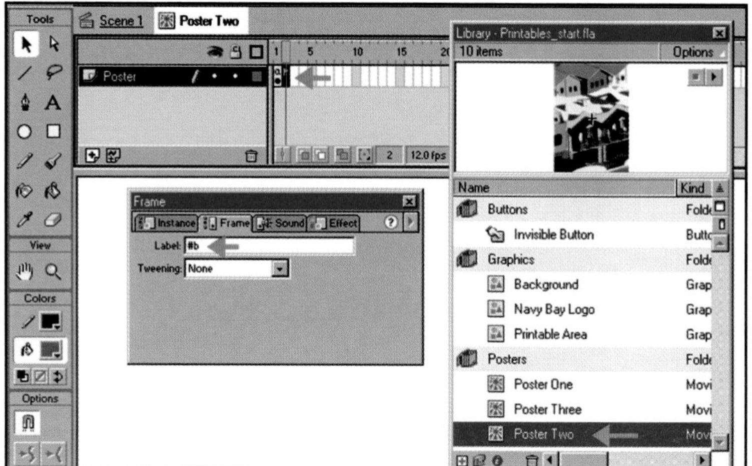

Give the blank key frame at position 2 the label **#b**.

Note: Only one key frame per Timeline can be labeled #b because that specifies the print area for the entire Timeline, not just one frame. The #b label stands for "bounding" as in "bounding box" or "bounding area," and it is one of a series of available options for controlling the printable area. Whereas #b is a hands-on way of manipulating the bounding box of printable content, the other methods are options of the **print** action to be explored later.

4 From the Library, drag an instance of Printable Area onto the Stage. Use the Align panel to center it vertically and horizontally relative to the "page."

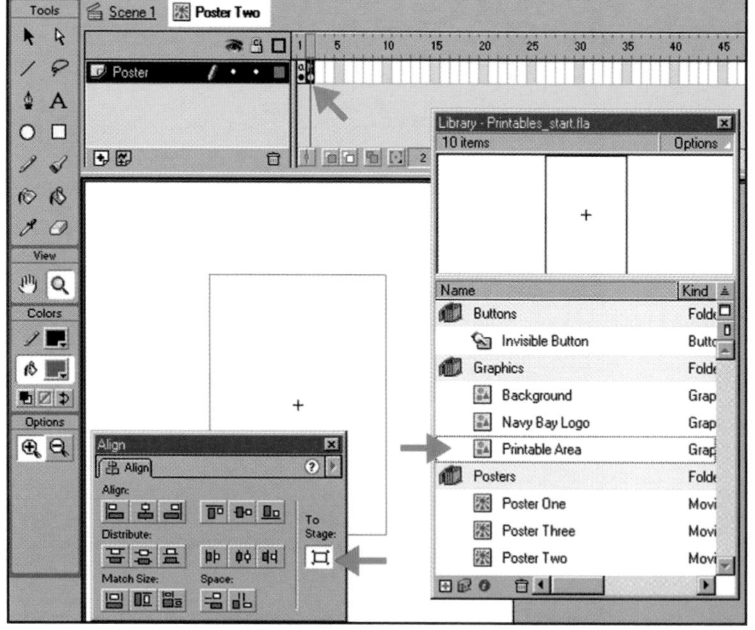

Add an instance of the Printable Area graphic symbol to the second frame of the Poster Two movie clip.

Now the graphics from frame 1 will be printed in the correct proportions, without the need for a border!

5 Return to the main Timeline.

Creating Print Buttons

Each of the poster movie clips is now prepared, so the next task is to create scripted buttons that the user will click to execute the **print** action. Each button will also check to ensure that printing capabilities are available in the version of Flash Player being used to display the movie.

1 Open the Library, locate the Invisible Button symbol, and drag three instances of it onto the Buttons layer. Position each instance over one of the poster symbols.

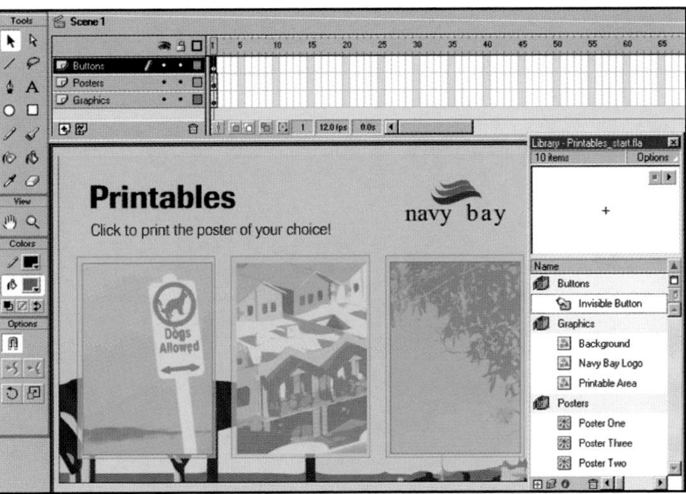

Place three instances of the Invisible Button symbol on the Buttons layer of the Poster images.

2 Click the first button, and then open the Actions panel. Insert the code for printing the poster.

When the user releases the mouse over this button, the print action is triggered. But first, the **if** action is used to make sure Flash Player is capable of printing. By coincidence, the first version of Flash Player to include the ***$version*** variable was also the first version to support printing. So, as long as the value of ***$version*** is not equal to nothing, it is okay to execute the **print** command.

Fast forward to the **print** action arguments, and you see that Poster One is the object to be printed, and **bframe** specifies that the frame contents are to be used to define the bounding box or printable area.

```
on (release) {
    if ($version != "") {
            print ("PosterOne", "bframe");
    }
}
```

The **print** action is used to print the Poster One Movie Clip instance.

Note: bframe is the most commonly used bounding box setting, but there are two others: **bmovie** and **bmax**. **bmovie** is used for printing frames on the main Timelines, where the Stage is used as the bounding area. **bmax**, on the other hand, is most useful for printing animated frames in succession. With **bmax**, all the frames on the Timeline are looked at to determine the maximum bounding box for all, which ensures that each successive page looks correct relative to the others.

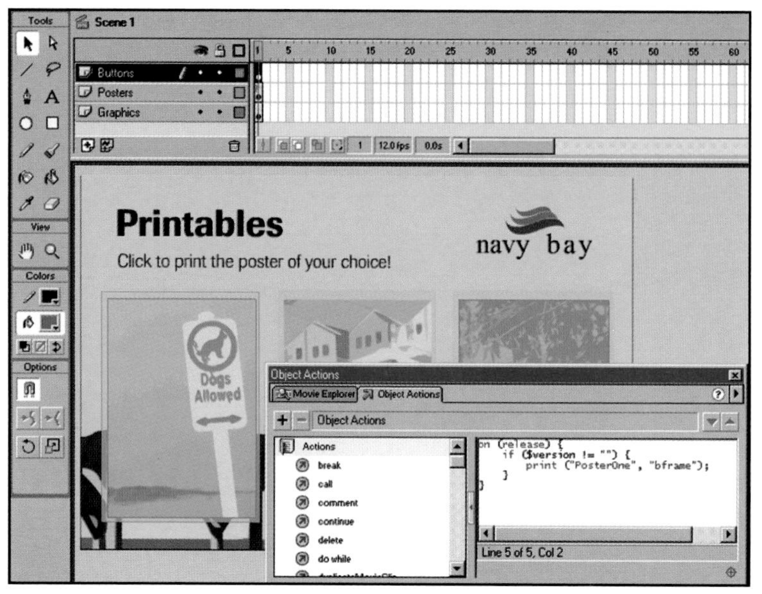

Apply the code that instigates the printing process to the Invisible Button instance that is over the Poster One movie clip.

3 Select the second button, and then insert the printing code with the Actions panel.

```
on (release) {
        if ($version != "") {
                print ("PosterTwo", "bframe");
        }
}
```

The **print** action is used to print the Poster Two Movie Clip instance.

4 Repeat step 3 for the third Invisible Button instance, specifying Poster Three as the print target value.

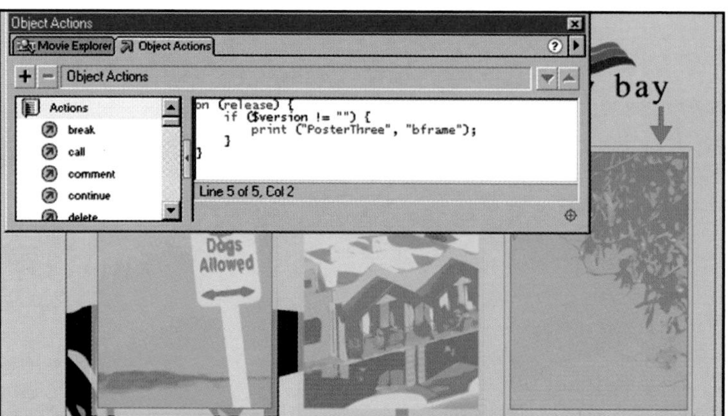

Assign the printing code to the third invisible button as shown.

How It Works

Flash Player includes a built-in printer driver that can convert graphical information from a .swf file and send it directly to the computer's printing system. This is useful for creating printable pamphlets, posters, data sheets, tests, and other material suited to paper format. Flash is a superior Web printing format because its vector graphics can scale to accommodate the highest resolution your printer is capable of.

A standard monitor can reproduce only 72 dots per inch; even an inexpensive inkjet printer can produce at least 300 dots per inch. Regular Web site bitmapped graphics will stretch and become pixelated at these higher resolutions, and a printed Web page can only reflect on paper what appears in the browser. A Flash Player movie, however, can have separate content for display and printing, making this a fantastic way to deliver paper-based material to viewers on the Web without using Acrobat and PDF files. Another advantage of Flash Player printing is that content can be personalized to the user with the use of dynamic text fields and even Macromedia Generator.

Flash can print high quality images, and it can even print content from dynamic text fields.

Smart Clips are a fantastic timesaving feature of Flash 5. They allow you to create what's known as *parameterized content*, or in other words, reusable components that you can quickly tailor for any number of different situations. Smart Clips differ from regular movie clips because each instance of a Smart Clip can be configured differently by setting its parameters—hence the term parameterized.

This chapter deals with the creation of a Smart Clip Calendar Control and its implementation as part of a Navy Bay character diary. The Smart Clip has a fairly generic function: to allow the user to select a particular date so it can be inserted into the movie and then customized using a special custom UI (or "user interface") that is actually built in Flash!

Once you've mastered this technique, you'll be able to create any number of Smart Clips of your own, complete with attractive Flash-based interfaces. These can then be used at your workplace, distributed free, or even sold to other Flash developers. Because Smart Clips are so flexible, you'll find that it's easier than ever to build modular, reusable Flash components.

3

CREATING A SMART CLIP CALENDAR CONTROL

by David Emberton

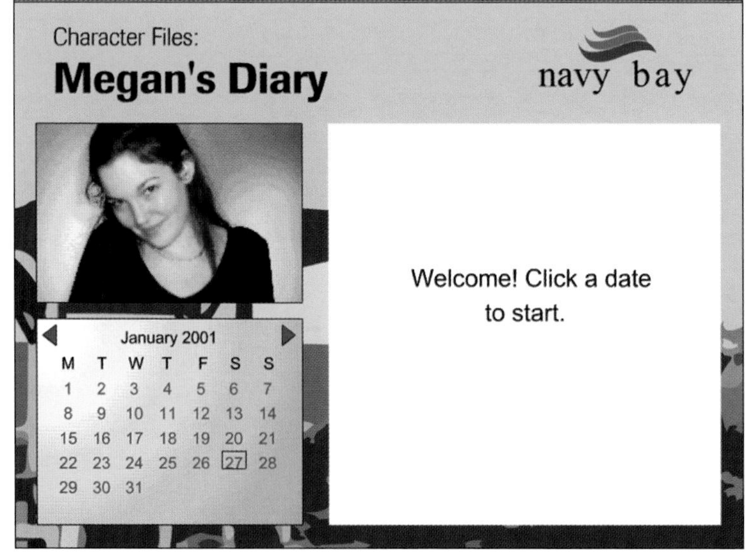

SCRIPTING THE CALENDAR

The Calendar Control begins its life as an ordinary Movie Clip symbol. It's actually constructed fairly simply, as a grid of text fields that are filled with numbers depending on the month and year currently being displayed. The fields and buttons have all been laid out for you, so the following steps will concentrate on the ActionScript code that makes the Calendar work.

1 Open the MegansDiary_start.fla file from the Chapter 03 folder and save it to your hard drive. The final file is MegansDiary_final.fla.

2 Open the Library window and locate the Calendar Control symbol. Double-click to edit it.

The symbol is made up of background graphics, a text field for displaying the current month and year, a grid of date fields, and two arrow buttons on either side for scrolling between months. Each of the date fields in the grid is an instance of the same movie clip, containing a text field for holding its date number, as well as a simple button that allows the user to click the selected date.

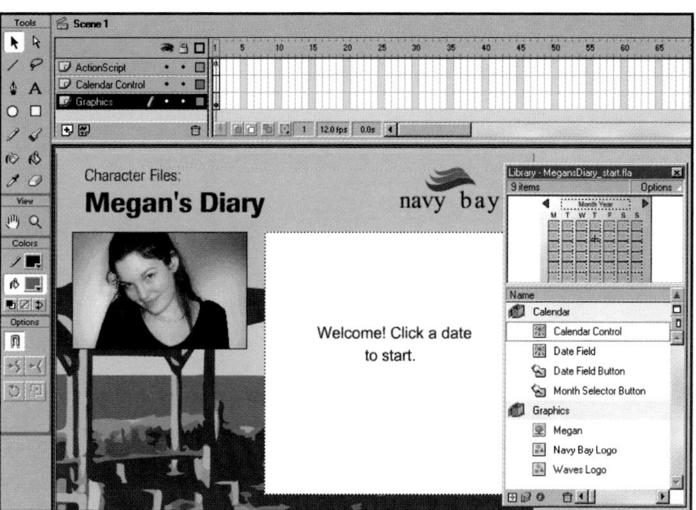

Locate the Calendar Control symbol in the library.

3 Select the empty keyframe on the ActionScript layer, and then open the Actions panel.

4 Insert the code to create an array of month names.

```
// Declare array of month names
Months = new Array("January","February","March","April","May","June",
➥"July","August","September","October","November","December");
```

Add the **Months** array, which contains a text name for each month of the year. Note that Flash keeps this code on one line. (The ➥ symbol you see here is used for editorial purposes only.)

You do this first to make sure the **Months** array is available to the other functions. ActionScript deals with dates as numbers and expresses months specifically as a number between 0 (for January) and 11 (for December). This zero-based counting system works perfectly with the Array object, because its first element is always numbered 0 also. So by creating an array of text strings that correspond to each of the twelve months, you have an easy way of taking any month number and plugging it into the **Months** array to get a text version. For example, if ActionScript gives you a date number 3, it's a simple matter to evaluate **Months[3]** to get the text string April.

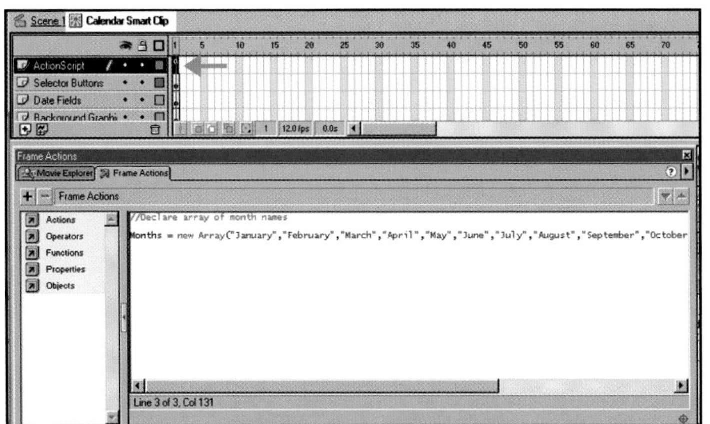

Notice that Flash keeps all the data for the **Months** array on one line.

> **Note:** Although ActionScript uses zero-based counting for months, it uses regular one-based counting for years and days. So even though the month 3 equals April, the day number 15 is just 15; there is no day 0.

5 Insert the ActionScript to initialize the calendar by creating a new Date object, and then setting its basic properties.

```
// Initialize Calendar
CalendarDate = new Date();
if (ShowYear != "Now") {
        CalendarDate.setYear(ShowYear);
}
if (ShowMonth != "Now") {
        CalendarDate.setMonth(ShowMonth);
}
DrawCalendar();
```

Insert the code to have the Smart Clip check its parameters to determine which date to display.

Date is one of the predefined ActionScript objects that's included so you don't have to design your own date-handling objects and all the methods that entails. When the new Date object, **CalendarDate**, is created here, it is set by default to the current time according to the system clock.

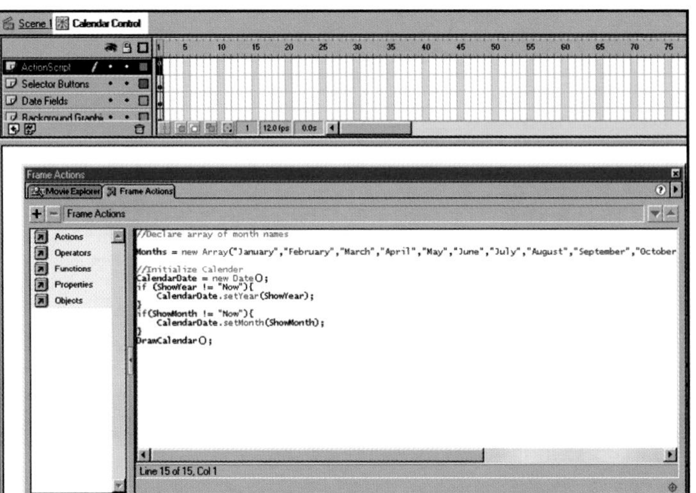

Make sure you have entered the Date object and initialized its properties correctly.

Part of the Smart Clip customization that will be added later, however, is the ability to override the default behavior and actually specify what month and year the calendar will display. So two **if** statements check to determine the value of the Smart Clip parameters **ShowYear** and **ShowMonth**. If they equal **Now**, nothing will be changed; otherwise the values are used as arguments for the **setYear** and **setMonth** methods of **CalendarDate** (inherited from the Date object).

The final line in this block invokes the function **DrawCalendar()**, which analyzes the current month and displays the correct information in each of the date fields in the grid. The **DrawCalendar()** function is added in step 7.

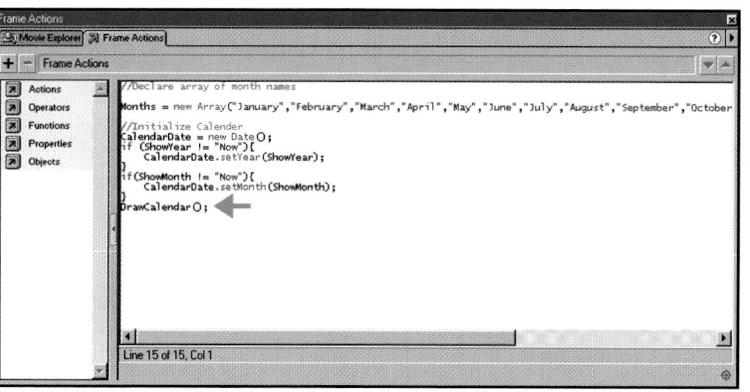

The **DrawCalendar()** function makes sure that each of the date fields accurately represent the current month.

6 Add this code to enable the calendar:

The calendar, invoked whenever the user clicks an individual date button, determines what date has been selected. That information is stored in a new Date object and passed to a function specified in another of the Smart Clip parameters, ***SendDateTo***. So even though ***SendDateTo*** is a variable, it can be used in conjunction with eval to point to a function.

```
// Send Date function
function SendDate(Day) {
    DateSelected = new Date(CurrentYear, CalendarDate.getMonth( ), Day);
    if (SendDateTo != "") {
        DateTarget = eval(SendDateTo);
        DateTarget(DateSelected);
    }
}
```

Add the **SendDate()** function to pass the selected date to the function specified by ***SendDateTo***.

7 To insert the **DrawCalendar()** function, which is required to update the calendar and its grid of date fields, insert this code next:

```
// Draw Calendar function
function DrawCalendar() {
    CurrentMonth = Months[CalendarDate.getMonth( )];
    CurrentYear = CalendarDate.getFullYear( );
    CalendarText = CurrentMonth + " " + CurrentYear;
```

Add the code for the **DrawCalendar()** function.

This first block of statements acts to convert numerical date information into a more readable text string displayed at the top of the calendar in "Month Year" format. The ***CurrentMonth*** variable is obtained by accessing the element of the **Months** array corresponding to the currently displayed month. **Calendar.getMonth()** returns a number equal to the current month of the CalendarDate object. This function call is used to access the corresponding element of the **Months** array, which is **Months[CalendarDate.getMonth()]**. The result is the text name of the current month.

Make sure the code for enabling the Calendar and the **DrawCalendar()** function is entered correctly.

8 Insert this code to determine the current year:

CurrentYear is slightly easier to determine; you use the fairly straightforward **getFullYear** method of CalendarDate. Then ***CalendarText***, the variable attached to the text field at the top of the calendar box, is set to the ***CurrentMonth*** text concatenated (or combined) with a space and ***CurrentYear***.

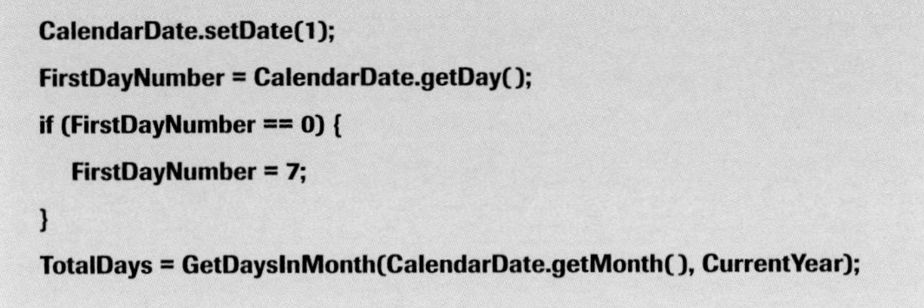

```
CalendarDate.setDate(1);
FirstDayNumber = CalendarDate.getDay();
if (FirstDayNumber == 0) {
    FirstDayNumber = 7;
}
TotalDays = GetDaysInMonth(CalendarDate.getMonth(), CurrentYear);
```

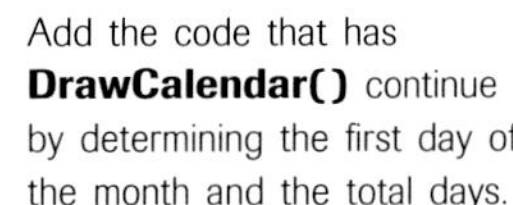

Add the code that has **DrawCalendar()** continue by determining the first day of the month and the total days.

This block of code is designed to figure out what day of the week the first day of the current month falls on. This is important for properly displaying the current month full of dates because they all need to line up correctly with the matching Mondays, Tuesdays, and Wednesdays. Because the **setDate()** method of CalendarDate sets the current date to 1 (the first of the month), the **getDay()** method can then be used to get the corresponding number of the first day in the current month. This number will determine whether the first day falls on a Monday, Tuesday, or whatever. (The total number of days in the current month, determined by a function that you add in a later step, makes sure that only the correct number of days is shown in each month.)

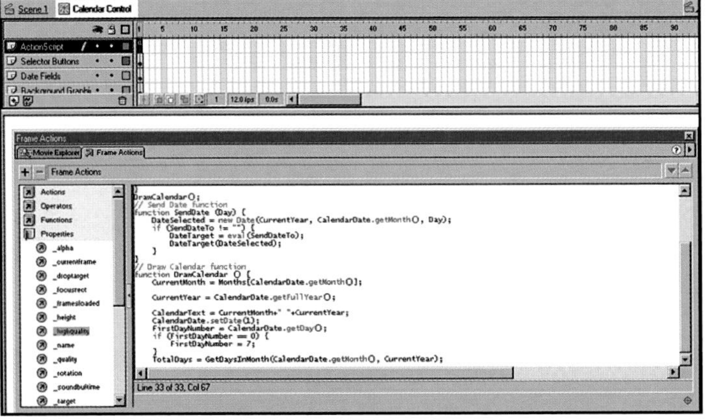

Make sure the code you inserted for determining the first day of the month is in the correct position.

9 Insert this code to create a **for** loop that paves the way for the fresh date information by looping through all the date field movie clips and setting their **_visible** properties to **false**.

```
for (Counter = 0; Counter <= 42; Counter ++) {
    eval("Field" + Counter)._visible = false;
}
```

Add this **for** loop to count through each of the 42 date fields, making them invisible.

This hides all the dates in the grid, and only the relevant ones will be reactivated in the next block of the code. The number 42 appears because that is the total number of fields in the grid. That's much more than 31, granted, but depending on the day of the week the first of the month falls on, all the dates following can be displaced further down the grid and past the 31st field.

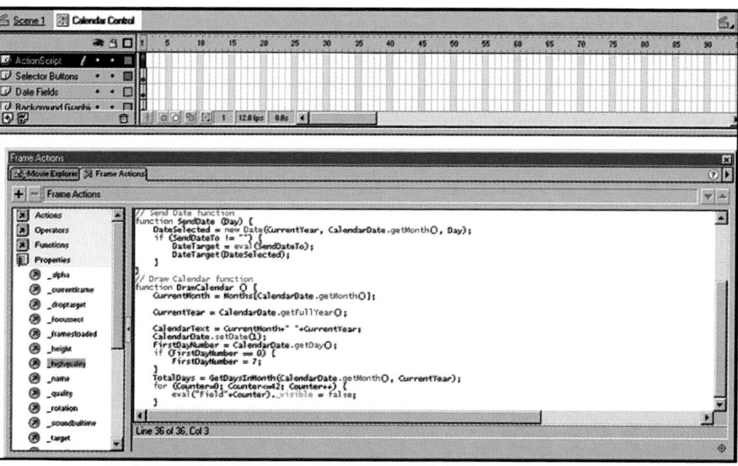

Make sure the **for** loop is inserted correctly.

10 Insert the code for a second **for** loop that counts through the **TotalDays** in the currently selected month, sets their **_visible** properties to **true**, and then sets the value of the **DateField** text field in each date in the grid. The **DateField** values are set to **Counter + 1**, because **Counter** starts at zero even though the first actual date number is one.

```
    for (Counter = 0; Counter < TotalDays; Counter ++) {
        eval("Field" + (FirstDayNumber + Counter))._visible = true;
        eval("Field" + (FirstDayNumber + Counter) + ".DateField") = Counter + 1;
    }
}
```

Add the code for the last section of **DrawCalendar()**, which inserts numbers into each of the date fields for the current month.

11 Insert the code for the first of two supplementary functions that calculate the correct number of days in any given month, based on what you already know about month lengths and leap years.

This function simply takes the **Month** and **Year** arguments passed to it and cycles through a series of **if** statements to determine the number of days in the month. The **Year** value is passed on to the next and final function, **IsLeapYear()**.

The double pipe **||** is another way of writing **or**, which allows for multiple arguments to be written into the same **if** statement. The **if** statement in this code block is the code equivalent of the old rhyme "30 days has September, April, June, and November. All the rest have 31, excepting February in a line, which in a leap year has 29."

The **return()** action is used to send values back to whatever object called the function. In this case, it returns the number of days in the specified month.

```
// Determine number of days in the month
function GetDaysInMonth(Month, Year) {
    if (Month==0 || Month==2 || Month==4 || Month==6 || Month==7 ||
    ➥Month==9 || Month==11) {
            Days = 31;
    } else if (Month==3 || Month==5 || Month==8 || Month==10) {
        Days = 30;
    } else if (Month==1) {
        if (IsLeapYear(Year)) {
            Days = 29;
        } else {
            Days = 28;
        }
    }
    return (Days);
}
```

GetDaysInMonth() takes a month and year value to determine the number of days in the specified month. (The ➥ symbol you see here is for editorial purposes only.)

12 Insert the last block of code to complete the Calendar Control.

This function uses a lesser-known operator called *modulo*. You can learn more about modulo in the ActionScript Reference that came with your software. In a nutshell, it divides one value by another and returns the remainder. This is the same process taught to schoolchildren as a precursor to short division. If **Year** can be divided by 4 and 400 and have no remainder, but when divided by 100 it *does have* a remainder, it's considered to be a leap year. The **return** action is then used to pass a **true** or **false** value back to the **GetDaysInMonth()** function from whence it was called.

```
// Check for leap years
function IsLeapYear (Year) {
    if (((Year % 4)==0) && ((Year % 100)!=0) || ((Year % 400)==0)) {
        return (true);
    } else {
return (false);
    }
}
```

Insert **IsLeapYear()** to check whether any given year is a leap year.

The Calendar Control symbol is effectively complete, but before you drag an instance of it onto the Stage, it needs to be set up as a Smart Clip, and part of that process is preparing the Custom User Interface.

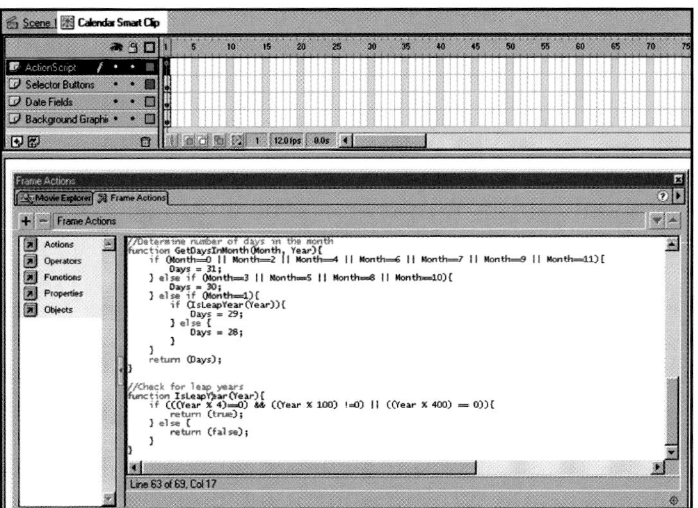

Make sure that the code that checks for leap years is inserted correctly.

PREPARING A CUSTOM USER INTERFACE

A Custom User Interface (UI) file isn't required as such, but it makes it easier for others to customize instances of your Smart Clip symbol and can make the whole process just a little more attractive. In addition, a Custom UI is a great way to display branding and copyright notices if you plan to distribute a Smart Clip to fellow developers.

If you don't use a Custom UI, Flash simply displays a standard-looking input box that looks a lot like the Generator panel. If you do use a Custom UI, you can include animations, artwork, and anything else Flash can manage. In this example, the CalendarUI file is quite basic—in fact it only contains some text and three input fields!

1 Open the CalendarUI.fla file from the Chapter 03 folder, save it to your hard drive, and open the XCH movie clip.

Within the CalendarUI file is a Movie Clip instance named XCH. This is the exchange clip, and it contains a text field for each of the three parameters that will be added to the Calendar Control Smart Clip. The process of getting the information entered into this UI to the actual Calendar Control itself isn't

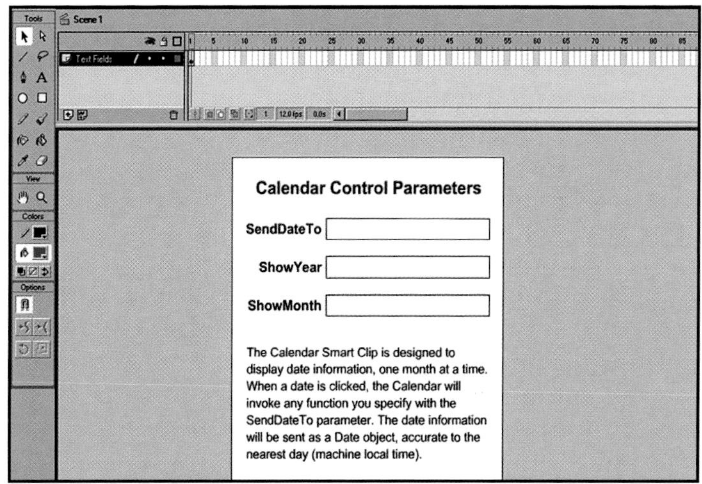

A Custom User Interface makes the task of customizing Smart Clip instances easier.

actually all that mysterious. The variables attached to each of the text fields in XCH are simply transferred inside the Calendar instance upon export. Then the functions you inserted earlier have access to that data as if those variables had always been there.

2 Click each of the text fields, and then use the Text Options panel to note the variable names.

3 Copy CalendarUI.fla to the same folder your MegansDiary file is located in, use Export Movie to export it, and then name it **CalendarUI.swf**.

The file CalendarUI.swf will now be available for use as the Custom UI.

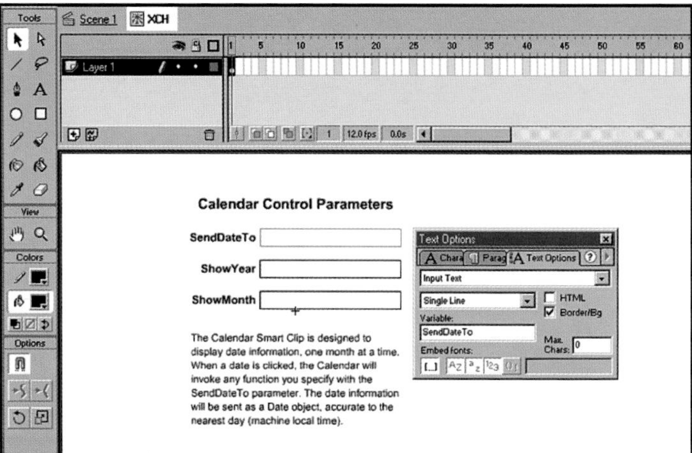

Use the Text Options panel to take note of the variable names assigned to each text field.

Moving from Movie Clip to Smart Clip

With the Custom UI all ready to go, it's time to turn the regular Movie Clip symbol Calendar Control into a Smart Clip. The method for doing this is a snap.

1 Return to your MegansDiary file, open the Library, and select the Calendar Control symbol.

2 Click the Options menu and select Define Clip Parameters.

3 In the Define Clip Parameters dialog box, add these three parameter names: **SendDateTo**, **ShowYear**, and **ShowMonth**.

Parameters can be Objects, Lists, and Arrays, but in this case the default plain text is just what you're after, so you can leave the Value and Type settings for each exactly as they are.

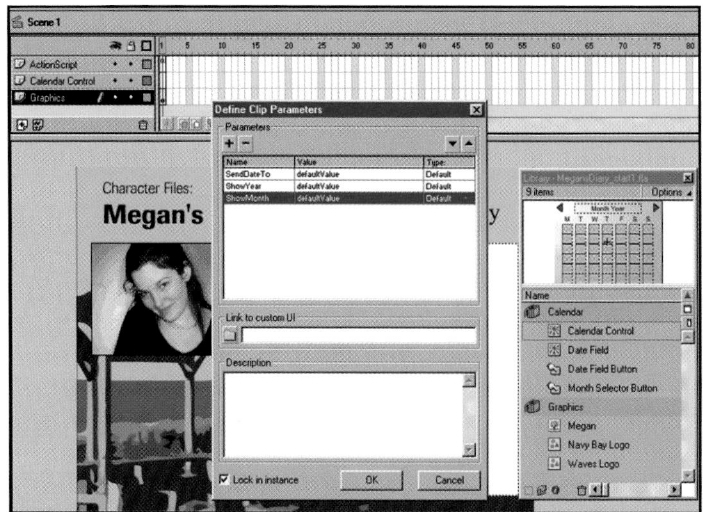

Use the Define Clip Parameters dialog box to add parameter names to the Calendar Control symbol.

4 In the Custom UI box below the Parameters list, type **CalendarUI.swf** to specify the Custom UI file you want associated with this Smart Clip.

5 Click OK to commit the changes.

The Library icon next to the Calendar Control should change from the standard movie clip graphic to the slightly different Smart Clip graphic. That's all there is to it!

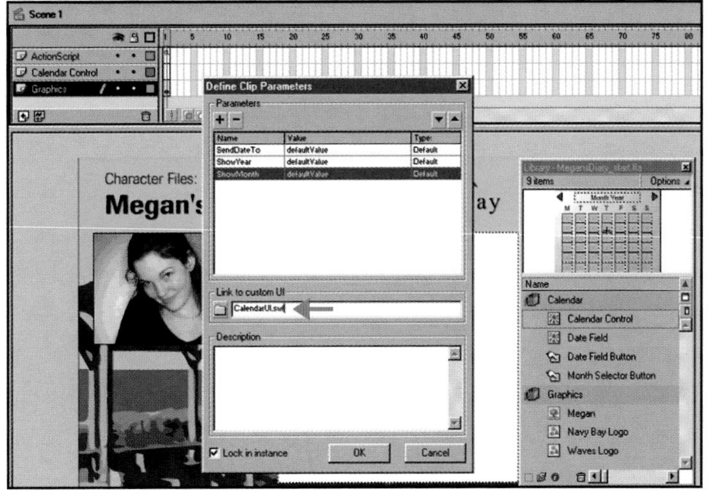

Specify the CalendarUI.swf file as the Custom User Interface.

Setting Smart Clip Parameters

Now that the Smart Clip is all set, you can add an instance of it to the Stage and set its parameters.

1 Select the Calendar Control layer, and then drag an instance of the Calendar Control symbol from the Library to the Stage. Position it at X: 18.8, Y: 230, which is under Megan's photo and to the left of the large white text area.

2 Open the Clip Parameters panel, and you'll see the CalendarUI.swf file displayed within the panel itself. Type **_root.GetDiaryEntry** in the SendDateTo field, **2001** in the ShowYear field, and **1** in the ShowMonth field.

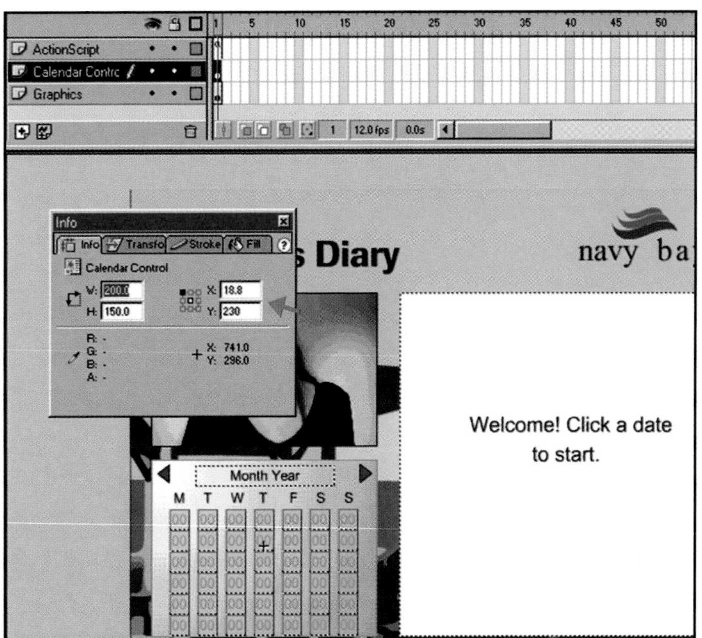

Use the Info panel to position the Calendar Control symbol.

3 Save the file and use Test Movie to export it.

The Calendar Control should display January of 2001, and you can click any of the dates and scroll between months.

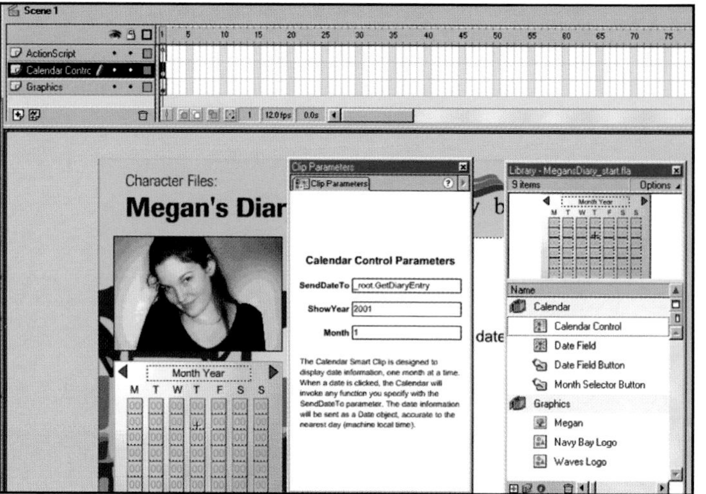

Use the Clip Parameters panel to specify which date will be displayed initially.

How It Works

Smart Clips are a great way of streamlining the creation of Flash content. Commonly used components, such as this calendar control, can be built once and then reused in a number of scenarios. The customization is achieved with the help of parameters that can be set using custom Flash interfaces to simplify the process.

Other examples of Smart Clips include various interface elements, such as drop-down menus and scrolling lists, as well as more sophisticated examples like animation controllers or interactive learning components (such as test questions). Although all this functionality could previously have been achieved with regular movie clip symbols, Smart Clips allow other developers to make use of your components without wasting time digging around inside and deciphering how they work in order to customize them for their needs.

The Calendar makes extensive use of the Date object and its methods to populate a grid of date fields. ActionScript is used to calculate the number of days in each month and lay out the information across the grid of text fields. The end user can then just click the date they choose. That date is then invisibly passed to a function specified in the Clip parameters. In this way, the Calendar is a lot like a regular button, because the user can just point and click. But it also does the job of a text field, where previously the user might've had to type the date he wanted to use.

At this point, the Megan's Diary file is incomplete. See Chapter 4 for more instructions on the project.

The calendar is now an editable Smart Clip.

USING EXTERNAL SCRIPT FILES AND THE DEBUGGER

by David Emberton

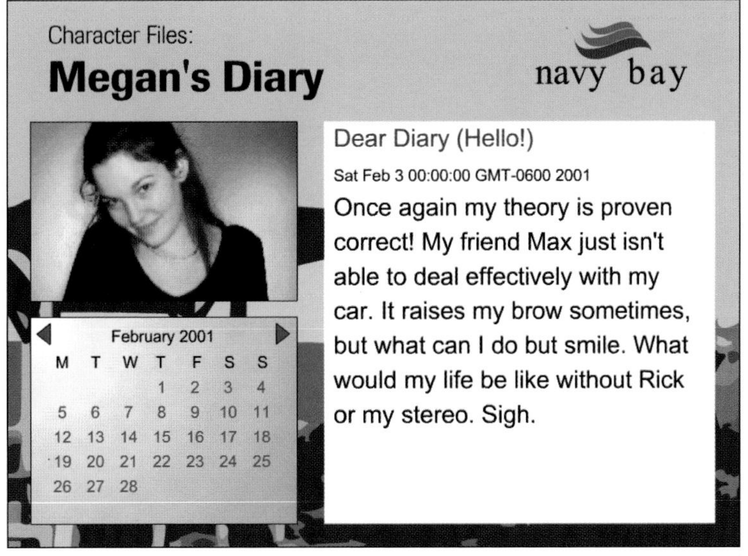

This chapter covers two of the more workflow-oriented Flash 5 features: the **#include** action for using external script files, and the Debugger panel. In this chapter, you will use the **#include** action and the Debugger to add the remaining parts of the Megan's Diary project to the application.

The aim of this chapter is to take date information from the Calendar Control Smart Clip and use it to display text in the **DiaryEntry** text field. In the process, external script files will be used, and the Debugger will be called in to diagnose errors—so don't be alarmed if you test the file early and it doesn't work as expected.

USING THE #include DIRECTIVE

The **#include** action, or directive as it is also known, is used to specify an external script file. **#include** acts as a placeholder, and when the movie is exported or tested, the contents of the text file are parsed as ActionScript code and included in the compressed .swf file. External scripts behave just like any scripts you enter regularly.

1 If you've completed Chapter 3, open the MegansDiary.fla file you were working with previously. Otherwise, open the MegansDiary_start.fla file from the Chapter 4 folder and save a copy to your hard disk.

To recap, the Calendar Control Smart Clip has been configured to invoke the **GetDiaryEntry()** function whenever the user clicks a date, and then to pass to that function a Date object representing the date clicked.

2 Select the first key frame of the ActionScript layer, and then open the Actions panel.

As you can see, the body of the **GetDiaryEntry()** function is missing. This is where you use the **#include** directive to specify the external script file containing the missing code.

Inspect the code assigned to the first frame on the ActionScript layer.

3 Delete the text that reads **// To be added in Chapter 4** and insert this code:

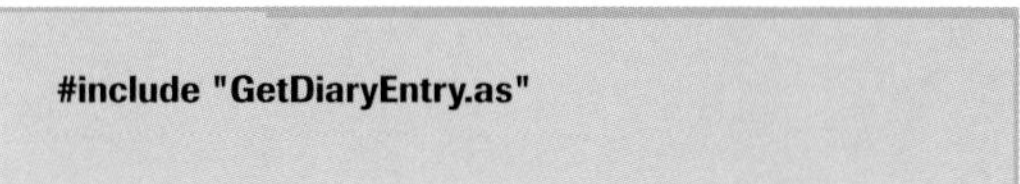

```
#include "GetDiaryEntry.as"
```

The **#include** directive allows for external script files to be imported upon export or testing.

GetDiaryEntry() calls on a number of supporting functions defined below it on the same key frame.

Megan's Diary is actually a new twist on the well-known madlibs concept. If the diary were a real person's diary, the data for each individual date could be loaded from a database or external file, but in this case, each entry is a freshly shuffled combination of random elements.

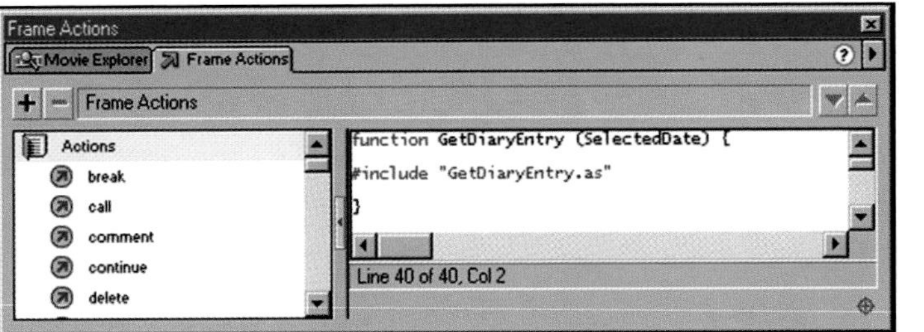

Remove the comment line and replace it with the preceding code.

The **PickOne()** function can take any array and select a random element from it. This is used to combine random elements from arrays of names, phrases, and things into sentences. These sentences are laid out in the Paragraphs array, a dynamic madlib of sorts that gives the illusion that a diary entry is attached to each date even though it isn't.

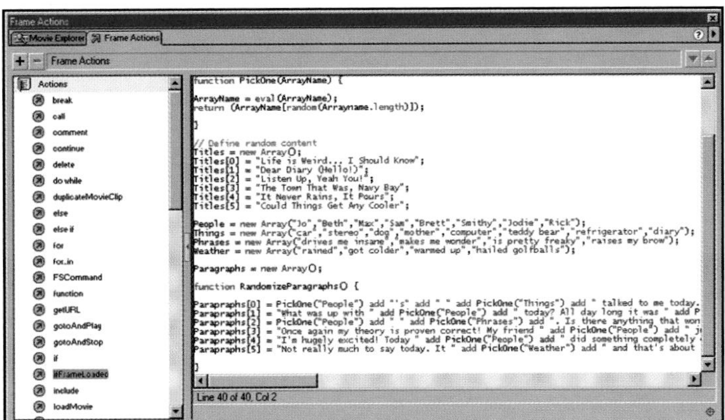

The pre-existing code in the ActionScript layer includes the **PickOne** function and a series of arrays.

Creating External Scripts

Although the Actions panel offers a great way to do your ActionScript work, under certain circumstances, you might want to create scripts in a text editor. This is particularly true for workgroups because only one person can work on an .fla file at a time. If you're waiting on that .fla to edit a script, hello bottleneck!

By using the **#include** action, however, you can keep your scripts separated from the main .fla and store them as text files. Then, when the movie is exported, the contents of those files are drawn on as if you'd entered them directly into Flash.

1. For something completely different, open your favorite text editor and create a new file. You can use any text editor that can save plain text files.

2 Name the file **GetDiaryEntry.as** and save it in the same folder where you plan to store the rest of your work files for this chapter. The file extension can really be anything, but .as is the recommended standard for ActionScript files.

If you've already completed Chapter 3, you'll remember that the Calendar Control Smart Clip is set up to call the function **GetDiaryEntry()** whenever it is clicked, so the next step is to enter the body of that function into your text editor.

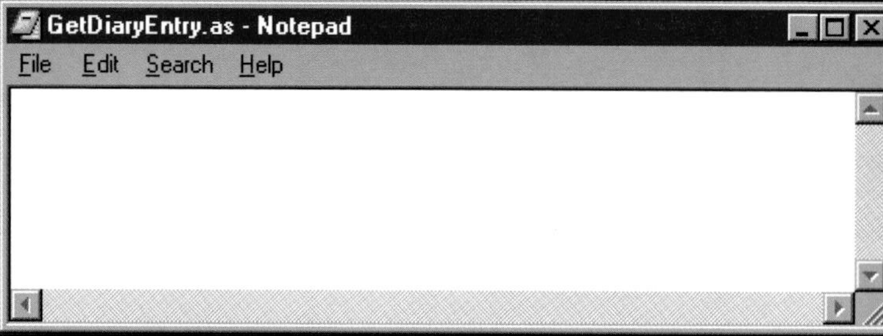

Use a text editor to create a new file called **GetDiaryEntry.as**.

Note: If you work in Windows, be aware that it may be set to hide the extensions of known file types. What you think is GetDiaryEntry.as could in fact be saved as GetDiaryEntry.as.doc or GetDiaryEntry.as.txt without your knowing it. You can display the hidden file extensions by opening an Explorer window and choosing View, Folder Options. In the Folder Options dialog box, select the View tab. Then disable the Hide Extensions for Known File Types option.

3 At the beginning of the file, enter the first two lines of code comprising the **GetDiaryEntry()** function:

```
// Process date information
DateText = SelectedDate.toString();
```

The **toString** method converts the SelectedDate object to a text string.

Megan's Diary works by allowing the user to click a date on the calendar and view the diary entry for that given day. The Calendar Smart Clip passes this date information to the **GetDiaryEntry** function as a Date object. The Date object is a built-in ActionScript function that has specific date-related methods and properties. The value of a Date object can be quickly extracted as a text string with the **toString** method. The plain text date can then be used as part of the diary text, underneath the title. For example, **SelectedDate.toString()** outputs something like this:

Tue Oct 3 23:13:56 GMT+0900 2000.

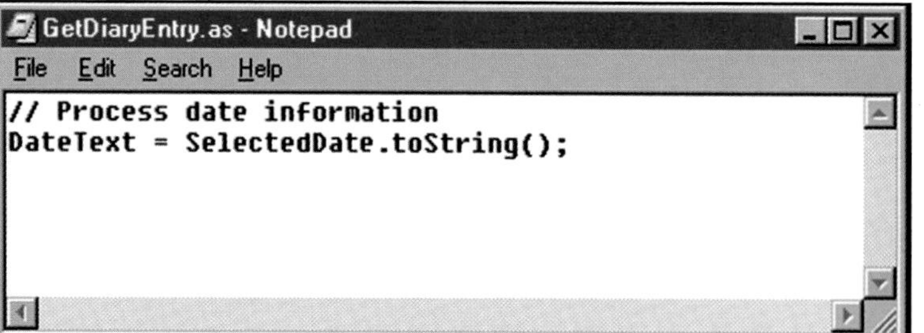

Enter the first two lines of code into your text editor.

4 Insert the following two lines of code into your text editor:

```
// Mix up paragraphs
_root.RandomizeParagraphs();
```

The **RandomizeParagraphs()** function shuffles around the available content, madlibs style.

In this code, the **GetDiaryEntry()** function invokes another function called **RandomizeParagraphs()** that is attached to the main Timeline, or **_root.RandomizeParagraphs()** takes a selection of prewritten words and shuffles them up to produce a new set of sentences, which can then be formatted and displayed in the **DiaryEntry** text field by this function. The **RandomizeParagraphs()** function is already present in the MegansDiary Flash file, so even though this is an external script file, you can call functions exactly the same way you could if you were editing the script directly in Flash.

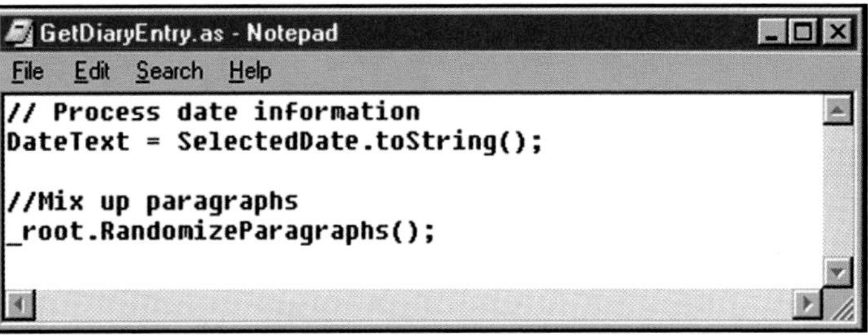

Enter the next two lines of code into your text editor.

The last statement in the **GetDiaryEntry()** function takes a random entry title, the selected date, and any of the newly shuffled paragraphs, and then sets it to display in the **DiaryEntry** text field.

5 Add this HTML code to liven up the look of the diary text:

```
// Assemble HTML
_root.DiaryEntry = "<font color='#003366'>" add _root.PickOne("Titles")
➥add "</font><br><font size='12'>" add DateText add "</font><br>" add
➥_root.PickOne("Paragraphs");
```

A **for** loop creates instances of the Color object for each palette selector. (The ➥ symbol you see here is for editorial purposes only.)

The **_root.DiaryEntry** is the text field to the right of the Stage that displays the text for each fictional diary entry. The contents of the text field are set just like a variable. The **add** operator is used to join several pieces of text together to form one long string of characters. Some of the text pieces are HTML code for formatting, and some are variables and function calls.

In particular, **PickOne()** is a custom function that has already been added to the MegansDiary file and is used here by **GetDiaryEntry()** to choose an element from whatever array you specify as its argument—first **Titles** and then **Paragraphs**. Here is a sample of the diary output:

Could Things Get Any Cooler

Sat Jan 13 00:00:00 GMT+0600 2001

Not really much to say today. It hailed golfballs and that's about it. Smithy rattled on about refrigerators but you know how that drives me insane. More tomorrow... I guess.

6 Save the file again, and make sure it is stored in the same folder as your MegansDiary file. Close the document and return to Flash.

This text file can now be inserted into the Flash Player file upon export, at the location of the **#include** directive.

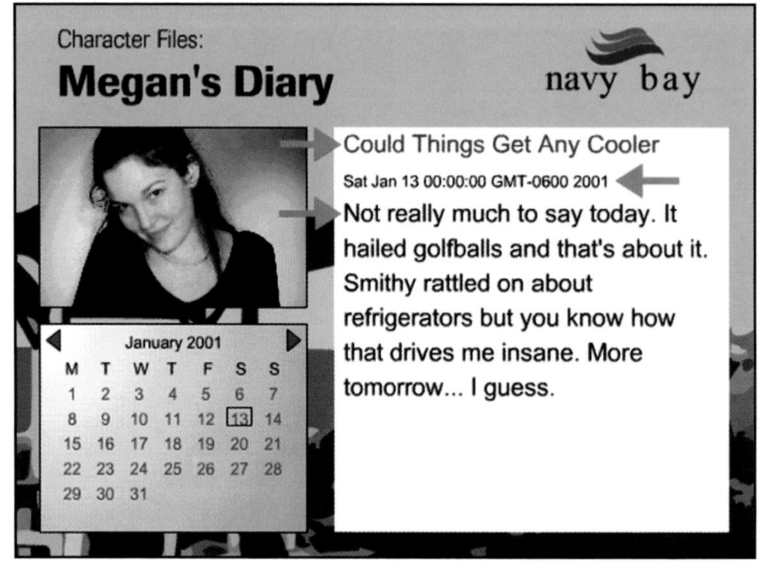

The **PickOne()** function chooses items in some of the pre-existing arrays to define a diary entry.

Working with the Flash Debugger

If you're used to using Test Movie, you may not have noticed the new Debug Movie option in the Control menu. The Debugger Panel can be used to monitor variables and properties, but how is it activated? The implementation of the feature is a little quirky, so while you can always access the Debugger from Debug Movie mode, whether or not you can activate it in Test Movie mode depends on your Publish settings. Specifically, whether the Remote Debugging feature is enabled. Remote Debugging is a feature that can be used to Debug files outside the authoring environment, using the special Debug Flash Player. Whether or not you want Remote Debugging activated, here are all the ways you can activate the Debugger Panel from within Flash:

With Remote Debugging Enabled

1 Choose File > Publish Settings, click the Flash tab and select Debugging Permitted.

You are ready to activate the Debugger panel.

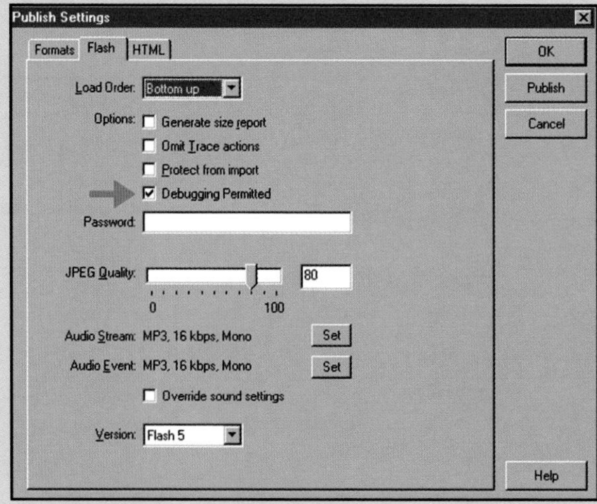

Turn on the Debugging Permitted option.

2 Select Control > Debug Movie

or

Select Control > Test Movie, right-click, and select Debug.

With Remote Debugging Disabled

1 Use File > Publish Settings > Flash tab to deactivate debugging.

You are ready to activate the Debugger panel.

2 Select Control > Debug Movie.

(In Test Movie mode, the Debug option will be grayed and unavailable.)

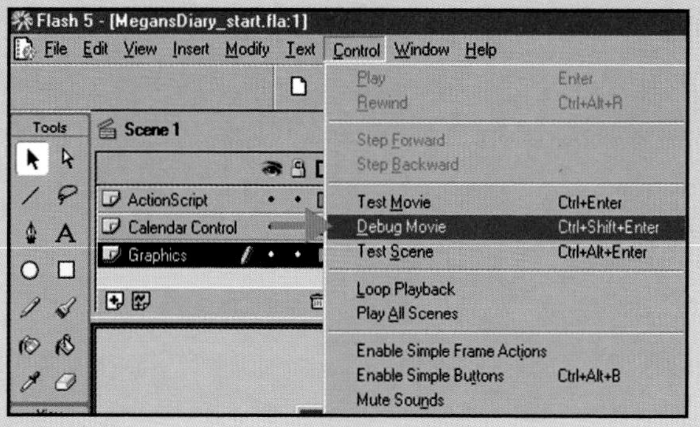

Select the Debug Movie option from the Control menu.

Troubleshooting the Debugger

If the Debugger is active but doesn't show any variables or properties, you can kick-start it by right-clicking the movie (in Test Movie or Debug Movie mode) and selecting Debug to deactivate the Debugger. Then, right-click and select Debug again. This will refresh the Debugger panel and the variables and properties should show as normal.

What Remote Debugging Means

Remote Debugging allows for a Flash Player Movie (swf) to be debugged outside of the author environment, even in a browser. Whether or not this feature is enabled depends on the settings in the File > Publish Settings> Flash tab.

Diagnosing Errors with the Debugger Panel

Now that all the code is in place, the movie can be tested. Click any date though, and all that shows up is the title and date! The diary entry paragraphs *should* show up, but they don't! How can you find the problem? Enter the Debugger panel—your new best friend.

1 To access the Debugger panel, return to your Flash movie and click the Control Movie. Select Debug Movie instead of the usual Test Movie. The Debug Movie option activates the debug tools.

The first step to eliminating a bug is to examine all the symptoms. In this case, everything seems to be working except for the missing paragraph text, which is stored as a variable on the _root Timeline or _level0.

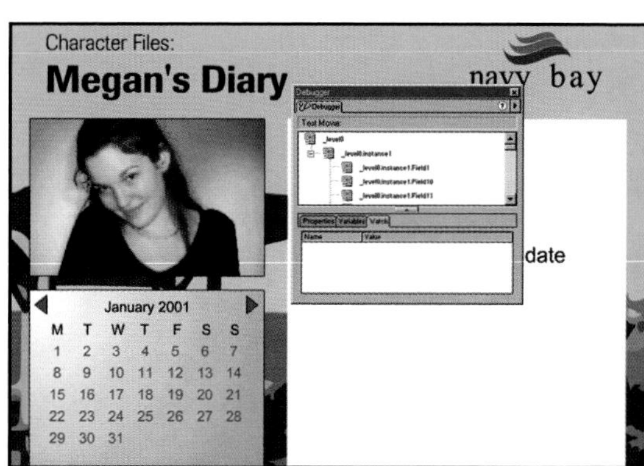

Open the Debugger panel in Flash 5.

2 Select _level0 in the Display list (the uppermost pane), and then click the Variable tab.

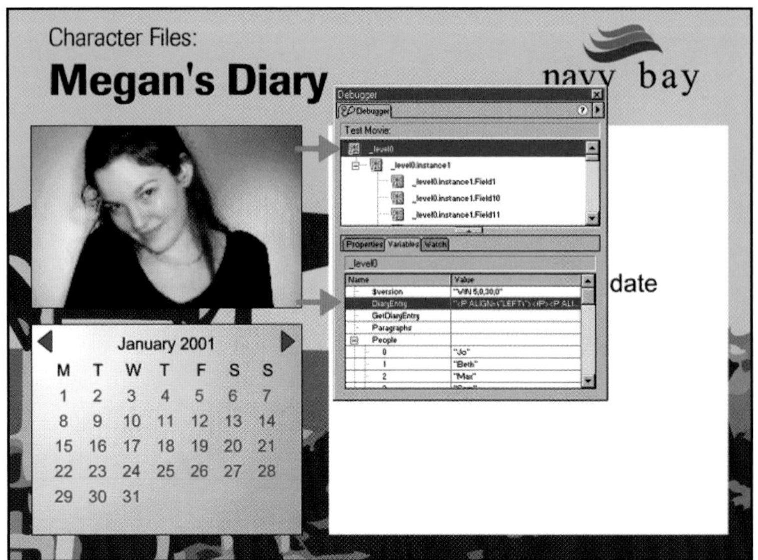

Select _level0 in the Debugger window, and then select the Variable tab.

3 Take a look at all the variables currently associated with the _root Timeline to try to determine the cause of the problem. Paragraph text is *supposed* to be appended to the end of **Diary Entry**, so it's possible that it's there but is not being displayed for some unknown reason.

4 Select **DiaryEntry** in the list of variables, and then use the right arrow button to scroll to its end.

No paragraph text is shown there, just the title, the date, and the HTML formatting. Something is preventing the data from being accessed in the first place.

Where is the paragraph information coming from? All the data used to construct the diary entries is stored in a series of arrays: Titles, People, Things, Phrases, Weather, and Paragraphs.

5 Scroll down the Variables list, and you'll see each of the arrays and their associated elements—except for Paragraphs!

It appears as though Paragraphs is an empty array, which doesn't make much sense because it is defined quite clearly back on the main Timeline.

6 Close the Debugger panel and the test movie. Then return to the Flash document for a closer look.

7 Select the first key frame of the ActionScript layer and open the Actions panel. Scroll down to the end of the script, where the Paragraphs array elements are defined.

Do you see the problem? Thanks to ever-reliable human error, each of the lines used to define the various paragraphs has a spelling mistake! Instead of defining elements of the array Paragraphs, they're mistakenly trying to reference Parapraphs.

8 Change each of the incorrect 'p' characters to a 'g,' save your file, and then test once again.

Everything should work! Amazingly, this bug is not a work of fiction; it actually occurred during the preparation of this chapter. Spelling errors and other small mistakes can quickly propagate, especially if they are copied and pasted around a document. Using the Debugger panel however, to track down the problem is relatively simple.

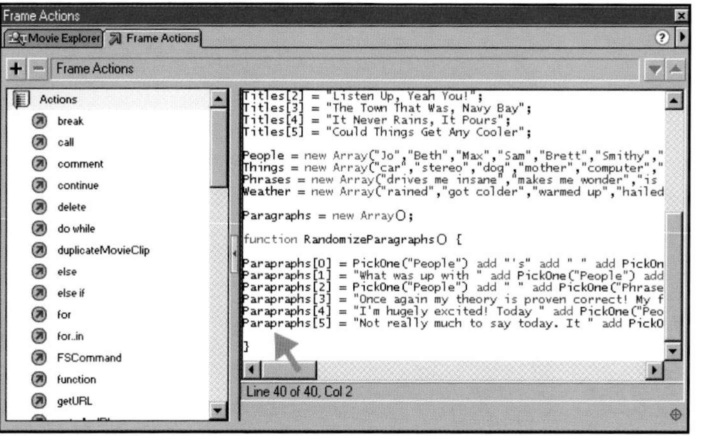

Use the Debugger to help you find the root of the problem—a misspelling in the code.

How It Works

These techniques build on work completed during Chapter 3 and incorporate a broad range of Flash and ActionScript features. In a nutshell, Megan's Diary is an entertainment application that presents a fictionalized set of information driven by a calendar control.

The calendar itself is a Smart Clip and is configured to produce an ActionScript Date object any time a date field is click, and then to pass that object to the function **GetDiaryEntry()**. The purpose of **GetDiaryEntry()** is to set the contents of the text field **DiaryEntry**, which it does by randomly selecting pieces of text, assembling them into sentences, and then displaying the result in the **DiaryEntry** text field.

The ActionScript for assembling the **DiaryEntry** contents is stored in an external text file named GetDiaryEntry.as. External files can be substituted for regularly entered ActionScript using the **#include** directive. The actual data used to compose the diary entries is stored in a series of arrays on the main Timeline. A custom function called **PickOne()** determines the length of any array it is given to work with and then uses **random()** to select any of the elements in that array. So, from the list of people's names that appear in the fictional diary, a random name can be chosen and included each time—which allows the stories to change even though the basic structure is the same.

NAVY BAY ENTERTAINMENT

Chapter 1

Chapter 2

Chapter 3

Chapter 4

"Listen good Todd, it's either education or elimination."

—BIG MAMA, IN DISNEY'S THE FOX AND THE HOUND (1981)

FISHSTIK EDUCATIONAL SOFTWARE

Even from the early days of the Web, the Internet has always been largely about accessible information. When the Web's bandwidth began to support entertainment as well, it was only natural to combine entertainment and information to create educational games. Educational games add a new layer of value to online entertainment by infusing real value to the entertainment experience. Not only are players amused, but also they often learn something in the bargain. Furthermore, the Web affords a bigger classroom and more advanced dynamics, such as the ability to monitor trends in individual scores and even how long it takes students to answer questions or complete a given challenge.

The FishStick Educational Software section of this book explores invaluable techniques such as randomizing arrays, working with keyboard input, implementing basic game setup, working with trigonometry in Flash, using collision detection, and setting up custom cursors.

5

WORKING WITH ARRAYS

By Jennifer S. Hall

This chapter demonstrates the use of the new Flash 5 array methods. Arrays are used to store related information that is used later in the program. All the related information is stored in an array, and the programmer needs to remember only the name of the array instead of the names of all the different variables.

The project in this chapter features a simple game of "select which one matches." A question is written *and* spoken, and the player chooses the correct one of four answer choices. The project illustrates several techniques involved in using arrays: loading an array while defining it, loading an array after it is defined, using one- and two-dimensional arrays, and randomizing arrays. For example, you use arrays to store *x* and *y* coordinates for Movie Clip placement later. You could use a variable for each stored coordinate (***Place1x***, ***Place1y***), or you could create an array (***Place1***) and put the *x* coordinate in index 1 (***Place1[1]***) and the *y* coordinate in index 2 (***Place1[2]***). The ***Place1*** array just described is a one-dimensional array.

A two-dimensional array stores information that has two items that need to be saved for each variable, such as rows and columns. Instead of using the one-dimensional ***Place1*** array, you can use a two-dimensional array named ***Place***. You can have Flash store the ***Place1*** *x* coordinates in ***Place[1][1]*** and the *y* coordinates in ***Place[1][2]***. (The first number in square brackets is the place's number (1), and the second number in square brackets is the *x* or *y* coordinate number.)

Positioning One- and Two-Dimensional Arrays

In this section, you create arrays to hold the *x* and *y* coordinates. You need to know the coordinates for the four choices, the question, and the talking man, and you create an array for each.

1 Open Select_Start.fla, which contains all the placed and named movies and graphics, and save it to your hard drive. (If you want to see the finished file, open Select_Final.fla.)

2 To open the **Init** code found in the Code layer, select the frame titled Init, open the pull-down menu at the top, and select Window > Actions.

This will allow you to view and edit the **Init** code. Notice the code already there. The sounds (**CorrectSound** and **InCorrectSound**) and some variables for the choice definitions (***Picture1-4***) are initialized. Notice too that the placeholders for the question and the choices (***PlaceHolderQuestion*** and ***Place1-4***) have their visibility set to false so they will be invisible when the program starts.

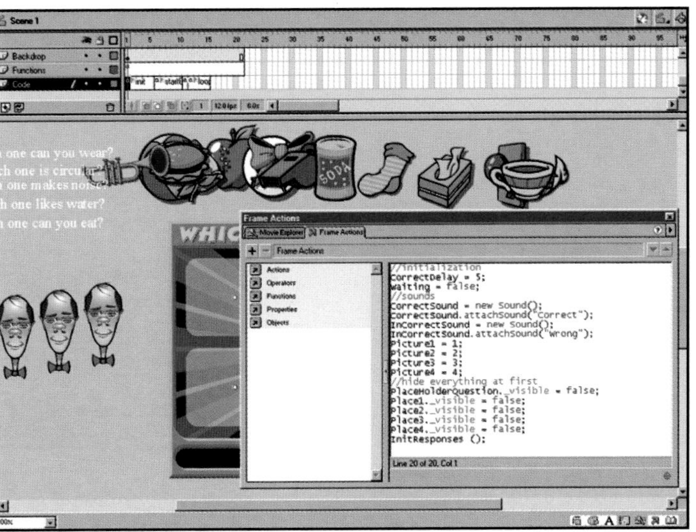

Take a moment to inspect the pre-existing code.

3 At the bottom of the **Init** code, add this code (you'll probably find it easiest to add if you use Expert Mode—Ctrl+E):

The following code creates a new array (**QuestionXY**):

```
QuestionXY = new Array();
```

This code loads the new array with the current *x* and *y* coordinates of the PlaceHolderQuestion movie clip.

```
QuestionXY[1] = PlaceHolderQuestion._x;
QuestionXY[2] = PlaceHolderQuestion._y;
```

```
// store places for questions
QuestionXY = new Array();
QuestionXY[1] = PlaceHolderQuestion._x;
QuestionXY[2] = PlaceHolderQuestion._y;
// store places for Audio man
TalkingManXY = new Array();
TalkingManXY[1] = TalkingMan._x;
TalkingManXY[2] = TalkingMan._y;
```

Add these arrays to the bottom of the **Init** code on the Code layer.

Flash uses this code later to place the appropriate written question in the appropriate place on the stage.

The following code creates a new array (**TalkingManXY**):

```
TalkingManXY = new Array();
```

This code loads the new array with the current *x* and *y* coordinates of the TalkingMan movie clip, which contains the audio for the question synched with mouth movements.

```
TalkingManXY[1] = TalkingMan._x;
TalkingManXY[2] = TalkingMan._y;
```

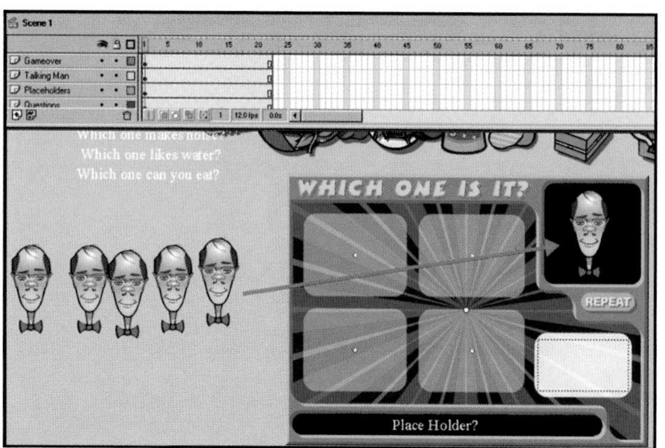

The code records the position of the TalkingMan movie clip so that the other TalkingMan movie clips will be in the correct position when swapped in during game play.

4 Add this code to **Init**:

This code creates a new array for each space in which an answer is going to appear (**AreaXY1,2,3,4**).

```
AreaXY1 = new Array();
```

This code loads the new arrays with the current *x* and *y* coordinates of the appropriate **Place1(2,3,4)** movie clip. The following line of code tells Flash to save the *x* coordinate for **Place1** (where answer 1 will be on the stage) in index 1 of the array **AreaXY1**.

```
AreaXY1[1] = Place1._x;
```

All the arrays created so far have been one-dimensional arrays. Now you will create a two-dimensional array. Then you can find any of the answer positions, but you have to reference only one array.

```
// arrays for items
AreaXY1 = new Array();
AreaXY1[1] = Place1._x;
AreaXY1[2] = Place1._y;
AreaXY2 = new Array();
AreaXY2[1] = Place2._x;
AreaXY2[2] = Place2._y;
AreaXY3 = new Array();
AreaXY3[1] = Place3._x;
AreaXY3[2] = Place3._y;
AreaXY4 = new Array();
AreaXY4[1] = Place4._x;
AreaXY4[2] = Place4._y;
```

Add these arrays to the **Init** code. This code positions the four selectable objects for the Activity.

5 Add this two-dimensional array to **Init**:

This code loads each of the arrays you just created for the answer's *x* and *y* coordinates into the **AreaXYArray** array. This makes it very easy to reference. If you want to find the *y* coordinate for answer 3, you simply use **AreaXYArray[3][2]**. The first number is the answer number, and the second number is the *x* or *y* coordinate.

```
// array to hold all the positions
AreaXYArray = new Array();
AreaXYArray[1] = AreaXY1;
AreaXYArray[2] = AreaXY2;
AreaXYArray[3] = AreaXY3;
AreaXYArray[4] = AreaXY4;
```

Add this array to the **Init** code. This code makes it easier to reference the coordinates of all the objects.

Creating Question and Answer Arrays

You currently have arrays that tell Flash where to put the information; now you need arrays that contain the information. Arrays are used here as a simple way of keeping track of a list of items—in this case, the question and matching answer, as well as the red herring answers.

1 Create a function called **InitQuestionArray** at the top of the function code on the Function layer.

This function will initialize the question and answer arrays. The functions are located in the Functions layer. You will not create all the functions that are used in this program; some of them are already created and are in the Functions layer. The function you've just created does nothing yet.

```
// Initialize the question and answer arrays
function InitQuestionArray () {
}
```

Initialize the **InitQuestionArray** function.

2 Add this code within the curly brackets of the **InitQuestionArray** function:

This code defines a new **Questions** array to hold the questions and fills it with the key question word. The movie clips containing both the written and audio questions are named with this key question word, so you can keep track of the questions for both written and audio in one array. For example, WearQuestion is the Instance name of the movie clip for the written portion, and Wearman is the Instance name of the movie clip for the audio portion for the question, "Which one do you wear?"

```
// questions array
Questions = new Array();
Questions[1] = "Wear";
Questions[2] = "Eat";
Questions[3] = "Water";
Questions[4] = "Noise";
Questions[5] = "Circular";
```

Create an array for each question.

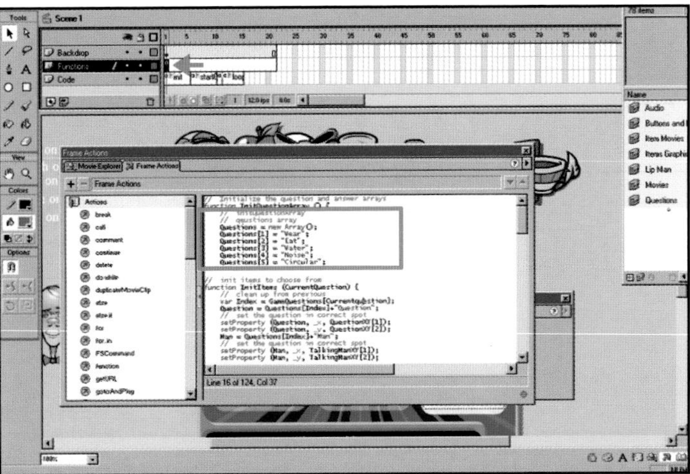

Add the **Questions** array to the code on the Functions layer within the **InitQuestionArray()** function.

3 Add this code below the previous code but still within the brackets of the **InitQuestionArray** function:

Each question has two possible answers, so the array for the answers must be a two-dimensional array. The index for the **Answers** array must correspond to the index in the **Questions** array. In other words, the question and the appropriate answer must be located in the same place in the two arrays. For example, the question about what to eat is in index 2 in the **Questions** array, so the answer must be in index 2 in the **Answers** array. Also notice the array called **TempAnswers**. This array defines the array and loads it at the same time.

```
var TempAnswers = new Array("Trumpet", "Whistle");
```

This two-dimensional array is used only in this function and only to fill the **Answers** array.

```
// answers array order dependent
// index must match questions array above
Answers = new Array();
// wear
var TempAnswers = new Array("Sock", "Ribbon");
Answers[1] = TempAnswers;
// eat
var TempAnswers = new Array("Hamburger", "Apple");
Answers[2] = TempAnswers;
// water
var TempAnswers = new Array("Flower", "Fish");
Answers[3] = TempAnswers;
// noise
var TempAnswers = new Array("Trumpet", "Whistle");
Answers[4] = TempAnswers;
// circular
var TempAnswers = new Array("Baseball", "Beachball");
Answers[5] = TempAnswers;
```

Add this array to specify which objects answer each question. There are two correct answers or objects for each question.

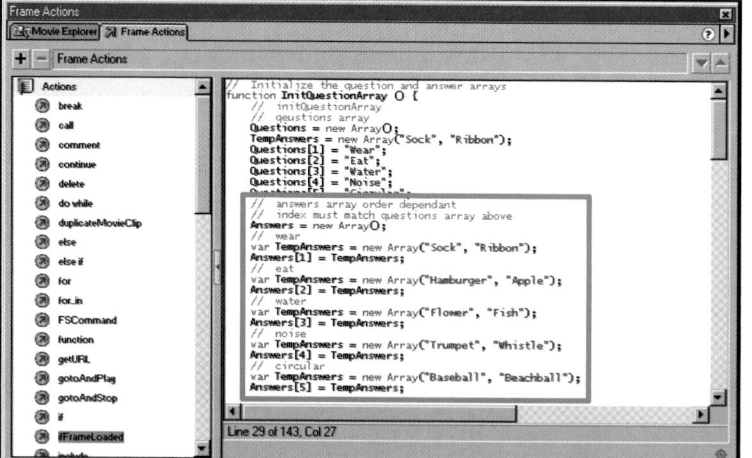

The array of **match questions** is added to the **InitQuestionArray()** function.

4 Add the red herring answers, placing them inside the bracket at the end of the **InitQuestionArray** function.

These are all the possible items to choose from, including the answers. The game can use the answers from one question as red herring answers for another question. The names, such as **Cup** and **Doorknob**, are also the names of the movie clips that have the actual items or graphics in them.

```
Items = new Array();
Items[1] = "Cup";
Items[2] = "Doorknob";
Items[3] = "Feather";
Items[4] = "Tissue";
Items[5] = "Ribbon";
Items[6] = "Sock";
Items[7] = "Flower";
Items[8] = "Fish";
Items[9] = "Baseball";
Items[10] = "Beachball";
Items[11] = "Apple";
Items[12] = "Hamburger";
Items[13] = "Trumpet";
Items[14] = "Whistle";
Items[15] = "Soda";
```

Add this array to specify a series of red herring objects.

> **Note:** You have created the entire function, which needs to be called only once at the start of the program. The information set up in the function does not change, no matter how many times the player repeats the game.

5 Add this code to the end of the **Init** code:

First the code calls the function **InitQuestionArray()**, which sets up the questions, answers, and red herrings, or items. Then the code determines the number of questions and choices of items by using the length of the arrays. You need to subtract 1 from the length because you started the arrays at index 1, but the array object assumes they start at index 0. This is standard JavaScript code indexing. All arrays start at 0 unless specified otherwise. Please note that you can create an array and start it anywhere within the index, but the Length method for this object assumes index 0.

```
InitQuestionArray();
NumberItems = Items.length - 1;
NumberQuestions = Answers.length - 1;
```

Add this code to the **Init** code, which is on the frame labeled Init on the Code layer.

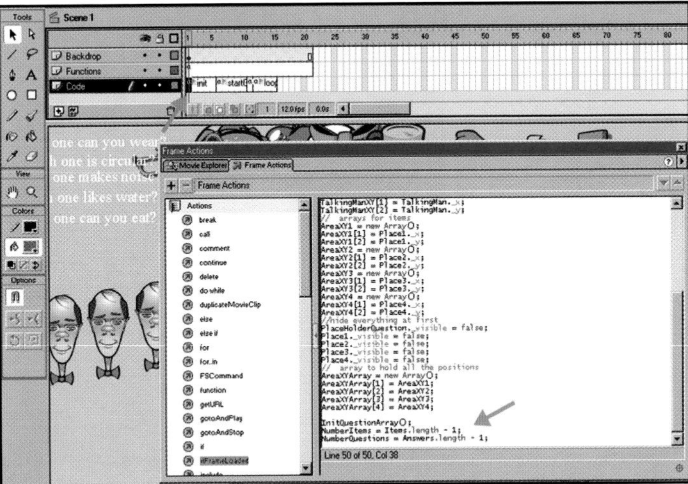

Return to the frame labeled Init on the Code layer, and then add the lines to the bottom as shown.

Randomizing an Array

You could use the game just as it is to this point, but the questions would always appear in the same order. In this section, you create a randomization function to randomize the **Questions** array.

1 Use this code to create a function in the **Functions** code called **InitQuestions**:

This code will randomize the questions each time the game is played.

```
function InitQuestions () {
}
```

Initiate the **InitQuestions()** function within the code on the Functions layer.

2 Add this code within the function:

The **GameQuestions** array is the array used to hold the order of the questions each time a visitor plays the game. Because the questions and corresponding answers have the same index (you made sure of that), you only need to store the indexes and then randomize the indexes. The ***TempQArray*** variable is used to hold these indexes to start with and to make sure no question is duplicated. ***TempQArray*** is loaded in the **for** loop. You use the ***QuestionsLeft*** variable as a counter, which also ensures that you don't duplicate questions.

The **for** loop is a way to do loops and counters that is new to Flash 5. This is standard JavaScript. It is a counting loop that continues until a condition is met. The **for** loop allows for an initialization of a counter, the test for when to finish, and the increment of the counter. A semi-colon (;) divides each section.

```
for (var Count = 0; Count<=NumberQuestions; Count++) {
```

```
GameQuestions = new Array();
var TempQArray = new Array();
for (var Count = 0; Count<=NumberQuestions; Count++) {
    TempQArray[Count] = Count;
}
var QuestionsLeft = NumberQuestions;
```

Add the array, the **for** loop, and variables to the **InitQuestions()** function.

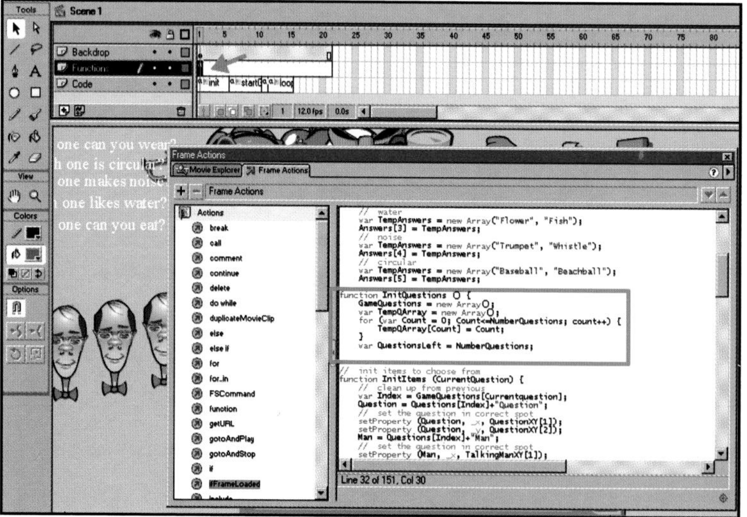

Return to the Functions layer code to enter the **InitQuestions()** function.

Notice in this **for** loop that the initialization of the counter ***Count*** is set to 0. This happens only the first time in the loop. The loop continues as long as ***Count*** is less than or equal to the number of questions (***NumberQuestions***). Each time this loop is executed, the ***Count*** is incremented by one (***Count++***). This is the same as the following code:

```
var Count = 0;
while(Count<=NumberQuestions)
{
        Count = Count + 1;
}
```

This figure shows the same question (Which one can you eat?) with four different random arrays of possible answers. The order of questions is also random.

3 Add this code within the function and below the previous code:

This code randomizes the questions. Remember that you are really randomizing only the indexes. The code loops until ***Count*** is equal to ***NumberQuestions***. You use the ***QuestionsLeft*** to generate the random number (***QuestionPlace***).

```
var QuestionPlace = random(QuestionsLeft)+1;
```

This index (***QuestionPlace***) is used to access the ***TempQArray*** and place what is in ***TempQArray*** in the **GameQuestion** array at index ***Count***.

```
GameQuestions[Count] = TempQArray[QuestionPlace];
```

```
    for (var Count = 1; Count<=NumberQuestions; Count++) {
        var QuestionPlace = random(QuestionsLeft)+1;
        GameQuestions[Count] = TempQArray[QuestionPlace];
        if (QuestionPlace<>QuestionsLeft) {
            TempQArray[QuestionPlace] = TempQArray[QuestionsLeft];
        }
        QuestionsLeft = QuestionsLeft-1;
    }
}
```

Add this code, which is responsible for randomizing the questions to the **InitQuestions()** function.

The last item in the ***TempQArray*** is moved into the place you just used. Therefore, the ***TempQArray*** is always getting smaller and adjusting for already used items, and there is no duplication.

```
TempQArray[QuestionPlace] =
➥TempQArray[QuestionsLeft];
```

(The ➥ symbol you see here is for editorial purposes only.)

Each loop through subtracts 1 from the ***QuestionsLeft*** variable.

```
QuestionsLeft = QuestionsLeft-1;
```

When the loop is finished, the **GameQuestion** array has a randomized list of numbers ranging from 1 to the total number of questions.

You have created a function to randomize the questions. Now you need to call it each time the game is started or restarted.

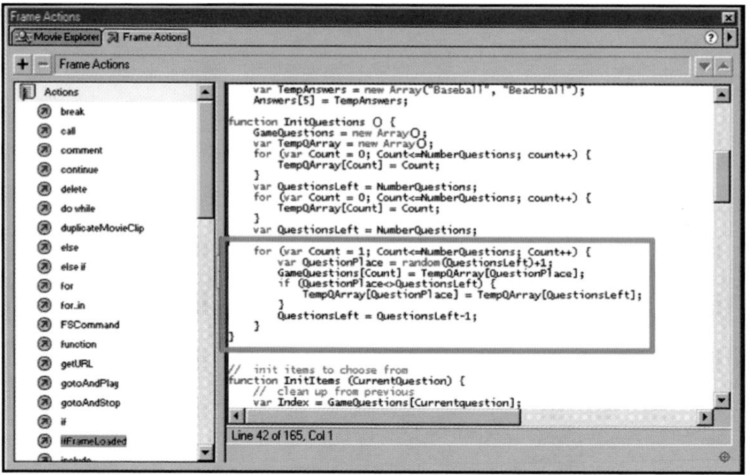

Complete the **InitQuestions()** function as shown.

4 Add this code in the StartGame frame before the **InitItems** function call:

```
InitQuestions();
```

Add a call to the **InitQuestions()** function to the frame labeled StartGame on the Code layer.

The **InitQuestions** function is the function you just created that randomizes the questions. This needs to happen before the game starts. So you place the call to the function before **InitItems**, which is the function that starts the answer choices.

5 Test the game.

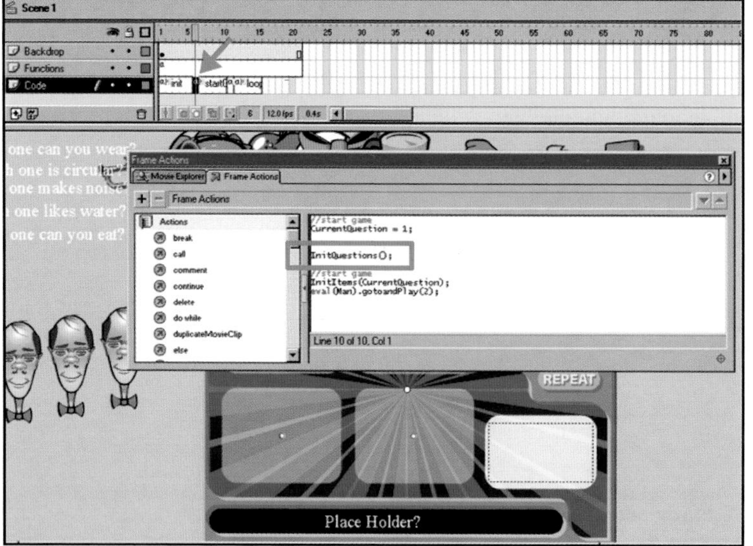

Insert a call to the **InitQuestions()** function on the StartGame frame located on the Code layer.

How It Works

As you can tell from the code you've entered, this simple "which is it" game is not so simple to code. Naming the movie clips consistently during the setup of this game is very important. The written question movie clips are named WearQuestion, EatQuestion, and so on, and the audio question movie clips are named WearMan, EatMan, and so on. This way the key word (Wear, Eat, and so on) can be used to access each of the appropriate movie clips. Also remember that the key word was loaded in the **Questions** array.

The movie clips for the items to choose from are simply named the same name as the item, and you stored the names in the **Items** array.

```
Items = new Array();
    Items[1] = "Cup";
    Items[2] = "Doorknob";
```

In the initialization section, you set up the arrays with the names of the questions, answers, and items. This code to initialize the sounds to play for correct and incorrect selections was already set up:

```
CorrectSound = new Sound();
CorrectSound.attachSound("Correct");
InCorrectSound = new Sound();
InCorrectSound.attachSound("Wrong");
```

This code to initialize the written response in the ***InitResponses*** function also was already set up:

```
CorrectResponseArray = new Array();
    CorrectResponseArray[0] = "You are so smart!";
    InCorrectResponseArray = new Array();
    InCorrectResponseArray[0] = "Duh!";
```

When all the game setup is done, the movie progresses to the StartGame frame. The game is designed to be played over and over again with a different order of questions and different answer selections each time. To create a randomized order of questions, you created the **InitQuestions** function, starting at the beginning of the list of questions.

Then **InitItems** is called, which determines the placement of a correct answer and the other three choices. Remember the question has two possible correct answers, so **InitItems** chooses one and places it randomly in the four answer areas.

One of several randomly chosen affirmative responses is displayed when the player selects the correct answer.

```
var AnswerPlace = random(2);
Answer = Answers[Index][AnswerPlace];
AnswerPosition = random(4)+1;
```

InitItems also makes sure the other possible answer to this question doesn't show up.

```
if (AnswerPlace == 0) {
        var AnswerDont = Answers[Index][1];
    } else {
        var AnswerDont = Answers[Index][0];
    }
```

InitItems then places the appropriate written and audio question. Finally, the audio question is started with this code:

```
eval(Man).gotoandPlay(2);
```

When the question is displayed, Flash goes into a frame loop until the user selects the correct answer. The loop goes from the Play frame to the Loop frame and back to Play. Play does nothing while the user is selecting an answer. The only action in the loop is to go to the Play frame, as shown in this code:

```
gotoAndPlay ("Play");
```

When the visitor plays the game, the answer choices are displayed: The visitor hears the question and sees the question. The visitor can click the Repeat button to hear the question again. If the visitor selects the wrong item, this action occurs:

```
InCorrectSound.start();
    Response = InCorrectResponseArray[random(5)];
```

InCorrectSound plays, and a randomly selected "incorrect" response is displayed in the text feedback. When the visitor selects the correct item, this action occurs:

```
// correct
    InCorrectSound.stop();
    CorrectSound.start();
    Response = CorrectResponseArray[random(5)];
    Waiting = true;
    StartWait = getTimer();
```

The **CorrectSound** plays, and a randomly selected "correct" response is displayed in the text feedback. After the user selects the correct answer, there is a time delay of five seconds to give the visitor time to read the response.

Each question has a corresponding character that is "lip synched" to an audio track. The key to lip synching in Flash is to set the Sync option to Stream in the Sound panel. This will force the Flash Player to do its best to keep the audio in sync with the playback of the animation.

The bald man character appears to mouth out the question as the player hears the question.

This delay is created by the **Waiting** flag. The **Waiting** flag is set to true. The **StartWait** timer is started when the user selects the correct answer, and Flash continues to loop between playing and looping until five seconds have passed. The **Waiting** flag disables each of the answer choices while the visitor is waiting for the next question.

As soon as the five-second waiting period is over, Flash cleans up everything and gets ready for a new question. This code moves the question and answer choices off the Stage and clears the text response box:

```
var cleanup = -200;
    setProperty (Picture1, _x, cleanup);
    setProperty (Picture2, _x, cleanup);
    setProperty (Picture3, _x, cleanup);
    setProperty (Answer, _x, cleanup);
    setProperty (Question, _x, cleanup);
    setProperty (Man, _x, cleanup);
    Response = "";
```

This code then displays the next question and starts the answering process:

```
InitItems(CurrentQuestion);
    eval(Man).gotoandPlay(2);
```

When the last question is answered correctly, Flash asks the visitor to play again using a full screen movie clip (Final Movie). If the visitor chooses to play again, this code causes Flash to go back to the StartGame frame and start the process again:

```
_root.cleanup( );
_root.gotoandPlay("startGame");
```

After the correct answer is selected a positive message is displayed for a short time, and then the question and answers are automatically reset.

6

HANDLING KEYBOARD INPUT

By Jennifer S. Hall

The Letters game is a typing game with a twist. The player must catch (type) each letter as it falls down the screen, before it reaches the bottom. There are three invisible clues at the bottom of the screen. As each letter is captured, if it belongs to one of the clues, that letter is made visible. At the end of the allotted time, the player is asked a question. Only the letters that the player has captured show up as clues. If the player selects the correct answer, she can advance to the next level. There are two levels with different speeds of letter dropping.

The techniques this game showcases are capturing keys typed on the keyboard and then processing the key captures.

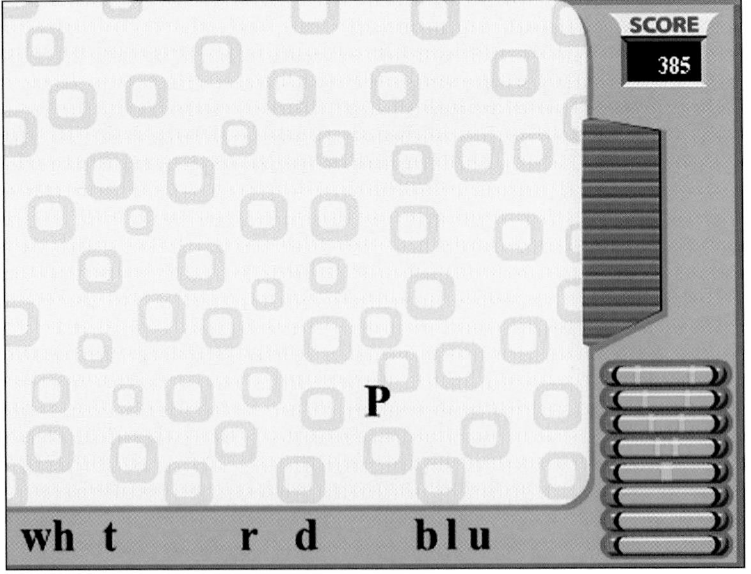

Placing the Letters

In this section, you set up the Letters layer that holds the lower- and uppercase letters used in the game. The letters need to be placed off Stage so the player doesn't see them until they drop down. Because they are moving, they cannot be simple graphics. Each letter has to be a movie clip.

1. Open Letters_Start.fla located in the Chapter 06 folder on the companion CD, save the file to your local hard drive, and remember to save periodically as you work through this technique. (If you want to see the finished file, open Letters_Final.fla.)

   Letters_Start.fla contains all the art and most of the ActionScript used in the game. Notice the layer named Letters that already contains all the lower- and uppercase letters except a, b, and c.

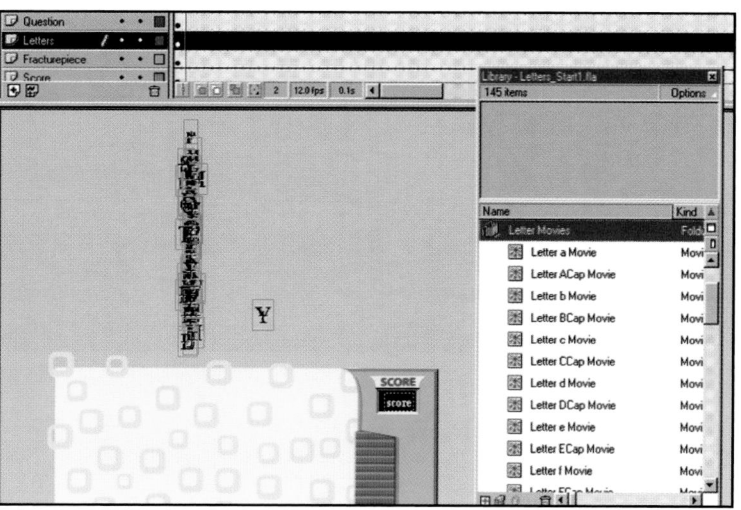

Position the movie clips off the Stage area.

2. Open the Library folder named Letter Movies, which has movies for both the lower- and the uppercase letters. Make sure the Letters layer is selected and select the following movie clips: Letter a Movie, Letter b Movie, Letter c Movie, Letter ACap Movie, Letter BCap Movie, and Letter CCap Movie. Drag the movies into the Stage area but not onto the Stage. Place them off the Stage in a group with the other letters.

   In the next few steps, you use the Movie Explorer (a new feature) to name each movie clip instance so you can refer to it in the ActionScript.

3. Make sure the Movie Explorer window is open. (To access it, choose Window > Movie Explorer.) The Movie Explorer window has a tab for the Movie Explorer and for the Object Actions. Make sure the Movie Explorer tab is selected.

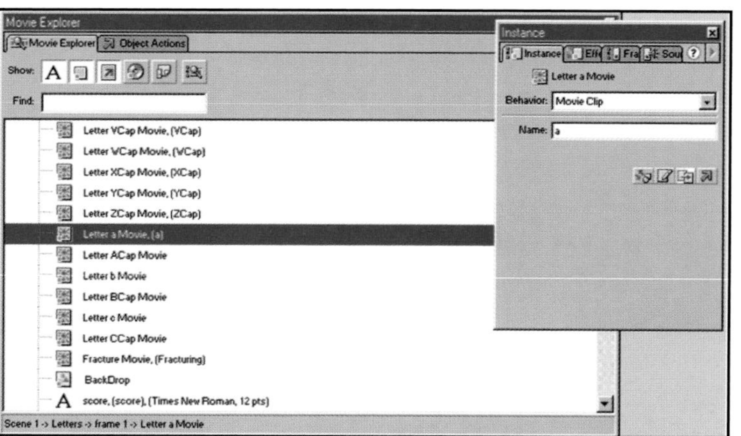

Select the Movie Explorer tab within the Movie Explorer panel.

4 In the Movie Explorer, select the Letter a Movie you just placed on the Stage and then, using the Instance panel, name it **A**. Repeat this process with Letter b Movie and Letter c Movie.

5 Select Letter ACap Movie and name it **Acap**. Then repeat this process with Letter BCap Movie and Letter CCap Movie.

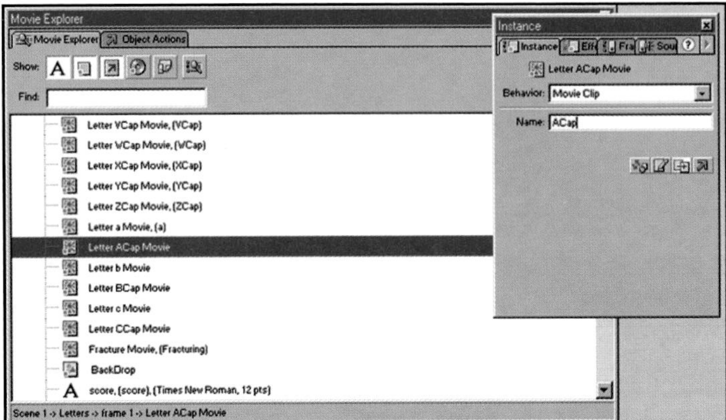

Use the Movie Explorer and the Instance panel to name the Letter xCap movie clips.

Creating the Key Captures for All the Letters

One way to set up a Key Capture is to use a button that isn't visible to the player. The layer called Letter Capture has two round green buttons at the upper-right, just off the Stage. One button captures the lowercase letters, and the other captures the uppercase letters.

Instead of using an **on release** call (for a mouse release) with these buttons, you use an **on keyPress** call. The key-capturing ActionScript must establish which key has been pressed and whether the letter pressed is the falling letter. If the key the visitor presses is the correct letter, the code hides the letter. If the key the visitor presses is the wrong letter, the code ignores the key press. You could create ActionScript for this entire process inside the **on keyPress** brackets and repeat it for every lower- and uppercase letter, but an easier, more efficient method is to create a function called **letterPressed** that does the processing and calls the function from within the on **KeyPress** brackets.

1 Select one of the round buttons in the Letter Capture layer, open the Object Actions window, and notice the code attached to the button. You want to work with the lowercase buttons first, so make sure the code at the top looks like the code in this figure:

Again, make sure you're not working with the code for the uppercase letters.

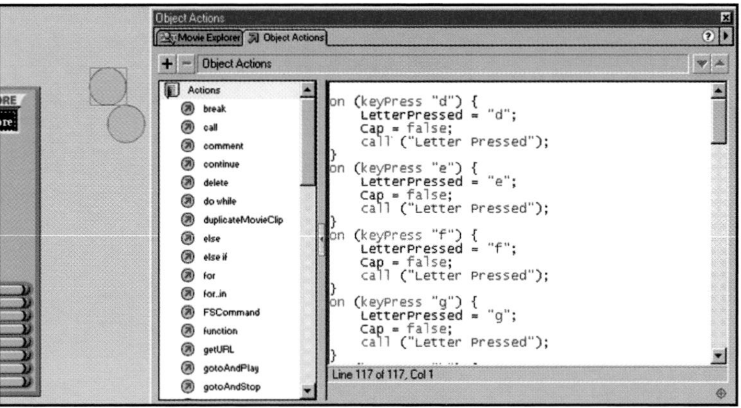

Select the round light green button that has the **keyPress** code for lowercase letters.

2 Within Basic Actions and at the top of the existing code, double-click **OnMouse** Event to insert an ActionScript for the Key Capture, deselect Release (the default), select KeyPress, and type **a** in the box next to KeyPress.

Any script within the brackets associated with the **KeyPress OnMouse** Event will be executed when the player presses the letter a.

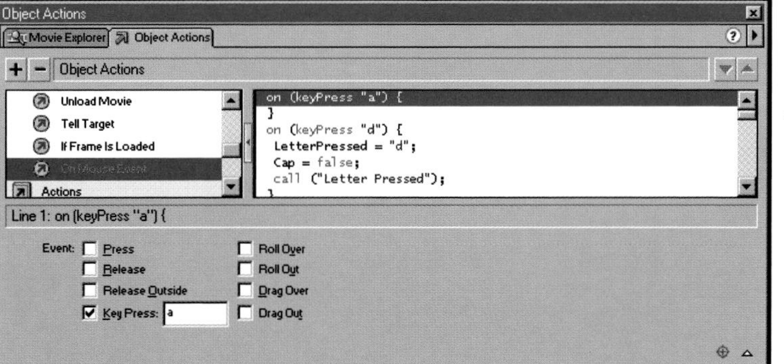

Use the Object Actions window in Normal mode to select **OnMouse** Event from Basic Actions.

3 Within the brackets, set the variable ***LetterPressed* = "a"** and set the variable ***Cap*** to **false** so that **LetterPressed** knows whether the letter is upper- or lowercase. Then call the function **LetterPressed**. Your code should look like this:

```
on (keyPress "a") {
    LetterPressed = "a";
    Cap = false;
    call ("Letter Pressed");
}
```

Enter this **keyPress** code for the lowercase a.

The code within the brackets is executed only when the visitor presses the letter a. Don't confuse the variable ***LetterPressed*** with the call to the ActionScript Letter Pressed. The ActionScript Letter Pressed compares the variable ***LetterPressed*** with the active letter (which is the letter dropping down on the screen during the game). The variable ***LetterPressed*** simply stores information about which letter is being pressed at a given time.

4 Click the arrow in the upper-right corner of the Actions panel to display the pop-up menu, and choose Expert Mode to enter the additional code.

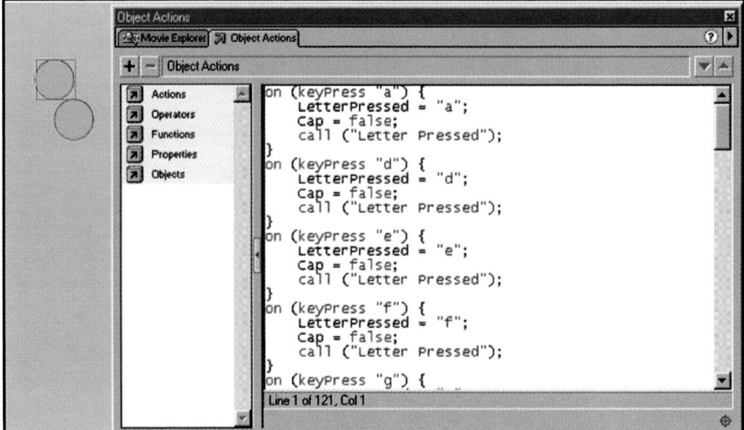

Switch to Expert Mode to enter the additional code.

5 Repeat steps 1 through 3 for the lowercase b and c, changing only the lowercase letter representing the key by using this code:

```
on (keyPress "b") {
  LetterPressed = "b";
  Cap = false;
  call ("Letter Pressed");
}......
on (keyPress "c") {
  LetterPressed = "c";
  Cap = false;
  call ("Letter Pressed");
}......
```

Enter this **keyPress** code for the lowercase b and c letters.

6 Repeat steps 1 through 4 for the capital letters A, B, and C, but use this ActionScript:

Notice that in the uppercase button, this line handles the uppercase A correctly:

```
on (keyPress "A") {
```

From then on, there is a designator for uppercase letters. This is because Flash is not case sensitive.

```
on (keyPress "A") {
   LetterPressed = "ACap";
   Cap = true;
   call ("Letter Pressed");
}
on (keyPress "B") {
   LetterPressed = "BCap";
   Cap = true;
   call ("Letter Pressed");
}.....
on (keyPress "C") {
   LetterPressed = "CCap";
   Cap = true;
   call ("Letter Pressed");
}.....
```

Enter this **keyPress** code for the uppercase A, B, and C.

Creating a Lookup Array

You now have a way to capture the letters, but you need to set them up to randomly fall down the screen. Flash has a **random** function for numbers. If you put the letters in an array, you can use the array to randomize the order in which the letters appear simply by randomizing on the total number of letters in the array. You use the new Flash 5 Array object to accomplish this.

1 Create a key frame on the Code layer and label the frame **ArrayLetters**.

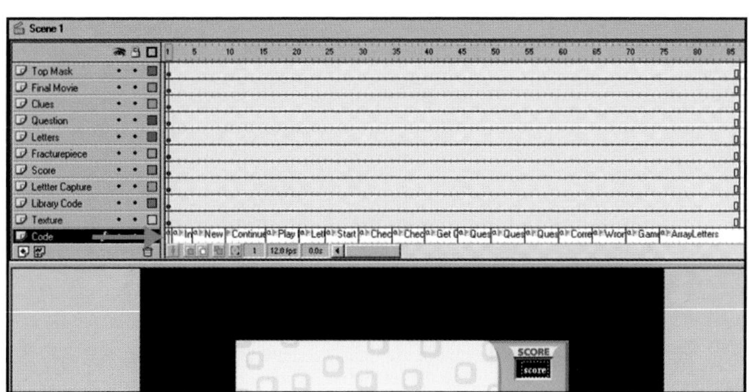

Place the new ArrayLetters frame on the Code layer, along with several keyframes that have pre-existing code.

2 In the Object Actions window, create a new array using this code:

```
LetterLookUp = new Array();
```

Enter this code to create the array that plays a role in randomizing the order of the falling letters.

This creates an empty array called **LetterLookUp**. Next you fill it with the letters.

3 On a new line that follows the code you just created, insert this code for each lower- and uppercase letter:

```
LetterLookUp [1] = "a";
LetterLookUp [2] = "b";
LetterLookUp [3] = "c";
LetterLookUp [4] = "d";
.
.
.
LetterLookUp [27] = "ACap";
LetterLookUp [28] = "BCap";
LetterLookUp [29] = "CCap";
.
.
.
```

Populate the **LetterLookUp** array with this code. (Note that not all lines of code have been printed here.)

> **Note:** None of the code you're adding should be inside the parentheses in **NewArray()**.

The letters do not need to be in any specific order, but all the letters need to be there, and each must have a unique indexed number. You will end up with an array of 52 letters indexed to specific numbers from 1 to 52. For example, to place the letter a in the LetterLookUp array at index 1, use this line of code:

```
LetterLookUp[1] = "a";
```

4 Place a call to **ArrayLetters** in the **Init** code right before the call to **NewGame**.

```
call("ArrayLetters");
gotoAndPlay ("NewGame");
```

Use this code to initialize the Letters array.

This calls **ArrayLetters** (the code you just wrote) to initialize the letters array.

5 Save the file and play it.

How It Works

In this section, you looked briefly at the pre-existing code to give you an idea of how the code you just entered relates to it. The movie is laid out in several different layers:

- The Final layer holds the Final movie clip.
- The Clues layer holds the clue letters that show up at the bottom of the screen (not covered in this technique).
- The Question layer contains the Question movie clip (not covered in this technique).

- The Letters layer holds the letters that drift on the screen.
- The Fracturepiece layer contains the FracturePiece movie that breaks apart for each letter that's missed.
- The Score layer holds the score and other graphics.
- The Library Code layer containing the Library code.
- The Code layer contains most of the ActionScripts.

The Code layer is where you will find the ActionScripts. They are spanned out over five frames each for the sake of readability. They also could have all been included in a movie clip, or they could have been written as functions.

The **Init** code, shown in the figure, initializes variables that will be used later in the movie. The following code designates the ***ActiveLetter*** variable to be nothing and calls ArrayLetters to initialize the lookup table of letters. Then Init calls **NewGame**.

```
ActiveLetter = "none";
Clues = "cluesflag";
call ("Array Letters");
gotoAndPlay ("New Game");
```

This game has two levels, and the **NewGame** code is called each time a new level is reached. The code does not reset the score, but it does update the levels. It also starts the game timer, as instructed by this code:

```
GameStart = int(GetTimer()/1000);
```

With the call to **StartLetter**, ActionScript plays an important role. It drops the initial letter from the top, as shown here:

```
if (Level == 1) {
      Change = 20;
      call ("Start Letter");
} else if (Level >=2) {
      Change = 30;
      call ("Start Letter");
}
```

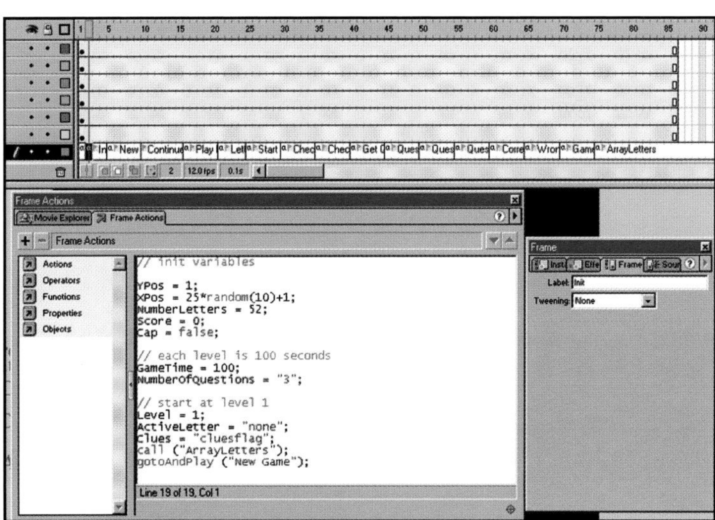

The frame labeled **Init** on the Code layer initializes several key variables.

StartLetter is called each time a new letter is needed. The following code randomly selects the letter.

```
var LetterNum = random(NumberLetters)+1;
Activeletter = LetterLookUp[LetterNum];
```

This code gives the letter a ***y*** starting position (off the Stage):

```
YPos1 = -10;
```

The following code gives the letter a random ***x*** position:

```
XPos = 25*(random(10)+1);
setProperty (ActiveLetter, _x, XPos);
setProperty (ActiveLetter, _y, YPos1);
```

The code then uses **gotoAndPlay** to call the **PlayLevel** script. ***ActiveLetter*** is the variable used to store the actual moving letter. This variable is used to compare with the key captures, as in this example:

```
gotoAndPlay ("Play Level");
```

The **PlayLevel** script, shown below and in the figure, is the guts of the letter capture process. It checks whether the game time is over.

```
CurrentTime = int(getTimer()/1000);
DiffTime = CurrentTime-GameStart;
// times up!!!
if (DiffTime>=GameTime) {
```

If the game time is up, the player gets a chance to play again. **PlayLevel** also moves the letter, using this code:

```
if (ActiveLetter<>"none") {
        YPos1 = YPos1+Change;
        if (YPos1>240) {
                LetterMissed = true;
        }
        setProperty (ActiveLetter, _y, YPos1);
```

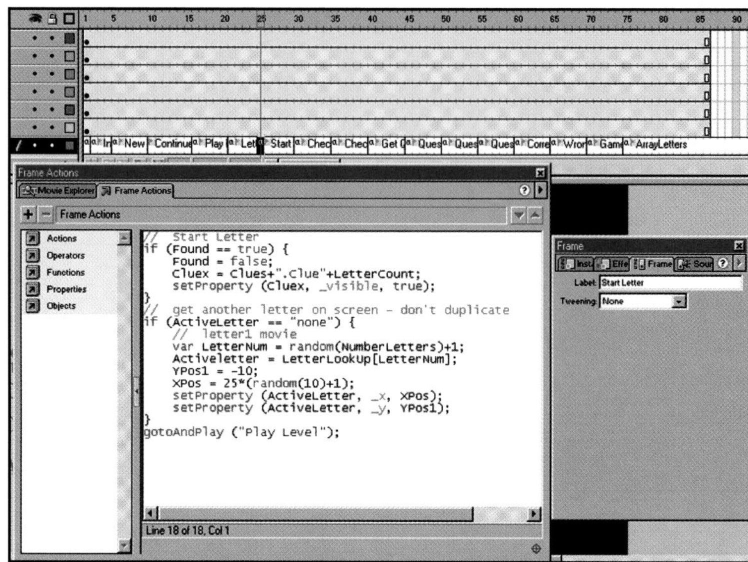

The code on the frame labeled StartLetter randomly positions each new letter.

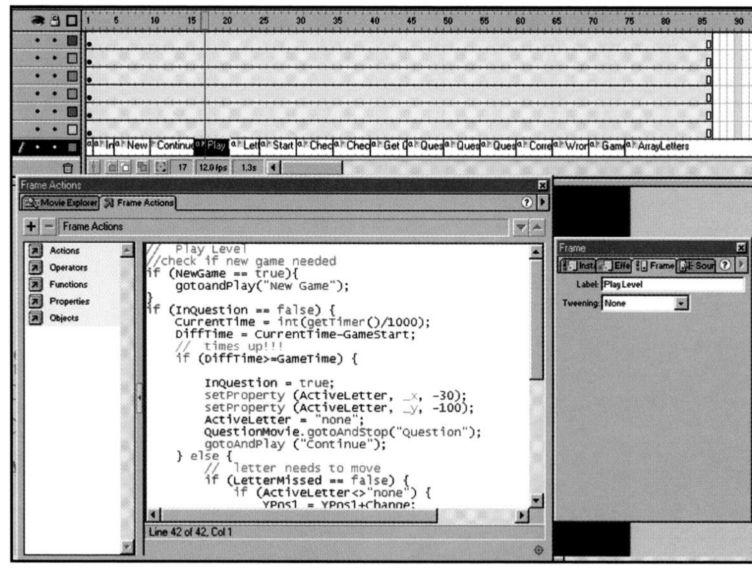

The code on the frame labeled PlayLevel contains the LetterCapture engine.

```
}
gotoAndPlay ("Continue");
```

PlayLevel then checks whether the letter is at the bottom of the screen (letter is missed). If a letter is missed, **StartLetter** is called. Otherwise, it loops around on itself, as shown in this code:

```
// missed letter - fell to bottom
if (ActiveLetter<>"none") {
        setProperty (ActiveLetter, _x, -30);
        setProperty (ActiveLetter, _y, -100);
        ActiveLetter = "none";
        Fracturing.nextframe();
        LetterMissed = false;
        call ("Start Letter");
```

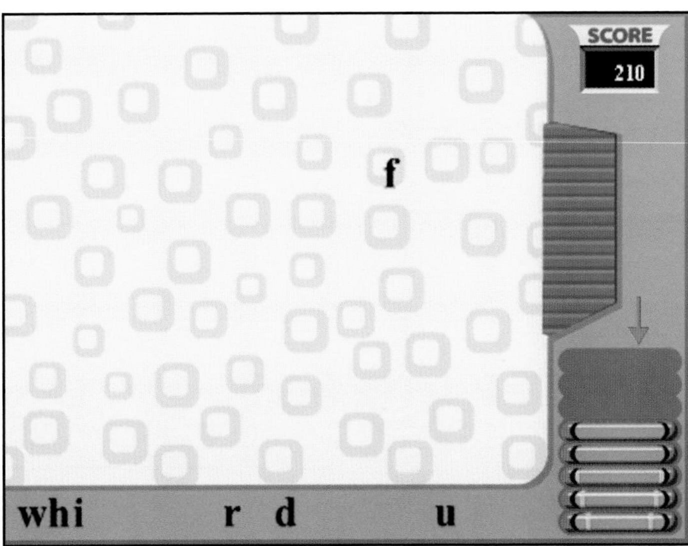

Every time the player misses a letter one of the "power cells" is removed. The player loses if all power cells are gone.

The **LetterPressed** code is called within the catch for the keyboard input. It compares the ***LetterPressed*** variable with the ***ActiveLetter*** variable:

```
if (ActiveLetter == LetterPressed) {
```

If the two are the same, the score is incremented by 5 points.

```
Score = Score+5;
```

It then checks to see if the letter is in one of the clue words.

```
if (Cap==true) {
        call ("Check Cap Clue Letter");
} else {
        call ("Check Clue Letter");
}
```

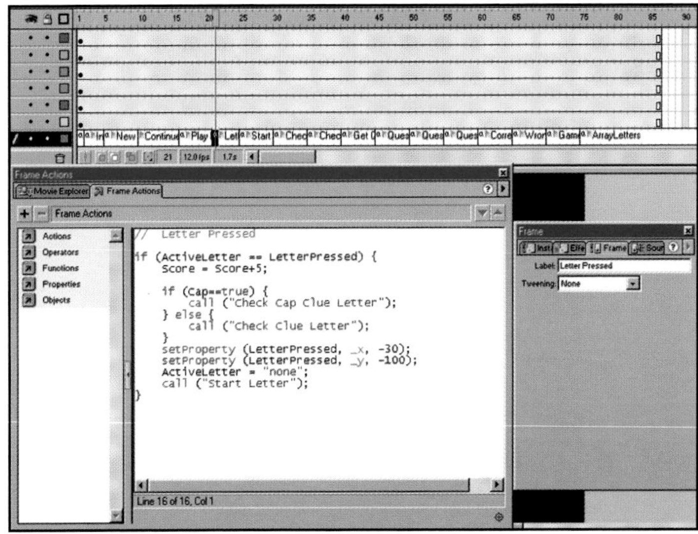

The code on the keyframe labeled LetterPressed compares the ***LetterPressed*** variable with the ***ActiveLetter*** variable.

It also stops the letter from drifting and places it off the stage.

```
setProperty (LetterPressed, _x, -30);
setProperty (LetterPressed, _y, -100);
```

Finally, it starts a new letter by calling **StartLetter**.

```
    ActiveLetter = "none";
    call ("Start Letter");
}
```

The rest of the code deals with the questions and clues that aren't covered in this technique.

> **Note:** The CD includes a Flash program called letters_3, which is the same game but has six levels and can drop up to three letters at one time.

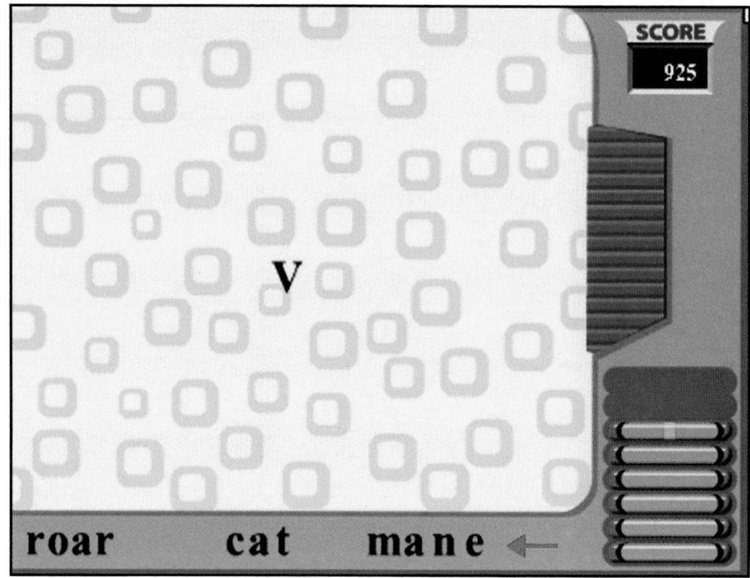

Letters that are typed correctly appear below as clues for the question at the end of each round.

USING A MODULAR APPROACH TO PROGRAMMING GAMES

By Samuel Wan

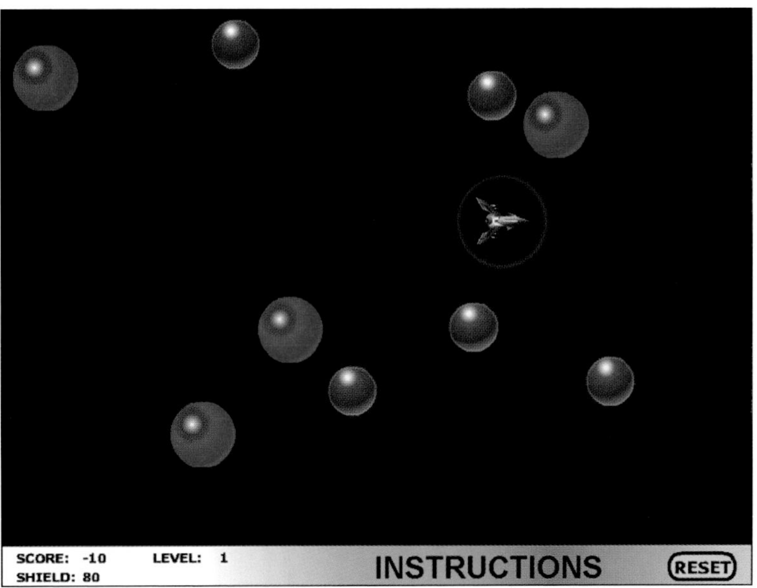

The Bubble Fighter uses many techniques, such as collision detection and trigonometry, that are often implemented in programming games and other types of interactive projects. Some of these techniques are interesting in their own right, but you should take a look at the overall structure to learn how to approach a complex project through modular programming.

Modular programming is a style of programming that allows you to break down a complex project into simple parts called "modules." By breaking down complicated projects into smaller parts, you can concentrate on building one module at a time instead of worrying about building a single giant system in one step. If something goes wrong, it's much easier to figure out which module isn't working properly and make the appropriate adjustments. Another advantage to modular programming is the ability to reuse different parts for future projects.

For Bubble Fighter, we've built four main movie clip modules, and each movie clip contains a complete set of ActionScript code, graphics, and animation needed to function independently:

- *Ship Module:* A spaceship flies around the screen, steered by the player who uses the arrow keys on the keyboard. The spaceship contains the hull of the ship, rocket thrusters, and a shield that sparks when hit by a blue bubble.

- *Bad Bubble Module:* Blue bubbles float around. If they hit the spaceship, they pop, reduce the spaceship's shields, and take a few points away from the score. Each time a bad bubble hits the ship, the bad bubble module checks the ship's shield. If the ship's shields reach zero, the player loses the game. The blue bubble contains a graphic that "pops."
- *Good Bubble Module:* Clear bubbles also float around. If they get hit by the ship, they pop and add points to the score. If the spaceship pops all the clear bubbles, a UFO appears. This also contains a "pop" graphic.

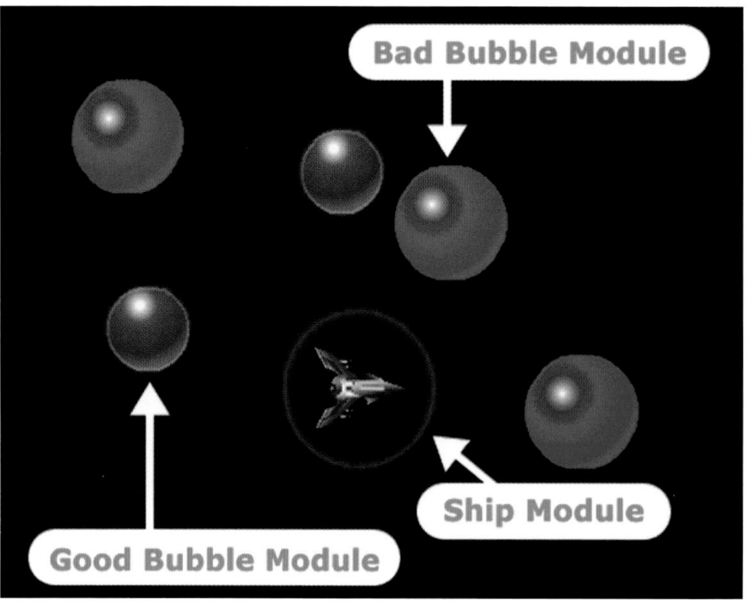

The Good Bubble Module, the Bad Bubble Module, and the Ship Module are the main elements for game play.

- *Big Boss Module:* A "Big Boss" UFO appears onscreen after all the clear bubbles have been popped. The UFO displays a question and five possible answers (in the form of five bubbles). When the ship pops the correct bubble, bonus points are added to the score, and the blue bubbles and clear bubbles appear again. The Big Boss module contains floating Answer bubbles, a UFO with animated rocket thrusters and winking lights, and a Question panel to display questions.

Other minor modules include the Preloader and the instruction button, but the main functionality of the game is built into the four major modules.

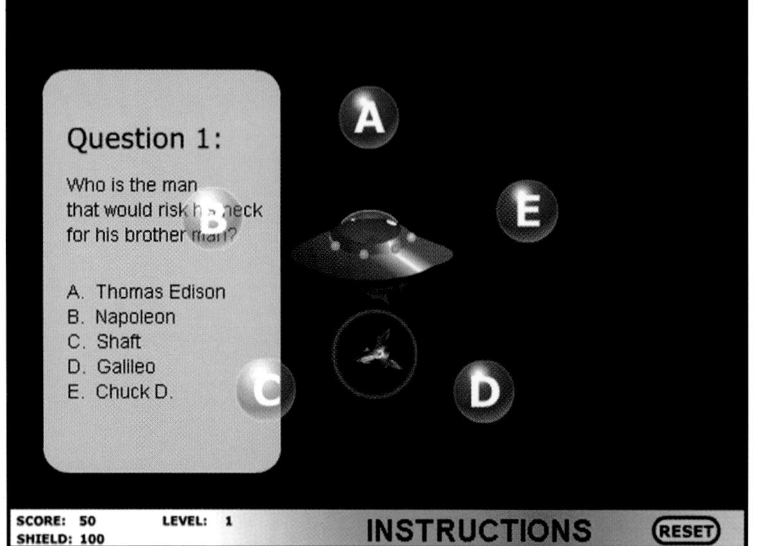

The Big Boss Module features a quiz question.

Initializing the Game

For this game, you need to prevent the movie from playing too soon. The game might not function properly if some of the graphics and sounds aren't loaded when game play commences. So, you employ a Preloader splash screen that's displayed until the whole movie has loaded. That allows you to ensure all the necessary assets are in place before game play begins.

1 Open BubbleFighter1_start.fla located in the Chapter 07 folder on the accompanying CD, save the file to your hard drive, and remember to save periodically as you work through this technique. (If you want to see the finished file, open BubbleFighter_final.fla.)

Notice that the Control layer contains only ActionScript—no graphics or sound.

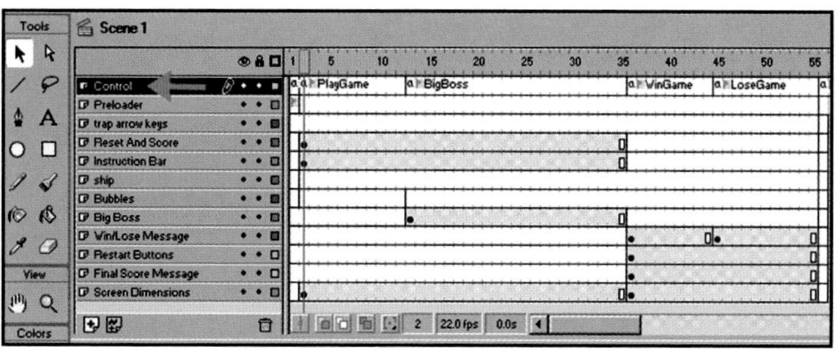

The Control layer contains only ActionScript.

2 To prevent the movie from playing any further, assign ActionScript to the first frame in the Control layer:

Note that two variables, ***Level*** and ***Score***, were also initialized in the main timeline and were set to zero. Now you can build the Preloader movie.

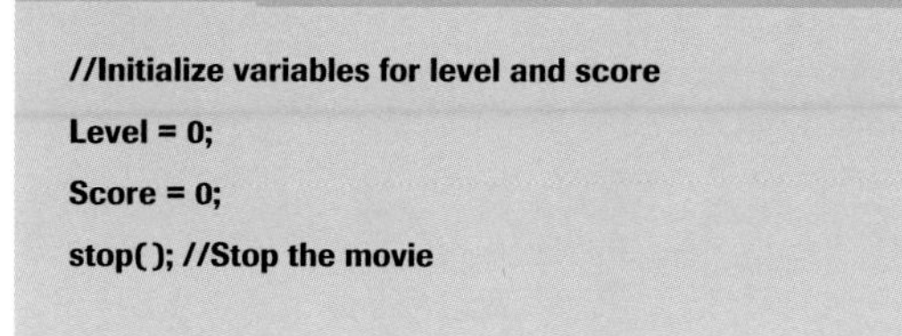

```
//Initialize variables for level and score
Level = 0;
Score = 0;
stop(); //Stop the movie
```

Assign the initialization code to prevent the movie from playing further.

Note: If possible, it's always a good idea to put all your ActionScript inside a separate layer at the top and label it Control (or something to that effect) to keep your code organized, easy to access, and easy to manage. You should also label the keyframes in your Control layer to reflect the purpose of the ActionScript in that keyframe.

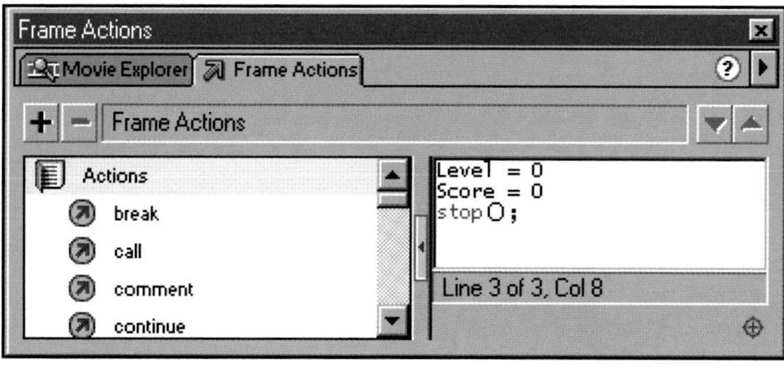

Use the Frame Actions window to add the initialization code to the frame labeled Initialize Variables (the first frame) on the Control layer.

3 Highlight the Preloader layer, open the Main Screen Elements folder in the Library, and drag the Preloader movie clip onto the center of the main Stage.

A quick peek inside the Preloader movie clip reveals three layers with two frames. The top Control layer contains code to stop the Preloader at each frame, and the Art layer contains the bubble artwork and title over both frames. The Message layer contains two different keyframes: Frame 1 has a "loading game" message, and frame 2 has a Go button that will tell the main timeline to go to the PlayGame keyframe when clicked.

If you were to compile the movie right now, you would see only the Preloader splash screen with the "LOADING GAME" message. For Flash to detect whether the game has been loaded, you have to add some detection ActionScript.

Use the Align panel to center the Preload movie Clip to the stage.

4 Open the Actions panel and select the Preloader movie clip in the main timeline. Assign the ActionScript to the Preloader movie clip:

```
onClipEvent (enterFrame) {
    if(_root._framesloaded == _root._totalframes and _root.totalframes > 0 ) {
        gotoAndStop(2);
    }
}
```

Use this code to verify that the entire movie is loaded before the player moves on to game play.

This code consists of a continually looping **onClipEvent(enterFrame)** handler that contains an **if** statement to detect whether the movie has loaded. If the movie is loaded, the movie proceeds to frame 2 and stops. The **onClipEvent** handler is the equivalent of the two-frame loop in Flash 4. Although the main timeline has stopped on frame 1, all the ActionScript within the **onClipEvent** handler runs continuously in a loop because the Flash Player sees the movie clip as an object that re-enters the frame again and again.

Don't confuse the **enterFrame** event with the **load** event because the code inside those two events are executed at different times. To illustrate the difference between the two events, look at an example of each. Here is the **load** event:

```
onClipEvent(load) {
    //code inside the "load" event handler will only run once
    ➥after the movieclip has completely loaded.
}
```

(The ➥ symbol you see here is for editorial purposes only.)

Here is the **enterFrame** event:

```
onClipEvent(enterFrame) {
    //code inside the "enterFrame" event handler will run again
    ➥and again (continuously) as long as the movieclip exists in
    ➥the timeline.
}
```

(The ➥ symbol you see here is for editorial purposes only.)

Also, remember that all ActionScript within Movie Clip event handlers is considered to be stored inside the movie clip, so the current scope will also be considered to be inside the clip. For example, if you created a variable inside the **load** event handler for a movie clip called **MyMovieclip** on the main timeline like this

```
OnClipEvent(load) {
    MyName = "Sam";
}
```

the scope of the variable ***MyName*** would be **_root.MyMovieclip.MyName**. Therefore, the variable's scope, or reference path, is considered "inside" the movie clip even though it was created within the event handler. You couldn't reference ***myName*** with the path **_root.MyName** because the path doesn't go into the MyMovieclip first. Any reference to the root (or main) timeline from within the clip handler requires a **_root** prefix to signify a reference to the root timeline.

Now that you've explored the **onClipEvent()** handlers for **load** and **enterFrame**, take a look at the **if** statement used in the **enterFrame** handler of the preloader. Here's the code:

```
onClipEvent (enterFrame) {
    if(_root._framesloaded == _root._totalframes and
    ➥_root.totalframes > 0 ) {
            gotoAndStop(2);
    }
}
```

(The ➥ symbol you see here is for editorial purposes only.)

Here, the **if** statement inside the **onClipEvent()** handler loops continuously. The logic inside the **if** statement can be broken down into two separate components. The first piece of logic is this:

```
_root._framesloaded == _root._totalframes
```

This code compares the number of frames in the main timeline loaded into the browser to the total number of frames in the root timeline. The second piece of logic is this:

```
_root._totalframes > 0
```

It determines whether the total number of frames in the main timeline is greater than zero.

Sometimes this looping detection runs before the first frame of the movie is completely loaded, and it mistakenly assumes that the movie has zero number of frames and zero number of frames loaded, which would accidentally trick the Preloader to think it's finished. To prevent this problem, you can add another condition to the detection, so the Preloader will not be triggered unless the total number of frames in the root timeline is greater than zero (**_root.totalframes > 0**).

Joining the two conditional logic statements means that this condition must be met: "If the number of frames loaded from the main timeline is equal to the total number of frames and if the total number of frames in the main timeline is greater than zero, then the Preloader tells its own timeline to go to frame 2 and stop." Just remember, movie clip event handlers are considered inside the scope of the movie clip, so when you refer to the main timeline, you must use the **_root** prefix.

When the detection has determined that the movie is completely loaded, the Preloader goes to the second frame and stops. The second frame is different from the first frame because it contains a Go! button instead of a "LOADING TEXT" message. The button's ActionScript tells the root timeline to go to and stop at the PlayGame frame when clicked.

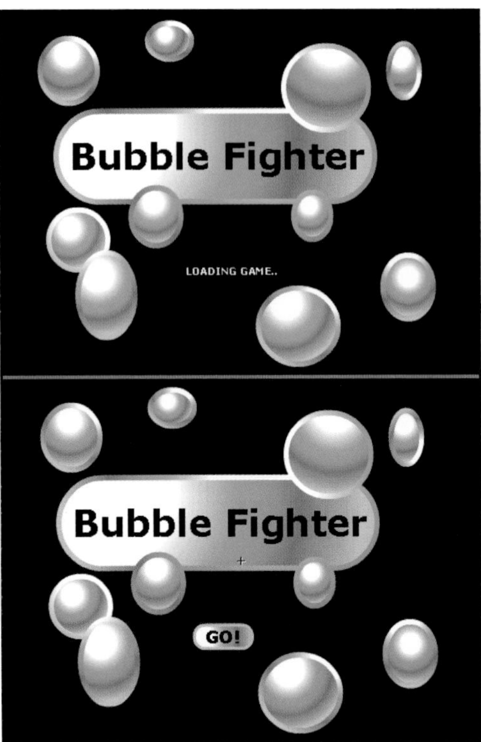

The Preload screen shows the text "LOADING GAME" until the game is fully loaded, at which time the text is replaced with a button labeled "Go!"

Trapping Keys for the Standalone Player

The first frame of the Control layer contains a **Stop()** command to prevent the movie from playing before it has loaded. However, movies running on the standalone player can accidentally move backward or forward one frame if the user hits the left or right arrow key. Because this game uses arrow keys to control the ship, it's absolutely essential that you "trap" those keystrokes to prevent them from moving the player to the wrong frame. Here's how to do that:

1 In the first frame of the Trap Arrow Keys layer (just beneath the Preloader layer), drag the Trap Key Button from the Main Screen Elements directory in the Library onto the Stage. Reposition the Trap Key Button anywhere off the stage.

Position the Trap Key button off the Stage area.

2 Apply ActionScript to capture the key events:

The assignment of **waldo** doesn't do anything except intercept the **keyPress** event for left and right arrow keys to prevent them from reaching the standalone player. Assigning a value to a variable defined with **var** also means that the variable exists only locally within the **{ }** bracket signs. In other words, defining a variable with the prefix **var** ensures that the variable will only exist inside the brackets of the event handler. This means that you cannot access the value of **waldo** from any other part of the script because it doesn't have any meaning outside of those brackets.

```
on (keyPress "<Left>") {
       var  waldo = 0;
}
on (keyPress "<Right>") {
       var waldo = 0;
}
```

Include this code to make sure the game won't be disturbed when the player presses the left or right arrow key on the keyboard.

SETTING VARIABLES

Before you begin constructing the first main module, you should read the instructions for the game (found within the game) and play the final version of the game to get a feel for how the spaceship functions. In this section, you set up the spaceship for the game. The left and right arrows turn the ship counterclockwise and clockwise. The up and down arrows accelerate the ship forward and backward, and the End and PgUp keys accelerate the ship left and right. Every time a player presses one of the acceleration keys, corresponding thrusters on the ship fire.

1 Open the SpaceShip folder in the Library, drag the SpaceshipModule movie clip onto the second frame of the ship layer on the main Stage, and give the movie clip the instance name of **ship**.

Thanks to the modular programming style, you don't need to specify the exact location of the ship on the stage; it will position itself, as you will see later in this technique.

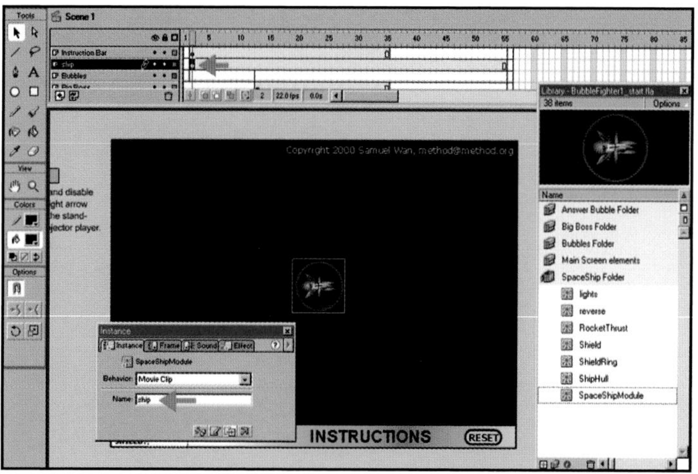

Place the SpaceShipModule movie clip on the stage and give it the instance name **ship**.

2 Edit on the Spaceship movie clip.

The movie clip contains six movie clips with these instance names: shield, hull (the actual body of the spaceship), leftthrust, rightthrust, reversethrust, and thrust. Exit Edit mode.

Next you need to set up a few of the ship's properties before you give it power. You begin by assigning the script to the **onClipEvent(load)** handler.

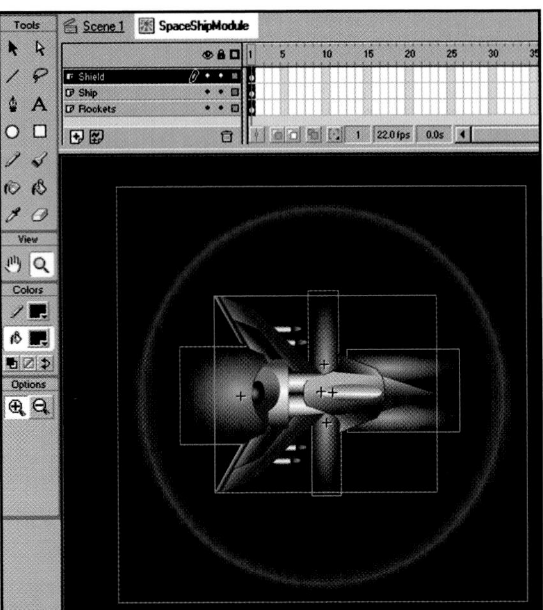

The Ship movie clip is composed of six movie clips, each of which already has an assigned instance name.

Tip: Specifying important variables all at once and placing them at the top of your code allows you to make simple and quick changes to a program's behavior without having to look through many lines of code.

3 Open the Actions panel for the Ship movie clip on the main timeline and add the code at right to initialize the variables for the ship module:

```
onClipEvent (load) {
    turnspeed = 15;
    xspeed = 0;
    yspeed = 0;
    acceleration = 1;
    _root.ship.Hitpoints = 100;
    PI = Math.PI
    this.thrust._visible = 0;
    this.reversethrust._visible = 0;
    this.leftthrust._visible = 0;
    this.rightthrust._visible = 0;
    this._rotation = -90;
}
```

Use this code to initialize a number of variables for the ship.

The **load** event for a movie clip runs all the code within its brackets once—and only once—after the movie clip is completely loaded into the Flash Player. Here, you've initialized several variables to describe how the ship will behave at first. Each variable describes a different attribute of the ship.

The variable ***turnspeed*** in

```
turnspeed = 15;
```

specifies that the ship will turn at 15 degrees per frame (running at 22 frames per second). You also set the horizontal speed in this line:

```
xspeed = 0;
```

You set the vertical speed in the following line:

```
yspeed = 0;
```

Setting the speeds to zero means that the ship won't be in motion when the game starts.

In the following line of code

```
acceleration = 1;
```

the acceleration is set to 1 so that the thrusters will increase the ship's speed in any direction by a value of 1. In this line of code

```
_root.ship.Hitpoints = 100;
```

the variable ***Hitpoints*** keeps track of the ship's health. Every time the ship hits a blue bubble, its shields and ***Hitpoints*** decrease by 20. That's why you set the variable ***HitPoints*** to a value of 100.

In the following line of code

```
PI = Math.PI
```

Math.PI is a constant value stored inside the Flash Player, and its value of 3.14159265358979 is a necessary ingredient in calculations with trigonometry and angles. You use the value of **PI** often during this game, so instead of typing out the constant **Math.PI** every time, assign the value of **Math.PI** to a variable named ***PI***.

Finally, the four lines of code that contain

```
visible = 0;
```

set the visibility of all the rocket thrusters to zero (or false). Remember, Flash considers all ActionScript inside the **onClipEvent** handlers to exist inside the movie clip, so the reference of this refers to whatever movie clip contains the code. In the case of the ship, **this.thrust** refers to the forward thrusting rockets inside the Ship movie clip instance.

The line of code

```
this._rotation = -90;
```

sets the rotation of the ship to –90 degrees so it is pointed in the right direction when the Ship movie clip is completely loaded into the player.

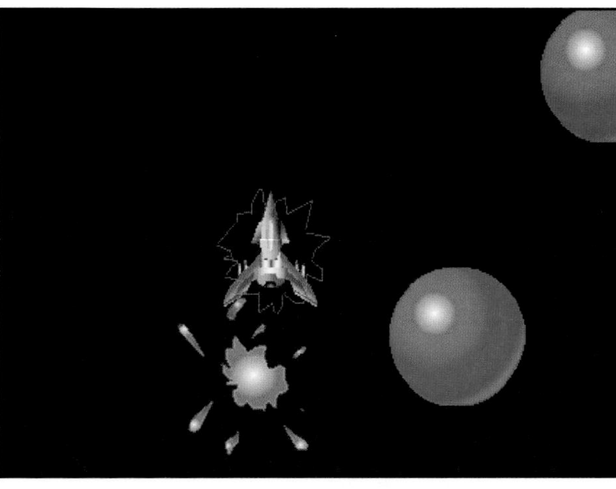

When a bubble collides with the ship's shield it causes damage.

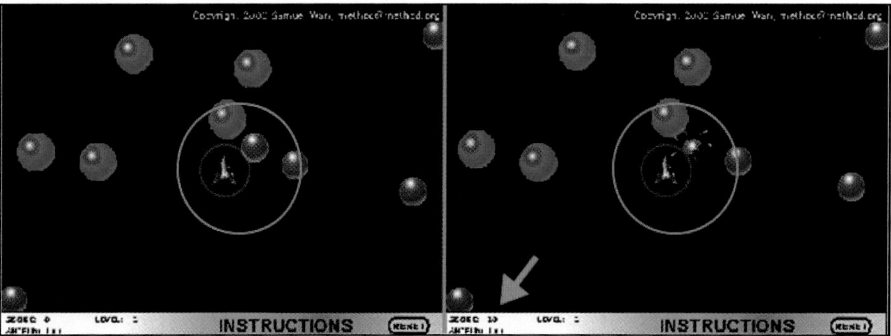

When the player hits the smaller bubble, he gets 10 points.

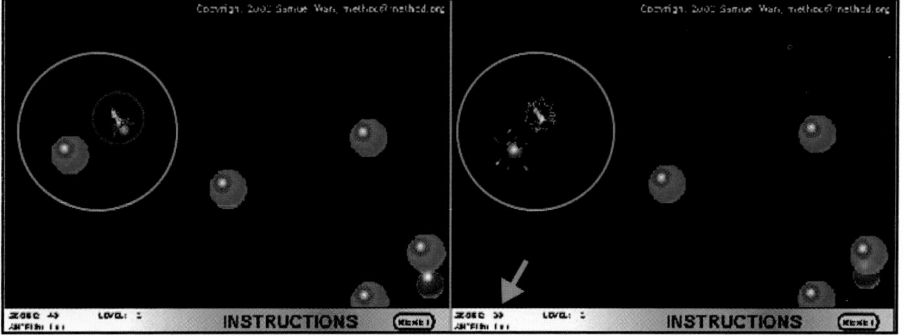

When the player hits the larger bubble, he loses 10 points and the shield strength is reduced by 20.

Setting Up Keyboard-Controlled Steering

As explained previously in the Preloader section, the **onClipEvent(enterFrame)** handler works as a continuous loop. All the code inside the **enterFrame** handler will run again and again as long as the movie clip exists. In programming terms, every cycle through a looping piece of code is called an iteration of the code. The ability to reiterate, or loop, through the same piece of code is important in arcade games because the game has to recalculate the position and velocity of an object for every frame per second.

For example, when a player holds down the left arrow to turn the ship counterclockwise, you don't want the ship to turn once and stop. You want the game to detect that the left arrow key is still down so the ship will continue to turn counterclockwise until the key is released.

1 In the main timeline, open the Actions panel for the ship movie clip again, and then apply this ActionScript after the code for the **onClipEvent(enterFrame)** handler:

```
onClipEvent (enterFrame) {
    _root.shields = _root.ship.Hitpoints;      //Display shields
    if (Key.isDown(39)){ //Turn right
        this._rotation = this._rotation + turnspeed;
    }
    if (Key.isDown(37)){ //Turn left
        this._rotation = this._rotation - turnspeed;
    }
}
```

Use this code to turn the ship left and right when the player presses the left and right arrow keys (respectively).

In the code

```
root.shields = _root.ship.Hitpoints;   //Display shields
```

you assign the **hitpoints** of the ship to the text field named shields in the main timeline to show the current health of the shields.

Then you use two conditional **if** statements that detect whether a key is being pressed down using the **Key.isDown()** method. The first conditional statement

```
if (Key.isDown(39)){ //Turn right
```

is for the right arrow key.

The **Key.isDown(39)** method returns a **true** value if the key corresponding to the **keycode 39** is pressed down; otherwise, it returns a **false** value. So if the user presses down on the right arrow (**keycode 39**), this code

```
this._rotation = this._rotation + turnspeed;
```

adds the value of ***turnspeed*** to turn the ship clockwise.

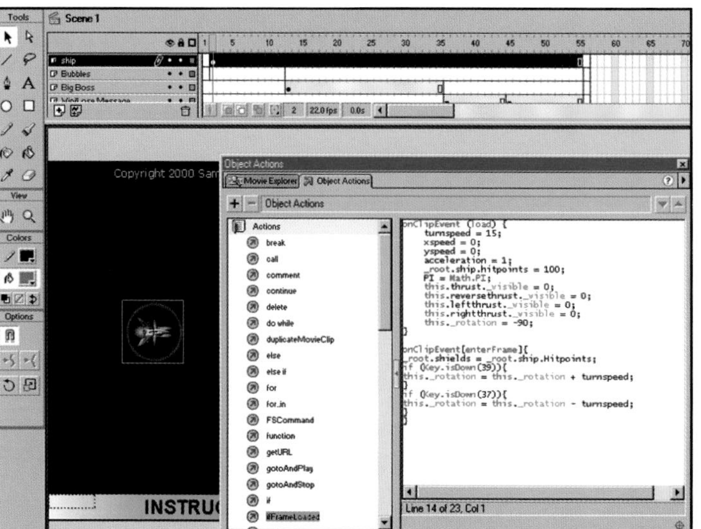

Apply the code to the Ship movie clip using the Object Actions window.

Remember, you assigned a value of **15** to ***turnspeed*** so the ship would rotate 15 degrees clockwise every iteration at 22 frames per second if the right arrow key is pressed down. You also rotate the ship 15 degrees counterclockwise if the left arrow is down by subtracting the value of ***turnspeed*** from the current rotation of the ship.

2 Use the same capturing **keyPress** technique to set up the code that toggles the visibility of the rocket thrusters:

```
if (Key.isDown(38)){ //up arrow
    this.thrust._visible = 1;
} else {
    this.thrust._visible = 0;
}
```

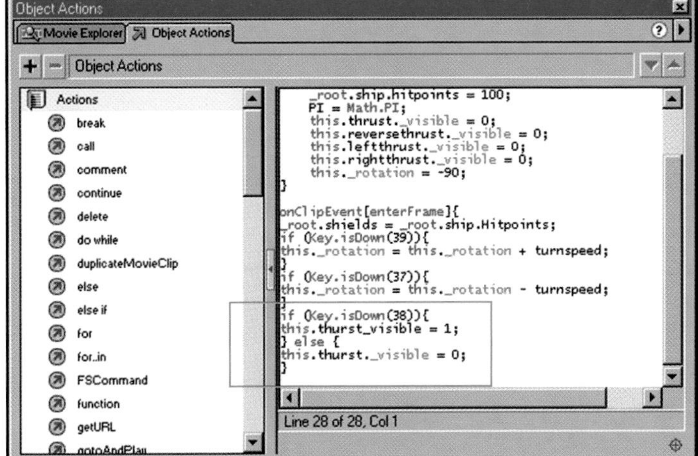

Add the code to toggle on and off the visibility of the rocket thrusters.

Note the similarity between this code for toggling the visibility of the rocket thrusters and the preceding code for turning the ship. The line of code given here

```
if (Key.isDown(38)){ //up arrow
```

checks to see if the up arrow key is pressed. If it is, this line of code

```
this.thrust._visible = 1;
```

makes the thrust movie clip visible. If the up arrow key isn't pressed, the **else** statement makes the thrust movie clip invisible.

3 Apply the same principle for all the other direction keys by adding this code:

```
if (Key.isDown(40)){ //down arrow
    this.reversethrust._visible = 1;
} else {
        this.reversethrust._visible = 0;
}
if (Key.isDown(34)){ //End Key = leftthrust
        this.leftthrust._visible = 1;
```

Apply this code to turn on and off the visibility of all the other thrusters.

continues

4 Preview the movie and experiment with the arrow keys to see how the thrusters turn on and off. Also, try turning the ship left and right.

continued

```
} else {
        this.leftthrust._visible = 0;
}
if (Key.isDown(35)){ //PgDn Key = rightthrust
        this.rightthrust._visible = 1;
} else {
        this.rightthrust._visible = 0;
}
```

How It Works

To place this chapter in perspective, what you've done here is lay the foundation of the arcade game by building the preloader and the ship module and by initializing variables to control the game play. You followed the modular approach to programming by constructing movie clips that contained all the functional source code and graphics inside.

The ship is now modular because it contains ActionScript code to capture key presses on the keyboard and to use those key presses to rotate the ship and toggle the visibility of the rocket thrusters—all without having to rely on code from another movie clip. Thus, you can say that the ship is an independent module that functions on its own. Now that you can control the rotation of the ship and visually display the rockets when a direction key is pressed, the next step is to add more functionality to the ship module by moving the ship in whatever direction it is pointing.

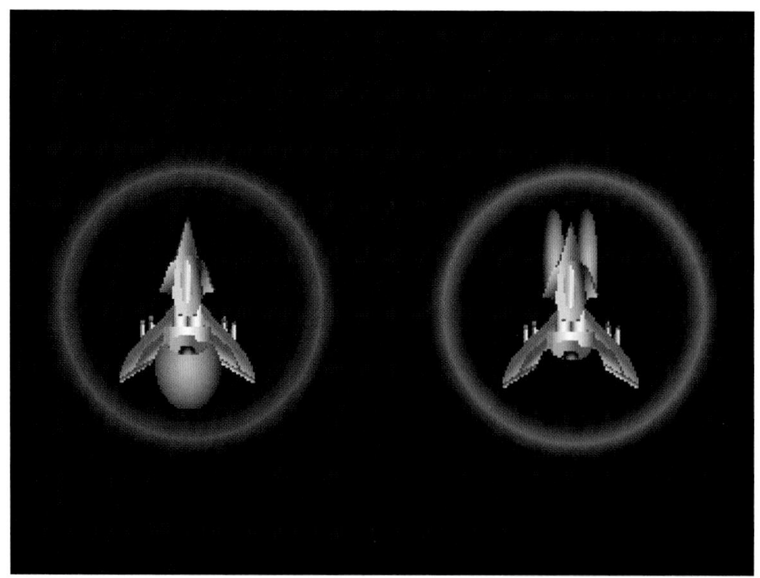

When the up arrow button on the keyboard is pressed, a thruster appears on the bottom of the ship to propel it forward (left) and when the down arrow button on the keyboard is pressed a thruster appears on the top of the ship to propel it backward (right).

PROGRAMMING WITH TRIGONOMETRY

By Samuel Wan

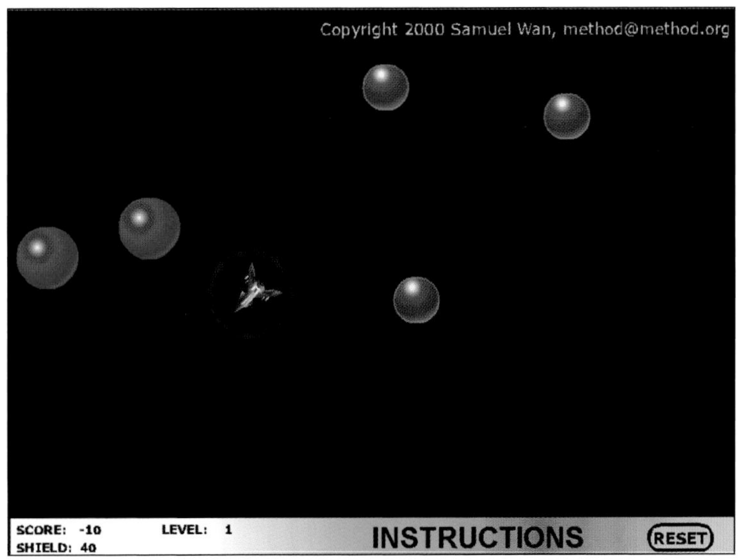

The previous chapter introduced the modular approach to building projects in Flash. You started to build an arcade game by constructing a preloader module step by step. The preloader introduced the concepts of scope and **onClipEvent** handlers. Then, you began putting together the basic structure of a spaceship module. In the first step of the spaceship's construction, you added ActionScript code to the spaceship's Actions panel to initialize its variables. Then you wrote ActionScript that would turn the ship left or right, depending on whether you used the left or right arrow key.

Now that the ship can turn left and right, it's time to make it move according to its rotation. As spaceships usually do, this spaceship should be able to move forward, backward, left, and right because it has rocket thrusters facing all four directions. This chapter introduces basic concepts of trigonometry to calculate how far the ship should move in any of the four directions, based on its degree of rotation. This chapter will help you gain a better understanding of the magic of mathematics and provide a starting point for learning more about advanced ActionScript techniques.

Using Trigonometry to Calculate Movement

Before you can add the ActionScript code to move the ship in the direction of its rocket thrusters, you need to understand the role of trigonometry in calculating the amount of movement in a particular direction based on the rotation of the ship.

1 Study the diagram shown here.

Trigonometry is based on the concept of a circle with a radius of 1 unit of distance, usually referred to as the *unit circle*. This unit can be measured in centimeters, pixels, feet, or miles; it doesn't matter, as long as the radius is equal to a unit of 1. The radius is the length of distance from the origin (or center) of a circle to the edge of the circle.

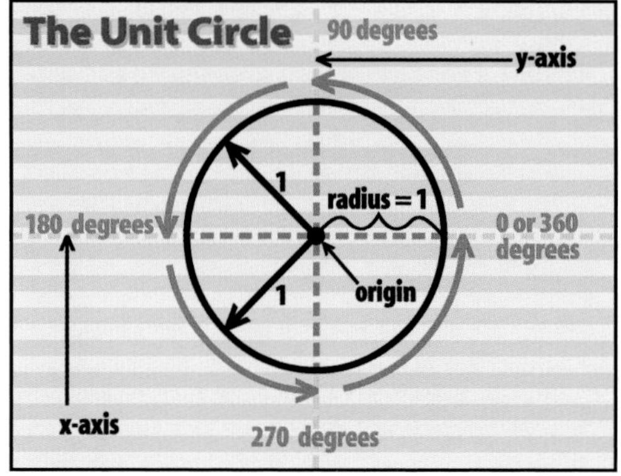

This diagram illustrates a basic concept in trigonometry: the unit circle.

2 Open BubbleFighter2_start.fla on the accompanying CD and save it to your hard drive. (If you want to see the finished file, open BubbleFighter2_final.fla.)

To calculate the direction of the ship's movement, you must use trigonometry to find the rotation of the ship (how far left or right did the ship spin?). After you calculate the rotation, you use the rotation value to break down the ship's movement into horizontal and vertical components. (In other words, how far does the ship move left/right and up/down on the screen?)

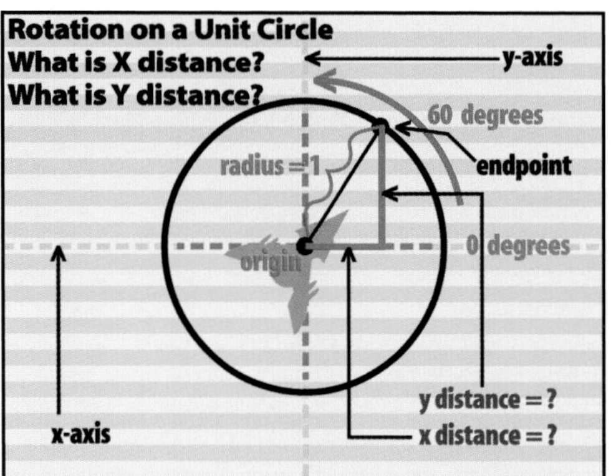

In this example, the ship rotates 60 degrees.

This diagram illustrates an example of a ship rotated 60 degrees. Although the ship points in a straight diagonal line from the origin to the endpoint, you can break down the diagonal line into two lines: a horizontal line along the x-axis with a length of x-distance and a vertical line along the y-axis with a length of y-distance.

The new rotated radius—from origin to the endpoint of the unit circle at 60 degrees—still has a distance of 1 inside the unit circle. If you draw a vertical line from the endpoint to the x-axis, you find the vertical (y) distance of the endpoint from the origin. If you draw a horizontal line from the origin to the new vertical line, you find the horizontal (x) distance of the endpoint from the origin. The combination of rotated radius, x-distance, and y-distance form a triangle.

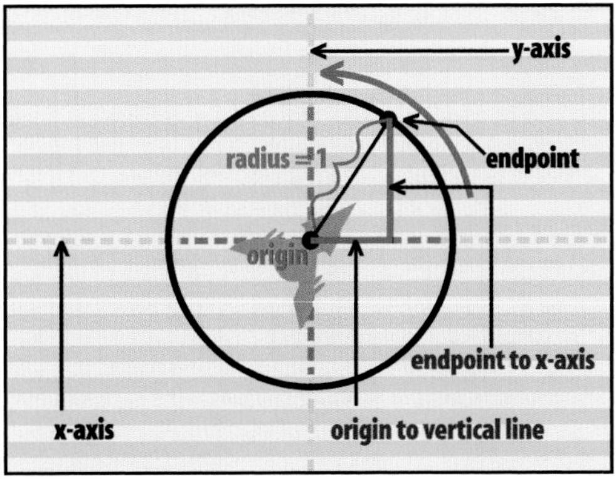

When the ship moves in the direction of 60 degrees, the movement along the y-axis is greater than the movement along the x-axis.

Look closely at the ship's direction again. If you picture the ship moving in the direction of 60 degrees according to the unit circle, notice that movement can be expressed in terms of distance along the x- and y-axes. There's a correlation between these two observations. The x-distance and y-distance reflect how fast the ship will move on the x-axis and y-axis, so you can break down the movement of an object into its horizontal and vertical movements. In this case, the ship moves further or faster along the y-axis.

Now if the ship were rotated 30 degrees instead, you could picture in your mind that the imaginary x-distance would be greater than the y-distance, which means that the ship would move faster horizontally than vertically. You could then conclude that the rotation of the ship directly affects how fast it will move in the horizontal and vertical directions. The question is, how fast and in what direction? You can answer these two questions next. Depending on how a ship is rotated, sometimes it will move faster horizontally than vertically, and sometimes it will move faster vertically than horizontally.

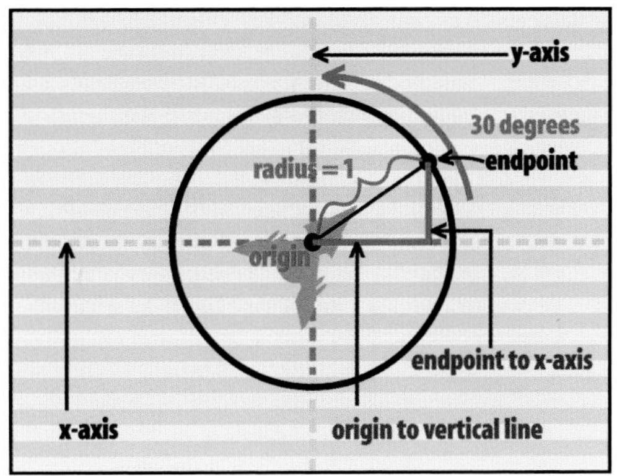

When the ship moves in the direction of 30 degrees, the movement along the x-axis is greater than the movement along the y-axis.

Note: I wish I could write more on this fascinating topic, but the objective here is to move the ship according to its direction, so we must move on. To learn more about the wonderful world of trigonometry, consult any number of trigonometry tutorials on the Web. Here are three excellent sites:

http://ww.math.com/tables/algebra/functions/trig/overview.htm

http://mathforum.com/dr.math/

http://were-here.com/forum/articles/FlashMath101/links.index.html

Using Cosine and Sine Functions

Your next task is to find the x-distance and y-distance of an endpoint on a unit circle given the degree of rotation. To find these values, you need to use two trigonometric functions: Cosine and Sine. Cosine calculates the x-distance given the amount of rotation, and Sine calculates the y-distance given the amount of rotation. In the previous example, you rotated the ship by 60 degrees, so you would use Cosine(60) and Sine(60) to calculate the x-distance and y-distance. The ActionScript equivalent of Cosine and Sine are methods of the Math object called **Math.cos()** and **Math.sin()**. These two math methods do not accept values in degrees. Instead, you must convert degrees to a measurement called a *radian*. Radians are beyond the scope of this book, but you can convert all the degrees you'll ever use in programming into radians by applying this simple formula:

```
Rad = degree * PI/180; //PI is a variable to which we earlier assigned the constant value, Math.PI
```

1 Locate the **enterFrame** handler you created in the previous chapter, attached to the ship movie clip.

In the **enterFrame** handler, you used the **Key.isDown()** method to detect whether a key is pressed down and, therefore, to turn the ship left or right and to make the directional rockets become visible/invisible with the other arrow keys.

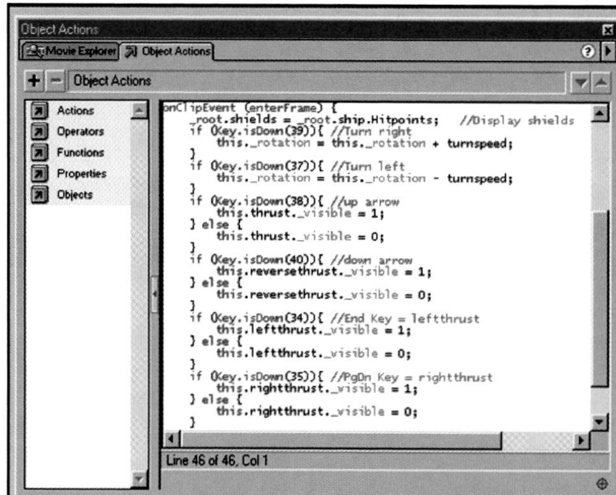

Object Actions
Movie Explorer
Object Actions
Object Actions
Actions
Operators
Functions
Properties
Objects
onClipEvent (enterFrame) {
_root.shields = _root.ship.Hitpoints; //Display shields
if (Key.isDown(39)){ //Turn right
this._rotation = this._rotation + turnspeed;
}
if (Key.isDown(37)){ //Turn left
this._rotation = this._rotation - turnspeed;
}
if (Key.isDown(38)){ //up arrow
this.thrust._visible = 1;
} else {
this.thrust._visible = 0;
}
if (Key.isDown(40)){ //down arrow
this.reversethrust._visible = 1;
} else {
this.reversethrust._visible = 0;
}
if (Key.isDown(34)){ //End Key = leftthrust
this.leftthrust._visible = 1;
} else {
this.leftthrust._visible = 0;
}
if (Key.isDown(35)){ //PgDn Key = rightthrust
this.rightthrust._visible = 1;
} else {
this.rightthrust._visible = 0;
}
Line 46 of 46, Col 1

Open the Object Actions window with the ship selected and scroll down to the **enterFrame** handler.

2 After the **(Key.isDown(38)** line, type the code that multiplies the ship's degrees of rotation (in radians) by the ship's acceleration to calculate the horizontal acceleration of the ship along the x-axis:

```
xspeed += Math.cos(PI/180 * this._rotation) * acceleration;
```

Enter this code to calculate acceleration on the x-axis.

Math.cos(PI/180 * this._rotation) provides the radian conversion of the ship's degrees in terms of horizontal (x-axis) direction.

The **** acceleration*** provides the rate of acceleration to be multiplied in the horizontal direction.

The ***xspeed* +=** means that you are adding the results of the calculation back into the current value of ***xspeed***. In other words, you can break down the entire line of code into three phrases: "Get the current value of ***xspeed*** and add it to the results of multiplying the radian conversion of direction by the rate of acceleration." Don't be confused by the **+=** sign. In plain English, it simply means: add the value of the following calculation to the current value of this variable called ***xspeed***." It's just like writing the following line of code, only more elegantly:

```
xspeed = xspeed + Math.cos(PI/180 * this._rotation) *
➥acceleration;
```

(The ➥ symbol you see here is for editorial purposes only.)

The horizontal speed has been calculated.

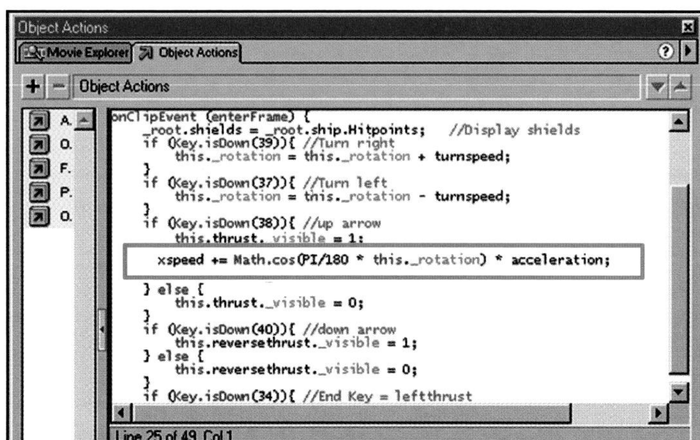

The horizontal acceleration code appears in the **(Key.isDown(38)** line.

3 To calculate the vertical speed, you use a similar equation, entering this code next:

```
yspeed += Math.sin(PI/180 * this._rotation) * acceleration;
```

Use this code to calculate the acceleration on the y-axis.

This code uses the same concept as the ***xspeed*** calculation. The only difference is that you are using the **Sin** function to calculate the vertical (y) direction of movement instead of the horizontal (x) direction of movement.

You inserted the calculation within a keypress for the up arrow key so that the calculation runs while the up arrow key is pressed down. This is how the code looks when the two calculations are added to the keypress for the up arrow key:

```
if (Key.isDown(38)){ //up arrow
    this.thrust._visible = 1;
    xspeed += Math.cos(PI/180 * this._rotation) *
    ➥acceleration;
    yspeed += Math.sin(PI/180 * this._rotation) *
    ➥acceleration;
} else {
    this.thrust._visible = 0;
}
```

(The ➥ symbol you see here is for editorial purposes only.)

So within the continually looping **enterFrame** handler, the ***xspeed*** and ***yspeed*** are calculated whenever the up arrow key is pressed, and the ship moves by the amount of ***xspeed*** and ***yspeed*** whenever the up arrow key is pressed. The thrust movie clip is visible so that the ship's main rocket thruster becomes visible.

The last **else** section simply sets the thrust movie clip's visibility to false, or 0, if Key 38 is not pressed, so that the rocket doesn't appear to fire when the up arrow key isn't pressed.

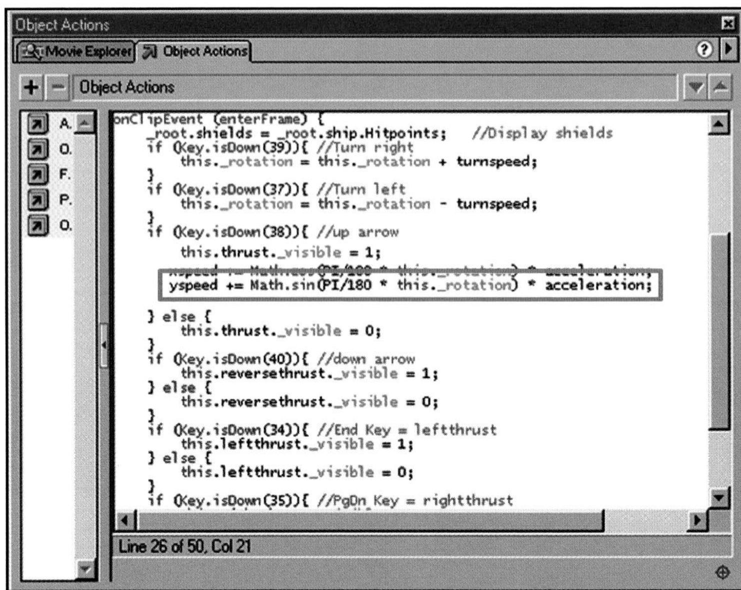

The vertical acceleration code is added to the **(Key.isDown(38))** line.

4 To calculate movement for ***xspeed*** and ***yspeed*** in the reverse direction, subtract the value of both calculations from their variables, ***xspeed*** and ***yspeed***, instead of adding them. Hence, you use the operator **-=** instead of **+=** to subtract the results of the calculations from the current value of ***xspeed*** and ***yspeed***. Place this code after the **(Key.isDown(40))** line:

```
xspeed -= Math.cos(PI/180 * this._rotation) * acceleration;
yspeed -= Math.sin(PI/180 * this._rotation) * acceleration;
```

Use the code to calculate the acceleration for a reverse thrust.

Note again that the movie clip, reversethrust, which shows the rockets thrusting the ship backward, is set to visible when the down arrow key is pressed and set to invisible when the down arrow key is *not* pressed. The next figure shows how the code looks when the two calculations are added to the keypress for the down arrow key.

```
if (Key.isDown(40)){ //down
    xspeed -= Math.cos(PI/180 * this._rotation) *
    ➥acceleration;
    yspeed -= Math.sin(PI/180 * this._rotation) *
    ➥acceleration;
    this.reversethrust._visible = 1;
} else {
    this.reversethrust._visible = 0;
}
```

(The ➥ symbol you see here is for editorial purposes only.)

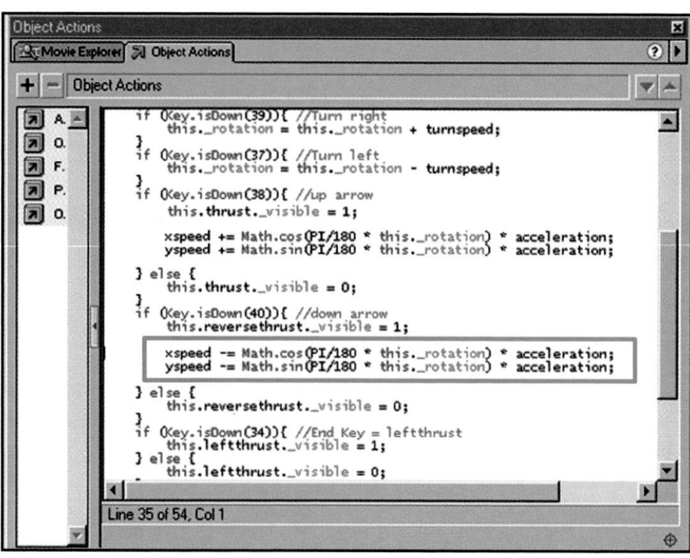

The deceleration code is added to the **(Key.isDown(40)** code.

5 To calculate movement of the ship toward the right, perpendicular to its current direction, add 90 degrees to the current rotation (refer to the unit circle diagram to see the relationship between degrees and direction) by placing this code after the **(KeyisDown(34)** line:

```
xspeed += Math.cos(PI/180 * (this._rotation + 90)) * acceleration;
yspeed += Math.sin(PI/180 * (this._rotation + 90)) * acceleration;
```

Use this code to calculate thrust or movement to the right.

This figure shows how the code looks when the two calculations are added to the keypress for the left arrow key:

```
if (Key.isDown(34)){ //pgdn = leftthrust
    xspeed += Math.cos(PI/180 * (this._rotation + 90)) *
    ➥acceleration;
    yspeed += Math.sin(PI/180 * (this._rotation + 90)) *
    ➥acceleration;
    this.leftthrust._visible = 1;
} else {
    this.leftthrust._visible = 0;
}
```

(The ➥ symbol you see here is for editorial purposes only.)

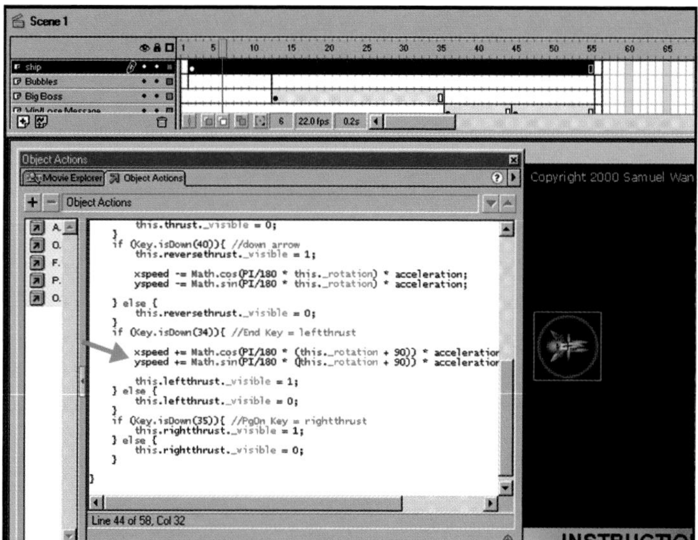

The right acceleration code is added to the **(Key.isDown(34)** line.

The code looks exactly the same, the only differences being the addition of 90 degrees to the value of the ship's rotation and the reference to the leftthrust movie clip for the rocket graphics. The instance name Leftthrust is used even though the ship is moving toward the right because the graphics for the rocket that moves the ship in that direction is located on the left side of the ship. (The opposite is true for the calculation moving the ship to the left.)

6 To accelerate toward the left, simply subtract the same 90 degrees (instead of adding 90 degrees toward the right) by placing this code after **(KeyisDown(35)**:

```
xspeed += Math.cos(PI/180 * (this._rotation - 90)) * acceleration;
yspeed += Math.sin(PI/180 * (this._rotation - 90)) * acceleration;
```

Use this code to calculate thrust or movement to the left.

Again, the only differences are the subtraction instead of addition of 90 degrees and the reference to the Rightthrust movie clip. This is how the code looks when the two calculations are added to the keypress for the right arrow key:

```
if (Key.isDown(35)){ //end = rightthrust
    xspeed += Math.cos(PI/180 * (this._rotation - 90)) *
    ➥acceleration;
    yspeed += Math.sin(PI/180 * (this._rotation - 90)) *
    ➥acceleration;
    this.rightthrust._visible = 1;
} else {
    this.rightthrust._visible = 0;
}
```

(The ➥ symbol you see here is for editorial purposes only.)

Note: Remember, **this** refers to the movie clip in which the ActionScript is stored, so **this._rotation** refers to the rotation of the ship, which you manipulated earlier when you added some ActionScript to turn the ship left and right.

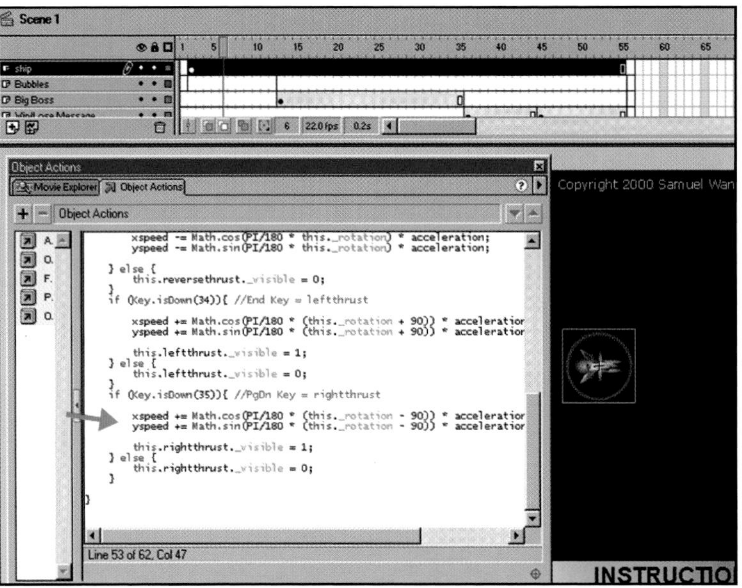

The left acceleration code is added to the **(Key.isDown(35)** line.

Even though you've run all these possible calculations for ***xspeed*** and ***yspeed*** according to whichever key the user presses, you still need to actually apply the value of ***xspeed*** and ***yspeed*** to the position of the ship on the screen.

7 To move the ship according to its new horizontal and vertical speed, enter the ActionScript right after all the calculations, at the end of the code inside the **enterFrame** handler.

```
//Propulsion
this._x = this._x + xspeed;
this._y = this._y + yspeed;
```

Enter the code that handles propulsion according to the new horizontal and vertical speed.

Here, you take the current value of the ship's x and y position, referenced by **this**, and add their respective ***xspeed*** and ***yspeed*** to the positions. You could, of course, use the **+=** notation previously used in the other calculations like so:

```
this._x += xspeed;
    this._y += yspeed;
```

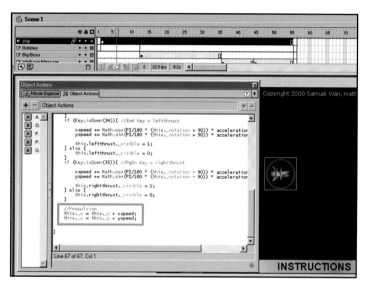

The propulsion acceleration code is added to the end of the **enterFrame** handler.

But I want to show that either way of expressing these calculations will work. The important thing is to show the reason why you added the ***xspeed*** and ***yspeed*** to the x position and y position. You only set the position of the ship at the very end so that you can calculate all possible combinations of keys inside the **enterFrame** loop *before* applying the final values of ***xspeed*** and ***yspeed*** to the ship's position. Thus, your final code should look like this:

```
onClipEvent (load) {
    turnspeed = 15;
    xspeed = 0;
    yspeed = 0;
    acceleration = 1;
    _root.ship.Hitpoints = 100;
    PI = Math.PI
    this.thrust._visible = 0;
    this.reversethrust._visible = 0;
    this.leftthrust._visible = 0;
    this.rightthrust._visible = 0;
    this._rotation = -90;
}

onClipEvent (enterFrame) {
    _root.shields = _root.ship.Hitpoints; //Display
    ➥shields
    if (Key.isDown(39)){ //Turn right
        this._rotation = this._rotation + turnspeed;
```

continues

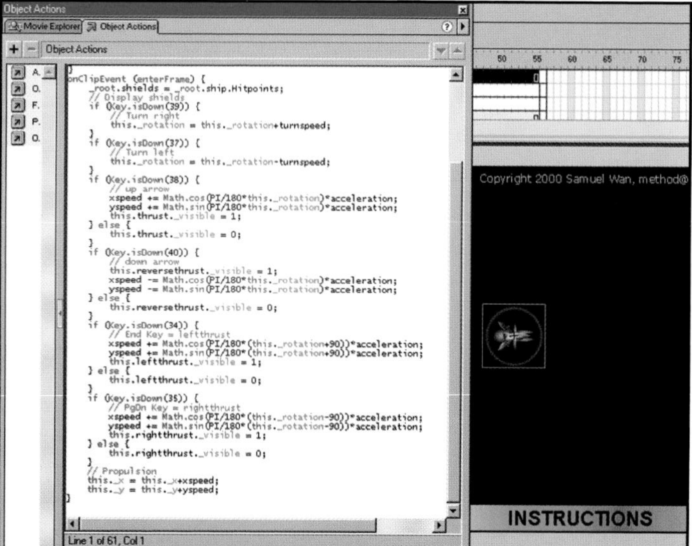

Take a look at the final **enterFrame** code.

continued

```
    }
    if (Key.isDown(37)){ //Turn left
        this._rotation = this._rotation - turnspeed;
    }
    if (Key.isDown(38)){ //up arrow
        this.thrust._visible = 1;
        xspeed += Math.cos(PI/180 * this._rotation) * acceleration;
        yspeed += Math.sin(PI/180 * this._rotation) * acceleration;
    } else {
        this.thrust._visible = 0;
    }
    if (Key.isDown(40)){ //down arrow
        this.reversethrust._visible = 1;
        xspeed -= Math.cos(PI/180 * this._rotation) * acceleration;
        yspeed -= Math.sin(PI/180 * this._rotation) * acceleration;
    } else {
        this.reversethrust._visible = 0;
    }
    if (Key.isDown(34)){ //End Key = leftthrust
        this.leftthrust._visible = 1;
        xspeed += Math.cos(PI/180 * (this._rotation + 90)) * acceleration;
        yspeed += Math.sin(PI/180 * (this._rotation + 90)) * acceleration;
    } else {
        this.leftthrust._visible = 0;
    }
    if (Key.isDown(35)){ //PgDn Key = rightthrust
        this.rightthrust._visible = 1;
        xspeed += Math.cos(PI/180 * (this._rotation - 90)) * acceleration;
        yspeed += Math.sin(PI/180 * (this._rotation - 90)) * acceleration;
    } else {
        this.rightthrust._visible = 0;
    }
    //Propulsion
    this._x = this._x + xspeed;
    this._y = this._y + yspeed;
}
```

(The ➥ symbol you see here is for editorial purposes only.)

Try it, and you'll see that the ship now moves according to the arrow keys on the keyboard. But what happens if the ship flies off the screen? You'll tackle that issue next…

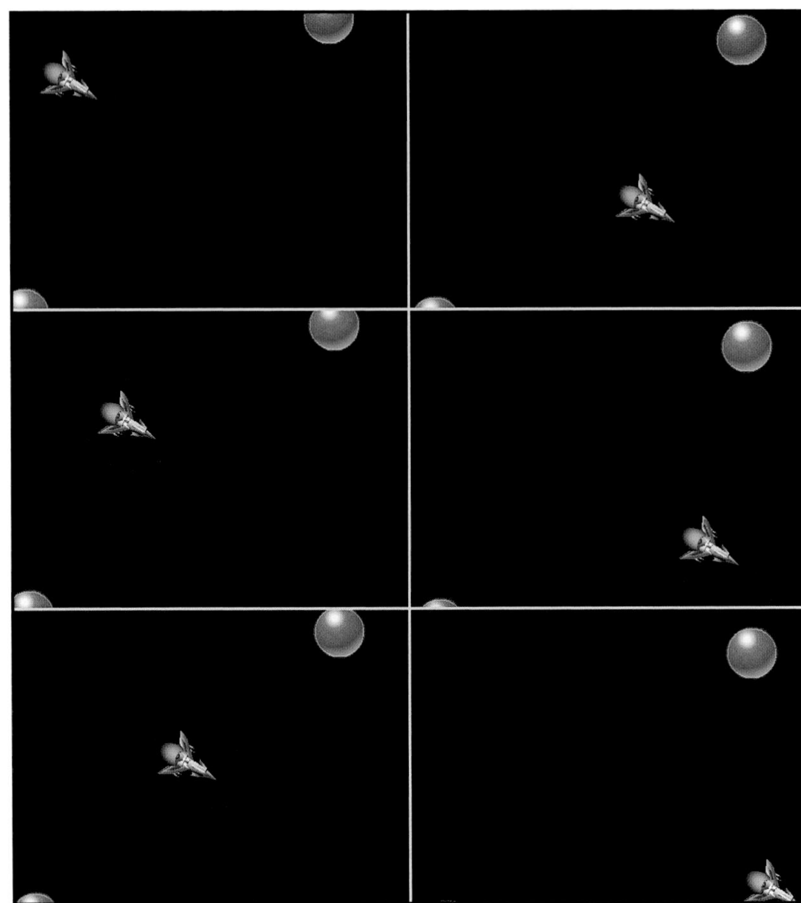

These frames show how the ship continues to accelerate when a direction key is held down.

Note: The explanation of trigonometric functions and their identities is beyond the scope of this book, but this subject is worth studying, especially for those interested in highly advanced programming techniques. I strongly recommend the *Black Art of 3d Game Programming: Writing Your Own High-Speed 3-D Polygon Video Games* by Andre LaMothe (Waite Group Press, Madera, CA), as well as *Computer Graphics: Principles and Practice in C, Second Edition* by James D. Foley, Andries Van Dam, Steven K. Feiner, and John F. Hughes (Addison Wesley, Reading, MA). Both books are based on the C language and require some interpretation.

USING SCREEN WRAPPING

As a final touch, you want to keep the ship inside the screen. To do so, wrap the ship's movements from one edge of the screen to the other. The code discussed in the following steps is assigned after the **Propulsion** code inside the **enterFrame** handler, which is assigned to the ship movie clip.

1 Retrieve the coordinates of the ship's edges, as if it were a box, by getting the ship's bounds according to its position in the **_root** coordinates.

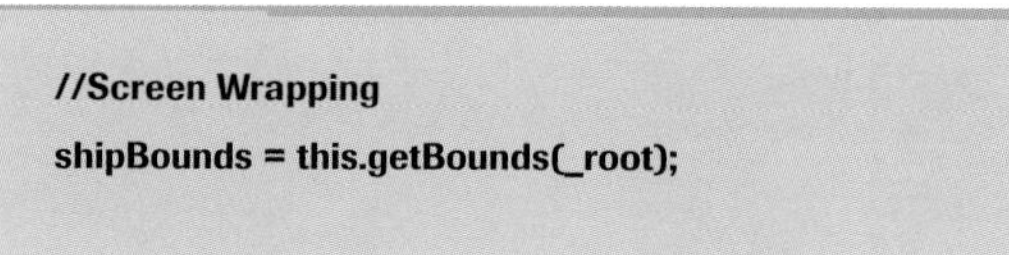

Use this code to get the coordinates of the edges of the ship.

The **getBounds(_root)** method allows you to retrieve the x and y coordinates of the four boundaries of the ship movie clip, by telling the movie clip to refer to itself as **this**. By assigning the value of **this.getBounds(_root)** to the variable ***shipBounds***, you create a new object called ***shipBounds*** that contains four properties: ***shipBounds.xMin***, ***shipBounds.xMax***, ***shipBounds.yMax***, and ***shipBounds.yMin***. These four properties provide the coordinates of the left border (***xMin***), the right border (***xMax***), the top border (***yMin***), and the bottom border (***yMax***). Refer to the diagram below for a visual representation of the ship's bounds.

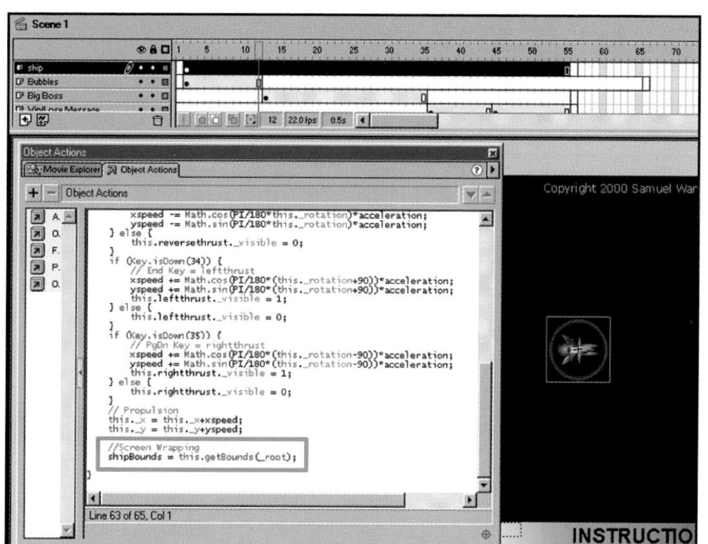

The line of code added to the **enterFrame** handler retrieves the coordinates of the ship movie clip.

You also specified the parameter **_root** to specify that you want the coordinates to be based on the global coordinates of the main timeline instead of the local coordinates inside the movie clip. It's important to use **_root** as the reference point of the bounds because it allows you to compare the bounds of other movie clips in the same global space, which you'll do in the next step.

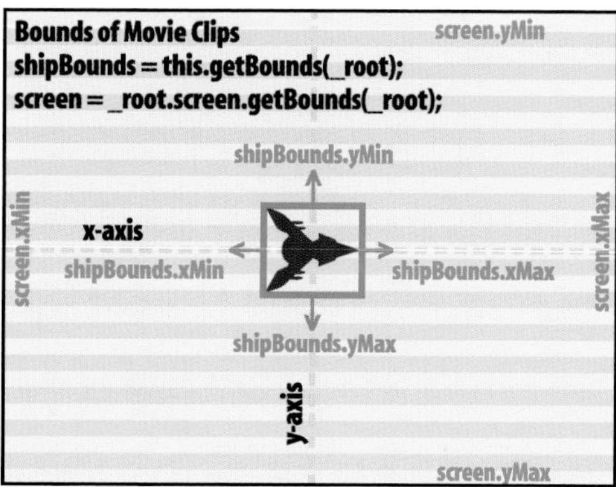

This diagram illustrates the programmatic reference for the boundaries of the ship and the screen.

2 Now that you've got the bounds of the ship in the **_root** global space, retrieve the bounds of the white rectangle movie clip on the main timeline by using this code:

```
screen = _root.screen.getBounds(_root);
```

Use this code to get the bounds of the edges of the screen.

The movie clip has an instance name of screen, and its dimensions match those of the game area. The reason for using the screen movie clip is that it allows you to specify the boundaries of where the game takes place on the screen.

Again you use the **getBounds(_root)** method with **_root** as the parameter. The difference here is that the code is *inside* the scope of the ship movie clip, so you have to provide an object path to the screen movie clip on the **_root** main timeline: **_root.screen.**

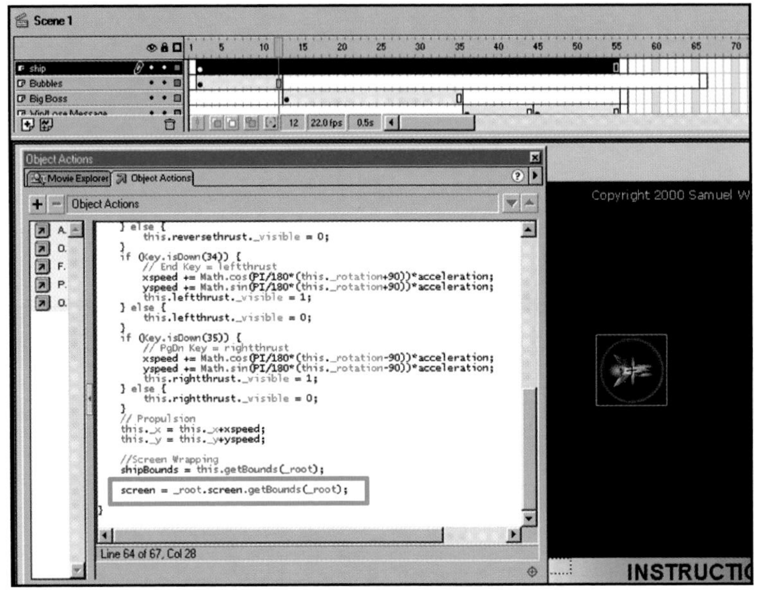

The line added to the **enterFrame** handler retrieves the bounds for the screen.

3 Check for the screen limits by using this code:

```
if (shipBounds.yMax < screen.yMin) {
    this._y = screen.yMax;
}
if (shipBounds.yMin > screen.yMax) {
    this._y = screen.yMin;
}
if (shipBounds.xMax < screen.xMin) {
    this._x = screen.xMax;
}
if (shipBounds.xMin > screen.xMax) {
    this._x = screen.xMin;
}
```

Add the code that provides an object path to the screen movie clip on the **_root** main timeline: **_root.screen**.

In the first portion of the newly added code, you test to see if the ship's bottom-most border, **shipBounds.yMax**, is above the screen's uppermost border, **screen.yMin**. To do so, you use this if statement:

```
if (shipBounds.yMax < screen.yMin) {
```

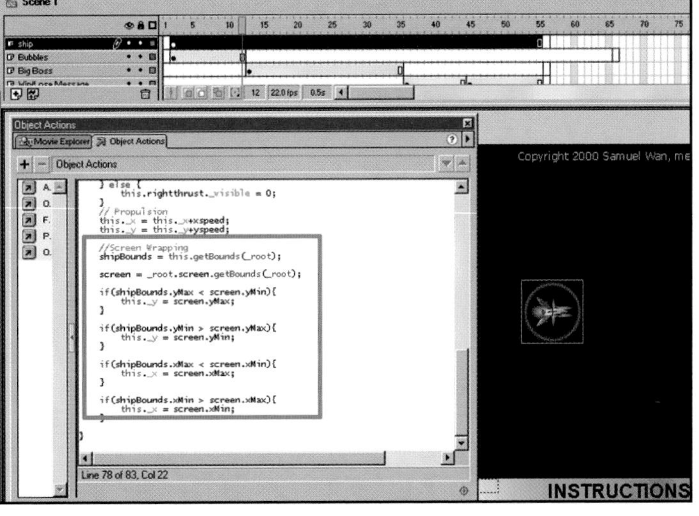

The lines added to the **enterFrame** handler provide an object path to the screen movie clip.

If the comparison is true, you know that the ship is *completely* out of the screen. If you simply compared the ship's position to the screen bounds, the ship would be considered "out of bounds" even though half the movie clip is still inside the screen. This is because the position of a movie clip is determined by the coordinates at the center of the movie clip. That's why you're using **getBounds** to make sure the ship doesn't seem to pop off the screen suddenly.

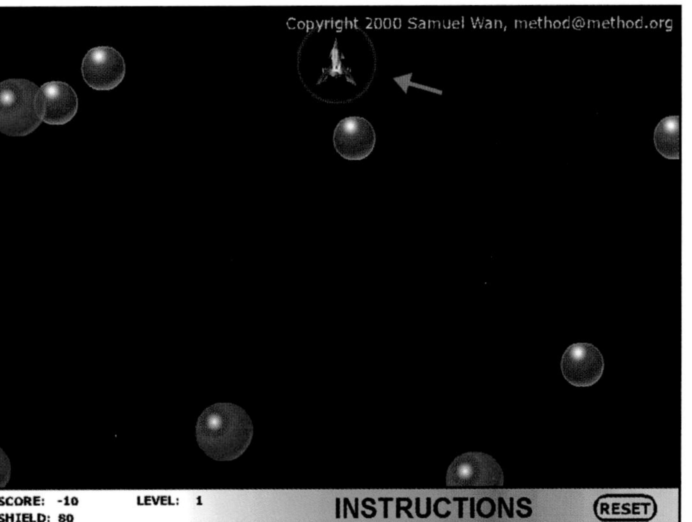

The ship exits off the Stage area.

Note: For those who still remember their x- and y-axes from algebra class, you might be confused about whether y increases up or down the screen. Remember that in the Flash environment, the top of the screen has a y coordinate of zero, and the y position increases downward, so the value of the y position increases from the top of the screen downward. The value of the x position increases from the left side of the screen (zero) toward the right side of the screen.

So what happens if the ship has moved completely off of the screen? You simply move it to the opposite bound of the screen, to make it seem as if the ship has wrapped around the screen like an airplane sailing around the world. You use the following code, where **this** refers to the ship movie clip, and where you set the y position of the ship to the bottom boundary of the screen movie clip on the **_root** main timeline.

```
this._y = screen.yMax;
```

This allows the ship to move continuously, yet prevents it from flying out of view. It also makes the game more fun and challenging. Now enter the following code to wrap the ship from the top of the screen to the bottom of the screen like so:

```
if (shipBounds.yMax < screen.yMin) {
    this._y = screen.yMax;
}
```

Then it becomes a simple matter of figuring out the other three portions of code to wrap the ship from bottom to top, left to right, and right to left.

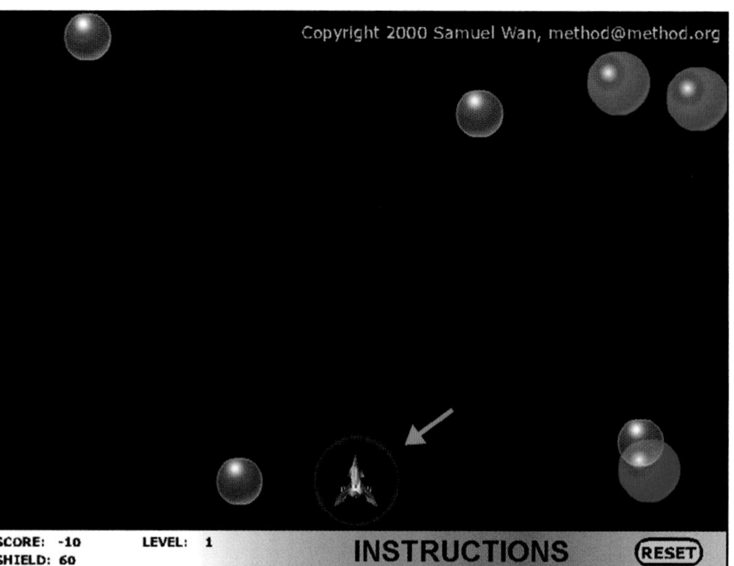

The ship then appears on the opposite side of the screen.

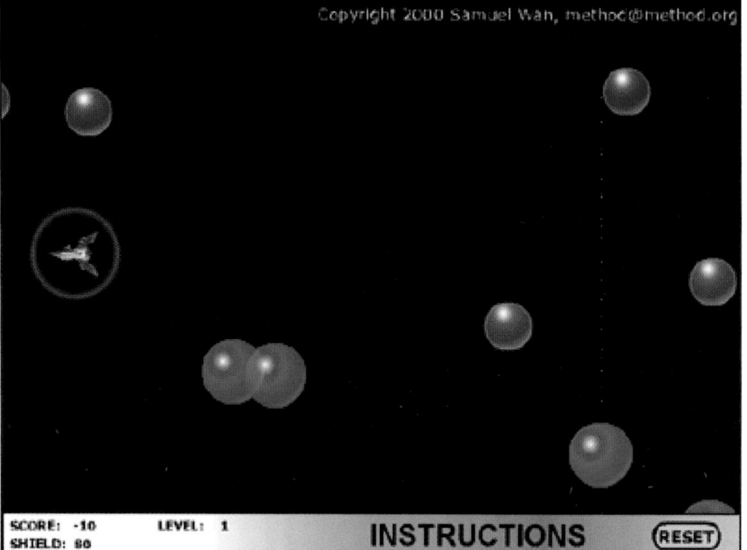

The ship wraps around the opposite side of the screen no matter where it exits the screen.

To reiterate the purpose of the screen wrapping code, consider what would happen if the ship moved toward the left. If the right-most edge of the ship is to the left of the left-most side of the screen, you would simply move the ship to the right side of the screen, so the ship appeared to "wrap" around the screen as it moves.

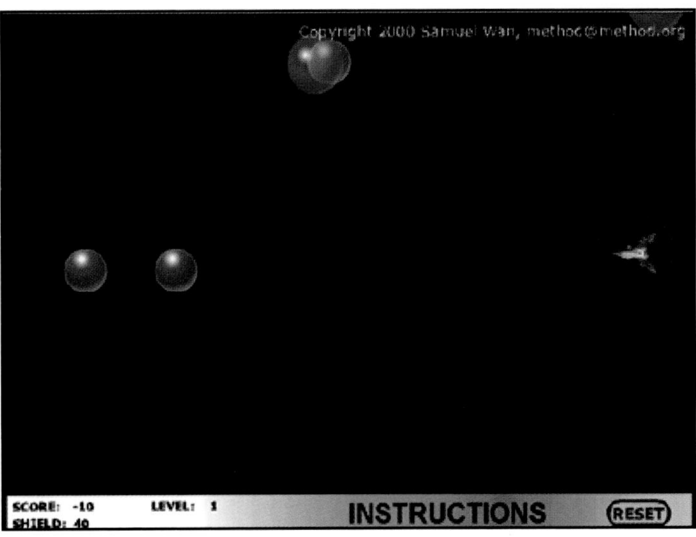

The ship exits off the Stage area.

How It Works

Wow, you've certainly written a lot of code to cover several concepts, so take a look at the whole code for the ship movie clip and review the concepts in each portion. In the **onClipEvent(load)** handler, you initialized all the variables as soon as the movie clip loaded into the Flash player. You also set the rocket thrusters for the ship to invisible and set the ship to point toward the top of the screen by default.

The **onClipEvent(enterFrame)** handler contains code that loops continually after the **load** handler code has been executed. This portion of the code contains separate sections that detect whether specific keys on the keyboard are being pressed by using the corresponding key numbers. If a specific key is pressed, ***xspeed*** and ***yspeed*** are calculated, and the corresponding rocket thruster graphic is made visible.

The left and right arrow keys cause the ship to turn left and right; its speed is determined by the ***turnspeed*** variable initialized at the top of the code. The other direction keys trigger calculations with Cosine and Sine to find how far the ship should move toward the x and y directions using ***xspeed*** and ***yspeed***.

Then the propulsion section of the code moves the ship by the value of ***xspeed*** and ***yspeed***. The final section handles screen wrapping, so the ship will wrap to the other side of the screen if it flies outside of the screen boundaries.

9

PROGRAMMING THE COLLISION DETECTION OF MULTIPLE PROJECTILES

By Samuel Wan

The concept of collision detection is easy enough to understand: Compare the areas of two movie clips to see if they overlap. The **hitTest** function in ActionScript makes the detection of colliding movie clips simple enough by comparing two objects to see if they overlap. If they do overlap at some point, the two movie clips are considered to have collided against one another. The **hitTest()** function in Actionscript is a very convenient method of collision detection. This function compares the bounding boxes of two movie clips to see if they overlap. Bounding boxes are like imaginary rectangles around the edges of a movie clip that define its left edge, right edge, top edge, and bottom edge. For example, if you were to compare the collision of two movie clips, bubble and ship, you would simply call the **hitTest** method of one movie clip and insert the instance name of the other movie clip as the parameter. The method returns a true or false: true if a collision was detected, or false if no collision was detected.

```
IsCollided = Bubble.hitTest("ship");
```

In the preceding line, the bubble movie clip's hitTest method is called to compare against the ship movie clip. If the bubble movie clip

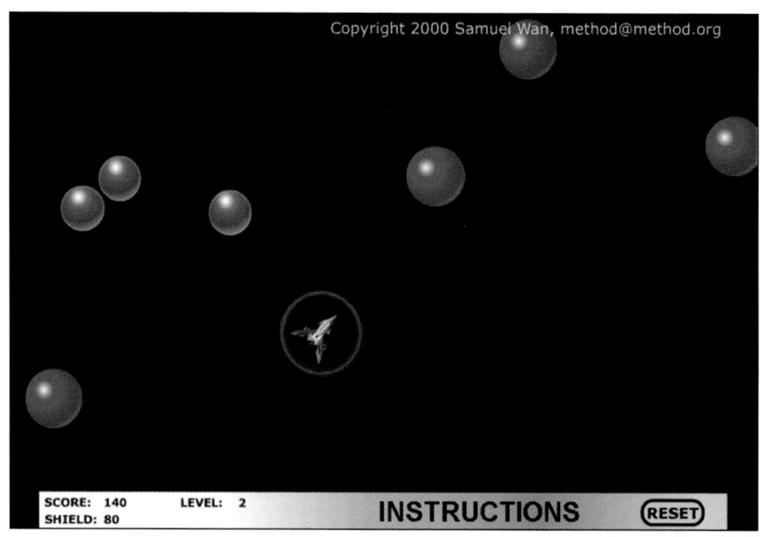

overlaps with the ship movie clip, the **hitTest** function will return a **true** to the ***IsCollided*** variable. Otherwise, the function will return a **false** if they don't overlap. This line of code is simple enough, but unlike the ship module, which contains only one ship, the bubble module contains many bubbles. How do you use the **hitTest** function to detect collision of the ship against more than one bubble? Objects in constant motion, also referred to as projectiles, change their position after every iteration of ActionScript. You could take a very crude approach and write code to compare the collision of each bubble to the ship like so:

```
IsCollided = Bubble1.hitTest("ship");
IsCollided = Bubble2.hitTest("ship");
IsCollided = Bubble3.hitTest("ship");
IsCollided = Bubble4.hitTest("ship");
```

However, writing out a line of code for every single projectile in the game is not only an inefficient way to program, but it's also tough on your fingers. So the question remains: How do you apply collision detection to multiple projectiles in an efficient, elegant way? To answer this question, you need to come up with a way to associate all the bubbles into a single, easy-to-use catalog system.

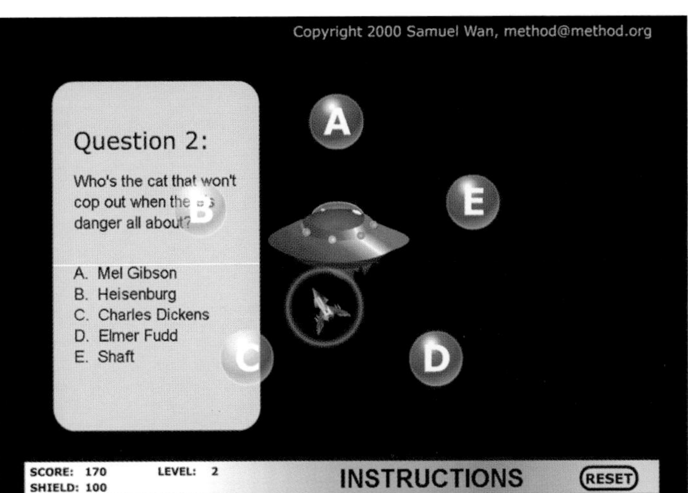

This scene has several bubbles that must be able to detect a collision with the ship.

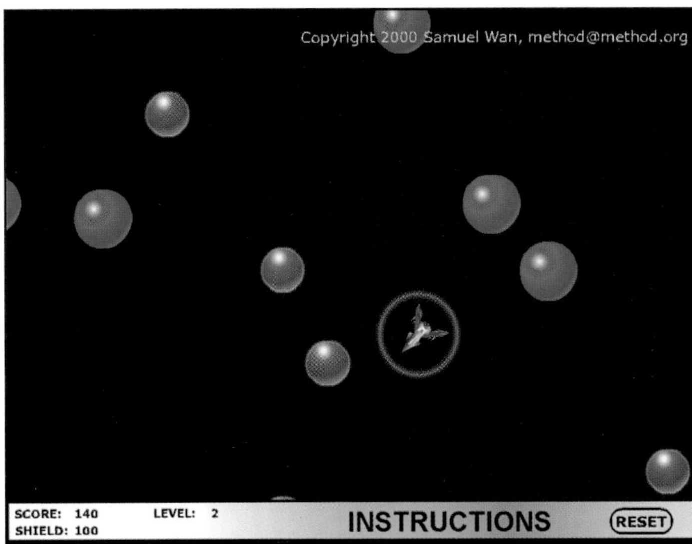

Multiple copies of the same two bubbles must be able to detect a collision with the ship in this scene.

Preparing for Associative Arrays

A catalog system is a handy way to reference objects—like the drawers of alphabetically organized cards that provide information about books in a library. In the same way, associative arrays allow us to build a small box of cards that are "associated" with objects, such as movie clips. If an associative array is like a box of reference cards, the card inside the box would be the equivalent of an "element" inside the associative array. This element could refer to an object, a variable, a value, and so on, but in this case, you want to build an array and associate its elements to movie clips. Let's walk through the construction of an associative array of bubbles in the game.

1 Open the BubbleFighter_Start3.fla file in the Chapter 09 folder and save it to your local hard drive. (The final file is BubbleFighter_Final3.fla.)

2 In the main timeline, look for the layer named Bubbles and select the second frame (frame 2) on that layer. Open the Bubbles Folder in the Library and drag the Good Bubble Module movie clip onto the Stage.

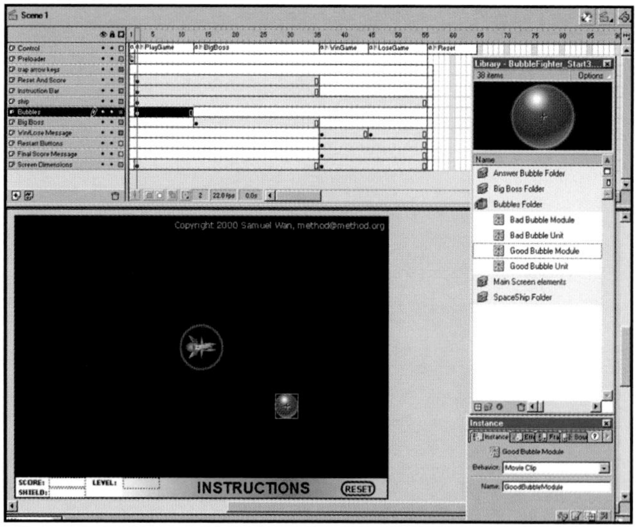

Drag the GoodBubbleModule movie clip onto the Stage at the second frame of the Bubbles layer.

3 Give the movie clip an instance name of **GoodBubbleModule**, and double-click on it to take a quick peek inside.

You'll notice that the movie clip contains another movie clip with an instance name called original-bubble. This movie clip contains the graphics that draw a bubble, and it acts as a template from which you can duplicate more bubbles.

4 Go back to the original timeline and open up the Actions panel of the GoodBubbleModule movie clip. Apply this ActionScript to initialize the bubble module:

```
onClipEvent (load) {
    maxBubbles = 5;
    bubble = new Array();
}
```

Apply the **onClipEvent (load)** code to the GoodBubbleModule movie clip.

> **Note:** As explained in previous chapters of this arcade game, **onClipEvent(load)** is an event handler that will execute all the code within its brackets one time after the movie clip has loaded.

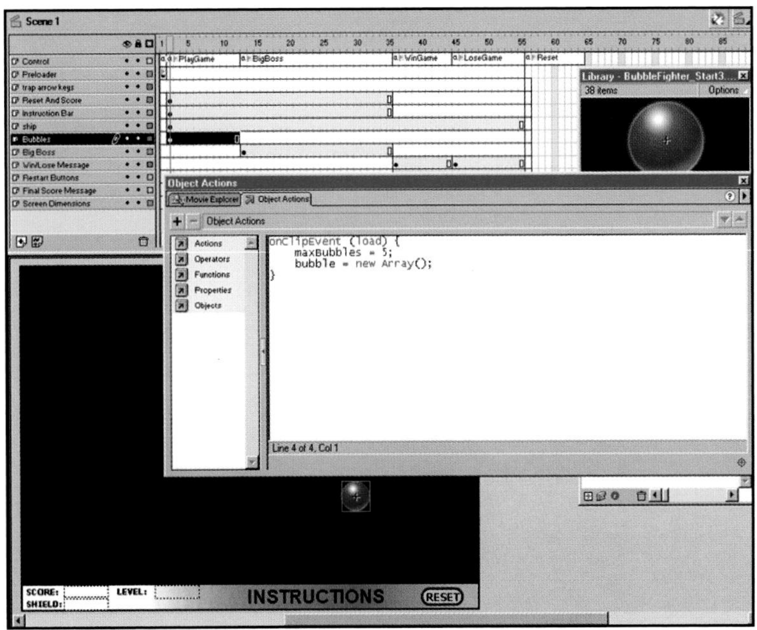

The Object Actions window shows the **onClipEvent(load)** code assigned to the GoodBubbleModule movie clip.

You created one variable and one array as soon as the GoodBubbles movie clip was loaded into the Flash player. The variable ***maxBubbles*** stores the maximum number of bubbles needed for the GoodBubbles module. The **bubbles** array will act as the cataloging box to keep track of all the bubbles.

Duplicating Bubbles and Associating Them to an Array

Now that you've initialized this module, you're ready to work with the bubble array. In this section, you add the ActionScript to accomplish three tasks. The first task is to duplicate the original Bubble movie clip inside the GoodBubbleModule movie clip into a new bubble movie clip with an appended number (such as bubble0, bubble1, bubble2, bubble3, and so on). The second task is to associate an element of the **bubbles** array to each new bubble instance. The third task is to assign random speed, direction, and original position of the new bubbles.

1. After the code that creates the new bubble array, insert this code:

```
var screen = _root.screen.getBounds(_root);
```

Add the ***screen*** variable to the GoodBubbleModule movie clip.

This code creates an object called screen that holds the left, right, upper, and lower bounds of the game area on the main timeline. Thus, the screen object contains properties of ***screen.xMin***, ***screen.xMax***, ***screen.yMin***, and ***screen.yMax***.

Note: See the previous chapter for more information about bounds and how you use the screen movie clip to get the bounds of the game area.

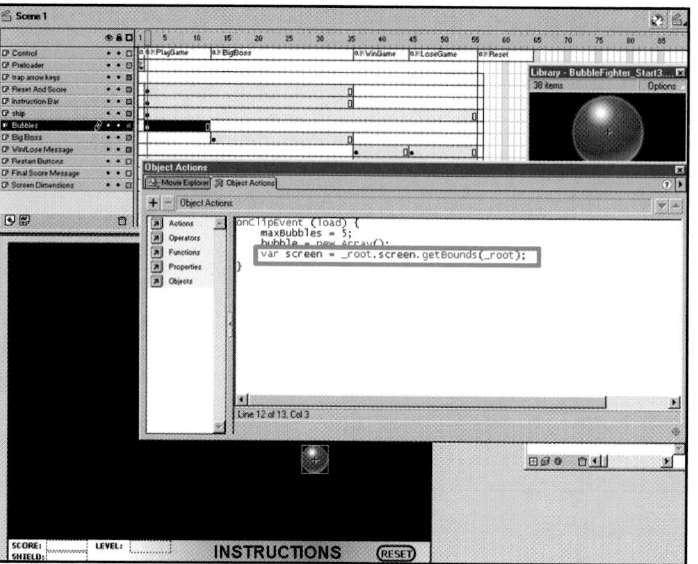

The ***screen*** variable is added to the GoodBubbleModule movie clip.

2 Use this code to duplicate to create a new instance of the original Bubble movie clip, and then assign that instance to the **bubble[]** array:

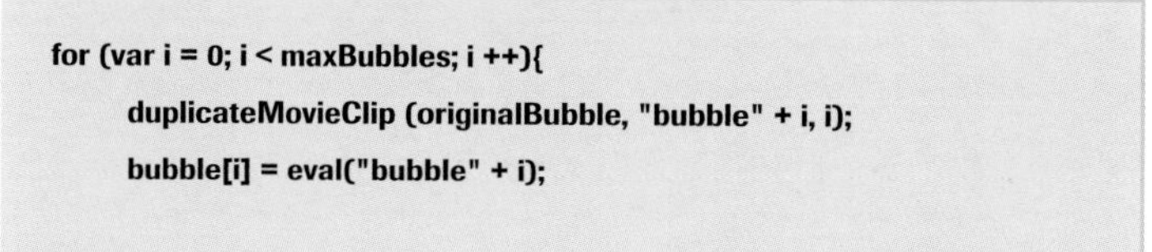

```
for (var i = 0; i < maxBubbles; i ++){
    duplicateMovieClip (originalBubble, "bubble" + i, i);
    bubble[i] = eval("bubble" + i);
```

Continue adding to the **onClipEvent(load)** code on the GoodBubbleModule movie clip.

To do this many times without writing many lines of code, you use a **for** loop to run through the whole process as many times as specified by the value of **maxBubbles**. The first line of code in the **load** event handler gave **maxBubbles** a value of **5**, so you loop through the duplication and array assignment five times.

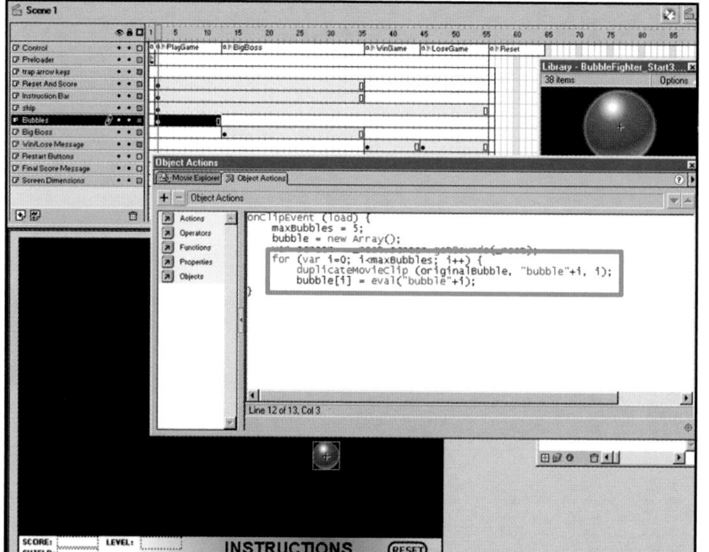

The **for** loop is added to the GoodBubbleModule movie clip.

Note that the variable ***i*** will increment from 0 through 4, for a total of five times (counting 0, 1, 2, 3, and 4). This code creates a new instance with the name bubble followed by the value of ***i***, so that you create four duplicated movie instances with the names bubble0, bubble1, bubble2, bubble3, and bubble4, at depths from 0 through 4, respectively.

3 Set the bubble's location to a random *x* and *y* position, within the *x* and *y* bounds of the screen movie clip, using this code:

```
bubble[i]._x = random(screen.xMax);
bubble[i]._y = random(screen.yMax);
```

Use this code to set a random location for each of the duplicate bubbles.

If all the bubbles moved at the same speed in the same direction, the game would feel too artificial, so you want to assign two variables, one for horizontal ***xspeed*** and one for vertical ***yspeed***, inside each bubble's movie clip.

4 Use this code to assign the variables:

```
bubble[i].xspeed = (int(random(5)) + 2) * (1 - (random(2)* 2));
bubble[i].yspeed = (int(random(5)) + 2) * (1 - (random(2)* 2));
}
```

Insert this code to set a random speed for each of the duplicate bubbles.

The formula in the two lines actually works in two parts to generate a random value for the ***xspeed*** and ***yspeed*** directions. The first part of the formula, **(int(random(5) + 2))**, generates a random number from 2 through 6.

The second part of this formula, **(1 - (random(2)* 2))**, returns a value of either **1** or –**1**. Its actual function is a bit more complicated than the first part, but it's much more worthy of a closer look. Note that the expression **random(2)** will return either zero or one (**0** or **1**). When you multiply that random expression by 2 to express **(random(2) * 2)**, you receive a value of either zero or 2 (**0** or **2**). The results are limited to these two values because zero times two is still zero (0 ⋆ 2 = 0), whereas one times two is equal to two (1 ⋆ 2 = 2). Subtracting this random expression of either zero or 2 from a number of 1 will produce only two possible calculations:

(1 - (random(2)* 2))
First possible calculation: 1 – 0 = 1
Second possible calculation: 1 – 2 = -1

Multiplying both parts of the formula results in random values from **–6** through **–2** or **2** through **6**. This allows us to tell the bubble to move randomly at a speed ranging from two through six in either a forward or backward direction. Because you use the same formula to set the values for ***xspeed*** and

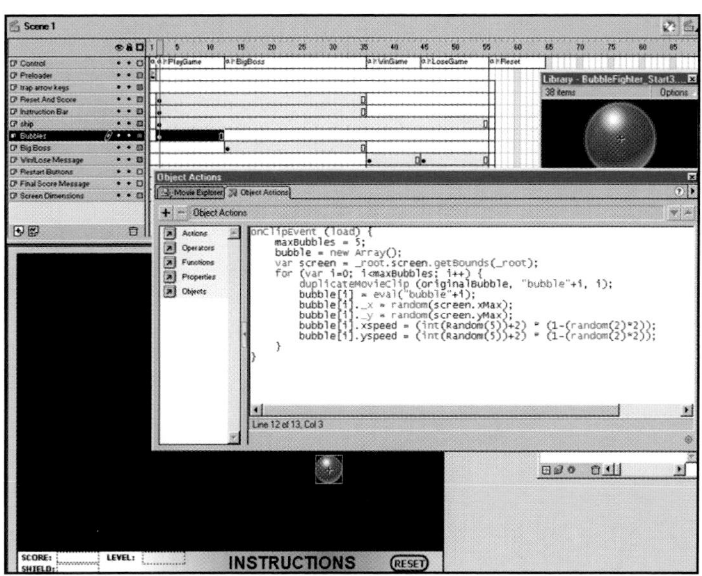

The additional code is added to the **onClipEvent(load)** code.

yspeed, those two lines of code will make the bubble move forward or backward, upward or downward, within a specific range of random numbers.

After all the duplication, positioning, and randomizing of speed has been completed, you no longer need the originalBubble movie clip, so you simply make it invisible.

> **Note:** For more detailed explanations about the mechanics inside the **random** function, refer to the Macromedia Flash documentation under the keyword "Random".

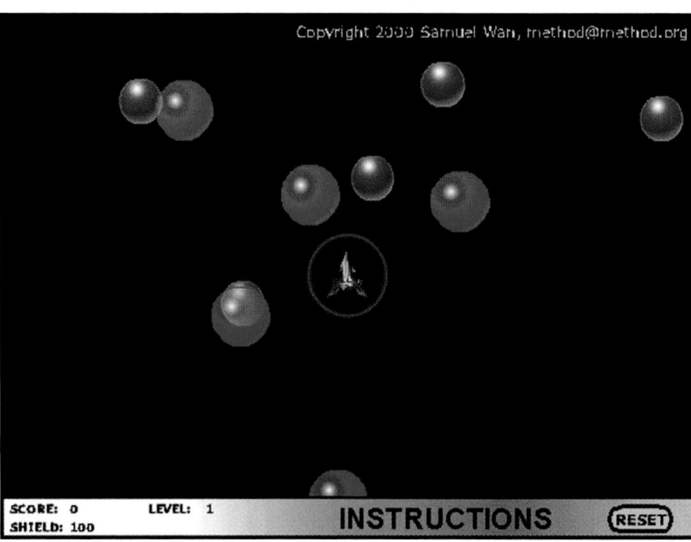

The bubbles appear randomly on the stage and move in random directions and at random speeds.

5 Use this code to make the movie clip invisible and close out the **onClipEvent(load)** event handler with a closing bracket:

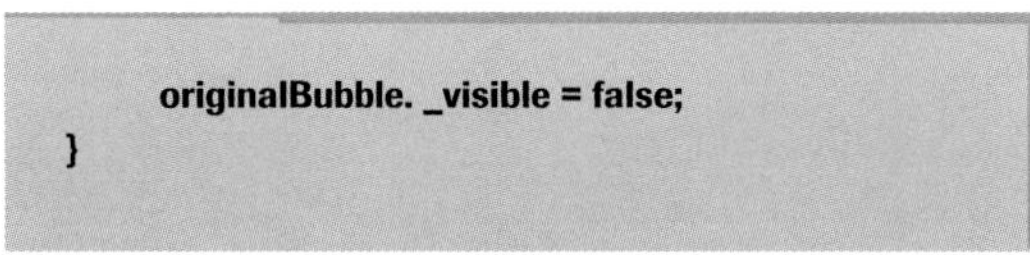

```
    originalBubble. _visible = false;
}
```

Insert the code that makes the originalBubble movie clip invisible.

Your final code for the **onClipEvent(load)** event handler for the goodbubble module should look like this:

```
onClipEvent (load) {
    maxBubbles = 5;
    bubble = new Array();
    var screen = _root.screen.getBounds(_root);
    for (var i = 0; i < maxBubbles; i ++){
        duplicateMovieClip (originalBubble, "bubble" +
        ➥i, i);
        bubble[i] = eval("bubble" + i);
        bubble[i]._x = random(screen.xMax);
        bubble[i]._y = random(screen.yMax);
        bubble[i].xspeed = (int(Random(5)) + 2) *
        ➥(1 - (random(2)* 2));
        bubble[i].yspeed = (int(Random(5)) + 2) *
        ➥(1 - (random(2)* 2));
    }
    originalBubble. _visible = false;
}
```

(The ➥ symbol you see here is for editorial purposes only.)

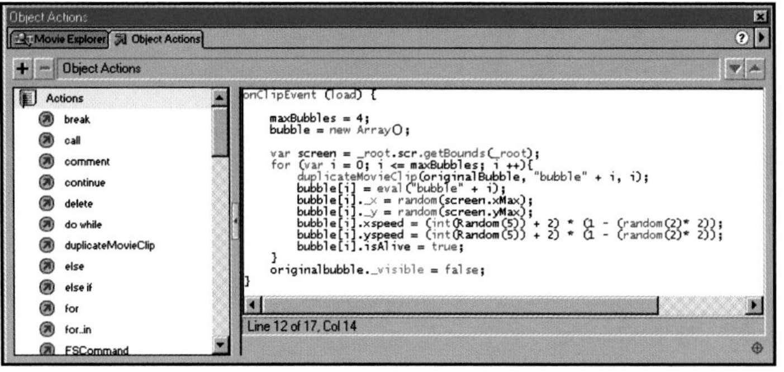

The **onClipEvent(load)** code now turns the original Bubble movie clip invisible.

The steps you've taken to initialize the bubble module during the **load** event handler reflect an essential concept in advanced Flash programming. Let's go over it one more time to make sure all the concepts are understood…

You create a loop with a counter variable called ***i*** that counts from zero to a number right below the number stored in ***maxBubbles***.

You start with the number zero because the first element in an array is counted as the zero element instead of the first element.

Every time the loop iterates, a new duplicate of the originalBubble Movie Clip is created, and it is dynamically given an instance name of "bubble" with the increasing value of variable ***i*** attached at the end (for example bubble0, bubble1, bubble2, bubble3 and so on). The new duplicate movie is also given a depth of ***i***, because two duplicate movies cannot occupy the same depth in the same timeline.

You assign the new bubble instance to an element of the **bubbles** array according to the increasing ***i*** variable. You then have to use the **eval()** statement to reference an object with the name bubble + ***i*** instead of simply creating a string value. The result of running through the **for** loop and associating objects will produce an array with associated bubble instances. For example, the first four elements of the array will be associated like so:

```
Bubble[0] = bubble0;
Bubble[1] = bubble1;
Bubble[2] = bubble2;
Bubble[3] = bubble3;
```

Note: Even though you started with zero as the first element in the array **(bubble[0])**, it's perfectly acceptable to duplicate a movie into a depth of 0, but not a depth with a negative number.

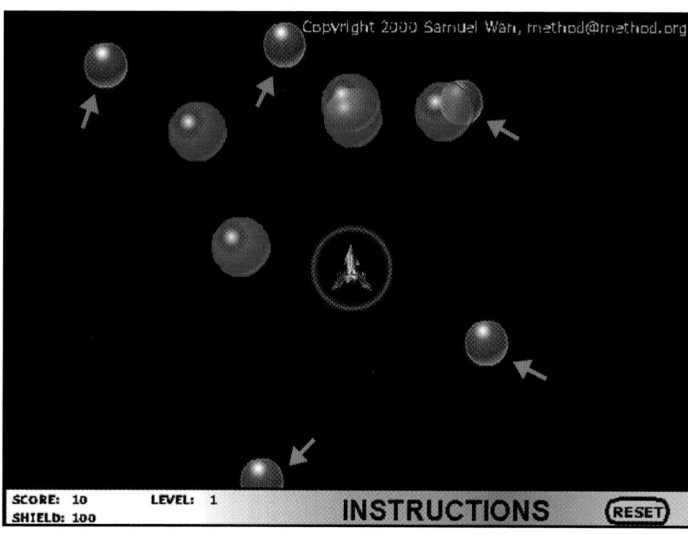

The **onClipEvent(load)** code uses duplicate movie clips to make several copies of the GoodBubble movie clip.

To set the location of the bubbles, you assign a random value between zero and the maximum bounds of the screen movie clip in the main timeline to the *_x* and *_y* values of the bubble instance.

```
bubble[i]._x = random(screen.xMax);
bubble[i]._y = random(screen.yMax);
```

To set the initial speed, you create two variables inside the duplicated movie clip: one for the horizontal speed (***xspeed***) and one for the vertical speed (***yspeed***). Use the formula **(1 - (random(2)* 2)** with the variables to generate a random number between 2 and 6.

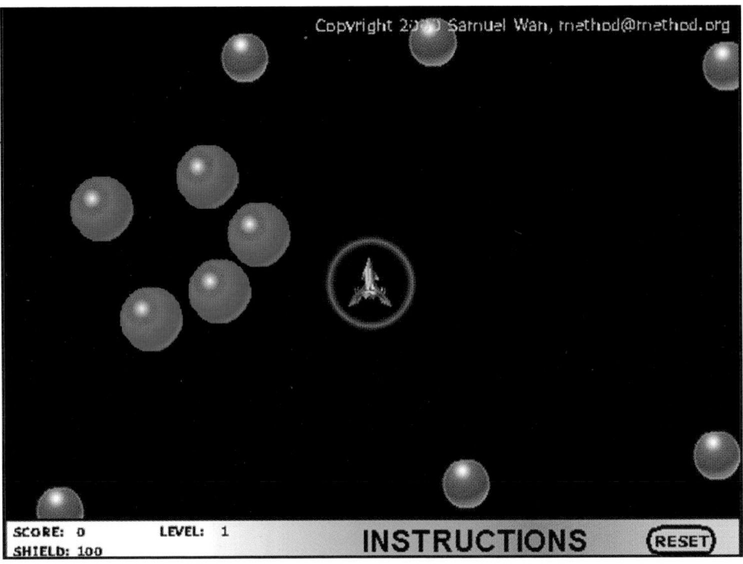

Compare this figure to the previous figure (both were shot at the beginning of game play), and you see that the bubbles are randomly positioned at the beginning of the game.

By varying the horizontal and vertical speed of the bubbles, each bubble's direction is likely to be unique. You can add more variety to a bubble's direction by multiplying ***xspeed*** and ***yspeed*** by a positive 1 or –1.

You set the original Bubble to invisible because you need only the new duplicated instances.

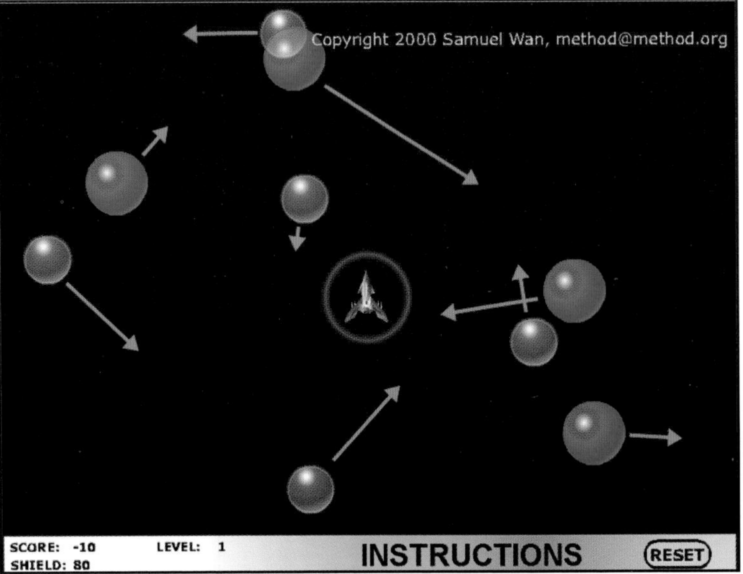

Although it's difficult to tell on the printed page, the Bubbles movie offers a variety of different directions and speeds.

MOVING THE BUBBLES

As far as the movement and screen-wrapping goes, the code for the bubble and ship are quite similar. Again, you insert code inside the looping **onClipEvent (enterframe)** event handler to continuously update the position of each bubble and to monitor for any collisions against the ship. The only difference is that the movement and screen-wrapping algorithms refer to elements of an associative array inside a **for** loop instead of a single object. The **for** loop uses the variable ***i*** for a counter again, and the loop iterates until the value of ***i*** reaches the maximum number of elements in the **bubbles** array. We are using the array length as the maximum number of iterations in the loop for a very important reason, which is revealed near the end of this chapter.

1 After the **onClipEvent (load)** handler, add this code to begin the **onClipEvent (enterframe)** handler and the looping:

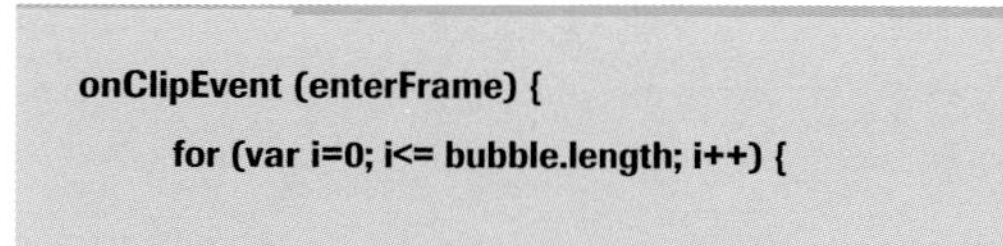

```
onClipEvent (enterFrame) {
    for (var i=0; i<= bubble.length; i++) {
```

Instantiate the **onClipEvent(enterFrame)** handler and add a **for** loop.

In the previous section, during the **load** event handler, you associated each new duplicated instance of the originalBubble movie clip with an element in the **bubble** array, where bubble0 is associated with **bubble[0]**, bubble1 is associated with **bubble[1]**, bubble2 is associated with **bubble[2]**, and so on. Now you're looping through each array and moving each associated bubble movie clip. Looping from 0 through the length of the **bubble** array will also loop through each element in the **bubble** array.

As you loop through each bubble, you want to move it in the *x* and *y* direction according to its unique randomized speed that you assigned during the **load** event handler (explained at the beginning of this chapter).

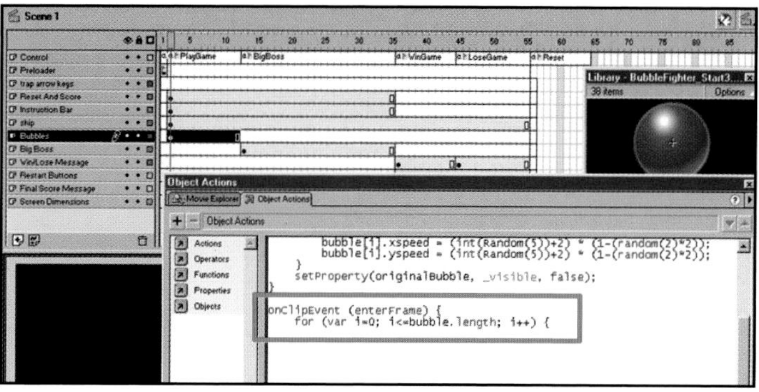

The **onClipEvent(enterFrame)** code begins after the **onClipEvent(load)** code.

2 Add the bubble's ***xspeed*** and ***yspeed*** to the bubble's current *x* and *y* position.

```
//Propulsion
bubble[i]._x = bubble[i]._x + bubble[i].xspeed;
bubble[i]._y = bubble[i]._y + bubble[i].yspeed;
```

Insert the code that handles movement or propulsion.

3 Next, you need to apply the exact same screen wrap technique that was explained in Chapter 7. The only difference is that instead of screen-wrapping the ship, you'll simply replace all references to the ship with references to the current bubble element, **bubble[i]**.

Remember, when you use the reference to an array element as **bubble[i]**, the value of variable ***i*** increments (increases by 1) during each loop, so all the code within the loop will affect all the duplicated instances of the bubble movie clips.

```
//Screen wrap
var screen = _root.screen.getBounds(_root);
var bubbleBounds = bubble[i].getBounds(_root);
var localscreen = _root.screen.getBounds(this);
if (bubbleBounds.yMax < screen.yMin) {
    bubble[i]._y = localscreen.yMax;
}
if (bubbleBounds.yMin > screen.yMax) {
    bubble[i]._y = localscreen.yMin;
}
if (bubbleBounds.xMax < screen.xMin) {
    bubble[i]._x = localscreen.xMax;
}
if (bubbleBounds.xMin > screen.xMax) {
    bubble[i]._x = localscreen.xMin;
}
}
}
```

Add the code that handles the screen wrapping for the bubbles.

Inserting the ActionScript for the Actual Collision Detection

Now that you have a way to conveniently reference all the bubbles within the module, you can also apply the **hitTest()** method within the **for** loop to detect for collision detection of each of the bubbles against the ship.

1 Apply this ActionScript right after the screen-wrap code inside the **enterframe** event handler:

The code goes into the bottom of the **enterFrame** event handler code so it fits like this:

```
onClipEvent (enterFrame) {
for (var i=0; i<= bubble.length; i++) {
    //Propulsion
    bubble[i]._x = bubble[i]._x + bubble[i].xspeed;
    bubble[i]._y = bubble[i]._y + bubble[i].yspeed;
```

```
//Collision Detection
if (bubble[i].hitTest(_root.ship.Hull)) {
    bubble[i].gotoAndPlay(2); // pop bubble
}
```

Add the beginning of the collision detection code to the **onClipEvent(enterFrame)** handler.

```
        //Screen wrap
        var screen = _root.screen.getBounds(_root);
        var bubbleBounds = bubble[i].getBounds(_root);
        var localscreen = _root.screen.getBounds(this);
        .
        .
        .
        if (bubbleBounds.xMin > screen.xMax) {
            bubble[i]._x = localscreen.xMin;
        }
        //Collision Detection
        if (bubble[i].hitTest(_root.ship.Hull)) {
            bubble[i].gotoAndPlay(2); // pop bubble
        }
    }
```

Each iteration of the loop causes each bubble instance to run a **hitTest** against the ship's main structure, the Hull. If a collision is detected, the bubble movie clip goes to a frame with the pop graphics. If you take a peek inside the Good Bubble Unit, which has an instance name of originalBubble, you will see that the second frame, which contains the popping bubble image, begins to play until the third frame. The third frame contains the command **removeMovieClip (this)**, which deletes that instance of the duplicated bubble movie clip. This structure allows you to choose how many frames to display the popped image before removing the bubble itself. Keep in mind that an original movie clip (one that wasn't duplicated from another clip) cannot be removed using the **removeMovieClip** command.

In the code you just inserted, there is an **if** conditional with a **hitTest** function that determines whether the bubble collided with the ship. The line of code inside that **if** conditional tells the bubble movie clip to go to the second frame.

```
bubble[i].gotoAndPlay(2); // pop bubble
```

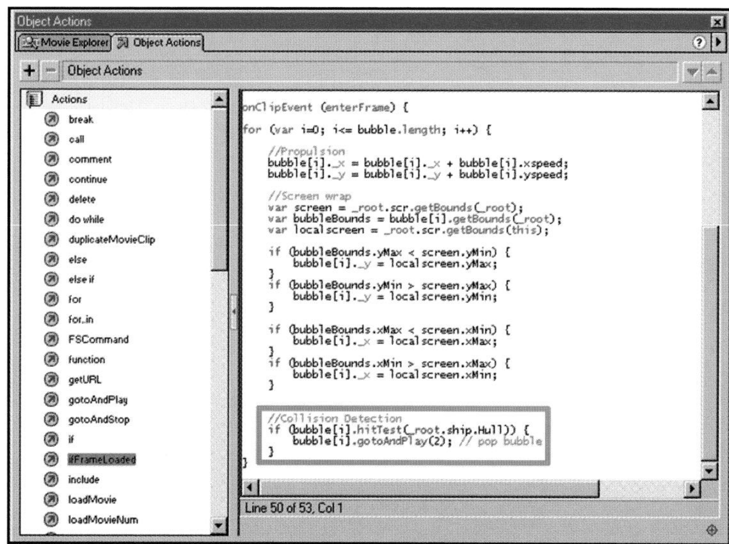

The first few lines of the collision detection code are entered.

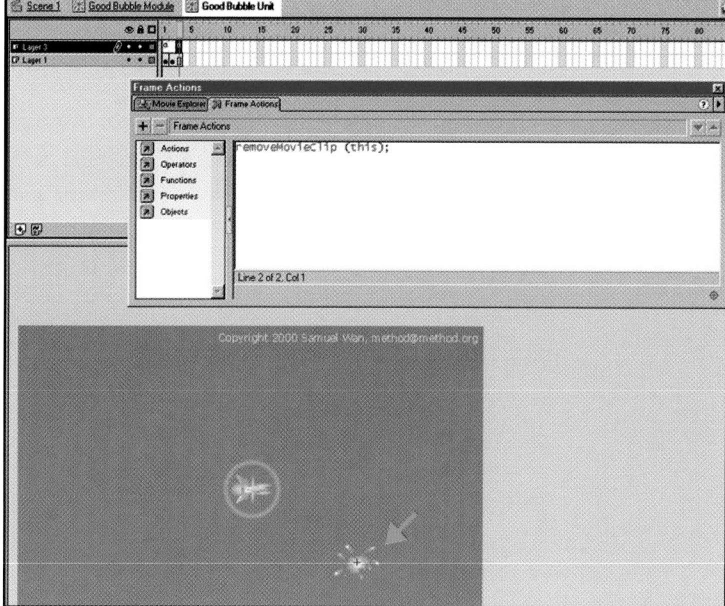

The third frame of the GoodBubbleModel movie clip contains a pop graphic and code that removes or deletes the movie clip.

2 Just below that **gotoAndPlay** command, inside the **if** conditional, add a **splice** method to remove that associated element from the array.

```
bubble.splice(i, 1); //remove associated element from the array
```

Add the **bubble.splice** code to the **Collision Detection** code within the **onClipEvent(enterFrame)** handler.

The **splice** method simply removes an element from an array and decreases the length of the array by the number of elements removed. You remove the element from the array because that bubble is popped, so it saves the CPU power if it doesn't have to check bubbles that have been popped already. Because you've already set the loop to stop as soon as the ***i*** counter reaches the array length, the number of iterations in the loop will decrease as the bubbles are removed from the array. A gradually reduced number of iterations allows the game to run more smoothly because the CPU gradually has to do less work.

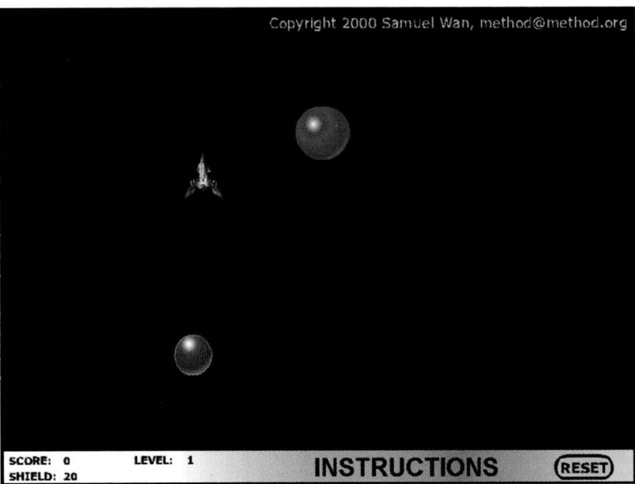

Removing bubbles as the ship collides with them saves CPU power because they no longer have to continually be accounted for.

3 Add one more line of code after the **splice** command to add ten points to the score if the good bubble is hit.

```
    _root.score = _root.score + 10;
}
```

Add the **_root.score** code to the **Collision Detection** code.

4 Add some code to check whether the game is over. If the **bubbles** array has reached zero, that means that all the bubbles have been popped, and all the associated elements in the array have been spliced out.

```
    //Is Game Over?
    if (bubble.length == 0) {
        _root.gotoAndStop("BigBoss");
    }
```

Add this code to the **onClipEvent(enterFrame)** handler below the **Collision Detection** code.

Your complete script for the GoodBubble Module should look like this:

```
onClipEvent(load){
        maxBubbles = 5;
        bubble = new Array();
        var screen = _root.screen.getBounds(_root);
        ➥onClipEvent (load) {
        for (var i = 0; i < maxBubbles; i ++){
                duplicateMovieClip (originalBubble,
                ➥"bubble" + i, i);
```

```
                bubble[i] = eval("bubble" + i);
                bubble[i]._x = random(screen.xMax);
                bubble[i]._y = random(screen.yMax);
                bubble[i].xspeed = (int(Random(5)) + 2) * (1 -
                ➥(random(2)* 2));
                bubble[i].yspeed = (int(Random(5)) + 2) * (1 -
                ➥(random(2)* 2));
        }
        originalBubble. _visible = false;
}
onClipEvent (enterFrame) {
        for (var i=0; i<= bubble.length; i++) {
                //Propulsion
                bubble[i]._x = bubble[i]._x + bubble[i].xspeed;
                bubble[i]._y = bubble[i]._y + bubble[i].yspeed;

                //Screen wrap
                var screen = _root.screen.getBounds(_root);
                var bubbleBounds = bubble[i].getBounds(_root);
                var localscreen = _root.screen.getBounds(this);
                if (bubbleBounds.yMax < screen.yMin) {
                        bubble[i]._y = localscreen.yMax;
                }
                if (bubbleBounds.yMin > screen.yMax) {
                        bubble[i]._y = localscreen.yMin;
                }
                if (bubbleBounds.xMax < screen.xMin) {
                        bubble[i]._x = localscreen.xMax;
                }
                if (bubbleBounds.xMin > screen.xMax) {
                        bubble[i]._x = localscreen.xMin;
                }
                //Collision Detection
                if (bubble[i].hitTest(_root.ship.Hull)) {
                        bubble[i].gotoAndPlay(2); // pop bubble
                        bubble.splice(i, 1);
                        _root.score = _root.score + 10;
                }

                //Is Game Over?
                if (bubble.length == 0) {
                        _root.gotoAndStop("BigBoss");
                }
        }
}
```

(The ➥ symbol you see here is for editorial purposes only.)

Note: The ActionScript for the good bubble module and the bad bubble module look nearly identical except for the code triggered by a collision detection, because hitting either kind of bubble with the ship will have different consequences in the game. This is a good example of how solid modular programming allows the same portions of script to be reused for similar tasks.

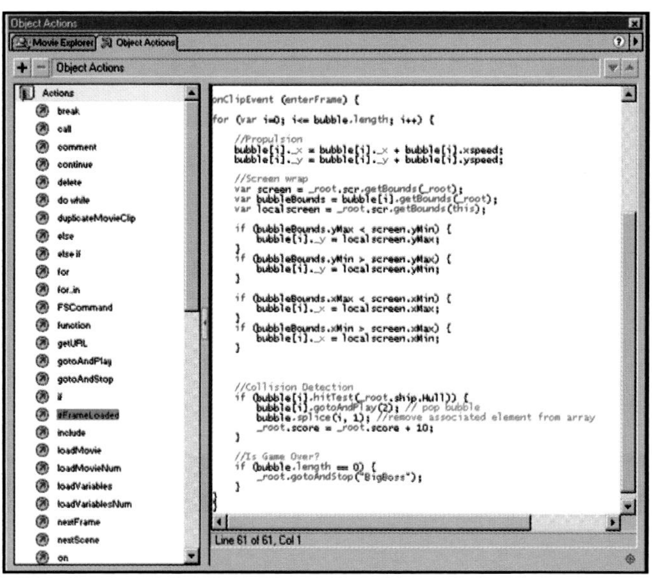

Your completed **onClipEvent(enterFrame)** handler should look like this after you add the **Game Over** code.

Reusing Code

In this section, you quickly and painlessly copy, paste, and modify that same code for the BadBubble module.

1 Select all the code in the Action panel for the Good Bubble Module, and then copy the code into the Clipboard by using Edit > Copy. Close the ActionScript panel.

2 Open the library and locate the Bad Bubble Module in the Bubbles Folder. Select the second frame of the Bubbles layer on the same timeline, the same frame that contains the Good Bubbles Module. Drag a copy of this movie clip onto the Stage and give it an instance name of **BadBubbleModule**.

3 Open the Action panel for the BadBubbleModule instance, put the cursor inside the Action panel, and choose Edit > Paste.

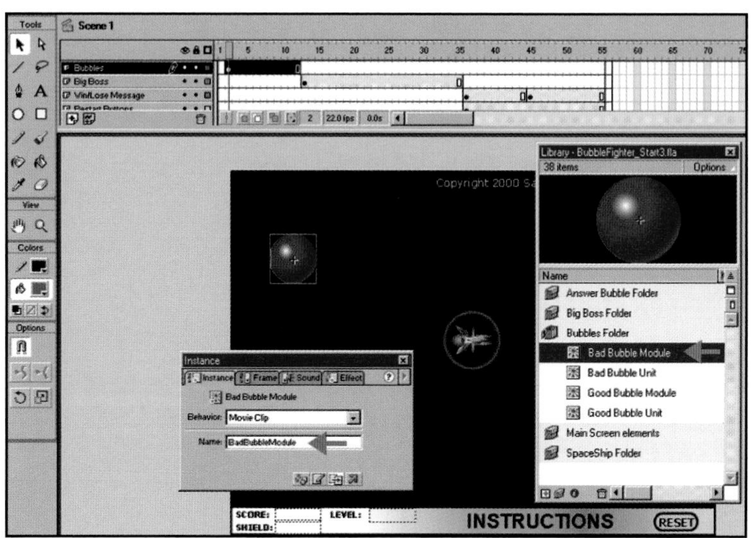

Drag an instance of the Bad Bubble Module movie clip onto the Stage on the Bubbles layer and give it an instance name of **BadBubbleModule**.

Voila, you have just copied and pasted all the code from the Good Bubble Module into the Bad Bubble Module.

4 Look at the **if** statement inside the **//Collision Detection** section. Instead of adding points each time a bubble is popped, you need to cause some damage to the ship. Right after the **splice** method, add code to show that the shield "sparks" a bit, because these are "bad" bubbles that are supposed to damage the ship. Because it damages the ship, you also have to reduce the shield transparency to show that it's weakening the shield. To do so, reduce the shield transparency by 10, and then reduce the hitpoints by 20.

```
//Collision Detection
if (bubble[i].hitTest(_root.ship.Hull)) {
      bubble[i].gotoAndPlay(2); // pop bubble
      bubble.splice(i, 1);

      //Reduce shields
      _root.ship.shield.gotoAndPlay(2); //Show shield sparks
      _root.ship.shield._alpha -= 20; //Reduce shield transparency
      _root.score = _root.score - 10; //Reduce score by 10 points.
      _root.ship.hitpoints -= 20;
}

//Is Game Over?
if (bubble.length == 0) {
      _root.gotoAndStop("BigBoss");
}
```

Modify the code that you copied and pasted from the GoodBubbleModule movie clip instance to reduce the shield and reduce points.

If the bad bubbles (the bigger blue bubbles) hit the ship too many times, the ship should lose its shield, and the player loses the game. If the player loses the game, the Flash movie goes to a frame called LoseGame that informs the player of the bad news. Because the LoseGame frame is text, you should also toggle the movie to high quality, so the text will show up anti-aliased and will be easy to read. You will make such changes to the **//Is Game Over?** section of the code.

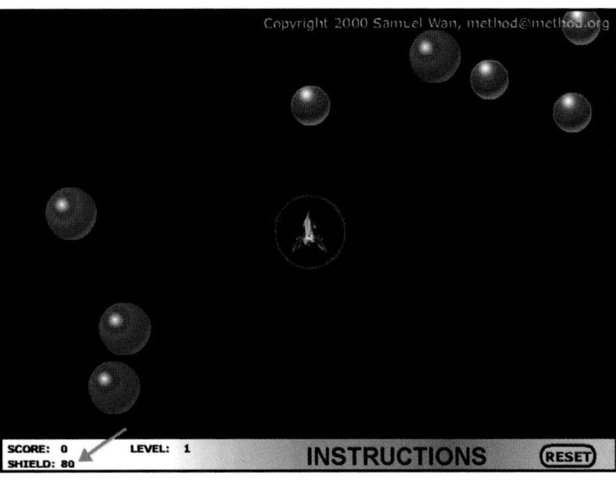

The Shield value is reduced every time the ship collides with a bad bubble.

5 Find the following code from the original Good Bubble Module version:

```
//Is Game Over?
if (_root.ship.hitpoints <= 0) { //Remember to change to
➥reflect shield strength
    _root._highquality = 1;
    _root.gotoAndStop("LoseGame");
}
```

(The ➥ symbol you see here is for editorial purposes only.)

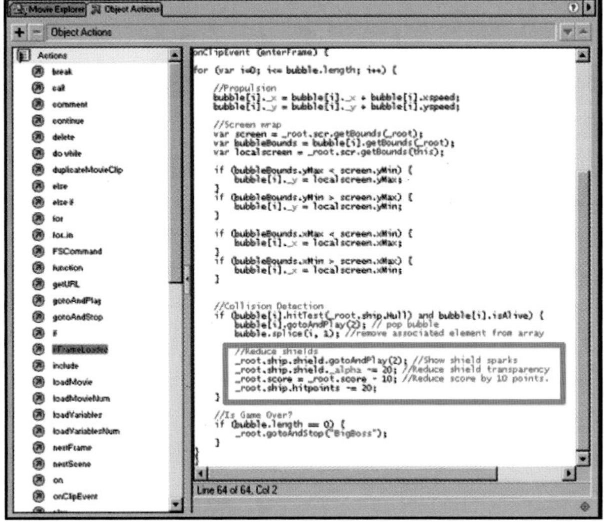

Modify the **Collision Detection** code as shown.

6 Replace the selected code with the Bad Bubble Module version:

```
//Is Game Over?
if (_root.ship.hitpoints <= 0) {
    //Remember to change to reflect shield strength
    _root._highquality = 1;
    _root.gotoAndStop("LoseGame");
}
```

Modify the **Game Over** code to ensure high-quality viewing and to display the LoseGame frame instead of BigBoss.

The final code for the BadBubbleModule should look like this:

```
onClipEvent (load) {
    maxBubbles = 5;
    bubble = new Array( );
    var screen = _root.screen.getBounds(_root);
    for (var i = 0; i < maxBubbles; i ++){
        duplicateMovieClip (originalBubble, "bubble" + i, i);
        bubble[i] = eval("bubble" + i);
        bubble[i]._x = random(screen.xMax);
        bubble[i]._y = random(screen.yMax);
        bubble[i].xspeed = (int(Random(5)) + 2) * (1 - (random(2)* 2));
        bubble[i].yspeed = (int(Random(5)) + 2) * (1 - (random(2)* 2));
    }
    originalBubble. _visible = false;
}

onClipEvent (enterFrame) {
    for (var i=0; i<= bubble.length; i++) {
            //Propulsion
            bubble[i]._x = bubble[i]._x + bubble[i].xspeed;
            bubble[i]._y = bubble[i]._y + bubble[i].yspeed;

            //Screen wrap
            var screen = _root.screen.getBounds(_root);
            var bubbleBounds = bubble[i].getBounds(_root);
            var localscreen = _root.screen.getBounds(this);
            if (bubbleBounds.yMax < screen.yMin) {
                bubble[i]._y = localscreen.yMax;
            }
            if (bubbleBounds.yMin > screen.yMax) {
                bubble[i]._y = localscreen.yMin;
            }
            if (bubbleBounds.xMax < screen.xMin) {
                bubble[i]._x = localscreen.xMax;
            }
            if (bubbleBounds.xMin > screen.xMax) {
                bubble[i]._x = localscreen.xMin;
            }
            //Collision Detection
            if (bubble[i].hitTest(_root.ship.Hull)) {
                bubble[i].gotoAndPlay(2); // pop bubble
                bubble.splice(i, 1);
                //Reduce shields
                _root.ship.shield.gotoAndPlay(2); //Show shield sparks
                _root.ship.shield._alpha -= 20; //Reduce shield transparency
                _root.score = _root.score - 10; //Reduce score by 10 points.
                _root.ship.hitpoints -= 20;
            }

            //Is Game Over?
            if (_root.ship.hitpoints <= 0) { //Remember to change to reflect shield strength
                _root._highquality = 1;
                _root.gotoAndStop("LoseGame");
            }
    }
```

How It Works

If this chapter were simply titled "Collision Detection," it would require only a paragraph explaining the **hitTest(target)** method. What makes this chapter worth reading is the fact that we've written code to detect collisions for multiple projectiles. To program algorithms for multiple objects (such as many bubbles flying around at once), you used a technique called "associative arrays." This type of array contains an element that refers to another object, such as a movie clip, and it is an elegant way to apply the same block of code to many associated movie clips by running through each element of the array inside a loop.

The two steps happened simultaneously to duplicate the originalBubble movie clip and to associate each duplicate instance to an element in the **bubbles** array. These two steps occurred inside the **onClipEvent(load)** event handler so they would execute only once, right after the bubble modules had loaded into the Flash Player. You initialized each movie clip by assigning it a randomized ***xspeed*** and ***yspeed***, and then you set each movie clip to a random location on the screen.

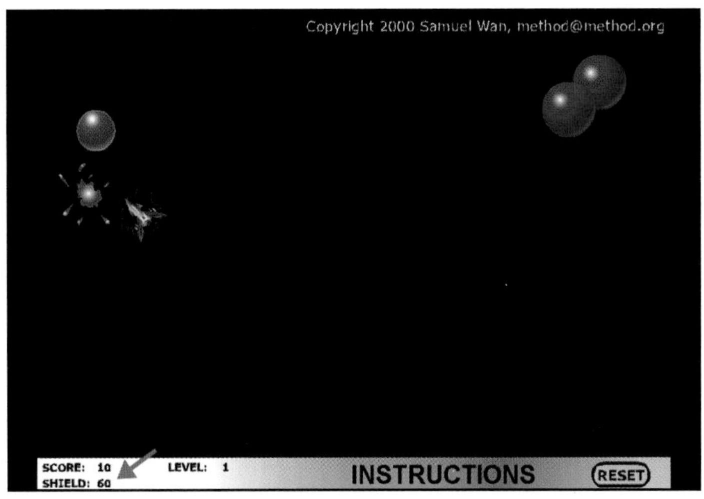

The ship's shield loses strength when you collide with a bad bubble.

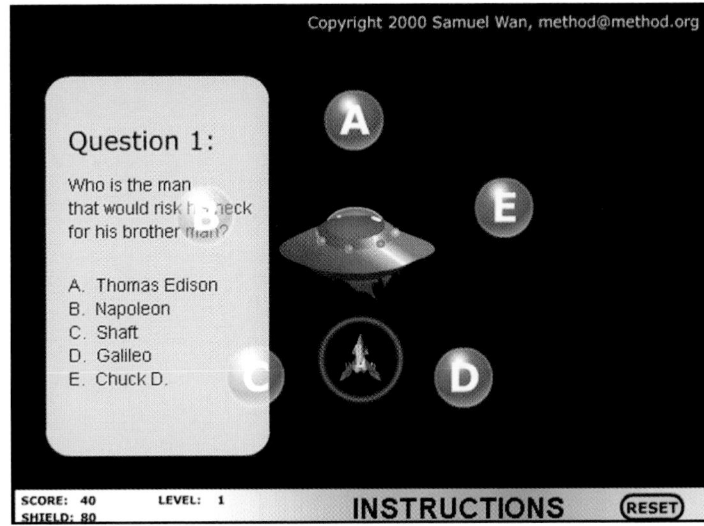

The player gets to go to the Big Boss screen if he removes all the good bubbles (the green ones).

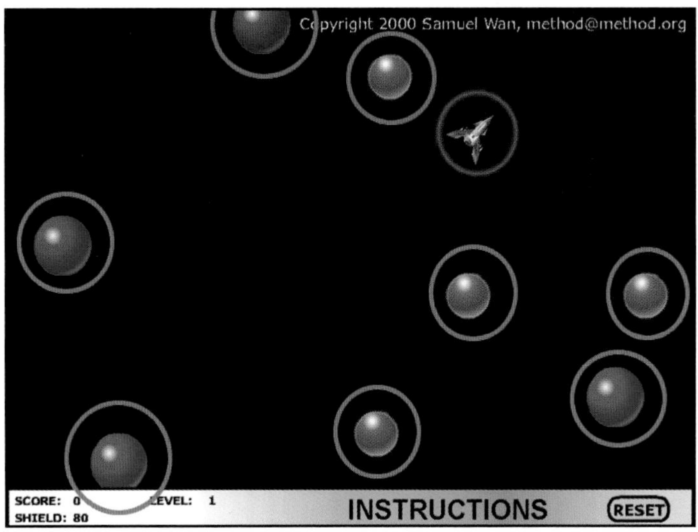

The Collision Detection engine must account for a number of objects or an array of objects.

The **onClipEvent(enterFrame)** handler contained all the code executed continually to move the bubbles and detect for collision. You used the same screen-wrap code with slight modification for the bubbles, too.

Several events occur in sequence when a collision is detected between a bubble and the ship's hull:

1. The bubble's associated element in the **bubbles** array is spliced (or removed) from the array.
2. The bubble goes to frame two and begins playing until frame three.
3. The ActionScript in frame three causes the bubble movie clip to remove itself.

If the ship has collided with a "good" bubble, the collision adds 10 points to the score. If it has collided with a "bad" bubble, the collision reduces the shield by 20 points.

Finally, you copied and pasted the complete code from the GoodBubbleModule to the BadBubbleModule and made certain adjustments to the code to reflect the behavior of the two different kinds of bubbles.

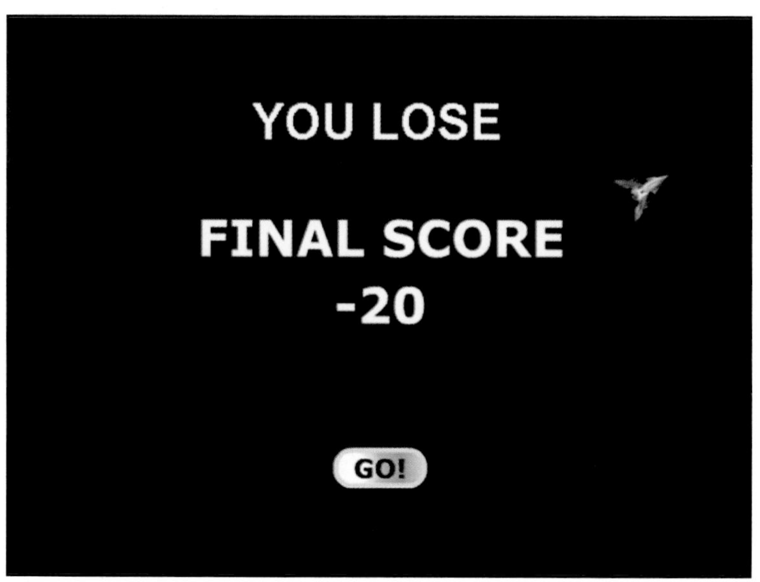

The player is sent to the Loser screen if he removes all the bad bubbles (the blue ones).

10

WORKING WITH THE COLOR OBJECT AND CURSORS

By David Emberton

Art Courtesy of Learning Soft
www.gamebrain.com
www.learningsoft.com

Coloring applications are a perennial favorite with children and are especially useful for developing hand-eye coordination and mousing skills. This particular example combines a raft of Flash 5 features to create a coloring application that's robust *and* compact. This chapter covers the use of the Color object, the **attachMovie** action, symbol linkage, and the Mouse object.

Throughout the course of the chapter, you will assign scripts to various keyframes and will set properties in the Library. The main tasks to be completed are setting up the paint program, creating the sliding color chooser, scripting the tool buttons, and scripting the paint tools themselves.

Initializing the Paint Program

Roughly half the ActionScript for SpacePainter is located on the first keyframe of the movie. It consists of three main sections: initialization, setup, and the creation of three custom functions that check the position of the mouse, adjust the current color display, and reset the picture. In this section, that script will be added to the Flash file, and the Linkage property of various symbols will be set to allow import.

1 Open SpacePainter_Start.fla in the Chapter 10 folder on the CD and save it to your hard drive. The file contains all the movies and graphics placed and named. (If you want to see the finished file, open SpacePainter_Final.fla.)

The first task is to hide the real cursor, and then call up an instance of the Pointer symbol from the Library to replace the cursor. The **attachMovie** action creates this instance of Pointer and places it in a very high level, so that it will always appear over top of other shapes drawn by the user. The code for making Pointer "stick" to the mouse will be added in the next section.

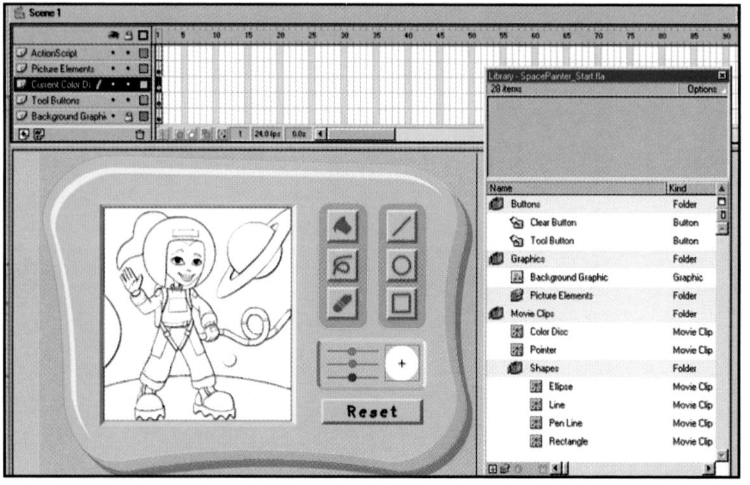

Open the SpacePainter_Start.fla file and save it to your local hard drive.

2 Open the Actions panel, select the first keyframe of the ActionScript layer, and insert this code:

```
// Change the Mouse Cursor
Mouse.hide();
_root.attachMovie("Pointer", "Pointer", 10000000);
```

Enter the code for the Mouse object that controls the visibility of the standard cursor.

This application makes extensive use of the Color object, which is a special kind of data object used to control the color of Movie Clip instances. The Color object works with RGB values, which are also commonly used in Web pages to set the color of various elements.

RGB stands for Red, Green, Blue, and an RGB value is used to describe a particular mix of those three colors onscreen. Flash can understand and display millions of different RGB combinations, each expressed as a hexadecimal number.

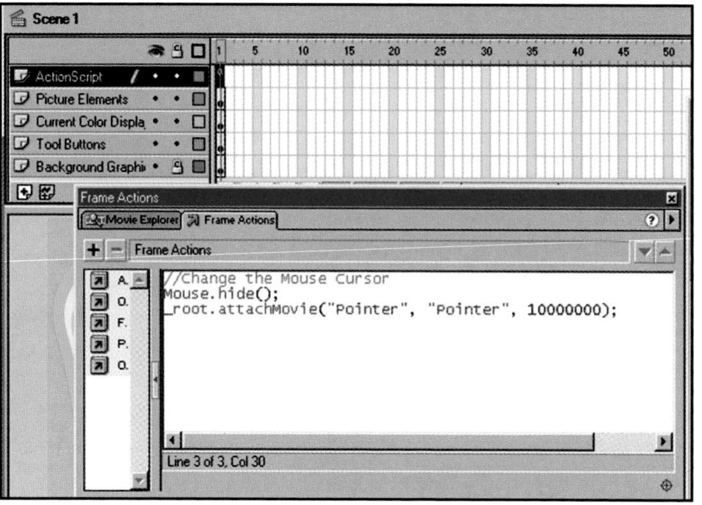

Mouse.hide() is added to the first frame of the ActionScript layer.

3 Use the Actions panel to insert this code:

Whereas a regular decimal number must switch to double digits after nine, in the hexadecimal number system, letters are used to create more single-digit numbers. This means that a single-digit hexadecimal number series includes 0, 1, 2, 3, 4, 5, 6, 7, 8, 9, A, B, C, D, E, and F. A through F stand for 10 through 15. This system allows millions of color combinations to be expressed in six digits.

The catch is to translate the positions of the sliders in the color chooser to hexadecimal, so an array of hex numbers must be set up.

First, an array of the single-digit hex numbers is created. Then two nested **for** loops populate a second array (**HexTable**) with all 256 two-digit hex combinations. Although each element in **HexTable** is a two-digit hex number, the actual elements are numbered as decimals from 0 to 255.

```
// Create Hexadecimal Number Array
HexSeries = new Array
➥("0","1","2","3","4","5","6","7","8","9","A","B","C","D","E","F");
HexTable = new Array();
CounterC = 0;
for (CounterA = 0; CounterA < 16; CounterA ++) {
    for (CounterB = 0; CounterB < 16; CounterB ++) {
        HexTable[CounterC] = HexSeries[CounterA] +
        ➥HexSeries[CounterB];
        CounterC ++;


    }

}
```

Use **for** loops to create a hexadecimal lookup table for number conversion. (The ➥ symbol you see here is for editorial purposes only.)

4 Add this code to create **CurrentColor**:

```
// Create Color object for Current Color Display
CurrentColor = new Color(CurrentColorDisplay);
AdjustColor();
```

Create a new Color object to control the appearance of **CurrentColorDisplay**, the Movie Clip instance.

Here the Color object creates **CurrentColor**, which will act as the color controller of the movie clip instance **CurrentColorDisplay**. **CurrentColorDisplay** is the larger circle to the right of the color sliders and displays the shade of color that's currently chosen.

Whereas most other objects have properties that are set directly (like *_x* and *_y*), to set the color of a movie clip, you must wrap it in an instance of Color.

Also in this code block, **AdjustColor()** is called. This is a function that will be defined later in this frame, and its job is to look at the three color sliders and change the properties of **CurrentColor** to reflect their positions.

The picture that comes with SpacePainter consists of fifteen elements, each of which is a different Movie Clip instance. To alter their appearances programmatically, an instance of the Color object must be created for each.

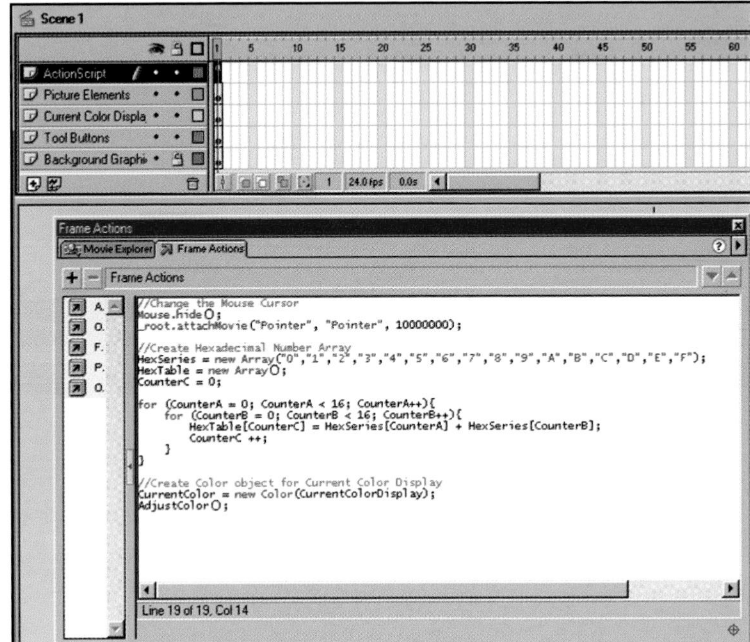

The **CurrentColor** code and the call to **AdjustColor()** are added to the script on the ActionScript layer.

In this code block, a **for** loop is used to count through each of the separate elements. The **eval** action is used to combine the value of ***Counter*** with some text to get the instance name of each element instance. Then all the new Color instances have their color set with the **setRGB** method. 0xFFFFFF is a hexadecimal number that stands for full-strength red, blue, and green (remember, FF is the highest two-digit hexadecimal number), and all three colors mixed at full intensity produces onscreen white.

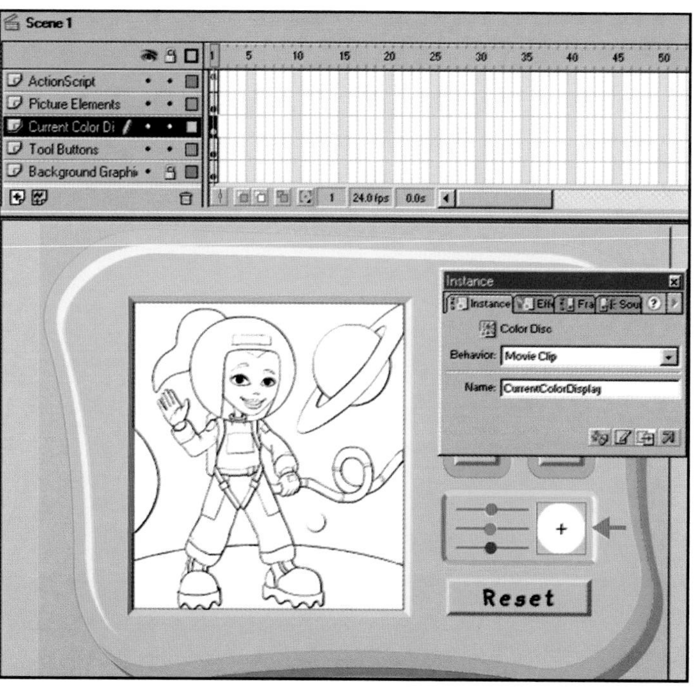

The ColorDisc movie clip already has an instance name of **CurrentColorDisplay**, which is reference in the code.

5 To complete the initialization section of this script, insert the following code:

Having entered the run-once section of the script, you will define the reusable custom functions. The first is **AdjustColor()**, which was called in step 3.

```
// Create Color objects for each Picture Element
for (Counter = 0; Counter < 15; Counter ++) {

    eval("Element" + Counter + "Color") = new Color(eval("Element" +
    ➥Counter));
    eval("Element" + Counter + "Color").setRGB(0xFFFFFF);

}
```

Use a **for** loop to create a Color instance for each of the 15 picture elements and color them white. (The ➥ symbol you see here is for editorial purposes only.)

6 To add the function, insert this code:

```
// Adjust Color Function
function AdjustColor() {

    // Get Color Mix
    RedValue = int(((RedSlider._x - 365) / 60) * 255);
    GreenValue = int(((GreenSlider._x - 365) / 60) * 255);
    BlueValue = int(((BlueSlider._x - 365) / 60) * 255);

    // Set Current Color
    CurrentColor.setRGB(parseInt(HexTable[RedValue] +
    ➥HexTable[GreenValue] + HexTable[BlueValue], 16));
}
```

AdjustColor() is a custom function that sets the appearance of the current color display. (The ➥ symbol you see here is for editorial purposes only.)

Note: How can a custom function be called before it has even been defined? Flash won't execute any code on a keyframe until it is completely loaded and the graphics have been drawn. Therefore, because **AdjustColor()** is defined on the same frame it is being called on, there will be no error.

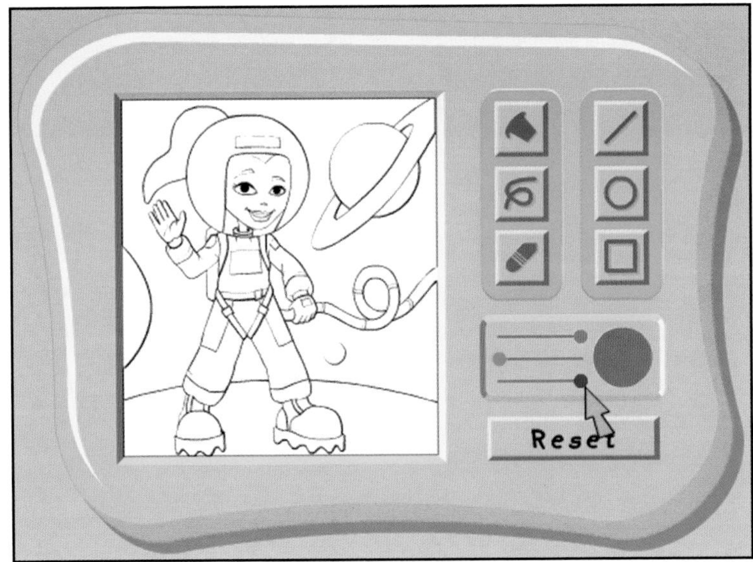

The **AdjustColor()** function evaulates the position of the sidebars and designates a color accordingly.

AdjustColor() evaluates the horizontal positioning of each of the three sliders in the color chooser. The sliders visually represent the amount of red, green, and blue (respectively) in the current color. So **AdjustColor()** calculates that mix and changes the appearance of **CurrentColorDisplay** in response.

The first part of the function creates three variables: ***RedValue***, ***GreenValue***, and ***BlueValue***. Each of these variables is assigned a value from 0 to 255, reflecting the *_x* position of its corresponding color slider. The sliders have a sixty pixel range of motion starting at X: 365, hence the numbers involved. For each slider, 365 is subtracted from the slider's *_x* position to arrive at a value from 0 to 60. That value is divided by 60 to get a percentage and then multiplied by 255 to equate that percentage value with a two-digit hexadecimal number. The equation doesn't tend to produce whole numbers, so the **int()** function is used to convert the result into an integer.

When all three values have been calculated, the resulting color is used to alter the appearance of **CurrentColorDisplay**. **CurrentColor** is the color object attached to that instance, so its **setRGB** method is used to set the shade. **parseInt()** is an ActionScript function that can work with numbers of bases other than 10, so it is used to combine all three color values as a hexadecimal number (base 16). Referencing an element in the **HexTable** array results in the two-digit hex numbers, and the + operator concatenates (joins) them.

The second custom function on this keyframe is **MouseInBounds()**, which is used to see if the mouse is currently being held over the picture area. The function returns a **true** or **false** value that is used by the drawing tool routines to decide whether or not they should draw. So if the mouse is outside the drawing area, **MouseInBounds()** will return **false**, and nothing will be drawn. Conversely, if the mouse *is* over the drawing area, **MouseInBounds()** will return **true**, and the operation will continue.

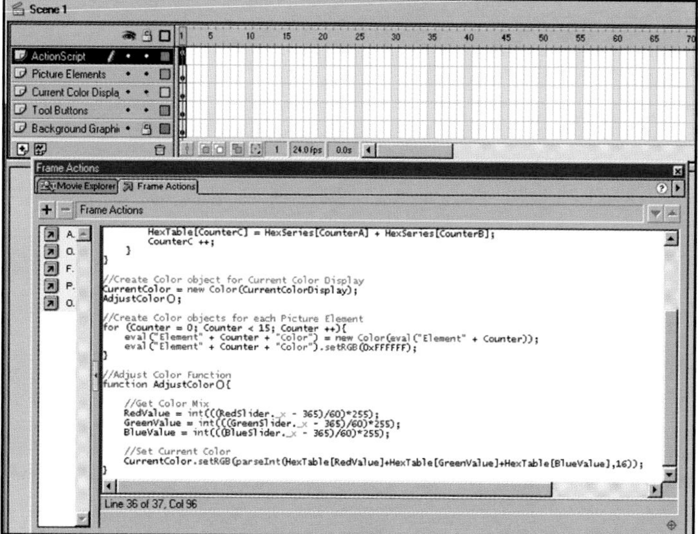

The **AdjustColor()** function is added to the code on the ActionScript layer.

7 Input this code to define the **MouseInBounds()** function:

```
// Check mouse position for draw operation
function MouseInBounds() {
    if (_xmouse > 83 && _xmouse < 317 && _ymouse > 67 && _ymouse < 323) {
        return(true);
    } else {
        return(false);
}
}
```

Enter the **MouseInBounds()** function, a custom function that checks for the position of the mouse cursor and returns **true** or **false**.

Note: Functions that return a value are very useful when creating programs. Whereas most functions perform some action, these types check a condition or make a calculation and return the result. There are several built-in ActionScript functions of this type; most of them are mathematical in nature like **int()** for calculating integers and **random()** for random numbers.

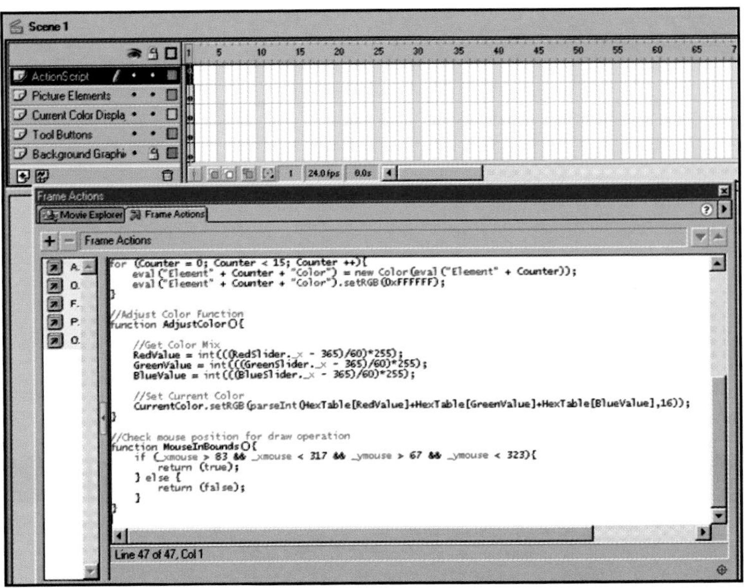

The **MouseInBounds()** function is added to the code on the ActionScript layer.

8 Insert the code for the third and final custom function, **Reset()**:

Reset() comprises two parts. The first resets the color of each of the picture elements back to white. This is similar to the code that appeared earlier, using the **for** loop to count through each of the element numbers while **eval** calculates their addresses.

The second part removes all the lines, ellipses, or rectangles the user may have drawn inside the picture area. The variable ***CurrentColorDisplay.ShapeCount*** keeps a count of all those objects while they're being drawn. A **for** loop counts from **0** to the value of ***ShapeCount***, using the **removeMovieClip** action to remove each one.

Throughout the SpacePainter application, the **attachMovie** action is used to instance symbols from the Library that are not manually placed on the Stage.

```
function Reset() {
    // Reset color of each Picture Element
    for (Counter = 0; Counter < 15; Counter ++) {
        eval("Element" + Counter + "Color").setRGB(0xFFFFFF);
    }
    // Remove all shapes
    for (Counter = 0; Counter <= CurrentColorDisplay.ShapeCount; Counter ++) {
        removeMovieClip("Shape" + Counter);
    }

    ShapeCount = 0;
}
```

Enter the **Reset()** function, which deletes all drawn shapes and recolors each picture element white.

To make sure these symbols are exported and available, you must set their Linkage properties.

9 To do that, select the specified symbol, and then choose Linkage from the Library's Options menu. In the Linkage dialog box, click the Export This Symbol option and type in the appropriate Identifier text (see the following table). The Identifier must be unique for each symbol and is used in the **attachMovie** action.

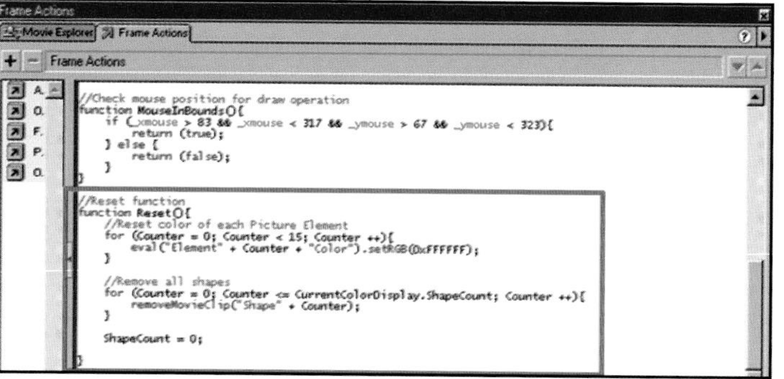

The **Reset()** function is added to the code on the ActionScript layer.

Symbol Name	Identifier
Movie Clips > Pointer	**Pointer**
Movie Clips > Shapes > Ellipse	**Ellipse**
Movie Clips > Shapes > Line	**Line**
Movie Clips > Shapes > Pen Line	**PenLine**
Movie Clips > Shapes > Rectangle	**Rectangle**

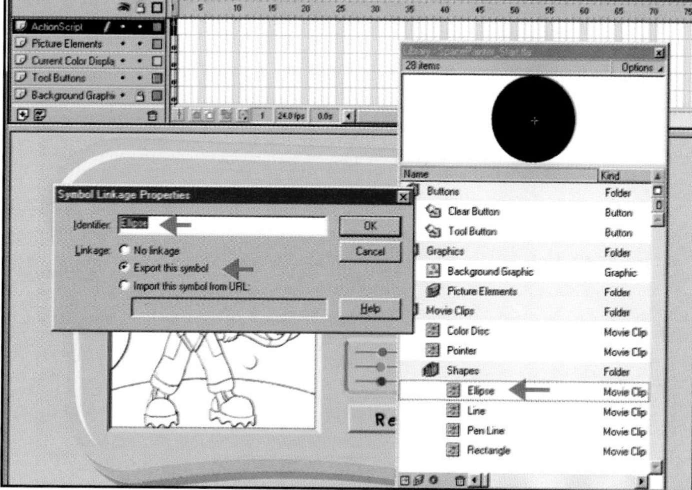

The **Linkage** properties for the specified movie clips are changed as indicated.

Creating the Sliding Color Chooser

In the first section, the **AdjustColor()** function was defined, allowing the position of each of the three color sliders to be converted into color information. But as they stand, the sliders themselves are just ordinary movie clip instances. To allow them to be dragged, more scripting is needed. In this section, ClipEvents will be used to respond to mouse actions, as an alternative to using buttons. The instance names of each of the slider clips have been assigned for you; they are RedSlider, BlueSlider, and GreenSlider, respectively.

1 Select the red colored slider handle, and bring up the Actions panel. Add the code for the first ClipEvent handler:

```
onClipEvent (mouseDown) {
    if (this.hitTest(_root._xmouse, _root._ymouse, true)) {
        Dragging = true;
    }
}
```

Enter the **onClipEvent mouseDown** handler that is executed when the mouse button is clicked anywhere in the movie.

In this block of code, some actions are being tagged for execution anytime the mouse button is clicked over the entire movie. Because ClipEvents are global and affect the whole movie (unlike button actions that relate to only that button instance), more code is required to see if the user is actually clicking this slider handle.

The **hitTest** action performs basic collision detection in Flash, and given a set of X and Y coordinates, it can let you know if a particular object exists there. So, **hitTest** can be applied to the slider using the current mouse coordinates. If **hitTest** returns **true**, it is known that the user is in fact clicking the slider, and the rest of the code is run. In this case, a variable named ***Dragging*** is set to **true** to indicate that the user is dragging the slider.

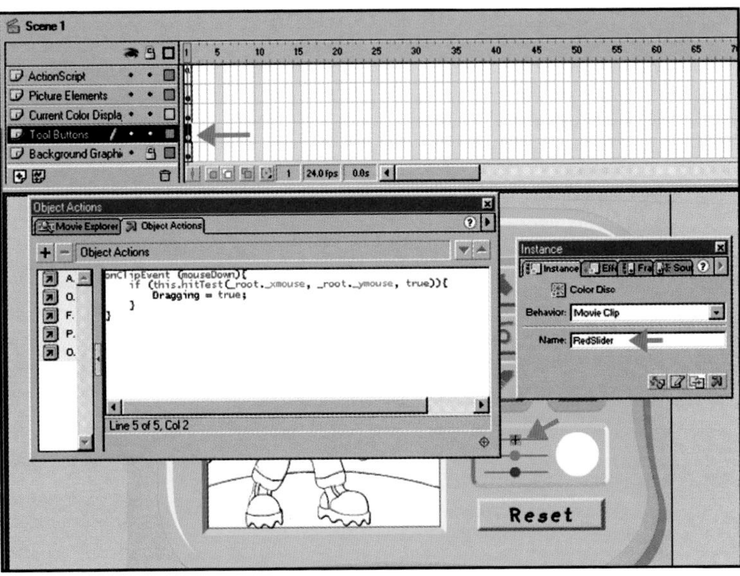

The **onClipEvent (MouseDown)** code is added to the red slider handle.

2 Insert this code:

```
onClipEvent (mouseUp) {
    Dragging = false;
}
```

Add the code that sets the ***Dragging*** variable to **false** when the mouse button is released.

This code has the opposite effect of the code in step 1. This time, the **mouseUp ClipEvent** is being captured. Logically, when the user releases the mouse button, he can no longer be dragging the slider (or anything else for that matter), so ***Dragging*** is set to **false**. No **if** statement is required because it doesn't matter where the mouse is released—all that counts here is that the user is no longer dragging.

The final section of the slider code is a ClipEvent handler for **enterFrame**. The **enterFrame** event fires every time the Stage is refreshed. It is a global event, so it doesn't matter whether the movie clip it is attached to is playing. Therefore, **enterFrame** is used in this technique as an "engine driver" event that allows for actions to be repeated continuously even though the movie itself comprises only one frame.

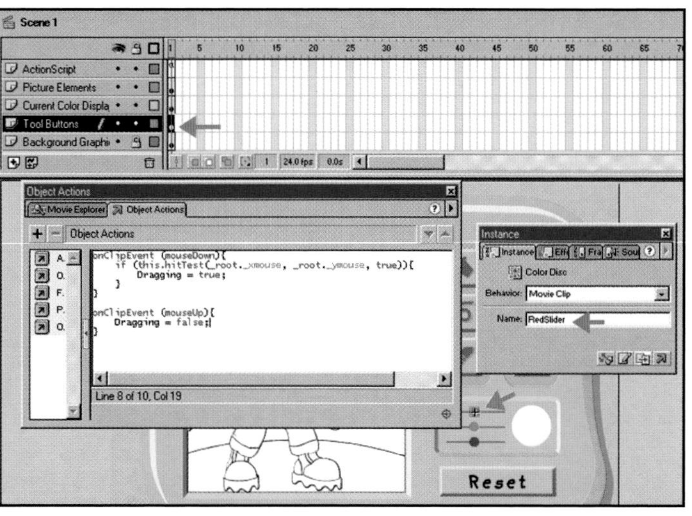

The **onClipEvent (MouseUp)** code is added to the red slider handle.

3 Add the final handler code:

```
onClipEvent (enterFrame) {
    if (Dragging && _root._xmouse > 425) {
        _x = 425;
    } else if (Dragging && _root._xmouse < 365) {
        _x = 365;
    } else if (Dragging && _root._xmouse < 425 && _root._xmouse > 365) {
        _x = _root._xmouse;
    }
    _root.AdjustColor();
}
```

The **onClipEvent (enterFrame)** handler is activated every time the Stage is refreshed, according to the movie's frame rate.

Note: Why are all the **_root**'s necessary? Clip Event scripts are a little misleading because you appear to attach them to the *outside* of a Movie Clip instance. In fact, they are stored and run from inside the clip's unique Timeline. So any references to variables or objects need to be written as though you were assigning them to a keyframe *inside* the movie clip—hence, all the _roots appended to the object references in this **enterFrame** handler.

The aim of all the scripts in this section is to make the slider behave a particular way. The desired behavior is that the slider should stick to the mouse cursor when clicked and move left or right within a range of sixty pixels. So the code in this step alters the position of the slider object to reflect the *X* coordinate of the mouse but *only* if that position is between X: 365 (the leftmost point) and X: 425 (the rightmost point). If the mouse is outside that range but the mouse button is still pressed, the slider is forced to stay put at either end of its invisible tether.

This effect is achieved with a set of **if** statements, each written to check two things: first, that ***Dragging*** still equals true, and second, the position of the mouse. The *_x* property of the slider is altered accordingly, being set to 365, 425, or the *X* coordinate of the cursor.

The scripts assigned to the red slider are identical to those needed on the other two sliders.

4 Copy the code from the Actions panel that you just entered, select each of the other sliders in turn, and paste the code back into the Panel. Now all three sliders are active.

Note: Where do the slider clips come from? Because ClipEvent scripts are assigned to instances individually, rather than via the parent symbol, it's possible to reuse movie clips and have each instance perform a unique set of tasks. So these sliders are just instances of the same symbol used to create the CurrentColorDisplay object, with color effects applied to make them red, blue, and green.

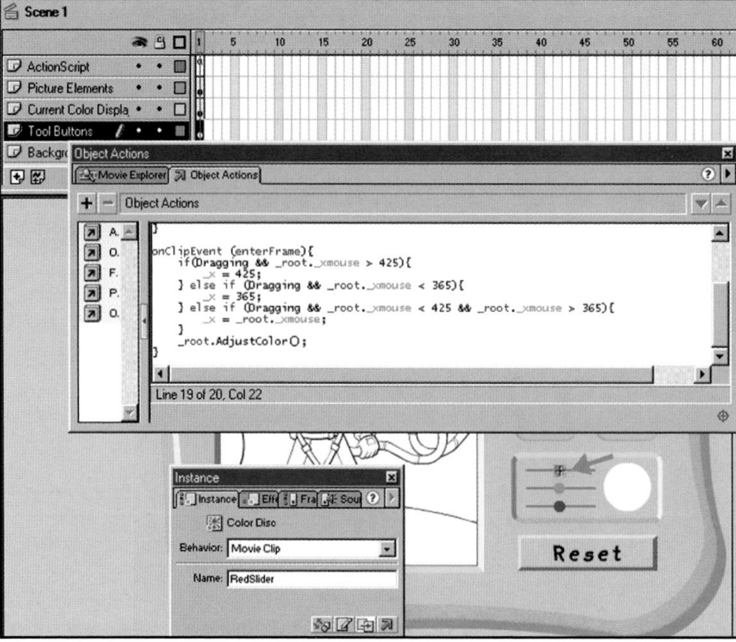

The **onClipEvent (enterFrame)** code is added to the red slider handle.

Scripting the Tool Buttons

SpacePainter features six different tools, plus a Reset button. When pressed, each of the tool buttons sets a variable named ***ToolType*** to a different text value to reflect which tool is currently active. The drawing scripts created in the next section control their behavior and then use this text value. Each of the tools and the Reset button are prescripted for convenience, and the code is displayed in the next seven figures:

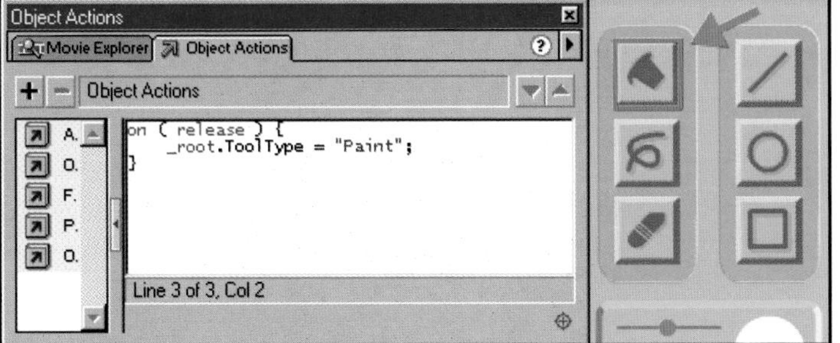

Paint tool and script.

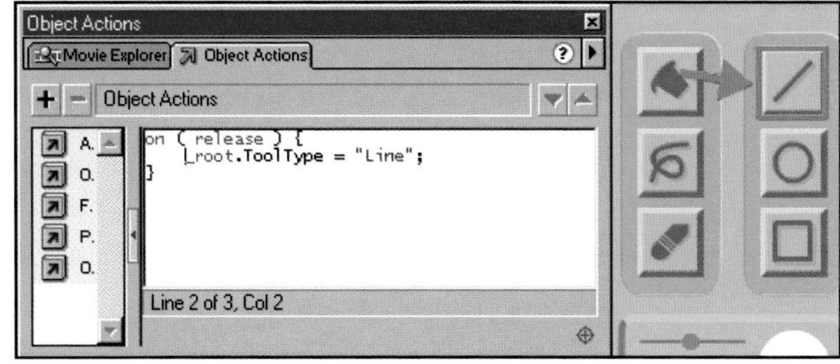

Line tool and script.

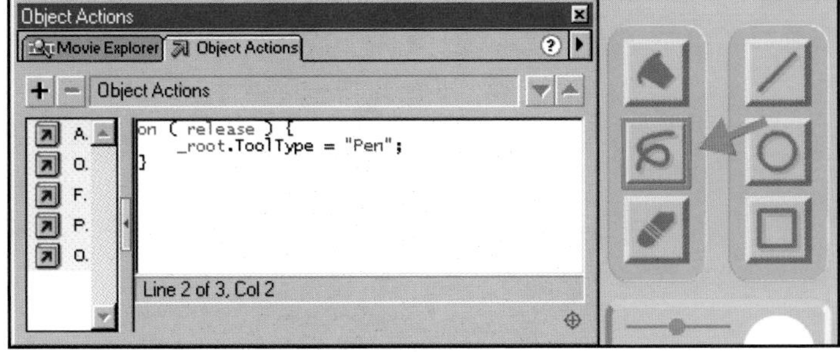

Pen tool and script.

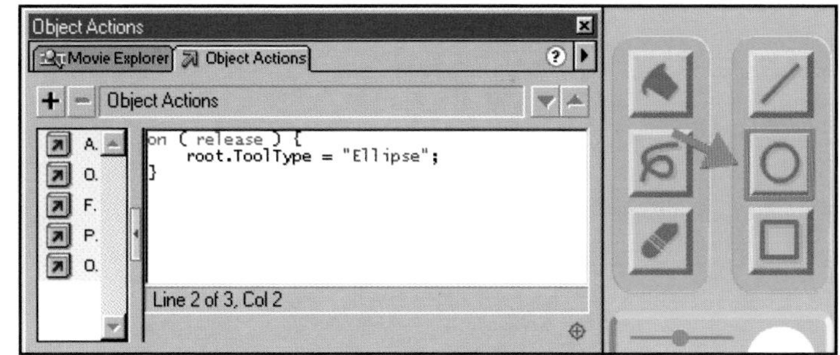

Ellipse tool and script.

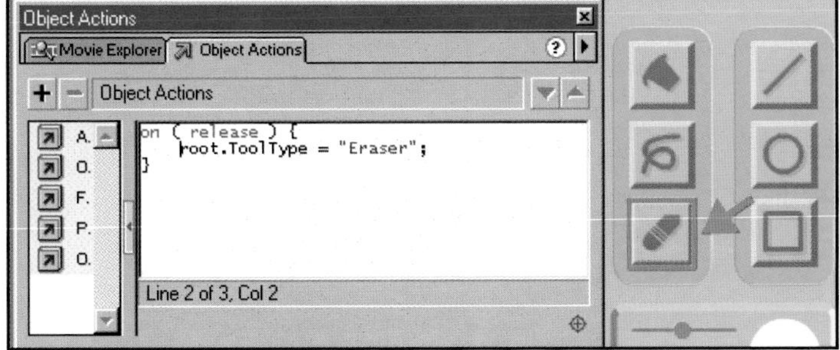

Eraser tool and script.

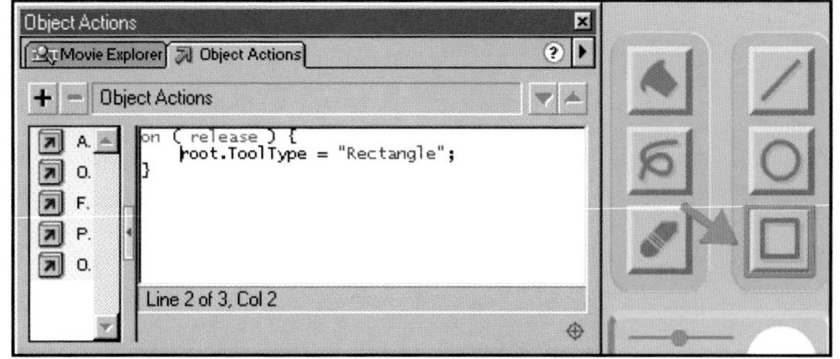

Rectangle tool and script

Here's a quick recap of what's been achieved so far. You've created Color objects and number conversion tables for altering the appearance of shapes, picture elements, and the current color display. You hid the mouse cursor and attached an instance of the Pointer symbol to the Stage, setting it to await instructions to follow the mouse. You created a **Reset** function to delete other visitor-drawn shapes and to return the color of the picture elements to white. Finally, you scripted and activated the color sliders and all the tool buttons.

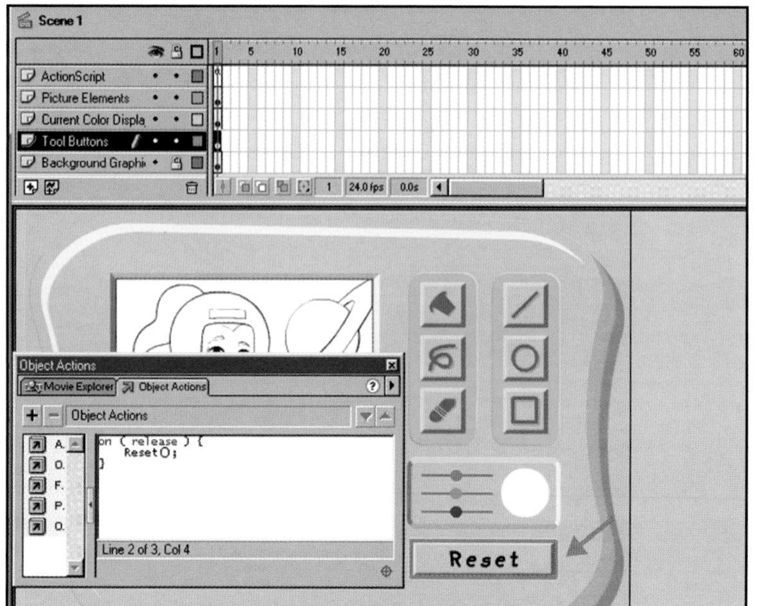

Reset button and script.

SCRIPTING THE PAINT TOOLS

Now that all the setup work is done, it's time to build the script that will actually make the custom pointer follow the mouse, color the picture elements, and draw the lines and shapes. These tasks are best performed with the help of ClipEvent handlers, and because any movie clip will do, the script will be assigned to the Current Color Display (the larger white circle to the lower-right in the diagram).

As in the previous set of ClipEvents, you will work with **mouseDown** first, setting it to capture all mouse clicks. In SpacePainter, several things might happen on a mouse click, depending on what the current tool is and the position of the cursor. So, each ClipEvent handler consists of a number of **if** statements that check the current state of things and react appropriately. In these first few lines of code, an **if** statement checks to see if the current tool is the Paint Tool.

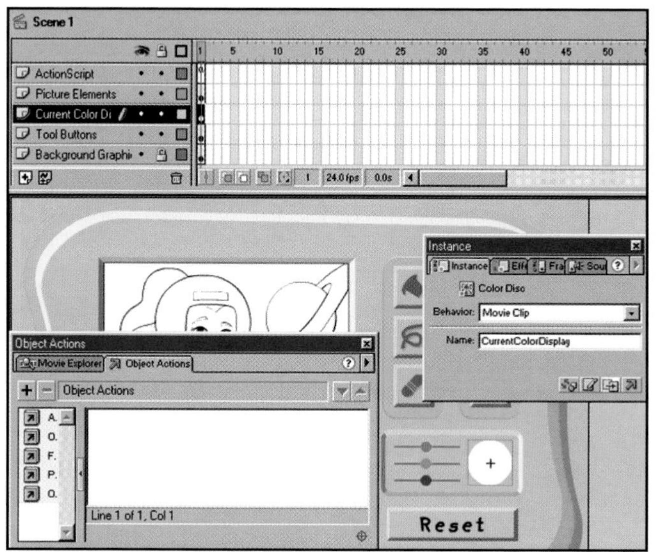

In this section, you apply the scripts to the ColorDisc movie clip (which has an instance name of CurrentColorDisplay).

1 Select the Current Color Display instance, open the Actions panel, and assign this code:

If ***ToolType*** does equal Paint and the returned value of the **MouseInBounds()** function is **true**, **eval** and the **setRGB** methods are used to alter the color of whatever object is being clicked. The address of the object being clicked is determined using the **_drop-target** property of Pointer.

The next tool to be accommodated is the Eraser. Eraser behaves differently depending on whether it is applied to a drawn shape or a picture element. If the user clicks a picture element with the Eraser, the element turns white. If the user clicks a shape, the shape is removed using the **removeMovieClip** action.

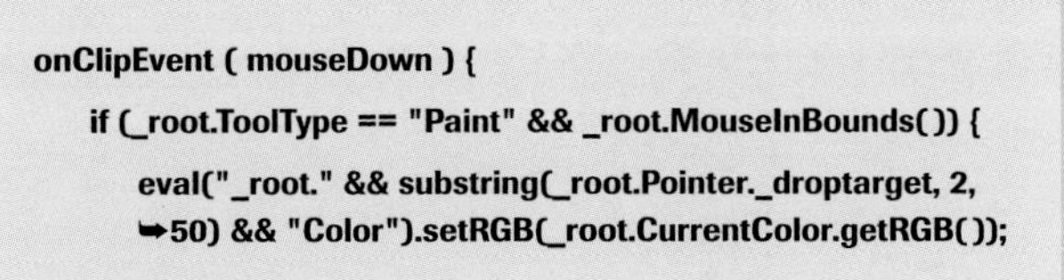

```
onClipEvent ( mouseDown ) {
    if (_root.ToolType == "Paint" && _root.MouseInBounds()) {
        eval("_root." && substring(_root.Pointer._droptarget, 2,
        ➥50) && "Color").setRGB(_root.CurrentColor.getRGB());
```

Enter this code so that the object being clicked has its color changed to reflect the currently selected color when the Paint tool is active. (The ➥ symbol you see here is for editorial purposes only.)

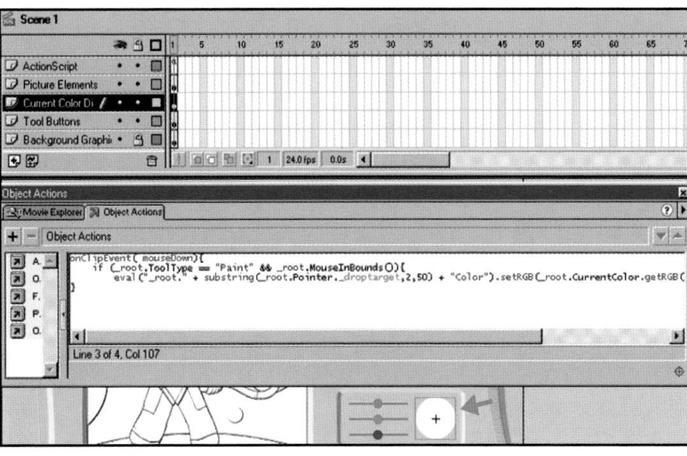

The code for the **onClipEvent(MouseDown)** code is assigned to the CurrentColorDisplay instance.

2 Insert the Eraser tool code:

It's known that picture elements have instance names like "Element1" and "Element2," and drawn shapes are named "Shape1" and "Shape2." So if the first five letters of the clicked object's name spell "Shape," the script knows how to react.

```
} else if (_root.ToolType == "Eraser" && _root.MouseInBounds()) {
    if (substring(_root.Pointer._droptarget, 2, 5) == "Shape") {
        eval("_root." && substring(_root.Pointer._droptarget, 2,
        ➥50)).removeMovieClip();
    } else {
        eval("_root." && substring(_root.Pointer._droptarget, 2,
        ➥50) && "Color").setRGB(0xFFFFFF);
    }
```

Enter the code that makes the Eraser tool behave differently depending on whether a shape or picture element is clicked. (The ➥ symbol you see here is for editorial purposes only.)

3 Add this code:

```
} else if (_root.ToolType == "Pen" && _root.MouseInBounds()) {
    PenDown = true;
```

Insert the code that sets the variable ***PenDown*** to **true** when the user clicks and the current tool is the Pen.

Paint and Eraser are "click" tools, because you click the object you want to change and that's it. The Pen and the shape tools are "click and drag" tools, whereby you click and then move the mouse around. So when the mouse is clicked with the Pen tool active, the ***PenDown*** variable is set to **true** to indicate that the dragging action has now begun. The remainder of the Pen script will be added in the **enterFrame** handler.

So far, the Paint, Eraser, and Pen tools have been accommodated for in this **mouseDown** handler. The last ones to add are the shape tools.

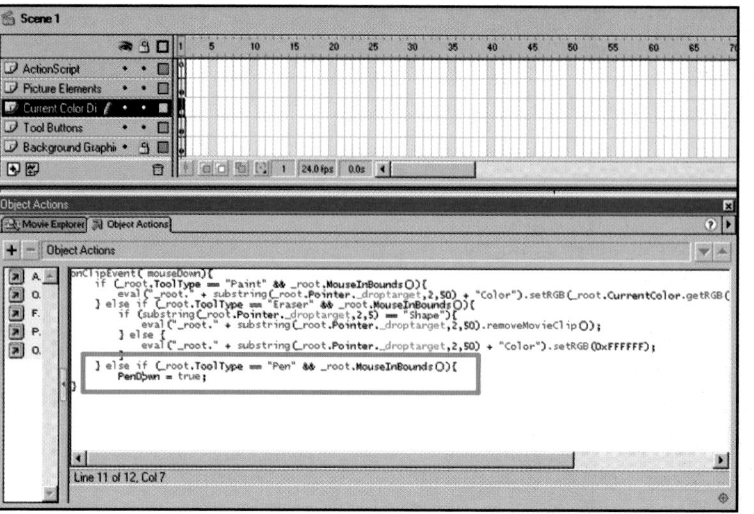

The code is added to the CurrentColorDisplay() movie clip instance.

4 To complete the **mouseDown** handler, insert this code:

This block of code creates a new instance of the currently selected shape tool, positions it at the same coordinates as the mouse cursor, and then changes its color to reflect the currently selected shade.

Now that all the **mouseDown** possibilities have been taken care of, the next handler to add is **mouseUp**. This code is executed whenever the user releases the mouse button.

```
} else if ((_root.ToolType == "Line" || _root.ToolType == "Ellipse" ||
➥_root.ToolType == "Rectangle") && _root.MouseInBounds()) {
    PenDown = true;
    ShapeCount ++;
    X1 = _root._xmouse;
    Y1 = _root._ymouse;
    _root.attachMovie(_root.ToolType,"Shape" + ShapeCount, ShapeCount +
    ➥100);
    eval("_root.Shape" + ShapeCount + "Color") = new Color("_root.Shape"
    ➥+ ShapeCount);
    eval("_root.Shape" + ShapeCount +
    ➥"Color").setRGB(_root.CurrentColor.getRGB());
}
}
```

If the user clicks when any of the shape tools is selected, a single instance of the appropriate shape is created and placed on the Stage. (The ➥ symbol you see here is for editorial purposes only.)

5 Insert the following code:

This event handler is rather short because its only job is to set ***PenDown*** to **false**, indicating that the user is no longer dragging. The handler doesn't need to check which tool is active, because ***PenDown*** would be **false** anyway (because the user released the button).

```
onClipEvent ( mouseUp ) {
    PenDown = false;
}
```

Enter the code that sets **PenDown** to **false** when the mouse button is released.

6 Moving right along, the next ClipEvent to be captured is **enterFrame**. This code is executed many times every second, so it is the appropriate place to put instructions for resizing shapes and drawing pen lines—all the things that need to appear as though they're reacting fairly snappily to the user's mouse movement. Input this code to begin the **enterFrame** handler:

```
onClipEvent ( enterFrame ) {
    FrameCount ++;
    if (FrameCount % 2 != 0 && _root.ToolType == "Pen") {
      X1 = _root._xmouse;
      Y1 = _root._ymouse;
    } else {
      X2 = _root._xmouse;
      Y2 = _root._ymouse;
    }

}
```

Insert the code that tracks the motion of the mouse cursor by maintaining two pairs of coordinates.

The aim of this first block of code is to record two pairs of coordinate points: one on odd frames and the other on even frames. The Pen tool uses these two coordinate pairs to follow the movement of the mouse. Of particular interest here is the use of the Modulo (%) operator to determine whether a frame is odd or even. **FrameCount** is incremented after every frame draw, so if **FrameCount % 2** equals **0**, the value of **FrameCount** is divisible by two without any remainder—making that value an even number such as 2, 4, or 6. If **FrameCount % 2** does not equal **0** (denoted by the code **!= 0**), the value of **FrameCount** is an odd number.

Notice that only the first pair of coordinates requires that the ***ToolType*** be Pen. This is because the other shape tools are anchored once at a particular point, but then the second point changes as the mouse is dragged. When the Pen is active however, both points change constantly.

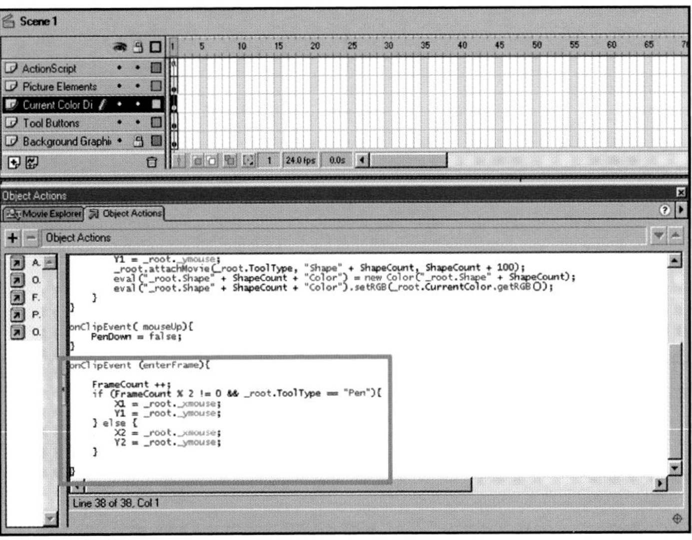

The code for the **onClipEvent(enterFrame)** code is added to the script assigned to the CurrentColorDisplay( ) movie clip instance.

Drawing the no-math way! The Pen tool script could be quite an involved process of calculating angles with trigonometry; but thanks to a clever technique, it's actually quite simple. The **enterFrame** handler constantly tracks mouse movement by maintaining two pairs of X and Y coordinates, each one updated on alternate keyframes. So if the cursor is moving, there will always be a gap between points X1, Y1 and X2, Y2. **attachMovie** is then used to create a new copy of the Pen Line symbol, and it is squeezed into that gap, creating a continuous line that traces all the points covered by the user's mouse motion. The same Pen Line symbol is copied multiple times and then stretched to fit between the points the user has traced with the mouse. No math is required other than to calculate the **_xscale**, **_yscale** and position of each Pen Line instance.

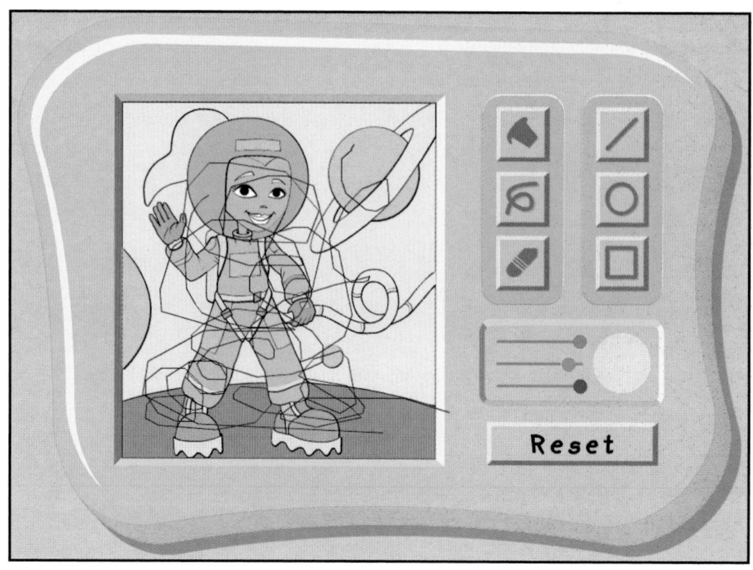

The Pen tool works by duplicating copies of the Pen Line symbol between two points on a continual basis (or at least until the visitor releases the mouse button).

7 Complete the **enterFrame** handler script by adding this code:

```
        if (PenDown && _root.MouseInBounds()) {
            if (_root.ToolType == "Pen") {
                ShapeCount ++
                _root.attachMovie(_root.ToolType,"Shape" + ShapeCount, ShapeCount + 100);
            }
            with (eval("_root.Shape" + ShapeCount)) {
                _x = ((X2 - X1) / 2) + X1;
                _y = ((Y2 - Y1) / 2) + Y1;
                _xscale = X1 - X2;
                _yscale = Y1 - Y2;
            }
        }
    }
```

Use the Pen tool code to create copies of the Pen Line symbol and to then position and resize the copies according to the values of X1, Y1 and X2, Y2.

This block of code serves a dual purpose. The first part is specific to the Pen tool and is responsible for creating multiple copies of the Pen Line symbol. The second part works for all the drawing tools, resizing the current shape depending on the values of X1, Y1 and X2, Y2. The effect is to squeeze the shape so that it fits between its anchor point and the current mouse position.

The code for making the custom mouse cursor move (the **mouseMove** event) is used in conjunction with the **startDrag** action to force the Pointer symbol to "stick" to the mouse cursor. The **updateAfterEvent( )** action is added to allow the cursor to be updated independent of the movie's frame rate. This eliminates a lot of the sluggishness usually associated with the **startDrag** action.

8 Insert the following code:

The SpacePainter application is now complete!

9 Use Test Movie to export the file.

```
onClipEvent (mouseMove) {
    startDrag("_root.Pointer", true);
    updateAfterEvent();
}
```

Enter the **updateAfterEvent()** action to allow the cursor to be updated independently of the movie's frame rate.

How It Works

The SpacePainter application relies heavily on the Color object, Flash's built-in mouse tools, and Clip Events. Instances of the Color object are created for any drawn shaped, picture elements, and the current color display. Manipulating the movie clip graphics with scripting allows for the creation of many colored copies of the same symbol. In addition, because the colors of various objects are set with script, they can be changed at any time in response to user input.

The Red, Green, and Blue sliders can be manipulated to produce millions of colors.

When it comes to colors, unless you're already familiar with RGB values, deciphering this number system can be confusing. All colors on the screen are reproduced using a mix of red, green, and blue. To describe a color, all you have to do is determine what proportion of those three basic colors to display. The numbers appear strange because they're hexadecimal. (Hexadecimal numbers have a base of 16 rather than 10, which is what we're accustomed to. The series of single-digit decimal numbers is 0, 1, 2, 3, 4, 5, 6, 7, 8, and 9. The hexadecimal single-digit series is 0, 1, 2, 3, 4, 5, 6, 7, 8, 9, A, B, C, D, E, and F, in which A through F are equivalent to 10 through 15 as double-digit numbers.) By using hexadecimal numbers of just six digits, it's possible to express millions of different color mixes in the form RRGGBB.

The other significant technique covered in this project is the creation of custom mouse cursors. Thanks to the Mouse object, you can now use ActionScript to hide or show the normal mouse cursor at will. Combine that with the draggable movie clip, and you have the ability to create your own cursors. This allows the user experience to be tailored to reflect the mood of your Flash movie and makes possible all sorts of creative animation effects.

To create the custom cursor effect, the Mouse object is used to hide the regular arrow/hand cursor. A movie clip instance is then created on-the-fly by using the **attachMovie** action and by scripting that instance to "drag" or follow the mouse movement—and the illusion of a custom cursor is complete.

SpacePainter is tied together with a series of ClipEvent handler scripts, applied to movie clip instances. ClipEvents are used here primarily as a substitute for buttons, and they make it possible to create such an application in the most simple way possible. And because different Clip-Event scripts can be added to individual instances of a movie clip, the file can be slimmer, too.

The SpacePainter also features a custom cursor and the ability to draw shapes like circles and squares.

FISHSTIK EDUCATIONAL SOFTWARE

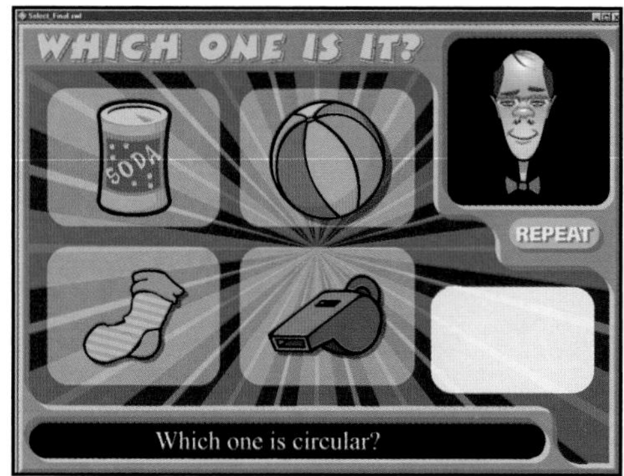

Chapter 5

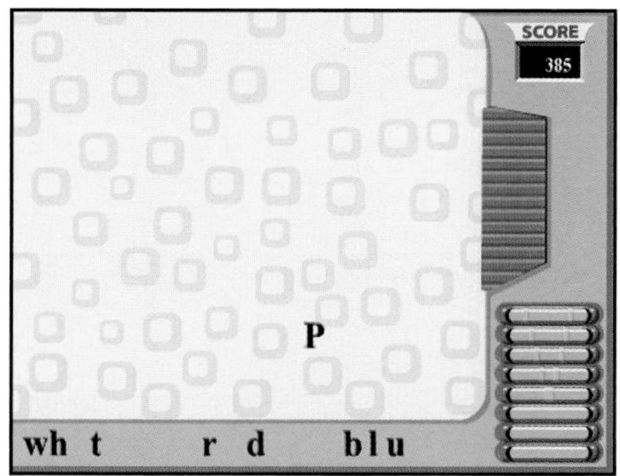

Chapter 6

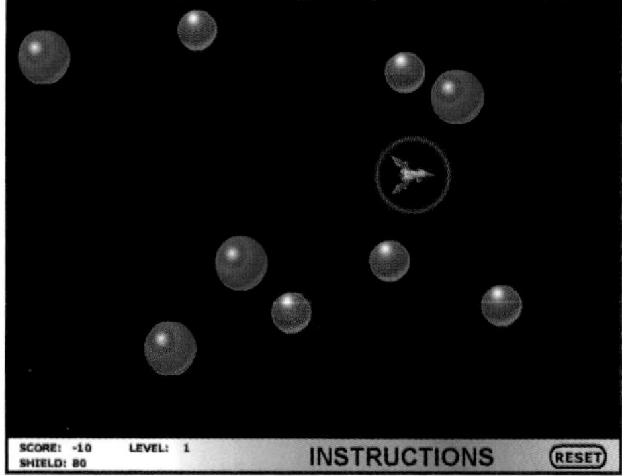

Chapter 7

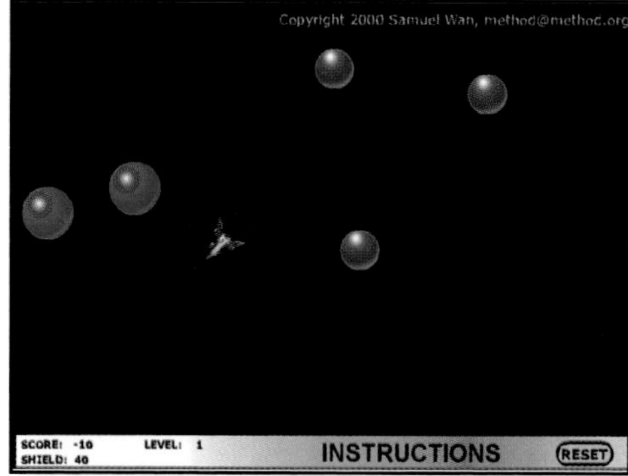

Chapter 8

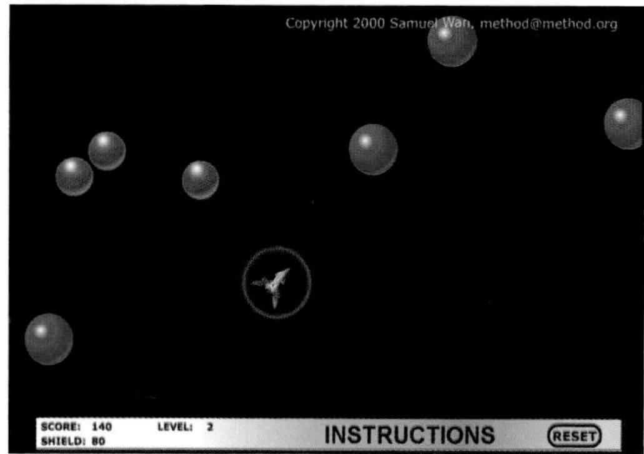

Chapter 9

Chapter 10

"The philosophy behind much advertising is based on the old observation that every man is really two men—the man he is and the man he wants to be."

—WILLIAM FEATHER

SPLENDOS

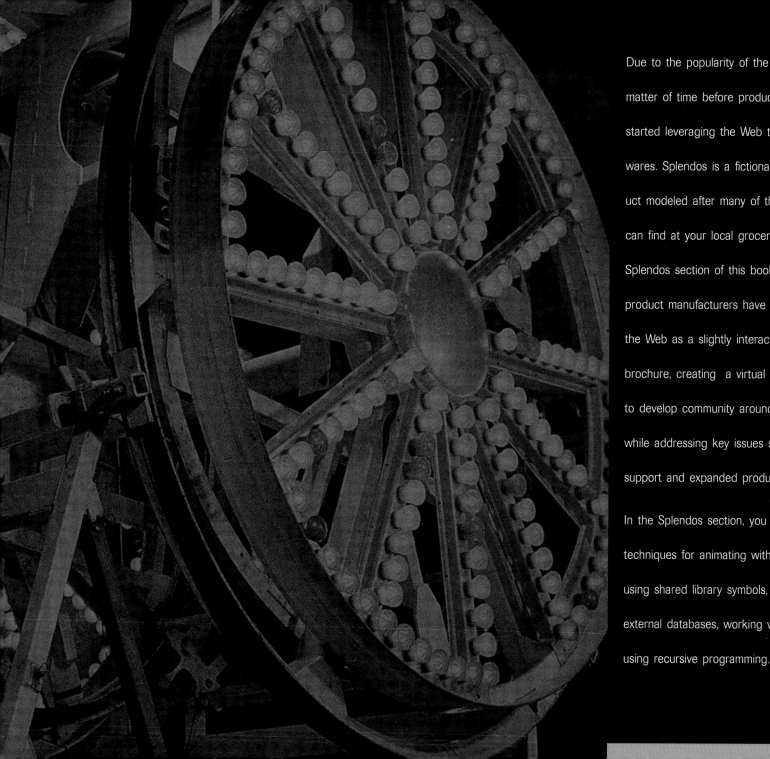

Due to the popularity of the Web, it was only a matter of time before product manufacturers started leveraging the Web to show off their wares. Splendos is a fictional spray-bottle product modeled after many of the products you can find at your local grocery store. The Splendos section of this book reflects how product manufacturers have gone beyond using the Web as a slightly interactive product brochure, creating a virtual presence designed to develop community around their offerings while addressing key issues such as customer support and expanded product information.

In the Splendos section, you will find valuable techniques for animating with ActionScript, using shared library symbols, interacting with external databases, working with functions, and using recursive programming.

11

CREATING SCRIPTED ANIMATIONS

By Jennifer S. Hall

This chapter demonstrates using ActionScript instead of tweening to give life to a project. In the project, the BottleMovie movie clip already has some action attached to it. When you select the Splendos bottle, it plays a spray animation, created by both tweening and keyframe-based animation. With ActionScript, you will create zooms, rotations, and tints for the movie clip of the Splendos bottle. To create visual interest, you will also add an ever-changing background.

When designing a program, it is standard to break down the project into smaller pieces to make it easier to design, test, and debug. This chapter follows that practice, adding the ActionScript in logical segments. Make sure you save and test the file at the end of each segment.

Using ActionScript to Make an Object Zoom In and Out

In this section, you write the code to zoom in and out on the bottle. You assign the code to buttons and place them on the lower left by using ActionScript, not tweening.

1 If you haven't already, open Animated_Demo_Start.fla and save it to your local hard drive. Remember to save it frequently throughout this chapter. (If you want to see the finished file, open Animated_Demo_Final.fla.)

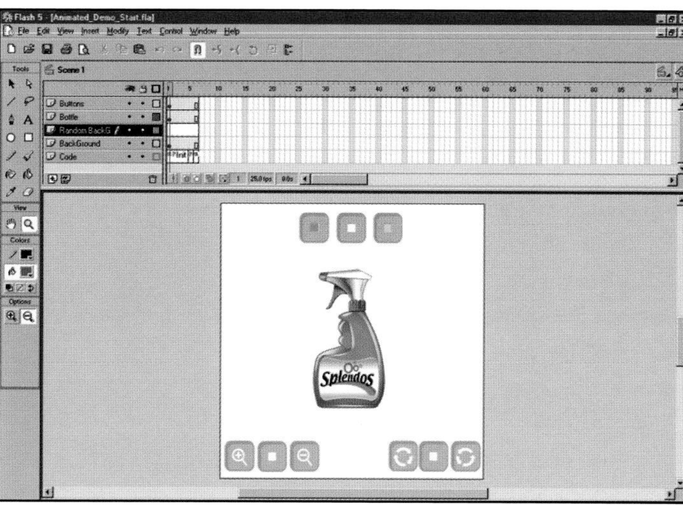

The Animated_Demo_Start.fla file has five layers with most of the art already positioned. Some basic code has already been added to the "Code" layer.

2 Look at the five layers in the file.

Each layer has a descriptive name. When you are programming, naming a layer helps you keep things separated and lets you turn related graphics on or off.

The bottom layer, labeled Code, has no graphics on it and contains only ActionScript and labels. Creating a separate layer and placing it at either the top or the bottom of the layers is a standard practice for Flash programming for several reasons:

- It allows the programmer to easily see, edit, and even delete ActionScript without worrying about the graphics.
- You can get very confused if the labels and ActionScript are attached to different graphics on different layers. Having all the labels for the program operation on one layer allows you to easily view where the program will jump to based on a

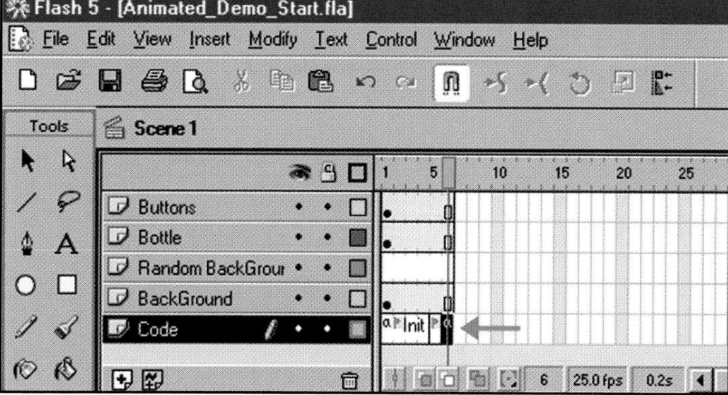

Notice that the code is placed on a its own layer for ease of editing.

label, and it keeps everything code related in one place.

- When you make a practice of putting the code layer at the top or bottom, you know exactly where to look and can easily find it later.

3 Select the frame labeled Init in the Code layer (the first frame), open the Frame Actions window by choosing Window > Actions, and view the initialization code for the movie already in place.

```
//Initialization
MovieDimensions = Screen.getBounds(_root);
```

A movie clip named Screen covers the entire Stage and is used with **getBounds** to get the boundaries of the movie, which are stored in the variable ***MovieDimensions***. The **getBounds** method is a new Flash method you can use for any movie clip. This method returns the ***xMin***, ***xMax***, ***yMin***, and ***yMax*** of the movie clip in reference to the parameter passed. In this example, because the Screen movie clip covers the whole Stage and the parameter that was passed is the **root(_root)**, you are actually determining the size of the Stage on-the-fly. (The term **_root** is the same thing as **_level0**.)

> **Tip:** Opening the movie properties, finding the movie dimensions, and storing them in the ***MovieDimensions*** variable is very simple. However, if you changed the Stage size later, you must edit the variable's ***MovieDimensions*** with the new Stage size. When you use a movie clip that covers the entire Stage and the **getBounds** method, you can change the Stage size without editing a variable.

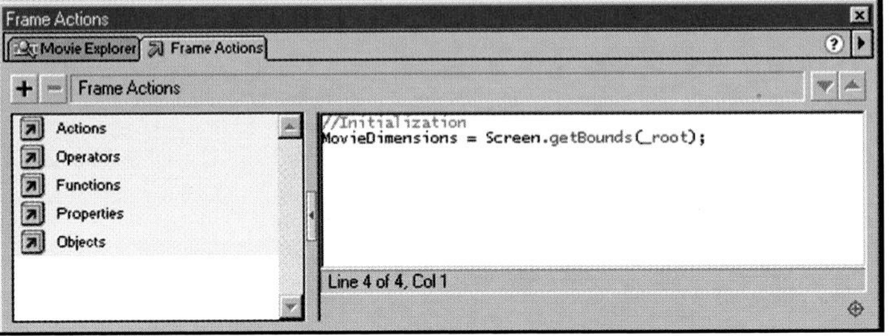

Open the Frame Actions window to view the initialization code that is already in place.

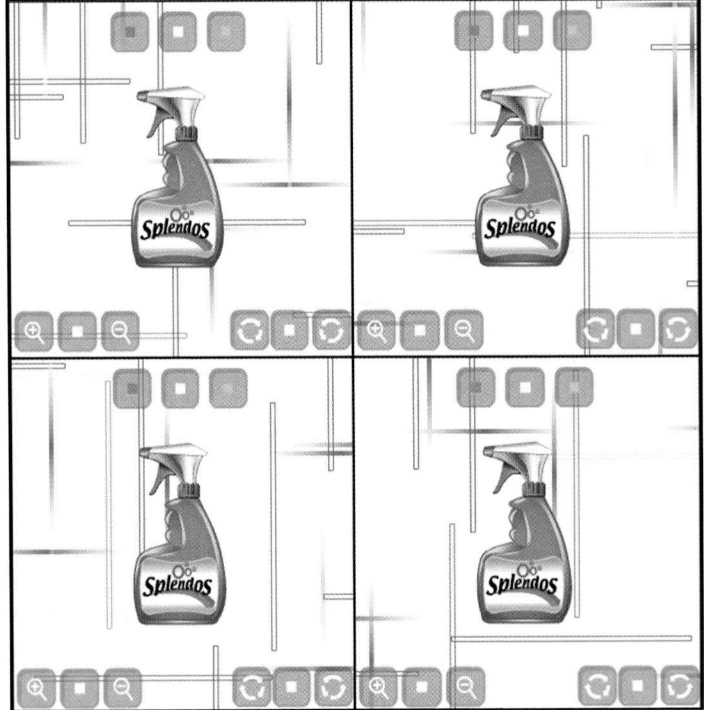

Later in this technique, you will create an animated background. The elements will include animation off the screen, which is why it will be important to know the Stage size.

4 In the **Init** code, set the variable ***ZoomRate*** and a flag to tell the program whether it's in Zoom Mode by using this code.

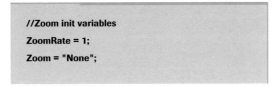

```
//Zoom init variables
ZoomRate = 1;
Zoom = "None";
```

Add this code to establish two variables for the Zooming animation. Note that you do not need to enter the comment line.

This code sets the variable ***ZoomRate*** to 1 so that Flash zooms at a rate of 1%. The variable ***Zoom*** establishes a flag that determines whether the visitor has the bottle zooming, and, if it is, which way—in or out. The code sets the **Zoom** flag to None so that the program isn't zoomed when it starts. (You cannot use true/false (boolean) with this variable because it has only two settings, true or false, and you need three settings—zoom in, zoom out, or not zoomed at all. An alternative is to use a string for the **Zoom** flag setting.) Now that you have the zoom settings initialized, you're ready to set up the Zoom buttons. Start with the Zoom In button.

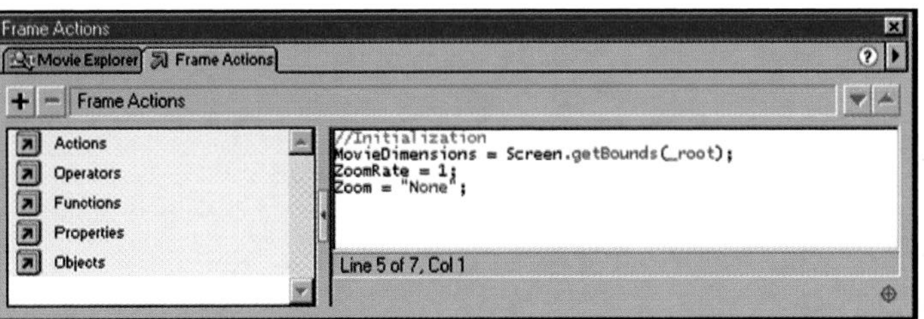

Enter the ***Zoom*** variables beneath the MovieDimensions line in the Frame Actions window.

5 With the Frame Actions window still open, select the Zoom In button and insert this code:

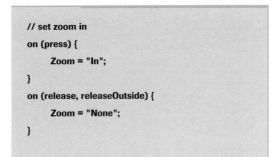

```
// set zoom in
on (press) {
    Zoom = "In";
}
on (release, releaseOutside) {
    Zoom = "None";
}
```

Include this code for the Zoom In button, the button with the icon that has a plus sign on a magnifying glass.

As soon as you selected the button, the Frame Actions window changed to an empty Object Actions window. When you inserted the code, Flash automatically attached it to the object that was selected, in this case, the Zoom In button.

This code sets ***Zoom*** to **In** when the visitor presses the mouse button and the cursor is on the Zoom In button. When the visitor releases the mouse button, Flash sets ***Zoom*** to None. Notice ***Zoom*** is set to **None** on **release** and **on releaseOutside**, which ensures that the zooming stops when the visitor releases the mouse button. The change doesn't depend on where the cursor is located. If you *hadn't* included the **releaseOutside** check, the visitor could click the Zoom In button to start the zooming, continue to press the mouse button, move the cursor off the Zoom In button, and then release the mouse button, and the zooming would continue. (This code only sets the variable. You actually process the ***Zoom*** flag and do the zooming later in this section.)

Enter the code for the Zoom In button, located on the Buttons layer, using the Object Actions window.

6 Select the Zoom Out button and attach this code to it:

```
// set zoom out
on (press) {
    Zoom = "Out";
}
on (release, releaseOutside) {
    Zoom = "None";
}
```

Include this code for the Zoom Out button.

This code sets the ***Zoom*** flag to **Out** when the visitor presses the mouse button and the cursor is on the Zoom Out button. When the visitor releases the mouse button, no matter where the cursor is, the ***Zoom*** flag is set to **None**.

7 Select the Zoom Revert button and attach this code to it:

```
//reset the bottle to original size
on (release) {

    BottleMovie._xscale = 100;
    BottleMovie._yscale = 100;
}
```

Enter the code for the Zoom Revert button, the button between the Zoom In button and the Zoom Out button.

Notice that this code doesn't have an **on press**, only an **on release**. Setting up the button this way makes it a forgiving button, allowing the visitor to change his mind. Flash completes the action only if the visitor releases the mouse button while the cursor is still over Zoom Revert. If the visitor presses the mouse button, moves off the Zoom Revert button, and then releases the mouse button, nothing will happen.

The two lines with ***BottleMovie._xscale*** and ***BottleMovie._yscale*** set the BottleMovie movie clip back to its original size (100%). Notice you have to set both the ***_xscale*** and the ***_yscale***, which are properties of the Flash 5 MovieClip object. These two lines of code are the equivalent of the following **SetProperty** code:

```
SetProperty(BottleMovie, _xscale, 100);
SetProperty(BottleMovie, _yscale, 100);
```

If you were to test the movie and the Zoom buttons, nothing would happen. That is because you need to process the ***Zoom*** flag and write the ActionScript that tells Flash to zoom in or out.

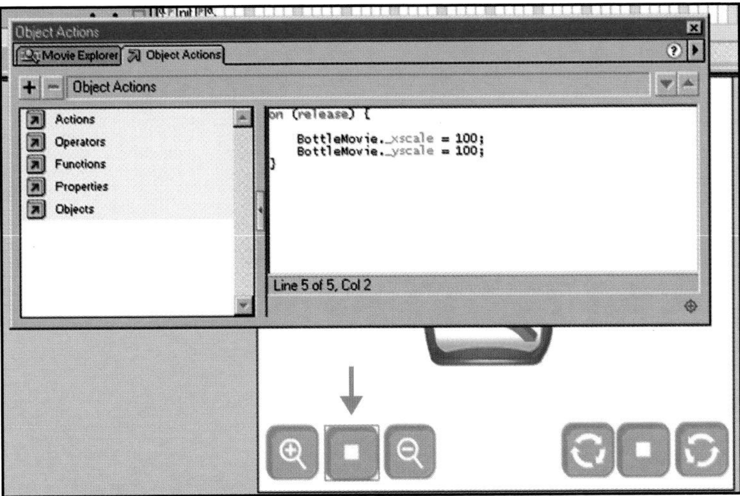

Enter the code for the Zoom Revert button.

8 In the Code layer, select the Play frame label and attach this code:

```
// check Zoom
if (Zoom == "In") {
        if (BottleMovie._xscale<175) {
                BottleMovie._xscale = BottleMovie._Xscale+ZoomRate;
                BottleMovie._yscale = BottleMovie._yscale+ZoomRate;
        }
} else if (Zoom == "Out") {
        if (BottleMovie._xscale>25) {
                BottleMovie._xscale = BottleMovie._Xscale-ZoomRate;
                BottleMovie._yscale = BottleMovie._yscale-ZoomRate;
        }
};
```

Use this code to run the Zoom animations.

The Play frame has a loop frame the next frame over. These frames make a simple two-frame loop to continuously check and update the Stage.

To make the Splendos bottle movie continuously zoom in or out, you really need a check for whether the mouse button is still down. Flash does not have this type of a check, so you must use the ***Zoom*** flag to implement this. Setting a ***Zoom*** flag allows the zoom to be continuous as long as the visitor presses the mouse button. You already have the code that sets up a detection for presses and releasees to change the flag. If you want something to program an action to occur for as long as the user continues to press a button you can use a flag to detect the key press. The flag is set to **true** when the user presses the mouse button; the flag is set to **false** when the user releases the mouse button. As long as the ***Zoom*** flag is set to **In** or **Out**, the Splendos bottle continues to zoom.

This code checks the ***Zoom*** flag:

```
if (Zoom == "In") {
    BottleMovie._xscale =
    ➥BottleMovie._Xscale+ZoomRate;
    BottleMovie._yscale =
    ➥BottleMovie._yscale+ZoomRate;
```

(The ➥ symbol you see here is for editorial purposes only.)

If it is set to **In**, Flash zooms the BottleMovie in by the ***ZoomRate*** that you set in the **Init** ActionScript. The ***ZoomRate*** variable, which you set in the **Init** ActionScript, determines the rate at which to zoom in or out. To get a proportionate zoom, you must set both the ***BottleMovie._xscale*** and ***BottleMovie._yscale***.

Notice that the ***BottleMovie._xScale*** and ***BottleMovie._yScale*** variables are on both the right and left side of the equals sign. This is a programming practice allowed in Flash 5. It lets you add to an existing variable without having to create a temporary variable to hold the new value. You could have written it this way:

```
temp = BottleMovie._Xscale+ZoomRate;
BottleMovie._xscale = temp;
```

There is nothing wrong with the preceding code. It does the exact same thing, but in two lines instead of one.

If the visitor isn't pressing the Zoom In button, this code sets the ***Zoom*** flag to **Out**, and Flash zooms out.

```
} else if (Zoom == "Out") {
    BottleMovie._xscale = BottleMovie._Xscale-
    ➥ZoomRate;
    BottleMovie._yscale = BottleMovie._yscale-
    ➥ZoomRate;
```

(The ➥ symbol you see here is for editorial purposes only.)

Notice that this code also has a check for the maximum and minimum amounts to zoom in or out:

```
if (BottleMovie._xscale<175) {
if (BottleMovie._xscale>25) {
```

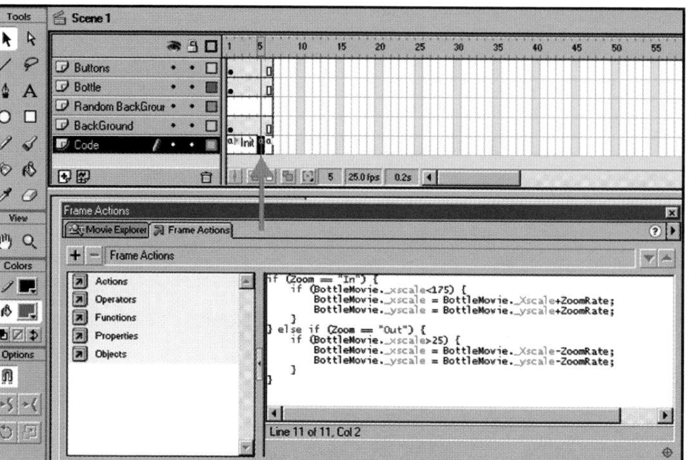

Enter the code on the frame labeled Play on the Code layer. The framed labeled Play is on frame 5.

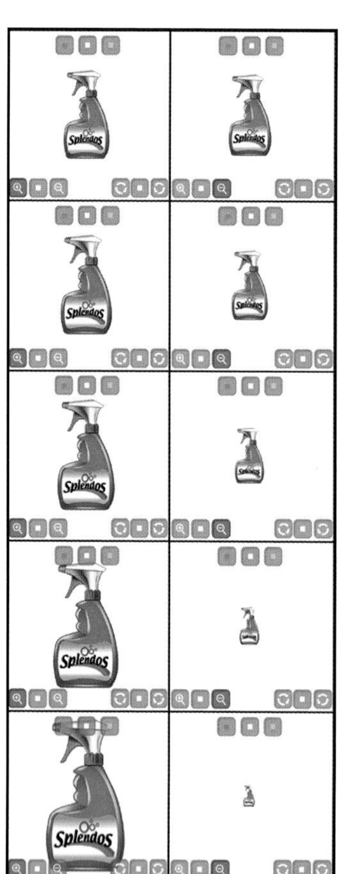

Zooming in or out continues as long as the respective button is pressed, creating a simple zooming animation.

This is an arbitrary limit and is unnecessary in the working of the program. Also notice that nothing is done when the ***Zoom*** flag is set to **None**.

9 Choose Control > Test Movie to test the buttons with Test Movie.

The Zoom In and Out buttons zoom the Splendos bottle in or out as long as the buttons are held down. Then the Zoom Revert button reverts the bottle back to its original size. Also test the forgiving Revert button and the **releaseOutside** of the Zoom buttons. If you want the bottle to zoom in and out faster, change the ***ZoomRate*** variable.

The middle button reverts the Splendor bottle to its original size.

SETTING UP ROTATION UPON COMMAND

In this section, you set up the code that makes the bottle rotate on command. You will use buttons and flags as you did in the previous zooming code.

1 Set the rotation rate and a flag to tell the program whether or not the file is in Rotating Mode, inserting the code in the **Init** code after the Zoom code added earlier:

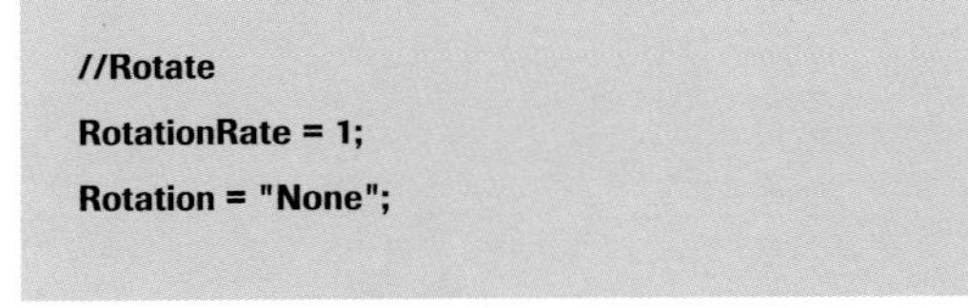

```
//Rotate
RotationRate = 1;
Rotation = "None";
```

Use this code to initialize a few variables for the Rotation animation.

This code looks very similar to the Zoom code. In fact, you are going to do the exact same thing you did with the Zoom code except with rotation. The ***RotationRate***, which determines how fast the Splendos bottle rotates around, is set to **1**, so the bottle rotates by 1 degree. The variable ***Rotation*** is a flag that determines whether the bottle rotates, and which way it rotates—right or left. To begin, the ***Rotation*** flag is set to **None**, so the bottle isn't rotating when the program starts. Once again, because the ***Rotation*** flag represents whether the bottle is rotating right, left, or not at all, you cannot use a boolean.

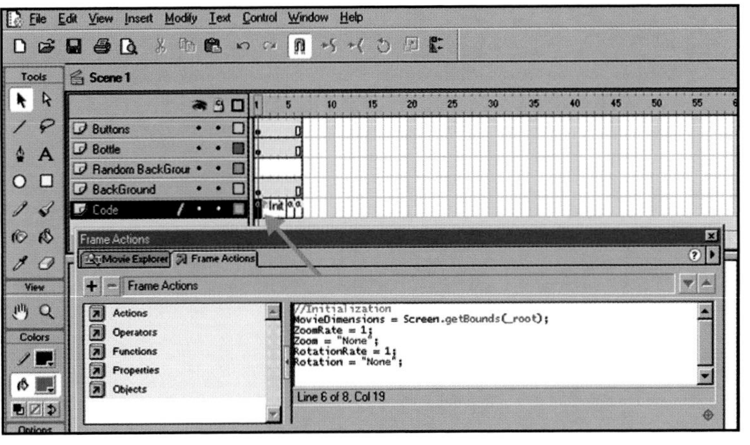

Enter the ***Rotation*** variables on the frame labeled Init (frame 1) on the Code layer by using the Frame Actions window.

2 To set the Rotate Right button, select the Rotate Right button and attach this code to it:

This code sets the ***Rotation*** flag to **Right** when the visitor places the mouse cursor on the Rotate Right button and presses the mouse button. When the visitor releases the mouse button, the ***Rotation*** flag is set to **None**.

```
// rotate right
on (press) {
    Rotation = "Right";
}
on (release, releaseOutside) {
    Rotation = "None";
}
```

Assign this code to the Rotate Right button, which is the button with the clockwise-pointing arrows on it.

3 Select the Rotate Left button and attach this code to it:

This code sets the ***Rotation*** flag to **Left** when the visitor places the mouse cursor on the Rotate Left button and presses the mouse button. When the visitor releases the mouse button, the ***Rotation*** flag is set to **None**.

```
// rotate left
on (press) {
    Rotation = "Left";
}
on (release, releaseOutside) {
    Rotation = "None";
}
```

Assign this code to the Rotate Left button, which is the button with the counterclockwise-pointing arrows on it.

4 Select the Rotate Revert button and attach this code to it:

This code sets the BottleMovie back to its original rotation (0 degrees). Notice the action is done on release of the mouse button, so this also is a forgiving button, as is the Zoom Revert button.

```
// revert movie to upright
on (release) {
    BottleMovie._rotation = 0;
}
```

Assign this code to the button between the two Rotation buttons.

5 To process the ***Rotate*** flag and actually rotate the Splendos bottle right or left, select the Play frame label in the Code layer and insert the following code:

You are doing the same thing you did in the Zoom code. Using a ***Rotation*** flag allows the rotation to be continuous as long as the button is held down, the same as the Zoom feature.

```
//  check rotation
if (Rotation == "Right") {
    BottleMovie._rotation = BottleMovie._rotation+RotationRate;
} else if (Rotation == "Left") {
    BottleMovie._rotation = BottleMovie._rotation-RotationRate;
}
```

Include this code to control the Rotation animation.

This code checks the ***Rotation*** flag:

```
if (Rotation == "Right") {
    BottleMovie._rotation =
    ➥BottleMovie._rotation+RotationRate;
```

(The ➥ symbol you see here is for editorial purposes only.)

If it is set to **Right**, Flash rotates the bottle to the right by the degrees set in ***RotationRate***. The movie clip **property _rotation** sets the ***BottleMovie._rotation*** the same way it did with ***Zoom***. You also add the ***RotationRate*** to the current rotation. If the ***Rotate*** flag is set to **Left**, Flash rotates the bottle to the left, using this code:

```
} else if (Rotation == "Left") {
    BottleMovie._rotation = BottleMovie._rotation-
    ➥RotationRate;
```

(The ➥ symbol you see here is for editorial purposes only.)

Notice that nothing happens when the ***Rotation*** flag is set to **None**.

6 Choose Control > Test Movie to test the buttons with Test Movie.

The Rotate Right and Left buttons rotate the Splendos bottle right or left as long as they are held down. The Rotate Revert button reverts the bottle back to its original position. Notice that when you hold down one of the Rotate buttons, the bottle continues to rotate around and around. If you want the bottle to rotate faster, simply change the ***RotationRate*** variable.

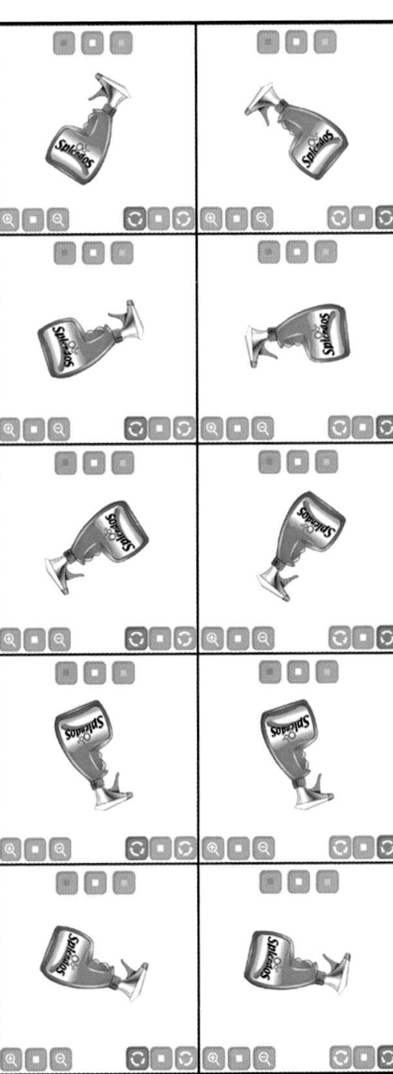

The Splendos bottle rotates continually while the Rotate Right button (clockwise) or Rotate Left button (counterclockwise) is pressed, creating a basic rotation animation.

Using ActionScript to Tint a Movie Clip

Flash 5 now has ways to change the look of any graphic on-the-fly in code without creating different graphics. This reduces the file size of the final product, and for Web work, you want it as small as possible. You will now set the bottle to different tints.

1 Select the Tint button on the left and enter this code:

```
on (release) {
    // tint bottle green
    var Green = new color(BottleMovie);
    var ColorTrans = new Object();
    ColorTrans = {ra:'100', rb:'0', ga:'80', gb:'129', ba:'18', bb:'-153', aa:'100', ab:'0'};
    Green.setTransform(ColorTrans);
}
```

Add this code to tint the Spendos bottle green.

This code tints the bottle a green color. This code uses the Flash 5 defined color Class to create the Green object:

```
var Green = new color(BottleMovie);
```

The color Class takes as a parameter the BottleMovie movie clip that you want to tint. This code defines your own generic object for the actual tinting:

```
var ColorTrans = new Object();
```

If the bottle were a solid color graphic, you could use the **SetRGB** method of the Green object already defined (**Green.setRGB()**), and you wouldn't need to define a new object. (For a demonstration of the **SetRGB** method, see Chapter 10.) Because the bottle is multicolored, you must use this **setTransform** method, which requires a defined object to hold the tinting information:

```
ColorTrans = {ra:'100', rb:'0', ga:'80', gb:'129', ba:'18',
➥bb:'-153', aa:'100', ab:'0'};
Green.setTransform(ColorTrans);
```

(The ➥ symbol you see here is for editorial purposes only.)

Each of these numbers in the **ColorTrans** object represents a tinting and percentage of the color. The ***ra*** and ***rb*** are for the reds, the ***ga*** and ***gb*** are for the greens, the ***ba*** and ***bb*** are for the blues, and the ***aa*** and ***ab*** are for the alpha transparency. You'll learn more about these numbers later in this section.

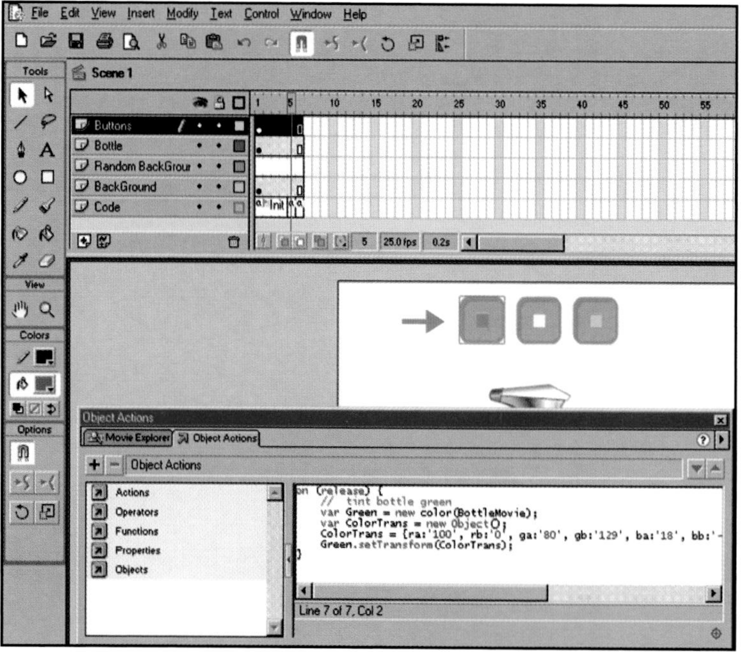

Assign the code for tinting the bottle green to the button with the green square on it.

2 Select the Revert Tint button and attach this code to it:

```
on (release) {
// tint bottle original
var Original = new color(BottleMovie);
    var ColorTrans = new Object();
    ColorTrans = {ra:'100', rb:'0', ga:'100', gb:'0', ba:'100', bb:'0', aa:'100', ab:'0'};
        Original.setTransform(ColorTrans);
}
```

Use this code to revert the bottle to its original color.

Notice that this code is identical to the code attached to the Green button, with the exception of the name of the object (*Green* vs. *Original*) and the numbers in the **ColorTrans** object. This code reverts the bottle back to its original color. Notice the ***ra***, ***ga***, ***ba***, and ***aa*** variables are all 100 (100%), and the ***rb***, ***gb***, ***bb***, and ***ab*** settings are all 0. This sets all the colors (red, green, blue, and alpha) to 0 tint at 100%. In other words, they have no tint.

3 Select the Tint button on the right and attach this code:

```
on (release) {
    // tint bottle yellow
    var Yellow = new color(BottleMovie);
    var ColorTrans = new Object();
    ColorTrans = {ra:'18', rb:'4', ga:'49', gb:'139', ba:'100', bb:'0', aa:'100', ab:'0'};
    Yellow.setTransform(ColorTrans);
}
```

Use this code to tint the Splendos bottle yellow.

This code is also identical to the other two tint buttons except for the different names for the objects (*Green* vs. *Yellow*) and different numbers in the **ColorTrans** object.

4 To make sure the bottle starts out in the original color, add this code to the **Init** code:

```
// tint bottle original
var Original = new color(BottleMovie);
    var ColorTrans = new Object();
    ColorTrans = {ra:'100', rb:'0', ga:'100', gb:'0', ba:'100', bb:'0', aa:'100', ab:'0'};
Original.setTransform(ColorTrans);
```

Include this code to ensure that the bottle will have its original color when the movie begins playing.

Notice that this is the same exact code attached to the Revert Tint button. You are ensuring that the BottleMovie starts with no tint applied to it.

5 Test the buttons.

The bottle should change tint. This tint remains even in Zoom and/or Rotate Mode.

6 To determine the numbers used in the **ColorTrans** object, select the BottleMovie movie clip and choose Window > Panels > Effect to open the Effect window. From the pull-down menu within the Effect window, select Advanced.

Notice the eight boxes—two boxes for each color (Red, Green, Blue) and two boxes for the Alpha setting. Each of these boxes contains information used in the **setTransform** method.

Notice that as you adjust the numbers, the BottleMovie movie clip changes color and opacity.

7 Adjust the settings to a color you like, and then enter the settings for the **setTransform** method.

The boxes on the left side are the percentages and apply to the ***ra***, ***ga***, ***ba***, and ***aa*** variables in the **setTransform** method. The boxes on the right side are the amount of color that will be applied and apply to the ***rb***, ***gb***, ***bb***, and ***ab*** variables in the **setTransform** method.

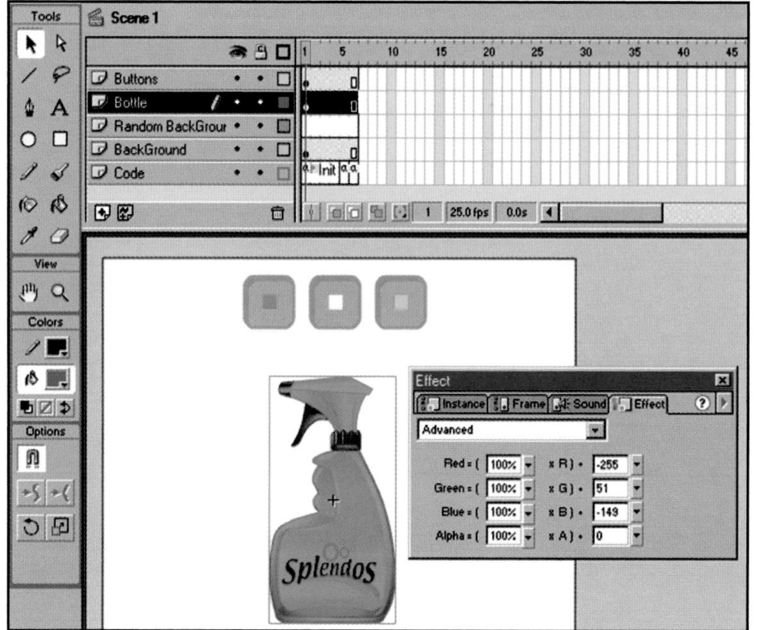

Use the Advanced feature in the Effect panel to come up with values for the **setTransform** method.

Creating a Random Background Animation

In this section, you add the final touch: the background. The code for the background consists of four line graphics, duplicated numerous times, that move across the screen at various speeds, directions, and locations. This technique is very useful for adding variety to a simple page.

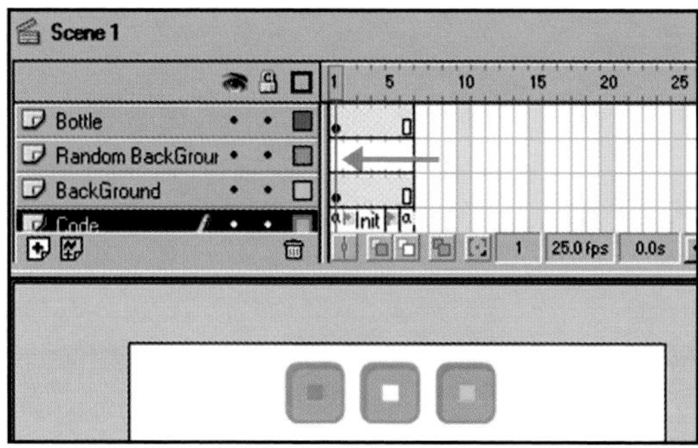

The resources for the Random Background animation will work best if they are placed on their own layer.

1 Notice the layer between the Background layer and the Bottle layer that's called Random Background.

You want the background to be on a separate layer for two reasons:

- You will know all the background graphics are in one layer and nothing else.

- You want to be able to actually physically place the graphics behind all the other graphics.

2 From within the Background folder in the Library, place the Line 1 Holding Movie on the Stage in the new layer and name this instance **Line1X**. Place it close to the upper-left corner of the Stage. The Line1X movie clip can even be off the Stage a little. You just want the movie clip to be as close to the 0,0 coordinate of the Stage as possible. This way when the ActionScript moves it, the ActionScript doesn't have to compensate for the actual starting position of the movie clip.

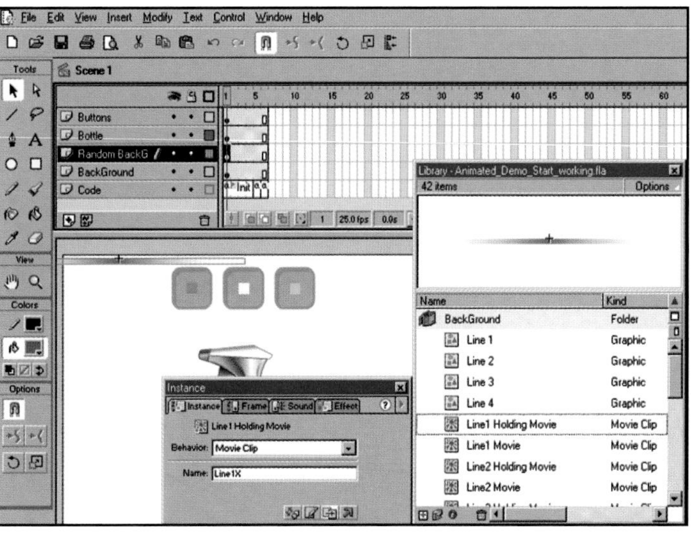

Place the Line 1 Holding movie clip on the stage and name it **Line1X**. Be sure to place the Line 1 Holding movie clip on the Random Background layer.

3 In frame 1 of the Code layer, enter the code in the **Init** code:

```
var ClipDimensions = Line1X.getBounds(_root);
//top,left,bottom,right
var Line1xLength = ClipDimensions.XMax - ClipDimensions.XMin;
Boundary = new Array();
Boundary[0] = 0 - Line1xLength;
Boundary[1] = 0 - Line1xLength;
Boundary[2] = MovieDimensions.YMax + Line1xLength;
Boundary[3] = MovieDimensions.XMax + Line1xLength
MaxEachLine = 5;
AlphaChange = 10;
```

Use this initialization code for the random background animation.

This code sets the boundary for the movement of the lines. You want the lines to move off the screen, and when they are gone, you want them to restart somewhere else so you always have movement. To make the lines move completely off the screen before restarting them, you calculate the boundary for the line movement based on the length of the line and the Stage boundaries. The length of the line is determined by the **getbounds** method used in this line:

```
var ClipDimensions = Line1X.getBounds(_root);
```

getBounds returns the maximum and minimum coordinates of both axes of the movie clip. The movie clip you selected runs horizontally, so to get the length of the line, you must subtract the maximum x coordinate from the minimum x coordinate, as shown in this line:

```
var Line1xLength = ClipDimensions.XMax -
➥ClipDimensions.XMin;
```

(The ➥ symbol you see here is for editorial purposes only.)

This line creates an array to contain the boundaries for the background lines, so you have to compute them only once instead of each time you need them:

```
Boundary = new Array();
```

You must adjust each boundary using the screen dimensions and the Line length. The top of the screen is denoted as 0, so you must subtract the length of the line from 0 and store the new top in the **Boundary** array in index 0, using this line:

```
Boundary[0] = 0 - Line1xLength;
```

The left side of the screen is also **0**, so you must subtract the length of the line from **0** and store the new left in the **Boundary** array in index 1, as shown in this code:

```
Boundary[1] = 0 - Line1xLength;
```

The bottom of the screen is determined by the ***MovieDimensions*** that you calculated earlier in the line:

```
(MovieDimensions = Screen.getBounds(_root);)
```

Then you add the length of the line to the ***Ymax*** in the ***MovieDimensions*** and store the new bottom in the **Boundary** array in index 2.

```
Boundary[2] = MovieDimensions.YMax + Line1xLength;
```

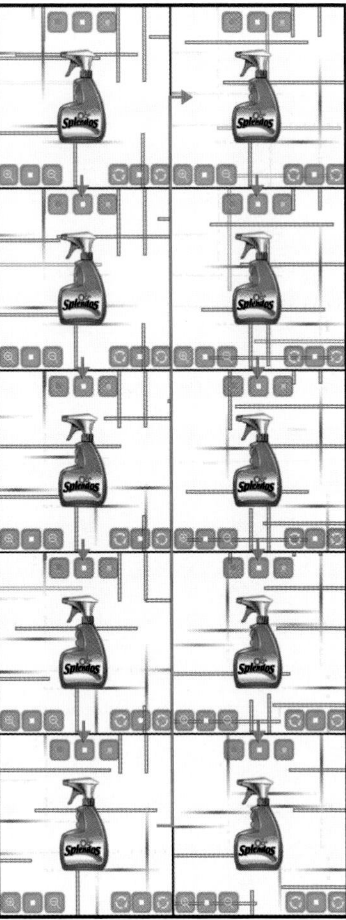

The remainder of this technique shows you how to create a random background animation using four simple objects. The objects (contained in movie clips) are randomly positioned on the screen, and they fade into view as they move off the screen. This process goes on continually with multiple instances of each object.

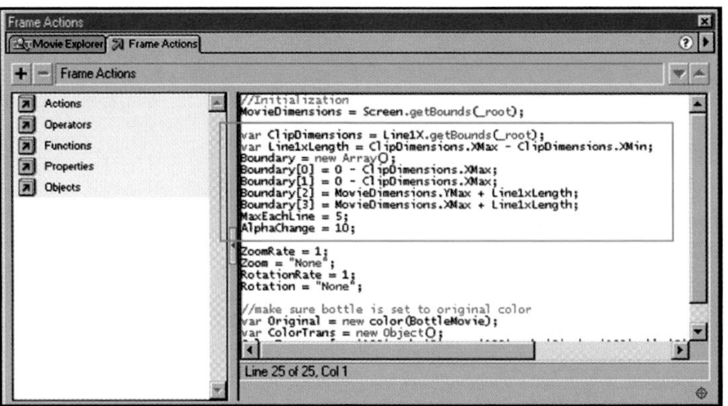

Assign the initialization code for the random background animation to the frame named Init on the Code layer.

The right side of the screen is also determined by the ***MovieDimensions***. To get it, you add the length of the line to the ***Xmax*** in the ***MovieDimensions*** and store the new right in the **Boundary** array in index 3.

```
Boundary[3] = MovieDimensions.XMax + Line1xLength;
```

The variable ***MaxEachLine*** determines how many lines of each type are on the screen. In this case, you want five lines of each type, so you use this code:

```
MaxEachLine = 5;
```

The variable ***AlphaChange*** fades the lines in by the specified percentage during each loop. In this case, you fade the lines in by 10% each loop, so it will take 10 loops to get the lines to their full opacity:

```
AlphaChange = 10;
```

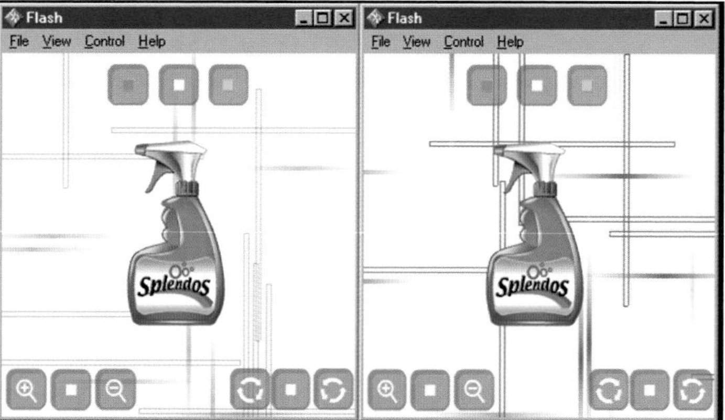

The movie clips fade into view and then they are animated off the screen as defined by the **MovieDimensions** code.

4 Without closing the Object Actions window, select the line that you placed on the Stage, and add the code to be done on the loading of this movie clip:

This code executes during the loading of this movie clip, the Line1X movie clip:

```
onClipEvent (load) {
```

You use a **for** loop to loop through and duplicate the Line1X movie clip. The number of times through the loop is determined by ***MaxEachLine***:

```
for (var Layer = 1; Layer<=_root.MaxEachLine; Layer++)
```

The **for** loop is an easy way to create loops. The counter is initialized in the first section of the for loop **(var Layer = 1;)**. Notice the semi-colon that separates the sections of the **for** loop. The semicolon is mandatory.

```
onClipEvent (load) {
    for (var Layer = 1; Layer<=_root.MaxEachLine; Layer++) {
        var NewMovieName = "LineX"+Layer;
        Line1X.duplicateMovieClip(NewMovieName, Layer);
        var YPos = random(_root.MovieDimensions.xMax);
        var XPos = random(_root.MovieDimensions.YMax);
        // offset for movie clip placement on the stage
        setProperty (eval(NewMovieName), _x, XPos);
        setProperty (eval(NewMovieName), _y, YPos);
    }
    Line1X._visible = false;
}
```

Add this code to control the animation of the Line1X movie clip.

The counter in this case is the variable ***Layer***, and it is initialized to 1. The loop continues as long as the second part of the section (**Layer<=_root.MaxEachLine;**) is true. As long as the *Layer* counter is less than ***MaxEachLine***, the loop will continue. In the third section, the counter variable (***Layer***) is incremented by one each time the loop loops (***Layer++***). The **++** is a standard Java way of incrementing a counter. If you wanted to decrease a variable by one, you would write ***Layer--***.

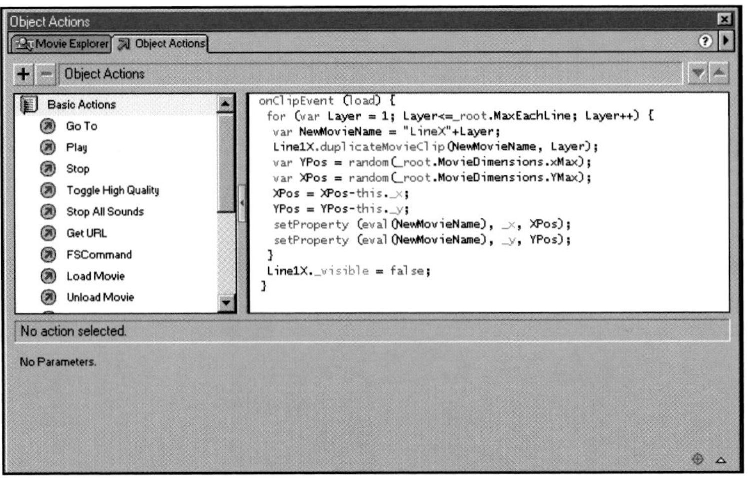

Assign the code to the Line1X movie clip instance using the Object Actions window.

To duplicate a movie clip, the movie clip you want to duplicate must have a unique name and must be on its own layer (thus one of the reasons for naming the counter in the **for** loop ***Layer***). A standard practice for naming duplicate movie clips is to use the layer number appended to the original movie clip name. This is basically what you do in the variable ***NewMovieName***:

```
var NewMovieName = "LineX"+Layer;
```

The **duplicateMovieClip** call is part of Flash 5's movie clip methods. You want to duplicate the Line1x movie clip, so the **duplicateMovieClip** call is attached to Line1x. The parameters that the **duplicateMovieClip** method requires are the new movie name (NewMovieName) and the layer that the movie will be on (Layer):

```
Line1X.duplicateMovieClip(NewMovieName, Layer);
```

Now you have two movies, the original Line1x and the new Line1X (LineX1), that look and act the same.

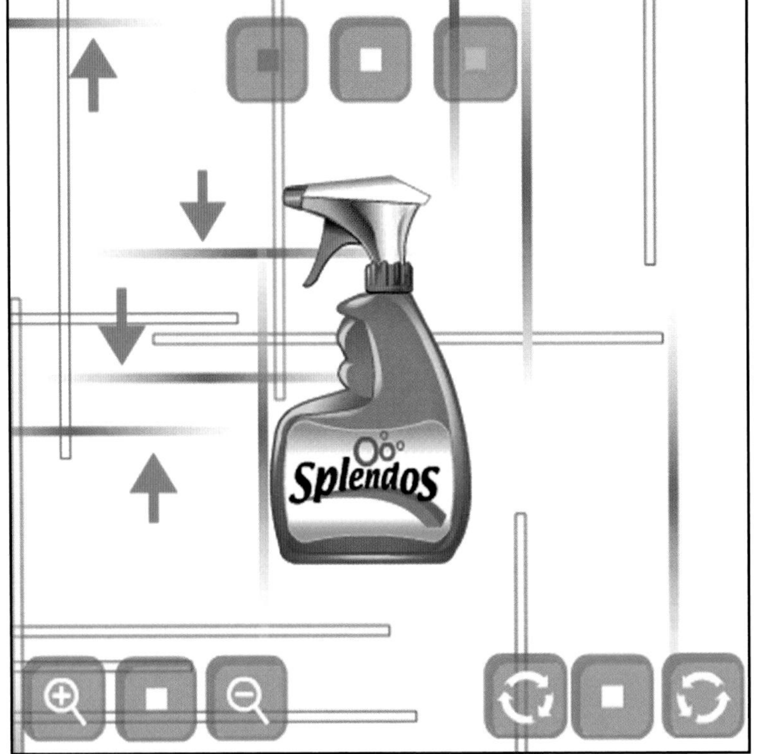

The code will be used to animate multiple instances of the Line1X movie clip using the **duplicateMovieClip** method.

The new line movie (LineX1) needs to be randomly placed on the screen based on the ***MovieDimensions***. The ***YPos*** and ***XPos*** are computed using the random function and the ***XMax*** and ***YMax*** of the screen:

```
var YPos = random(_root.MovieDimensions.YMax);
var XPos = random(_root.MovieDimensions.XMax);
```

Then the new line movie is placed using the new positions (***YPos*** and ***XPos***):

```
setProperty (eval(NewMovieName), _x, XPos);
setProperty (eval(NewMovieName), _y, YPos);
```

This is done with the **setProperty** call. The ***NewMovieName*** is a variable that contains the actual name of the movie clip, so you must evaluate the variable in order to set the *_x* and *_y* properties (**eval(newMovieName)**). The movie clip has both its *_x* and *_y* coordinates set.

This is done five times, the maximum for each line (***MaxEachLine***). When the for loop has finished, you need to hide the original movie clip by setting its visibility to **false**:

```
Line1X._visible = false;
```

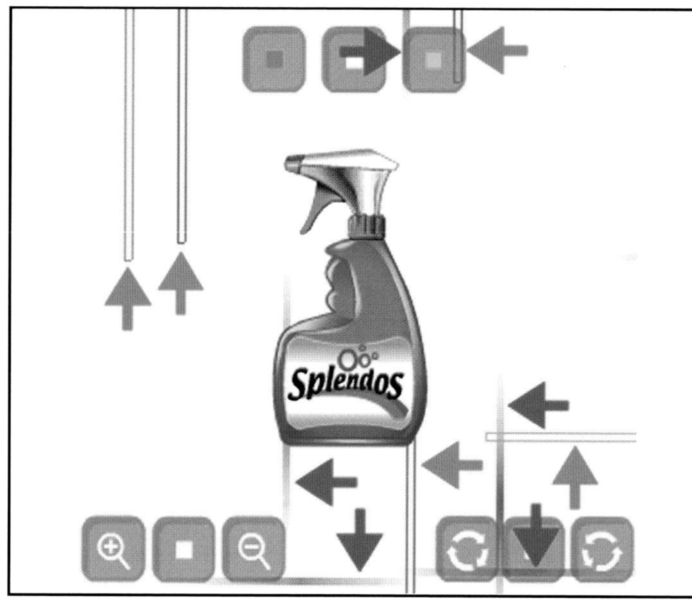

Five copies of each line are randomly positioned on the stage and then animated off the screen.

5 Open the Line 1 movie clip from the Library folder Background (located in the Line 1 Holding Movie you placed on the Stage), and enter this code in the Init frame label:

```
//init stuff
Speed = 2*(random(5)+1);
Direction = random(2);
// reverse direction
if (Direction == 1) {
Speed = 0-Speed;
}
//start fade
this._alpha = _root.AlphaChange;
```

Use this code to randomize the speed and direction, as well as to initiate the fade, of each Line1X movie clip instance.

You want the Line movie clips to move across the Stage. This code randomly sets the movement speed (between 5 and 10 pixels) for each duplicated movie clip. This way, each line will move at a slightly different speed:

```
Speed = 2*(random(5)+1);
```

You also want the lines to move in both directions, so the code determines the direction:

```
Direction = random(2);
```

The direction will either be a 0 or a 1 (Random always starts on 0). If ***Direction*** is equal to 0, you let the speed be positive. If ***Direction*** is equal to 1, you want to reverse the direction, so set the speed to a negative:

```
// reverse direction
if (Direction == 1) {
    Speed = 0-Speed;
}
```

You initialize the alpha transparency at which the ***this*** movie clip starts. Notice the use of the word ***this***. It is a standard reference to whatever movie clip this code is attached to. The following code changes the **_alpha** of ***this*** to ***_root.AlphaChange***:

```
this._alpha = _root.AlphaChange;
```

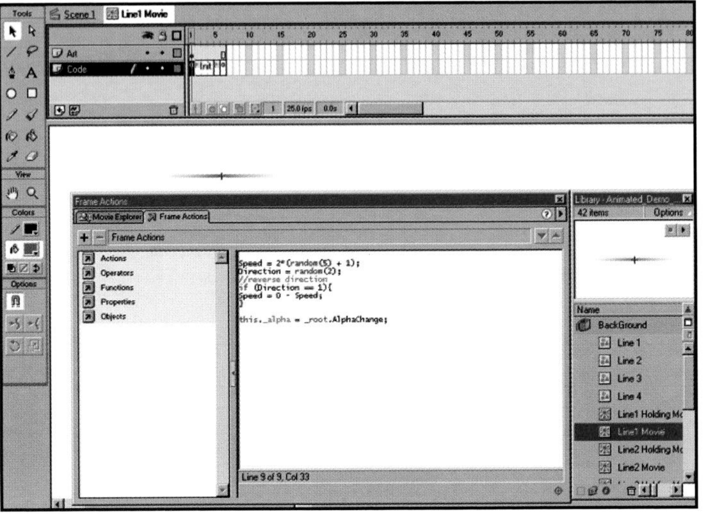

Assign the code to the frame labeled Init within the Line 1 movie clip. Don't look for the Line 1 movie clip on the Stage. You will find it only in the Library within the Background folder.

6 Still within the Line 1 Movie, add this code to the frame labeled Play:

You don't want to waste time moving the original movie clip, which is invisible, so you check for it right at the start. You know the name of the original movie clip (Line1X), so you compare the name of this movie clip (*this*) with the original movie clip name. You are currently in a movie clip called Line1X, which is in a movie clip called Line1x, which is on the root (**_root.Line1x.Line1X**):

```
if (this<>_root.Line1x.Line1X) {
```

Then you check for the Boundary of the screen. Because this line is horizontal, you need to check for the boundary conditions only in the x-axis (or the right and left). Notice that you are using *x*. This is the same thing as saying ***this._x***:

```
if (_x > _root.Boundary[3] or _x < _root.Boundary[1])
```

```
// don't move original
if (this<>_root.Line1x.Line1X) {
        if (_x > _root.Boundary[3] or _x < _root.Boundary[1]) {
        _root.Line1X.NewPosition(this);
        gotoandPlay("Init");
    } else {
        _x = _x+Speed;
    }

//change alpha
    if (_alpha>=100.0) {
        _alpha = 100;
    } else {
        _alpha = _alpha+_root.AlphaChange;
    }
}
```

Use this code to keep the original movie clip from being animated, as well as to help control the fade.

If the line has moved outside of the boundary conditions, you want to start the line movement over and give it a new starting position. You do this with the function **NewPosition**, which is explained later in this section:

```
_root.Line1X.NewPosition(this);
```

In the **NewPosition** code, you restart the line to a new position. You also want to give it a different speed and direction and to fade it in again. So the movie needs to go back to the Init frame"

```
gotoandPlay("Init");
```

As long as the line is within the screen boundaries, you move it the desired speed by adding the *Speed* to the current *_x* position of this movie clip:

```
_x = _x+Speed;
```

In the alpha transparency codes, the movie fades in only until you are at full transparency (100%), and then you don't want the movie to bother with the fade-in anymore:

```
if (_alpha>=100.0) {
_alpha = 100;
```

Until the movie has not reached 100% opacity, the movie needs to fade in some more:

```
_alpha = _alpha+_root.AlphaChange;
```

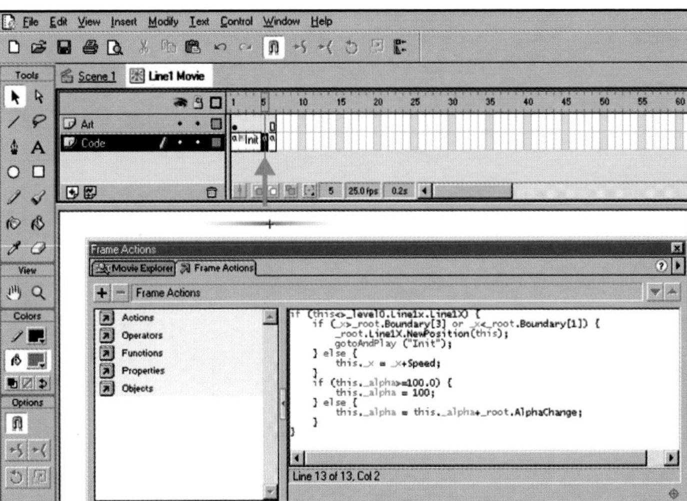

Assign the code to the frame labeled Play (frame 5) within the Line 1 movie clip.

7 To create the **NewPosition** function, which sets the new position called when the movie went out of bounds, go to the Holding Line 1 Movie and add this function in frame 1:

This function takes the ***MovieObject***, which is passed in from the calling movie. Remember that when you called this function, you also passed in the parameter ***this***. This tells the function what movie clip (***MovieObject***) to apply the changes to:

```
function NewPosition (MovieObject){
```

```
function NewPosition (MovieObject)
{
    var YPos = random(_root.MovieDimensions.xMax);
    var XPos = random(_root.MovieDimensions.YMax);
    setProperty (eval(MovieObject), _x, XPos);
    setProperty (eval(MovieObject), _y, YPos);
}
```

Use this code to randomly reposition the movie clip instance on the screen.

The function computes a random *y* position (***YPos***) and a random *x* position (***XPos***) based on the Stage size stored in ***MovieDimensions***:

```
var YPos = random(_root.MovieDimensions.YMax);
var XPos = random(_root.MovieDimensions.XMax);
```

Flash applies the new positions to the movie clip that was passed in. Notice that the variable ***MovieObject*** is not the actual name of the movie clip, but it contains the name of it, so you must use **eval(MovieObject)** to evaluate the ***MovieObject*** variable to determine the name.

```
setProperty (eval(MovieObject), _x, XPos);
setProperty (eval(MovieObject), _y, YPos);
```

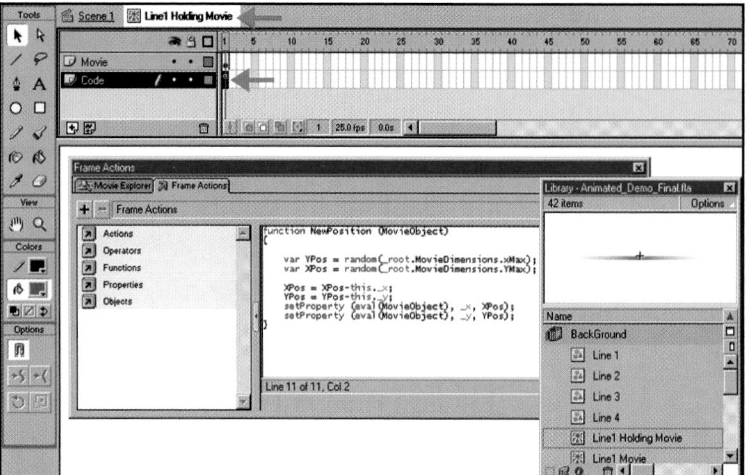

Assign this code to frame 1 of the "Holding Line 1 Movie" movie clip on the Code layer.

8 Test the movie using Control > Test Movie. Watch how the lines appear in random places all over the screen, fade in, and move in both directions.

Three other lines are available in the Library for adding more variety to the background. The code to make the lines move is already embedded in each one. All you need to do is attach the code to the **onclipEvent(Load)**. If you want to add them, you will need to place them in the upper-left corner of the Stage in the Random Background layer.

9 Name the instances this way: Line2 Holding Movie is named **Line2X**; Line3 Holding Movie is named **Line3X**; and Line 4 Holding Movie is named **Line4X**.

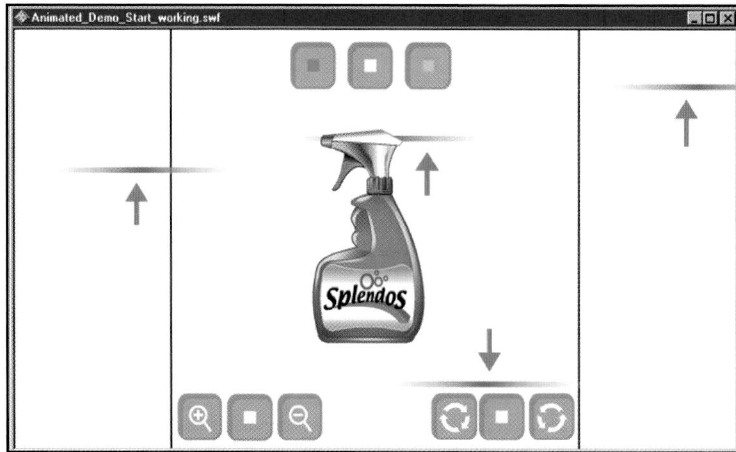

When you run the test movie, you should see multiple instances of the Line1X movie clip moving left and right.

10 Attach the code to each instance, changing the **?** to the appropriate movie number:

This is the same code attached to the Line1X movie clip (see step 3 for explanation). However, the number 1 has been replaced by a **?**. You need to replace the **?** with the appropriate movie clip number. For example, if the movie clip the code is attached to is named Line3X, the **?** needs to be replaced by a 3. All the other code for moving the line(s) is in the movie clips.

```
onClipEvent (load) {
    for (var Layer = 1; Layer<=_root.MaxEachLine; Layer++) {
        var NewMovieName = "LineX"+Layer;
        Line?X.duplicateMovieClip(NewMovieName, Layer);
        var YPos = random(_root.MovieDimensions.xMax);
        var XPos = random(_root.MovieDimensions.YMax);
        // offset for movie clip placement on the stage
        XPos = XPos-this._x;
        YPos = YPos-this._y;
        setProperty (eval(NewMovieName), _x, XPos);
        setProperty (eval(NewMovieName), _y, YPos);
    }
    Line?X._visible = false;
}
```

Add this code to the Line2X, Line 3X, and Line 4X movie clip instances. Substitute the question marks for the respective number of each movie clip.

11 After adding as many of the three line movies as you desire, test the movie. Notice that the bottle reacts slower due to the amount of processing required for all the lines.

How It Works

You have created all the functionality in this program. The main purpose of this movie is to demonstrate animation using ActionScript. During initialization, the size of the movie is determined, as are the boundaries that the random background can travel over. You also set the ***Zoom*** and ***Rotation*** variables and made sure the Splendos bottle was not tinted at the start of the product demo.

While the demo is running, the visitor can select from the nine buttons or the bottle. If the visitor selects the bottle, the BottleMovie does a tweening animation. When the visitor selects a button, it performs its function.

The tint buttons change the tint of the Splendos bottle by using the new Flash 5 color object. This tint remains even while the visitor zooms and rotates.

When the visitor selects a Rotation or Zoom button, Flash sets the appropriate flag. Then within the Play label, the code checks for any and all possible flag settings and performs the appropriate action based on the flag. The code in the Play label is in a one-frame loop that allows changes to the rotation and the zoom to be made as quickly as possible.

The background animation starts at the beginning. The visitor has no interaction with the background. Each line movie that is on the Stage executes the code in the **onclipEvent(load)**, which is where each line movie is duplicated. When all the line movies have been duplicated, the movement, fading, and resetting of the line movie are handled within each duplicated line's code.

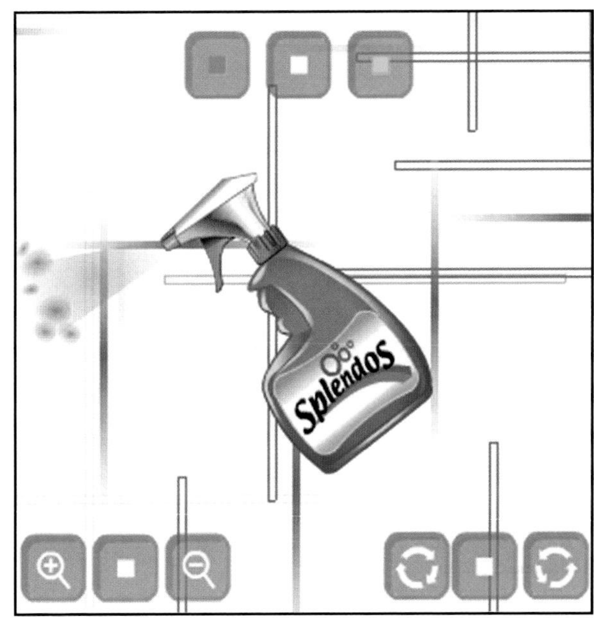

The Splendos bottle sprays and plays a spraying sound when you click on it.

12

USING SHARED LIBRARIES TO MANAGE ASSETS

By David Emberton

The task of planning, creating, and updating Flash content can be intimidating, especially if you are part of a workgroup or have many different projects with similar content. Shared Libraries alleviate a great deal of this difficulty by allowing you to aggregate common assets and then use them in as many different projects as you want.

One advantage of Shared Libraries is simplified updating. Just as the symbol Library in a regular Flash movie makes it simple to update a symbol across the whole movie, a Shared Library lets you achieve the same thing across entire groups of movies! Just change the asset in the Shared Library, export it again, and publish—and any related movie will automatically grab the latest version whenever it is run.

When you create a Shared Library, you use it to store assets that are common across a number of projects. For example, Splendos.com contents share common logos, sounds, and decorative symbols. Rather than managing multiple copies of those assets in every individual source file used in the Splendos Web site, they can be stored once in the Shared Library and then managed centrally.

The process revolves around a modified version of the **LoadMovie** action. When you're editing a movie with shared assets, you see a placeholder instead of the shared asset. When the movie is exported, those placeholders are replaced with pointers to the shared assets and the URLs where they can be located. When a visitor plays the exported movie, all the shared assets are loaded from their respective URLs before the first frame is streamed. This

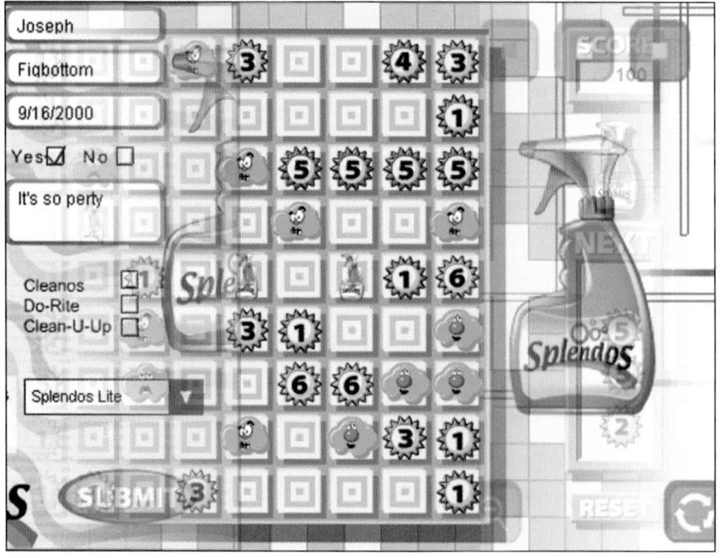

ensures that all the shared symbols are available when needed, and the flow of the animation will not be disrupted, nor will there be script problems should the shared symbol contain vital ActionScript.

Note: If you are creating a Shared Library for projects distributed on CD-ROM or other non-networked media, it's a good idea to include the exporter Shared Library files on the CD itself and link to it with a local URL. Forcing Flash Player to load assets over the network from your Web server, for example, will fail if the user doesn't have a connection—and any movies using the shared assets will not play.

Designing a Shared Library

Designing a Shared Library is not difficult, but it does require planning. This section describes the process you can follow when developing the Library. First, you must identify a set of commonly used elements. Then it's a matter of collecting them, assigning each one a unique ID, and setting linkage properties to ensure each asset is included upon export.

1 Decide what common elements you use most often and want to include.

Shared Libraries are useful for storing the following elements:

- *Logos and artwork.* Part of creating a consistent visual identity and strengthening brand recognition across your projects is to make sure logos, lettering, and supporting graphics all look similar. But what if the company you work for decides to change its logo? Instead of updating a hundred movies by hand, you can make the change in the Shared Library and have the changes reflected across the board—and you won't even have to re-export those other files! The shared assets are loaded upon playback, so the latest versions are always used automatically.
- *ActionScript and scripted components.* If you've ever spent time working with HTML and JavaScript (or even other application development environments like Visual Basic), you'll appreciate just how handy centralized scripts can be. For example, suppose you use a similar animated menu across a series of Flash movies. If something ever needs to be changed or debugged in that menu system, it will involve a lot of work! If that script is encapsulated in a shared symbol, however, updating multiple instances of it becomes a simple task.

- *Audio music and sound effects.* By far, these types of files are the most bandwidth-intensive parts of any Flash work. Aside from the task of updating, Shared Libraries can actually speed up the process of loading common audio data used in multiple files. Because the Shared Library .swf file containing the audio gets cached, opening a new file that uses those same shared symbols would be a matter of pulling it from the browser cache in most cases rather than loading a fresh copy over the network.

2 Determine the required bandwidth, taking into consideration just how often each of the assets in the list will be used.

The reason for this is that a Shared Library is exported as a single .swf file containing *all* the symbols in it. For another movie to access one of these symbols, it streams the entire Shared Library .swf before beginning playback. So if a particular 200KB sound file is going to be used only once or twice, you should put it in a separate Shared Library file.

Of course, when a Shared Library .swf file is downloaded, it is stored in your browser's cache. So reusing symbols from it after it's loaded isn't such a problem.

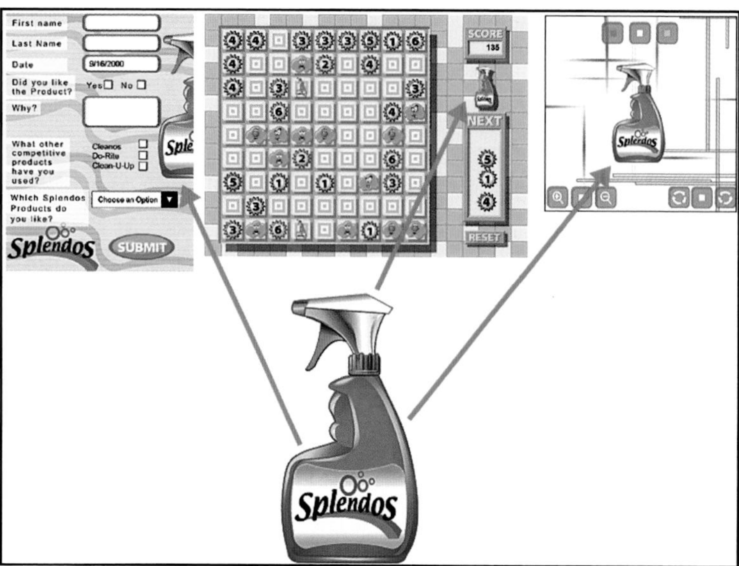

Resources that are used repetitively in different files for a project are good candidates for Shared Libraries.

Tip: Group large symbols or those you use less often into separate Shared Libraries. That way you still get the benefit of centrally updated symbols, but without making people wait unnecessarily to download data that a particular movie might not even use.

Don't go crazy separating Shared Libraries too much, however, because Flash Player will experience performance problems if it attempts to stream too many external files at once. It's best to stick with one, two, or even three Shared Libraries of varying importance—taking care to keep each one as lean as possible to avoid onerous downloading delays.

SETTING UP A SHARED LIBRARY

To maintain a consistent approach to brand recognition across the Splendos Web site, you'll use the following common assets. These assets need to be shared across all the site's Flash content: the Splendos logo, the Spray bottle graphic, the Splendos "swoosh" sound, the Squeegee and spray sound effects for buttons and transitions, and a pair of supporting graphics for backgrounds and decoration.

To prepare this otherwise fairly ordinary Flash file for use as a Shared Library, you need to decide on a unique identifier for each symbol and then set the linkage properties for each.

1. Open the file SplendosAssets_speed.fla in the Chapter 12 folder of the accompanying CD, save it to your hard drive, and display the Library window.

2. One by one, select each of the symbols indicated below from the Library, choose Library Options > Linkage, and set each symbol's linkage properties in the resulting dialog box. Select Export This Symbol and use these Identifiers:

   Audio:

   Spray Sound – **SpraySound**

   Graphics:

   Splendos Logo - **SplendosLogo**

   Splendos Bottle - **SplendosBottle**

   Supporting Graphic 1 - **Swoosh**

   Supporting Graphic 2 – **Bubbles**

   The Shared Library is now ready for export to .swf format.

3. Use Test Movie, and then select File > Export Movie or File > Publish to export the movie in Flash 5 Player format.

4. Save and close the file.

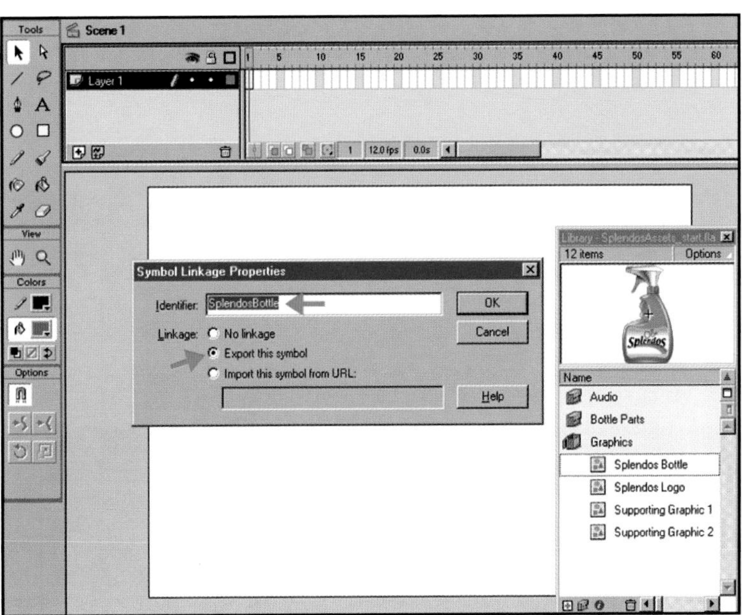

Set the linkage properties for each of the symbols.

Adding Shared Symbols to a New File

After you prepare the Shared Library, you can use it with any of the following projects. Here is the procedure for using a shared asset.

1 Open a new file.

2 Use the File > Open As Shared Library command to open SplendosAssets_start.fla as a Shared Library.

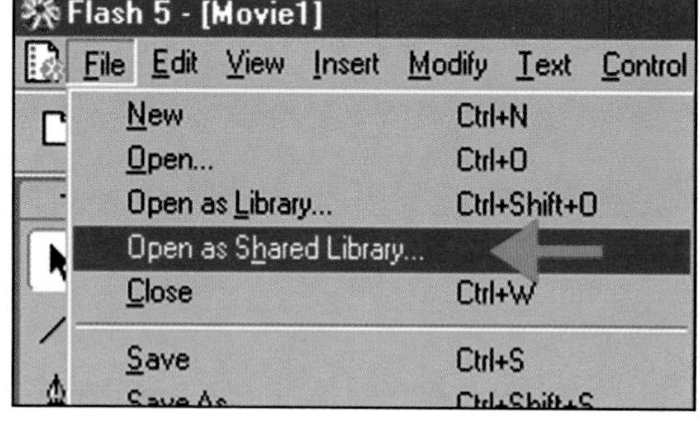

Select the Open As Shared Library command.

> **Note:** It's important to use the Open As Shared Library command here, and not the regular Open As Library option. Only the Open As Shared Library command will allow you to drag and drop symbols into your new movie with the linkage properties intact.

3 Bring up the Library window for your new file and drag one of the symbols from the Shared Library into it.

If you click the newly added symbol in your movie's Library and check its linkage properties, you'll see the identifier, as well as a URL specifying the location of the Shared Library's .swf file. If you move that .swf file, you must update this URL field for the linkage to work.

4 Drag the symbol from your movie's Library onto the Stage. You can resize, rotate, and otherwise transform it just like any regular instance.

5 Save your file, and then export it using Test Movie. If you activate the Bandwidth Profiler, you'll see that the file is very tiny—because the graphics are being imported from the Shared Library .swf file.

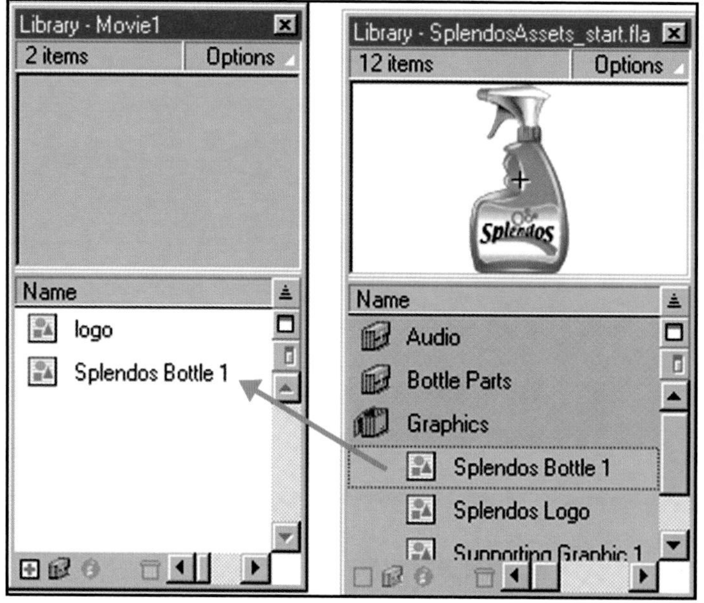

Drag the files from the Shared Library to the new library. Some symbols have other symbols associated with them.

Note: It's vital that you save your file before you try to test it. If the file is not saved, the linkage URLs don't work properly. If you attempt to test the movie before saving it, you will receive an error message in the Output window.

Replacing Existing Symbols with Shared Ones

Now you know how to add shared symbols to your Library, but what if you want to replace a symbol already in an existing project's Library with a shared asset? It's actually a lot simpler. All you have to know is the identifier of the shared asset and the URL of the .swf file that contains it.

1. Open the database_final.fla file from Chapter 13 of the accompanying CD and save it to your hard drive. For the sake of this exercise, save a copy of it into the same folder that contains SplendosAssets_start.fla (on your local hard drive—not on the CD, of course).
2. Bring up the Library window for that file and select the Splendos logo.
3. Use the Options menu to open the symbol's linkage properties.
4. In the Identifier field, type **SplendosLogo**, and then click the Import This Symbol from URL: option. Type **SplendosAssets_start.swf** in the URL field.
5. Save the file and use Test Movie to check the results. All uses of the logo will now be dynamically loaded from the SplendosAssets_start.swf file. To test the effect further, go back to the SplendosAssets_start source file, change the logo symbol, and then export again. Play the example file you've been working with, and the new logo will be displayed instead of the old one.

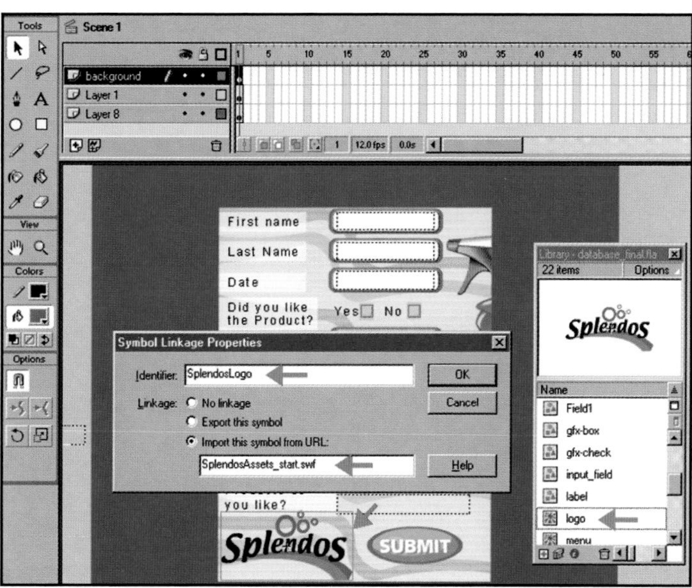

Use the Linkage option to refer to the Splendos logo from the Shared Assets file.

That's all there is to it! With planning and practice, Shared Libraries can make your updating and maintenance tasks a breeze—and you won't have to manually code **LoadMovie** actions and loading solutions.

How It Works

Creating numerous Flash movies or even one large Flash movie takes some careful bandwidth planning. The .swf format is already optimized for low bandwidth connections, having support for symbols so elements can be defined once and used often. But what about symbols, fonts, and sounds that are common to several movies? In the past, these common assets had to be downloaded for each movie.

Flash 4 introduced the **LoadMovie** action, which was used by keen developers to solve these redundancies to an extent. However, this involved managing the loading and positioning of each individual shared file, and having to simply "know" during the authoring process how everything would turn out in the end. And of course, font sets were not supported in that scheme either.

The Shared Libraries feature of Flash 5 was inspired directly by the Load Movie techniques developers were already using. It added support for asset management right into the authoring environment, so positioning and previewing was no longer a matter of luck. Now Flash can export multiple symbols as a single shared .swf file instead of having to manage each one separately, even though they might be very small. And, the shared asset files are conveniently loaded before anything else, so nothing is left to chance.

All in all, the Shared Libraries feature—when used mindfully—can speed up production, ease updating, and most of all, make the development process just a little bit more organized.

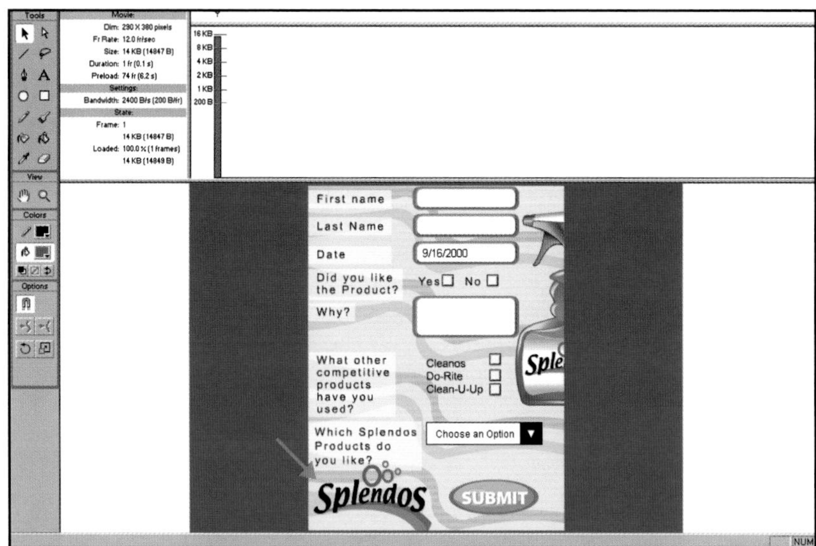

Now the database file uses the logo from the Shared Assets file.

13

WORKING WITH FORM ELEMENTS AND ASP

By Matthew David

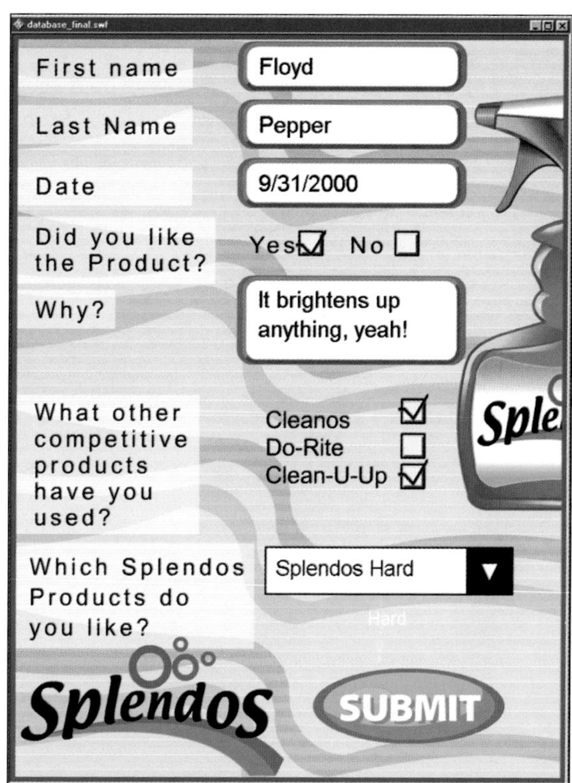

Flash is now capable of integrating databases within ActionScript. That is, you can now program ActionScript to both load content to and deliver content from a database. To enable Flash to do this, however, you must employ Server Side Scripting. Flash now supports Perl, PHP, Cold Fusion, JavaServer Pages (JSP), and Microsoft's Active Server Pages (ASP).

This technique uses Microsoft's Active Server Pages in conjunction with Flash to send a completed survey from a Flash movie to an Access database. Splendos, the ultimate cure-all product, is the subject for the survey.

Creating a Basic Form in Flash

Passing data from Flash to the server is relatively easy. All you need is a simple Flash form. A Flash movie consisting of one layer and one frame can comprise a basic form. In this section, you create a simple form in Flash to cover the basics and demonstrate how easy and unintimidating it is.

1 Open a new Flash file and draw a text field approximately 45 characters long on the Stage. In the Text field, select Dynamic Text. Select the Border/Bg option to make the field easier to see.

This creates a field to which a user can add data. Because you chose Dynamic Text, the field can be dynamically updated.

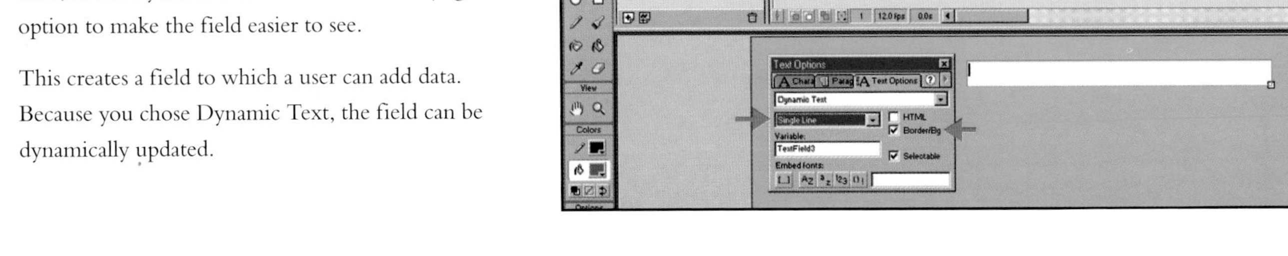

Create a text field, change the option to Dynamic Text, and turn on the Border/Bg option.

2 Hold down the Alt key, drag to create five more instances of the text field, and align the fields.

You should now have six instances of the text input field with a solid border color.

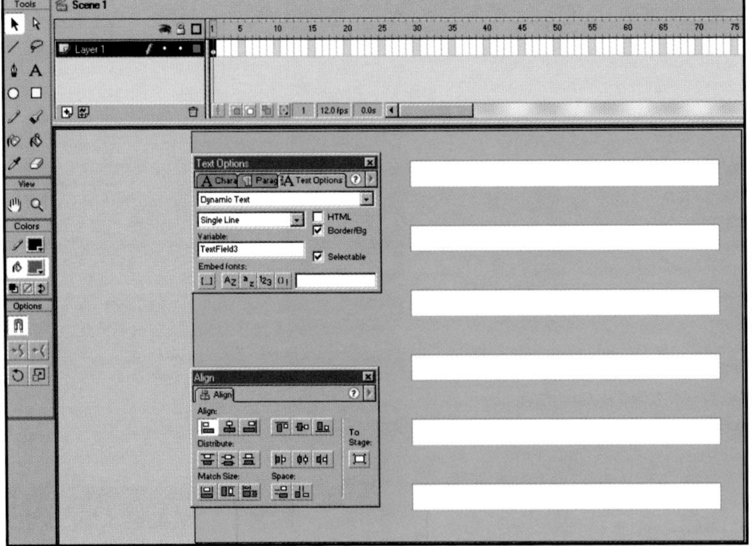

Make five copies of the text field, and then align and distribute the text fields to one another.

3 So that Flash and the Server pages know where the content in the forms is being passed to, enter a variable name for each instance of the text field to match the name of the database field. For example, the first field should have the variable ***FirstName***; the second, ***LastName***; the third, ***Date***; the fourth, ***LikeProduct***; the fifth, ***Why***; and the sixth, ***Samples***. These names match references in the ASP file used later.

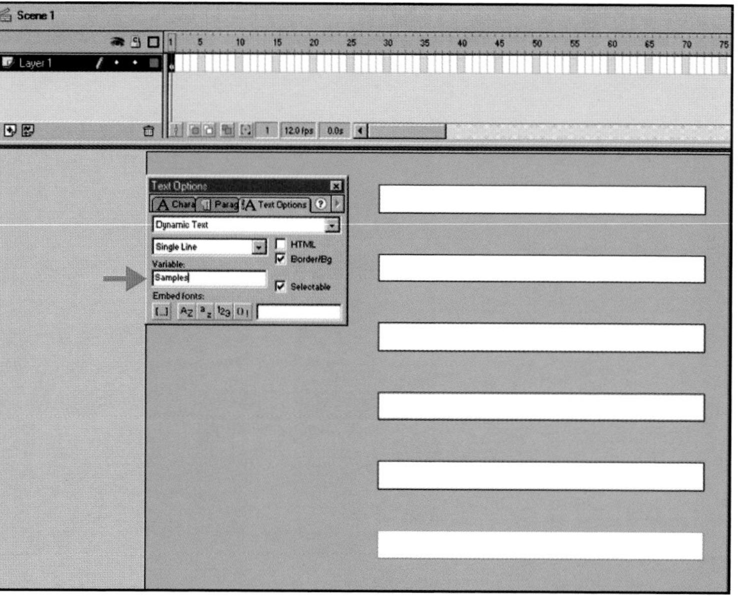

Each text field has a variable name.

4 Along the left side of the input fields, add descriptions for what you would like the customer to enter. You could use the following:

Variable Name for Input Field	Static Text Description
FirstName	**Your First Name**
LastName	**Your Last Name**
Date	**Today's Date**
LikeProduct	**Do you like this product? Yes or No.**
Why	**What was the reason for your answer?**
Samples	**What competitors' products have you used?**

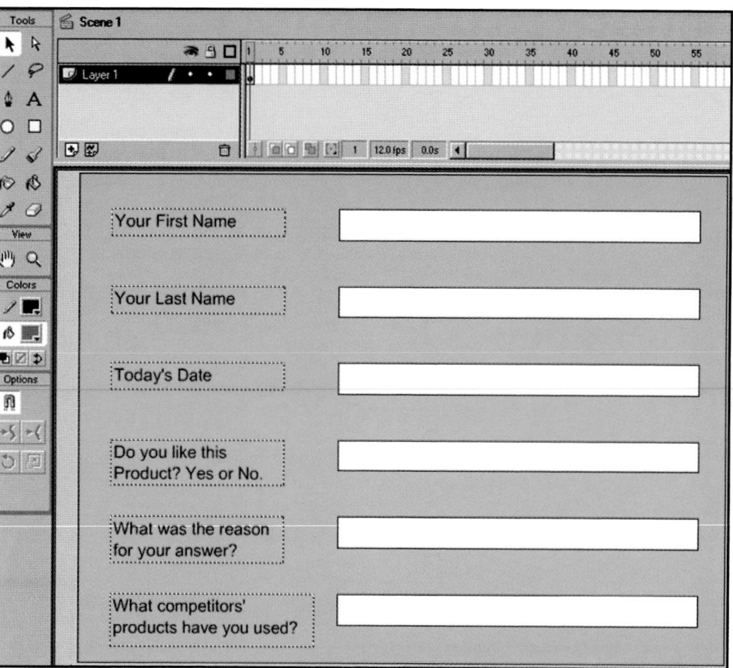

Each text field has a corresponding text description.

5 To make it possible for customers to submit the form, drag an instance of a button onto the Stage and add this action to it:

```
on (release) {
    mm_insert = "true";
    loadVariables ("\"submit.asp\"", "", "POST");
    getURL ("thankyou.htm", "_self");
}
```

Add this code to the instance of the button.

mm_insert, which has to be set to **true** for the submit.asp file to work correctly, is a variable inside the Server page—in this case, a Microsoft Active Server Pages (ASP)—that is requesting a **true** or **false** value. By adding the value as **true** in Flash, you can guarantee the next steps will work.

The next step for Flash is to load the ASP file. The ASP file that will be loaded into the Flash movie is located on the CD.

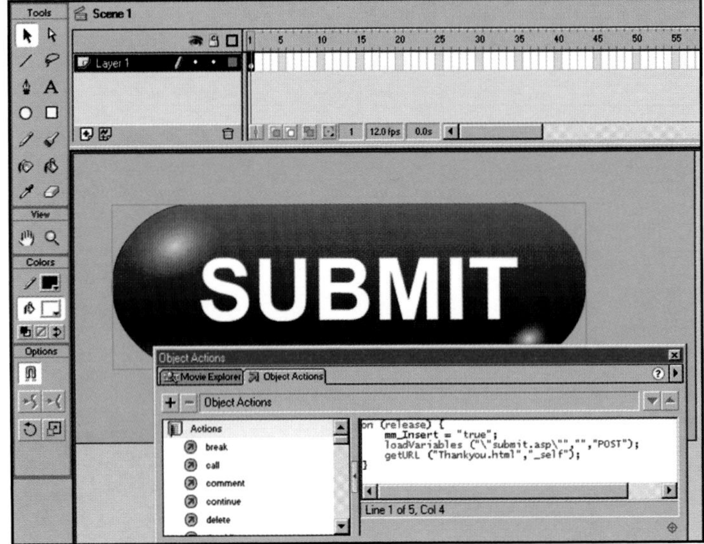

The code is assigned to the button.

Tip: For the ASP to work, you need to be running Microsoft's Internet Information Server, IIS, (version 3.0+) or Microsoft's Personal Web Server, PSW. On your Web server, create a directory (such as http://localhost/flash). Place the Flash movies you've created in this chapter (the .swf file), along with the ASP page, into that directory. When you browse with your Web browser to this directory, the Active Server Page will be activated by the Web server. For more information on Microsoft's Internet Information Server or Personal Web Server for the PC or Macintosh, go to http://www.microsoft.com/windows20000/guide/server/features/appsvcs.asp.

The file is submit.asp. Because the server reads that a value for ***mm_insert*** has been set to **true**, it can load the form fields in the ASP file with the values collected from the Flash form. The **POST** command sends the data to the Web server.

The current movie uses an ASP and an .swf file stored in the same directory. You can load Active Web pages from different Web servers if your company has many different Microsoft Web servers. What you will need to change is the file that is being loaded into the Flash movie. Where you have

```
Loadvariables ("\"submit.asp\"","","POST"
```

you will need to change the script to load the full Web path to the file, such as

```
Loadvariables ("\"http://www.servername.com/
directory/load.asp\"","","POST")
```

This allows an ASP file anywhere in the company to be loaded into your Flash movie.

The final step is to send the user a thank you after the data has been successfully uploaded. That is managed with the following line:

```
getURL ("thankyou.htm", "_self");
```

The **getURL** retrieves the thank you page, in this case thankyou.htm, and loads it into the Web browser window.

The form created here is the most basic version of a survey. All the user has to do is fill in the blanks. Flash allows for a rich collection of form objects, such as multilined text fields, check boxes, and drop-down boxes. In the following sections, you will see how to employ these elements in Flash.

Creating a Single or Multilined Text Field

User response fields often require more than one line. For example, when you ask customers why they use Splendos, it is a good idea to give them more than one line to answer the question. In this section, you convert a text field from one that accepts only a single line to one that accepts multiple lines.

1 Open the Database_Start.fla file from the Chapter13 folder and save it to your local hard drive. See Database_Final.fla for the finished version.

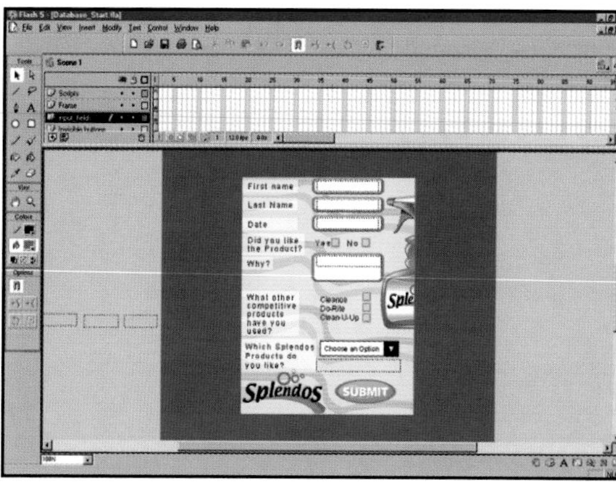

Open the Database_Start.fla file and save it to your local drive.

2 Select the Why text field, open the Text Options panel, and change the setting in the second field from Single Line to Multiline.

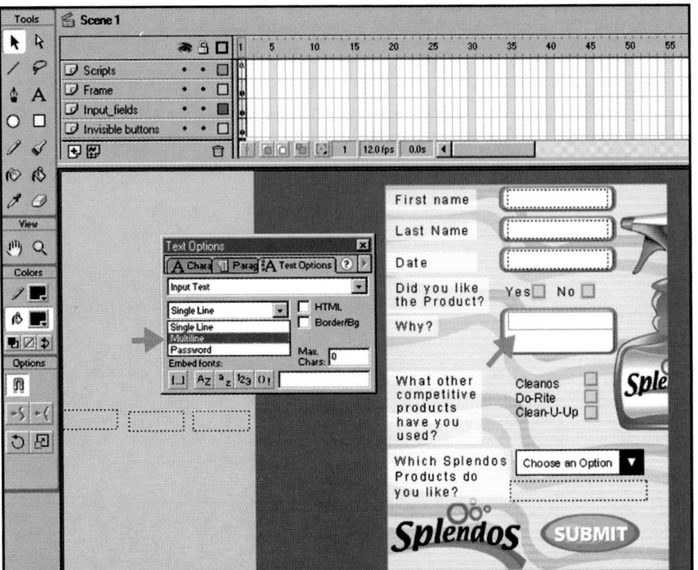

Select the text field next to the field labeled Why and use the Text Options panel to change it to Multiline.

3 Resize the text field to allow a user to add paragraphs of text.

A feature unique to Flash and not possible with HTML forms is the ability to limit the number of characters a user can add to a multiline text field. In the Text Options panel, a field called Max Chars is available for Input Text fields. Here, you can add a number to limit the amount of input a user adds to the form.

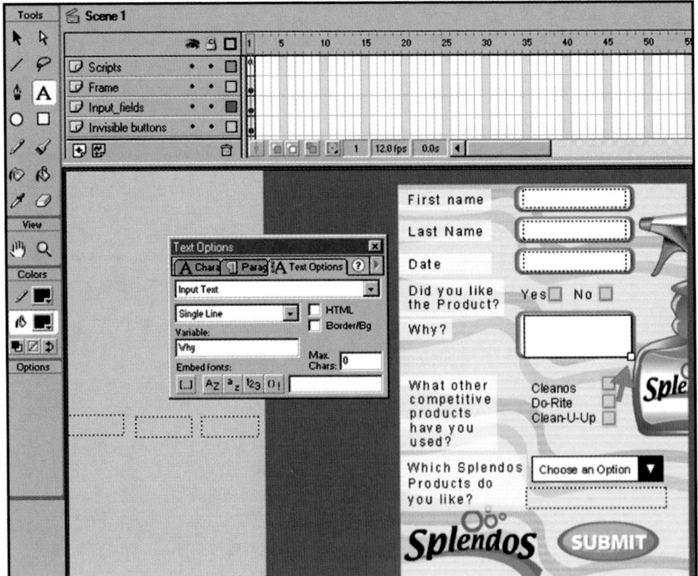

Resize the Why text field.

ADDING THE DATE OBJECT

It is often important to know the date on which a user submitted a form to a Web server. To do this, you can use the Date object in Flash 5. The Date object must be loaded as the movie is loaded. For this reason, you will insert the variable that calls the date in the first frame of the movie.

1 Select the Scripts layer.

2 Select the first frame in the Scripts layer and assign this code to it:

```
now = new Date();
date = (now.getMonth()+"/"+now.getDate()+"/"+now.getFullYear());
```

Add this code to the Scripts layer.

Here two variables are being managed. The first variable, called ***now***, allows you to calculate the date. This variable is going to calculate the value of the variable ***new Date()***, which gets the date from the computer system clock.

The date also has to be formatted. To do this, the script leverages a set of new date objects with Flash: **getMonth**, **getDate**, and **getFullYear**.

The ***now*** variable has already accessed the computer's system clock to retrieve the date. The format is used to parse the correct information from this date to the Flash movie.

The **getMonth** object retrieves the numeric value of the month from the ***now*** variable, the **getDate** object retrieves today's day of the month, and **getFullYear** retrieves the year as a four-figure year. A forward slash (/) formats the space between objects.

Now the date has to be put somewhere. In the form, you have a dynamic text field with the variable name of ***date***. The text field is going to be dynamically populated with the date from your survey form.

You know the value of ***now*** is today's date, but this value has not been formatted as month, day, and year. This formatting is done using the Date objects. The value for the current month is taken from **getMonth**,

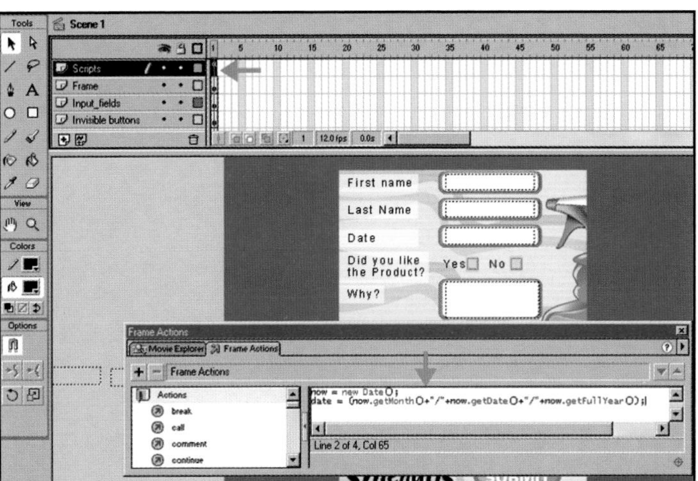

The date generation code is added to the Scripts layer.

the value of the current day is **getDate**, and the value of the current year is **getFullYear**.

The date can be easily modified. For example, outside of the USA, time is calculated as day/month/year, in which case the ActionScript for the date would be written like this:

```
now = new Date();
date =
(now.getDate()+"/"+now.getMonth()+"/"+now.getFullY
➥ear());
```

(The ➥ symbol you see here is for editorial purposes only.)

Without having to resort to external JavaScripts through the **FS** command (which is the only way to get the date in Flash 4), you can now easily insert a date into your Flash 5 movies.

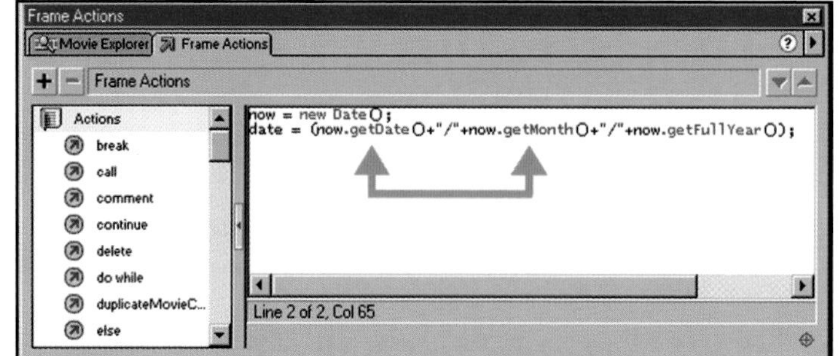

You can easily change the order of the date elements.

Creating Check Boxes

A checkbox is a useful tool in any form. With it, you can get a definitive yes or no response. For example, a form can ask, "Do you have a computer?" The responder either does or doesn't.

The trick in Flash is to get a value and be able to pass it along to a Web server. To demonstrate this, the survey you are building for Splendos asks if a customer has used any competitors' products. The customer can select from three products: Cleanos, Do-U-Rite, and Clean-U-Up. When a customer chooses any or all of these products, a value has to be recorded and sent to the Web server. This is done through the use of three objects you will create: checkbox movie, box button, and a dynamic text field.

The checkbox movie is comprised of two frames, both with a **Stop** action. The first frame of the movie shows the checkbox as blank, and the second frame of the movie shows the check in the check box, allowing the user to see that a value has been entered.

1 Temporarily turn off the visibility of the Invisible buttons layer, select the small check box graphic symbol next to the Cleanos text, and name the instance **checkbox1**.

2 Turn on the visibility of the Invisible buttons layer and select the light blue box or square (which is a button) directly on top of the instance of the check box graphic symbol you just named checkbox1.

The box button is light blue because it is a button that is invisible. Only the "hit" area, which defines the clickable area for the button, contains the square graphic used to give substance to the button. You will apply ActionScript to this button in a moment.

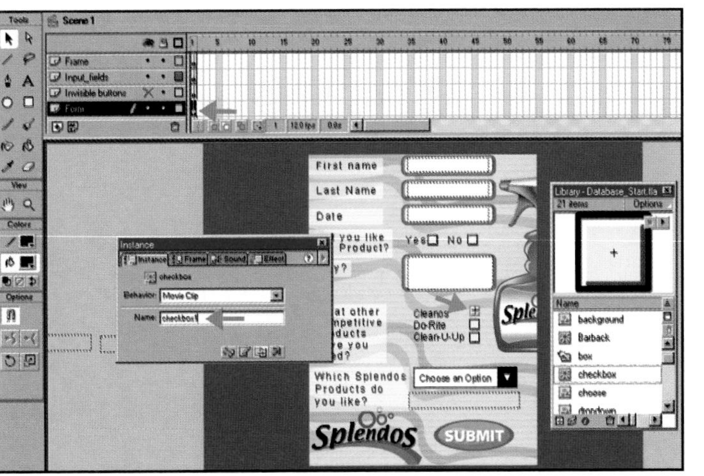

Give the checkbox graphic symbol an instance name.

3 Before adding the script, notice the four dynamic text fields off the side of the screen.

4 Select the second field from the left and notice that it has the variable name ***samples1***.

The text field is used in the form to capture the value of the check box. The value of the text field will be sent to the Web server after the customer clicks on the Submit button. The variable name of the text field will be called from the ActionScript, and a value will be inserted.

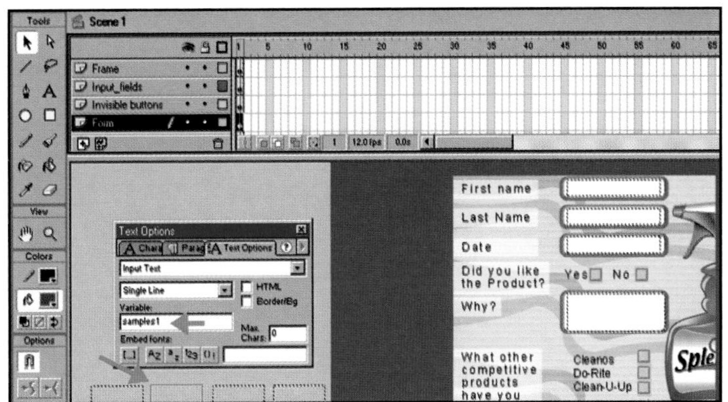

Notice the ***samples1*** text field off the edge of the viewable Stage area.

5 Select the invisible instance of the box button, open the ActionScript window, and assign this script:

```
on (press) {
    if (Number(Checked) == 0) {
        tellTarget ("/checkbox1") {
            gotoAndStop (2);
        }
```

Assign this code to the invisible button that holds the meat of the script. When a user selects the button with the mouse, the script reacts.

continues

continued

```
            checked = 1;
            samples1 = "Cleanos";
        } else {
            tellTarget ("/checkbox1") {
                gotoAndStop (1);
            }
            checked = 0;
            samples1 = "";
        }
    }
```

By default, the movie is stopped on frame 1. This is the blank check box. When the user selects it, the **if** statement is invoked.

The first task for **if** is to evaluate the value of the variable named ***checked***. Earlier in the movie, the ***checked*** variable was created in frame 1. The default value was set to **0**. When the **if** statement sees that the value is **0**, it proceeds to the next line.

This line of code is a **tellTarget** command to send Flash to the movie instance on the main Stage called checkbox1:

tellTarget ("/checkbox1") {

When the instance is found, the player goes to and stops at frame 2. This shows the user a check.

Two more actions take place. The value for ***checked*** is now changed from **0** to **1**, and a text string is passed to the dynamic text field with the variable name ***samples1***. This populates the dynamic text field.

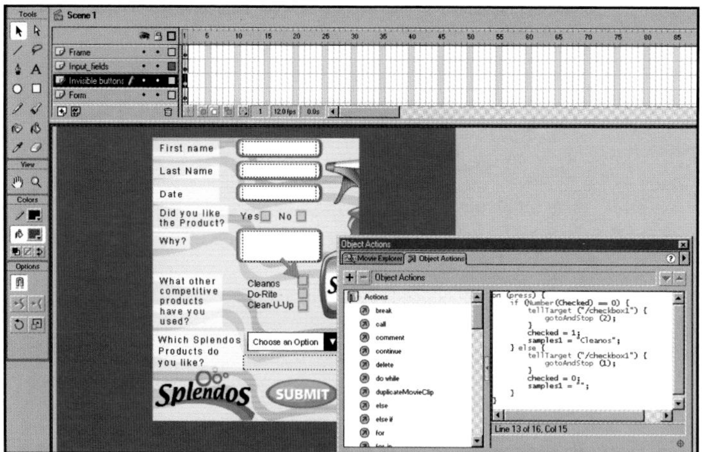

The code is applied to the invisible button.

Users can change their minds and deselect a check box if necessary. When the value of ***checked*** is set to **1**,the second half of the **if** statement, the **else**, can be triggered. The Flash player is sent to frame 1 of the checkbox1 movie instance, and the value of ***checked*** is restored to **0**. To show the change in input, the value sent to the dynamic text field is also changed. Here the new value is blank; however, you could easily change it to a null value.

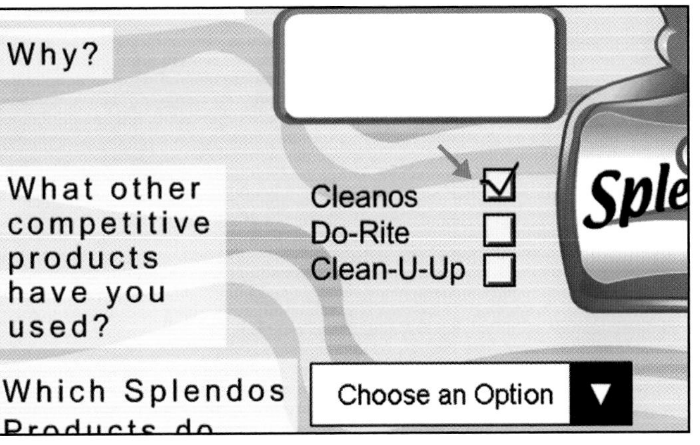

A check appears on the check-box when the user clicks it.

The script is a basic **if/else** statement. Essentially, the script says that when a user clicks on (presses) the box button, the movie instance named checkbox1 is sent to frame 2 of the movie. At the same time, a value of **Cleanos** is placed in the dynamic text field samples1. The end result is that you can have a user enter a value into a check box, which can then be captured and sent to a database via the Active Server Pages script.

6 Copy the code that you assigned to the first invisible button (the one next to the Cleanos label) and assign it to the second invisible button (next to the Do-Rite label) directly below the first. Modify the script so that every reference to **checkbox1** reads **checkbox2**. Repeat this process for the third invisible button (next to the Clean-U-Up label) below the previous two invisible buttons, only change all references from **checkbox1** to **checkbox3**.

```
on (press) {
    if (Number(Checked) == 0) {
        tellTarget ("/checkbox2") {
            gotoAndStop (2);
        }
        CB_1 = 1;
        samples2 = "Do-Rite";
    } else {
        tellTarget ("/checkbox2") {
            gotoAndStop (1);
        }
        CB_1 = 0;
        samples2 = "Blank";
    }
}
```

Modify the code for checkbox1 to work for checkbox2 and checkbox3.

The corresponding check box graphic symbols have already had their respective instance names applied to them, and the dynamic text fields for **checkbox2** and **checkbox3** are already created.

You can see how a check box can now be added to your forms.

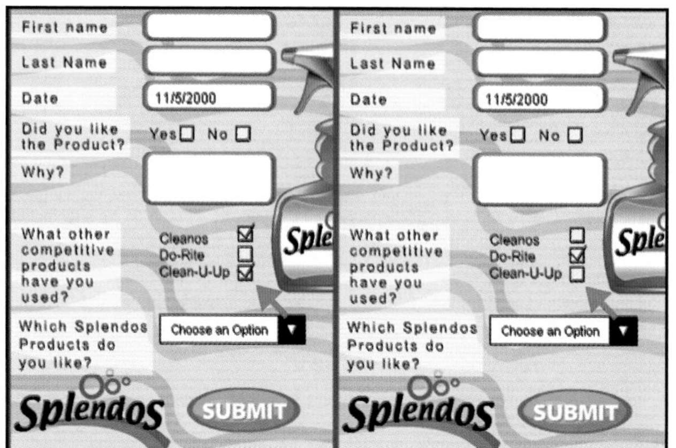

The user can check and uncheck the boxes before they submit the form.

7 To allow this check box and the following radio button script to operate smoothly, add this code to frame 1 of the main movie:

```
Checked = 0;
```

This script stops users from having to double-click an option.

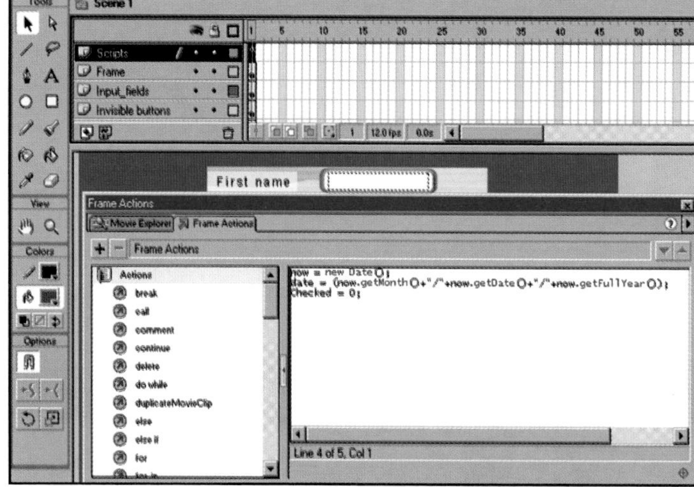

Add a line of code to the ActionScript on the Scripts layer.

Adding Radio Buttons

Radio buttons are very similar to check boxes. The only difference is that you can have only one true value for a group of buttons. For example, in the question "Are you male or female?" there can be only one answer. You cannot be both male and female.

To set up the radio button, you modify the scripts written for the check box. Essentially, the same principles still apply: The user sees a box, an invisible button over the box manages the value being selected, and a dynamic text box collects the value and sends it to a Web server when the user clicks the Submit button.

For this exercise, the customer completing the Splendos questionnaire is asked, "Did you like the product?," to which the answer is either yes or no.

1 Turn off the visibility of the Invisible buttons layer and select the radio box symbol next to the words Yes and No to the right of the question "Do you like the Product?" With the radio box symbol selected, open the Instance panel.

The radio box movie, unlike the check box, is made up of three frames. The first frame has both radio boxes empty, the second frame has only the left box selected, and the third frame has only the right box selected. The ActionScript is going to direct the input from the user to either frame 2 or frame 3, depending on the user's choice.

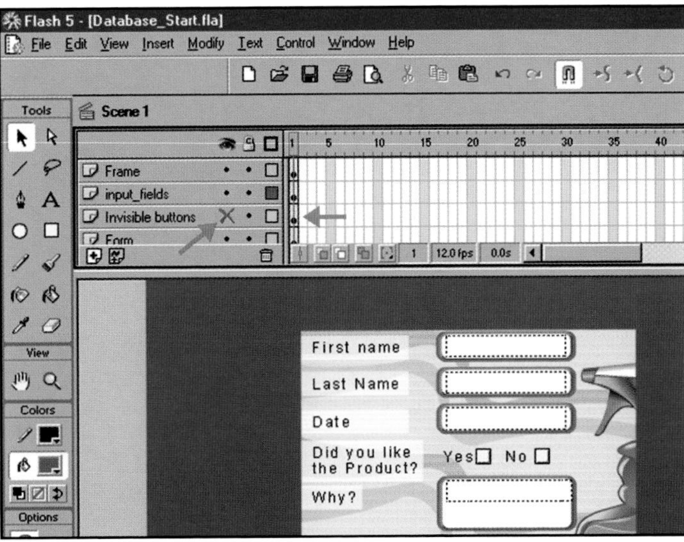

Turn off the visibility of the Invisible buttons layer so that you can get to the radio box signals.

2 Name the radio box movie clip instance **radiobox**.

3 Select the third dynamic text field from the right off the edge of the viewable Stage area and notice that its variable name is ***LikeProduct***.

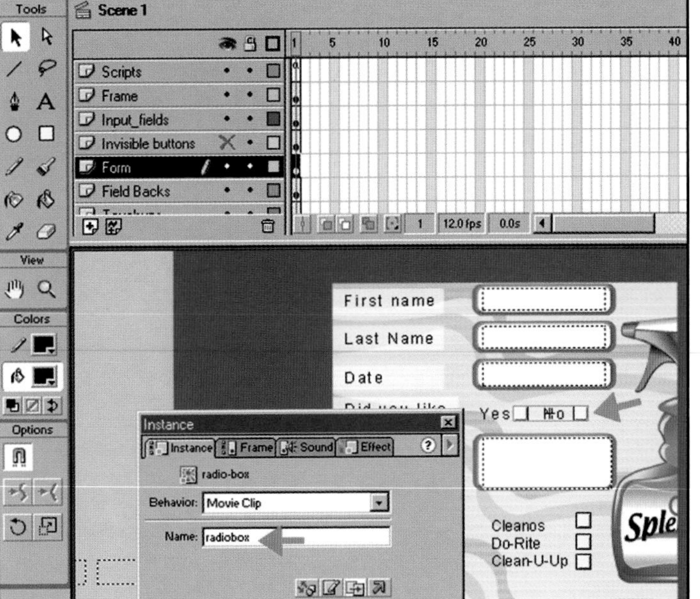

Use the Instance panel to name the movie clip instance **radiobox**.

4 Turn on the visibility of the Invisible buttons layer and select the invisible button to the right of the word "Yes." Add this code to the invisible button:

The script is very similar to that for the check box. The exceptions are that **tellTarget** points to the movie instance radiobutton and passes a value of **Yes** to the dynamic text field called LikeProduct.

```
on (press) {
    if (Number(Checked) == 0) {
        tellTarget ("/radiobox") {
            gotoAndStop (2);
        }
        checked = 1;
        LikeProduct = "Yes";
    } else {
        tellTarget ("/radiobox") {
            gotoAndStop (1);
        }
        checked  = 0;
        LikeProduct = "";
    }
}
```

Assign this code to the invisible button to the right of the word "Yes."

5 Add this code to the invisible button to the right of the word "No:"

The difference here is that the button directs a user to a different frame, in this case frame 3. This provides for the illusion that a user is able to make only one choice. The value sent to the LikeProduct dynamic text field is also different.

```
on (press) {
    if (Number(Checked) == 0) {
        tellTarget ("/radiobox") {
            gotoAndStop (3);
        }
        CB_1 = 1;
        LikeProduct = "No";
    } else {
        tellTarget ("/radiobox") {
            gotoAndStop (1);
        }
        CB_1 = 0;
        LikeProduct = "";
    }
}
```

Assign this code to the invisible button to the right of the word "No."

Hiding Values in the Dynamic Text Fields

Capturing the values of the check boxes and radio buttons in the dynamic text boxes is the only way to submit a value to the Web server. This can look messy and out of place on a form. To prevent the user from seeing the data being added to the dynamic text fields, you can blend the font with the background of the movie. The following steps have already been completed in the example file:

1. Deselect Border/Bg in the Text Options dialog box.
2. Make the text color the same color as the background.

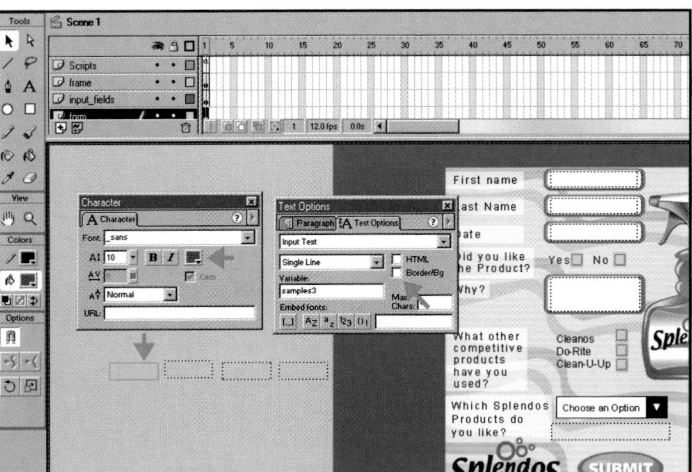

The Border/Bg option has been turned off, and the text color has been made gray to help keep the dynamic text field from showing.

Creating a Drop-Down Box

Drop-down menus are useful when you have a number of items from which to select, but only a small area to display them in. Drop-down menus help keep an interface manageable while offering an expanded list of options. A drop-down menu functions like a radio button in that the movie must be created to pass a value to a dynamic text field. The one significant difference is that the menu is placed within its own Movie within the Library. This provides two significant benefits when adding menu options to a movie:

- The menu movie's code is separated from the rest of the movie. If a bug within the menu is found, it is easier to find and resolve it.
- When the menu is saved as its own movie, it can be easily imported and reused in other Flash movies. Instead of having to cut and paste the ActionScript code, you can import the menu movie as a Library item and drop it into any new movie.

The drop-down menu works by assigning a variable to each option offered in the drop-down list. When an option is chosen, the menu movie goes to a frame that highlights that the option has been chosen and sends a variable (the name of the option) to a dynamic text box.

1 Edit the menu movie clip located to the right of the question "Which Splendos Products do you like?"

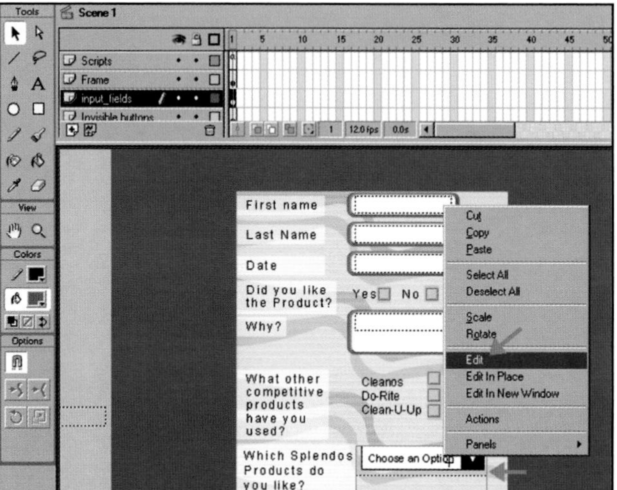

Edit the Menu movie clip.

2 In frame 1 of the dropdown layer, add this script:

Add this code to the first frame of the dropdown layer.

The ***checkbox*** variable has a default value set to **0**. When the script sees that the value is **0**, it proceeds to the next line. If the user has already made a selection from the drop-down menu, the value for the ***checkbox*** variable is programmatically changed. This allows for users to always have the option of changing their minds and choosing a second or third item from the drop-down menu. This stops the movie on the first frame and causes the user to interact with the movie.

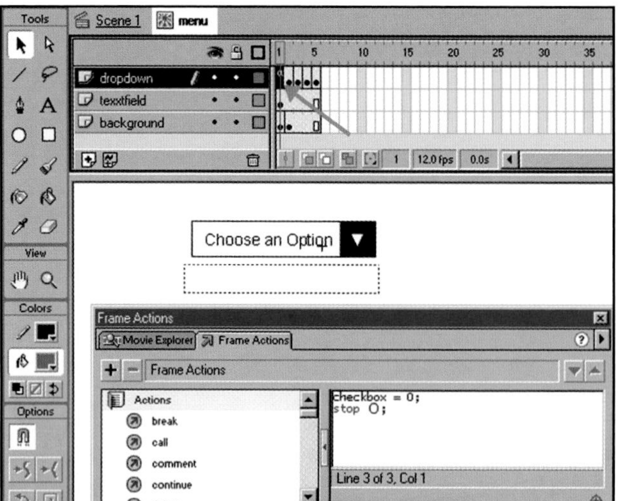

Add code to the first frame of the dropdown layer.

3 Select the dynamic text field on the textfield layer and give it the variable name ***menu***.

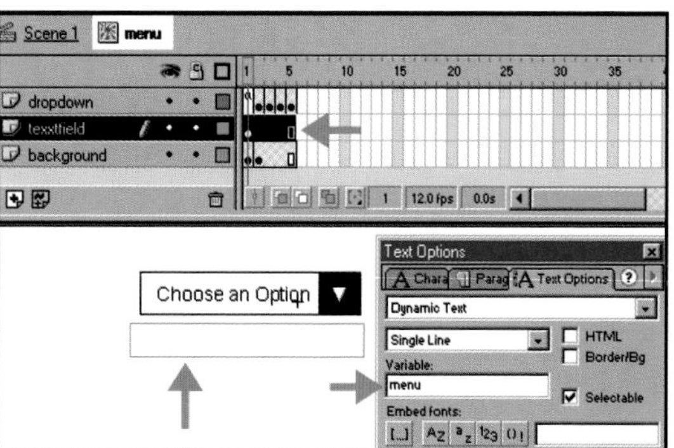

Assign the variable name.

4 Select the arrow button symbol and apply this script to it:

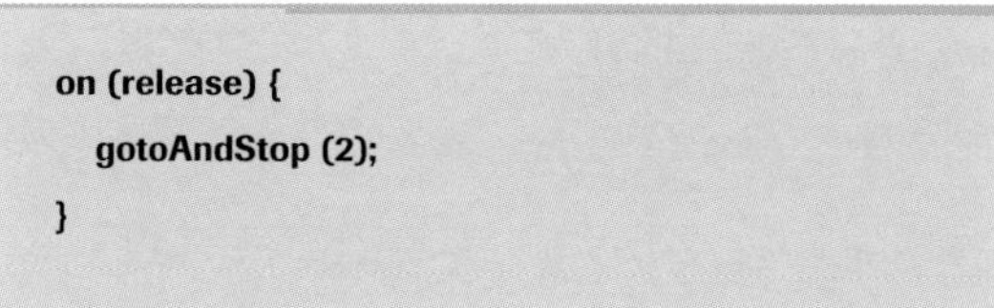

```
on (release) {
    gotoAndStop (2);
}
```

Assign this code to the arrow button.

This sends users to frame 2 when they click the button. The last three frames in the movie clip show that the user has made a selection. Next you add the code for accessing these frames.

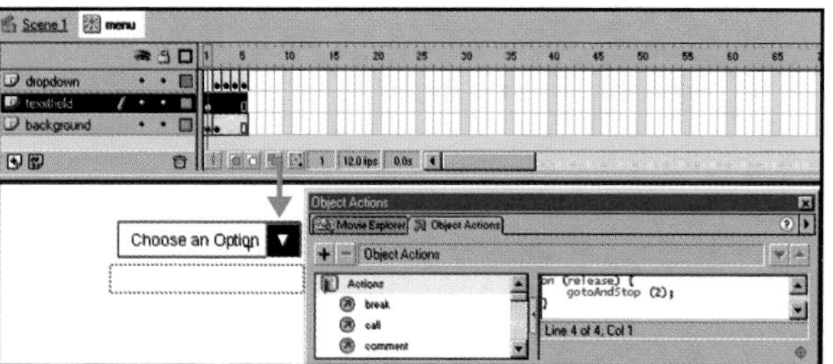

Add the code to the arrow button.

5 Select frame 2, select the Splendos Hard button, and add this script to the button:

You can see that the script is very similar to the check box and radio button. The only exception is that the **tellTarget** command has been removed.

```
on (press) {
    if (Number(Checked) == 0) {
        gotoAndStop (3);
        checkbox = 1;
        menu = "Hard";
    } else {
        gotoAndStop (1);
        checkbox = 0;
        menu = "";
    }
}
```

Add this script to the Spendos Hard button on frame 2.

6 Add this script to the Splendos Life button:

```
on (press) {
    if (Number(Checked) == 0) {
        gotoAndStop (4);
        checkbox = 1;
        menu = "Lite";
    } else {
        gotoAndStop (1);
        checkbox = 0;
        menu = "";
    }
}
```

Add this script to the Splendos Life button.

7 Add this script to the Splendos Clear button:

As you can see, drop-down menus are as flexible as check boxes and radio buttons. With them, you can create any number of forms. For example, you could extend the menu to list the names of the individual states in the United States. The choice in the drop-down menu can include a button with the state's name, such as Wisconsin, and the value for the state could be changed programmatically to:

```
menu = "WI"
```

```
on (press) {
    if (Number(Checked) == 0) {
        gotoAndStop (5);
        checkbox = 1;
        menu = "Clear";
    } else {
        gotoAndStop (1);
        checkbox = 0;
        menu = "";
    }
}
```

Add this script to the Splendos Clear button.

The menu can also be used for navigation. Instead of placing a value that needs to be sent to a dynamic text field, why not remove that line and have the **gotoAndStop** command send the user to another section of the movie. Equally, the **gotoAndStop** action could be replaced with a **getURL** action for another Web site.

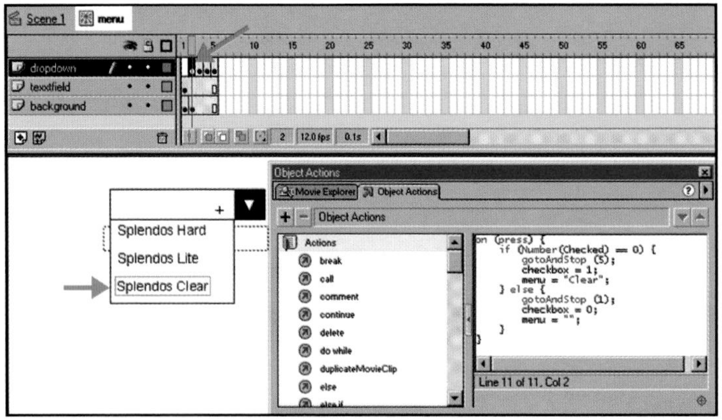

Assign the scripts to the drop-down buttons on frame 2.

Creating the Database (ODBC Talk)

ODBC, the Open Database Connector, is an industry standard that allows databases to be accessed by Web servers and other programs. The standard was created to allow programmers to write applications without having to install a specific copy of the database for each customer using the database. Applications written in C++, Visual Basic, and Java, along with Web server scripts such as Active Server Pages, could all access the database concurrently without having to duplicate the database and risk losing data.

1 Included in the files is an Access database that can be used with this program. In the supplied Access database, you will find only one table, called guest, which has the following fields:

Table Name	Stores
FirstName	The first name of the customer filling out the form.
LastName	The last name of the customer filling out the form.
Date	The date the form was completed.
LikeProduct	The Yes/No response from customers as to whether they liked the product.
Why	A text box in which the customers can explain their reasons for liking the product.
Samples1	The first item in a list of competitors' products that customers might buy.
Samples2	The second item in a list of competitors' products customers might buy.
Samples3	The third item in a list of competitors' products customers might buy.
Menu	A query asking the customers which Splendos product they like to buy.

You can use a different database. Microsoft Access, the most common database program, works very well with ASP; however, you could also very easily use a Microsoft SQL, Sybase, or Oracle database. If the database is large, use Microsoft SQL or Oracle. Both of these database programs can hold, manage, and support many hundreds of thousands of records.

When the database is complete, you must use ODBC to make a connection between the computer and the ASP pages. This is a commonly accepted solution for allowing information to be passed from a Web page to a database. The ODBC Data Sources (32-bit) program is located in the Control Panel for Windows computers.

2 Open the ODBC Data Sources program and create a System DNS link to the Access database created above, naming the connection **survey**.

The connection name will be important when the Microsoft's Active Server Pages (ASP) are created.

Creating the ASP Pages

ASP is a server scripting technology similar to Cold Fusion, Perl, and JavaServer Pages. The differences between the technologies lie in the Web servers supporting them. For example, ASP requires that the files be delivered from a Microsoft Internet Information Server. On the other hand, Cold Fusion mark-up pages must be delivered on a Web server that has the Cold Fusion Server installed. If these servers are not correctly installed, the scripts created with ASP or Cold Fusion simply will not work. Using server side pages provides a designer the freedom to control interaction with databases, updates of dynamic content, and the layout of a Web page without having to rely on a Web browser.

Flash leverages ASP to pass content to a database on the Web site to the Microsoft Internet Information Web server. The pages pass the data to the database using the ODBC connection created earlier. It is important to remember that the pages have to be served from a Microsoft Internet Information Web server, or the ASP will not work. A Web server, such as Apache, will not support ASP.

One of the easier ways to quickly create ASP pages is by using Macromedia's Dreamweaver UltraDev. In this example, you could use UltraDev to create a connection string to the ODBC source named survey. Using UltraDev is not the only solution for creating ASP pages. Other solutions include using Microsoft's IntraDev or Allaire's Homesite, and of course the old standby, Notepad.

This script will manage the connection to the database for the survey:

```
Set MM_insertCmd = Server.CreateObject("ADODB.Command")
MM_insertCmd.ActiveConnection = "dsn=Splendos_survey;"
MM_insertCmd.CommandText = MM_insertStr
MM_insertCmd.Execute
```

The dsn name refers to the ODBC name created earlier. **MM_insertStr** is a command to insert records passed from a form or a Flash movie. The data is told which table in the Microsoft Access database to place the content and to which field with the following statement:

```
MM_tableName = "guest"
    MM_fields = "FirstName,FirstName,',none,'',LastName,LastName,',none,''
    ➥,Date,Date,',none,'',LikeProduct,LikeProduct,',none,'',Why,Why,',none,'',Competition,
    ➥Competition,',none,''"
```

(The ➥ symbol you see here is for editorial purposes only.)

In this example, the table is called guest. This references the fields created earlier in the Flash movie. Therefore, the fields in the Flash movie are matched up with actual fields in the database. For example, you might see FirstName,FirstName, in which case the first FirstName is the name of the Flash movie form field, and the second FirstName is the corresponding field name in the Microsoft Access Database.

1. Open submit.asp with a text editor.

   Notice the following HTML form elements at the bottom of the page:

2. Close the submit.asp; do not save changes.

```
<form name="form1" method="post" action="<%=MM_editAction%>">
    <p>
        <input type="text" name="FirstName">
    </p>
    <p>
        <input type="text" name="LastName">
    </p>

    <p>
        <input type="text" name="Date">
    </p>
    <p>
        <input type="text" name="LikeProduct">
    </p>
    <p>
        <input type="text" name="Why">
    </p>
    <p>
        <input type="text" name="Competition">
    </p>
    <p>
        <input type="submit" name="Submit" value="Submit">
    </p>
    <input type="hidden" name="MM_insert" value="true">
</form>
        The form elements allow for variables in Flash file to be sent up to
        the database.
<insert ASP code – submit.asp>.
```

These HTML form elements reference the fields you named earlier in Flash.

Converting the Files to Work with Cold Fusion and JavaServer Page Servers

What you have created with Flash and ASPs can be easily converted to either Cold Fusion or JavaServer Pages. Dreamweaver UltraDev and ODBC forms can add content to a database in any of these formats. However, explaining this process is very code intensive. In the interest of saving space, we put the explanation for how to convert your ASPs to either Cold Fusion or JavaServer Pages on the CD accompanying this book. Look for the Cold_Java.doc file in the Chapter 13 directory for this extensive explanation.

Submitting information to a database can be critical for any type of application, from entering scores from an online game to tracking a student's pass rate for online training. Using Flash in conjunction with other technologies provides for a powerful and resourceful solution.

How It Works

The whole application is tightly integrated with the Web server, a database, and the Flash movie. This enables for a three-tiered distributed application—the core of every successful Internet site.

At the lowest level is the database. In the case, the database is a simple Microsoft Access 2000 database. The tables and fields are basic, flexible, and scalable. This demonstrates how the database can be populated with data collected from a Flash movie. This database could easily be replaced with one that is much larger or with more tables running on different systems, such as Oracle, Sybase, or Microsoft SQL Server.

In between the database and the Flash movie is the Web server. The Web server used for this chapter is Microsoft's Internet Information Server, running Active Server Pages. Active Server Pages, or ASP, provides an easy-to-use and flexible technology that allows a Web browser to integrate with a database. In this example, information is being passed to one table with a collection of fields. In more complex operations, there could be multiple tables.

The final section of the three-tiered application is the Flash movie. Flash is leveraged to build a rich set of form tools that collect data stored in Dynamic Text fields. The data is then sent to the Access database by loading the ASP page into the movie.

Flash by itself is a powerful development environment. When it is coupled with the strengths of Web server technologies, such as Active Server Pages, it becomes a tour de force solution for any Web site.

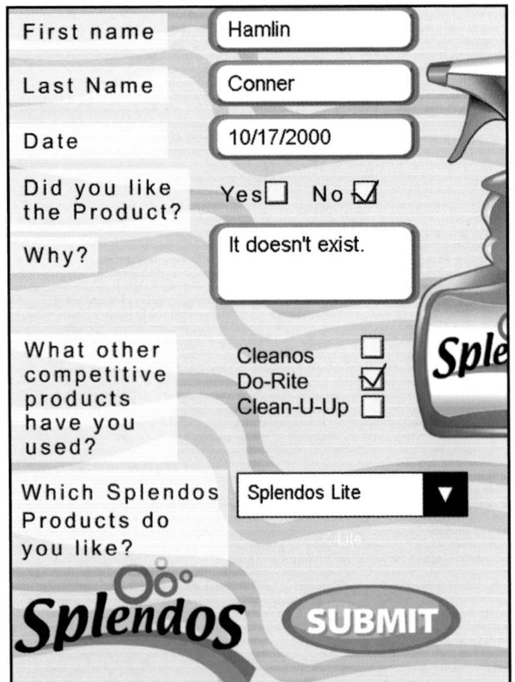

When the user clicks the Submit button, the Flash movie sends the contents in the form fields to a database on a Web server.

14

WORKING WITH FUNCTIONS

By Jennifer S. Hall

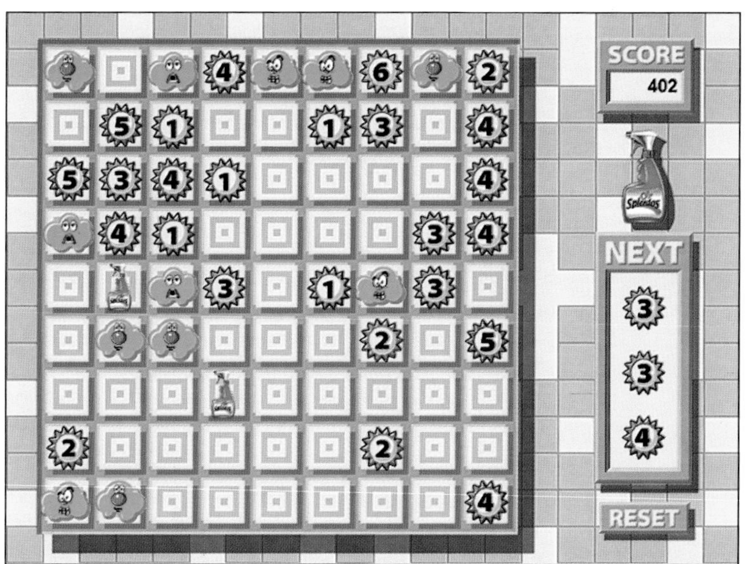

This chapter demonstrates the use of the new Flash 5 function capability, including the use of recursive functions, by means of a board game. Functions offer a helpful way of organizing and simplifying code. They can receive information (parameters) and return it even if the information is not in a global variable. A *recursive function* is a function that calls itself, creating the possibility for an endless loop. This looping is stopped when a predefined set of conditions is met.

The object of this game is to keep the board cleared for as long as possible. The player moves the colored pieces in an attempt to get five pieces of the same color in a row, at which point those five matching pieces disappear and points are awarded based on the number of pieces in a row and the numbers on the pieces (1–6).

Creating a Function for Checking on a Diagonal

In this game, the player clicks on a movable piece and then clicks on an empty space to indicate that the selected piece will move to that space. However, the player can't move to an empty space if the path is blocked. In this section, you create a function that checks for matching pieces from the upper left to the lower right.

1 Open the file GermFight_Start.fla in Chapter 14 on the CD and save it to your hard drive. To see the final file, open the file GermFight_Final.fla.

The game is already partially functional. If you were to play it, you'd notice that each time you moved a piece, three more pieces would appear somewhere on the board. The game also has two special pieces: the germ and the Splendos. Germs are unmovable; the only way to destroy one is to move a Splendos piece into an adjacent space. The Splendos destroys any and all pieces in adjacent spaces. The spaces on the game board are numbered as shown in this chart:

1	2	3	4	5	6	7	8	9
10	11	12	13	14	15	16	17	18
19	20	21	22	23	24	25	26	27
28	29	30	31	32	33	34	35	36
37	38	39	40	41	42	43	44	45
46	47	48	49	50	51	52	53	54
55	56	57	58	59	60	61	62	63
64	65	66	67	68	69	70	71	72
73	74	75	76	77	78	79	80	81

This chart shows how the spaces on the game board are numbered.

2 Choose Window > Actions to open the functions code located in the Scoring Functions layer.

Notice that this layer already has some functions: **CheckHorizontal**, **CheckVertical**, **CheckBackward**, **CheckMatching**, and **CheckForBonus**. These functions check for matching pieces in the appropriate directions.

Don't worry about this code at this point. Soon you will enter code that is almost exactly the same, so you'll know how this pre-existing code works when you finish this chapter.

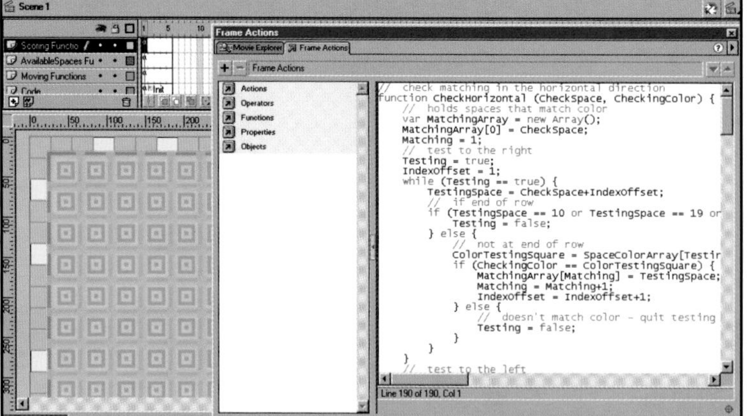

Notice the pre-existing functions on the Scoring Functions layer.

3 Add this code below the **CheckBackward** function:

The placement of this code is actually irrelevant. It works no matter where you place it as long as it is not within another function. The placement specified is for organizational clarity only; it keeps all the **Check** functions together.

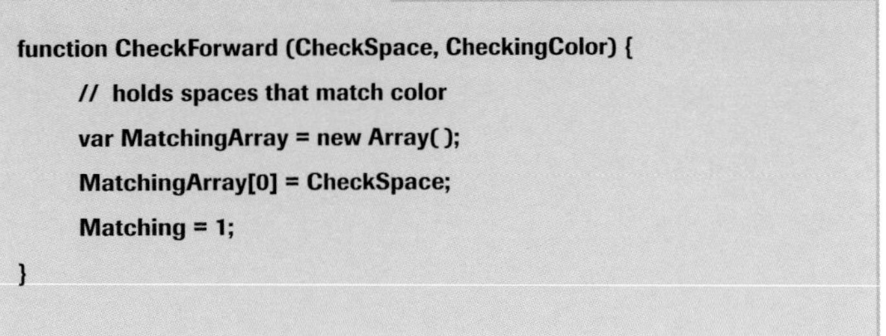

```
function CheckForward (CheckSpace, CheckingColor) {
    // holds spaces that match color
    var MatchingArray = new Array( );
    MatchingArray[0] = CheckSpace;
    Matching = 1;
}
```

Insert this first part of the **CheckForward** function.

The **CheckForward** function is going to check for matching pieces from upper left to lower right. Notice that two parameters are being passed in, **CheckSpace** and **CheckingColor**. The **CheckSpace** parameter is the space number that the code will be checking from, usually the space where the player just placed a piece. The **CheckingColor** parameter indicates the color of the piece in the **CheckSpace** space. The following line of code creates a new array to hold the space number of any pieces that match the color in the ***MatchingArray*** direction:

```
var MatchingArray = new Array( );
```

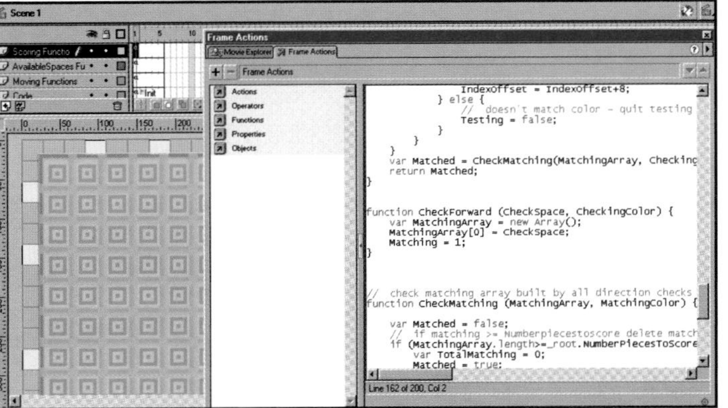

Add the **CheckForward( )** function to the code on the Scoring Functions layer.

The next line of code takes whatever is in the variable ***CheckSpace*** and places it in the first placeholder of the array called MatchingArray. (Remember that in the world of coding, 0 is often 1.)

```
MatchingArray[0] = CheckSpace;
```

The number of matching pieces (Matching) is initialized to 1. Matching will be used to count the number of matching pieces stored in the array.

```
Matching = 1;
```

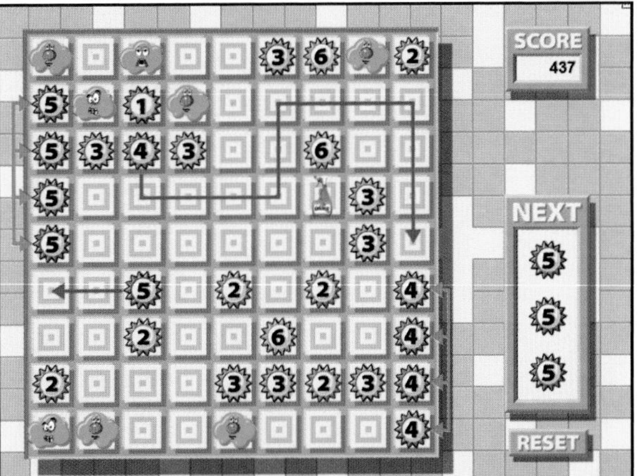

The **CheckForward( )** function is part of the code that checks to see whether certain pieces are adjacent. When five numbered pieces are set in a row (including diagonally), the player earns points.

4 Add this code within the function, but below the previous code and within the **CheckForward** brackets:

First the code tests toward the lower right of the board. The **Testing** flag, shown here, is used to indicate when to stop checking.

```
Testing = true;
```

As long as the **Testing** flag is set to true, the code continues to check for matching pieces in this direction. The **Testing** flag checks for two conditions that indicate it's time to stop checking: If the color is not the same, or if the space is off the end of the game board, the **Testing** flag changes to false.

The game board is a 9×9 board, so to move from upper right to lower left (down and over), add 10 to the current testing space, like this:

```
IndexOffset = 10;
```

These are all the initializations before the code starts checking. The code shown below establishes that, while *Testing* is equal to true, checking will continue to take place.

```
while (Testing == true) {
```

The first line in the **while** loop establishes that the space to be checked (**TestingSpace**) is computed based on two things: the offset (**IndexOffset**) and the space that was originally passed into the ***CheckSpace*** variable.

```
TestingSpace = CheckSpace+ IndexOffset;
```

If the space to be checked is in the far-left column of the board, the code has looped around the board and is trying to check off the board. If you look at the table with the numbered columns, you'll see that this code references the starting space of each new row:

```
// test to the mainPiece to lower right
Testing = true;
IndexOffset = 10;
while (Testing == true) {
    TestingSpace = CheckSpace+ IndexOffset;
    // if bottom of board or off to the right
    if (TestingSpace == 10 || TestingSpace == 19 || TestingSpace == 28 ||
    ➥TestingSpace == 37 || TestingSpace == 46 || TestingSpace == 55 or
    ➥TestingSpace == 64 || TestingSpace == 73 || TestingSpace>81) {
            Testing = false;
        } else {
            // not at bottom
            ColorTestingSpace = SpaceColorArray[TestingSpace];
            if (CheckingColor == ColorTestingSpace) {
                MatchingArray[Matching] = TestingSpace;
                Matching = Matching+1;
                IndexOffset = IndexOffset +10;
            } else {
                // doesn't match color - quit testing this direction
                Testing = false;
            }
        }
    }
```

Add the rest of the **CheckForward()** function. (The ➥ symbol you see here is for editorial purposes only.)

```
if (TestingSpace == 10 || TestingSpace == 19 ||
➥TestingSpace == 28 || TestingSpace == 37 ||
➥TestingSpace == 46 || TestingSpace == 55 or
➥TestingSpace == 64 || TestingSpace == 73 ||
➥TestingSpace>81) {
    Testing = false;
```

(The ➥ symbol you see here is for editorial purposes only.)

The game is designed to match without looping around the ends of the board, so **Testing** is set to **false** whenever the code finishes testing in this direction.

Next, the code determines what color piece is in the ***TestingSpace*** variable with this code:

```
ColorTestingSpace = SpaceColorArray[TestingSpace];
```

The SpaceColorArray array contains the color of every piece in the appropriate space/index relation. If a red piece is in space 10, the word "red" is stored in index 10 of SpaceColorArray. If there is not a piece in the space, the SpaceColorArray contains "none."

Then the code checks to see if the color (ColorTestingSpace) is the correct color, starting with this line of code:

```
if (CheckingColor == ColorTestingSpace) {
```

As long as the color is the same color, the checking continues. Each time the color is the same, the space number is saved in the MatchingArray, and the Matching index is incremented by 1, as specified by this code:

```
MatchingArray[Matching] = TestingSpace;
Matching = Matching+1;
```

The **IndexOffset** is then incremented by 10 according to the code shown below, which moves the space checking down one row and over one column. If the color is not the same, the **Testing** flag is set to **false**.

```
IndexOffset = IndexOffset +10;
Testing = false;
```

1	2	3	4	5	6	7	8	9
10	11	12	13	14	15	16	17	18
19	20	21	22	23	24	25	26	27
28	29	30	31	32	33	34	35	36
37	38	39	40	41	42	43	44	45
46	47	48	49	50	51	52	53	54
55	56	57	58	59	60	61	62	63
64	65	66	67	68	69	70	71	72
73	74	75	76	77	78	79	80	81

Refer to this chart for the numbered spaces on the game board.

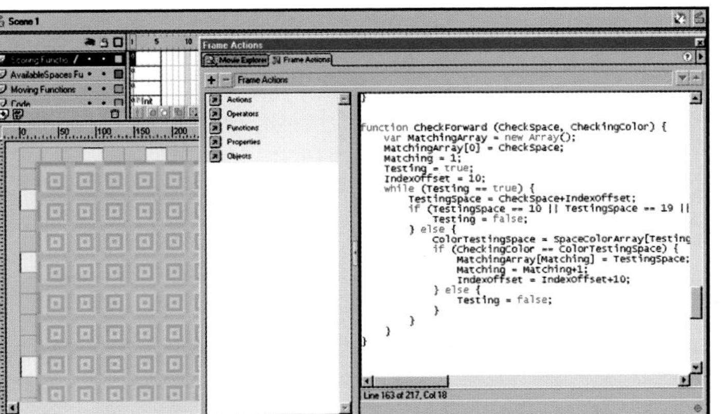

This figure shows the rest of the code for the **CheckForward()** function.

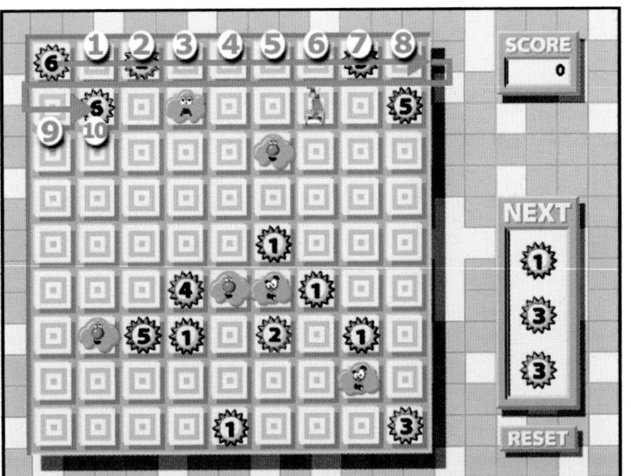

The code checks 10 spaces to the right for a matching color or piece.

3 To enter the code to check upward from lower right to upper left, add this code within the function but below the preceding code:

This does the exact same thing as the code you saw earlier, except that it tests toward the upper left of the board. The **Testing** flag is reset to **true**. Remember that, in the previous section, the code stopped only when the **Testing** flag was set to **false**.

The only difference between the previous section and this one is the direction the code is checking. So the TestingSpace will be decremented instead of incremented, as specified by this code:

```
TestingSpace = CheckSpace-IndexOffset;
```

Also, the check for going off the board has different spaces to check for, as shown in this code:

```
if (TestingSpace<1 or TestingSpace == 9 ||
➥TestingSpace == 18 || TestingSpace == 27 ||
➥TestingSpace == 36 || TestingSpace == 45 ||
➥TestingSpace == 54 || TestingSpace == 63 ||
➥TestingSpace == 72) {
```

(The ➥ symbol you see here is for editorial purposes only.)

Note that the Matching index and the MatchingArray were not reset. This means all the matches computed in the previous section are still there, and this section simply adds to it.

```
// test to from mainPiece to upper left
    Testing = true;
    IndexOffset = 10;
    while (Testing == true) {
        TestingSpace = CheckSpace-IndexOffset;
        // if end of column - off the top
        if (TestingSpace<1 or TestingSpace == 9 or TestingSpace == 18 or
        ➥TestingSpace == 27 or TestingSpace == 36 or TestingSpace == 45 or
        ➥TestingSpace == 54 or TestingSpace == 63 or TestingSpace == 72) {
            Testing = false;
        } else {
            // not at end
            ColorTestingSquare = SpaceColorArray[TestingSpace];
            if (CheckingColor == ColorTestingSquare) {
                MatchingArray[Matching] = TestingSpace;
                Matching = Matching+1;
                IndexOffset = IndexOffset+10;
            } else {
                // doesn't match color - quit testing this direction
                Testing = false;
            }
        }
    }
```

Use this code, which is similar to the code you already entered, to check the upper left of the game board. (The ➥ symbol you see here is for editorial purposes only.)

4 To add the call to check whether there is enough matching to score with, insert this code at the end of but within the closing bracket of the **CheckForward** function:

```
var Matched = CheckMatching(MatchingArray, CheckingColor);
return Matched;
```

Insert this code to check for scoring matches.

This code is a call to the **CheckMatching** function. The **CheckMatching** function needs the array of matching spaces (MatchingArray) and the color to be checked (CheckingColor). **CheckMatching** sees if there are enough matching pieces based on the number of pieces saved in the MatchingArray. If there are, the score is updated, the matching pieces are deleted, and the player gets a free move where no new pieces appear on the board. The variable ***Matched*** is **true** or **false** based on whether there were enough matching colors. This Boolean is used in the **MovePiece** function to determine if more pieces should be placed on the board.

Next you need to call the function.

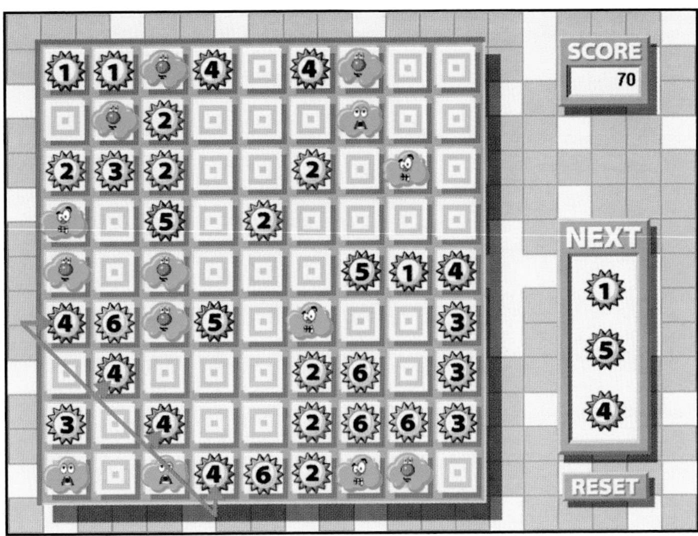

The **if TestingSpace** statement checks for matches that wrap around the game board, keeping them from scoring. With the **if TestingSpace** statement, the diagonal row of 4 would score.

5 Open the functions in the Moving Functions layer. (Notice that **GetNextBoardPieces** already has a call to three checks: **CheckVertical**, **CheckHorizontal**, and **CheckBackward**.) Add the call to the fourth check, the **CheckForward** function:

```
CheckForward(ChosenSpace, NewColor);
```

Insert this code to ensure that the player will get the score when the new pieces placed on the board form a scoring match.

These checks are used when the pieces first appear randomly on the board. The code checks to see if the piece happened to land perfectly to complete a scoring move. This calls the **CheckForward** function and passes it to the space the piece just appeared in (**ChosenSpace**) and the color of the piece (**NewColor**).

Next you add the function call for when the player actually moves the piece. In the function **MovePiece**, notice that the calls for **CheckVertical**, **CheckHorizontal**, and **CheckBackward** differ slightly. They catch the return variable. This is the Matched Boolean that returns whether this was a scoring move.

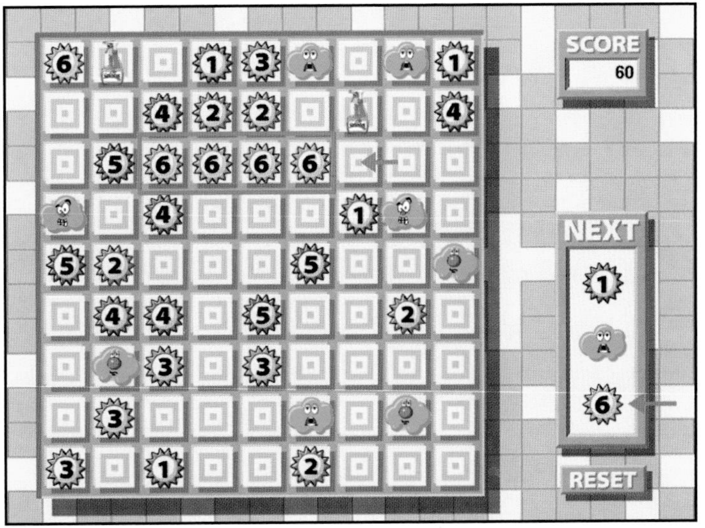

When the next pieces are place, the 6 piece could land next to the other four 6 pieces and complete a score.

6 Locate this code within the **MovePiece** function:

```
var MatchedHor = false;
var MatchedVer = false;
var MatchedBack = false;
```

7 Add this code for the **MatchedFor** flag under the **MatchedBack** line:

```
var MatchedFor = false;
```

Add this code to the **MovePiece** function.

This variable holds the return from the **CheckForward** function.

8 Locate this code further down within the same **MovePiece** function:

```
MatchedHor = CheckHorizontal(MoveToSpace,
➥NewColor);
    MatchedVer = CheckVertical(MoveToSpace,
    ➥NewColor);
    MatchedBack = CheckBackward(MoveToSpace,
    ➥NewColor);
```

(The ➥ symbol you see here is for editorial purposes only.)

9 Add this code under the **MatchedBack** line:

```
MatchedFor = CheckForward(MoveToSpace, NewColor);
```

Add this code under the **MatchedBack** line in the **MovePiece** function.

This code calls the **CheckForward** function and stores the return value in the ***MatchedFor*** variable. It passes in two parameters: ***MoveToSpace*** (the space the player just placed a piece to) and ***NewColor*** (the color of the piece).

10 To determine whether a score was made in any of the directions, locate this **if** statement

```
if ((MatchedHor == false) and (MatchedVer == false)
➥and (MatchedBack == false)) {
```

(The ➥ symbol you see here is for editorial purposes only.)

11 Within the **if** statement, add this check:

```
and (MatchedFor == false)
```

Add this code to the **if** statement.

The **if** statement should look like this:

```
if ((MatchedHor == false) and (MatchedVer == false)
➥and (MatchedFor == false) and (MatchedBack ==
➥false)) {
```

(The ➥ symbol you see here is for editorial purposes only.)

12 Test the game, particularly checking to see if the player can now score points in both diagonal directions.

Creating Recursive Functions

You could stop working and have a complete game at this point, but it's really not very challenging. To make it more complicated, add restrictions to the movement. Currently, the player can move a piece to any open space. You're going to make it so the player can move a piece to an empty space only if the move can be made using empty spaces (no filled space blocks the path).

In addition, you'll restrict the movement to horizontal or vertical, not diagonal. In other words, if a move to the empty space must move diagonally around pieces, the move is not allowed. See the example shown in this figure.

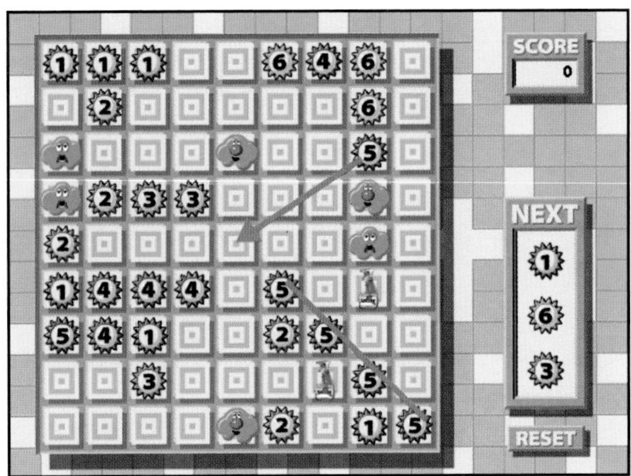

You should be able to score diagonally at this point.

The 6 piece and the 3 piece in the upper-left corner are trapped. There are three spaces to which they can move without making a diagonal move or jumping another piece. Also notice that the Splendos piece in the lower-right corner is blocked from moving out of the little square formed around it. This also works in reverse; no other pieces can move into these two blocked areas. The only way to fix this is for the player to move one of the blocking pieces out of the way to form a hole.

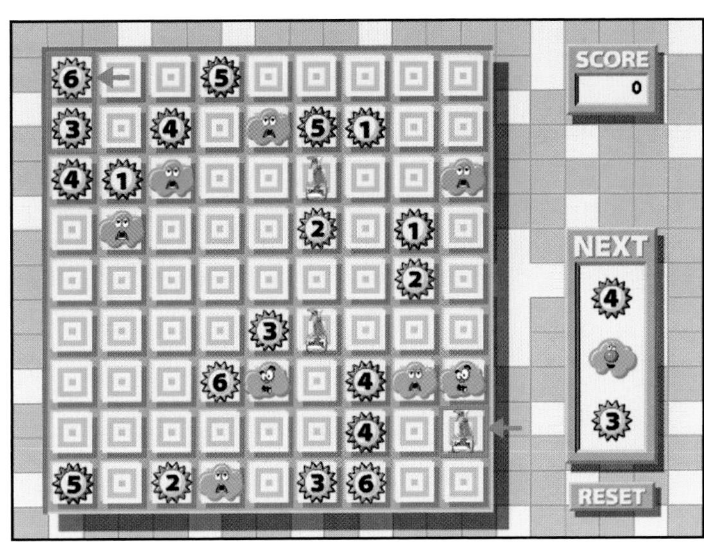

The 6 and 3 pieces are blocked, as is the Splendos bottle.

Although the player could move the 3 piece in the lower-right corner, that would not create a hole to move through because it would still mean a diagonal move for the Splendos piece. At this point, you can use recursive functions to determine the available moves.

1 In the **Init** code in the Code layer, add this code:

This array will be used to determine which moves are available.

```
// initialize array that holds the the available spaces
AvailableSpacesArray = new Array();
```

Initialize the **AvailableSpacesArray** array.

2 Because functions are already in place for restricting movement in this layer, add this function in the AvailableSpace Functions layer at the top:

```
function CheckAvailableSpaces () {
    // clear available array
    for (var Index = 1; Index<=NumberOfSpaces; Index++) {
        AvailableSpacesArray[Index] = false;
    }
    var SelectedSpace = int(substring(SelectedPiece, 14, 2));
    GetAvailableSpaces(SelectedSpace);
}
```

Insert this code to check for which spaces are not occupied with game pieces.

This function will be used to start the checks for which spaces are available. It is called each time a piece is selected. If you were to open the Pieces Movie and select a piece, you would see that the code attached to it already has the call to this function. It worked before because Flash 5 is smart enough to ignore a call to a function that does not exist. The ***AvailableSpacesArray*** is initialized to **false**.

```
for (var Index = 1; Index<=NumberOfSpaces; Index++) {
    AvailableSpacesArray[Index] = false;
}
```

This means there are no available moves. This is the best way to start out, because as the game progresses, in many cases, very few moves will be available. The ***SelectedSpace*** is the space number of the piece the player selected, and it is computed based on the name of the ***SelectedPiece***.

```
var SelectedSpace = int(substring(SelectedPiece, 14, 2));
```

In this code, the name of the ***SelectedPiece*** is based on the movie clip name of the piece, which has the space number as the last two characters of its name. The call to **GetAvailableSpaces** is where all the work starts. Note that the ***SelectedSpace*** number is passed into **GetAvailableSpaces**.

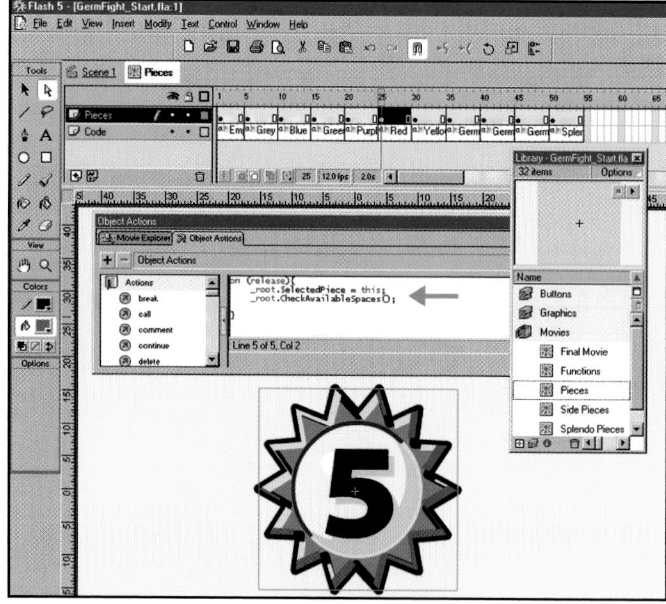

The call to **CheckAvailableSpaces** is assigned to each of the game pieces in the Pieces movie clip.

3 Create the **GetAvailableSpaces** function using this code:

```
// process through each four pieces touching
function GetAvailableSpaces (SelectedSpace) {
    CheckRight(SelectedSpace);
    CheckLeft(SelectedSpace);
    CheckUp(SelectedSpace);
    CheckDown(SelectedSpace);
}
```

Insert this code to call functions that will check for available spaces.

All the **GetAvailableSpaces** function does is call four other functions. Each of the four functions does a check for an available space in only one direction. In other words, the **CheckRight** function checks only the space to the right of the ***SelectedSpace***. The

SelectedSpace is passed into all four of the functions. Note that the functions only check in the horizontal and the vertical. A diagonal move is not allowed, so there is no need to check in that direction.

These functions are broken down into four separate functions for ease of readability only. All the code in the four functions could have been placed within the **GetAvailableSpaces** function.

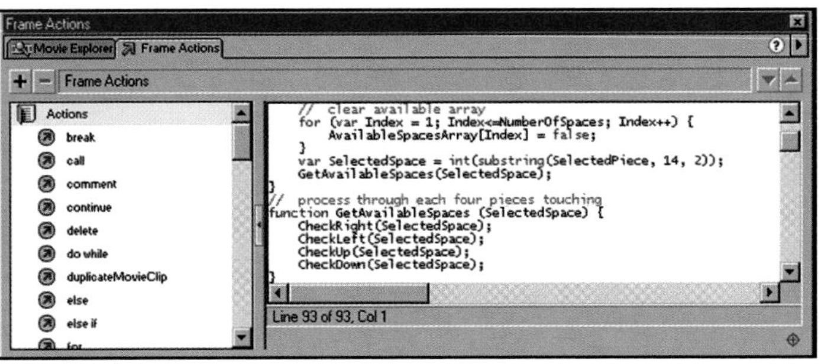

Add the **GetAvailableSpaces** function to the code on the AvailableSpaces Functions layer.

4 Create the **CheckRight** function, using this code:

The **CheckRight** function has the center space (***SelectedSpace***) passed in as a parameter. This is the space the code will check to the right of. First, however, the code must make sure there is an available right space.

```
if (SelectedSpace == 9 || SelectedSpace == 18 ||
➥SelectedSpace == 27 || SelectedSpace == 36 ||
➥SelectedSpace == 45 || SelectedSpace == 54 ||
➥SelectedSpace == 63 || SelectedSpace == 72 ||
➥SelectedSpace == 81) {
```

(The ➥ symbol you see here is for editorial purposes only.)

```
function CheckRight (SelectedSpace) {
    // check to make sure there is a right space
    if (SelectedSpace == 9 || SelectedSpace == 18 || SelectedSpace == 27 ||
    ➥SelectedSpace == 36 || SelectedSpace == 45 || SelectedSpace == 54 ||
    ➥SelectedSpace == 63 || SelectedSpace == 72 || SelectedSpace == 81) {
        // do nothing, nothing to be done
        return;
    } else {
        var NewSelectedSpace = SelectedSpace+1;
        // make sure hasen't been check yet
        if (AvailableSpacesArray[NewSelectedSpace] == false) {
            // found good place to move
            if (SpaceColorArray[NewSelectedSpace] == "none") {
                AvailableSpacesArray[NewSelectedSpace] = true;
                // test next right
                GetAvailableSpaces(NewSelectedSpace);
            }
        }
    }
}
```

Insert this code to check for available spaces to the right of the selected piece. (The ➥ symbol you see here is for editorial purposes only.)

If the ***SelectedSpace*** is already at the end of a row, there is no space to the right, so there is nothing to do except return out of this function. Otherwise, Flash gets the next space number (***NewSelectedSpace***) by adding 1 to the ***SelectedSpace***, as specified in this code:

```
var NewSelectedSpace = SelectedSpace+1;
```

Make sure the new space hasn't already been checked, using this code:

```
if (AvailableSpacesArray[NewSelectedSpace] == false) {
```

Remember that the ***AvailableSpacesArray*** is used to hold the list of available moves, and it starts out with all falses. So as long as it is still false, check it. Also, the new space must to be empty (none) in order for it to be an available move.

```
if (SpaceColorArray[NewSelectedSpace] == "none") {
```

If these are all true, Flash changes the setting in the ***AvailableSpacesArray*** at the new index (***NewSelectedSpace***) to **true**, making this space available to move to.

```
AvailableSpacesArray[NewSelectedSpace] = true;
```

Finally this code calls the **GetAvailableSpaces** for this new space:

```
GetAvailableSpaces(NewSelectedSpace);
```

This call to **GetAvailableSpaces** is what makes the function recursive. Now **GetAvailableSpaces** will check all the spaces around the new space.

The other functions in this layer are **CheckLeft**, **CheckUp**, and **CheckDown**. Each of these functions does the exact same thing as the function you just created (**CheckUp**), except that each works in a different direction.

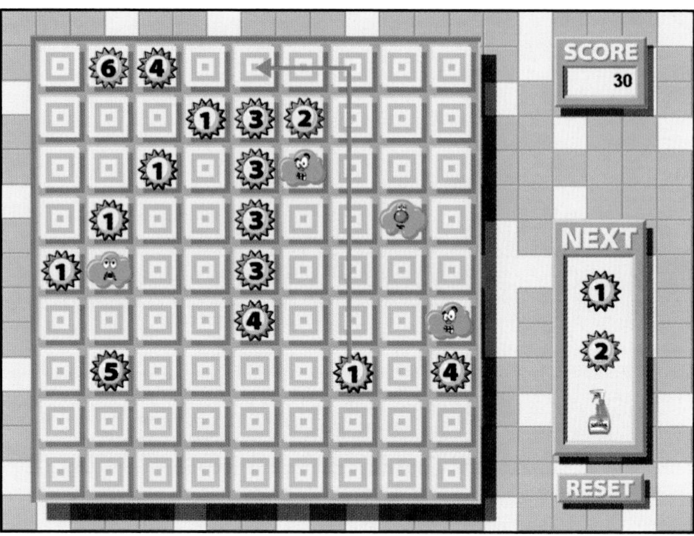

Insert the code that basically allows you to move pieces around corners.

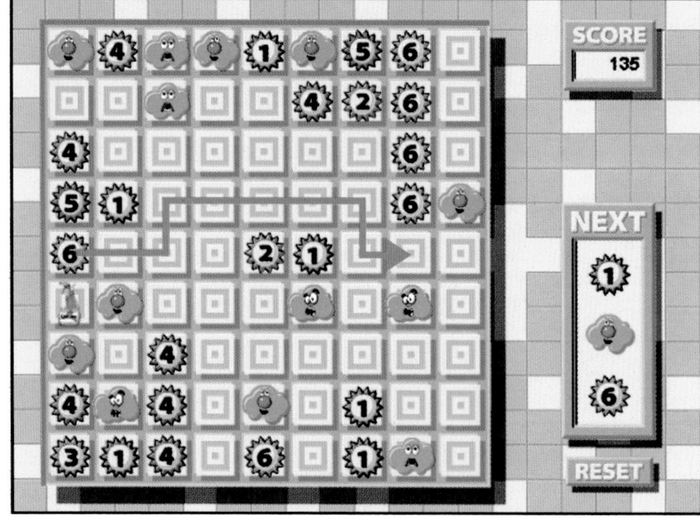

As long as there is an open path, the piece will turn as many corners as necessary to move to the specified available space.

Finally, you need to use the available move information in the actual move of the piece.

5 In the Moving Functions layer, within the function **MovePiece**, locate this code:

```
if (SpaceColorArray[MoveToSpace] == "none") {
```

6 Replace the code with this:

```
If (AvailableSpacesArray[MoveToSpace] == true){
```

Add this code to the **MovePiece** function.

Because the **GetAvailableSpaces** function already checks for an empty space, the first check is inherent in the available moves check.

You have now created a recursive function (**GetAvailableSpaces**). Each time a new space is checked and is available, it calls the check to **GetAvailableSpaces** around itself. This cycle of checking and calling continues until all the spaces are checked or until it reaches a dead end. In the case of the board example at the start of these steps, when the player selects the 6 piece in the upper left (space 1), **GetAvailableSpaces** gets called first on space 1. There is no left or upward movement, so the calls within **GetAvailableSpaces** to **CheckLeft** and **CheckUp** return without doing anything. **CheckDown** finds a piece in the space, so it also returns at that point.

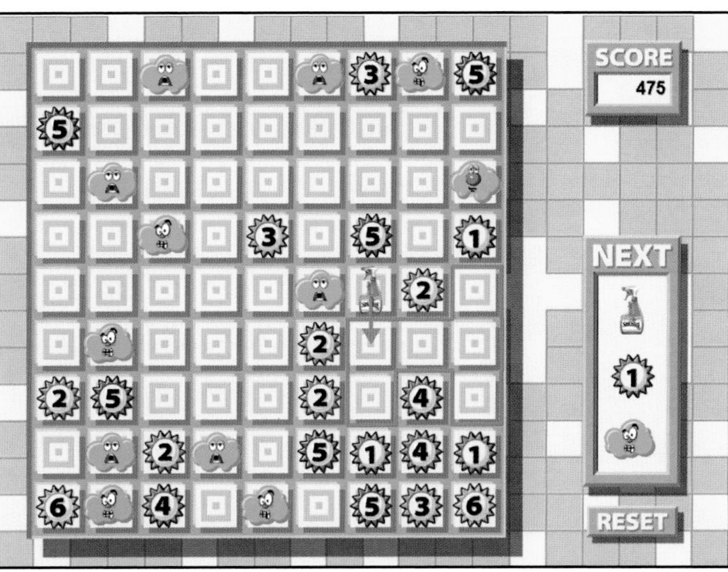

The Splendos bottle piece can be moved to one of only six available spaces because the rest of the spaces are blocked. Therefore, the Splendos bottle can't be used to get rid of any germ pieces during this turn.

CheckRight is the only function that can do anything. **CheckRight** finds an available space (space 2), so it calls **GetAvailableSpaces** on space 2. From space 2, **CheckLeft** has a piece in it, **CheckUp** doesn't exist, **CheckDown** is available, and so on, as shown in this code:

```
User selected : 1
    CheckRight of 1 (2) available
        CheckRight of 2 (3) – available
            CheckRight of 3 (4) – full
            CheckLeft of 3 (2) – already checked
            CheckUp of 3– doesn't exist
            CheckDown of 3 (12) – full
        CheckLeft of 2 (1) – full
        CheckUp of 2 – doesn't exist
        CheckDown of 2 (11) – available
            CheckRight of 11 (12) – full
            CheckLeft of 11 (10) – full
            CheckUp of 11 (2) – already checked
            CheckDown of 11 (20) – full
    CheckLeft of 1 – doesn't exist
    CheckUp of 1 – doesn't exist
    CheckDown of 1 – full
```

When the code finishes checking all available spaces, only three moves are available—spaces 2,3, and 11.

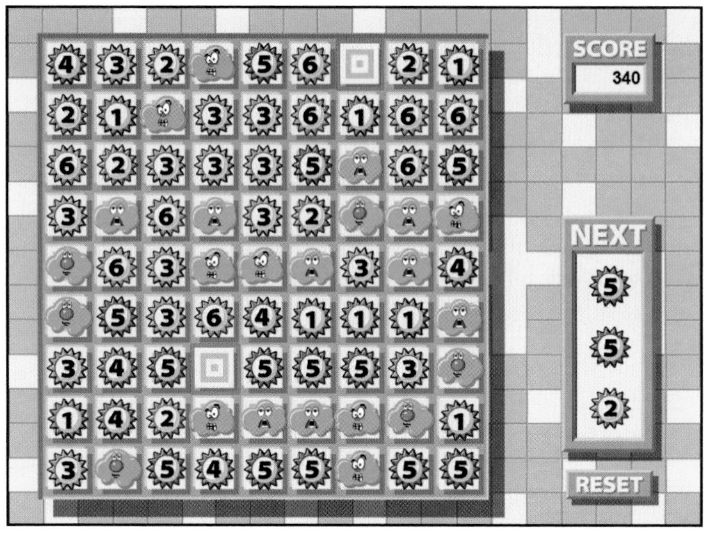

With only two spaces left, the **CleanUp** function will be called, ending the game.

How It Works

Each of the pieces on the board is a Piece movie clip named Space#, where the '#' is the space number that the actual Piece movie clip is sitting in. Because each Piece movie clip is named with the space in which it is located, the movie's board location can be determined from the name of the movie clip. Within each Piece Movie are all the pieces. So 81 copies of the Piece Movie exist in the appropriate spaces and are named for the appropriate spaces. The ActionScript tells the appropriate Piece movie clip to go to the color it needs to be.

Each of the side pieces is an almost exact duplicate of the Piece Movie, but the actions for selecting the piece are not available.

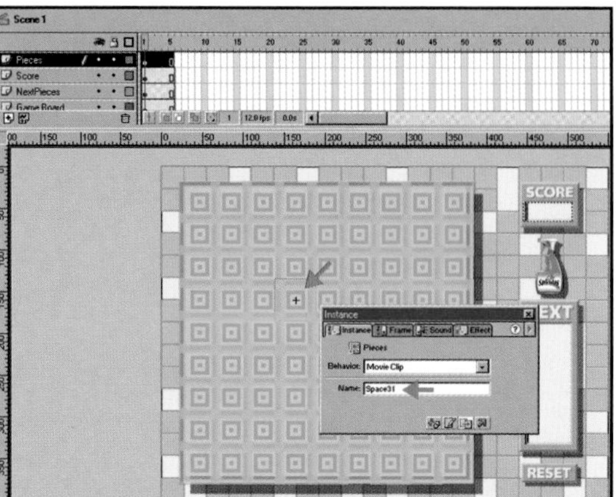

There are 81 instances of the Pieces movie clip each with an Instance name of Space1, Space2, and so on.

On initialization, the number of spaces is set to 81 (***NumberOfSpaces***), and the score to get a bonus is set to 100 (***BonusPoints***). Also, the score is set to 0 (***Score***), and the accumulated bonus points is set to 0 (***BonusTotal***). The number of pieces on the board is set to 0 (***TotalPieces***). ***TotalPieces*** is used to tell when the game can no longer be played because the board is full. The two arrays that keep track of the pieces are initialized. The function **ShowNextPieces** is called, and the next pieces appear on the side. Then the function **GetNextBoardPieces** is called, which moves the pieces from the side box to the board. And finally, **ShowNextPieces** is called again, which shows the next pieces that will be placed on the board.

Within the Pieces Movie, each piece is a button, with the exception of the germs, which are not movable. When a piece is selected, it sets the selected piece (***SelectedPiece***) to itself like this

```
_root.SelectedPiece = this;
```

and then calls **GetAvailableSpaces**. When a blank (which is also a button) is selected, it calls the **MovePiece** function. The piece is moved only if it has an available move as calculated by **GetAvailableSpaces**.

There are two special pieces: the Splendos piece and the germ. The germ does not move and cannot be selected. The only thing it can do is be destroyed by the Splendos. The Splendos piece can be selected and moved. When it is moved, it destroys everything it touches. Within the **MovePieces** function, there is a check to see if the piece is a Splendos, and if it is, the **DestroyAllAround** function is called.

A bonus Splendos is awarded at each accumulation of 100 points. That piece can be put in any empty space. When the player selects it, the ***SelectedPiece*** variable is set to **Bonus**, and when the player selects an empty space, the **MoveBonusPiece** function is called. A player is allowed to have only one bonus Splendos at a time; they do not accumulate.

The score is kept in an editable text field named Score. The variable ***Score*** is directly linked to the text field Score. Each time a piece is moved, a check is done to see if there are enough of the same colored pieces in a row to score. This is also done each time a piece appears on the board. The score is based on the number of matching pieces and their values. Scoring is calculated in the **CheckMatching** function.

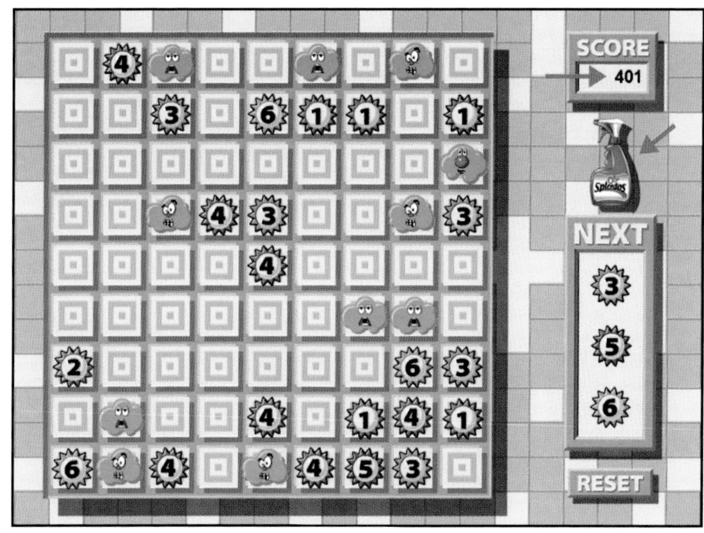

A bonus Splendos piece is awarded each time the player earns another 100 points. This piece can be placed in any available space.

Each time a piece is placed, the **MovePiece** checks to see if the moved piece scored. If it scored, nothing happens. If it did not score, the next three pieces are placed (**GetNextBoardPieces**) and then **ShowNextPieces** is called.

When the board is full, the player is asked if he wants to play again. If the player chooses to play again, the program executes the **CleanUp** function. The **CleanUp** function initializes both arrays (***SpaceColorArray*** and ***AvailableSpacesArray***) and loops through each piece and sets it to empty. The board then has no pieces left on it. **CleanUp** also resets all the scoring variables, and then it starts a new game by placing the first three pieces on the board (**GetNextBoardPieces**).

SPLENDOS

Chapter 11

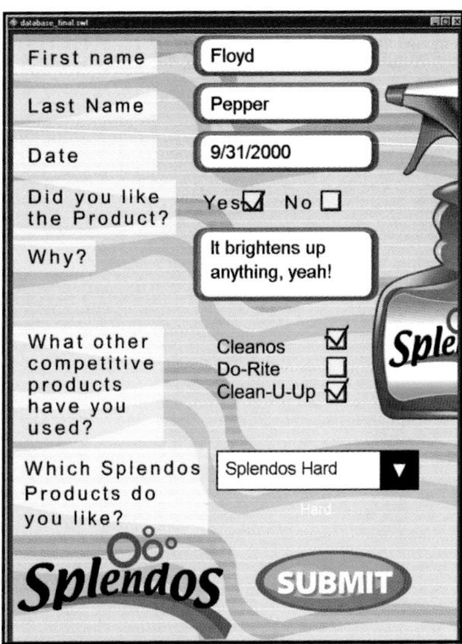

Chapter 13

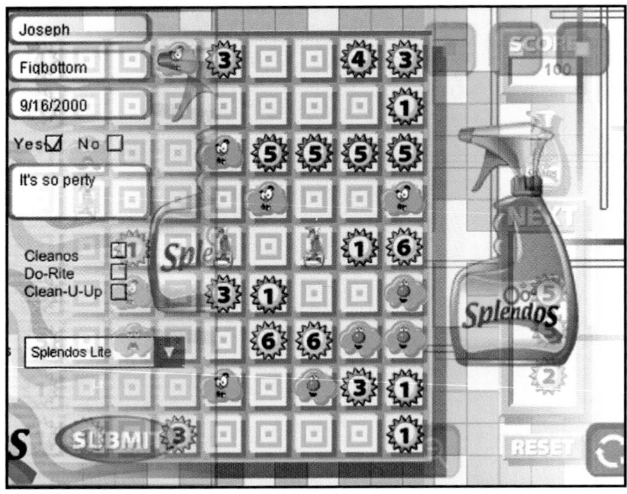

Chapter 12

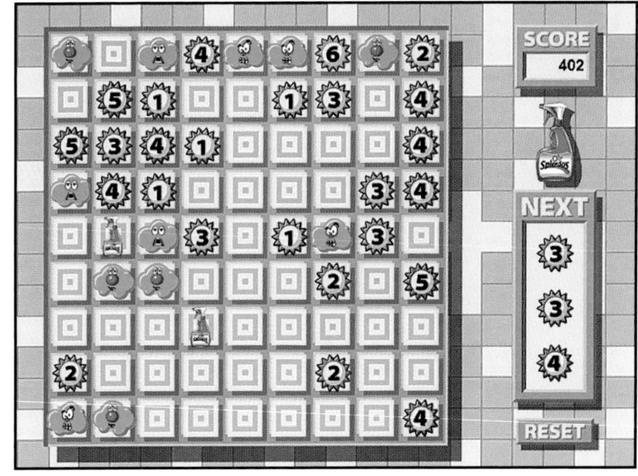

Chapter 14

PENNY DAVIS ONLINE RETAILING LLC

"Art produces ugly things which frequently become more beautiful with time. Fashion, on the other hand, produces beautiful things which always become ugly with time."

—JEAN COCTEAU

Even clothing manufacturers have found a niche on the Web. Although it's hard to try on clothes online, it can also be hard to find the right size of that outfit you fell in love with at the local retailers. The Web provides manufacturers of wearables several advantages, such as providing an interactive catalog and providing access to potential customers who don't have a retail outlet nearby. This section explores solutions to many of the key challenges that clothing manufacturers face when displaying their products online, such as dealing with ever-changing inventory and retail prices.

The Penny Davis Online Retailing LLC section of this book deals with such invaluable techniques as utilizing XML data, displaying rich text, and generating dynamic menus.

XML is a flexible data format, designed to be easily read by humans and easily interpreted by programs on all computing platforms. In particular, XML is tuned for transmitting information via the Internet. With Flash 5's built-in XML parsing capabilities, importing structured data into your .swf movies has never been easier.

This chapter covers the process of reading an external .xml file and extracting its contents to build a menu of categories and products. In turn, this menu drives a catalog, allowing users to peruse items from the Penny Davis women's wear section.

15

UTILIZING XML DATA

By David Emberton

EXAMINING AN XML FRAGMENT

To understand how XML and Flash work together, the best place to start is with XML. XML files are just text, so they can be edited with any word processing program that can export plain text format—for example, NotePad or SimpleText. This section takes a look at the PDCatalog.xml and PDCatalog.dtd files in the Chapter 15 folder on the CD-ROM. A .dtd file is a Document Type Definition, used by XML processors as a guide to interpreting any XML fragments based upon it. It lays out the structure and specifics of a particular type of document—in this case, the Penny Davis Catalog, or PDCatalog.xml.

> **Note:** Please be aware that Macromedia Flash 5 is not an industry standard XML parser and does not "validate" data. The XML solution detailed in this project was designed to work specifically with Flash Player 5. We recommend that you consider other XML resources to determine the appropriate form to use outside of Macromedia Flash 5.

1 Open the PDCatalog.xml and PDCatalog.dtd files in the Chapter 15 folder on the CD-ROM. Save them to your hard drive and open each file.

```
PDCatalog.xml - Notepad
File Edit Search Help Send
<?xml version = "1.0"?>
        <PDCatalog xmlns:PDCatalog = "PDCatalog.dtd">

                <Product>
                        <Name>ToeTap</Name>
                        <Category>Footwear</Category>
                        <Price>34.99</Price>
                        <ImageURL>toetap.swf</ImageURL>
                        <DescriptionURL>toetap.txt</DescriptionURL>
                </Product>

                <Product>
                        <Name>Evening Shade</Name>
                        <Category>Footwear</Category>
                        <Price>44.99</Price>
                        <ImageURL>eveningshade.swf</ImageURL>
                        <DescriptionURL>eveningshade.txt</DescriptionURL>
                </Product>

                <Product>
                        <Name>Comfort Sandals</Name>
                        <Category>Footwear</Category>
                        <Price>14.99</Price>
                        <ImageURL>comfortsandals.swf</ImageURL>
                        <DescriptionURL>comfortsandals.txt</DescriptionURL>
                </Product>

                <Product>
                        <Name>Stretch Jeans</Name>
                        <Category>Bottoms</Category>
                        <Price>14.99</Price>
```

Use a standard text editor to view an XML file.

2 In PDCatalog.xml, examine this XML fragment:

This code describes a single product, ToeTap shoes. Using ActionScript, it's possible to filter out each of the relevant tags (denoted by the brackets <>'s) and put the information to use.

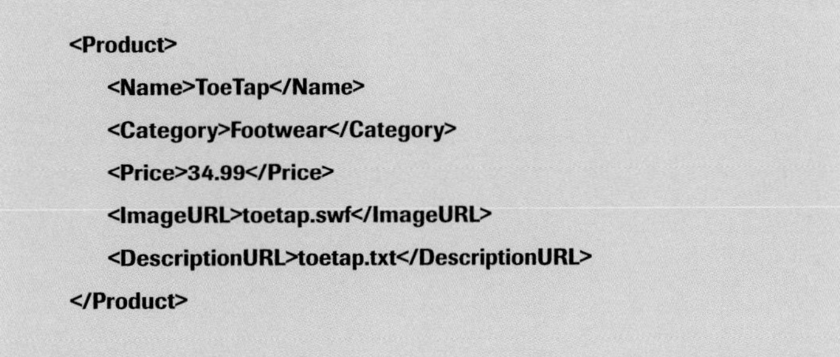

```
<Product>
    <Name>ToeTap</Name>
    <Category>Footwear</Category>
    <Price>34.99</Price>
    <ImageURL>toetap.swf</ImageURL>
    <DescriptionURL>toetap.txt</DescriptionURL>
</Product>
```

XML for the ToeTap product.

EXTRACTING DATA FROM PARSED XML

The first batch of code loads the file containing the XML fragment and invokes the **ExtractData()** function, which cycles through all the XML tags and redistributes the data they contain into arrays.

1 Open the file ProductCatalog_start.fla in the Chapter 15 folder and save it to your hard drive. To see the finished version, open the file ProductCatalog_final.fla.

2 Click the first keyframe of the ActionScript layer. Notice the code already in this frame. This code is used to display the menu and to make the menu scroll. Insert the initialization code before this existing code.

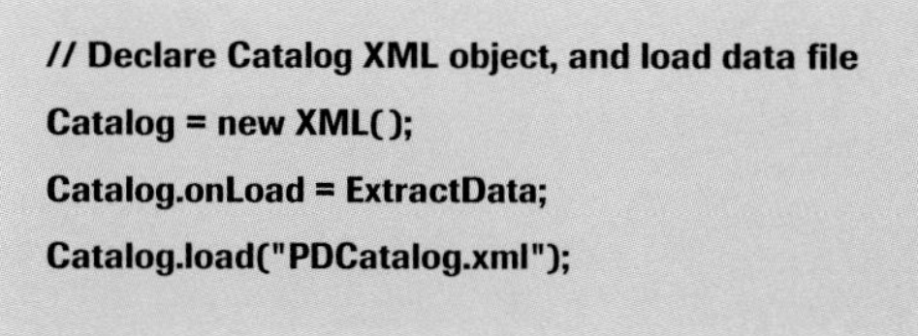

```
// Declare Catalog XML object, and load data file
Catalog = new XML();
Catalog.onLoad = ExtractData;
Catalog.load("PDCatalog.xml");
```

This code declares an XML object and specifies which XML file to load in order to populate it.

This code begins with the creation of a new XML object named Catalog. Catalog will be used to store the XML data from the file PDCatalog.xml. The XML object has an **onLoad** method, which can be set to any function you want executed after the XML data file is loaded. You don't have to manually verify that all the data in the XML file is loaded, because whatever function you specify as the **onLoad** method will automatically fire after Flash grabs the complete XML file. Another vital method of the XML object is **load**, which loads the specified file and parses its contents into the XML tree. In this case, the PDCatalog.xml file is specified, because it is the file that must be loaded and parsed into the Catalog object.

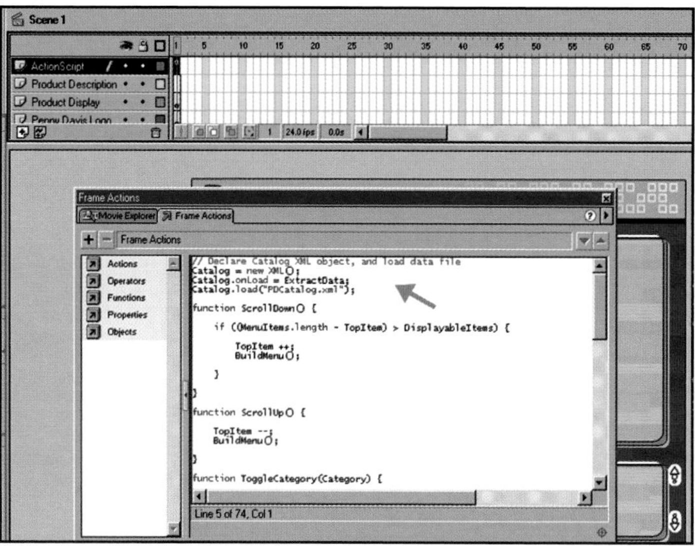

Add the XML object code to the ActionScript layer using the Frame Actions panel.

3 In the following six steps, insert the code that makes up the **ExtractData()** function:

```
// ExtractData Function
function ExtractData() {
    // Declare necessary arrays and variables
    Categories = new Array();
    Products = new Array();
    ProductTags = this.lastChild.childNodes;
    // Specify what tags to watch for
    ProductData = new Array("Name","Category","Price","ImageURL","DescriptionURL");
```

ExtractData creates the necessary arrays and variables and specifies which tags to watch for.

The **ExtractData()** function begins by declaring and defining some key objects. **Categories**, **Products**, **ProductTags**, and **ProductData** are all arrays, capable of storing and manipulating collections of data. **Categories** will be used to hold the product category names, which are extracted from the XML data. Similarly, **Products** will hold the names of the products extracted. **ProductTags** is another array, used to actually store the XML information, **this.lastChild.childNodes**.

To understand what **this.lastChild.childNodes** really means, look at the breakdown shown in this figure.

This is the object calling the function. It is an "invisible" argument passed during the function call, and in this case, it refers to the XML object Catalog.

this.lastChild is the <Catalog> tag in the PDCatalog.xml ➥file.

(The ➥ symbol you see here is for editorial purposes only.)

this.lastChild.childNodes is the array of **<Product>** tags nested within the **<Catalog>** tag.

ProductData is another array, comprising five text strings, each equaling the name of a tag nested inside **<Product>** that you want to extract. In other words, for each **<Product>** tag, the associated **<Name>**, **<Category>**, **<Price>**, **<ImageURL>**, and **<DescriptionURL>** information will be recorded.

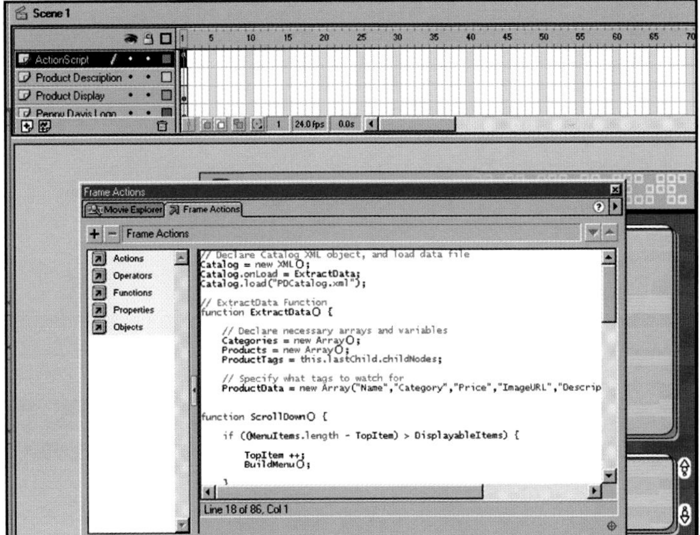

Add the **ExtractData()** function to the code on the ActionScript layer.

4 Continue the **ExtractData()** function by inserting this code:

```
// Cycle through all available XML tags, and extract node values
for (CounterA in ProductTags) {
    if (ProductTags[CounterA].nodeName == "Product") {
        Products[Products.length] = new Object();
```

This code cycles through the XML data and extracts node values.

Over the next few steps, a number of program loops will be started that will cycle through all the XML data and pull out the relevant details. Here, a **for**…**in** loop is started that will count through every element of **ProductTags**. ***CounterA*** is an arbitrary variable used as the counter for this loop. Next, an **if** action uses the value of ***CounterA*** to check for **<Product>** tags in the XML data. If the current node name is in fact Product, a brand new element is added to the **Products** array for retrieval later.

```
for (CounterA in ProductTags) {
```

Here, a **for**…**in** loop is initiated. It will execute all the statements enclosed in its curly braces once for every element in the **ProductTags** array. The current element number will be reflected in the value of ***CounterA***, the variable used to track the number of loops performed.

```
if (ProductTags[CounterA].nodeName == "Product") {
```

The elements of the **ProductTags** array can be referenced using the array access operators, []. ***CounterA*** is used inside the array access operators so that a new element is accessed every time. In other words, when ***CounterA*** = 1, **ProductTags[*CounterA*]** will evaluate as **ProductTags[1]**. Each element of ProductTags contains an XML data node, extracted from the PDCatalog.xml file. Every node can have a name and a value. Of particular interest are any nodes or tags named Product, which is why the **if** action checks the value of **ProductTags[*CounterA*].nodeName** to see if it equals **Product**.

```
Products[Products.length] = new Object();
```

This is the first line nested inside the **if** statement. Therefore, it is only executed when a **Product** tag is encountered. So when a new **Product** tag is found, a new element is added to the **Products** array.

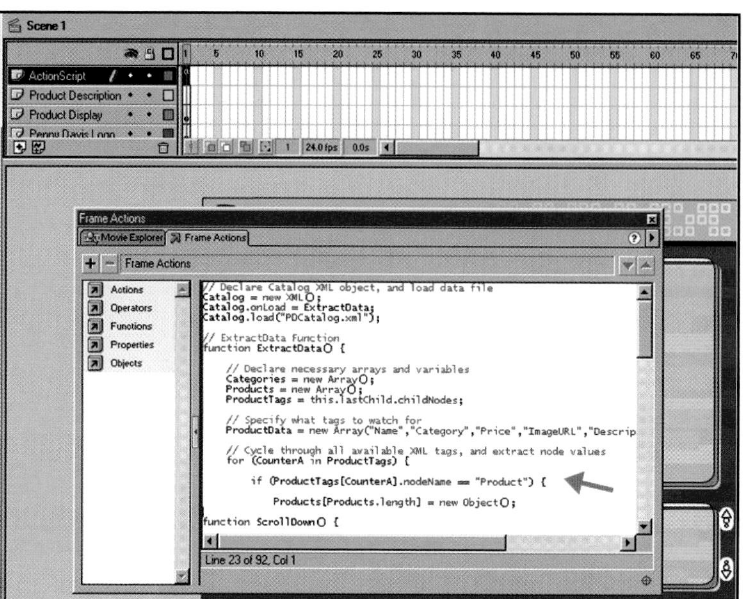

Add a **for** loop to the ActionScript layer.

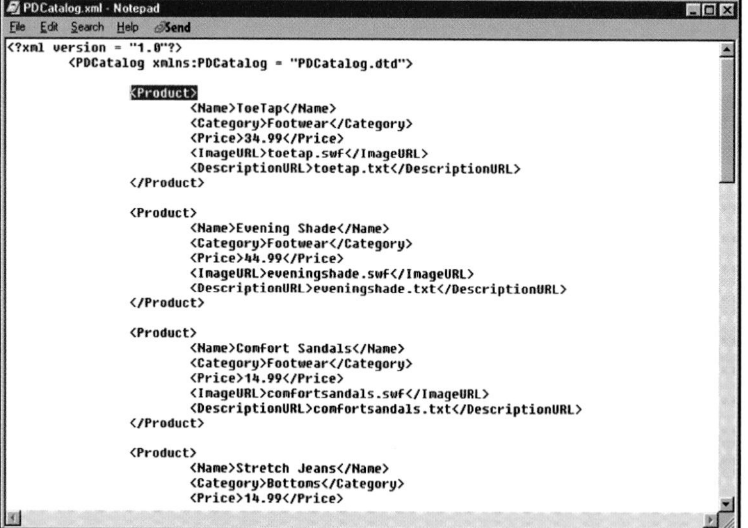

Each **Product** tag contains an XML data node.

5 Add the next block of code to the **ExtractData()** function.

This set of statements is executed once every time a **<Product>** tag is turned up by the code from step 4. A new **for**...**in** loop counts through all the tags nested under the **<Product>** tag and takes advantage of a second counter variable, ***CounterB***. So while ***CounterA*** is used to loop through the **<Product>** tags, ***CounterB*** loops through the child tags of each individual product. At the beginning of the **for**...**in** loop, a variable called ***CurrentNode*** holds whatever child tag is currently being inspected, and ***ChildValue*** holds the actual text the child tag contains. For example, ***CurrentNode*** may be a ***<Name>*** tag with the text value Knitted Sweater.

```
for (CounterB in ProductTags[CounterA].childNodes) {
```

Here, another **for**...**in** loop is used to count through the elements of an array. This time, however, the array is not the **ProductTags** themselves, but the children of a **Product** tag. In the catalog data file, descriptive information is nested inside the **Product** tag. Each of these "child" tags is accessible as an array **ProductTags[].childNodes**, and they contain information like product name, price, and so on.

```
CurrentNode =
➥ProductTags[CounterA].childNodes[CounterB].
➥nodeName;
ChildValue =
➥ProductTags[CounterA].childNodes[CounterB].
➥firstChild.nodeValue;
```

(The ➥ symbol you see here is for editorial purposes only.)

Both these statements are designed to clean up the code to come. The object addresses on the right are very long and unwieldy, so they are both assigned to variables with much shorter, more descriptive names. ***CurrentNode*** will always be a sub-detail of one of the products in the catalog, like price of category, and

```
for (CounterB in ProductTags[CounterA].childNodes) {
    CurrentNode = ProductTags[CounterA].childNodes[CounterB].nodeName;
    ChildValue = ProductTags[CounterA].childNodes[CounterB].firstChild.nodeValue;
```

This **for** loop works through the tags within each **<Product>** tag in the XML.

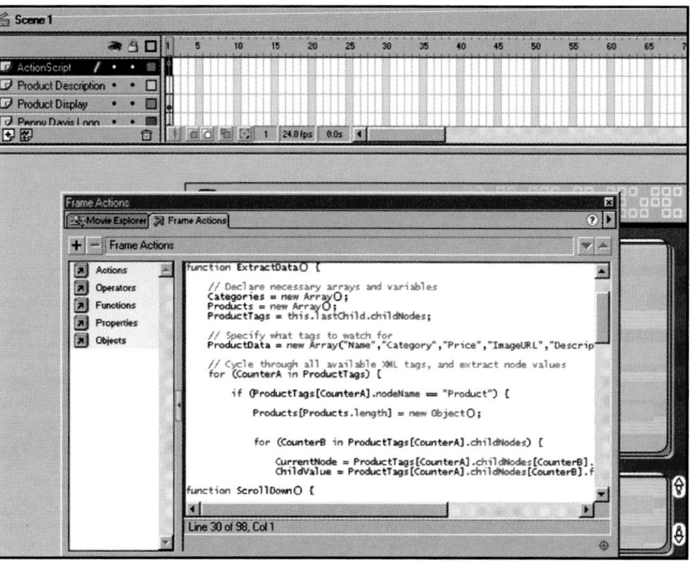

Add a **for** loop to cycle through the tags within each **<Product>** tag.

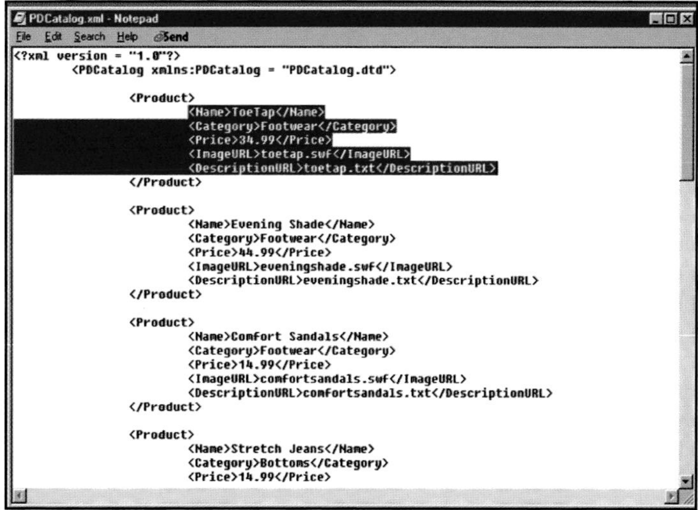

Each **Product** tag contains a **Name** tag, a **Category** tag, an **Image URL** tag, and a **Description URL** tag.

ChildValue is the actual value of those details, such as $19.95 or Tops. This information will be used to construct the catalog menu later in the chapter.

6 Add this code to the **ExtractData()** function:

This set of statements is the first part of the **ExtractData()** function that actually starts to store data taken from the XML object. The menu system organizes products from the catalog under categories. So it makes sense to keep an array of categories as well as products to optimize the process of creating the menus. Therefore, as the greater script loops over each of the tags nested inside each **<Product>** tag, each product's Category value is compared against the elements in the **Categories** array. Each new Category is added to the **Categories** array if it is unique.

```
for (Element in ProductData) {
    if (Element != "length" && CurrentNode == ProductData[Element]) {
        if (CurrentNode == "Category") {
            Matches = 0;
            for (CounterC = 0; CounterC < Categories.length; CounterC ++) {

                if (Categories[CounterC].Name == ChildValue) {
                    Matches ++;
                }
            }
            // If there are no matches, create a new category
            if (Matches == 0) {
                Categories[Categories.length] = new Object();
                Categories[Categories.length - 1].Name = ChildValue;
                Categories[Categories.length - 1].Expanded = false;
            }
        }
```

This code begins storing data from the XML object.

7 Complete the **ExtractData()** function with this code:

```
                    CurrentProduct = Products[Products.length - 1];
                    eval("CurrentProduct." + CurrentNode) = ChildValue;
                }
            }
        }
    }
}
BuildMenu();
}
```

Add this code to complete the **ExtractData** function.

Finally, now that the categories are all extracted, the rest of the product data is added to the **Products** array. A variable ***CurrentProduct*** is set to the most recently added element of the **Products** array, and then this variable is utilized in an **eval** action to populate the product's properties.

```
for (CounterC = 0; CounterC < Categories.length;
➥CounterC ++)
```

(The ➥ symbol you see here is for editorial purposes only.)

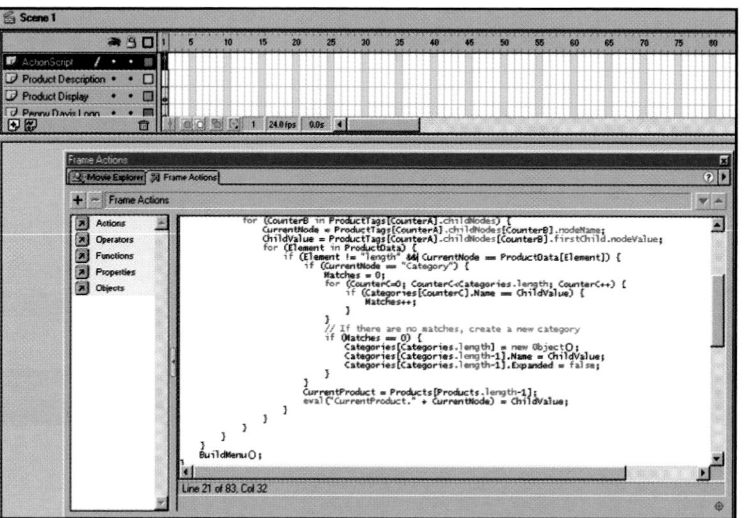

Add the code to complete the **ExtractData()** function.

Although **ExtractData()** looks complex, it's not. Upon further inspection, you'll notice that it contains a series of **for** and **for**...**in** actions that allow for the automated looping through elements of the various arrays involved. Using loops in this way is necessary whenever you are uncertain of just how much information you will have to deal with—as in this case, where the length of the PDCatalog.xml XML fragment is undetermined before playback.

The last statement in **ExtractData()** invokes a second custom function, **BuildMenu()**.

8 Insert the **BuildMenu()** function using this code:

```
// BuildMenu Function
function BuildMenu() {
    // Declare necessary arrays and variables
    MenuItems = new Array();
    DisplayableItems = 11;
    XOrigin = 87;
    YOrigin = 117;
    ItemHeight = 24;
```

Include this code to build menus using the data that was gathered with the **ExtractData()** function.

The **BuildMenu()** function is designed to take the arrays of data created by **ExtractData()** and use them to lay out a menu of buttons that accurately represents the categories and product names listed in the catalog. This first section of the function declares an array named **MenuItems** and defines some variables to be used later in the function. **MenuItems** will be used to hold the combined product and category information. **DisplayableItems** specifies just how many of the category/product buttons can be displayed in the space allotted on the Stage. ***XOrigin*** and ***YOrigin*** are coordinate values that specify the center point of the very first menu button. ***ItemHeight*** is the height in pixels of the menu button symbol itself, plus a small vertical margin for spacing.

9 Continue the **BuildMenu()** function with this code:

Because the number of displayable items is eleven, it's easy for a catalog to contain more than that amount of products and categories. So as the menu is scrollable, it's important to make sure that the list of items can't be scrolled in a way that doesn't make sense. The scrolling functions added later will manage a variable called ***TopItem*** by looking at the menu item in the top position and recording its element number in the **MenuItems** array. If the user tries to scroll up, this section of the script will ensure that the topmost element can't ever be less than zero because that is an element that would not exist.

```
// Normalize TopItem number to prevent scrolling past the beginning

if (TopItem < 0) {
	TopItem = 0;
}
```

Use this code to keep the scrollable menus from using illogical numbers.

10 Next in the **BuildMenu()** function, insert this code to populate the **MenuItems()** array:

Two nested **for** loops are used to cycle through each category, and then through each product that matches the current category, to build the **MenuItems** array. The **for** action works using three separate arguments. The first argument specifies the counter variable for the loop, and its initial value, as in this example:

```
CounterA = 0
```

The second argument specifies the condition under which the loop should continue, and the third argument dictates the amount by which the counter should be changed each time the loop completes itself.

```
// Create array of menu items
for (CounterA = 0; CounterA < Categories.length; CounterA ++) {

	MenuItems[MenuItems.length] = new Object();
	MenuItems[MenuItems.length - 1].Type = "Category";
	MenuItems[MenuItems.length - 1].ObjectSource = Categories[CounterA];
	if (Categories[CounterA].Expanded == true) {
	for (CounterB = 0; CounterB < Products.length; CounterB ++) {
			if (Products[CounterB].Category == Categories[CounterA].Name) {
				MenuItems[MenuItems.length] = new Object();
				MenuItems[MenuItems.length - 1].Type = "Product";
				MenuItems[MenuItems.length - 1].ObjectSource = Products[CounterB];
			}
		}
	}
}
```

Use this code to populate the **MenuItems** array.

```
for (CounterA = 0; CounterA < Categories.length; CounterA ++) {
    ^ Argument 1    ^ Argument 2                ^ Argument 3

    // Block of statements to be repeated while Argument 2 is true.

}
```

Argument 1: Initialize counter variable
Argument 2: "Keep looping" condition
Argument 3: Counter increment

The point of this script is that the user can click category buttons to collapse or expand them, thereby hiding or showing the products listed under each one. So, the actual products present in the menu can change, therefore making it necessary to go back over the Category and Product arrays each time the user clicks, to update the menu and ensure that only the right things are actually being shown. For each element in the **Categories** array, a variable named ***Expanded*** is used to track whether or not that category is expanded in the menu.

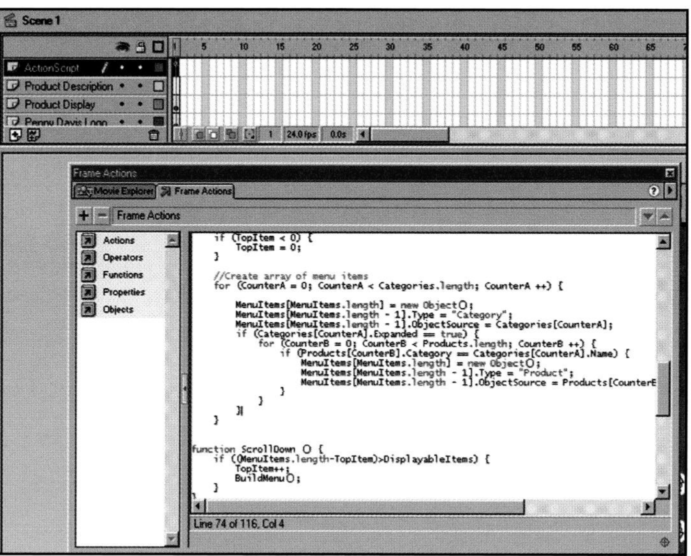

Add a **for** loop to the **BuildMenu()** function to populate the **MenuItems** array.

11 Insert this script to complete the **BuildMenu()** function:

Now for the business end of the function. After the housekeeping tasks of checking the correct composition of the menu and building an array containing all the necessary buttons has been done, that data is used as a guide for replicating and positioning all the menu buttons. Another **for** loop is used, counting up from zero to the value of **DisplayableItems** (11). Each

```
// Build menu
for (CounterA = 0; CounterA < DisplayableItems; CounterA ++) {
    eval("Item" + CounterA).removeMovieClip();
    _root.attachMovie(MenuItems[CounterA + TopItem].Type, "Item"
    ➥+ CounterA, CounterA + 100);
    eval("Item" + CounterA)._x = XOrigin;
    eval("Item" + CounterA)._y = YOrigin + (CounterA * ItemHeight);
    eval("Item" + CounterA).Name = MenuItems[CounterA +
    ➥TopItem].ObjectSource.Name;
}
}
```

Add this code to replicate and position all the menu buttons. (The ➥ symbol you see here is for editorial purposes only.)

cycle of the loop therefore corresponds to a particular button in the menu, so first of all, the **removeMovieClip** action clears away any existing symbol that might've previously occupied the current spot. Then the **attachMovie** action grabs either a category or product button from the Library and creates an instance of it on the Stage. ***XOrigin*** and ***YOrigin*** are used to position each successive button at its appropriate coordinates—each one lower than the previous one by the value of **ItemHeight**. Finally, the ***Name*** variable is set for each button so that it displays the correct label.

eval is used throughout this section of the function to dynamically reference objects, depending on the value of ***CounterA***. As the **for** action loops, the value of ***CounterA*** increases by one each time, which is key for using **eval** in a looping context. For example, if ***CounterA*** is equal to 4, **eval("Item" add *CounterA*)** will evaluate as the object Item4. If ***CounterA*** equals 5, the object referenced by **eval("Item" add *CounterA*)** changes to Item5.

```
CounterA = 4 -> eval("Item" add CounterA) = Item4
CounterA = 5 -> eval("Item" add CounterA) = Item5
```

So if the value of ***CounterA*** steadily increases, each of the different menu button objects can be manipulated in turn, even though the actual **eval** action never changes.

BuildMenu() is intended to be called anytime a user clicks to expand or contract a category, as well as each time the user scrolls the menu. It is the "engine" of the menu system and always operates on the latest data.

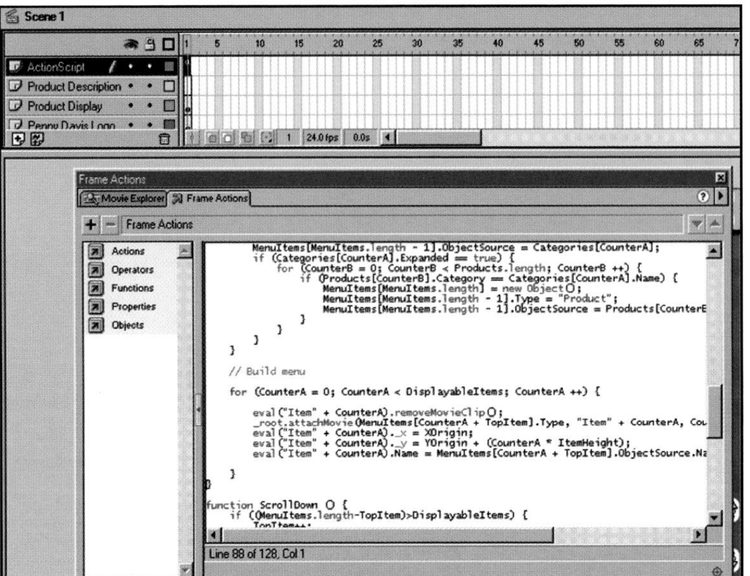

Add the remaining code for the **BuildMenu()** function.

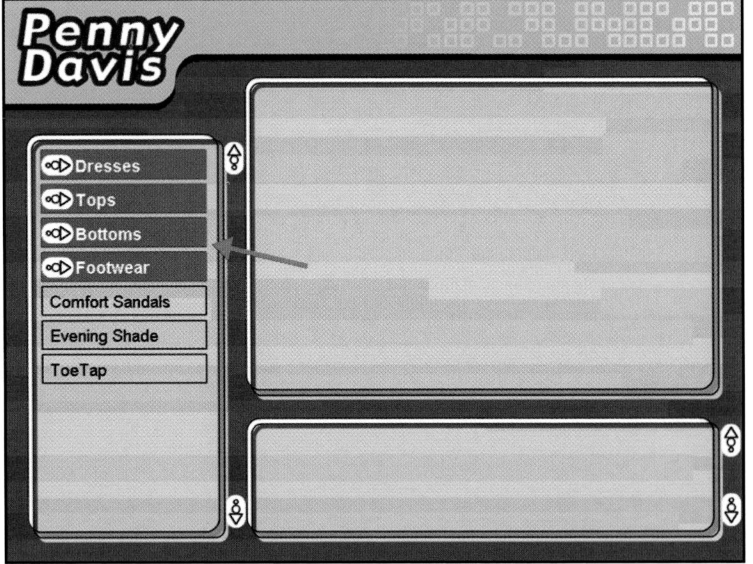

The **BuildMenu()** function positions the menu items and buttons.

Setting Symbol Linkage

The Category and Product symbols, which are both simple movie clips containing text fields and buttons, are attached dynamically during playback. So it's necessary to set their linkage properties and make certain they are exported with the other symbols.

1. Open the Library and locate Category in the Movie Clips folder.
2. Click Category to select it, and choose Linkage from the Library Options menu.

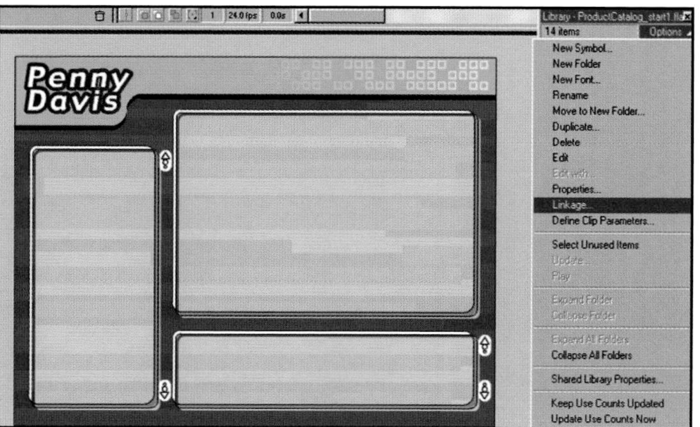

Select the Category movie clip and then choose Linkage from Library Options.

3. Select Export This Symbol and type Category in the Identifier field.
4. Repeat steps 1 through 3 for the Product symbol, using Product as the unique identifier.

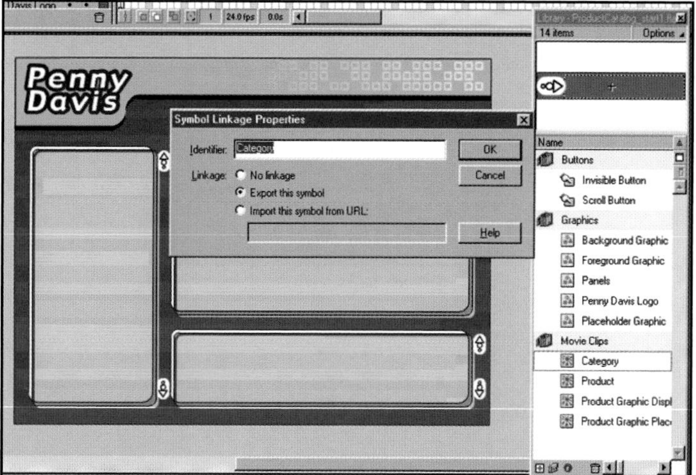

Specify the Identifier and the Linkage options for the Category movie clip.

> **Note:** When setting the Linkage properties of movie clips, be sure to take their size into account. All linked assets are loaded before the first frame of the movie to ensure they are available before any **attachMovie** actions might require them. So if you do take advantage of this feature, be frugal and plan ahead.

Passing Arguments in Function Calls

The Product Catalog has several clickable elements, including the menu scroll buttons and the Category and Product symbols. Rather than assigning full code blocks to each button, an event handler and a function call are used. This saves time and makes debugging simpler because all the primary code is in the same place. One of the key advantages of ActionScript in Flash 5 is that you can pass arguments to a function when you invoke it. To illustrate, here is the setup procedure for the button nested inside the Product symbol.

1 Locate the Product symbol in the Library's Movie Clips folder and double-click to edit it.

2 Click to select the button instance on the Invisible Button layer, and then open the Actions panel.

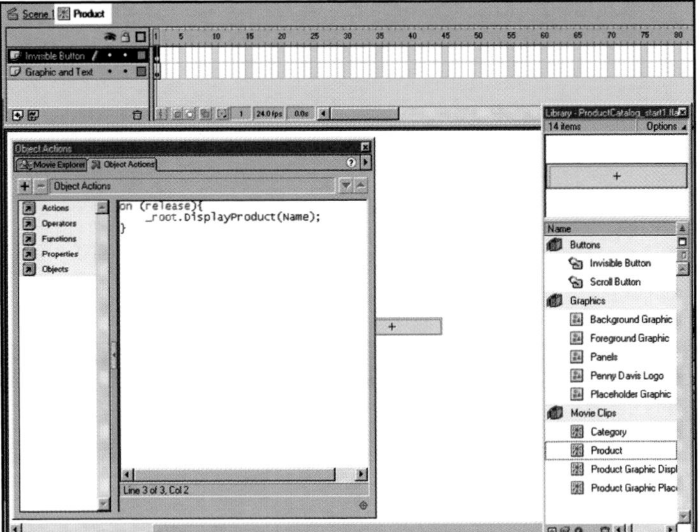

Assign the code that calls the **DisplayProduct()** function to the button on the Invisible Button layer in the Product movie clip.

3 Type the code for the button's event handler:

```
on (release) {
      _root.DisplayProduct(Name);
}
```

Use this code to launch the **DisplayProduct()** function after a mouse click on the button.

This is a simple **on release** handler that executes the code block it encloses anytime the user clicks and releases the mouse over the button. **DisplayProduct()** is a function attached to the _root Timeline and it accepts one argument, the name of the product being selected by the user. Each Product instance duplicated by the **BuildMenu()** function is assigned the variable ***Name***, which is used to populate the text field and also to identify the product being displayed. Passing ***Name*** to the **DisplayProduct()** function lets ActionScript know just which product to display.

How It Works

XML, or Extensible Markup Language, is an open standard for describing data structures and documents. A cousin of HTML, XML is designed to be ASCII or plain-text based and can be read by humans as well as computers. Flash has a built-in XML processor that can take these text files and parse them into an XML object.

<< Example? Sample XML Data

<Family>

<Surname>Smith</Surname>

<Members>4</Members>

</Family>

>>

XML fragments consist of nested groups of tags, a tag being a word enclosed by square braces, as in **<TagName>**. Flash translates each of these tags into a data node, which can be rearranged, inserted, or deleted using ActionScript. So a tag is the way XML data is written and stored, whereas a data node is a tag in its processed form that can be manipulated with script. A parsed XML fragment is like a tree of nodes, each one capable of having child nodes (nested tags), names, and values. In the Product Catalog chapter, the focus is on *reading* XML data rather than manipulating it and sending it back to a server. Using XML to transmit the product data is simply more flexible and simpler than using standard URL-encoded text that works with the **loadVariables** action.

The **ExtractData()** function is a nested series of loops. The top-level loop counts through all the nodes in the XML object and pays attention to ones named Product because those are the only tags of interest. Whenever a **Product** tag is located, the contents of the node are added to a new element in the **Products** array, which was created to store all the product data. Then a second loop counts through all the *child nodes* of the **Product** tag, which in the Penny Davis catalog include Name, Price, Category, and so on. Anytime one of these child nodes is located, it too is added to the **Products** array as a sub-element of the product it belongs to.

PDCatalog.xml - Notepad

File Edit Search Help Send

```
<?xml version = "1.0"?>
	<PDCatalog xmlns:PDCatalog = "PDCatalog.dtd">

		<Product>
			<Name>ToeTap</Name>
			<Category>Footwear</Category>
			<Price>34.99</Price>
			<ImageURL>toetap.swf</ImageURL>
			<DescriptionURL>toetap.txt</DescriptionURL>
		</Product>

		<Product>
			<Name>Evening Shade</Name>
			<Category>Footwear</Category>
			<Price>44.99</Price>
			<ImageURL>eveningshade.swf</ImageURL>
			<DescriptionURL>eveningshade.txt</DescriptionURL>
		</Product>

		<Product>
			<Name>Comfort Sandals</Name>
			<Category>Footwear</Category>
			<Price>14.99</Price>
			<ImageURL>comfortsandals.swf</ImageURL>
			<DescriptionURL>comfortsandals.txt</DescriptionURL>
		</Product>

		<Product>
			<Name>Stretch Jeans</Name>
			<Category>Bottoms</Category>
			<Price>14.99</Price>
```

Flash can parse XML data into an XML object.

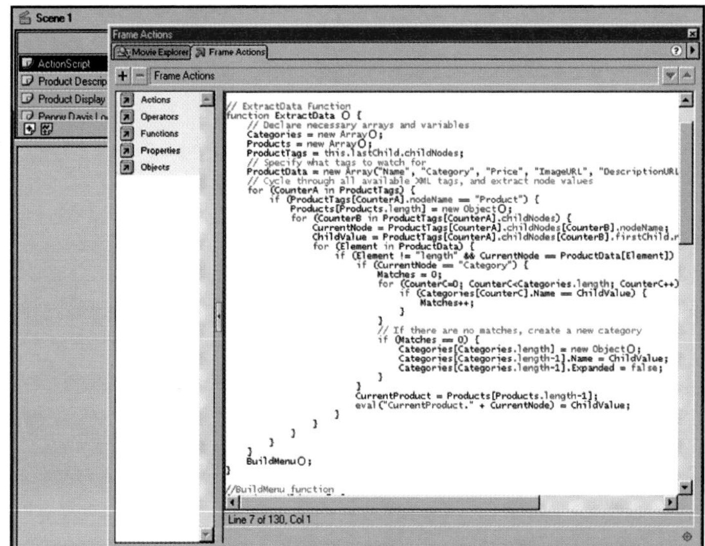

The **ExtractData()** function employs a series of loops to process the XML data.

Also at this point in the script, a second array, **Categories**, is populated. As each **Product** node is encountered, the script checks for **Category** child nodes and checks to see if each new category is unique. If it is, a new element is created for it in the **Categories** array. Having a separate array for categories makes managing the menu building process a lot simpler than if the data was only ordered by product name.

When all the data from the XML object has been examined and used in the various arrays created, the **BuildMenu()** function uses it to dynamically attach instances of the Category and Product symbols to the Stage. Each of these is seeded with the name of the category or product it represents so that information can be passed back to the functions doing the heavy lifting of collapsing and expanding categories or displaying the picture and description of any selected product.

XML is a powerful way of storing data because it can be easily transmitted via the Internet, and it can be processed, manipulated, and retransmitted by any properly equipped database or server, and yes, even the Flash Player. XML wins over other methods for sending data in and out of Flash Player because of its flexibility. You have the power to describe any kind of document you want with XML and then work with it in ActionScript and send it back to the server. This chapter gives you a sneak peek at some of the power of XML in combination with Flash. With practice, you can build data-enabled applications of greater and greater complexity.

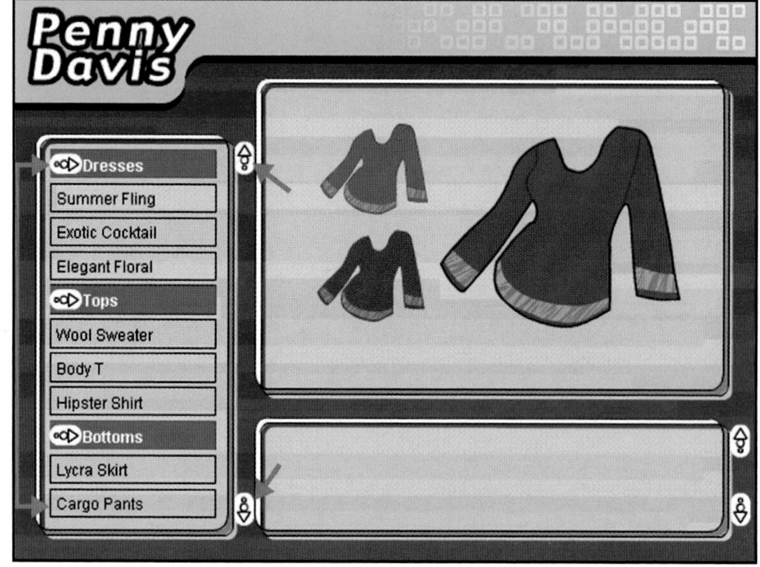

The view can scroll through menu options when they are all expanded.

16

DISPLAYING DYNAMIC TEXT AND HTML HYPERLINKS WITH SCROLLING

by David Emberton

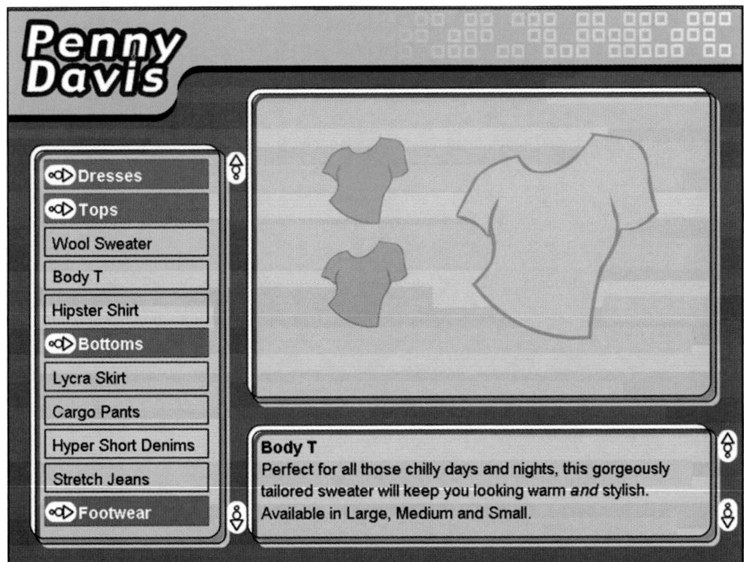

The Penny Davis online product catalog, being ever so refined, includes full-color pictures of various products, but also HTML-based descriptions of each. The ability to dynamically display HTML text is new to Flash 5 and is especially interesting because it also supports hyperlinks—which in this case you'll be using to link to hypothetical URLs related to products in the catalog.

When you open the starting file, the greater portion of the catalog application is already completed, including the variables to hold the HTML data. All that remains is to create the dynamic text field control and script the scrolling buttons in case the text takes up more than the space provided.

Dynamic Text Fields and Variables

In Chapter 15, XML was used to store information about the products in the catalog, including the location of picture and description files to be displayed on demand. When the user clicked a menu item corresponding to a particular product, this code was used to control the ***ProductDescription*** variable:

```
// Clear the ProductDescription variable
ProductDescription = "";
// Load the relevant file and extract any variables it contains
loadVariables (SelectedProductDescription, 0);
```

Because you set ***ProductDescription*** to an empty string, its contents are cleared so that irrelevant data is not displayed while the new product description is downloaded. The ***SelectedProductDescription*** variable holds the location of the text file containing the relevant HTML data you want to obtain.

A dynamic text field can be used to create a new variable or, as in this case, to display the contents of the existing one, ***ProductDescription***. The text file downloaded by the loadVariables action contains its own definition of ***ProductDescription***, so when it is loaded into the catalog movie, this new data overrides the old and thereby updates the dynamic text field.

1 Open the ProductCatalog2_Start.fla in the Chapter 16 folder of the accompanying CD and save to it to your hard drive.

2 Using the Text Tool, create a new text object on the Product Description layer and make sure it's sized and positioned so that it shows through the windowed area in the bottom right.

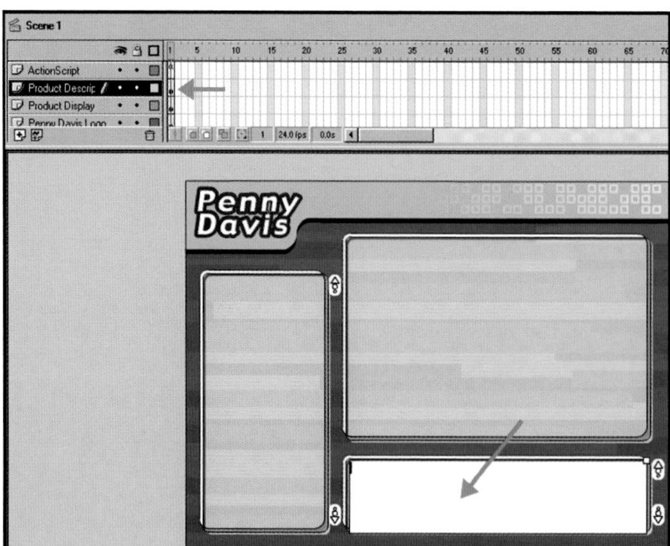

Create a new text object on the Product Description layer.

3 Bring up the Text Options panel, select Dynamic Text from the first drop-down list, and select Multiline from the second drop-down list. Check the HTML and Word Wrap options and make sure the Border/BG and Selectable options are left unchecked.

By selecting HTML, you are opting to have HTML formatting information such as paragraphs and font choice, as well as hyperlinks, preserved when the contents of ***ProductDescription*** are displayed. Otherwise, the data would be shown in plain text format.

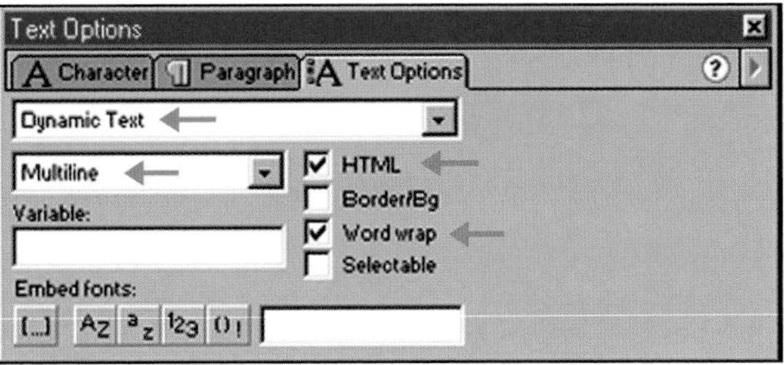

Use the Text Options panel to set the properties for the text object.

4 To link this new text field to the ***ProductDescription*** variable, type the address of the variable (in this case, ***ProductDescription***) into the Variable field of the Text Options panel.

This automatically joins the text field to the variable, and once it's exported, the contents of the field will be updated automatically whenever the variable's contents change.

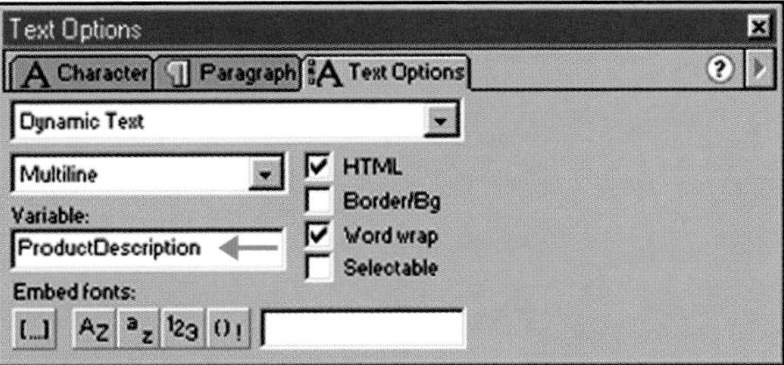

Link the text to the ***ProductDescription*** variable.

5 The next step in the text field creation process is to set the overall font attributes. Make sure the text field is still selected and access the Character panel. For the font, choose _sans, and for the point size, choose 12. The font called _sans and its siblings _serif and _keyboard are known as device fonts.

Because you've chosen a device font, no font outlines are exported, reducing overall file size. This is especially useful for HTML text, which might use bold or italic characters you hadn't planned on.

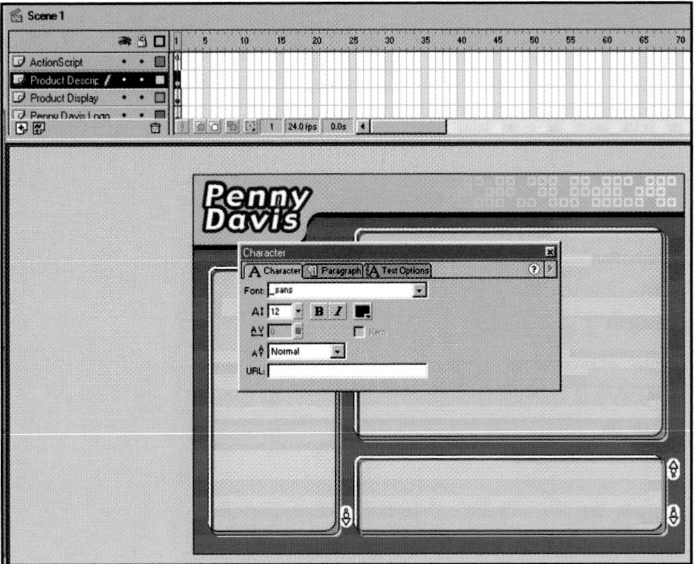

From the Character panel, assign text characteristics to the text field.

Scroll Controls

Any good text field deserves a set of scroll buttons—at least if the text displayed might take up more space than the field itself. In this case, HTML data is being loaded about a number of different products, so you can't exactly predict how long each description will be. Implementing scroll controls is a simple process of assigning Object Actions to the buttons that have already been included as part of the catalog's interface.

1 Select the scroll arrow pointing upward that's located to the right of the text field on the Scrolling Controls layer. Then open the Actions panel to edit the button's Object Actions.

2 Add an **on** handler, which will envelop all the actions you want executed in response to a mouse click.

```
on (release) {
}
```

The **on** action traps button events.

In fact, the specific event being handled is a mouse button release rather than a press; this is done to comply with standard user interface conventions about when a button's action takes place.

Now that you have an empty event handler, you can insert a block of code in it.

3 Create a conditional statement that scrolls the ***ProductDescription*** text field upward. The entire list of actions should look like this:

```
on (release) {
    if (ProductDescription.scroll > 0) {
        ProductDescription.scroll = ProductDescription.scroll-1;
    }
}
```

The **scroll** property can be set in order to change the top line of a text field.

The **if** statement insulates a set of actions from being executed, except when the supplied condition is met. That way, the text will be scrolled only if it isn't already at the top line—which is where the **scroll** property comes in. Specifically, the **if** action tests the value of **ProductDescription.scroll** to see if it is greater than 0. For the **scroll** property of a text field to equal 0, the first line must be the first line visible, meaning no scrolling up is possible. So if you assume the **if** condition is satisfied and it is possible to scroll up, the statement inside the **if** action is executed.

Text fields have two special ActionScript properties that other objects don't: **scroll** and **maxscroll**. When **ProductDescription.scroll** is decremented by one, the text field scrolls up one line.

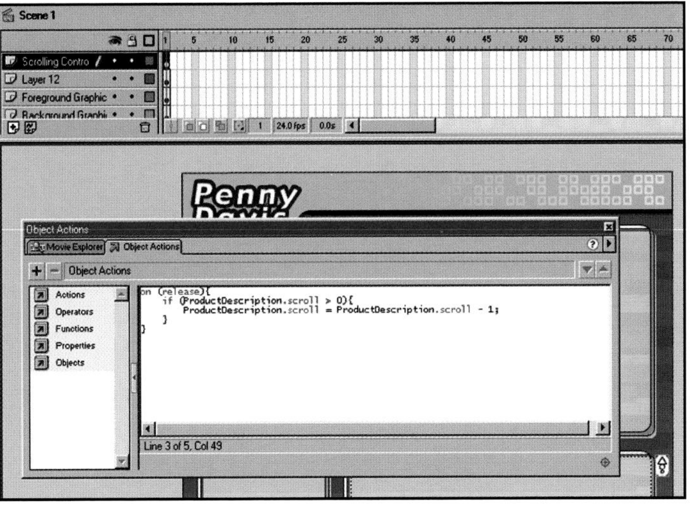

Add the scrolling script to the upward-pointing arrow button.

4 Select the down scrolling button, located to the right of the text field, to edit its Object Actions. Then create a new **on** event handler to respond to mouse clicks.

Observe the role that the **maxscroll** property plays in this **if** statement. Because the point here is to scroll down as far as possible, the value of **maxscroll** defines just how far down that is. Therefore, as long as the **scroll** property is less than **maxscroll**, the text will be scrolled down one line.

```
on (release)
    if (ProductDescription.scroll < ProductDescription.maxscroll) {
        ProductDescription.scroll = ProductDescription.scroll+1;

    }
}
```

The **scroll** property is incremented to scroll the text field downward.

How It Works

Ironic as it seems, displaying HTML within a plug-in that usually sits within an HTML document has its uses. Strictly speaking, dynamic text fields in Flash 5 can render only the most basic of HTML 1.0 tags, but even the most perfunctory rich text capability is better than boring plain text. Plus, the ability to embed hyperlinks in a text field is most useful because it's flexible and easy. The actual HTML itself can be either generated on-the-fly using ActionScript or prewritten and stored in a database or text file as in the catalog example.

Flash Player cannot actually read HTML files usually displayed by a Web browser, but as you learned in this example, HTML code can be assigned to a variable and then displayed in a text field. This capability was added as a response to requests by developers to be able to display richly formatted text. The formatting information needed to actually be embedded in the variable, so rather than using a proprietary set of formatting codes, Macromedia drew on standard HTML markup.

Scrolling in Flash 5 remains largely unchanged since it was introduced in version 4, except that now of course the updated syntax and the Actions panel make the whole process a lot easier to input. By working from the values of **scroll** and **maxscroll** and then setting the value of **scroll**, working with long text blocks becomes an easy task.

In particular, the **if** action is used to test the state of the scrolling text field to determine whether or not it can actually scroll any further up or down. When downward scrolling is possible, the **scroll** property of the text field is less than **maxscroll**, as set in this line:

```
if (ProductDescription.scroll < ProductDescription.maxscroll)
```

When upward scrolling is possible, the **scroll** property will be greater than zero, as set in this line:

```
if (ProductDescription.scroll > 0)
```

Once the state of the text field is determined, the value of **scroll** can be incremented or decremented to change the currently displayed top line in the field.

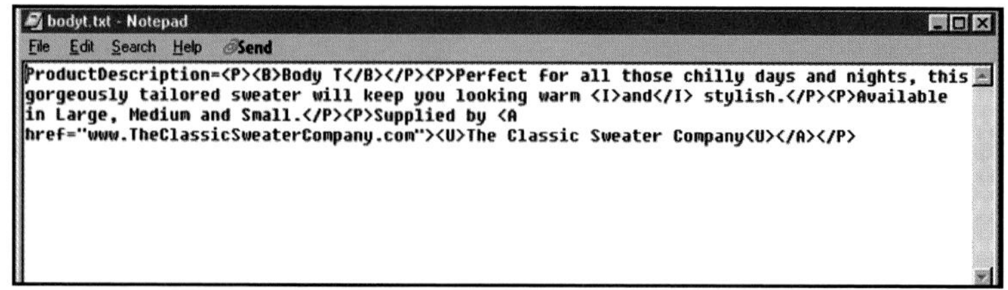

The description of each product is loaded from an external text file that is formatted with basic HTML 1.0.

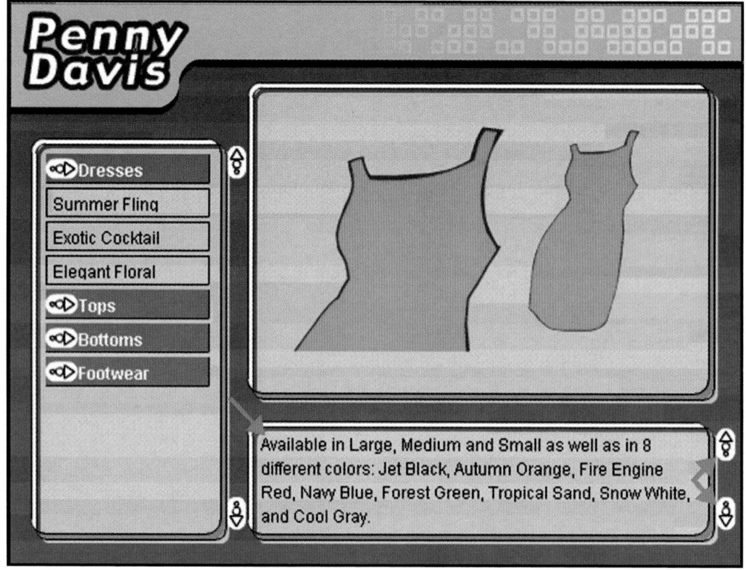

The description field is scrollable.

17

GENERATING DYNAMIC MENUS

by David Emberton

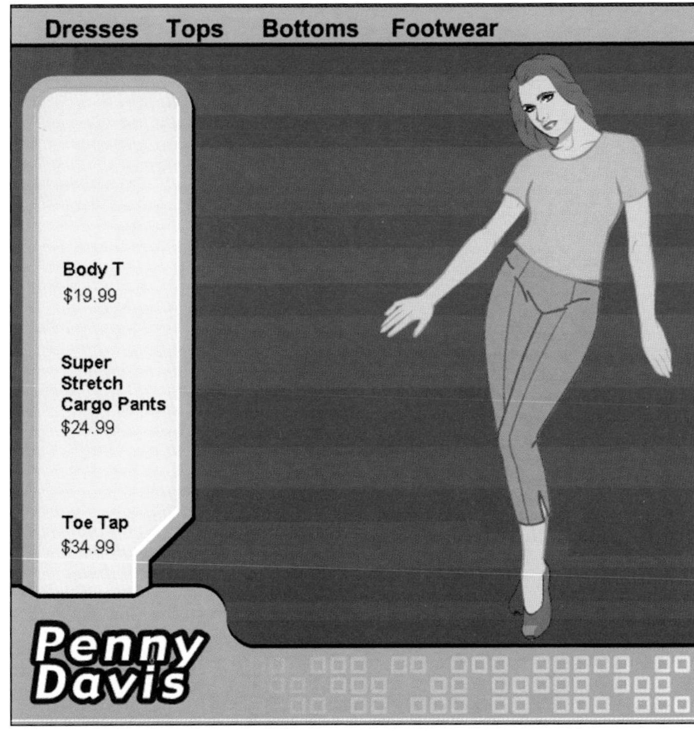

Flash is a great tool for creating interactive catalogs, interfaces, and demonstrations, and with a little careful planning, you can save yourself a lot of work by avoiding having to lay out and manage elements manually. This chapter brings together the power of the Array object with on-the-fly movie clip generation to create a powerful, and scalable, set of dynamic menus. The menus form part of the Penny Davis interactive product demonstration, allowing users to view a number of different garments and shoes in combination with one another, along with pricing information.

Setting Symbol Linkage Properties

This dynamic menu system uses the **attachMovie** action to make instances of the Menu and Item symbols, but which don't have to be physically placed on the Stage. It's important to do the necessary preparation so these symbols are exported along with the rest of the movie.

1 Open the file iMannequin_start.fla in the Chapter 17 folder on the CD and save it to your hard drive. (If you need to refer to the finished file, open iMannequin_final.fla.)

2 Open the Library, and locate the Menu symbol in the Movie Clips folder.

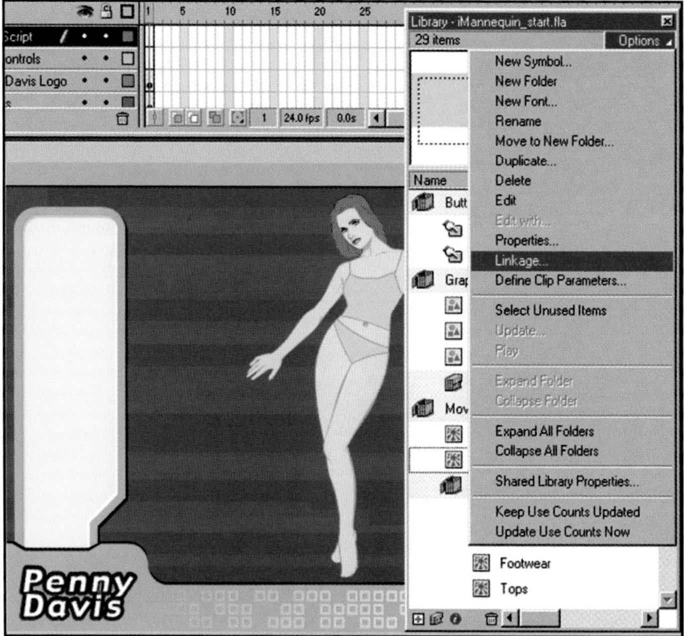

Select Linkage for the Menu symbol in the Movie Clips folder of the Library.

3 Click the Options menu and select Linkage. Click the Export This Symbol option and type **Menu** in the Identifier field.

If you force this symbol to be exported, it will be available to ActionScript after the movie has been exported.

4 Repeat steps 2 and 3 for the Item symbol. Again, make sure Export This Symbol is selected, and this time, type **Item** in the Identifier field.

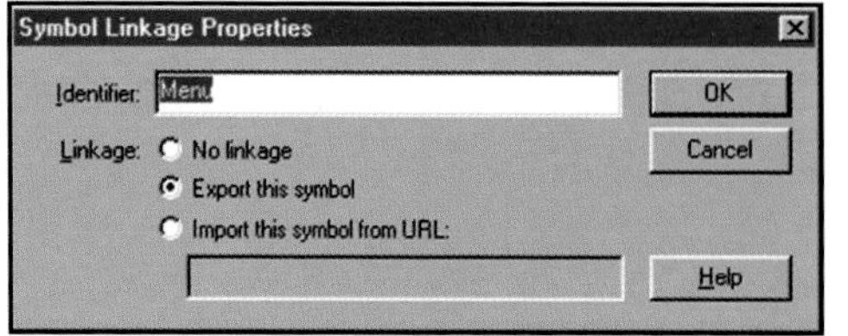

Set the properties for the Menu symbol in the Symbol Linkage Properties dialog box.

The other main consideration is to set aside space for the menu headings to appear in your movie. The Product Demonstration's menus are 20 pixels high, so a blue strip 20 pixels high appears at the top of the Background Graphic that shows where the menus will be placed.

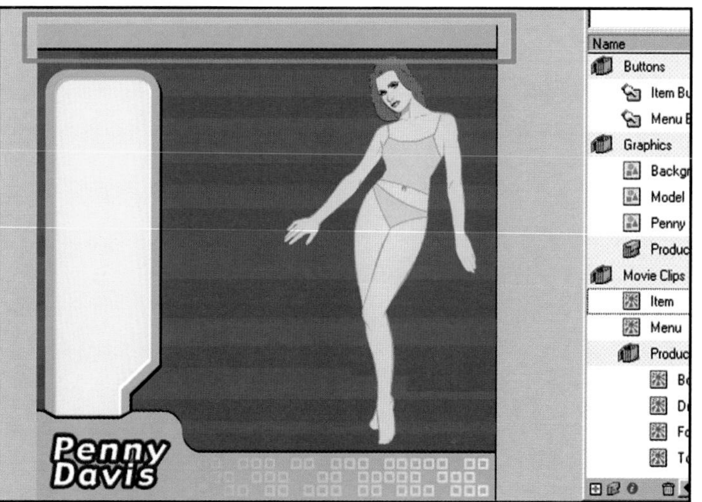

The menus appear along the top blue bar.

Preventing Movie Clips from Looping

The purpose of the Product Demonstration is to show off a variety of Penny Davis' most popular items. The user can select from among a number of different dresses, tops, shirts, pants, skirts, and shoes by choosing them from the menus. So, to make the menus useful, the product graphics must be put into place.

Each group of products is nested in its own Movie Clip symbol, arranged in a slideshow-type setup so that only one item from each group can be showing at a time. The product groups have already been placed in separate movie clips. Now you need to arrange them on the Stage and insert some actions in each to prevent them from looping!

1. Locate the Bottoms symbol in the Movie Clips > Product Groups Library folder and double-click to edit it.
2. Select the first keyframe and open the Actions panel.
3. To prevent the movie clip from playing when it appears on the Stage and looping inappropriately through each of the different products, use the **stop** action:

```
stop();
```

Prevent the movie clip from playing by using a **stop** action.

4 Repeat steps 1 through 3 with the remaining symbols in the Product Groups Library folder.

5 Return to Scene 1.

6 Notice that each of the Product Groups has already been assigned its own layer. Drag an instance of each group movie clip onto its particular layer, and then use the Info panel to set its location with these coordinates:

Tops:	x **317**, y **127**
Dresses:	x **313**, y **175**
Bottoms:	x **302**, y **211**
Footwear:	x **302**, y **335**

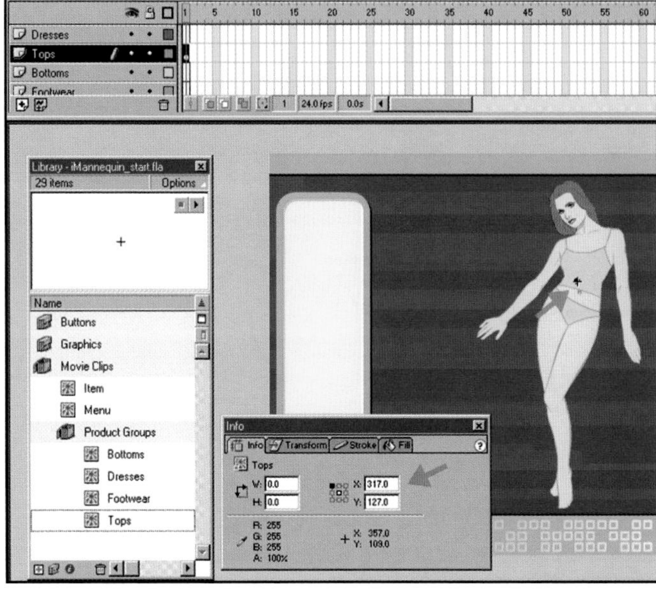

Use the Info panel to position the Tops, Dresses, Bottoms, and Footwear movie clips.

7 Select each instance, and then use the Instance panel to assign the following names:

Tops:	**Tops**
Dresses:	**Dresses**
Bottoms:	**Bottoms**
Footwear:	**Footwear**

Each of the movie clip instances needs a unique instance name so it will become an object that can be addressed with ActionScript.

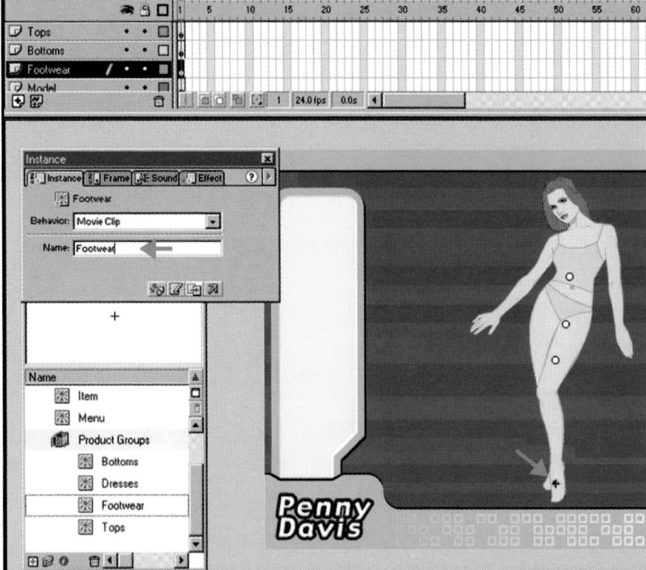

Give each movie clip an instance name.

> **Note:** Although the matching symbol and instance names seem obvious, they don't have to be the same. You'll make them match for the sake of simplicity in this example, but you don't have to do so in all cases.

Storing Data in Arrays

Now that the actual graphics are all laid out correctly, you need to create a data model that reflects each of the items in the demo. In addition to the individual item names, your data will include additional information about the menus, including the name and width (in pixels) of each menu. By creating a data object that stores all that information, Flash can quickly and easily generate the set of menus.

1 Select the first keyframe of the ActionScript layer, and then open the Actions panel. You'll see that the initialization code has already been entered; it refers to a function named **SetData()**, which you'll enter now.

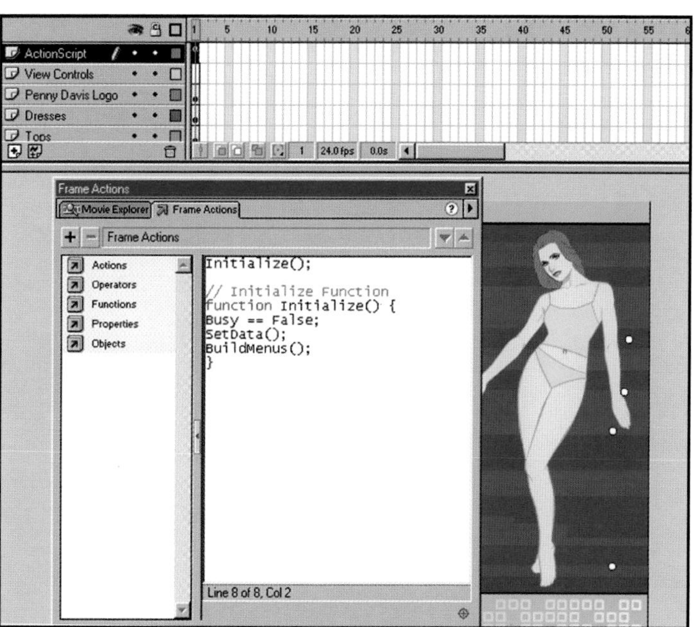

Look at the initialization code that has already been added to the ActionScript layer.

2 Define the function:

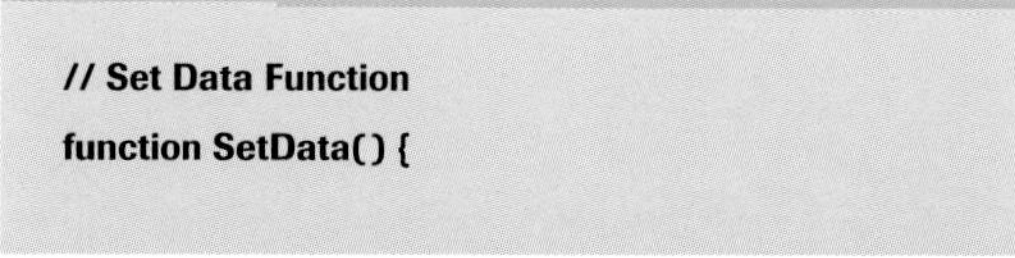

```
// Set Data Function
function SetData() {
```

Create the function called **SetData()**.

3 Create a set of Array objects to hold your menu set and the sets of items that will make up each of those menus.

The ActionScript Array object uses a zero-based counting system, which is why 3 is specified as the number of elements for menus instead of 4. The elements are numbered 0, 1, 2, and 3. You've been conditioned to start counting from one because you were taught that from the time you started numbering your fingers and toes. So in a zero-based system, your first finger would be zero, and the last one would be nine.

You now have an Array object named **Menus**, which will hold the data for all four of our menus. As it stands, **Menus** has four declared, empty elements, each of which can hold numbers or text strings. The data for each menu consists of more than a simple number or piece of text, so each of the array elements will be converted to an object for added flexibility. The simplest of all object classes or types is Object, so four new instances of that are created to populate the array.

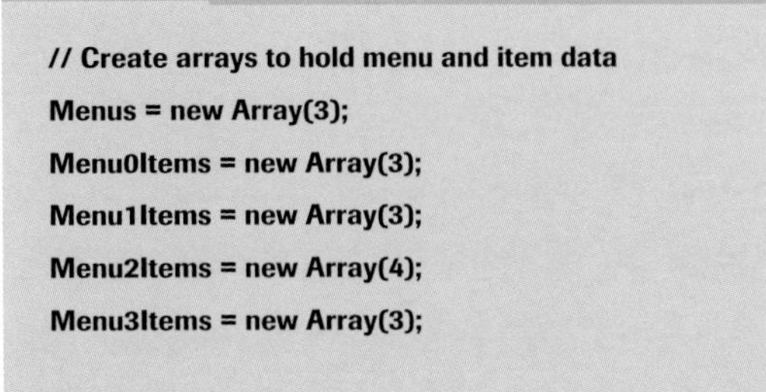

```
// Create arrays to hold menu and item data
Menus = new Array(3);
Menu0Items = new Array(3);
Menu1Items = new Array(3);
Menu2Items = new Array(4);
Menu3Items = new Array(3);
```

Insert the **SetData()** function and the **Menu** array to the ActionScript.

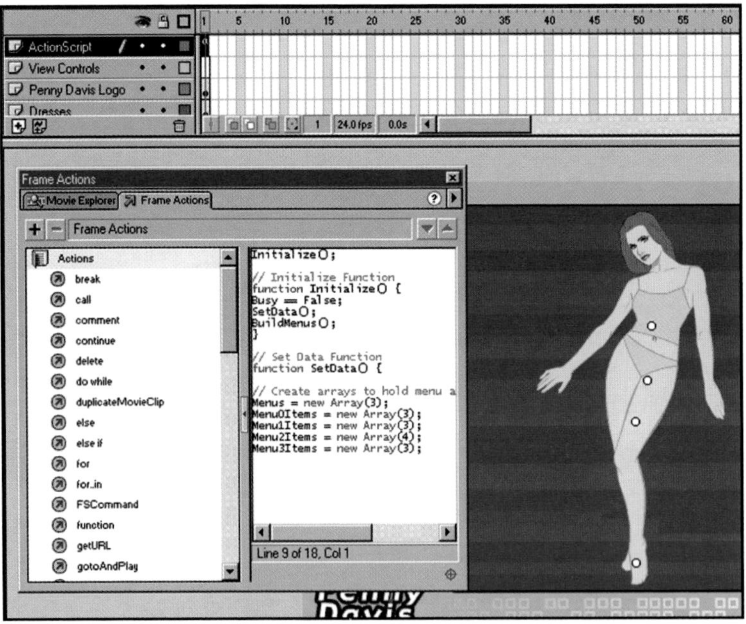

This figure shows the **SetData()** function and the Menu array you are inserting on the ActionScript layer.

4 Enter the ActionScript to make each Menu element an Object object.

Object is more flexible than numbers or text, and it can hold much more than just a single piece of information. Next you get into the actual menu data.

```
// Create an object for each element in the Menus array
Menus[0] = new Object();
Menus[1] = new Object();
Menus[2] = new Object();
Menus[3] = new Object();
```

Use this code to make each Menu element an Object object.

5 Add data to element 0 of the **Menus** array by using this ActionScript:

```
// Populate the menu and item data
Menus[0].Name = "Dresses";
Menus[0].Width = 65;
Menus[0].Items = Menu0Items;
```

Use this code to assign a specified date to the menu.

You began with element 0 of the **Menus** array. You just made element 0 an Object object, so you can add data to it by setting its properties.

The **Items** property of element 0 is set to the **Menu0Items** array created back in step 2. Linking objects and arrays in this way is useful because you can refer to a menu's items as sub-sections of the menu array itself instead of having to refer to totally separate arrays. For example, **Menu0Items[0]** and **Menus[0].Items[0]** now refer to the same piece of data. They are, for all practical purposes, interchangeable.

6 Still working with element 0 of the **Menus** array, you can now fill in the details of all the items that fall under the Dresses category.

```
with (Menus[0]) {
        Items[0] = "None";
        Items[1] = "Elegant Floral Motif";
        Items[2] = "Exotic Cocktail";
        Items[3] = "Summer Fling Frock";
}
```

The **with** action allows for a block of statements operating on the same object to be abbreviated.

The **with** action is a space-saving tool used to perform a number of operations on the same object. In this case, you're setting a number of properties of the **Menus[0]** object, and **with** saves you from having to type **Menus[0]** at the beginning of each line.

The figure shows what the ActionScript should look like for this menu. That's one menu down! Just three to go.

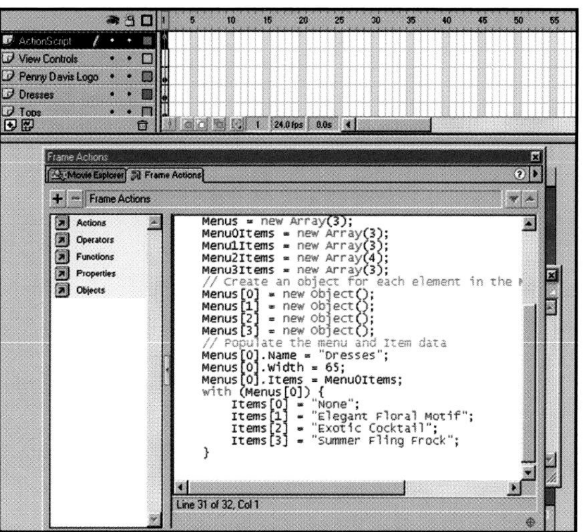

The code for the first menu on the ActionScript layer should match this figure.

7 To populate the remaining three menus, insert the script for each. Just be sure to close the **SetData()** function declaration at the end.

Now that all the menu data has been input, ActionScript has all the information it needs to build and manage the set of dynamic menus.

```
        Menus[1].Name = "Tops";
        Menus[1].Width = 70;
        Menus[1].Items = Menu1Items;
        with (Menus[1]) {
                Items[0] = "None";
                Items[1] = "Hipster Shirt";
                Items[2] = "Body T";
                Items[3] = "Classic Woollen Sweater";
        }
        Menus[2].Name = "Bottoms";
        Menus[2].Width = 55;
        Menus[2].Items = Menu2Items;
        with (Menus[2]) {
                Items[0] = "None";
                Items[1] = "Classic Stretch Jeans";
                Items[2] = "Hyper Short Denims";
                Items[3] = "Super Stretch Cargo Pants";
                Items[4] = "Lycra Cotton Blend Skirt";
        }
        Menus[3].Name = "Footwear";
        Menus[3].Width = 75;
        Menus[3].Items = Menu3Items;
        with (Menus[3]) {
                Items[0] = "None";
                Items[1] = "Toetap";
                Items[2] = "Evening Shade";
                Items[3] = "Classic Comfort Sandals";
        }
}
```

The menu data is stored in array elements for easy retrieval.

BUILDING, SHOWING, HIDING, AND SWITCHING

With all the necessary data in place, the next required function is **BuildMenus()**. **BuildMenus()** creates as many instances of the Menu symbol as needed and positions them according to the width attributes of each menu title.

1 Without leaving the first keyframe of the ActionScript layer, scroll to the bottom of the existing code and input the **BuildMenus()** function:

```
// Build Menus Function
function BuildMenus() {
    XPosition = 0;
    for (Counter = 0; Counter < Menus.Length; Counter ++) {
        XPosition = XPosition + Menus[Counter].Width;
        _root.AttachMovie("Menu", "Menu" add Counter, 100 + Counter);
        eval("Menu" add Counter).Name = Menus[Counter].Name;
        eval("Menu" add Counter)._x = XPosition;
        eval("Menu" add Counter)._y = 10;
    }
}
```

Add the **BuildMenus()** function to the ActionScript layer.

This function is invoked only once, during the **Initialize()** function, and it is designed to run off menu heading buttons for each element of the Menus array. The ***XPosition*** variable is used throughout to control the horizontal positioning of each menu. It starts at 0, the leftmost point of the Stage, and is increased after each loop according to how wide the current menu is. The vertical y coordinate of each menu is set to 10, but this value can be changed depending on how high or low the menu bar needs to appear.

The **for** action in this function repeats the enclosed set of actions as many times as the number of menus you have to build, which is equal to the value of **Menus.Length**. The **AttachMovie** action is used to create fresh instances of the Library's Menu symbol and attach them to the _root Timeline. Using the **eval** action to dynamically reference the newly created Menu instances, the ***Name*** variable and the ***_x*** and ***_y*** properties are set for each menu. Notice how elements of the **Menus** array can be specified not only by numbers, as in **Menus[2]**, but also by using variables, such as **Menus[Counter]**. This makes it easy to refer to a series of array elements in a loop, meaning that the **BuildMenus()** function can scale to any number of menu headings, all based on the value of **Menus.Length**.

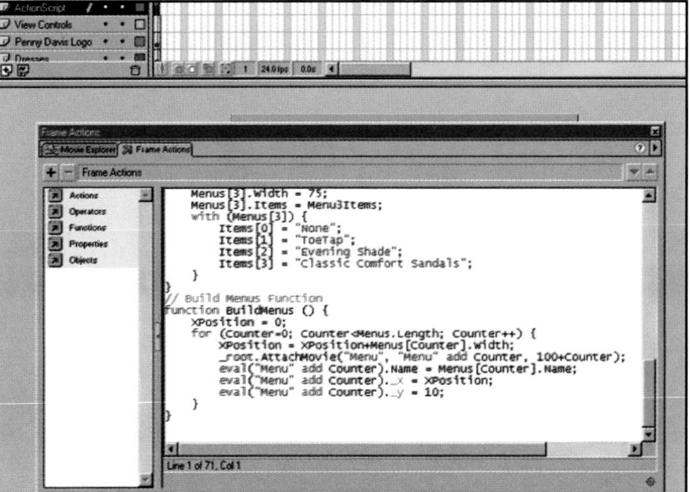

Counter ++ is the functional equivalent of **Counter = Counter + 1**. Using the double plus (**++**) or double minus (**--**) makes it easy to increment or decrement a value.

2 Define the next function, **ShowMenu()**.

```
// Show Menu Function
function ShowMenu() {
	for (Counter = 0; Counter < Menus[CurrentMenu].Items.Length; Counter ++) {
		_root.AttachMovie("Item", "Item" add Counter, 200 + Counter);
		eval("Item" add Counter).Name = Menus[CurrentMenu].Items[Counter];
		eval("Item" add Counter)._x = eval("Menu" add CurrentMenu)._x;
		eval("Item" add Counter)._y = (Counter * 20) + 30;
	}
	eval("Menu" add CurrentMenu).MenuOn = true;
}
```

The **ShowMenu()** function creates instances of Item, positions them, and sets their **MenuOn** variable to **true**.

ShowMenu() is similar to **BuildMenu()**, except that it is called when one of the menu headings is actually clicked. Rather than replicating Menu instances, **ShowMenu()** creates the correct number of Item instances and aligns them vertically under the corresponding menu heading.

Once again, the **for** action is used to count through a given number of elements in an array, this time the items in the menu being shown. First, the **attachMovie** action creates each new menu item, drawing on the Item symbol in the Library. Then the ***CurrentMenu*** variable is used in conjunction with the **eval** action to dynamically set the positioning of the items and the ***Name*** variable, which determines the text displayed on each item.

The ***MenuOn*** variable is a flag used to keep track of whether a menu is active. ***MenuOn*** is used when the menu button is clicked, the logic being that if you click a menu that is on already, you'll want to hide it, and that if it's off, you'll want to show it. It's crucial to keep the ***MenuOn*** variable in each Menu updated at all times in this manner to prevent the system from behaving oddly.

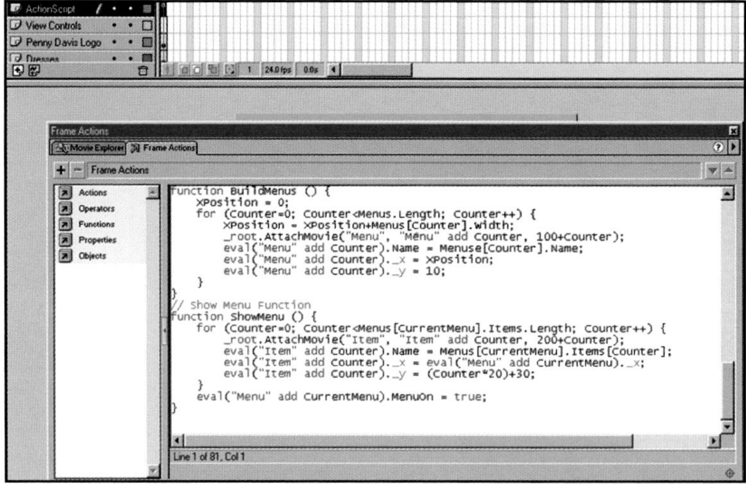

Add the **ShowMenu()** function to the ActionScript layer.

3 Add the ActionScript for **HideFunction()**, the last menu-related function.

HideFunction() is used to remove all the Item instances created by the function in step 2, acting as a menu "eraser." It essentially works in reverse of the **ShowMenu** function, using the **removeMovieClip** action to remove all the instances of Item belonging to the menu being deactivated.

```
// Hide Menu Function
function HideMenu() {
for (Counter = 0; Counter < Menus[CurrentMenu].Items.Length; Counter ++) {
        eval("_root.Item" add Counter).removeMovieClip();
}
eval("Menu" add CurrentMenu).MenuOn = false;
_root.Busy = false;
}
```

The **HideMenu()** function removes all instances of Item and sets the **MenuOn** variable of the current menu to false in order to deactivate it.

If you've run the final version of the Product Demonstration, you'll notice that the menu items flicker momentarily after you click them. This is added feedback to the visitor indicating that the click has actually done something, but while the flicker is happening, ***_root.Busy*** *is* set to **true** so that the other menu buttons know not to do anything! The **HideMenu()** function returns **_root.Busy** back to **false** so that the menu buttons can continue accepting input.

4 Add the ActionScript that defines **SwitchItems()**, the final function on this keyframe.

```
// Switch Items Function
function SwitchItems(Item) {
eval(Menus[CurrentMenu].Name).gotoAndStop(Item);
}
```

Add the **SwitchItems()** function to the ActionScript layer.

This function is invoked every time the user clicks an individual menu item and is designed to "switch" the product group movie clips so they display the correct frame. The **eval** action is used to take a piece of text such as **_root.theObject** and substitute it for a reference to the object during playback. **eval** is useful in situations such as this where the object being referred to changes depending on the information passed in the function arguments.

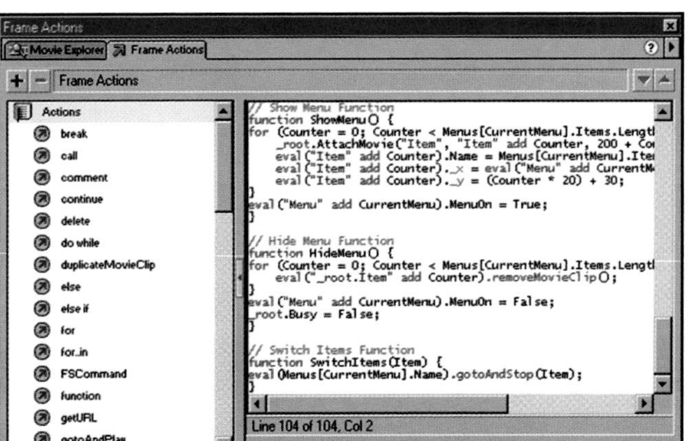

In the **SwitchItems()** function, the Item argument is passed from the menu item button and specifies the frame number to go to in the appropriate product clip.

How It Works

The code you've entered so far is really the backbone of the dynamic menu system, but the Menu and Item symbols are like the limbs that help it do something useful. If you take a look inside each, you'll see a dynamic text field and a button. The text fields are both named Name, and they display the menu and item Name text set out in our object definitions. The Menu button calls **ShowMenu()** and **HideMenu()** in response to various mouse input, and the Item button calls **SwitchItem()**, causing the user's chosen product to appear in the demonstration.

The dynamic menu system takes full advantage of object-oriented ActionScript features such as the Array and Object objects, as well as functions, event, and symbol linkage. When you model a set of menus and menu items as data, ActionScript can use that data as a kind of map for generating the actual text and buttons the user interacts with.

In particular, the Array object can store a stack of related objects and variables that can be accessed numerically, simplifying the process of looping through all the menu data. Using that data, the **AttachMovie** action generates the right number of instances of symbols stored in the Library—alleviating the need to lay out menu buttons and labels by hand.

Because array elements are numbered, looping actions such as for can be used to repeat a set of actions from element 0 to element *n*, where *n* is the last element. **AttachMovieClip** and **removeMovieClip** either add or remove instances of the Menu and Item symbols from the Library, allowing for menus to be built, shown, or hidden on-the-fly. This gives the impression that the menus have been hand-arranged, when in fact they are created, positioned, and labeled according to the data in the menu arrays.

Manipulating the ***_x*** and ***_y*** properties of each new instance controls its positioning, and a dynamic text field Name in both Menu and Item allows for the setting of its "label." Finally, **eval** makes it easy to refer to a *different* object every time the **for** loop cycles through a new array element, by allowing text to be combined with the current value of ***Counter*** and then evaluated as a reference to the desired Menu or Item instance.

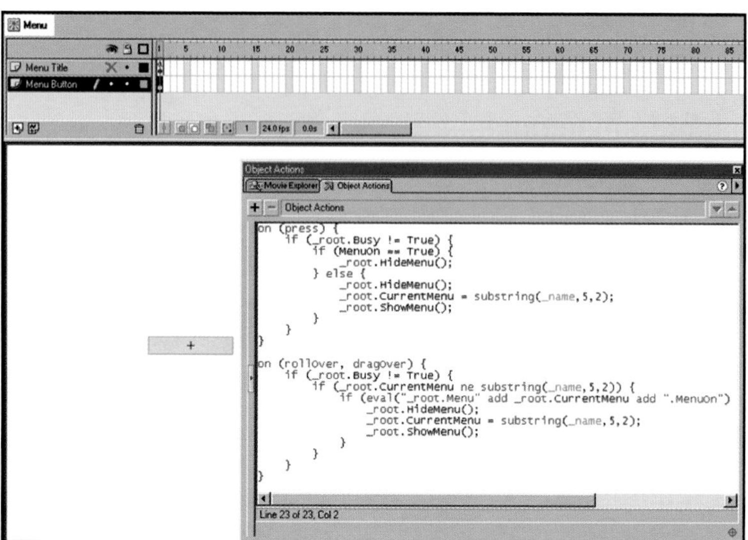

The code assigned to the menu button calls the **ShowMenu()** and **HideMenu()** functions.

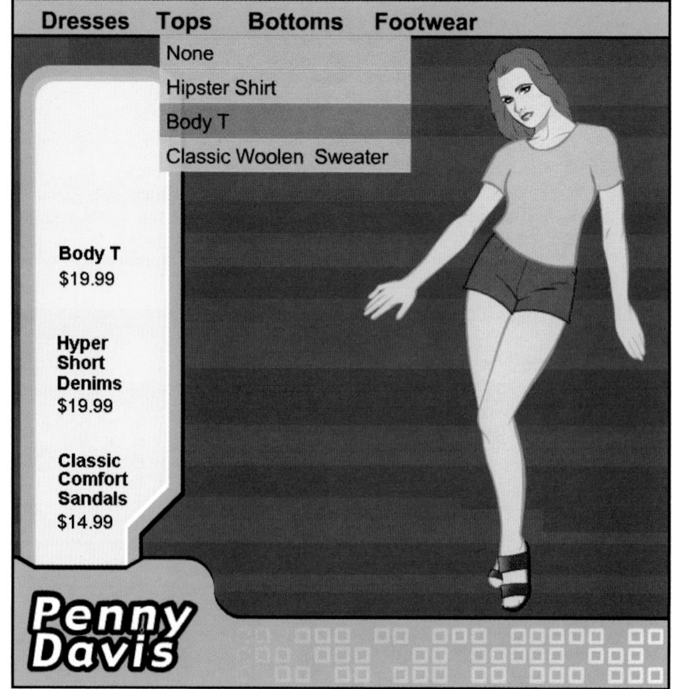

Dress the mannequin by selecting items from the menu.

PENNY DAVIS ONLINE RETAILING LLC

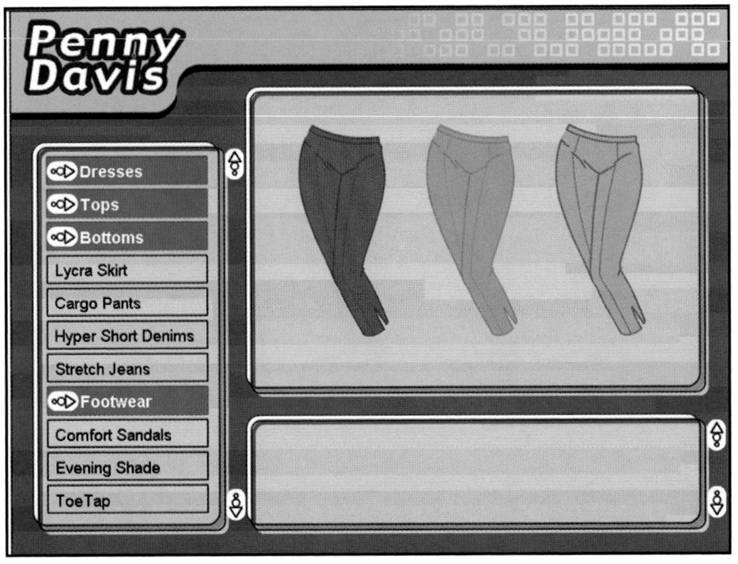

Chapter 15

Chapter 16

Chapter 17

"You've got to take the initiative and play your game. In a decisive set, confidence is the difference."

—CHRIS EVERT

PIYK'S WEBFOLIO

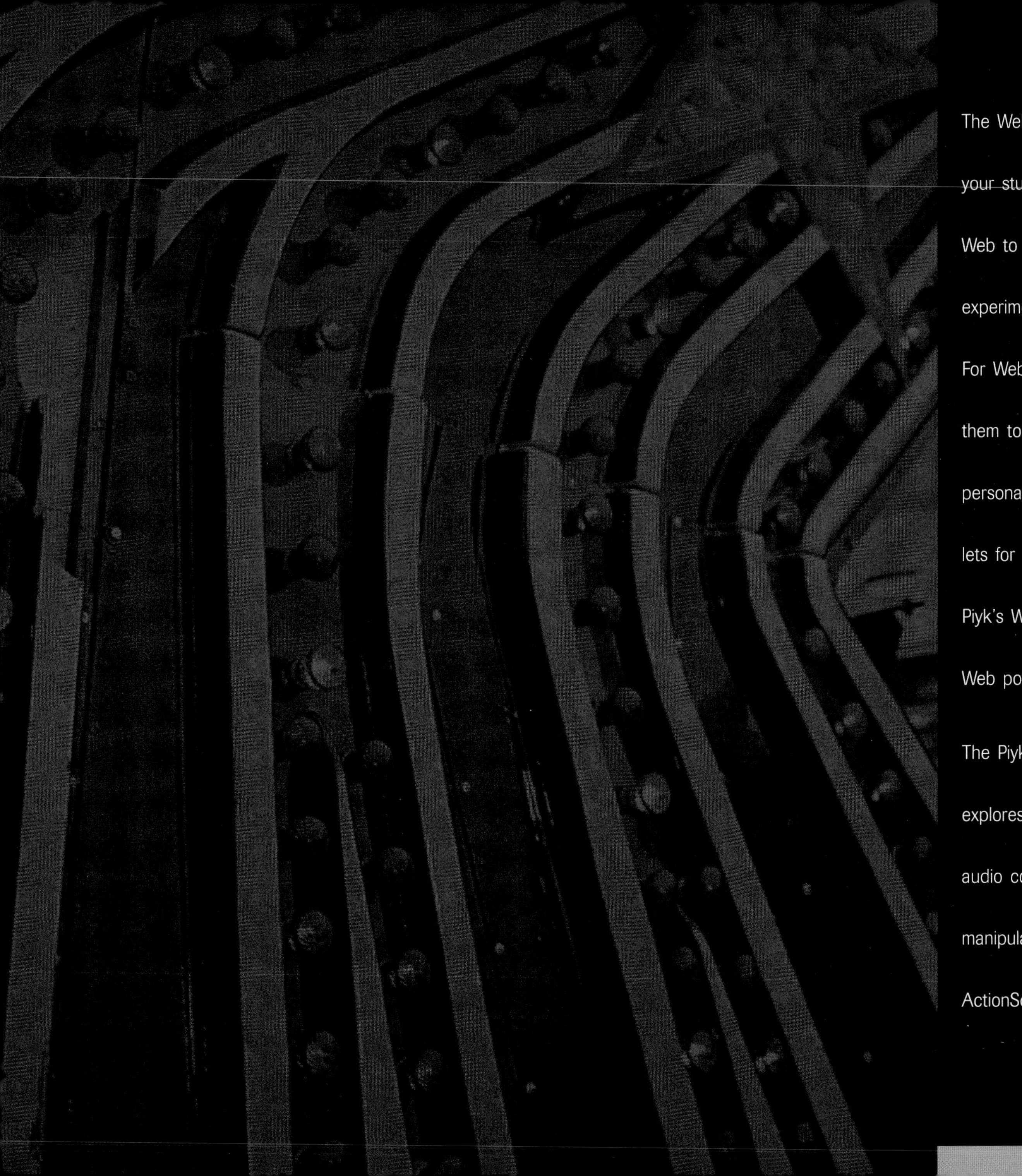

The Web is nothing if not a great place to strut your stuff. Web designers naturally turn to the Web to display their portfolios and conduct experiments to develop and hone their skills. For Web designers whose normal work forces them to stick to more mundane pursuits, the personal Web site can be one of the few outlets for more rewarding and even fun pursuits. Piyk's Webfolio is a fictional Web designer's Web portfolio site.

The Piyk's Webfolio section of this book explores techniques such as programming audio controls, generating mouse effects, and manipulating movie clip attributes with ActionScript.

This chapter demonstrates the new Flash 5 sound methods, such as selecting a sound or song, playing it, stopping it, pausing it, and rewinding it. In this chapter, you also see how to use a dial to change the volume and a slider to change the speaker balance (pan).

18

SETTING UP AUDIO CONTROLS

By Jennifer S. Hall

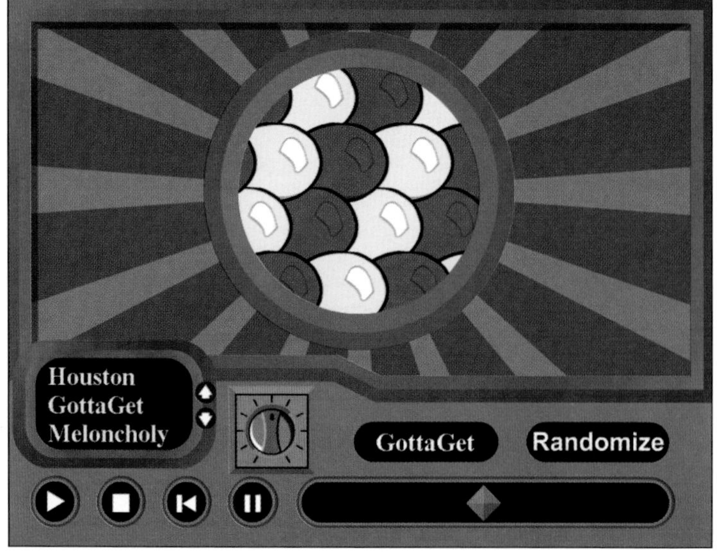

PLAYING AND STOPPING SOUNDS

In this section, you write the code to play a sound and to stop a sound by using a new feature in Flash 5: the Sound object. This object lets you easily control sound without actually placing it in a layer. It can be controlled while the sound exists only in the Library.

1 Open the file VolumeControls_Start.fla in the Chapter 18 folder on the CD and save it to your hard drive.

The technique starts with the volume controls already placed but not working. The capability to select a song is working. For a final version of what you will create in this section, see Volume Controls_Final.fla.

2 Open the **Init** code, which already has the code that names the sounds. Enter this code at the bottom above the **Stop()** command:

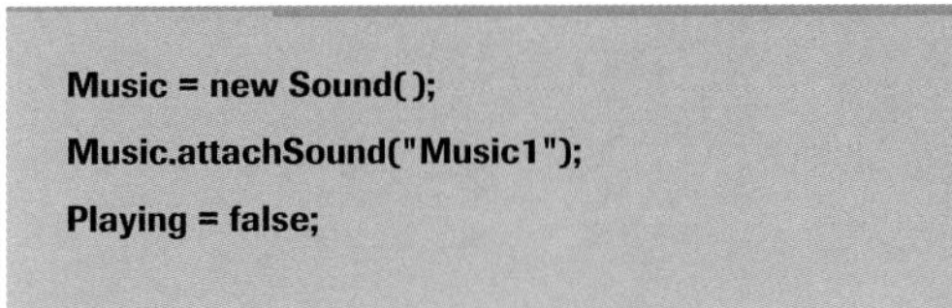

```
Music = new Sound();
Music.attachSound("Music1");
Playing = false;
```

Add three lines of code to the **Init** code on the Code layer.

This code creates a new Sound object (from the Flash 5 Library) called Music:

Music = new Sound();

It also attaches a sound to it called Music1 using the **attachSound** method of the sound class.

Music.attachSound("Music1");

The ***Playing*** flag is used later to determine if a sound is playing while the visitor selects a new sound.

Playing = false;

In the next step, you will use the Linkage window to name the sound.

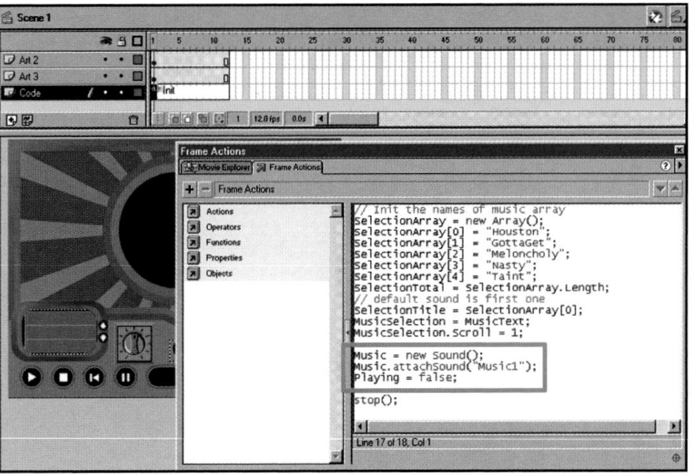

The three new lines are inserted in the **Init** code on the Code layer.

3 Select Cominhouston_lr.wav from the Audio folder in the Library. Select the Options pull-down menu (in the Library window) and select Linkage. Select the Export This Symbol button and type **Music1** in the Name field (no quotes and no space).

This allows the sound to be linked to the code and played. The name in the Linkage window must be the same as the name used in the **attachSound** call.

```
Music.attachSound("Music1");
```

4 Select the Play button and attach this code:

```
// start music playing
on (release) {
        Music.start();
        Playing = true;
}
```

Attach this code to the Play button to initiate playback of the music.

When a visitor clicks the Play button, this code starts the selected music and sets the ***Playing*** flag to **true**. The music starts with the code:

```
Music.start();
```

The **Playing = true;** code sets a flag for later use and has nothing to do with the music starting or stopping. Notice that you did all this on a mouse release instead of a mouse press. This is called a forgiving button, and it allows the visitor a chance to change his or her mind. If the mouse is pressed and released while it is located on top of the Play button, the music will start. However, if the mouse is pressed while on top of the Play button but released somewhere else, nothing will happen. Now you need to stop it.

5 Select the Stop button and attach this code:

```
// stop music playing
on (release) {
        Music.stop();
        Playing = false;
}
```

Attach this code to the Stop button to halt playback of the music.

This code stops the music when the visitor clicks and releases the Stop button:

```
Music.stop();
```

This code sets the ***Playing*** flag to **false**.

```
Playing = false;
```

Right now the reason for using the ***Playing*** flag is not obvious. It will be used when the visitor selects other sounds to play.

6 Test and play the program. Stop and start the sound, and then choose a different selection. Notice that you can choose a selection even when another selection is already playing. The visitor must click Play to hear the new selection.

Rewinding and Pausing on Command

You will now set the music to rewind and pause on command. These actions are not built into the Sound object code as the start and stop commands were.

1 Select the Rewind button, enter this code, and then test it:

This code stops the music.

Music.stop();

This code restarts the music from the beginning, creating an easy rewind.

Music.start();

Next you set up the pausing. This code is a little trickier because you want to resume playing the music at the same place it was paused. You can use the **getTimer** ActionScript for this.

```
on (release) {
	Music.stop();
	Music.start();
}
```

Set up the code that rewinds the music to the beginning of the song.

2 Add this code to **Init** in the Code layer:

This global variable will keep track of the pause time—where the music was when the visitor clicked the Pause button.

```
PauseMusicTime = 0;
```

Enter the global variable that helps keep track of where the song was when paused.

3 Select the Play button and replace this line

Music.start();

with this code:

The **Music.start** command passes in two parameters. The first parameter is where to start the music (in seconds), and the second parameter is how many times to loop. You have set the loop (the second parameter) to **100** so that it will loop 100 times, over and over again.

Music.start(0, 100);

```
//check if music paused
	if (PauseMusicTime == 0) {
		Music.start(0, 100);
	} else {
		Music.start(PauseMusicTime, 1);
	}
	startMusicTime = getTimer();
	PauseMusicTime = 0;
	Paused = false;
```

Edit the code assigned to the Play button.

If ***PauseMusicTime*** is set to **0** (in other words, if the visitor has not paused the music), you want to start the music at the beginning. So the time to start the music is **0**, which is the first parameter.

```
Music.start(0, 100);
```

Otherwise, start the music at the paused point in the music and set the loop to **1**. If the loop is set to **100**, the music repeats itself 100 times from the paused point to the end, so it doesn't repeat from the beginning. If the loop is set to **1**, as soon as the sound is finished playing, it stops, and the visitor has to restart the music again by selecting the Play button.

```
Music.start(PauseMusicTime, 1);
```

The ***StartMusicTime*** variable keeps track of how many seconds the music has played, and it is started with the **getTimer()** call.

```
startMusicTime = getTimer();
```

The ***PausedMusicTime*** variable is set to **0** because you are not paused. Remember, this code is attached to the Play button and is activated when the visitor selects Play (so not paused).

```
PauseMusicTime = 0;
```

The ***Paused*** flag is set to **false** for the same reason as above.

```
Paused = false;
```

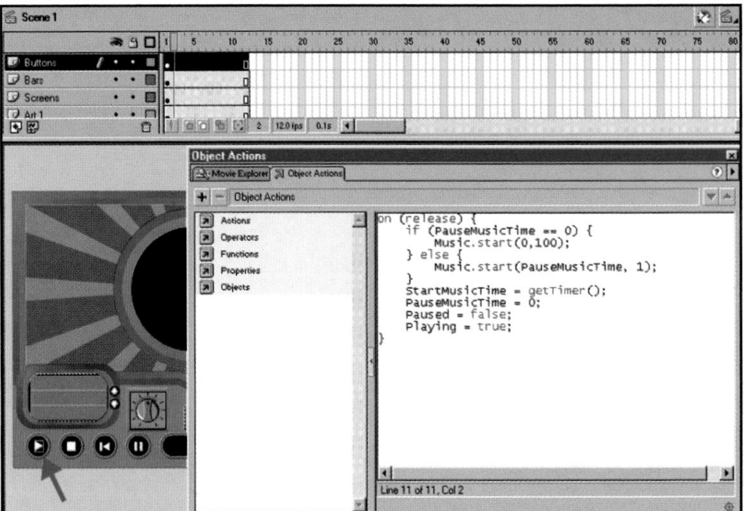

The Play button code is edited.

4 Add this code to the Stop button within the release brackets:

```
PauseMusicTime = 0;
Paused = false;
```

Add this code to the Stop button to accommodate pausing.

This code is used if the visitor has the sound paused and then clicks the Stop button. The code turns off the pause, both ***PauseMusicTime*** and the ***Paused*** flag, which allows the music to start at the beginning of the sound when the visitor selects Play.

5 Select the Rewind button and replace the line

Music.start();

with:

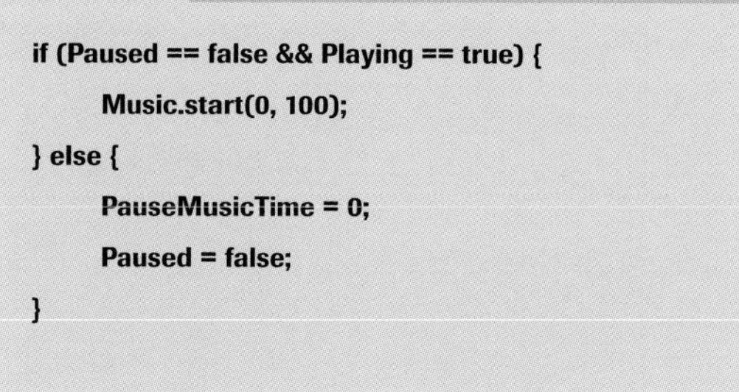

```
if (Paused == false && Playing == true) {
        Music.start(0, 100);
} else {
        PauseMusicTime = 0;
        Paused = false;
}
```

Edit the Rewind button to accommodate pausing.

You add a check for the paused music. If the music is not paused and the music is playing, as determined by this line:

if (Paused == false and Playing == true)

Flash starts the music at the beginning and loops 100 times, as indicated in this line:

Music.start(0, 100);

Otherwise, the music is either stopped or paused. When the music is paused, you want Flash to reset the paused settings. (Remember that this code is attached to the Rewind button.) These lines reset ***PauseMusicTime*** and the **Paused** flag.

PauseMusicTime = 0;
Paused = false;

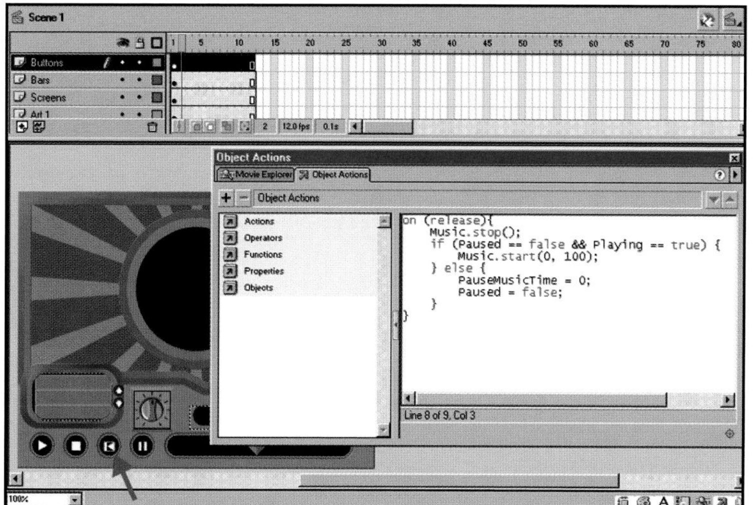

The code for the Rewind button is edited.

6 Select the Pause button and attach this code:

```
// pause music playing
on (release) {
        Music.stop();
        PauseMusicTime = (getTimer()-StartMusicTime)/1000;
        Paused = true;
        Playing = false;
}
```

Assign this code to the Pause button.

This code stops the music:

Music.stop();

Flash then uses **getTimer** and the ***StartMusicTime*** variable (which specifies when the music started playing) to compute how long the music has been playing:

PauseMusicTime = (getTimer()-StartMusicTime)/1000;

The script subtracts the current time (**getTimer**) from the time the music started (***StartMusicTime***), and to get seconds (**getTimer** is in milliseconds), you divide by 1000.

This line sets the ***Paused*** flag to **true**:

```
Paused = true;
```

This line sets the ***Playing*** flag to **false**:

```
Playing = false;
```

7 Test this code and play with the Pause and Rewind buttons.

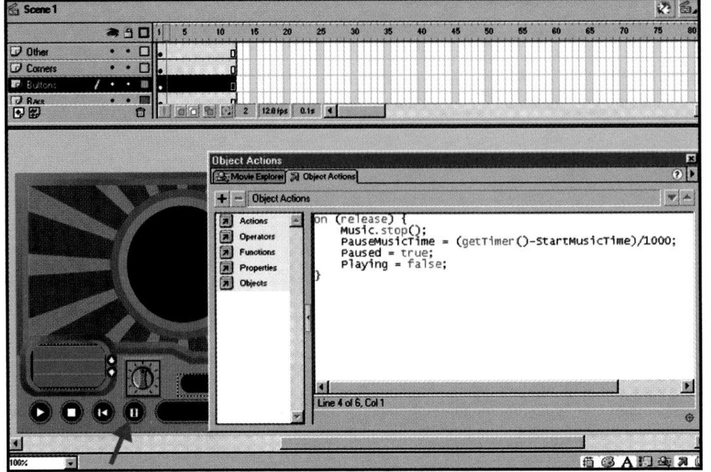

The code for the Pause button is applied.

Creating the Speaker Balance Control

Speaker balance (pan) is also included in Flash 5. You can use a slider bar to control the pan of the speakers. The slider button slides on a line 200 pixels long.

1 Select the Slider button and attach this code to the button:

After this movie clip is loaded in the **onClipEvent (load)**, the script defines an array to hold the drag constrain (**Constrain**).

```
Constrain = new Array(_x-100, _y, _x+100, _y);
```

The array consists of left, top, right, and bottom values for the constrain box (a box to which the Slider button is constrained). Because you want the slider to slide in a straight line horizontally, the top and bottom are the same (_*y*). You know that the bar to slide on is 200 pixels long, and the slider button is centered on the bar. So the left and right constrains are computed based on this. Right is equal to _x–100, and left is equal to _x+100. These constrains are computed using the starting position of the Slider button, assuming it is centered on the slider bar.

```
// set drag constraint on load
// compute the percentage of pixels for 100% pan
onClipEvent (load) {
    Constrain = new Array(_x-100, _y, _x+100, _y);
    PanFactor = (Constrain[2]-Constrain[0])/100;
    _root.Pan = ((_x-Constrain[0])/PanFactor)*2-100;
}
// test for dragging and change the balance
onClipEvent (enterFrame) {
    if (Drag == true) {
        _root.Pan = ((_x-Constrain[0])/PanFactor;
        _root.Music.setPan(_root.Pan);
    }
}
```

Add the Slider button code for dragging and panning.

Remember, based on this code, the Slider button needs to be centered in both directions on the slider bar.

The pan setting runs from 0 to 100. The **PanFactor** is a percentage used to compute how much 1 pixel of movement along the slider bar changes the pan setting. **PanFactor** starts with the length of the slider bar (in pixels) and divides it by 100 (the maximum the pan can be set to) to get a percentage of pan change per pixel change.

```
PanFactor = (Constrain[2]-Constrain[0])/100;
```

Finally, you set the **_root.Pan** to the current pan setting so that at the start of the program, the pan setting matches the location of the pan button.

```
_root.Pan = (_(x-Constrain[0])/PanFactor)*2-100;
```

This calculates the position of the pan button in pixels along the slider by using the *x* position of the pan button (_x) and subtracting from it the furthest left position of the slider. The result is a number of pixels and needs to be in the form of a number from –100 to 100. So you divide that number by the **PanFactor**.

During the **enterFrame** of the movie clip (**onClipEvent (enterFrame)**), you determine if dragging is occurring (**Drag = true**). ***Drag*** is a flag that will be set when the visitor presses the mouse button on the pan button (you will do this in the next step). If the visitor is dragging the pan button, the actual pan for the speakers is determined by the position of the pan button on the slider.

Finally the pan is set in the Sound object (**Music**) using the **setPan** method and passing in as a parameter the new pan setting (**_root.Pan**).

```
_root.Music.setPan(_root.Pan);
```

The code for dragging and panning is assigned to the Slider button.

When the slider is moved to the right, only the right stereo signal plays.

2 Select the Diamond button inside the **SliderButton** movie. This is the pan button. Attach this code to it:

```
// catch press and start dragging
on (press) {
    startDrag (this, true, Constrain[0], Constrain[1], Constrain[2], Constrain[3]);
    Drag = true;
}
on (release, releaseOutside) {
    stopDrag ();
    Drag = false;
}
```

Assign this code to the Diamond button, which is inside the Slider Button movie clip.

When the visitor selects the pan button, the drag of this button is enabled and constrained to the **Constrain** array you defined with the **onClipEvent(load)** code above.

```
startDrag (this, true, Constrain[0], Constrain[1],
➥Constrain[2], Constrain[3]);
```

(The ➥ symbol you see here is for editorial purposes only.)

Because this array was defined during the loading of this movie clip, it is local to this movie clip. You also need to set the ***Drag*** flag to **true**.

```
Drag = true;
```

On release of the button, you disable the dragging:

```
stopDrag ();
```

This line sets the **Drag** flag to **false**:

```
Drag = false;
```

As long as the visitor holds the mouse button down over the pan button, the button will slide back and forth, constrained to the pan slider. Also, because of the **onClipEvent (enterFrame)** code that checks to see if the ***Drag*** flag is **true**, the pan setting for the speakers will be updated every time the pan button movie clip enters a frame, currently set to 12 frames per second (fps).

The **Constrain** code keeps the slider from moving up or down, even when the viewer's mouse moves up or down during a drag operation.

3 To make sure you get the correct balance each time a song starts, add a line of code to the beginning of the code attached to the Play button (which you set up in step 3 of the first section).

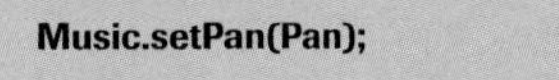

```
Music.setPan(Pan);
```

Insert the line of code that sets the **Pan** function when the visitor presses the Play button.

This code sets the pan of the music as the music starts. So even if the visitor changed the pan setting when no music was playing, the pan setting would take effect as soon as the visitor started playing music.

4 Test the movie and play with the pan feature. Sliding the button moves the sound balance from one speaker to the other. Also try starting and stopping a sound; note that the balance remains as you left it.

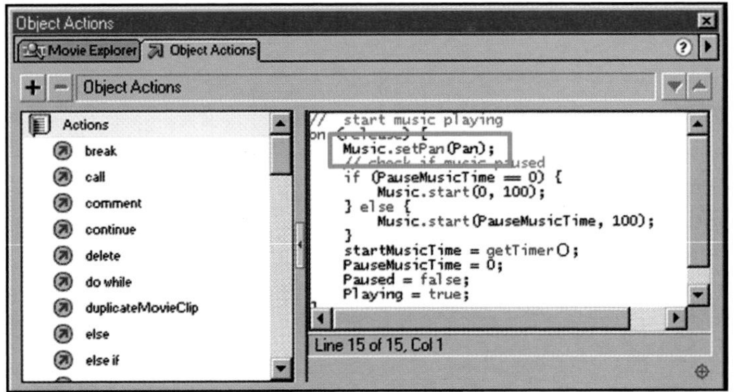

The call to the Panning code is added to the Play button code.

Using a Rotating Dial for the Volume Control

The volume control could be a slider similar to the pan control. However, for variety, a rotating dial is used here so you have to use a little math.

1 Attach this code to the Dial movie clip:

This code runs upon loading the Dial movie:

```
(onClipEvent (load))
```

This code initializes the volume to 50(%):

```
DialVolume = 50;
```

This code computes the **VolumeFactor**:

```
VolumeFactor = 100/300;
```

The dial has movement of 300 degrees, and the volume goes from 0 to 100. So you calculate a percentage of volume to degrees to get the **VolumeFactor**. This is used to calculate the volume based on the degree rotation it has on the dial. **RotAmount**, in this line, represents the degrees the dial rotates at one time, which is 5 degrees:

```
RotAmount = 5;
```

```
//load the variable for the volume dial
onClipEvent (load) {
    DialVolume = 50;
    // based on possiblity of 300 degrees with the dial
    VolumeFactor = 100/300;
    RotAmount = 5;
    var DialPointer = this.getBounds(_root);
    DialCenter = new Array();
    // dial middle
    DialCenter[0] = DialPointer.XMin+(DialPointer.Xmax-DialPointer.XMin)/2;
    DialCenter[1] = DialPointer.YMin+(DialPointer.Ymax-DialPointer.YMin)/2;
}
```

Enter this code, which should be assigned to the Dial movie clip. The code instantiates a series of variables for volume, control, and the dial functionality.

Determine the center point of the dial with respect to the Stage.

```
var DialPointer = this.getBounds(_root);
```

This value is used to compute where the mouse wants to move the dial to. You compute the center using the **getBounds** method of the Dial movie clip, and then you save the information in an array.

```
DialCenter = new Array();
```

The **DialCenter** array index 0 is the *x* center of the dial. You subtract the right side of the dial (***DialPointer.XMax***) from the left side of the dial (***DialPointer.XMin***) and divide it by 2 (halve it). Then add the result to the left side of the dial (***DialPointer.XMax***), and that gives you the center.

```
DialCenter[0] = DialPointer.XMin+(DialPointer.Xmax-
➥DialPointer.XMin)/2;
```

(The ➥ symbol you see here is for editorial purposes only.)

The **DialCenter** array index 1 is the *y* center of the dial. You perform the same calculations you did for the *x* center, but you use the top and bottom of the dial instead.

```
DialCenter[1] = DialPointer.YMin+(DialPointer.Ymax-
➥DialPointer.YMin)/2;
```

(The ➥ symbol you see here is for editorial purposes only.)

You calculate this so that no matter where the Dial is placed on the Stage during authoring mode, the code will still work. In other words, no hard coded numbers indicate that when the mouse is at *x* and *y* position, move the dial to ***x1*** and ***y1***. Instead, it is self-contained.

The dial and volume control codes are assigned to the Dial movie clip.

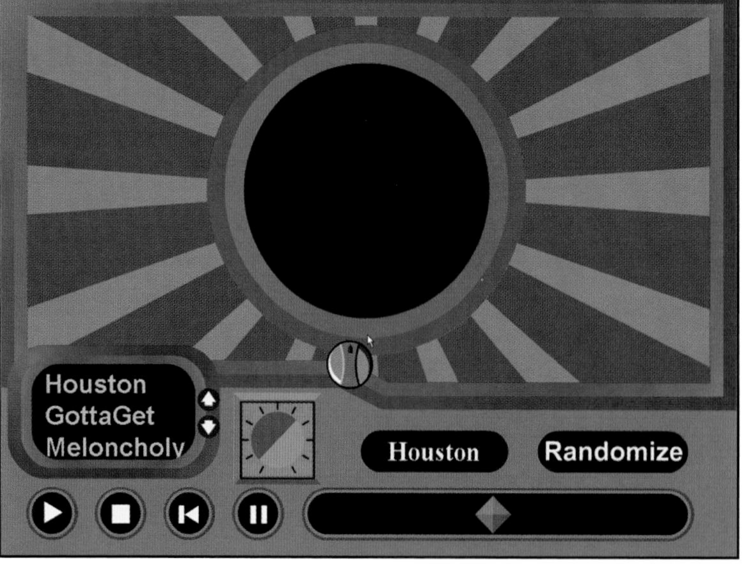

The Dial code works properly no matter where the Dial movie clip is positioned.

2 Attach the code to the Dial button within the Dial movie:

This code sets a flag to say the visitor is changing the volume. When the visitor presses the mouse button on the dial, the ***VolumeChange*** flag is set to **true**.

```
on (press) {
    VolumeChange = true;
}
```

When the visitor releases the mouse button, the ***VolumeChange*** flag is set to **false**.

```
on (release, releaseOutside) {
    .VolumeChange = false;
}
```

Notice the **on (release)** also has a catch for **on (releaseOutside)**. This way, if the visitor releases the mouse press outside the button, the code stops changing the volume also. If you didn't have the **on (releaseOutside)** catch, the dial would continue to rotate, and the volume would continue to change as the mouse moved around, even after the visitor had released the mouse button.

```
// set up for change volume
on (press) {
    VolumeChange = true;
}
on (release, releaseOutside) {
    .VolumeChange = false;
}
```

Edit the Dial movie clip and assign this code to the Dial button.

3 Add this code attached to the Dial movie clip but below the **onClipEvent (load)**. This is where the main action happens:

All of this code is done in **onClipEvent (enterFrame)** and only if the ***VolumeChange*** flag is set to **true**.

```
if (VolumeChange == true) {
```

Each time the Dial movie clip loops through a frame (12 fps) and the visitor has selected to change the volume by holding down the mouse button while pointing to the volume dial, all the ActionScript is executed. This ActionScript, which provides most of the **Dial** action, is a little more complicated than the Slider button. It will be broken down into smaller sections below.

```
//check every loop
onClipEvent (enterFrame) {
    // do if changing volume
    if (VolumeChange == true) {
        var DialRot = this._rotation;
        // compute new dial position
        var PosX = _root._xmouse-DialCenter[0];
        var PosY = DialCenter[1]-_root._ymouse;
        NewDial = (180/Math.PI)*Math.atan2(PosY, PosX);
        if (NewDial>-180 and NewDial<-90) {
            Newdial = NewDial+360;
        }
```

continues

Enter this code as the engine for the dial functionality and for the volume control.

```
var DialRot = this._rotation;
// compute new dial position
var PosX = _root._xmouse-DialCenter[0];
var PosY = DialCenter[1]-_root._ymouse;
```

This code sets the variable ***DialRot***, which is the rotation amount that the dial is currently rotated.

```
var DialRot = this._rotation;
```

This uses the **_rotation** property of the dial movie (***this***). The values ***PosX*** and ***PosY*** establish the mouse position in relation to the center of the dial.

```
var PosX = _root._xmouse-DialCenter[0];
var PosY = DialCenter[1]-_root._ymouse;
```

In other words, this code determines whether the mouse is to the right or left of the center of the dial, whether the mouse is above or below the center of the dial, and by how much in both cases.

```
    // convert to degrees
NewDial = (180/Math.PI)*Math.atan2(PosY, PosX);
    if (NewDial>-180 and NewDial<-90) {
        Newdial = NewDial+360;
    }
        // fix for compass coordinate
    NewDial = -(NewDial-90);
```

For ease of comparison, the mouse position and the rotation of the dial are converted into the same units (degrees). The rotation is already in degrees; however, the starting position of the dial is considered 0 degrees, which in this case is straight up. This is not where 0 degrees is when you compute the degrees of the mouse, so you will need to compensate for this difference. To compute the degree the mouse is compared to the center of the dial, you will use **atan2**. This is a new Flash 5 math routine that returns the angle of a point (***PosY***,***PosX***) with respect to the center (0,0).

```
Math.atan2(PosY,PosX);
```

continued

```
            // fix for compass coordinate
        NewDial = -(NewDial-90);
        // check for out of range
        if (NewDial>150) {
            NewDial = 150;
        }
        if (NewDial<-150) {
            NewDial = -150;
        }
        if (NewDial>DialRot) {
            this._rotation = DialRot+rotAmount;
        } else if (NewDial<DialRot) {
            this._rotation = DialRot-rotAmount;
        }
        DialVolume = (this._rotation+150)*VolumeFactor;
        _root.Music.setVolume(DialVolume);
    }
}
```

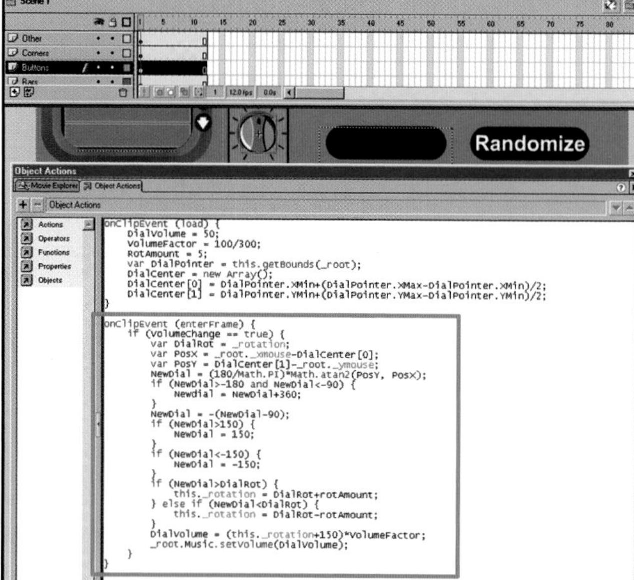

The dial and volume control engine is added to the Dial movie clip (not the Dial button within the Dial movie clip) after the **onClipEvent (load)** code.

atan2 gives the angle of the mouse position with respect to the center, but it is in radians. So you must multiply the angle by (180/pi) to convert it to degrees.

```
NewDial = (180/Math.PI)*Math.atan2(PosY, PosX);
```

This returns the angle of the mouse in degrees; however, the dial needs to move toward the mouse in a smooth fashion based on where the mouse is. The current ***NewDial*** variable is perfect for all areas of the dial except for the lower left. You need to make a slight adjustment in the computation to allow the dial to move toward the mouse even in this case.

```
if (NewDial>-180 and NewDial<-90) {
    Newdial = NewDial+360;
}
```

This checks to see whether the mouse position (***NewDial***) is in the lower left, and if it is, 360 (degrees) is added to it. Because a circle is 360 degrees, this doesn't change the degrees, it only changes the direction the degree was calculated from (clockwise or counterclockwise).

The Dial rotation is given in compass coordinates (0 degrees is at the top), and ***NewDial*** uses 0 degrees on the right. Setting up the code to subtract 90 from the final ***NewDial*** angle converts the ***NewDial*** angle into compass coordinates.

```
// check for out of range
if (NewDial>150) {
    NewDial = 150;
}
if (NewDial<-150) {
    NewDial = -150;
}
if (NewDial>DialRot) {
    this._rotation = DialRot+rotAmount;
} else if (NewDial<DialRot) {
    this._rotation = DialRot-rotAmount;
}
```

When the dial is moved to the far right or left, a slight amount of angle compensation is required.

The dial moves toward the cursor during a **mouseDown** event.

```
DialVolume = (this._rotation+150)*VolumeFactor;
_root.Music.setVolume(DialVolume);
```

This code checks to ensure that the dial does not rotate past the dial marks (–150 and 150). If the mouse is pointing to an area past the marks, ***NewDial*** is set to the end mark.

```
if (NewDial>150) {
    NewDial = 150;
}
if (NewDial<-150) {
    NewDial = -150;
}
```

Then it checks to see if the new setting is greater than or less than the current setting, and it changes does the rotation accordingly. In other words, if the new setting (***NewDial***) is greater than the old setting (***DialRot***), the rotation is adjusted in the positive direction; if the new setting is less than the old setting, the rotation is adjusted in the negative direction. Notice that the rotation is done in increments of the ***rotAmount***.

```
if (NewDial>DialRot) {
    this._rotation = DialRot+rotAmount;
} else if (NewDial<DialRot) {
    this._rotation = DialRot-rotAmount;
}
```

Finally the code computes the volume (***DialVolume***). The placement of the dial (***this._rotation***) is based on 0 being at the top. Because the volume dial needs to change the volume for 0 at the lower left, you add 150 to ***this._rotation*** and then multiply the ***VolumeFactor*** to get a number from 0 to 100.

```
DialVolume = (this._rotation+150)*VolumeFactor;
```

This line sets the music to the new volume using the new **setVolume** method.

```
_root.Music.setVolume(DialVolume);
```

4 Test this code by moving the volume control.

The dial does not rotate beyond the fixed points.

The volume control defaults to a medium volume. When the dial is turned to the far left there is no volume, and when the dial is turned to the far right it is set to the maximum volume.

HOW IT WORKS

You have built all the sound controls, but not the selections. The sound selection is based on the nine sounds in the library; each selection is linked and given the name Music with a number, such as Music1, Music2, and so on. Init has an array of sound names that corresponds to each of the sounds in the Library. Also notice that a text box off the Stage contains each of these names, in the same order, one on each line. This text box displays a list from which visitors can select the names of sounds.

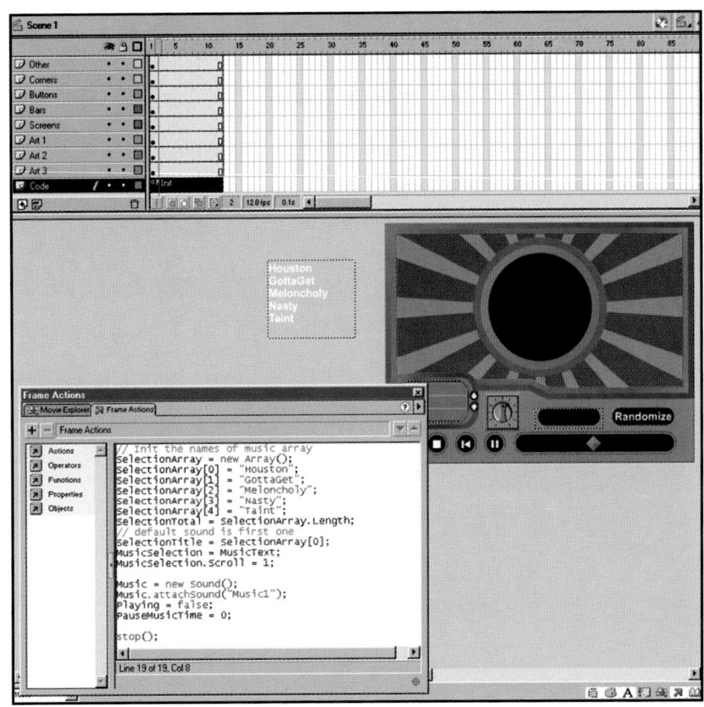

A text box over the Stage contains the names for all the songs.

When the movie starts, you do not want the selection buttons to show. To prevent that, each of the selection buttons, the scroll buttons, the selection text, and the rollover buttons has its **visibility** setting set to **false** on the **OnClipEvent (Load)** command, so each one must be a movie clip, not just a button.

When a visitor clicks the Selection button, the buttons are made visible, and the text from the list of names is put into the editable text box **MusicSelection**. This text box is big enough to show only three sounds at a time, so that's why it has the scroll buttons. The scroll buttons change the scroll setting in the **MusicSelection** to move either up or down the list.

Above the **MusicSelection** text box are three overlay buttons that show a graphic of a gray rectangle, only in the over and down frames. Because you want the letters below it to show through, the rectangle's alpha transparency is set to 60%. These buttons give the effect of a rollover selection, like menu bars.

When visitors select a sound to play, the overlay button executes the code:

```
// select the music
on (release) {
    Selection = _root.MusicSelection.Scroll;
    // check if playing
    if (_root.Playing == true) {
        _root.Music.Stop();
    }
//determine sound
    if (this == _root.HighLight2) {
        Selection = Selection+1;
    } else if (this == _root.HighLight3{
        Selection = Selection+2;
    }
//attach music
    _root.Music = new Sound();
```

```
        _root.Music.Attachsound("Music"+Selection);
        // clean up
        call (_root+".Clean Up");
        _root.SelectionTitle =
          _root.SelectionArray[Selection-1];
}
```

This code determines the **Selection**, actually the line number of the first line showing at the top of the text window. The code then figures out which sound was selected based on the name of this overlay movie. If any sound is playing, it is stopped. The new sound is attached to Music (the name of the sound object), and then the clean-up routine is called. The clean-up code hides all selection buttons again. To display the selection that is playing, the selection in the **SelectionArray** is passed to the text named **SelectionTitle**.

The Randomize button uses the **SelectionArray** to randomize the next song to play. If any sound is playing, it stops.

The names of the songs change color on rollover.

Each song has a corresponding animation.

19

CREATING MOUSE-DRIVEN ANIMATION EFFECTS

By Samuel Wan

This chapter covers three types of mouse effects: the graphical trailer, the text trailer, and sparkling stars. All three effects are based on the same fundamental algorithm, which goes to show that a bit of tweaking can squeeze a lot of mileage out of well-written modular ActionScript.

Before you write any actual code, consider what you're trying to accomplish here. The actual programming behind this graphical mouse effect requires you to work in three stages:

- As soon as the movie loads, create duplicate movies of the originalRoot movie clip, in which each subsequent duplicate is bigger and more transparent than the previous movie clip. Therefore, the _xscale and the _yscale increase for each duplicate, and _alpha decreases for each duplicate.
- Position each instance a bit closer to the previous instance in the series of duplicated movie clips so they move in a "floating chain" of duplicate movie clips.
- Allow the user to change each duplicated movie to a specified effect by clicking on a button.

Setting Up the Flash File to Create a Mouse Effect

1 Open the MouseEffects_Start1.fla in the Chapter 19 folder on the CD and save it to your local hard drive. (Look at the MouseEffects_Final1.fla file for the finished version.)

2 Unlock the MouseEffect layer and select the first frame of the layer.

3 Open the MouseEffects folder in the Library. Drag the movie clip named MouseEffectModule anywhere onto the main Stage. To see the movie clip, make the Mask layer invisible. Give the movie clip an instance name of **MouseEffectModule**.

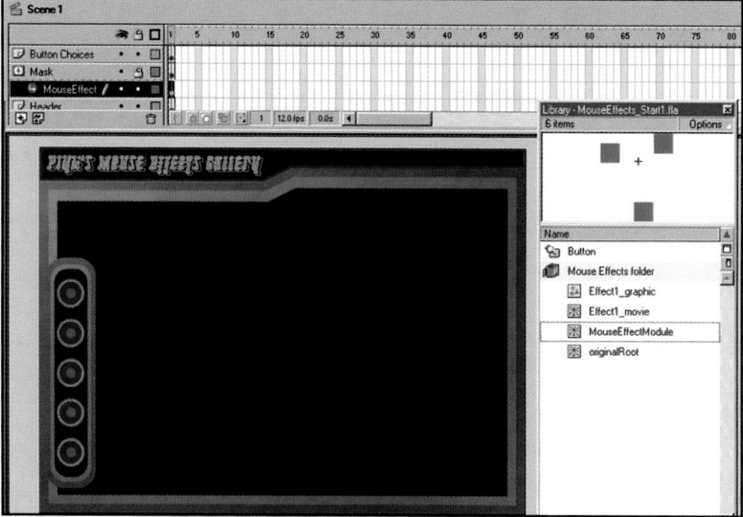

Locate the Mouse Effects layer on the timeline and the MouseEffectsModule movie clip in the Library.

Now all the graphical elements for the Fading Mouse Effect are contained within a single movie clip called MouseEffectModule that's located on the main Stage. The module itself contains a movie clip called originalRoot, and the originalRoot movie clip contains five frames. Each frame has a different graphic symbol that creates a different kind of fading mouse effect. On the screen, there are already five buttons, to which you will later add ActionScript that will change the mouse effect.

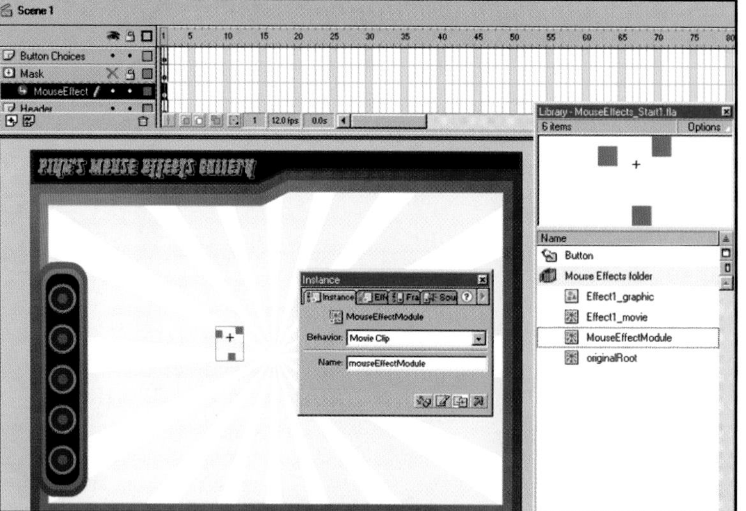

Place the MouseEffectModule movie clip on the MouseEffect layer. Because the MouseEffect layer is covered with a mask, you need to make the Mask layer invisible.

Initializing the Variables and Duplicating the Movie Clips

Defining important values at the top of the script allows you to easily access them if you want to make adjustments to the mouse effect later on. In this section, you define the variables at the top of the **onClipEvent(load)** handler of the MouseEffectModule movie clip. You also duplicate the movie clips.

1 Make sure you are in MouseEffects_start1.fla, select the MouseEffectsModule movie clip, and open its Action panel.

2 Set up this code to initialize each variable in the **onClipEvent(load)** event handler so the variables are initialized only once and as soon as the movie clip loads into the Flash player:

```
onClipEvent (load) {
    // init variables
    startSize = 20;
    max = 20;
    sizeIncrement = 15;
    effectChoice = 1;
    roots = new Array();
}
```

Initialize several variables in the **onClipEvent(load)** handler, which is assigned to the MouseEffectModule movie clip.

The variable ***StartSize*** defines the size of the first duplicate movie clip in percentages. Here, you set the initial size to 20 percent. The variable ***max*** defines how many duplicates the script will make. The variable ***sizeIncrement*** defines the percentage increase of each new duplicate movie clip. The variable ***effectChoice*** defines the default mouse effect as the first effect. **Roots** is a new array that you'll use to associate each duplicate. For more about associative arrays, read the detailed explanations in Chapter 9.

Now that you've established the parameters of this mouse effect, you can begin to duplicate the movie clips.

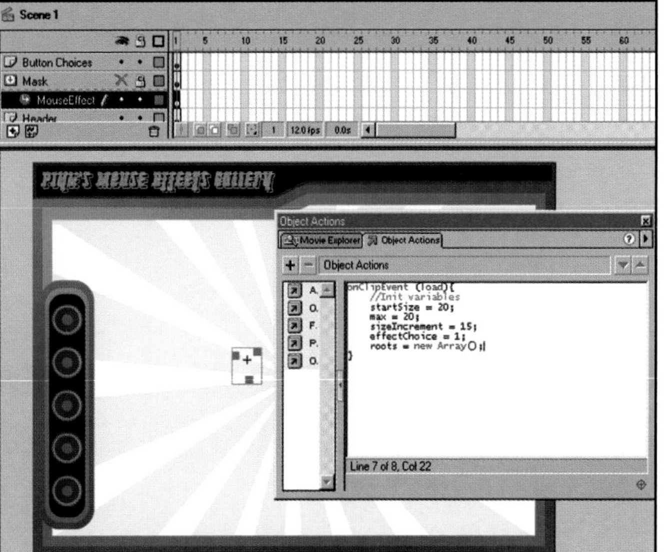

Enter the **onClipEvent(load)** code.

3 Assign this code right after the variable initialization portion, inside the **onClipEvent(load)** handler:

The duplication process runs as many times as specified by the ***max*** value by using ***max*** as the limit of the **for** loop:

```
for (var i = 0; i<max; i++) {
```

The first line of code inside the **for** loop

```
duplicateMovie Clip (originalRoot, "root"+i, i);
```

actually duplicates a movie clip from the movie clip named originalRoot and assigns the new duplicate an instance name of root + *i*, where *i* is a number between 0 and max–1.

```
duplicateMovie Clip (originalRoot, "root"+i, i);
```

For example, the first loop would create an instance with the name root0, the second loop would create an instance with the name root1, the third loop would create an instance with the name root2, and so on.

You associate the new duplicate movie clip to a corresponding element in the array **roots[i]**. (Refer to Chapter 9 for an explanation of associative arrays.) So root0 is assigned to roots[0], root1 is assigned to roots[1], root2 is assigned to roots[2], and so on.

```
roots[i] = eval("root"+i);
```

Resize the horizontal and vertical scales of the duplicate movie clip according to the formula *startSize* + (*i***sizeIncrement*).

```
roots[i]._xscale = startSize+(i*sizeIncrement);
roots[i]._yscale = startSize+(i*sizeIncrement);
```

```
// Duplication process
for (var i = 0; i<max; i++) {
    duplicateMovie Clip (originalRoot, "root"+i, i);
    roots[i] = eval("root"+i);
    roots[i]._xscale = startSize+(i*sizeIncrement);
    roots[i]._yscale = startSize+(i*sizeIncrement);
    roots[i]._alpha = 100-(100/max)*i;
    roots[i].gotoAndStop(effectChoice);
}
```

Add the duplication code to the **onClipEvent(load)** handler after the initialization code and variables.

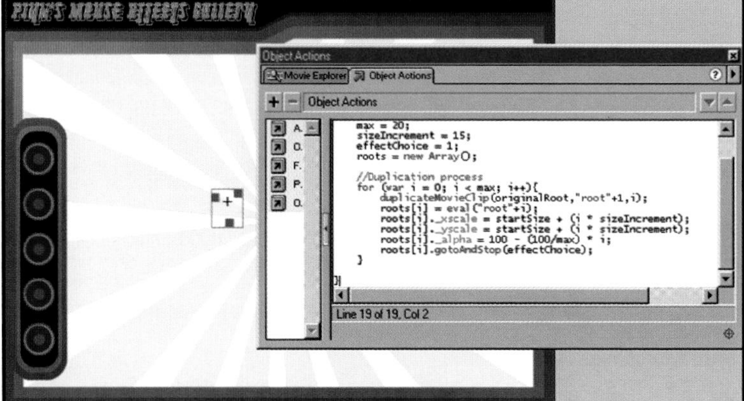

Enter the duplication process code.

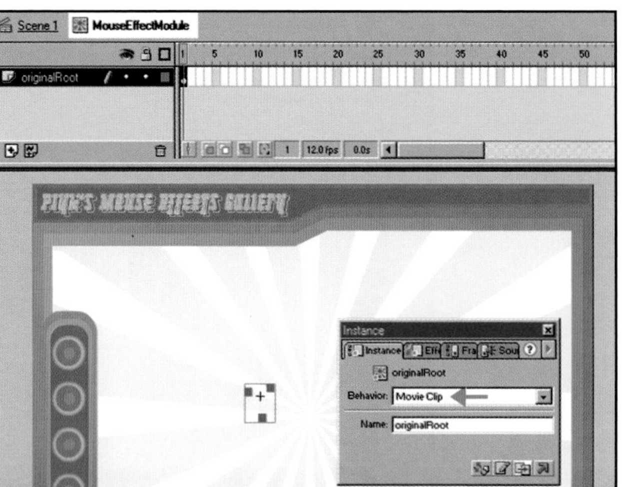

The original movie clip within the MouseEffectModule movie clip has an instance name of originalRoot, which is referenced in the code.

The ***startSize*** variable, which you had previously initialized to a value of 20 is added to a multiple of the ***sizeIncrement*** value. For example, the first loop would rescale the instance root0 to an *_xscale* and *_yscale* of 20 + (0*15), which means that you simply rescaled it to 20 percent because 0 times 15 equals 0. The second loop would rescale the instance root1 to an *_xscale* and *_yscale* of 20+(1*15), which equals 35 percent. The third loop would rescale to 20+(2*15), which equals 50 percent.

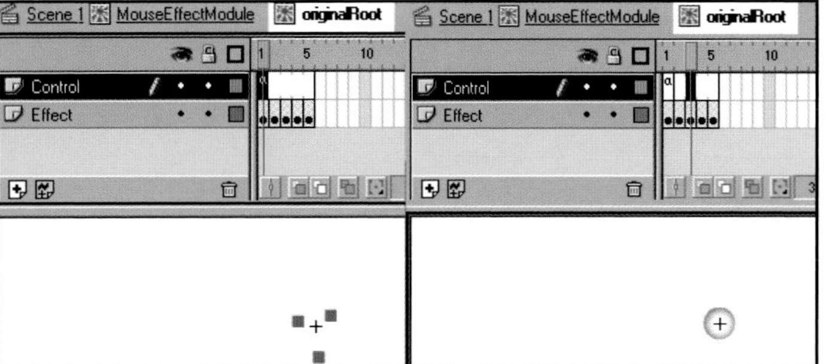

The MouseEffectModule movie clip contains a movie clip for each mouse effect on separate frames.

In the second to last line of the **for** loop code

```
roots[i]._alpha = 100-(100/max)*i;
```

you find the percentage of 100 divided by ***max***, multiply that by the increment *i*, and then subtract from 100. This formula allows you to calculate however many slices of percentage might exist from zero through 100. So if ***max*** = 20, the percentage slice would be 100, 80, 60, 40, 20, 0, and the result of subtracting from 100 would be 0, 20, 40, 60, 80, 100. The transparency alpha of each new duplicate movie clip would be 20 less than that of the previous duplicate.

Writing a Function to Change the Mouse Effect

Before you write the ActionScript to animate the mouse effect, you need to write a function that will change the mouse effect on-the-fly. The movie clip originalRoot contains five different graphics. If you created duplicate movie clips of originalRoot, you need a way to tell each duplicate to go to a specific frame.

1 Add this ActionScript after the duplication process section:

The parameter for the newly defined function, **ChooseNewEffect**, will pass a number to tell the duplicate movie clip to go to a specific frame. In the function definition, ***choice*** is the variable that holds the value of the passed number parameter.

```
function ChooseNewEffect(choice) {
```

Because there are only five frames and each contains a unique graphic, you need to make sure that the value of ***choice*** is a number that falls between 0 and 5. To do so, you make sure that ***choice*** is greater than 0 and less than or equal to the total number of frames in the originalRoot movie clip with the following conditional statement:

```
if (choice > 0 and choice <= originalRoot._totalframes){
```

The inner **for** loop runs through all the existing movie clips and tells them to go to the number value of the ***choice*** parameter.

```
roots[n].gotoAndStop(choice);
```

2 To make the originalRoot movie clip invisible, enter this code:

```
//A function that changes the mouse effect
function ChooseNewEffect(choice) {
	if (choice > 0 && choice <= originalRoot._totalframes){
		for (var n = 0; n < max; n ++) {
			roots[n].gotoAndStop(choice);
		}
	}
}
```

Add the **ChooseNewEffect(choice)** function to the **onClipEvent(load)** handler after the duplication code.

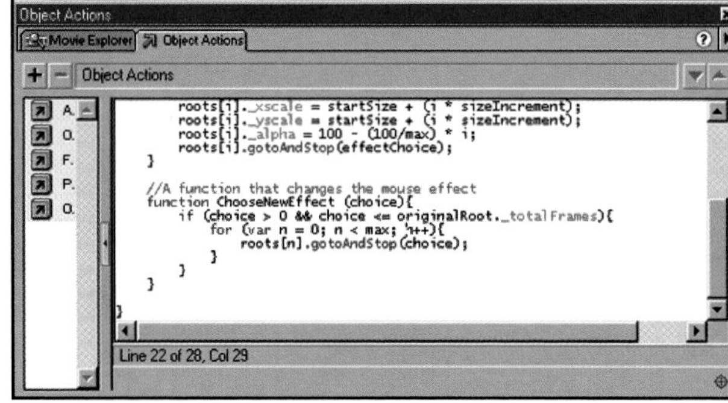

The **ChooseNewEffect(choice)** function of the **onClipEvent(load)** handler is placed beneath the duplication code.

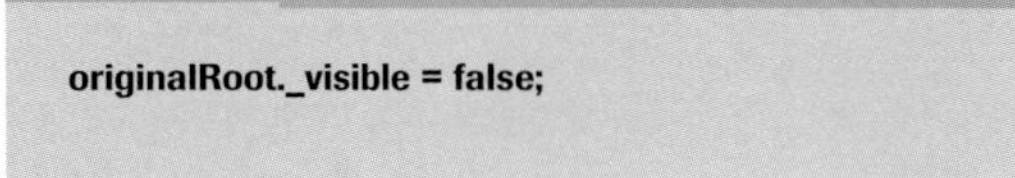

```
originalRoot._visible = false;
```

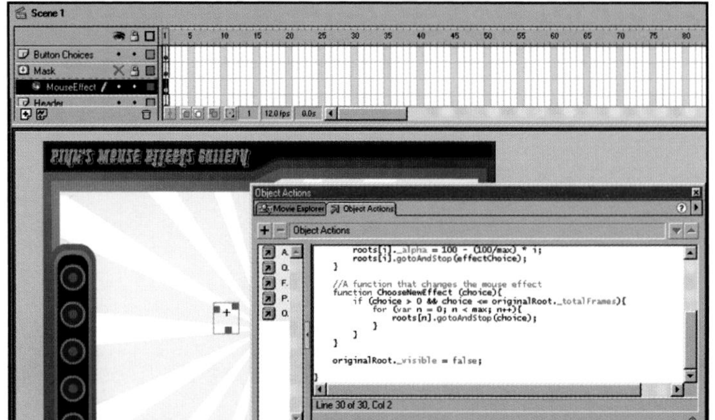

Add the code that makes the movie clip invisible.

ANIMATING THE MOUSE EFFECT WITH ACTIONSCRIPT

Take another overview look at how the mouse effect actually works before digging into the animation algorithms.

1 Open the source file, MouseEffects_Final1.fla, compile it, and observe how the mouse effect works.

This is actually a series of duplicated movie clips that follow one another in a "floating chain" of graphic symbols. In other words, the movie clip root3 moves towards root2, root2 moves towards root1, root1 moves towards root0, and root0 is positioned according to the mouse's *_xmouse* and *_ymouse* positions.

2 Add this ActionScript after the **onClipEvent(load)** section.

```
onClipEvent (enterFrame) {
    roots[0]._x = _xmouse;
    roots[0]._y = _ymouse;
    for (var i = 1; i<=roots.length; i++) {
        roots[i].xdistance = (roots[i-1]._x-roots[i]._x)/2+
        ➥(roots[i].xdistance*0.3);
        roots[i].ydistance = (roots[i-1]._y-roots[i]._y)/2+
        ➥(roots[i].ydistance*0.3);
        roots[i]._x += roots[i].xdistance;
        roots[i]._y += roots[i].ydistance;
    }
}
```

Add the **onClipEvent(enterFrame)** handler after the **onClipEvent(load)** handler. (The ➥ symbol you see here is for editorial purposes only.)

The code you just entered is the only code needed to run the graphical mouse trailer effect. This is an effect, not a game or application, so the code itself may appear simple. However, those eight lines of code contain some key concepts that are worth a more detailed study.

Remember that the ActionScript inside the **onClipEvent(enterFrame)** handler is executed continuously while the movie clip still exists in the timeline. Therefore, these lines of code

```
roots[0]._x = _xmouse;
```

and

```
roots[0]._y = _ymouse;
```

continuously reposition the movie instance associated with roots[0] (that is, the instance "root0") to wherever the mouse is currently located on the screen.

In each iteration of the **for** loop, a mathematical formula repositions the duplicate movie clips to achieve that "floating chain" effect.

Take a closer look at the code in the **onClipEvent(enterFrame)** handler. The effect you want to achieve is for each duplicated movie clip to be "attracted" to the next movie clip and move a little closer to the next movie clip's position. The following explanation uses the example of ***i=2***. In other words, the ***i*** in the **onClipEvent(enterFrame)** handler equals 2.

The code duplicates instances of the root movie clip according to the position of the mouse.

The movie clip instances are positioned close to one another to create a more elastic effect.

First, the code finds the horizontal position and distance between the current movie clip and the previous movie clip and assigns that value to the ***xdistance*** variable inside the movie clip. So in the third iteration of the **for** loop, the variable ***i*** equals 2, and the distance is calculated using this code:

```
Roots[2].xdistance = (roots[2-1]._x – roots[2]._x)
```

In plain English, this code calculates the difference in horizontal positions between the current movie clip associated with roots[2] and the previous movie clip associated with roots[1]. Then it assigns that distance value to a variable called ***xdistance*** inside the current movie clip associated with roots[2].

Next, the code finds the ***ydistance***, or vertical distance, using this code:

```
Roots[2].ydistance = (roots[2-1]._y – roots[2]._y)
```

This formula moves the movie clip to the same position as the previous movie clip. Moving it only a short distance makes the animation appear smoother and more liquid.

The next section of code divides the distance by 2, using this code:

```
Roots[2].xdistance = (roots[2-1]._x – roots[2]._x)/2
Roots[2].ydistance = (roots[2-1]._y – roots[2]._y)/2
```

The last two lines of code assign the x and y position of the movie clip according to its original position **plus** the *xdistance* and *ydistance*.

```
Roots[i]._x += roots[i].xdistance;
Roots[i]._y += roots[i].ydistance;
```

I'll use a joke to illustrate this important mathematical concept more clearly. Once an engineer and a mathematician were competing to determine who would enter a grove to wake Sleeping Beauty with a kiss. Unfortunately, a magic spell prevented people

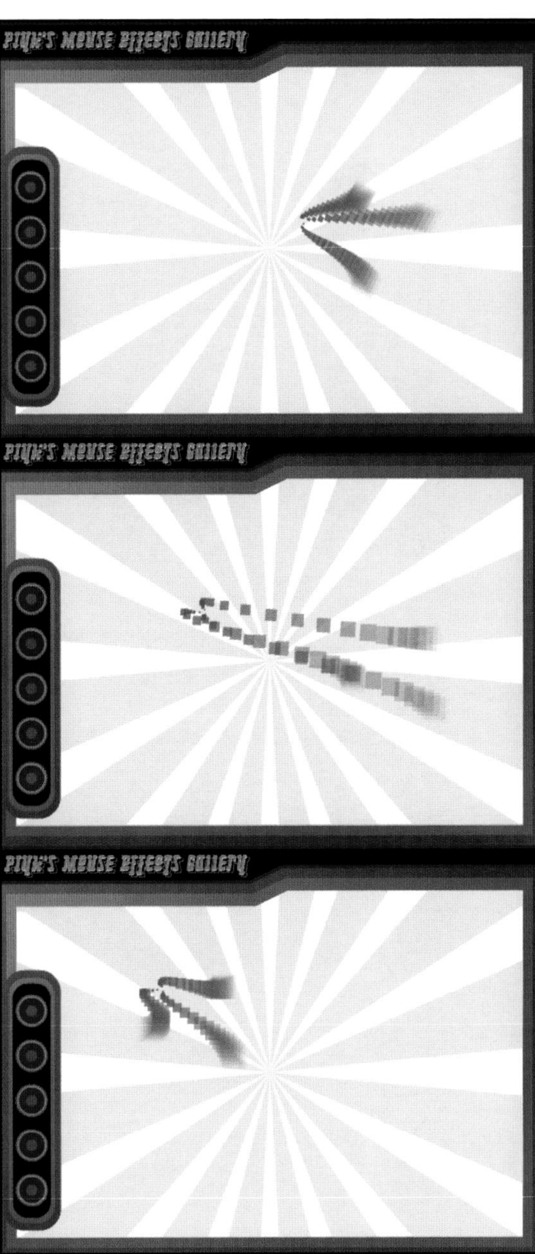

The mouse effect is described as elastic because when the mouse moves slowly, the movie clip duplicates are close together, as shown in the upper window.

When the mouse moves faster, the duplicates get further apart, as shown in the middle window.

When the mouse slows down, the duplicates snap back and are again close together, as shown in the lower window.

from moving more than half the distance toward the princess with each step. The mathematician tried to walk forward a few steps into the grove, but the distance he covered in each step would become shorter and shorter as the distance shrank. Eventually, he was moving at a snail's pace, almost but not quite reaching the Princess. He exclaimed, "I give up! Because of the magic spell, there will always be half a distance between the princess and me. Theoretically, I would never reach her." The engineer smiled and walked toward the sleeping princess as well. Each step he took became shorter and shorter until finally, he too was moving at a snail's pace. After a number of steps, however, he simply leaned over with the length of his whole body and reached out to kiss the princess. He said, "for all practical purposes, I was close enough."

To polish off the mathematical formula, add a tiny fraction of the previous distance to the new calculation of the distance, using this code:

```
Roots[2].xdistance = (roots[2-1]._x – roots[2]._x)/2 +
➥roots[i].xdistance*0.3;
Roots[2].ydistance = (roots[2-1]._y – roots[2]._y)/2 +
➥roots[i].ydistance*0.3;
```

(The ➥ symbol you see here is for editorial purposes only.)

In this code, you add a fraction of the previously calculated distance for that movie clip—in this case 30 (0.3) percent—to give the mouse effect some elasticity.

To understand why this elasticity occurs, think of the Sleeping Beauty scenario again, where the mathematician can move only half the distance toward the princess with each step. Then imagine the person moves half the distance plus a fraction of the previous half-distance for each step. If you think about it long enough, you will see that the mathematician will eventually overshoot the princess's location and have to move backward a half-distance step plus a fraction

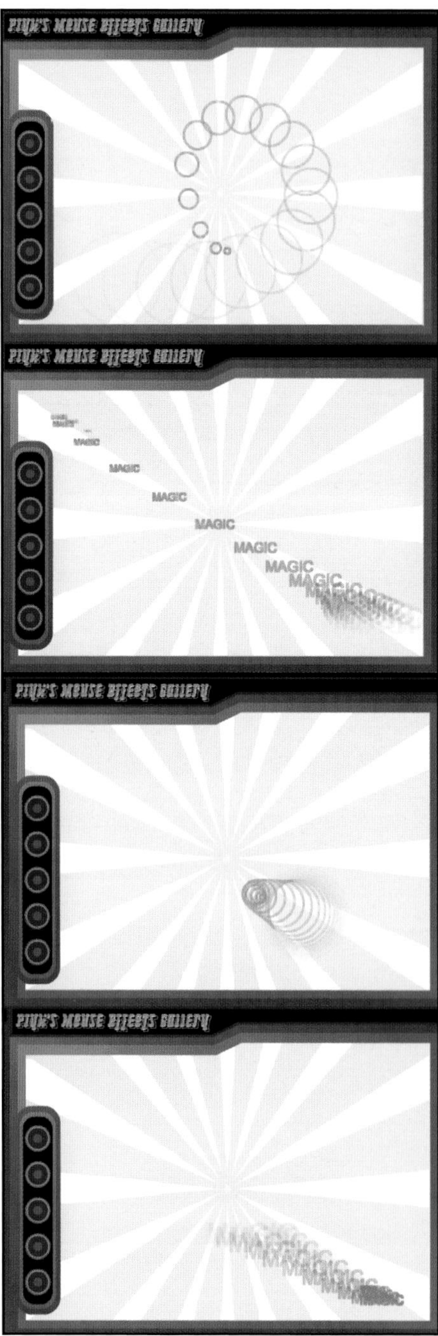

All the other mouse effect options share the same elastic properties.

of his previous half-distance step. If the fraction is large enough, his path of movement begins to look like an elastic ball bouncing back and forth over the coordinates of the princess, gradually decreasing until he reaches the princess's location.

3 Run the demo and move your mouse arrow around to see how this concept works visually.

Changing Effects On-the-Fly

Changing the graphics for the mouse effect is easy since you have already written the **ChooseNewEffect()** function (near the beginning of this chapter). To change the effect, simply call the function and pass a number from 1 to 5 as the parameter. In the demo, there are five buttons, each of which calls the function and passes a different number when the button is clicked:

```
on (release) {
    _root.mouseEffectModule.ChooseNewEffect(1);
}
```

For each of the buttons on the screen, select one and add the preceding code to change the mouse effect to a different graphic. In each function call on each button, make sure you call a different number, from 1 to 5, to select the full range of effects.

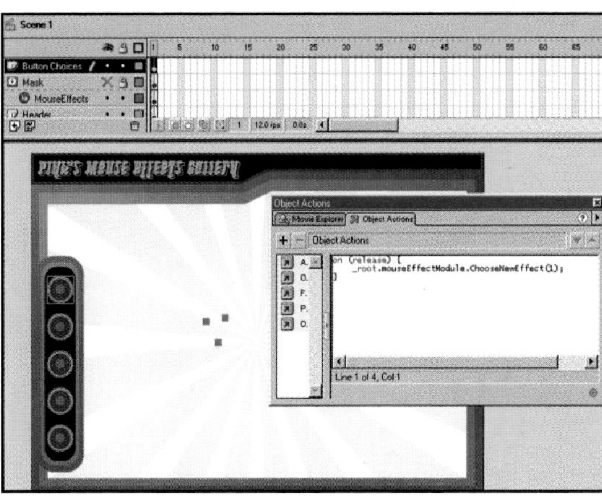

Each button passes a number to the MouseEffectModule movie clip to change the effect.

Setting Up the Mouse Trailer

The next effect in this chapter anchors to the mouse cursor a continually updated string of characters that show the current date and time. Although the algorithmic and mathematical concepts are very similar to those in the previous section, the structure of the code will look slightly different because you will make extensive use of functions. You'll be storing most of the code inside functions within the **onClipEvent** handlers instead of simply running the code directly within event handlers. You will take this approach for several reasons, which will become apparent as you dig deeper into the actual functionality of these mouse effects.

1 Open the MouseEffect_Start2.fla file located in the Chapter 19 folder on the companion CD and save it to your hard drive. (See MouseEffect_Final2.fla for the finished version.)

2 In the first layer, titled Mouse Trailer Module, select the first frame, which is empty.

The date and time follow the mouse movements.

3 Open the Library, and then open the Mouse Trailer folder. Drag the MouseEffectModule onto the stage and give it an instance name of **MouseEffectModule**.

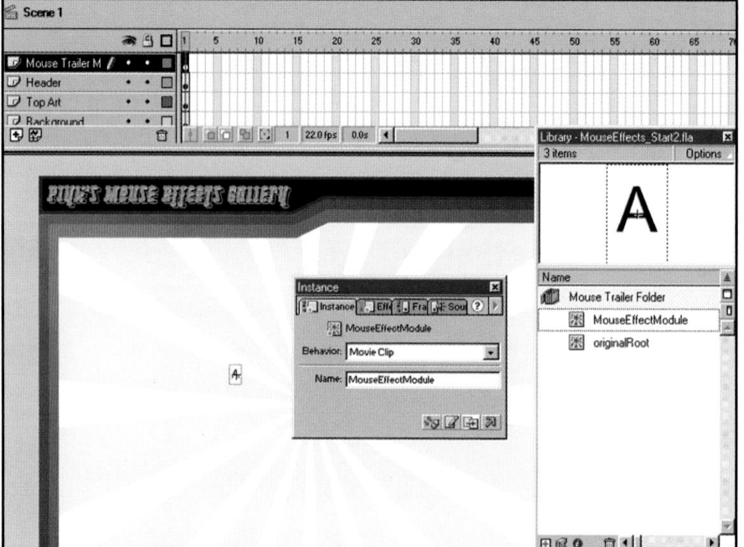

The instance of the MouseEffectModule movie clip goes on the Mouse Trailer Module layer.

4 Open the Action panel for the MouseEffectModule movie clip and assign this code.

```
onClipEvent (load) {
    function InitializeMouseTrail(message) {
        // init variables
        max = message.length;
        spacing = 4;
        letters = new Array();

        // Duplication process
        for (var i = 0; i < message.length; i++) {
            duplicateMovieClip (originalRoot, "letter"+i, i);
            letters[i] = eval("letter"+i);
            letters[i].textfield = message.substr(i,1);
        }
    }
```

Assign the **onClipEvent(load)** code to the MouseEffectModule movie clip.

In previous sections, variables are sometimes initialized inside the **onClipEvent(load)** event handler, to be initialized as soon as the movie clip has loaded into the Flash Player. Here, you still initialize the variables and array for the mouse effect, but you initialize them by calling a function called **InitializeMouseTrail(*message*)** that contains all the necessary code. Why? Because the function allows you to reinitialize the variables and array anytime you need to call this function, not just once in the **load** event handler. This approach is cleaner, more flexible, and easier to reuse.

So within the **InitializeMouseTrail(*message*)** function, ***message*** contains the string of characters you want to add to the mouse trailer. Then you get the number of characters in the ***message*** string variable by using the **message.length** method, and you assign that value to the ***max*** variable. Later on, the variable ***spacing*** will tell the script exactly how far apart to space the characters on the floating chain. The ***letters*** array will become an associated array that refers to each new duplicate movie in the effect.

The "duplication process" section of this function contains a **for** loop that will loop for the number of characters in the ***message*** string variable using the variable ***i*** as the counter variable. For example, if ***message*** had a value of **hello**, the **for** loop would loop five times as the ***i*** increments from 0 to 4. If ***message*** had a value of **goodbye**, the **for** loop would loop seven times as ***i*** increments from 0 to 6.

The first line inside the **for** loop

```
duplicateMovieClip (originalRoot, "letter"+i, i);
```

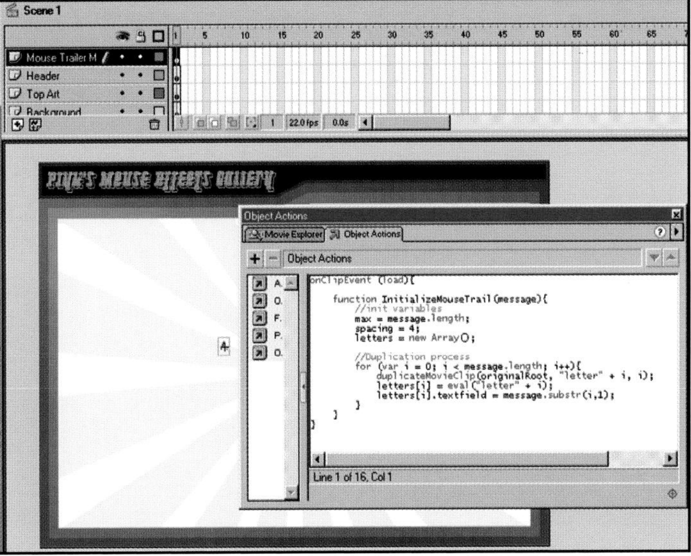

The **onClipEvent(load)** code looks like this.

actually duplicates the originalRoot movie clip (which contains a text field variable named ***textfield***) and then gives that duplicate an instance name of letter and the value of ***i*** (for example, **letter0**, **letter1**, **letter2**, and so on). In the next line, an element of the **letters** array is associated with the new duplicated movie clip:

```
letters[i] = eval("letter"+i);
```

And in the final line of code, you pull a character from the message string using the **substr** method and assign it to the text field of the duplicated movie clip. The technique of pulling out characters from a string piece by piece is called parsing, and the ***Substr*** variable allows you to parse out any number of characters in sequence, from a starting point in the string, where 0 is the position of the first character. For example, if ***message*** had a value of **hello**, **message.substr(0,1)** would parse out the letter h, and **message.substr(4,1)** would parse out the letter o.

```
letters[i].textfield = message.substr(i,1);
```

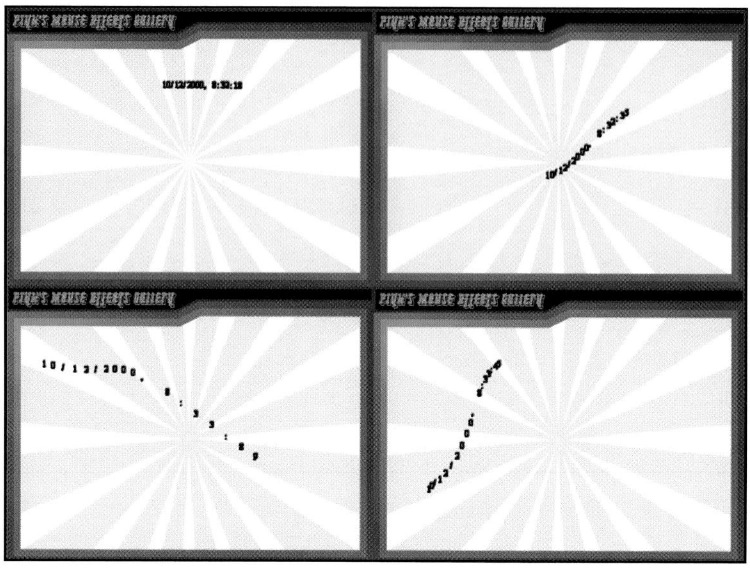

The numbers for the date and time follow the mouse with the same elastic effect discussed earlier.

5 Write the function that will update the characters in the mouse trailer with a new string value passed into the ***message*** variable parameter.

Here, you simply run through all the duplicated movie clips associated in the **letters[ ]** array and parse out each character in the new ***message*** variable into the text field of each duplicated movie.

```
function UpdateMouseTrail(message) {
    // Simple update process
    for (var i = 0; i < message.length; i++) {
        letters[i].textfield = message.substr(i,1);
    }
}
```

Add the **UpdateMouseTrail(message)** function to the **onClipEvent(load)** handler.

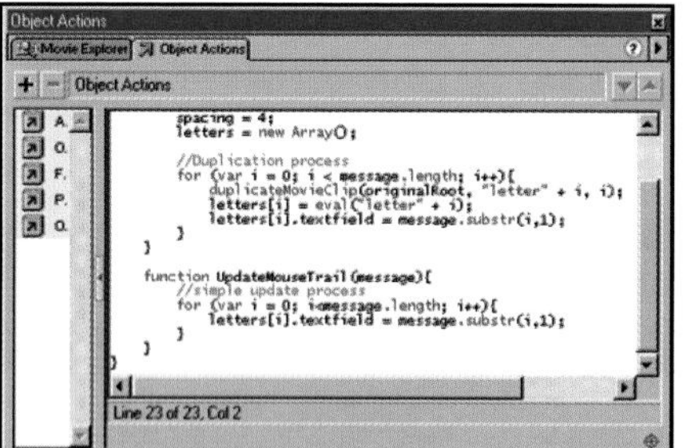

The **UpdateMouseTrail(message)** function appears in the **onClipEvent(load)** handler.

6 Add the **ShowTime()** function inside the **onClipEvent(load)** handler, which gets the value of the current month, date, year, hour, minutes, and seconds.

```
function ShowTime() {
    var now = new Date();
    var output =
        now.getMonth() + "/" +
        now.getDate() + "/" +
        now.getFullYear() + ", " +
        now.getHours() + ":" +
        now.getMinutes() + ":" +
        now.getSeconds();
    return output;
}
```

Add the **ShowTime** function to the **onClipEvent(load)** code.

This function creates a new Date object called now, concatenates the value of those properties of the object into a string called *output*, and then returns the string value in the variable ***output***. For example, if the internal clock of your computer is set to December 2, 2000 and it's one o'clock in the afternoon, the **ShowTime()** function would return this value:

12/2/2000, 13:00:00

At this point, you might ask the questions, "Why write all these functions?" and "When will I use them?"

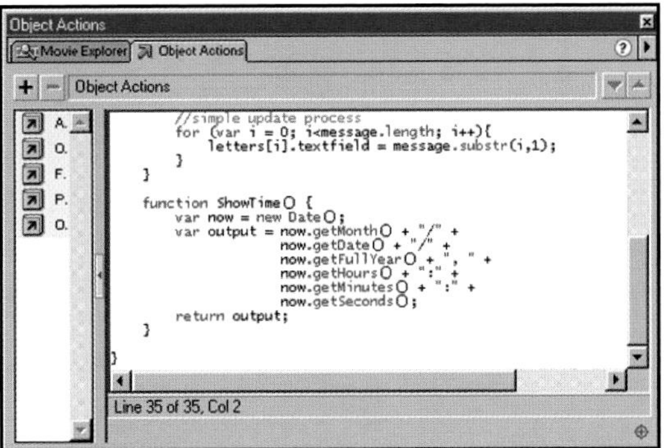

The **ShowTime** function appears in the **onClipEvent(load)** code.

7 At the end of the **load** event handler, add this line:

```
InitializeMouseTrail(ShowTime());
```

Add a function call to the **onClipEvent(load)** handler.

The **InitializeMouseTrail(ShowTime())** function call actually calls two functions. The inner function call gets the result of the ***ShowTime*** string to get the current date and time and passes that string to the **InitializeMouseTrail()** function. That function in turn initializes the mouse trailer and parses each character into a new duplicated movie clip.

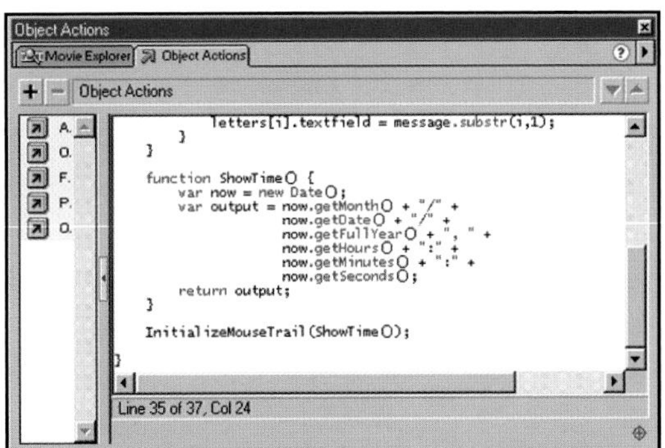

The function call appears in the code.

8 You no longer need the original MovieClip, so make it invisible, using this code:

```
originalRoot._visible = false;
```

Add this code to the **onClipEvent(load)** handler to make the original movie clip invisible.

Now that you've written the ActionScript for the **load** handler to set up those three functions and initialize the movie clip, finish up the mouse effect by writing ActionScript for the continually looping **enterFrame** event handler.

9 Insert this code:

```
onClipEvent (enterFrame) {
    UpdateMouseTrail(showTime());
    letters[0]._x = _xmouse;
    letters[0]._y = _ymouse;
    for (var i = 1; i <= letters.length; i++) {
    letters[i].xdistance = (letters[i-1]._x - letters[i]._x)/2+(letters[i].
    ➥xdistance*0.2);
        letters[i].ydistance = (letters[i-1]._y -
        ➥letters[i]._y)/2+(letters[i].ydistance*0.2);
    letters[i]._x += (letters[i].xdistance) + spacing;
    letters[i]._y += letters[i].ydistance;
    }
}
```

Assign the **onClipEvent(enterFrame)** handler. (The ➥ symbol you see here is for editorial purposes only.)

The ActionScript for mouse trailer movement is identical to the ActionScript for the floating effect in Mouse Effects 1, except for two differences. The most obvious difference is that you've renamed the **roots** array with the more appropriate name of **letters**. The second difference is the adding of the ***spacing*** variable (in this case, a value of 4) to the *x* position to space out the letters along a horizontal line as they would appear in a written sentence or phrase.

Take a minute to break down that block of code. The line of code

```
UpdateMouseTrail(showTime());
```

is a double function call. It calls the **ShowTime()** function to retrieve the current date and time and then passes that value into the **UpdateMouseTrail()** function, which updates the characters in each movie clip of the "floating chain." This line of code allows you to continually update the current date and time for the floating chain of letters.

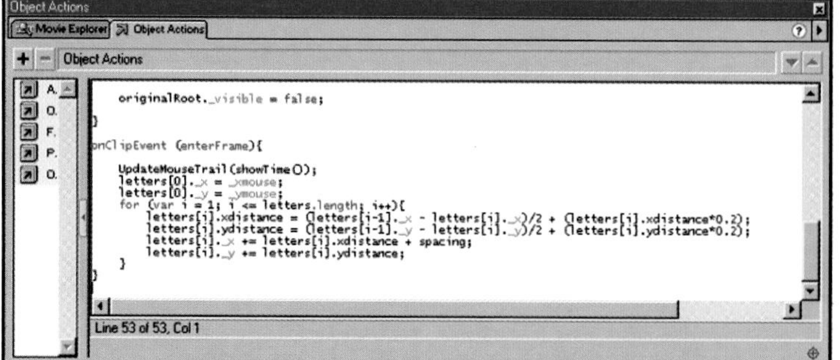

The **onClipEvent(enterFrame)** handler is assigned.

Next you set the position of the first duplicated movie clip to the local x and y position of the mouse.

```
letters[0]._x = _xmouse;
letters[0]._y = _ymouse;
```

Then you wrote a **for** loop to run through every associated movie clip in the **letters** array.

```
for (var i = 1; i <= letters.length; i++) {
    letters[i].xdistance = (letters[i-1]._x –
        letters[i]._x)/2+(letters[i].xdistance*0.2);
    letters[i].ydistance = (letters[i-1]._y –
        letters[i]._y)/2+(letters[i].ydistance*0.2);
    letters[i]._x += (letters[i].xdistance) + spacing;
    letters[i]._y += letters[i].ydistance;
}
```

The two "elastic" formulas look identical to the formulas explained earlier. The main difference is in this line:

```
letters[i]._x += (letters[i].xdistance) + spacing;
```

Adding the value of the ***spacing*** variable makes it string out the chain of movie clips toward the right instead of having them all centered as in the earlier example.

10 Test the file to observe the effect.

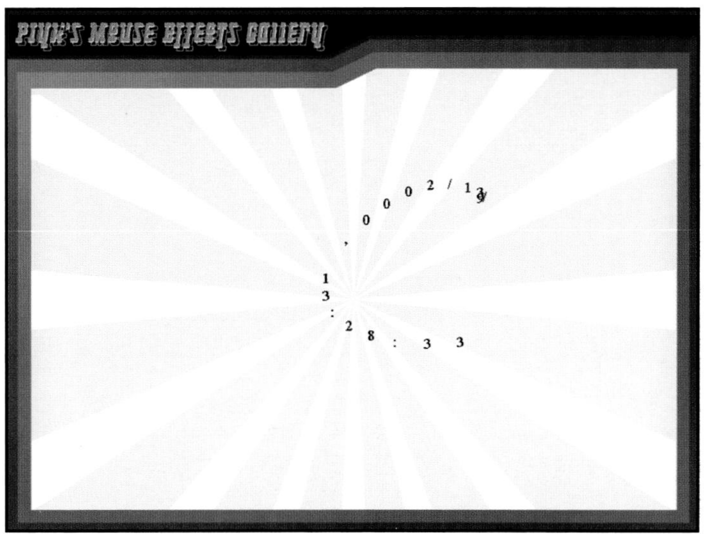

The elastic code has an additional line that tells the date and time to follow the mouse to the right of the cursor rather than at the center of the cursor.

Initializing Variables for a Pixel Dust Effect

In this section, you see an opposite mouse trailer, where duplicated movie clips fly away from the mouse instead of moving toward it. This effect duplicates movie clips continuously without a maximum limit and sends them flying off the screen according to the speed and direction of the mouse movement. The movie being duplicated inside the starModule is called **originalStar**, which contains an animation of a falling star, and the last frame contains a line of ActionScript to remove itself (assuming that the movie clip is a duplicated instance).

1 Open the MouseEffects_Start3.fla file located in the Chapter 19 folder on the companion CD and save it to your hard drive. Select the first frame of the Star Module layer. Then open the Library, open the Star Folder, and drag the StarModule movie clip onto the Stage. See MouseEffects_Final3.fla for the finished version.

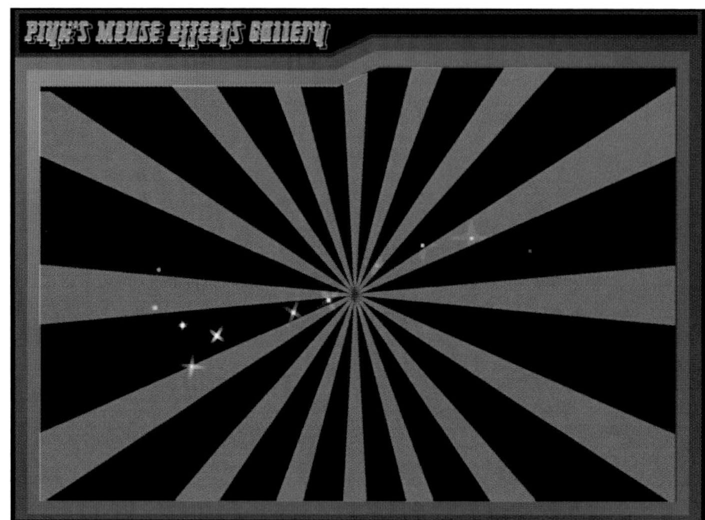

The star-shaped movie clips shoot out from the position of the mouse cursor.

2 Enter this code to initialize the variables inside the **onClipEvent(load)** handler:

```
onClipEvent(Load) {
    //Initialize variables for calculating inertia
    starTime = getTimer();
    xdistance = 0;
    ydistance = 0;
    inertiaSpeed = 10;
    xoriginal = _xmouse;
    yoriginal = _ymouse;
    //Initialize variables for duplicating star
    originalStar._visible = false;
    originalStar.stop();
    i = 0;
```

Assign the **onClipEvent(load)** handler to the StarModule movie clip.

The first set of variables initializes the horizontal and vertical speed of the mouse, which will be used to apply inertia to the stars. The second set of variables makes the original star invisible, tells it to stop on the first frame, and initializes the ***i*** counter for the duplication process.

By now, you should be familiar with the duplication process. But get a quick overview of the tasks performed by the **fallingStar()** function, which makes only **one** duplicate movie clip and assigns it to a new instance name and depth that increments by 1 each time the function is called. This increment is stored by the variable ***i***, which acts as a counter.

3 Enter this code to get the *x* and *y* coordinates of the mouse:

```
function fallingStar(){
    //Get mouse coordinates
    x = _xmouse;
    y = _ymouse;
```

Add this code for setting the mouse coordinates to the **onClipEvent(load)** handler.

4 Duplicate the movie clip and assign the instance to an easy-to-use reference variable called ***path***.

```
//Duplicate the star movieclip and assign the movie to the variable "path"
duplicateMovieClip ("originalStar", "Star" + i, i);
var path = eval("Star" + i);
```

Add the duplication code to the **onClipEvent(load)** handler.

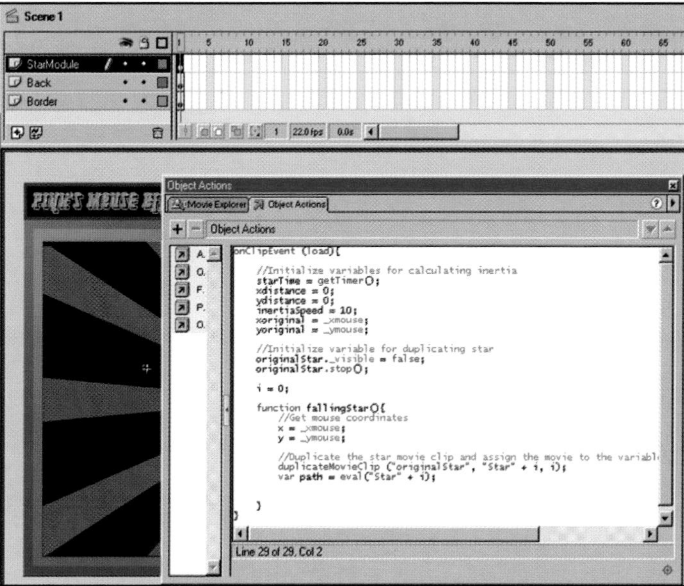

The **onClipEvent(load)** handler appears in the StarModule movie.

5 Using the path reference, resize the stars randomly to make them appear different sizes.

```
//Assign a random xscale and yscale to the movieclip

//between 30% and 60%.
newWidth = random(20)+40;
newHeight = random(20)+40;
newWidth *=  1 - (random(2)* 2); //Randomly flip the star horizontally
path._xscale = newWidth;
path._yscale = newHeight;
```

Add the code for random sizing to the **onClipEvent(load)** handler.

6 Position the star within –5 to +5 pixels of the mouse's *x* position and within 0 to +15 pixels of the mouse's *y* position by using this code:

```
path._x = x+(random(5)-random(10));
path._y = y+random(15);
```

Add the code for the star position relative to the mouse to the **onClipEvent(load)** handler.

7 Set the star's ***inertia*** variable according to the recorded speed of the mouse. (You learn how to record the speed of mouse movement within an **enterFrame** event handler a few steps later.) For now, just assume that the value of ***inertiaSpeed*** has been calculated for the speed of the mouse as it moves across the screen.

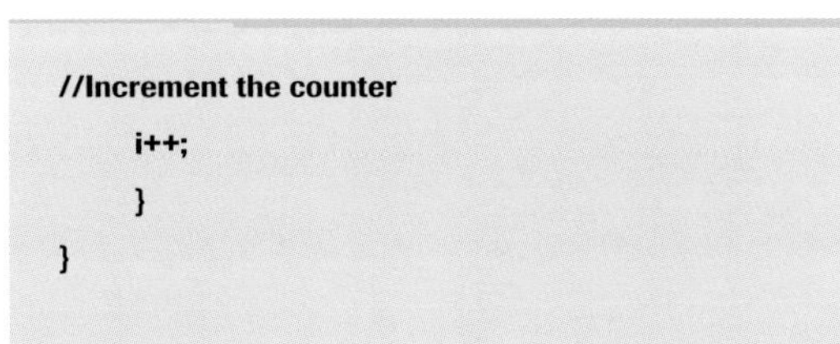

```
//Assign inertia
path.xinertia = xdistance * inertiaSpeed;
path.yinertia = ydistance * inertiaSpeed;
```

Add the inertia code to the **onClipEvent(load)** handler.

8 Increment the counter by 1, close out the function with a closing bracket, and close out the **load** event handler with a bracket.

```
//Increment the counter
        i++;
        }
}
```

Add the code for incrementing the counter to the **onClipEvent(load)** handler.

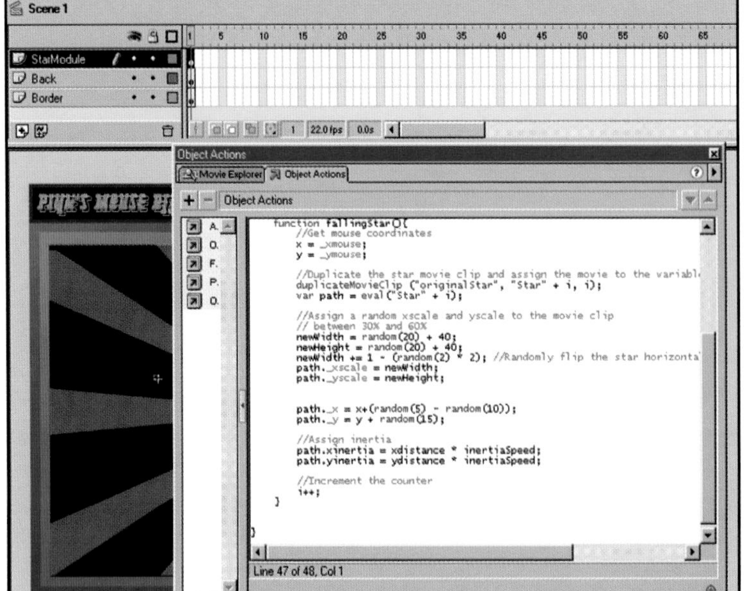

The code you added should match what's shown here.

9 You want to trigger the duplication process and inertia effect only when the mouse is moving, so instead of using the continually looping **onClipEvent(enterFrame)** event handler, use a different kind of event handler called **mouseMove**. This event handler will execute code inside its brackets only when the mouse is in motion.

```
onClipEvent(mouseMove) {
      fallingStar();
}
```

Add the **onClipEvent(mouseMove)** handler after the **onClipEvent(load)** handler.

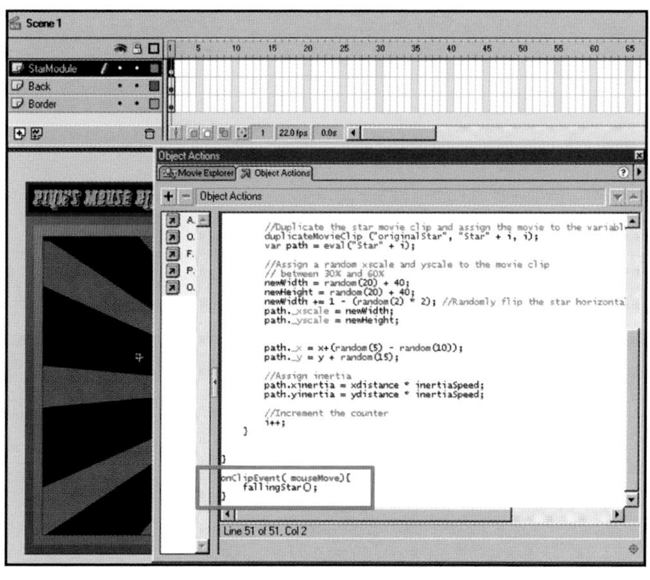

The **onClipEvent(mouseMove)** handler appears in the code.

Recording Mouse Speed

The code for calculating the mouse speed exists inside the **onClipevent(enterFrame)** handler, which loops continuously.

1 To calculate the mouse speed, enter this code for the **enterFrame** handler, below the **onClipEvent(mouseMove)** event handler:

This code takes a snapshot of three pieces of information and stores the information in three variables: the original *x* and *y* positions of the mouse, and the current timer of the Flash Player, which shows how many milliseconds have elapsed since the Flash movie started playing.

```
onClipEvent(enterFrame) {
      //Calculate inertia
      xoriginal = _xmouse;
      yoriginal = _ymouse;
      startTime = getTimer();
}
```

Add the **onClipEvent(enterFrame)** handler after the **onClipEvent(mouseMove)** handler.

2 Insert this code under the comment for calculating inertia to capture the mouse's speed per millisecond:

```
timeslice = getTimer() - startTime;
xdistance = (_xmouse - xoriginal)/timeslice;
ydistance = (_ymouse - yoriginal)/timeslice;
```

Add the code to calculate the mouse speed to the **onClipEvent(enterFrame)** handler.

In its entirety, the final version of the **enterFrame** code looks like this:

```
onClipEvent(enterFrame) {

    //Calculate inertia
    timeslice = getTimer() - startTime;
    xdistance = (_xmouse - xoriginal)/timeslice;
    ydistance = (_ymouse - yoriginal)/timeslice;
    xoriginal = _xmouse;
    yoriginal = _ymouse;
    startTime = getTimer();
}
```

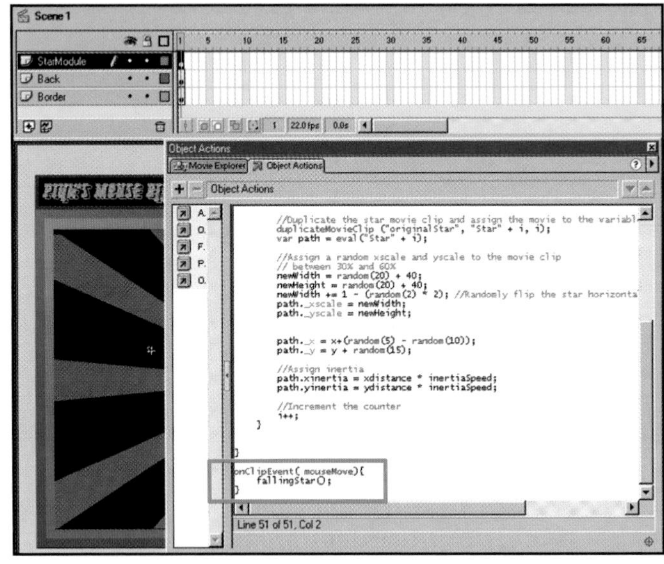

The **onClipEvent(enterFrame)** code appears.

The final version of the **enterFrame** code contains three new lines immediately below the **//Calculate Inertia** comments. The first new line finds out how much time has elapsed since capturing the position and timer, and it stores that elapsed time in the ***timeslice*** variable. The second and third new lines find the *x* and *y* distance from the old *x*,*y* mouse position and the new *x*,*y* position, and they divide the distance by the value of ***timeslice*** to capture the mouse's speed per millisecond (the Flash Player's **Timer** function is in milliseconds).

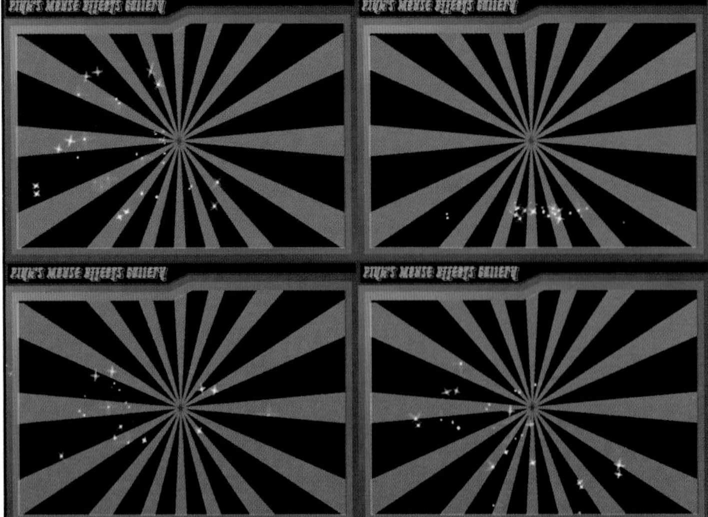

The stars shoot out from the mouse position. The faster the mouse moves, the farther the stars travel from the mouse.

3 Test the file to observe the effect.

The final source code for the StarModule should look like this:

```
onClipEvent (load) {

    //Initialize variables for calculating inertia
    starTime = getTimer( );
    xdistance = 0;
    ydistance = 0;
    inertiaSpeed = 10;
    xoriginal = _xmouse;
    yoriginal = _ymouse;

    //Initialize variables for duplicating star
    originalStar._visible = false;
    originalStar.stop( );
    i = 0;

    //Starmodule's main function
    function fallingStar( ) {
        //Get mouse coordinates
        x = _xmouse;
        y = _ymouse;

        //Duplicate the star movieclip and assign the movie to the variable "path"
        duplicateMovieClip ("originalStar", "Star" + i, i);
        var path = eval("Star" + i);

        //Assign a random xscale and yscale to the movieclip
        //between 30% and 60%.
        newWidth = random(20)+40;
        newHeight = random(20)+40;
        newWidth *=  1 - (random(2)* 2); //Randomly flip the star horizontally
        path._xscale = newWidth;
        path._yscale = newHeight;


        path._x = x+(random(5)-random(10));
        path._y = y+random(15);

        //Assign inertia
        path.xinertia = xdistance * inertiaSpeed;
        path.yinertia = ydistance * inertiaSpeed;

        //Increment the counter
        i++;
    }
}

onClipEvent(mouseMove) {
    fallingStar( );
}


onClipEvent(enterFrame) {

    //Calculate inertia
    timeslice = getTimer( ) - startTime;
    xdistance = (_xmouse - xoriginal)/timeslice;
    ydistance = (_ymouse - yoriginal)/timeslice;
    xoriginal = _xmouse;
    yoriginal = _ymouse;
    startTime = getTimer( );
}
```

How It Works

Overall, the graphical mouse trailer effect requires relatively little ActionScript code compared to effects in other chapters, but considering it is a simple "effect," this chapter contains several useful concepts for using ActionScript to create user-driven animation. Most of the code is in the **onClipEvent(load)** event handler to initialize variables, to duplicate and associate the originalRoot movie clip with an array, and to define a function to change each duplicated movie clip to a different frame.

In this chapter, you've learned how you can use the same idea, and often the same code, with a slight twist to create totally new effects. You can play around with the effects and learn more about how they work by adjusting some of the variables initialized in each movie.

By initializing variables at the top of the code, you save yourself time when you want to change the size, number, or speed of the mouse effect code later on. By defining a function to change the graphics of the mouse effect, you created a way for a button to call that function and quickly change the entire effect to any number choice, with the ***choice*** variable as the function parameter.

For the mouse trailer effect, you used basically the same code, but you applied it within functions, so you could call a single function both for initializing the movie clip and for updating the movie clip. New techniques were introduced in the mouse trailer, such as the use of the **Date()** object to retrieve the month, day, year, hour, minute, and seconds of the computer's internal cock. The mouse trailer also used the ***substr(a, b)*** string method to parse out each character in a string and assign it to a text field inside the duplicated movie clips. These two events are executed inside functions, so you could simply call the functions every time the **enterFrame** event handler runs through its loop.

For the pixie dust effect, you didn't use the same code, but you did use the same concepts about duplicating new movie clip instances and manipulating them through associative arrays and **for** loops. New concepts introduced in the pixie dust effect include the technique of calculating the speed of the mouse and the technique of using the **onClipEvent(mouseMove)** event handler, which called the **fallingStar()** function only when the mouse was in motion.

You can use ActionScript to create a mouse effect like the one shown here.

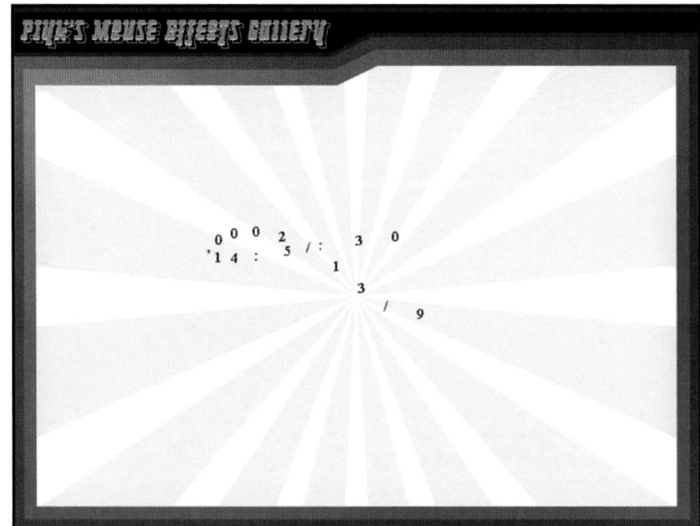

The mouse trailer consists of the date and time, which follow the mouse movement.

The key behind mouse-driven effects is creating special effects that move according to the user's actions. Using ActionScript to link the behavior of animation directly to a user's input can create a perception of true interactivity through motion.

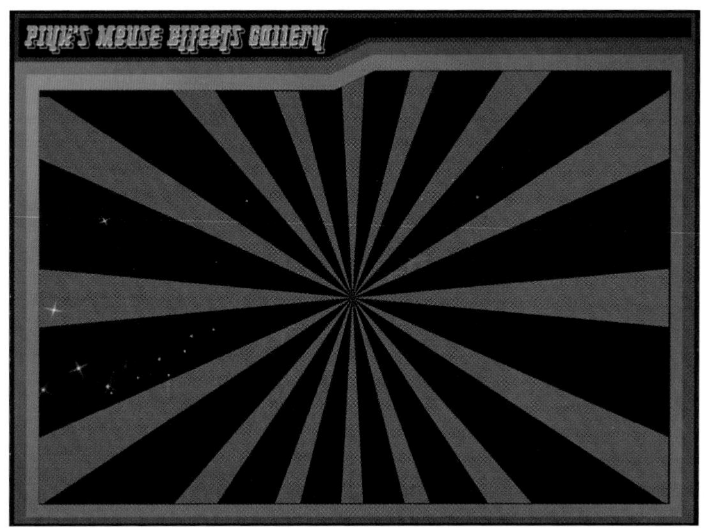

The movie clips fly away from the mouse, creating a pixel dust effect.

20

USING ACTIONSCRIPT TO MANIPULATE MOVIE CLIP ATTRIBUTES

By Jennifer S. Hall

This program demonstrates the use of on-the-fly calculations to determine placement of movie clips. It could be used as a changing background so that each time the program was run, the background would be different. This section includes many options: random rotation, random rotation within limits, random alpha transparency, random alpha transparency within a range, and quadrant constraint. We will demonstrate and create all these and learn how to turn them on and off easily.

Creating Random Tiling

1 Open Tiles_Start.fla. (If you want to see the finished file, open Tiles_Final.fla.)

You start with the tiles already in place and named. You can choose from two available tiling movie clips: circles and pills. For this example, you will work with the pills.

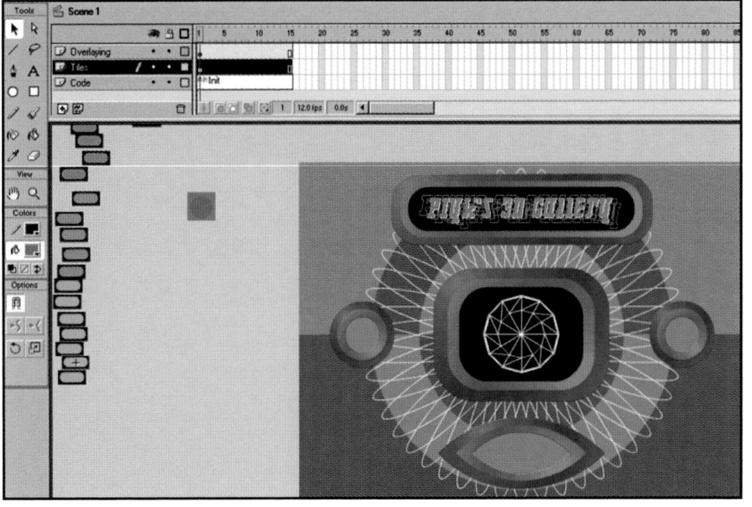

Notice that the movie clips are already placed off the Stage.

> **Note:** In order to create more movie clips for this tiling feature, the size of the movie clip is determined by the size of the Stage. The clip size needs to be an even multiple of the stage size. For example, if your stage size is 100 by 200, the tile size could be 10 by 10, but not 30 by 40, because 100 is not evenly divisible by 30, even though 200 is divisible by 40.

Notice that the tiles are placed off the Stage. This is because the ActionScript is going to place them on the stage.

2 Select one of the Pill tile movie clips and notice the name in the Instance window (Window > Panels > Instance).

The actual Pill movie clips are named in even numbers only (2, 4, 6, and so on). For ease of programming, each movie clip instance is named sequentially, starting with 1. For example, the instance of Pill 2 movie clip is named Pill1X. Each tile is named a specific number with an *X* at the end of the name.

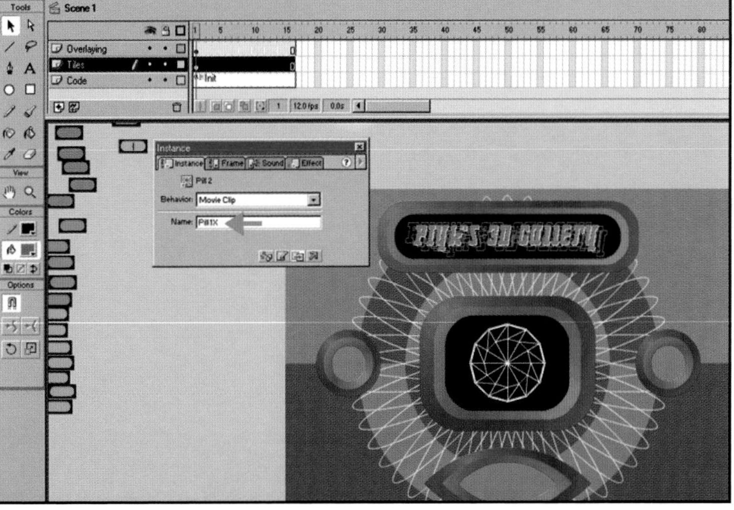

Check out the names of the movie clips. Each Pill movie clip has an instance name, such as Pill1X, Pill2X, Pill3X, and so on.

Because you are duplicating these tiles and giving them new names based on the layer, the *X* at the end of the name prevents two duplicate movies from having the same name. Think about what would happen if the tiles didn't have the *X* at the end and Pill1 tile were duplicated and placed on layer 21. Because the new name of the movie is created simply by adding the layer number to the original name, the new name would be Pill121 (Pill1 + 21—the layer). If Pill12 were placed on layer 1, the instance name would be Pill121, the exact same name as the instance on layer 21. When you duplicate movie clips, each movie clip must be on a separate layer and have a different name; otherwise they cancel each other out, as would happen in the case described, and the resulting tiles would not appear. However, because the names contain *X*s, the final names would be Pill1X21 and Pill12X1—two completely different names.

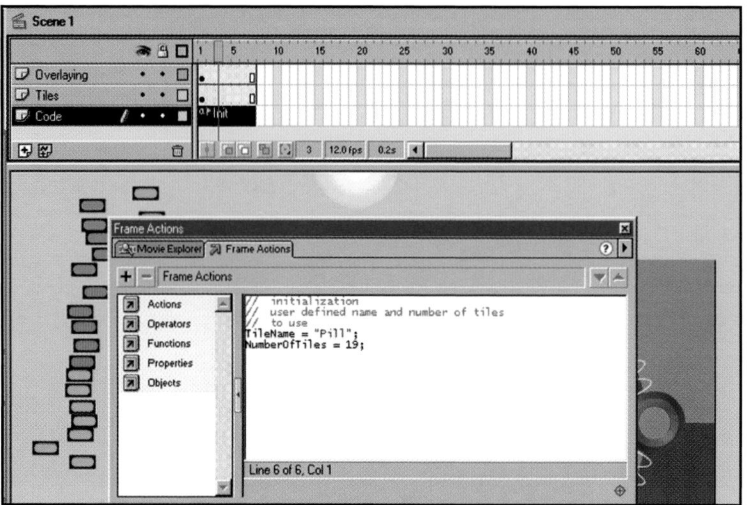

Notice that a few lines of initialization code are already on the code layer.

3 Select the Init frame on the Code layer. Open the ActionScript (Window > Actions) to view and edit it. There are already a couple of lines in the **Init** code.

The type of tile you are going to use for the background is ***TileName***, and the number of tiles of this type to use is ***NumberOfTiles***.

```
// initialization
// user defined name and number of tiles
// to use
TileName = "Pill";
NumberOfTiles = 19
```

Use the initialization code to set a few key variables.

4 Insert this code to determine the width of the stage to tile over:

```
//size of stage
StageSize = new Array(400,300);
```

Use this code to establish Stage size.

This puts the Stage size, which is 400 by 300, in an array called **StageSize**. This way if you want to change the size of the Stage, you need to change only one variable, which is in the **Init** code and is very easy to find.

5 Add this code below the ***StageSize*** variable in the **Init** code:

```
var Temp = TileName+"1X";
Width = getProperty(Temp, _width);
Height = getProperty(Temp, _height);
```

Include this code to get the width and height of the movie clips that the code will later tile onto the Stage.

The variable ***Temp*** is a temporary variable (notice the var in front) and is used to get the width and the height of appropriate tiles in this line:

```
var Temp = TileName+"1X";
```

It is assumed that any tiles that are used will follow the same naming convention already used in the circle and pill tiles (Pill1X and Circle1X). This means the code does not have to change, even though the size of the tiles used does change. The width of the tiles is determined by the **getProperty** command and stored in the ***Width*** variable in this line:

```
Width = getProperty(Temp, _width);
```

The height of the tiles is determined by the **getProperty** command and is stored in the ***Height*** variable.

```
Height = getProperty(Temp, _height);
```

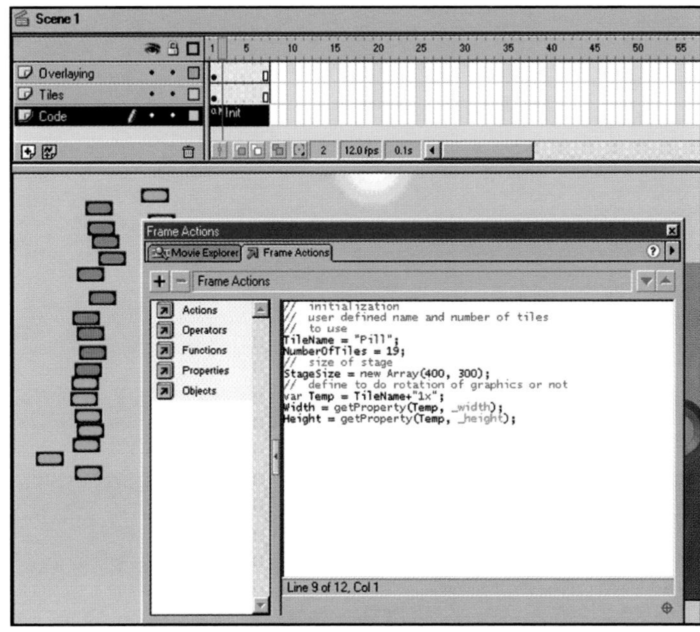

Add a variable and two **getProperty** commands to the frame labeled Init on the Code layer.

6 In the **Init** code at the bottom, add this code to determine the number of rows and columns that the selected tile will use to cover the stage area (probably easiest in Expert Mode):

```
Column = int((StageSize[0]/(Width)+0.5);
Row = int((StageSize[1]/(Height)+0.5);
NumberOfTilesOnScreen = Row*Column;
```

Add this code to determine the number of rows and columns the tiles will need to cover the specified stage area.

The ***Column*** variable is determined by dividing the Stage width (**StageSize[0]**) by the width of the movie clip (**Width**) in this line:

```
Column = int(StageSize[0]/(Width)+0.5);
```

The ***Row*** variable is determined by dividing the Stage height (**StageSize[1]**) by the height of the movie clip (**Height**).

```
Row = int(StageSize[1]/(Height)+0.5);
```

These variables should divide evenly, but just in case you can add a rounding up (**+0.5**) and make sure the result is an integer (**int**).

The number of tiles to be displayed on the screen (**NumberOfTilesOnScreen**) is computed by multiplying the ***Row*** and ***Column*** variables.

```
NumberOfTilesOnScreen = Row*Column;
```

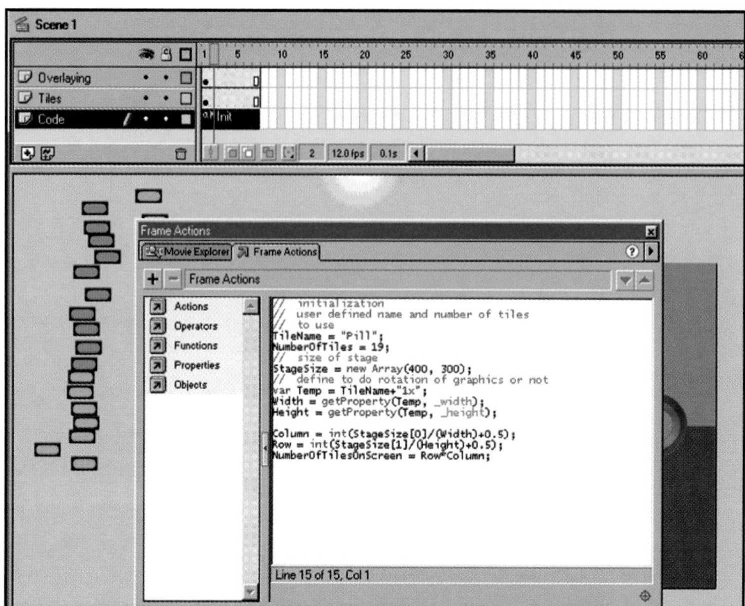

The code is added to the **Init** code on the Code layer.

7 At the bottom of the **Init** code, add a few counter variables to keep track of the looping:

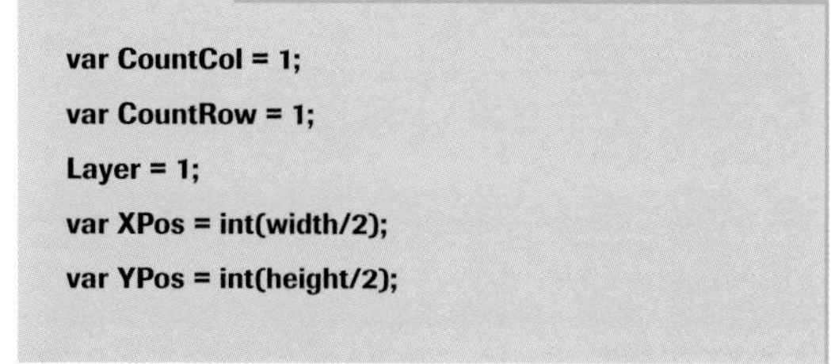

```
var CountCol = 1;
var CountRow = 1;
Layer = 1;
var XPos = int(width/2);
var YPos = int(height/2);
```

Use these variables to keep track of the looping.

CountCol will be used in the loop for placing the tiles as a counter to increment the column, and ***CountRow*** is used to increment the row. To have a movie clip that also starts off at 1 to make sure the first duplicated movie clip is placed in the first layer, you use this line:

```
Layer = 1;
```

The ***XPos*** and ***YPos*** are the starting positions for the movie clips. You want them to start off in the upper-left corner (**0**,**0**). The tiles' registration point is at the center of each of the tiles. To place the first tile at (**0**, **0**), you need to allow for the tile itself (or half of it). So you compensate for the tile itself by starting the tile placement, ½ a tile over and ½ a tile down.

```
var XPos = int(width/2);
var YPos = int(height/2);
```

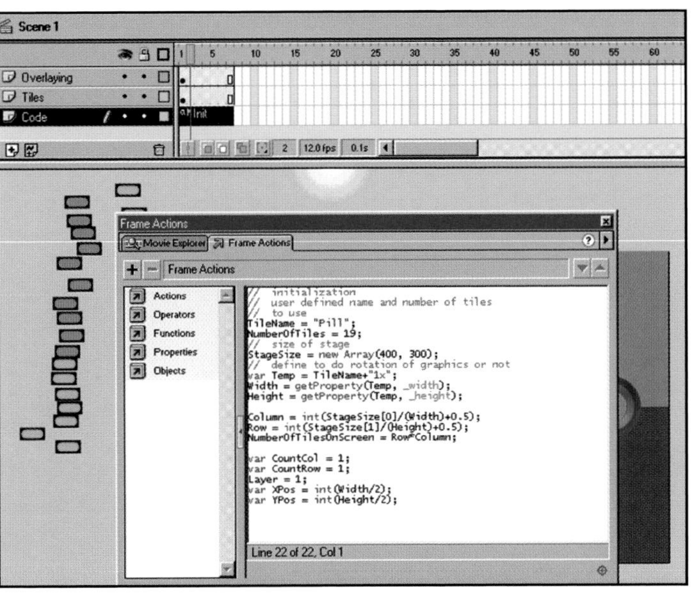

Add the ***counter*** variable that will keep track of the looping to the **Init** code on the Code layer.

8 Below all the code in the **Init** code, write the loop that places a random movie clip in each row and column.

This code establishes where the tiles are place. There needs to be a tile for each place, in each row and column. You initialized the ***CountRow*** and ***CountCol*** variables to **1** in the previous code. This code starts a **while** loop for the rows that will continue until all the rows have been done:

```
while (CountRow<=Row) {
```

Within the row loop, there is a column loop that continues its loop until all the columns are done. This means that for each row, you will place a tile in every column before going to the next row.

```
while (CountCol<=Column) {
```

```
while (CountRow<=Row) {
    while (CountCol<=Column) {
        var IPiece = random(NumberOfTiles)+1;
        Temp = TileName+IPiece+"X";
        NewName = Temp+Layer;
        duplicateMovieClip (Temp, NewName, Layer);
        setProperty (eval(NewName), _x, XPos);
        setProperty (eval(NewName), _y, YPos);
        CountCol = 1+CountCol;
        XPos = XPos+Width;
        Layer = Layer+1;
    }
    CountRow = CountRow+1;
    CountCol = 1;
    XPos = int(width/2);
    YPos = YPos+Height;
}
```

This code is a loop that tiles movie clips into rows and columns.

The movie clip is selected randomly for each row and column combination, based on the ***NumberOfTiles*** variable. ***IPiece*** is simply the number of the movie clip to be duplicated.

```
var IPiece = random(NumberOfTiles)+1;
```

Remember that the **random** function returns a number that includes **0**, thus the **+1** at the end of the **random** call.

Based on the number selected, the actual instance name of movie clip is determined and stored in the variable ***Temp***.

```
Temp = TileName+IPiece+"X";
```

The new name for the duplicated movie clip is based on the name of the tile piece plus the layer and is stored in the variable ***NewName***.

```
NewName = Temp+Layer;
```

Next the movie is actually duplicated using the **duplicateMovieClip** method. The first parameter is the name of the original movie clip—the one to be duplicated—(**Temp**), the second parameter is the new name of the duplicated movie (**NewName**), and the third parameter is the layer on which the new movie will be placed (**Layer**).

```
duplicateMovieClip (Temp, NewName, Layer);
```

The new movie is then placed in the correct *x* and *y* position using the **setProperty** command on the new duplicated movie and based on the *x* and *y* positions calculated.

```
setProperty (eval(NewName), _x, XPos);
setProperty (eval(NewName), _y, YPos);
```

Finally all the variables are incremented. The column counter (***CountCol***) is incremented by one (to move over one column).

```
CountCol = 1+CountCol;
```

XPos is incremented by the width of the tile (***Width***) in this line:

```
XPos = XPos+Width;
```

The layer (**Layer**) for duplicating the movies is incremented by 1.

```
Layer = Layer+1;
```

Once all the columns have been done in one row, the execution falls out of the column loop and increments the variables for the row loop. The row counter (***CountRow***) is incremented by 1, to go to the next row.

```
CountRow = CountRow+1;
```

The column counter (***CountCol***) is reset to 1, so you start back in the first column for the new row.

```
CountCol = 1;
```

The *x* position (***XPos***) is reset to its original position.

```
XPos = int(width/2);
```

The *y* position (***YPos***) is incremented by the height of the tile.

```
YPos = YPos+Height;
```

9 Test this and notice that each time you start the movie, it has a different look.

There is actually a problem with creating and placing duplicate movies this way. Notice that all the movie clips cover all the other graphics even though the layer that the tiled movie clips are on is below the layers the other graphics are on.

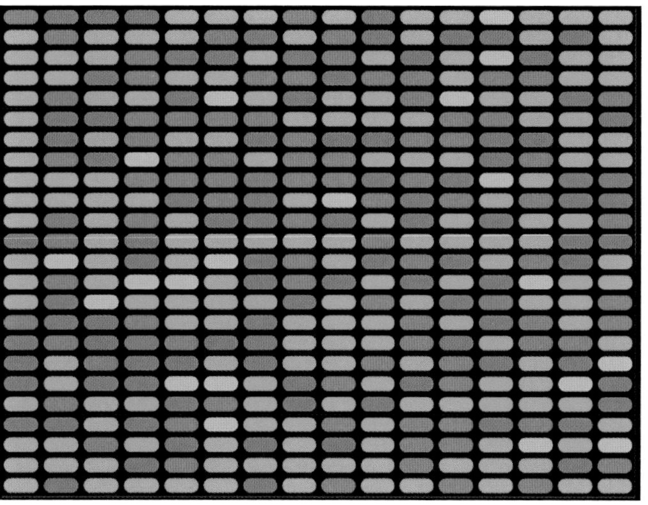

The Pill movie clips are selected at random and tiled onto the Stage, creating an animated pattern.

Duplicating Tiles to Create Better Random Tiling

To have the tiles always appear on the bottom, you could duplicate any and all graphics that you wanted on top of the tiles. A better way to do this is to duplicate each tile in its own movie.

1 Replace each of the Pill movies with the matching Holding movie. To do this, select a Pill movie on the Stage and press the Swap Symbol button in the Instance window (Window > Panels > Instance). Within the Swap Symbol window, select the appropriately numbered Holding movie.

For example, movie Pill 2, named Pill1X, is swapped with movie Holding Pill 2. When you use the Swap Symbol button to exchange movie clips, all the attached code becomes attached to the new symbol, but the instance name remains the same. The **Init** code still works the same way.

Use the Swap feature in the Instance panel to exchange movie clips.

2 Open any one of the Holding Pill movies. Each Holding movie contains the matching Pill movie named Pill and code. Open the ActionScript on the Code layer and look at this code:.

```
function CreateMovie (Xpos, Ypos) {
    XPos = XPos-this._x;
    YPos = YPos-this._y;
    Layer = Layer+1;
    NewName = "Pill"+Layer;
    duplicateMovieClip ("Pill", NewName, Layer);
    setProperty (eval(NewName), _x, XPos);
    setProperty (eval(NewName), _y, YPos);
    if (_root.Rotation==true) {
            setProperty (eval(NewName), _rotation,
            ➥random(4)*90);
    }
    if (_root.AlphaStart<>-1) {
setProperty (eval(NewName), _alpha,
➥random(_root.AlphaRange)+_root.AlphaStart);
    }
}
```

This code is very similar to the **Init** code within the row and column loop, but it is a function. The ***XPos*** and the ***YPos*** are passed as parameters.

XPos and ***YPos*** are compensated for where the original movie clip is placed on the main Stage in these lines:

```
XPos = XPos-this._x;
YPos = YPos-this._y;
```

The ***Layer*** variable local to this Holding movie

```
Layer = Layer+1;
```

is the same as setting ***Layer*** to **1** at the start and incrementing it later.

The next few lines of code are identical to the **Init** code, where you get a new name for the movie, duplicate it, and then place it.

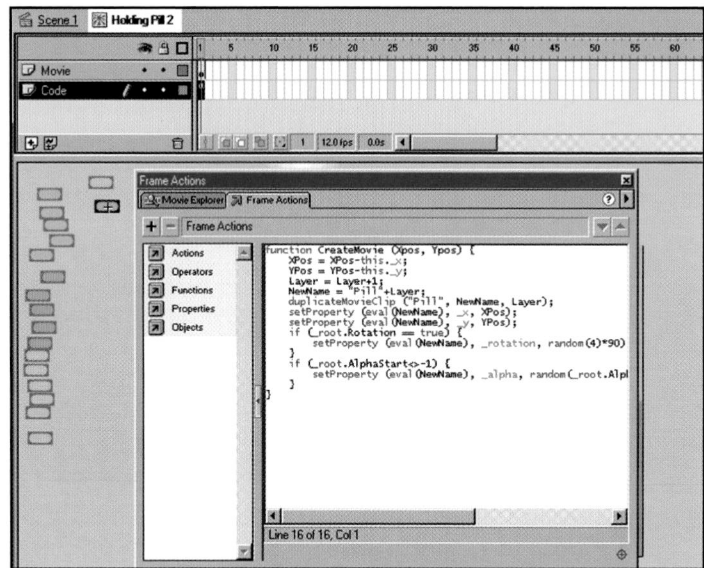

Check out the ActionScript within one of the Holding Pill movies.

Note: The code **Variable=Variable+1**, which increments a variable, is actually a Flash trick. If a variable doesn't exist when the code executes for the first time, Flash assumes that the variable is equal to 0 and adds 1 to it.

These final lines of code are for rotation and alpha transparency, which are not active and will be explained later:

```
if (_root.Rotation==true) {
    setProperty (eval(NewName), _rotation,
    ➥random(4)*90);
}
if (_root.AlphaStart<>-1) {
setProperty (eval(NewName), _alpha,
➥random(_root.AlphaRange)+_root.AlphaStart);
}
```

(The ➥ symbol you see here is for editorial purposes only.)

The rotation and alpha setting need to be turned off. This is done in the main scene in the **Init** code.

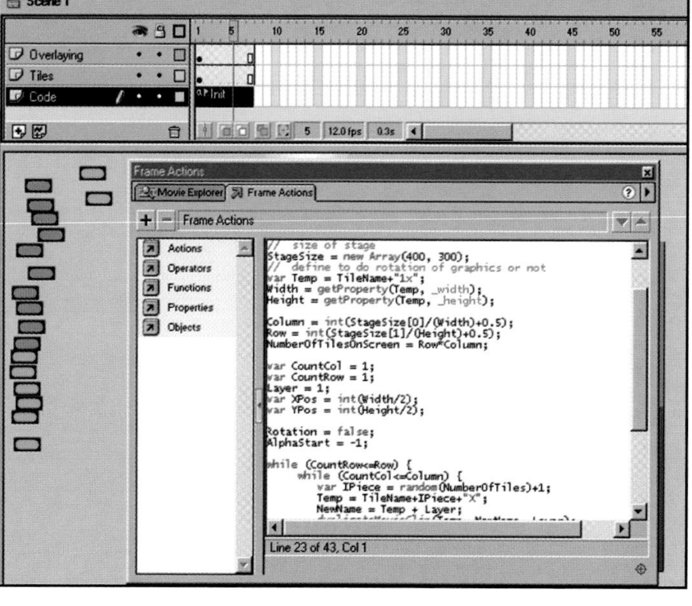

Continue the **Init** code on the Code layer, located on the Main timeline.

3 Close the Holding Pill movie clip and insert this code before the **while** loop in **Init** to turn off the rotation and alpha setting (you'll work with those settings later).

```
Rotation = false;
AlphaStart = -1;
```

Use this code to turn off rotation and random alpha transparency.

This sets a ***Rotation*** variable to **false** and the ***AlphaStart*** variable to **–1**. Now you can call the **CreateMovie** function from within this same loop in the **Init** code in scene 1.

4 Delete these lines of code in the **Init** code:

```
NewName = Temp+Layer;
duplicateMovieClip (Temp, NewName, Layer);
setProperty (eval(NewName), _x, XPos);
setProperty (eval(NewName), _y, YPos);
```

5 Replace the deleted code with a call to the **CreateMovie** code. Make sure this line of code goes in the same place:

```
eval(Temp).CreateMovie(XPos, YPos);
```

Use this code to call the **CreateMovie** code.

Remember that the **CreateMovie** function in each Holding Pill movie duplicates, names, and places the movie. Because this is done in the Holding Pill movie within the function, you replace the same code in the **_root** with the call to **CreateMovie**. Once the duplication of the movie clips within the movie clip is complete, the physical layers at the **_root** level will work.

```
eval(temp).CreateMovie(XPos, YPos);
```

This call to the **CreateMovie** function is within the row and column loops. So one movie is still duplicated, named, and placed for each row and column combination.

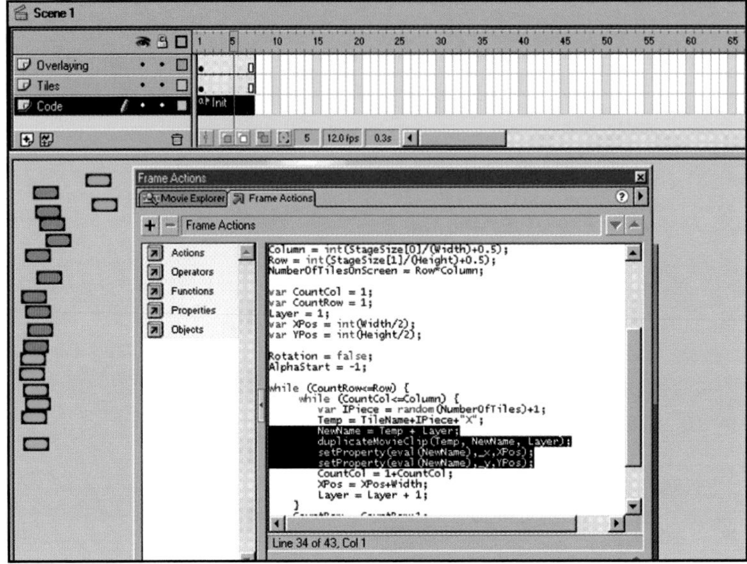

Delete four lines from the **Init** code.

6 Test this file and notice how each time you start the movie, it has a different look. In addition, you have fixed the problem. Draw a temporary box on the topmost layer and play the movie. The box now stays on top of the tiles as they change. Delete the box when you finish testing the file.

7 To understand how easily you can change the look, insert the Circle movie clips instead of the Pills:

```
TileName = "Circle";
NumberOfTiles = 9;
```

Change the look of the tiles simply by changing the movie clip.

8 Change the ***TileName*** from **Pill** to **Circle** and the ***NumberOfTiles*** from **19** to **9**. These simple changes to the variable name and variable number allow the look to be completely different by using other tiles. When you finish, test this.

9 Before continuing on to the next section, change the tiles to be used back to **Pill** and **19**.

Make sure the tiled movie clip appears below the graphics contained within the layers above.

Setting Up the Rotation and Alpha Transparency

You will now add some variation to the way the tiles look on the Stage. You will add a rotation of the tiles, in various rotations, and you will add a change to their alpha transparency. Each of these changes alone gives the movie a very different look.

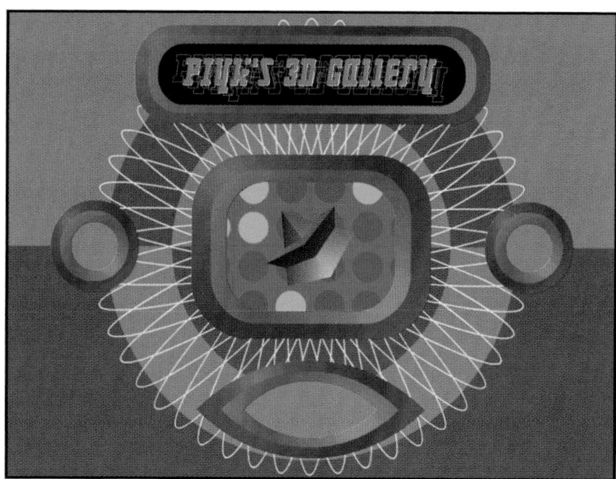

You can easily swap in other movie clips.

1 Change the random rotation flag (***Rotation***) to be true, so that rotation is enabled. This is found in the **Init** ActionScript.

```
Rotation = true;
```

Use this code to turn on rotation.

2 Test this. Notice that the tiles rotate, but only at 90 degree angles.

```
if (_root.Rotation==true) {
    setProperty (eval(NewName), _rotation,
    ➥random(4)*90);
}
```

(The ➥ symbol you see here is for editorial purposes only.)

Make sure that the movie clips are positioned in one of four degrees of rotation.

3 Open a Holding Pill movie and open the ActionScript on the Code layer (**CreateMovie** function). Notice this code:

```
if (_root.Rotation==true) {
    setProperty (eval(NewName), _rotation,
    ➥random(4)*90);
}
```

(The ➥ symbol you see here is for editorial purposes only.)

This checks to see if the **Rotation** flag is set to **true**. If it is, it proceeds to rotate the duplicated movie clip. It rotates the clip randomly but only based on **4**, because the rotation is only every 90 degrees (**random(4)*90**). This is applied to the new movie clip using the **setProperty** command with the **_rotation** property.

To set the rotation of the movie clips to be any degree, change the **CreateMovie** function within each Holding Pill movie clip to this:

```
setProperty (eval(NewName), _rotation, random(360));
```

This would rotate the new movie clip to a random degree based on 360 degrees. Note that, for this to take effect, you would have to change the code in all the Holding Pill movie clips.

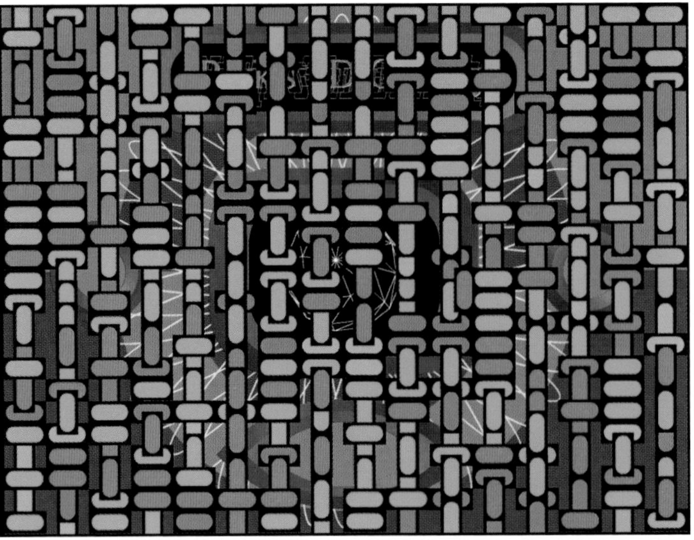

Here is the same file with the Tiles layer moved to the top so you can see the rotated movie clips better.

4 To randomly set the alpha transparency of each tiled movie clip within a range, replace the line of code **AlphaStart = -1;**, which is in Scene 1 **Init** code, with this code:

```
AlphaStart = 20;
AlphaRange = 30;
```

Add this code to establish a range of variable transparency for the movie clips.

The variable ***AlphaStart*** is the starting point for the alpha transparency. Remember in the **CreateMovie** function, the test for ***AlphaStart*** is ***AlphaStart* <> -1;**. So ***AlphaStart*** can be used as a flag to turn the transparency off by simply setting it to **-1**. The ***AlphaRange*** variable is used for the alpha transparency range. In this case, the alpha transparency for each movie clip will be set somewhere between 20% and 50%. The start is 20%, and the range is 30, so 20 + 30 = 50%. If you wanted the range to be the full 100%, the ***AlphaStart*** would be set to 0%, and the ***AlphaRange*** would be set to 100% (0 + 100 = 100).

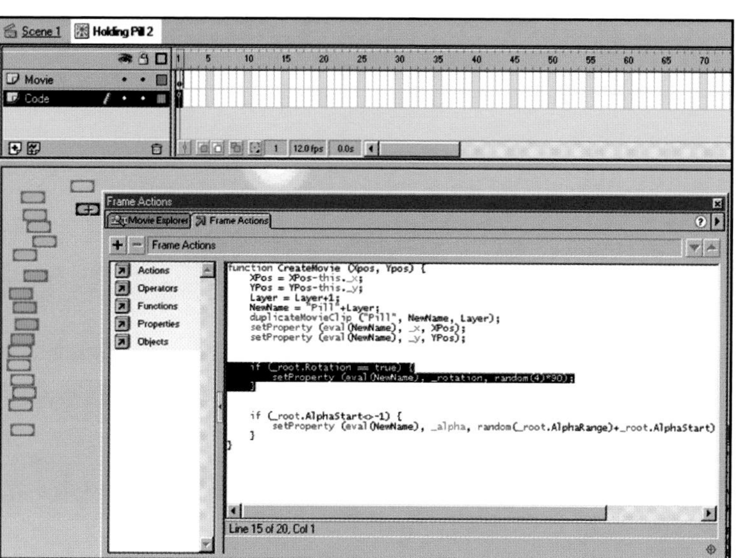

Inspect the code in one of the Holding Movies that randomizes the transparency of each of the movie clips.

5 Open a Holding Pill movie, open the ActionScript on the Code layer (**CreateMovie** function), and look at this code:

```
if (_root.AlphaStart<>-1) {
        setProperty (eval(NewName), _alpha, random
        ➥(_root.AlphaRange)+_root.AlphaStart);
    }
```

This code within the ***CreateMovie*** function checks to see if ***AlphaStart*** is equal to –1. If it is equal to –1, the alpha transparency is not changed in any of the Holding Tile movies. Otherwise, the new alpha transparency for each new movie is computed based on the randomizing ***AlphaRange***. The alpha transparency is set using the **setProperty** call on the new movie and the **_alpha** property.

6 Test to make sure that the transparency of each movie clip is different and that they are still rotated.

Make sure the movie clips are randomly transparent within a predefined range.

Restricting an Element to a Quadrant of the Stage

The tiling graphics and all their tricks can be restricted to a predefined section of the Stage. This way the graphics can be tiled either over the whole Stage or only over a section of the Stage.

1 Add this code before the loop in **Init** ActionScript in Scene 1:

```
TileQuadrant = new Array(100, 100, 300, 200);
```

Use this code to define the boundaries within which the movie clips will be tiled.

The **TileQuadrant** array is used to define the boundaries of the quadrant. The quadrant is loaded on the creation of the array. The quadrant must be smaller than the stage size. The first number in the array is the left boundary of the quadrant, the second is the top starting boundary, the third is the right boundary, and the fourth is the bottom boundary.

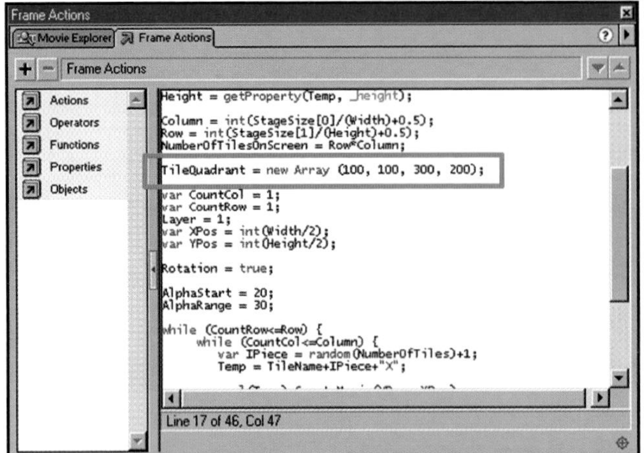

Insert the **TileQuadrant** array as shown.

2 Change the initial ***XPos*** and ***YPos*** variables to this code to allow for the quadrant:

You need to include the quadrant restrictions when you compute the placement of the tiles. The ***XPos*** variable is offset by the left side of the quadrant, which is stored in the **TileQuadrant** array index 0 (first place).

```
var XPos = TileQuadrant[0]+int(width/2);
```

The ***YPos*** variable is offset by the top of the quadrant, which is stored in the **TileQuadrant** array index 1 (second place):

```
var YPos = TileQuadrant[1]+int(height/2);
```

```
var XPos = TileQuadrant[0]+int(width/2);
var YPos = TileQuadrant[1]+int(height/2);
```

Change the **var xPos** and **var YPos** lines to accommodate the quadrant restriction.

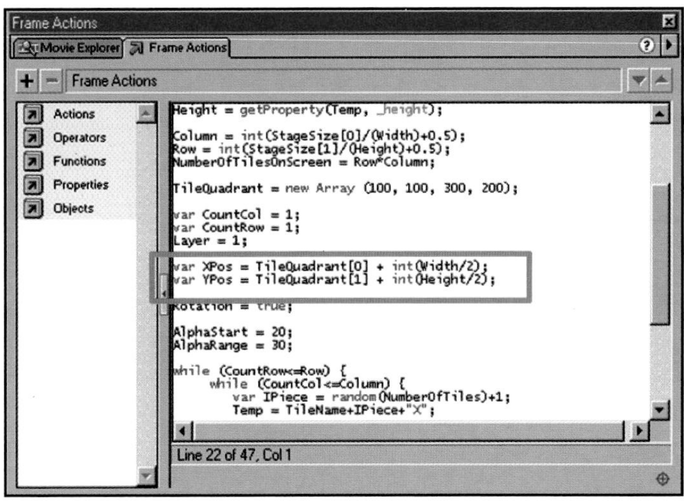

Edit the **var XPos** and **var YPos** lines as shown.

3 Change the **while** loops to keep the row and columns within the quadrant by deleting these lines:

```
while (CountRow<=Row) {
      while (CountCol<=Column) {
```

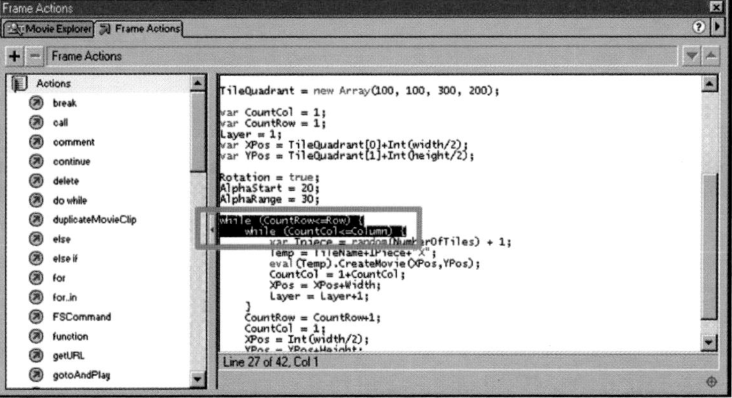

The highlighted two **while** lines are the lines you need to delete.

4 Replace the deleted lines with this code:

You are changing the check to be based on the quadrant instead of the whole screen. You set the starting positions of the ***XPos*** and **YPos** to be at the beginning of the quadrant, and you increment the ***XPos*** and ***YPos*** based on the height and width of the movies, so when the movie clips try to get outside of the quadrant, the appropriate **while** loop stops.

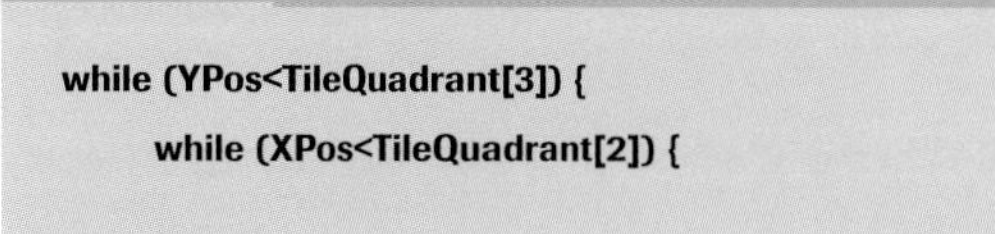

```
while (YPos<TileQuadrant[3]) {
    while (XPos<TileQuadrant[2]) {
```

Replace the code you deleted in step 3 with this code.

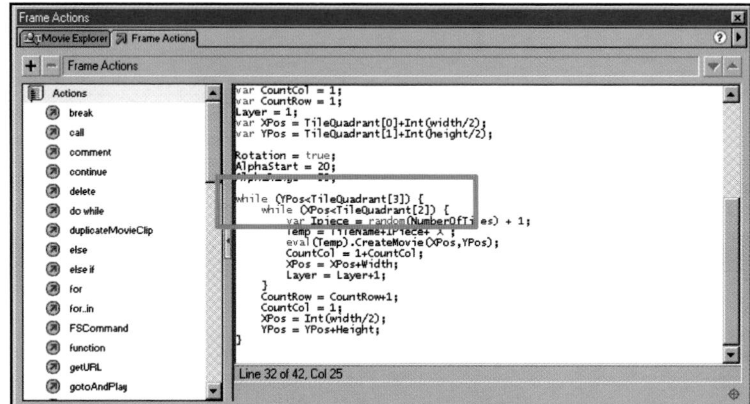

The highlighted area is where you replace lines with new code. Replace the deleted lines with the new code as shown.

5 Change the resetting of ***XPos*** at the end of the loop to compensate for the boundary on the left side.

Note that this is the same as when you initialized the ***XPos*** above.

```
var XPos = TileQuadrant[0]+int(width/2);
```

Add **TileQuadrant** to the variable close to the end of the **while** loop.

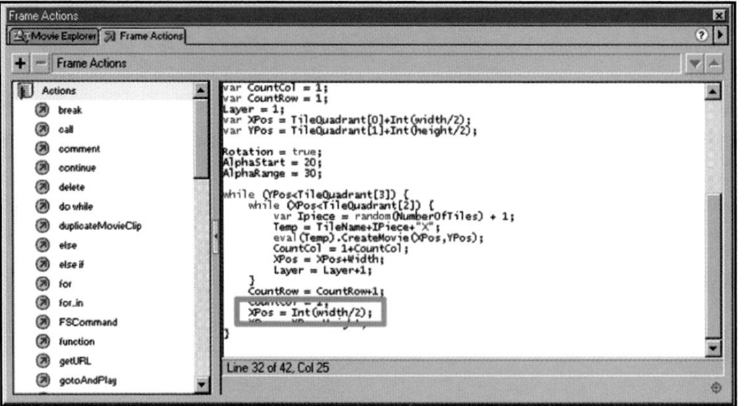

Edit this line.

6 Test the movie.

The tiles are restricted to the small rectangle defined in **TileQuadrant**. Now you have created code to compute the placement of movie clips randomly but within a predefined area on the screen.

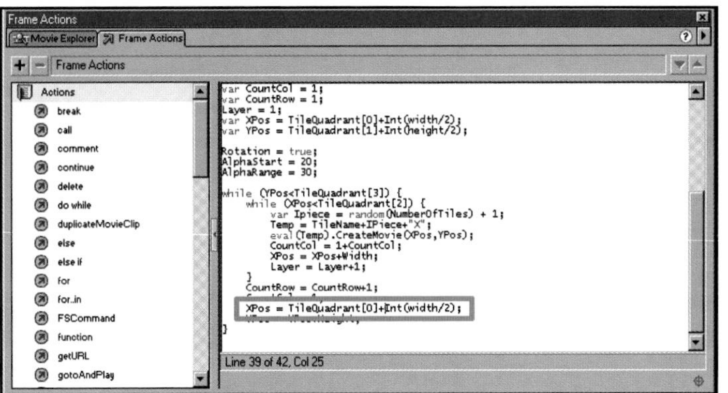

Add the **TileQuadrant** code.

How It Works

You have created most of the ActionScript for this program. The only looping is within the actual Pill movie clips. The main time line does not loop. The program achieves the movement in the Pill movie clips. Each of the different tiling Pill movie clips does the same sort of thing: It changes the dark yellow pill to a light yellow pill and then back to a dark yellow pill. However, each movie makes this change at a different frame number, which is what makes the randomization work. That is also why the movie clips are named the way they are; the number represents the frame at which the change takes place. The **Init** code sets up the variables for the loop and for all the variation, rotation, transparency, and quadrant restriction. It also places the tiles.

To use the same movie in different places at the same time, the **duplicateMovieClip** command is used. This is a method of class **MovieClip**. This will duplicate the selected movie clip with a new name and put it in the designated layer. There can be only one movie clip in each layer. If two movie clips are placed on the same layer, only one of them shows. Also, if two duplicated movies have the same name, only one shows on the Stage. This was explained in more detail at the start of this chapter in the explanation of the movie clip naming convention.

You cannot see the results of implementing the quadrant restriction very well. In this figure, the Tiles layer has been moved to the top to show that the movie clips are tiling only within the predefined quadrant.

Each movie was duplicated done within the Holding Pill movie clips. This way each Holding Pill movie clip took care of only the duplicate movie clips that were of its type. This also allows the physical layers in the **_root** movie to still be applicable.

The rotation and transparency changes are one-time changes. This was not a constant rotation or transparency change. Because of this, the ActionScript could compute the rotation and transparency only once, during the duplication of the movie clip (***CreateMovie***), and assign it.

The quadrant is based on a programmer-defined rectangle. During the placement of the tiles, as long as the ***XPos*** and ***YPos*** are within the quadrant, the tile is placed; otherwise, nothing happens.

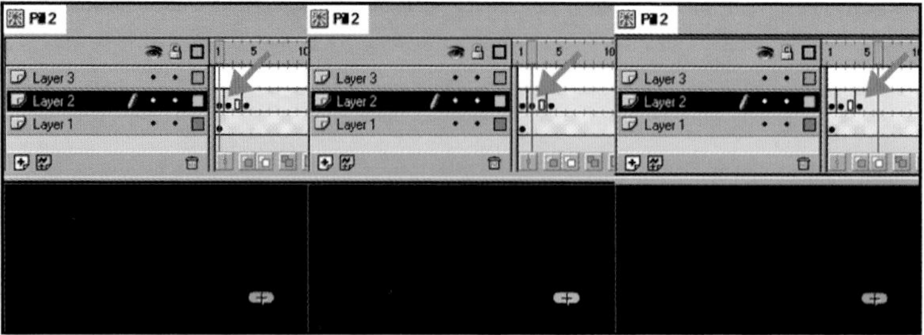

Each Pill movie changes to a different colored yellow pill on a different frame.

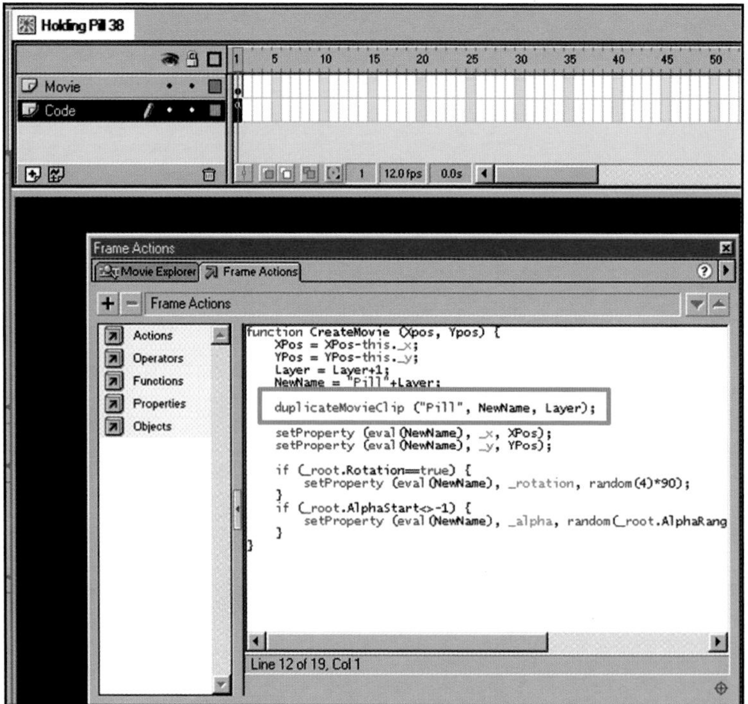

The **duplicateMovieClip** command provides for more than one instance of a movie clip to be used at a time.

PIYK'S WEBFOLIO

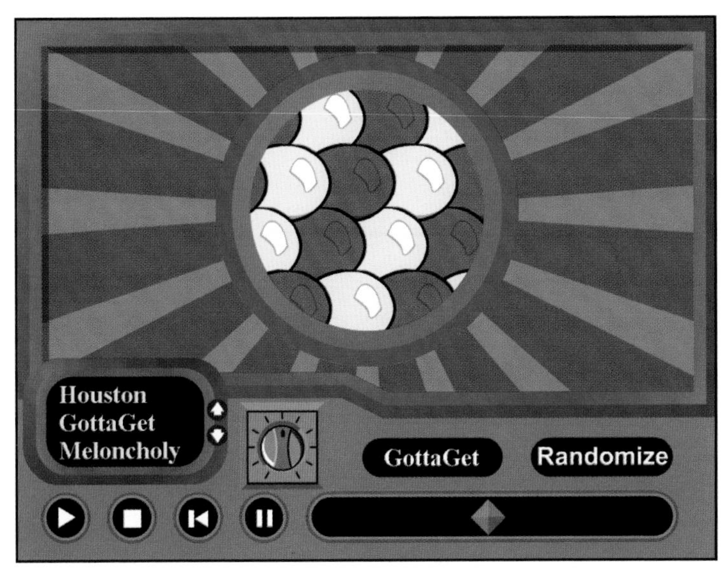

Chapter 18

Chapter 19

Chapter 20

"There was a time when the reader of an unexciting newspaper would remark, 'How dull is the world today!' Nowadays he says, 'What a dull newspaper!'"

—DANIEL J. BOORSTIN

DYNAMIK ACTION NEWS

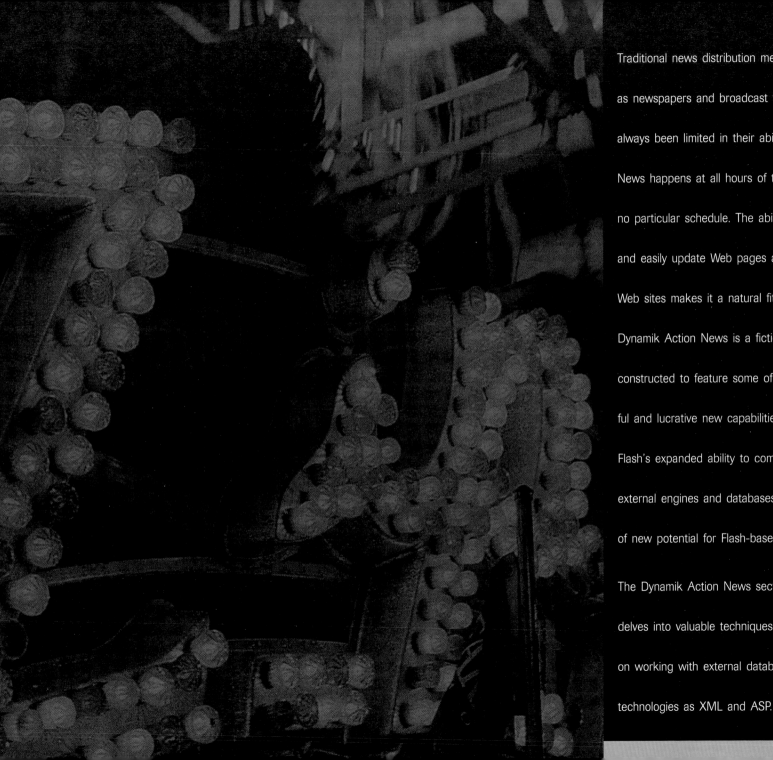

Traditional news distribution mechanisms, such as newspapers and broadcast television, have always been limited in their ability to be timely. News happens at all hours of the day and on no particular schedule. The ability to quickly and easily update Web pages and even whole Web sites makes it a natural fit for news. Dynamik Action News is a fictional news site constructed to feature some of the most powerful and lucrative new capabilities with Flash. Flash's expanded ability to communicate with external engines and databases opens a world of new potential for Flash-based production. The Dynamik Action News section of this book delves into valuable techniques and information on working with external databases using such technologies as XML and ASP.

21

IMPLEMENTING DATABASE INTEGRATION

By John Lenker

Macromedia has had the foresight and ingenuity to develop a suite of interconnected products that allow designers and developers to address the total experience of the individual user spatially (within an individual experience) and temporally (a series of experiences over time). These complementary products mainly deal with what is known as "back-end integration." The ability of Flash to integrate with external data systems allows it to incorporate not only dynamic content but also personalized content into the Web experience.

The purpose of this chapter and the next is to introduce you to the concepts and techniques that allow you to begin building Web experiences with Flash 5 in order to deliver this dynamic and personalized content to your online audience.

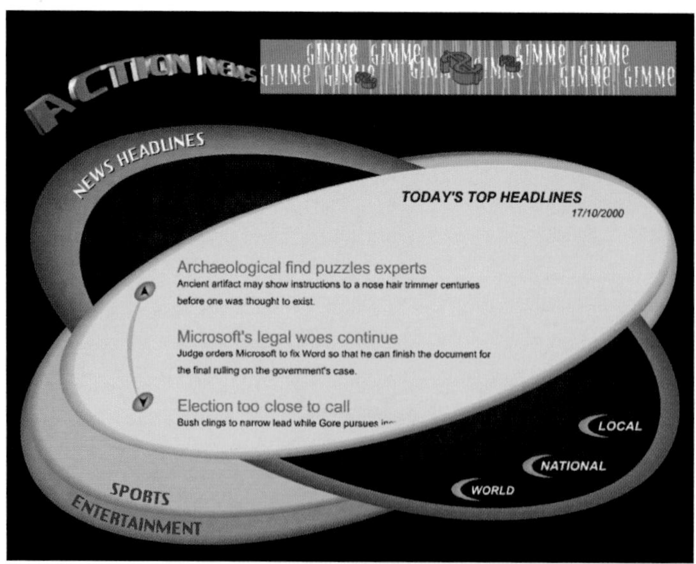

Integrating Back-End Data: The Whys and Wherefores

Instead of assuming that you understand the concepts and reasoning behind back-end data integration, this chapter focuses some attention on the rationale up front. Files are included on the companion CD for you to work with during these chapters. In addition, an example of the site built here is running at http://www.lenker.com/Flash5_Magic/. This URL contains working versions of the files discussed in these two chapters.

Note: Please be aware that Macromedia Flash 5 is not an industry standard XML parser and does not "validate" data. The XML solution detailed in this project was designed to work specifically with Flash Player 5. We recommend that you consider other XML resources to determine the appropriate form to use outside of Macromedia Flash 5.

1. Copy all the files from the 21and22 folder and save them to your hard drive.

   You can now open .fla files and generate .swf files. Also, the .swf files will read from external documents contained within this directory.

2. Open actionnews0.fla and generate the .swf to view the file.

   This type of presentation is a component of many types of Web sites. It could be the front page of a major online newspaper, or it could be the "newsletter" component of a corporate Web site.

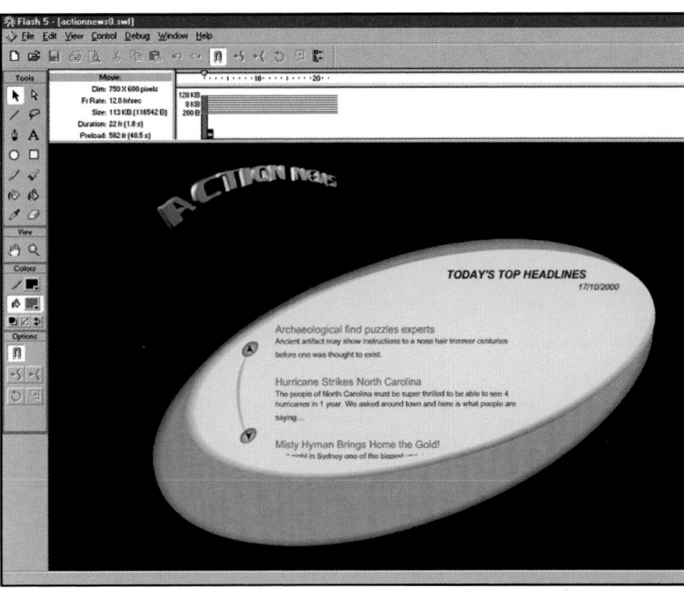

When you open actionnews0.fla and run a test movie, you can observe the output.

3 Close the .swf file and look at the .fla file.

Notice that there is a blank text field on the main stage. This text field is actually contained within a movie clip called news headline - summaries. If you select frame 1 in the actions layer and open the Actions panel, you will notice that the headlines, summaries, and links have been entered directly into the code. When the .swf is generated, this code builds a list of headlines coupled with the appropriate summary. When a headline is clicked, it opens the appropriate story by sending another movie clip, story ring, to the appropriate frame while populating the text field with the story text.

As you can see, the file runs correctly. All the headlines are present, and the links pull up the appropriate story. Although this may seem to be acceptable, this design is seriously flawed for several reasons:

- Every headline, summary, and link to a story has been manually entered, or "hard-coded," into this file. This means someone must make changes manually every time changes are necessary. If a typographical error is found, someone must make the correction. If a headline and story is added or deleted, someone must make that change as well. This is time consuming, costly, and monotonous.
- If there are more headlines than can fit on the screen, the client either will be forced to pick and choose between stories or will have to manually create a paging scheme. The problem with a non-dynamic paging scheme is that it does not lend itself well to content that changes often.

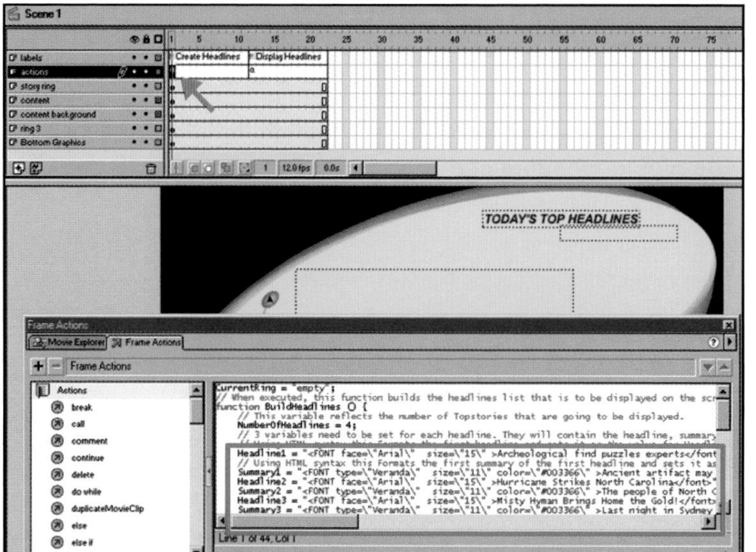

The headline and summary text is built into the Flash file.

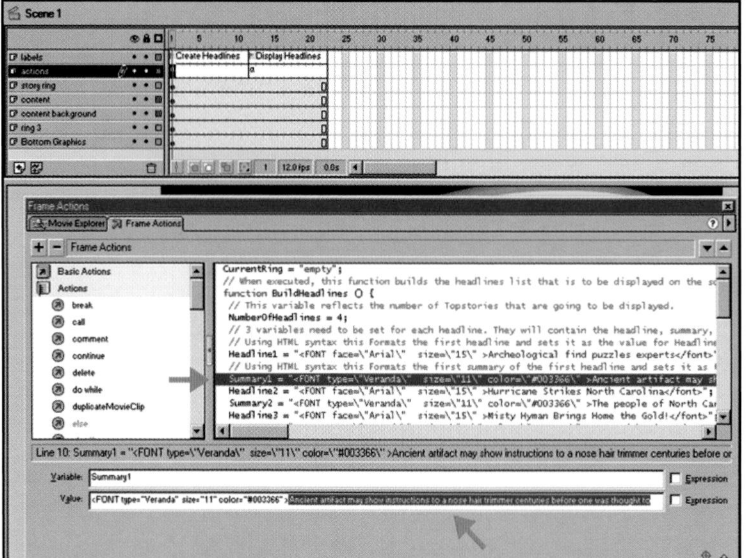

Changes to headline summaries and stories must be made inside the Flash file.

- Perhaps the most disregarded problem with this design is that everyone who enters this site sees exactly the same content. There is no personalization. Personalization is rapidly becoming a distinguishing factor among Web sites and represents a competitive advantage over non-personalized sites. Similarly, the advertising is not targeted to anyone in particular and is a major reason why most banner ads are all but ignored.

Aside from the personalization issue, these problems may seem to be minor details. One might assume that it would take just as long to enter this type of content into a database as it would to enter it into Flash. In a sense, this is a valid point—if the scope of the project was limited to this one list of stories. But multiply this by 10,000 stories (which many major newspapers deal with annually), and the problems compound themselves beyond what is reasonable to deal with.

How can the problems with the news story module be addressed? The answer is to separate the content from the code. In other words, you must externalize any displayed information that is not persistent. Usually, this means displayed information that is not part of the interface itself. "Displayed" information is specified because some navigational information is dynamic, such as certain variables that are loaded from external sources in order to make navigation function appropriately. This type of information is usually transparent to the user.

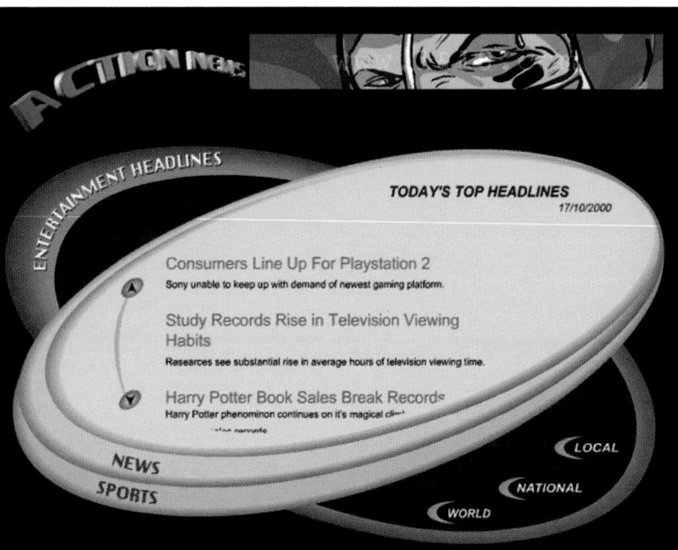

When the headlines, summaries, and stories are hard-coded into the Flash file, each visitor sees the same thing because the capability to personalize is severely limited.

EXTERNALIZING THE CONTENT

You're ready to begin the process of transforming this flawed example into a system that leverages back-end data systems to improve maintainability and personalization. Because the final solution is fairly sophisticated, you will add features and functionality in waves so that each wave brings you closer and closer to the final solution. This is known as the "iterative process of successive approximations." You will find it much easier to comprehend and retain the concepts involved in this way.

1. Open the file titled actionnews1.fla.
2. Notice that the actions attached to frame 1 in the actions layer have been modified to generate the headlines dynamically. This code will be dissected later in the chapter, after more background information is revealed.

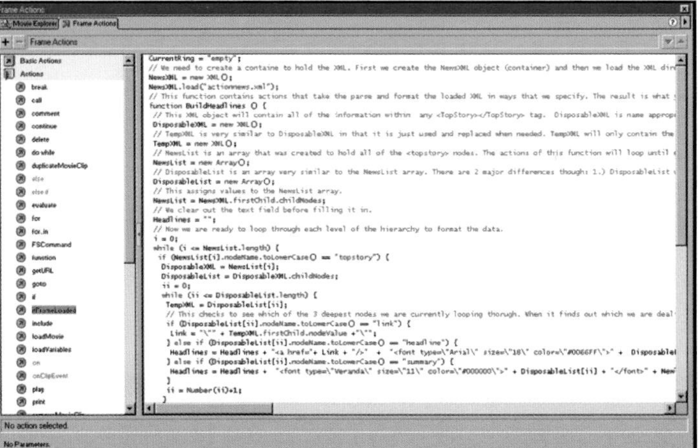

The headlines, summaries, and stories are not hard-coded into the Actionnews0.fla file.

READING AN EXTERNAL TEXT FILE

Before you jump right into using a server-side script, such as an Active Server Page (ASP) with a database, you'll begin by reading content from an external text file that is located right on your hard drive. This file is a text file with the .xml extension.

Knowing how to use local text files and making them part of your process is important because the workflow of your project may not allow you to access the server-side scripts and/or the database. Often the back-end work (server side) and the front-end work (Flash) are worked on (even finished) at different times. Because of this, you need something against which to test your ActionScript in place of the database itself. Using the text files in place of the server-side scripts that will eventually replace them allows the front-end Flash developer to work concurrently with the middleware (ASP, JSP, and so on) developer. When the middleware developer is ready, the server-side scripts will be designed to behave like the text files.

Understanding how to develop Flash front ends when a database, along with its server-side scripts, has already been developed is also important. You must design your ActionScript to tie into server-side script "hooks" that already exist. This means that sometimes it may not be efficient or cost effective to redesign the back end and middleware to fit Flash, and you will have to design your Flash front end to fit the pre-existing middleware and back end. It can sometimes be a challenge to track down and understand the ins and outs of a predesigned system.

1. Open actionnews.xml with a text editor such as Notepad.

2. Notice the basic nested hierarchical structure of the information displayed in this document. Some of the elements you see might not make sense. In the midst of these elements, you'll notice some text that is recognizable as headlines. These more recognizable elements are the bits of content that will eventually be read into the .swf file. The other elements (text that is enclosed by a < symbol on the left and a > symbol on the right) are known as "tags." These tags define the hierarchical relationships between the various data.

3. Look for the XML declaration that looks like this:

```
<?xml version=1.0"?>
```

The role of this initial tag is to identify the document as an XML document and to list the version of XML used for the document.

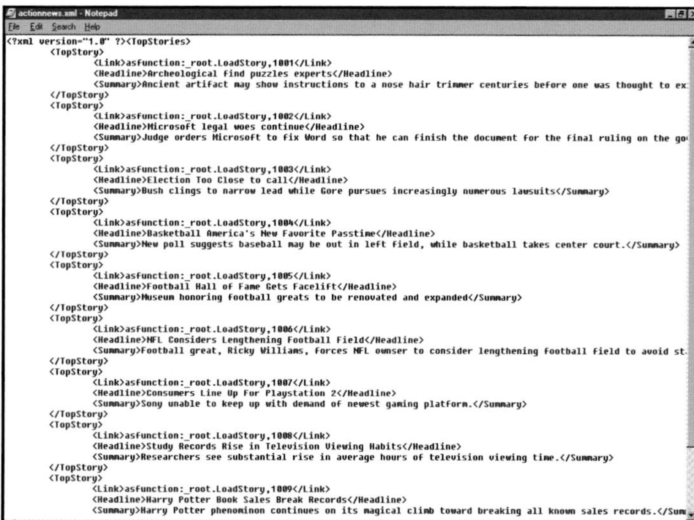


```
<?xml version="1.0" ?><TopStories>
	<TopStory>
		<Link>asfunction:_root.LoadStory,1001</Link>
		<Headline>Archeological find puzzles experts</Headline>
		<Summary>Ancient artifact may show instructions to a nose hair trimmer centuries before one was thought to ex
	</TopStory>
	<TopStory>
		<Link>asfunction:_root.LoadStory,1002</Link>
		<Headline>Microsoft legal woes continue</Headline>
		<Summary>Judge orders Microsoft to fix Word so that he can finish the document for the final ruling on the go
	</TopStory>
	<TopStory>
		<Link>asfunction:_root.LoadStory,1003</Link>
		<Headline>Election Too Close to call</Headline>
		<Summary>Bush clings to narrow lead while Gore pursues increasingly numerous lawsuits</Summary>
	</TopStory>
	<TopStory>
		<Link>asfunction:_root.LoadStory,1004</Link>
		<Headline>Basketball America's New Favorite Passtime</Headline>
		<Summary>New poll suggests baseball may be out in left field, while basketball takes center court.</Summary>
	</TopStory>
	<TopStory>
		<Link>asfunction:_root.LoadStory,1005</Link>
		<Headline>Football Hall of Fame Gets Facelift</Headline>
		<Summary>Museum honoring football greats to be renovated and expanded</Summary>
	</TopStory>
	<TopStory>
		<Link>asfunction:_root.LoadStory,1006</Link>
		<Headline>NFL Considers Lengthening Football Field</Headline>
		<Summary>Football great, Ricky Williams, forces NFL ownser to consider lengthening football field to avoid st
	</TopStory>
	<TopStory>
		<Link>asfunction:_root.LoadStory,1007</Link>
		<Headline>Consumers Line Up For Playstation 2</Headline>
		<Summary>Sony unable to keep up with demand of newest gaming platform.</Summary>
	</TopStory>
	<TopStory>
		<Link>asfunction:_root.LoadStory,1008</Link>
		<Headline>Study Records Rise in Television Viewing Habits</Headline>
		<Summary>Researchers see substantial rise in average hours of television viewing time.</Summary>
	</TopStory>
	<TopStory>
		<Link>asfunction:_root.LoadStory,1009</Link>
		<Headline>Harry Potter Book Sales Break Records</Headline>
		<Summary>Harry Potter phenominon continues on its magical climb toward breaking all known sales records.</Sum
```

The Actionnews.xml file contains the headline and summary information referenced by the code in the Actionnews0.fla file.

4 Notice the tag that marks the beginning of what is known as the "Parent" object:

```
<topstories>
```

5 Scroll to the bottom of the file and locate the end of the parent tag that looks like this:

```
</topstories>
```

With the declaration of this object, you do not actually define any content. You only establish a place where you can group individual chunks of content or other objects that in turn contain chunks of content.

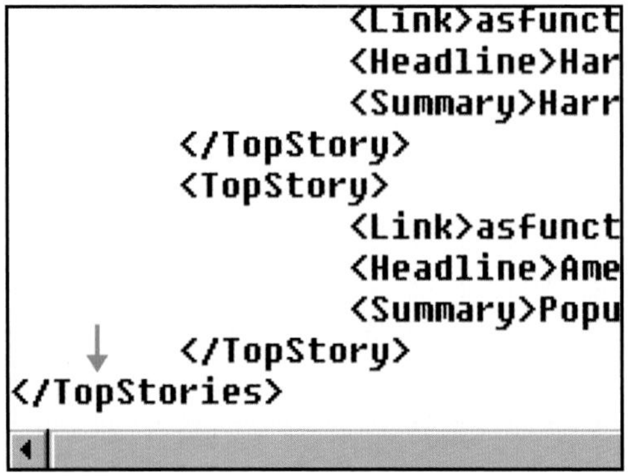

```
                <Link>asfunct
                <Headline>Har
                <Summary>Harr
        </TopStory>
        <TopStory>
                <Link>asfunct
                <Headline>Ame
                <Summary>Popu
        </TopStory>
</TopStories>
```

The <topstories> file contains the headline and summary information referenced by the code in the Actionnews0.fla file.

6 Look for the additional level to the hierarchy that contains several instances of a child object called "topstory." It looks like this:

```
<topstories>
<topstory>
</topstory>
<etc...>
</topstory>
</topstories>
```

The XML tags establish a hierarchy of parent/child objects.

Here, again, you've defined an object that has no actual content. You have merely created a subcontainer that has the potential to hold either more objects or chunks of content. So far we have a two-level hierarchy. The "topstories" tags define the parent object that has several instances of the "topstory" object as children.

7 The next level of the nested hierarchy will contain actual content.

This level of the nested hierarchy groups three types of information into one object. These three pieces of information are Headline, Summary, and Link. In context, they look like this:

```
|-Level 1-|
    |-Level 2-|
        |-Level 3-|

<topstories>
    <topstory>
        <headline>This is a headline</headline>
        <summary>This is a summary</summary>
        <link>asfunction:_root.LoadStory,1010</link>
    </topstory>
</topstories>
```

Note: It is important to note that any given XML file can have only one top-level parent node. (To think about the parent tag, imagine it as a large plastic container that holds other smaller containers, which in turn can hold progressively smaller containers.) As was mentioned earlier, each of these nested containers is known as a "child" of the hierarchical level directly above it. A child is actually a parent to any container nested within it.

8 Examine this structure more closely to understand why this kind of structure is needed.

This Web site provides the user with a list of news headlines and summaries he can click in order to read the full text of the stories. With only one list of headlines, it's easy to see how that singular list ties in with the singular top-level parent object called "topstories." The ActionScript within the .swf file is programmed to know that there is only one list of headlines, accompanied by related summaries and links. What the FLA file does not know is how many groupings of these headlines, summaries, and links there are. That's why the number of second-level child objects as defined by the <topstory> tag is indefinite. There can be as many occurrences of the <topstory> objects as necessary. Several possible stories equal several possible <topstory> objects.

The third level of the nested object hierarchy is more defined. Three content elements are always necessary to build the list of top stories. This third-level node can have one of three names: "Link," "Headline," or "Summary." This is the only level in the XML document that contains more than one node name. Each of these three nodes contains one of the following: the headline for the story, the story summary, or the link to be executed when the headline is clicked.

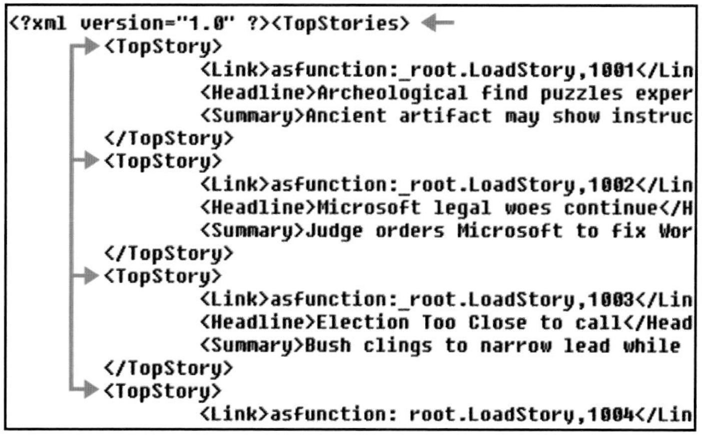

```
<?xml version="1.0" ?><TopStories>
     <TopStory>
               <Link>asfunction:_root.LoadStory,1001</Lin
               <Headline>Archeological find puzzles exper
               <Summary>Ancient artifact may show instruc
     </TopStory>
     <TopStory>
               <Link>asfunction:_root.LoadStory,1002</Lin
               <Headline>Microsoft legal woes continue</H
               <Summary>Judge orders Microsoft to fix Wor
     </TopStory>
     <TopStory>
               <Link>asfunction:_root.LoadStory,1003</Lin
               <Headline>Election Too Close to call</Head
               <Summary>Bush clings to narrow lead while
     </TopStory>
     <TopStory>
               <Link>asfunction: root.LoadStory,1004</Lin
```

Multiple <topstory> tags are nested within the <topstories> tag.

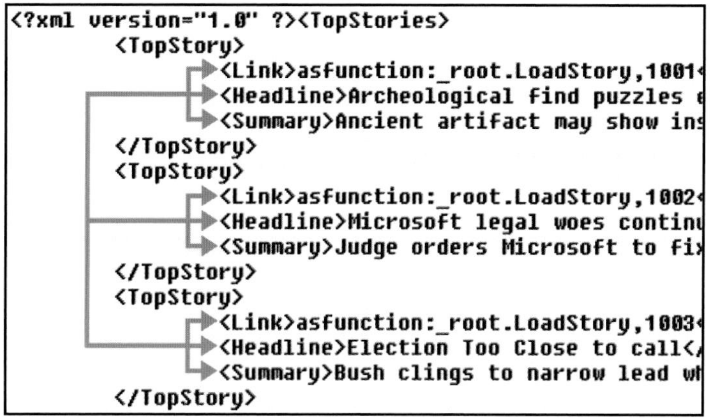

```
<?xml version="1.0" ?><TopStories>
     <TopStory>
               <Link>asfunction:_root.LoadStory,1001
               <Headline>Archeological find puzzles e
               <Summary>Ancient artifact may show ins
     </TopStory>
     <TopStory>
               <Link>asfunction:_root.LoadStory,1002
               <Headline>Microsoft legal woes contin
               <Summary>Judge orders Microsoft to fi
     </TopStory>
     <TopStory>
               <Link>asfunction:_root.LoadStory,1003
               <Headline>Election Too Close to call</
               <Summary>Bush clings to narrow lead wh
     </TopStory>
```

The hierarchy within each <topstory> tag is consistent.

ADDING CONTENT TO AN XML DOCUMENT

Add some content to this XML document to help burn these ideas into your mind. In the process, you will gain a better understanding of the format of the third level of the nested object hierarchy. To do this, you are going to add one more headline grouping to this document. You will also create a text file to contain the actual story.

1 Insert the cursor on the LAST blank line before the </topstories> tag.

2 You need to create a new topstory object. To do so, type **<topstory>**, taking care to tab in such a way as to position the cursor correctly within the hierarchy of the rest of the document, and then press Enter to make a line break. (Note: Incorrect tabbing will not result in error, just a confusing document. The tabbing convention is used to help visualize the structure.) The last tag you must type when creating a new entry is </topstory>.

```
<topstory>
```

This opens a new second-level child object within the "topstories" object.

```
		<Headline>Harry Pot
		<Summary>Harry Pott
	</TopStory>
	<TopStory>
		<Link>asfunction:_r
		<Headline>America V
		<Summary>Popularity
	</TopStory>
	<TopStory>
	</TopStory>
</TopStories>
```

Add a new set of <topstory> tags at the bottom of the actionnews.xml file.

3 Tab to the third-level position, type this headline object, and press Enter to make a line break:

You have just added a new headline to the XML file. It is enclosed within a new <topstory> tag.

```
<headline>(Enter your name here) wins the lottery and
➥becomes the richest multimillionaire of all time</headline>
```

Add this headline to the new <topstory> tag. (The ➥ symbol you see here is for editorial purposes only.)

4 Tab to the third-level position, type this summary object, and press Enter to make a line break:

This summary will be associated with the headline you created. It, too, is enclosed within the new "topstory" object.

```
<summary>This seems like news of a lifetime for (enter you
➥name here); however, authorities are investigating whether
➥or not the winning lottery ticket might have been
➥stolen.</summary>
```

Add this summary to the new <topstory> tag. (The ➥ symbol you see here is for editorial purposes only.)

5 Tab to the third-level position and add the link object.

```
<link>asfunction:_root.LoadStory,1011</link>)
```

Add this link tag to the new <topstory> tag.

This link tag works very similar to the Link tag (<a href=whatever.html) in HTML. Ultimately, this XML will be parsed, interpreted, and put into an HTML-enabled text field in the actionnews.swf file. Each headline will become a hyperlink. The **a href** parameter value will be what was enclosed within the link tags in the XML document. For example, if <link>http://www.lenker.com</link> was in your XML document, that URL would be visited when the associated headline was clicked. But in this case, you are using **asfunction** instead of a URL. When the link is clicked, Flash recognizes that **asfunction** is calling the ActionScript function that appears after the colon. So **asfunction:_root.LoadStory,1010** calls the function called "LoadStory" located in the root and passes it the parameter 1010. This function was written to load a story depending on the parameter passed to it. So 1010 loads Story1010.txt.

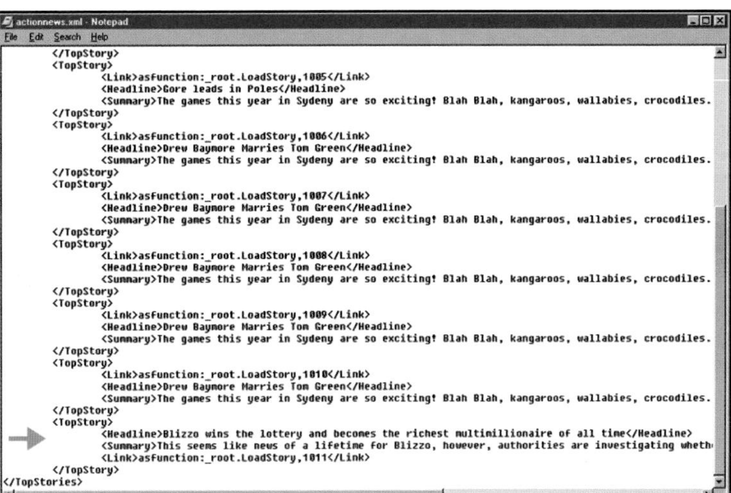

Add a new set of tags for another story to the actionnews.xml file.

6 Save your XML file to your local hard drive (into the current working directory) and switch to Flash. Then open actionnews1.fla. When you build a preview by pressing Ctrl+Enter, a new .swf file is built that incorporates the content you just appended to the actionnews.xml document. In addition, the headline you just built appears at the bottom of the scrolling text field. If you click on the headline, no story loads because you have not written a story yet.

7 Switch to a text editor. Type this into the new text document, adding more text if you want:

```
Story=(Your Name) is pretty happy about winning the lottery.
```

In any text editor, create a new file and type this text.

8 Save this file in your current working directory as Story1011.txt. Then test the .swf file again and click on your headline. The story you wrote should now appear in the story window.

Analyzing the ActionScript That Loads, Interprets, and Formats the XML

Our next task is to break down the ActionScript that deals with this XML file.

1. Return to actionnews1.fla.

2. Click on the first frame within the Actions layer for the file.

3. Switch to the Frame Actions editor and look at the code.

   You will dissect the code needed to deal with the XML line by line. Begin by taking a quick overview of Entire Frame. This frame contains actions that load, parse, and format the XML contained within the actionnews.xml file. It also contains actions that will be called when a hyperlink is clicked. When all this code has been either defined or executed, the frame is then told to leave and go to another frame.

   The first major block of code (lines 1–44) loads XML-formatted information from a file with the .xml extension, and then parses and reformats this information to fit your needs (HTML). The end result is a text field containing clickable headlines, each of which has its own summary. Now look at the individual line or lines of code.

```
NewsXML = new XML();
NewsXML.load("actionnews.xml");
```

Lines 3 and 4.

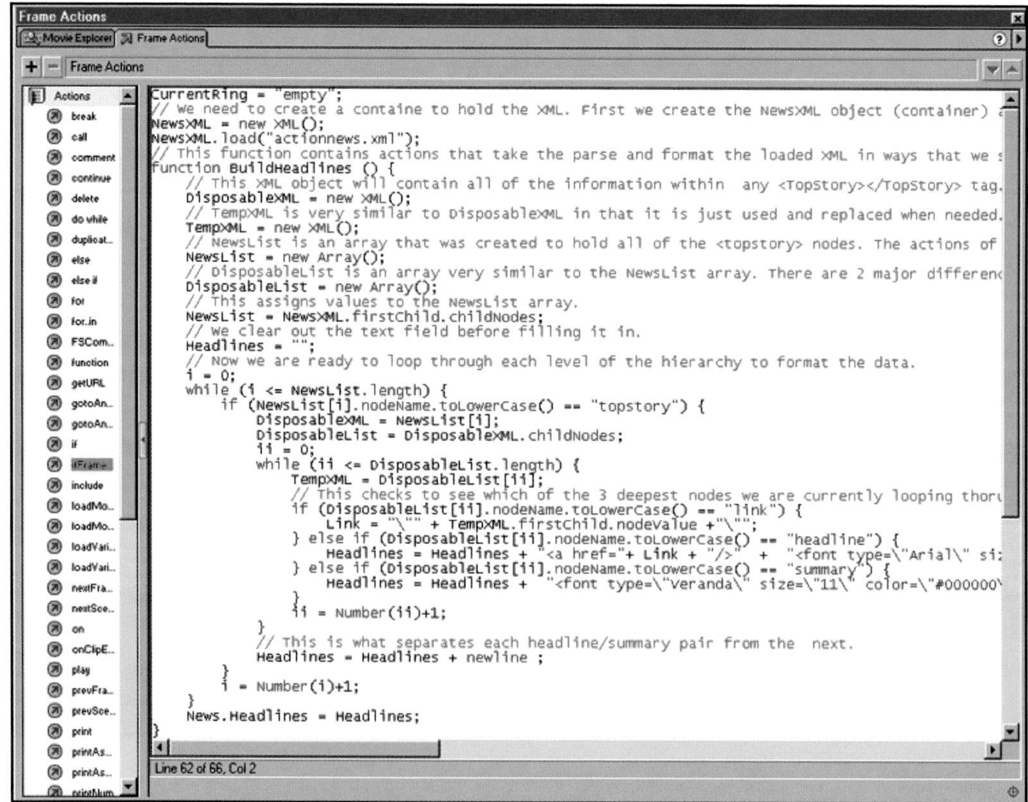

The following pages offer an in-depth look at the code on the first frame of the Actions layer.

You want to load the information from an XML file into your .swf. Before you do that, however, you need to create a container for it. This container is called an XML object and is created using the syntax shown in line 3. "NewsXML" is the name for this XML object. Line 4 of this code tells Flash to load a file called "actionnews.xml" into the NewsXML object you just created.

```
function BuildHeadlines () {
```

Line 6.

This line gives a name to the function you are building with all the code between the {} braces. This function has the name **BuildHeadlines** because its duty is to take the XML that has been loaded into NewsXML, dissect it, and format it in such a way as to build the headlines. Functions are not executed until told to. So by building this function, you can use this code as frequently as you would like without having to write any more code. This will be very useful if you ever need headlines to be updated frequently (on the order of minutes).

Here is a brief synopsis of **BuildHeadlines()**. The XML document is set up to have 1 parent node and approximately 10 child nodes (as the file comes off the CD), each of which will have 3 child nodes. **BuildHeadlines()** takes the information stored in NewsXML, determines how many child nodes there are (10), and then stores the information from childnode1 in a new XML object you create. It then takes the first child node of that XML object and stores it in another XML object. This function then determines the name of that node and formats the information accordingly. For example, if the name of that deepest node is "headline," it makes it a certain font size with a certain color, both of which are specified within the code. The function then loops through the other two deepest nodes, then backs out one level to move on to the roots second child node and proceeds from there. So if you have 10 "topstory" child nodes with 3 child nodes each, this function will perform 30 loops (using two nested loops) to format all the information contained within this document.

```
DisposableXML = new XML();
    TempXML = new XML();
```

Lines 8 and 10.

As you learned earlier in this chapter, the XML document called actionnews.xml contains information formatted according to a hierarchy. You have already created an XML container to hold the entire XML document (NewsXML). Now you will create an XML container to hold information that is two levels deep and one for information that is three levels deep.

DisposableXML is the name of the XML object created to hold second-level information—everything between the <topstory> and </topstory> tags. It will hold the child nodes for only one set of topstory tags at a time. So you will loop through the 10 sets of topstory tags and replace DisposableXML with new child node information as necessary. To recap, DisposableXML will contain the child nodes for each set of topstory tags (headlines, link, and summary), one set at a time.

TempXML is very similar to DisposableXML in its duty. It was created to hold third-level (the actual content level) nodes. It is also similar to DisposableXML in that it will hold only one node at a time. So you will loop through the deepest level three times to extract the needed information.

```
NewsList = new Array();
    DisposableList = new Array();
```

Lines 12 and 14.

You just learned that DisposableXML and TempXML will not hold more than one node at a time. So where can you store all the other nodes for future use? In arrays. You create two arrays, one for the level 2 elements and one for the level 3 elements. You do not have to create one for level 1 because it contains only one node, so there is nothing left over to store it in an array. These two arrays are called **NewsList** and **Disposable**, and they correspond to level 2 and level 3 of the hierarchy, respectively. Here is an example: NewsList[0] (the first item in the **NewsList** array) contains everything between the first set of <topstory></topstory> tags. DisposableList[0] contains everything between the first tags of the level 3 content (the <link></link> tags).

In the example XML file provided, **NewsList** contains 10 items: NewsList[0] through NewsList[9]. DisposableList contains three items: DisposableList[0] through DisposableList[2].

The entries in **NewsList** will not change, but DisposableList contains "disposable" entries.

```
NewsList = NewsXML.firstChild.childNodes;
```

Line 16.

This line of code fills the **NewsList** array that you created. It tells Flash to take the childNodes of the firstChild and set them as sequential entries in the array. The firstChild is the first node of the document <topstories></topstories>. The childNodes of the **NewsXML** firstChild include all the <topstory></topstory> nodes.

```
Headlines = "";
```

Line 18.

The text field in which you will load your XML is called "Headlines." The line of code shown here clears this text field so you can start with a clean field. If you didn't do this, any text already residing in this text field would be appended with your headlines.

```
i = 0;
while (i<=NewsList.length) {
```

Lines 20 and 21.

You now begin the first loop of the two nested loops. First you set your loop variable ***i*** to **0** as a convenient starting place. Then you add a **while** statement with an argument to ensure that you perform this loop only the required number of time. **NewsList.length** returns the number of items in the array called **NewsList**. So the **while** loop loops through until all entries in the **NewsList** array have been addressed.

```
if (NewsList[i].nodeName.toLowerCase() == "topstory") {
        DisposableXML = NewsList[i];
        DisposableList = DisposableXML.childNodes;
```

Lines 22 through 24.

The **if** statement is used to verify that you are dealing with the correct node. Some problems can occur if this is not done because Flash can read a carriage return as a node. So to make sure you are not trying to format a carriage return, you add the **if** statement. **nodeName** returns the name contained within the < and > of the node. The **.toLowerCase()** code is not necessary to function properly, but it makes your comparison more likely to succeed. If a back-end programmer decides to call the tag "Topstories" instead of "TopStories" (or even "TOPSTORIES"), this will force it to lowercase so you can verify the name regardless of previous case.

As was stated earlier in the dissection of this code, DisposableXML takes only one set of contents at a time. Line 23 assigns the correct item from the **NewsList** array to DisposableXML.

DisposableList is an array that will change its contents every time you loop through the main loop. Its contents are always going to be the 3 child nodes of the <topstory></topstory> tag you are dealing with at that time.

```
ii = 0;
while (ii<=DisposableList.length) {
        TempXML = DisposableList[ii];
```

Lines 25 through 27.

To start the nested loop, the first thing you do is set **ii = 0** for convenience. The argument of the **while** loop tells Flash to loop through the following actions while **ii** is less than or equal to the number of elements in the **DisposableList** array (in other words, three times). This is the loop that will move through each of the three deepest nodes (headlines, link, and summary).

Line 27 tells Flash to set contents of TempXML to item **ii** of **DisposableList**. Remember that we said earlier that TempXML will hold only one node at a time. So TempXML first contains node 1, then node 2, then node 3, and then you will leave the loop, and the main loop will increment and start over.

```
if (DisposableList[ii].nodeName.toLowerCase() == "link") {
                        Link = "\""+TempXML.firstChild.nodeValue+"\"";
} else if (DisposableList[ii].nodeName.toLowerCase() == "headline") {
Headlines = Headlines+"<a href="+Link+"/>"+"<font type=\"Arial\"
size=\"18\"
➥color=\"#666633\">"+DisposableList[ii]+"</font></a>"+newline;
} else if (DisposableList[ii].nodeName.toLowerCase() == "summary") {
Headlines = Headlines+"<font type=\"Veranda\" size=\"11\"
➥color=\"#ffcc33\">"+DisposableList[ii]+"</font>"+newline;
                }
                ii = Number(ii)+1;
            }
            Headlines = Headlines+newline;
        }
        i = Number(i)+1;
    }
    News.Headlines=Haedlines;
}
```

Lines 29 through 44. (The ➥ symbol you see here is for editorial purposes only.)

The main function of this next block of code is to determine which of the three level 2 tags you are dealing with. Once that is established, format the information accordingly and append it to the Headlines text field. Then increment the loop. If you are at the end of the loop, you will move on to the next headline. So you will add a blank line to what you already have. Take a closer look.

Line 29 checks to see if you are dealing with the node named "link." If you are, it sets that node value as the value for a variable you will conveniently call "link." With some forethought, you also enclose this link in double quotation marks to be directly inserted when needed into the HTML <a href></a> tags.

The first **else if** statement checks to see if the node name is "headline." If that statement is satisfied, you append the Headlines text field by using HTML syntax, and you give the value of that node a certain font type, color, and size and enclose it with <a href> tags with the link you just created.

The second **else if** statement is a more simple version of the first. If the **nodename** is verified as being "summary," you append the Headlines text field with an HTML-formatted version of that node value. When these loops are finished, the function is done doing what you designed it to do.

Lines 45 through 50 make up the second major block of code. This block of code is called when a hyperlink in the text field is clicked. When it's clicked, a parameter is passed to the **LoadStory** function, and an appropriate story is loaded as a result.

```
function LoadStory () {
```

Line 46.

This line defines a function called **LoadStory**. Everything contained with in the {} braces will be executed when called. This function will be called when a link is clicked.

The <link></link> tags of the XML document provide information in this form:

```
Asfunction:_root.LoadStory,1001
```

An example link result of the formatted text above in its html form is:

```
<font type="Arial" color="b#446699">
➥<a href="asfunction:_root.LoadStory,1001">USA Wins Another Gold
➥Medal</font></a>
```

(The ➥ symbol you see here is for editorial purposes only.)

When this is clicked, Flash interprets **asfunction** as "Execute an Actionscript function with this name." What appears after the comma is what you pass to that function in a built-in array called **arguments**.

```
    StoryNumber = arguments[0];
```

Line 47.

What appears after the comma in the **asfunction** statement (for example, 1001) is passed to the function as the zeroth element in an array called **arguments**. This is not an array that you create; it is created automatically by Flash. You set a variable called ***StoryNumber*** equal to the passed argument.

```
loadVariables ("Story"+StoryNumber+".txt", "StoryContainer");
```
Line 48.

You have included 10 text files with names story1001.txt through story1010.txt. So the ***StoryNumber*** corresponds to the name of the story you would like to load. When the user specifies which story to load, you concatenate that ID number between "Story" and ".txt" to build the name of the story to load. The StoryContainer movie clip was built to display these news stories, use it as the destination for the file being loaded.

```
    StoryContainer.gotoAndPlay("View Story");
}
```
Lines 49 and 50.

The text field that will contain the loaded story is on the ViewStory frame in the StoryContainer movie clip . This action tells StoryContainer to go to the ViewStory frame and stop there. That is the end of this function.

```
NewsXML.onLoad = BuildHeadlines;
gotoAndStop ("Display Headlines");
```
Lines 62 and 65.

These two lines of code do not reside in a function, which means they will be executed when this frame is visited. The first of the two lines tells Flash to execute the function **BuildHeadlines()**. This action could very well have been assigned to a button (and still can be). After this action has been executed, Flash goes to another frame and stops.

By completing these exercises, you have gained a basic framework on which you can build. You have learned the fundamentals of using XML documents to separate a project's content from the code. The next step is to learn how to tap into back-end database systems that can manage larger volumes of content than you can manage yourself with external text documents.

Note: John Lenker provides an area on his Web site where you can go to test out these files: http://www.lenker.com/Flash5_Magic. If you use a PC and have Windows 98 installed, you can test locally if you prefer (read below). If you use a Macintosh, you will have to upload all your ASP files to a Web server capable of executing ASP pages, or you can visit the provided URL at Allen Interactions.

Windows 98 users have the ability to build and test ASP files locally (on their own hard drives). Usually server-side scripts (such as ASP, JSP, CGI, and PHP) have to be uploaded to a server for testing. The Windows 98 CD comes bundled with Personal Web Server (PWS). It installs to the directory C:\Inetpub. ASP files that are accessed through your Web browser pointing to the ASP files located in C:\Inetpub\wwwroot will be executed. Some ASP components are not supported with PWS, which would cause errors, such as the CDONTS component. Overall, PWS proves to be the quicker way to test ASP files for two main reasons: It requires no upload time, and the files can be edited in their directory.

To get PWS up and running on your Windows 98 machine, put the Windows 98 CD into your CD-ROM drive and go to the directory D:\add-ons\pws. Run setup.exe to install PWS. After PWS is installed, you can test to make sure it is working properly. You access PWS through the browser by using this URL as the starting point: http://localhost. You should be able to type that into your browser to test if PWS is working properly. If you see a Web page, it worked; if you do not see a Web page, PWS is not functioning properly. If you have trouble, please visit the provided Allen Interactions URL for troubleshooting.

Now if you were to create a directory called actionnews in C:\Inetpub\wwwroot\ and add all the Action News files to that directory, you would be able to access them through the browser with a starting point URL of http://localhost/actionnews/. This will be necessary to test any ASP files locally.

Tapping into Server-Side Scripts (ASP) with Flash

Now that you understand how to externalize text, take a look at what goes into assigning the values you established in your XML file to an Active Server Page (ASP) file.

The important thing to understand is that the .asp file is simply a liaison between Flash and the database. In fact, as far as Flash is concerned, the .asp file behaves in the exact same manner as the .XML file did. The only difference is that the .asp derives all its content from a database and then formats it into the XML structure you learned about in the previous section. So the ASP page is a server-side script whose final output should look very similar to the file actionnews.xml. Generally it is not the Flash programmer's job to build the ASP pages; it is a back-end programmer's job.

1 Look at this side-by-side comparison of what the .swf file sees when looking at an XML verses an ASP document:

XML Text File	ASP Published File
<topstories> <topstory> <headline>This is a headline</headline> <summary>This is a summary</summary> <link>asfunction:_root. </topstory> </topstories>	<topstories> <topstory> <headline>This is a headline</headline> <summary>This is a summary</summary> <link>asfunction:_root.LoadStory,1010</link> </topstory> </topstories>

2 Take a look at a full ASP file.

In reality, the file looks much more complex than the XML file you looked at earlier. The added complexity is the scripting that's necessary for the .asp to communicate with the database. The added complexity is in the form of Visual Basic and Structured Query Language.

```
<%@ Language=VBScript %>
<%

dim conn,rs,SQLstr,rscount
dim times, ddate
dim output
dim doc
dim xmlProcess
dim rootElement
dim xmlElement
dim chldElement
```

The ASP source.

continues

The goal here is to understand the role of the server-side script and to know how to get the .swf file to communicate with it.

The ActionScript you developed in the previous section to communicate with an external text file is the same ActionScript that communicates with the ASP file. Only one line needs to be modified.

Note: It is beyond the scope of this chapter to teach server-side scripting. For one thing, as you shall see in the next chapter, there are several types of server-side scripts to choose from, depending on the environment your .swf file will live in.

continued

```
set conn = server.CreateObject("ADODB.Connection")
conn.Open(Application("connectionStr"))

SQLstr = "SELECT * FROM tblHeadline WHERE CatergoryID = " & Request("catergory")
set rs = conn.Execute(SQLstr)

if not rs.eof then
    set doc = server.CreateObject("Microsoft.XMLDOM")
    doc.async = False

    Set xmlProcess = doc.createProcessingInstruction("xml", "version=""1.0""")
    doc.insertBefore xmlProcess, doc.childNodes.item(0)

    Set rootElement = doc.appendChild(doc.createElement("TopStories"))

    do while not rs.eof
        set xmlElement = rootElement.appendChild(doc.createElement("TopStory"))

        set chldElement = xmlElement.appendChild(doc.createElement("Link"))
        chldElement.text = "asfunction:LoadStory," & rs("HeadlineID")

        set chldElement = xmlElement.appendChild(doc.createElement("Headline"))
        chldElement.text = server.URLEncode(rs("Title"))

        set chldElement = xmlElement.appendChild(doc.createElement("Summary"))
        chldElement.text = server.URLEncode(rs("Summary"))

        rs.movenext
    loop
end if

rs.close
set rs = nothing
conn.Close
set conn = nothing

Response.Write(doc.xml)
```

3 Open actionnews2.fla. Click on the first frame in the actions layer and open the Actions panel.

There's one important difference between this file and actionnews1.fla. This line (the third line of code, or fourth counting the comment):

```
NewsXML.load("actionnews.xml")
```

has been changed to this:

```
NewsXML.load("Headlines.asp?Category=1")
```

That line is the only difference between this .fla file and the previous one. All you did was change **"actionnews.xml"** to **"headlines.asp?Category=1"**.

Variables can be passed to an external script by the method shown here, which appends the variable to the name of the script. So if you wanted to pass three variables, your code would look like this:

```
Headlines.asp?variable1=something&variable2=
➥somethingelse&variable3=anotherthing
```

(The ➥ symbol you see here is for editorial purposes only.)

You passed the variable ***Category*** with a value of **1** to the script. That tells the script to load the default headlines. When the other three sections are activated (when the user presses their respective buttons), a similar load variable command is executed, replacing the value of **1** with **2**, **3**, or **4**.

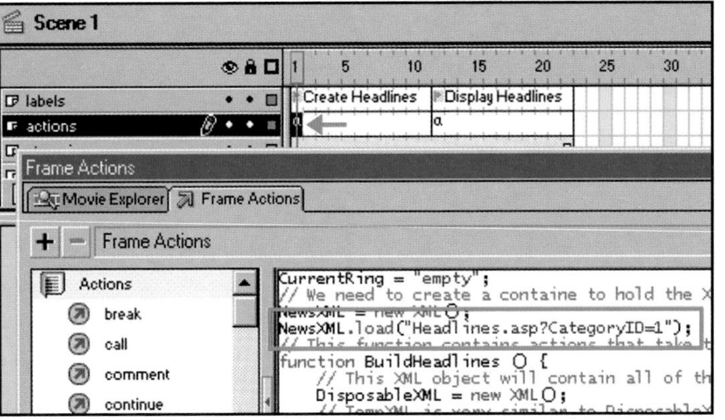

Notice the difference in the **NewsXML.load** line between the actionnews1.fla file and the actionnews2.fla file.

Note: This is a very common way of doing things. A Flash file is created and tested locally with premade XML documents, and then when the back-end work is done (the database and server-side scripting), it is an easy change. Usually this is the most efficient way to work because the back end and front end will be under construction simultaneously.

UNDERSTANDING DATABASE DESIGN FUNDAMENTALS

Before you go deeper into the complexity of ActionScript as it relates to communicating with server-side scripts, it will be helpful for you to understand some basics regarding the database itself. The goal is to compare the roles of the database and the ActionScript. Common sense would imply that the database is the information warehouse and that Flash is where the decisions are made regarding what information to retrieve from the information warehouse. This is actually not the case. The roles are somewhat more blurred, as you shall see.

Although many brands of database software are available, most of the databases you will encounter are based on Structured Query Language (SQL). SQL is the protocol, or the mechanism if you will, that database programmers use to access, retrieve, and return information from a series of related tables, which are set up like spreadsheets within the database itself. Because of the relationships between the data tables, databases that utilize the SQL protocol are known as *relational* databases. The "Query" part of SQL simply refers to the act of asking the database to look up values that are stored in a table at a certain location, and then returning those values to the source making the request. Here is an example of what a data table, or grid, might look like:

Name=UserInfo			
UserName	**UserID**	**Password**	**eMail**
PhilNelson	PNelson14	Pizzasauce14	pnelson@myco.com
JackNimble	Jnimble	GreenTree11	jnimble@netco.com

The Name=UserInfo identifies the table within the database. The column headers define specific categories for each record. The specific information represents the content for each record.

The way a query works is that the SQL locates a specific piece of data within a record. To understand this process, picture the grid as having an X-Y coordinate system. The headers in the top row represent the X-axis, and the array of specific data within a column represents the Y-axis. The idea is pick a row and pick a column. The result of the query will be where the crosshairs converge. Here is a simplified explanation of how a query of this data table might look:

```
Select "Password" from "UserInfo" Where UserID = "Jnimble"
```

The "relational" part comes into play when data from one table is associated with data from another table. For example, if Phil Nelson had made a product purchase online, his UserID would be associated with another table that tracked the transaction. Rather than redundantly storing personal information about Mr. Nelson in more than one location, each data table is designed to contain only information specific to its function in the overall information architecture. When an interface designed to display Mr. Nelson's recent purchase makes a query of the database, it pulls contact information, transaction information, product information, and shipping information from separate tables and combines them into one format.

The server-side scripts, such as ASP, JSP, PHP, and Cold Fusion play the role of liaison between the .swf file and the SQL database. Here is how these scripts function:

1. Receive the request for data from the .swf file.
2. Query the database for requested data using the SQL.
3. Receive the data back from the database.
4. Format the data into an XML object hierarchy that corresponds to the specific XML object ActionScripting in the .swf.
5. Send the XML-formatted information to the .swf file.

> **Note:** The server-side script can also send data to be stored in a record in the database.

These scripts are referred to as "server-side" scripts because the script is not downloaded to the user's computer like.swf and .html files are. Instead, they stay resident on the server. The server-side script is executed on the server every time the page is requested.

MAKING THE FLASH ARCHITECTURE DATABASE-FRIENDLY

It is very important to plan projects with information architecture in mind. Projects have a way of growing out of control. What begins as a simple project often keeps having features added to it. This has the effect of decentralizing code, which makes the project harder to maintain over time. Here is a list of simple rules to follow that will make things run more smoothly:

1. Plan content extensively so as to eliminate duplication of information requests.
2. Develop ActionScript functions that can be repurposed throughout a project. You will see that in actionnews1.swf and higher, more than one function is defined in the first frame. That means if later on in the user experience you want to refresh the headlines with the most up-to-date headlines, you can just call the **BuildHealines()** function without having to write another block of code.
3. When faced with a project that has been repeatedly repurposed and that has changed fundamentally from the original information blueprint, opt to re-engineer the ActionScript rather than altering the original idea.
4. Create data clips that store related sets of local variables so that the waters of the global variables-ocean are not muddied. It makes it much easier to fetch user input and send it to the database without a mess of stowaway variables tagging along.

> **Note:** A data clip is an empty movie clip created only to store variables. The advantage of putting variables in a movie clip is that you can later destroy, relink, or duplicate the movie clip to dynamically flush out all the variables. In addition, it makes the variables easy to find.

5. Test the functionality of your ActionScript with the aid of XML text files before you invest heavily in back-end integration. In many cases, an initial prototype will blow away assumptions in the initial information blueprint that would be costly to redesign on the back end. Once ideas have been validated in this way, progress can ensue on the back end with fewer iterations.
6. When problems become confusing, try breaking the code down into smaller, more manageable components.
7. When variables don't seem to be loading into a file correctly, type the URL for the server-side script into a Web browser to determine if variables are in fact being passed back to the .swf file. If they are not, the problem lies in the back end. If they do, a round of troubleshooting can begin within the .fla file. Note on how to do this: If you are, for example, dealing with an ASP file called actionnews.asp whose output should be similar to the content of the sample actionnews.xml file and you suspect a problem, follow these instructions. Type **http://pathtofile/actionnews.asp** into your browser. You should be able to view the output in the browser window. Does it look correct? If so, the problem is in Flash; if not, wake up the back-end programmer.
8. Add comments frequently in your code to quickly explain what it does. This will help make future .fla edits more manageable, especially if someone else has to do the editing.

How It Works

Building Flash to be a dynamic front end and building the efficient back-end components can be a very confusing process. What has been covered in this chapter should help you organize a similar project or should at least help you understand what it takes to accomplish such an application.

Essentially, this chapter has covered how to dynamically create content in a Flash movie by having the movie talk to a database through server-side scripting (ASP). What happens is this:

1. A user visits the Web site.
2. In loading the page, the .swf requests information from an ASP page.
3. The ASP page is written in Visual Basic and is designed to extract data from a database and to format it in XML structure.
4. Flash runs this XML through an ActionScript function (discussed earlier), creates output in HTML format, and displays an HTML interpreting text field.

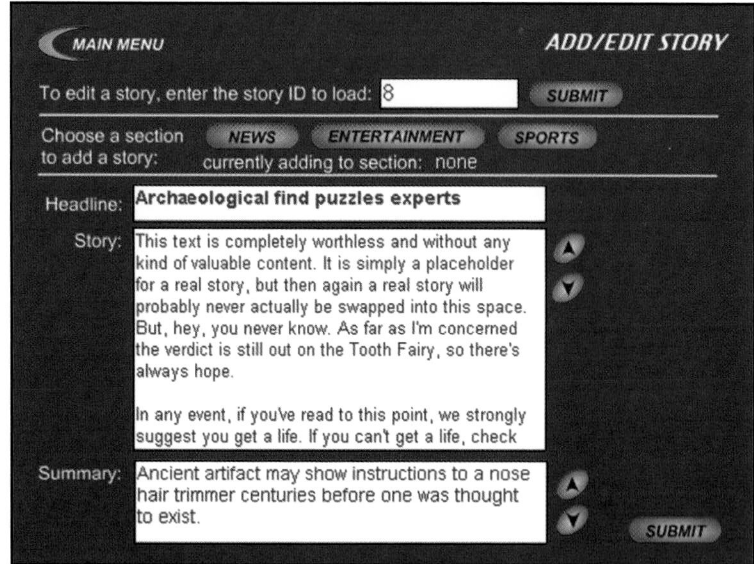

An advantage to working with external databases is that you can build a custom UI to make it easier to enter content.

XML is quickly becoming the Web standard for structuring chunks of data. If you learn to effectively use methods such as those outlined in this chapter, you will be better prepared to meet the increasing demand of creating front ends that display dynamic content. The initial time required to hard code a Flash site is short, but the time required to reedit FLA never ends when hard coded. The initial time required to build a complete database-driven Flash site is not short, but it is extremely easy to maintain with minimal or no FLA editing.

22

IMPLEMENTING COMPLEX DATABASE INTEGRATION

By John Lenker

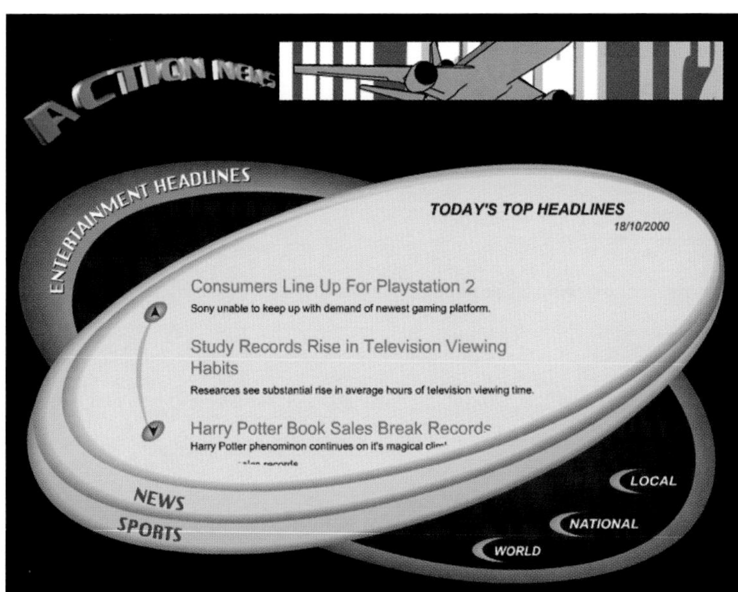

The Web's increasingly competitive nature is forcing site developers to design more meaningful features to increase the perceived value for both visitors and advertisers, as well as for the site's creators and maintainers. An increasingly popular way to augment a site's impact is to structure it so that it is dynamically personalized to each visitor's preferences and interests.

This chapter explores the true power of using a relational database to drive Flash content. Specifically, you will look at three value-added features that use advanced database integration:

- Feature #1: Built-in intelligence that progressively learns about user interests and filters content to match those specific interests.
- Feature #2: The ability to dynamically match banner ads with user interests.
- Feature #3: A Flash-based content input system that allows non-technical users to add stories and analyze user profiles.

All three of these features require the power that only a back-end database-driven solution can offer. The interesting thing about these new features is on the back end. Consequently, this chapter doesn't have much hands-on Flash development. However, a few interface enhancements will be necessary.

Understanding the Design of the Data Tables

When given the choice between building intelligence into the .swf or into the database, in most cases it is better to build the intelligence into the database. The reasons for this range from minimizing the number of times the Flash .swf file and the database need to exchange information, to minimizing development and revision time. It is always easier to make decisions about data on the server side. In addition, middleware scripting is far more powerful than ActionScripting.

Because the database will be making all the decisions, the information being passed to the .swf will be the same as it was in Chapter 21. The difference will be in the *nature* of the information being passed back. The database will now make some decisions it wasn't making before—namely, which headlines, summaries, and banner ads to send to the .swf based on individual user interests.

In order to make decisions, the database must contain two separate tables that *relate* to one another. (This is why the database is known as a *relational database*—because disparate chunks of information can relate to and inform one another in order to create information synergies.) The two necessary tables are described here:

- The existing data table that contains the records for each individual story
- A new table that contains records of individual user profiles

The database record for each story formerly contained only the headline, the byline, the summary, and the full text of the story. Now it will have the following details:

- A unique story ID number.
- A subcategory label, such as National, International, or Political for the News section; Film, Theater, or Literature for the Entertainment section; and Football, Baseball, or Basketball for the Sports section. (Note: When the site administrator creates a new record for a story, that person must categorize the story.)
- A date field, so that "yesterday's" top stories will be demoted in the list.

Adding these extra details to the record accomplishes a critical task: When the .swf sends a request to the database, in addition to returning the full text of the story, it can also inform the users' record in the "User Profile" table regarding the users' selection.

The new User Profile Table must contain these components of the individual records:

- A unique user ID number. (In a more "real-world" solution, the user would be enticed to reveal personal information over time, such as name and contact information. However, most users will not disclose personal information until the site's value has been established.)
- A matrix of the nine subcategories: National, International, and Political; Film, Theater, and Literature; and Football, Baseball, and Basketball.
- Accompanying check boxes for each of the nine subcategories to indicate whether or not a story within that subcategory has ever been read.
- Accompanying text fields for each of the nine subcategories to indicate the number of times a story within that subcategory has been read.
- Accompanying text fields for each of the nine subcategories to indicate the percentage of all stories read that fell under that specific subcategory. (This will be used to "weight" the number of stories returned to the .swf to favor stories that are of most interest to the user. It will also be used to determine the order from top to bottom in which the stories will be listed.)
- Accompanying text fields for each of the subcategories to indicate the most recent date on which a story under that particular subcategory was returned. This also will be used to "weight" the types of stories returned to the .swf.

Understanding the Personalization Process

Now that you understand the design of the database tables, you're ready to look at the structure of the process that uses them. Here is how the personalization process works:

1. The user comes to the site for the first time.
2. A cookie is set on the user's computer to assign the anonymous user a unique ID number that is associated with a record within the "user profile" section of the database. Even though the database does not know the user's specific identity, it will be able to track the user's interests in the background with this general tracking number.
3. The main list of headlines and summaries will be generic to all users the first time they come to the site. The database essentially sends everything in the "Today's Top Story" database to the .swf. (Now is where the fun begins.)
4. When the user clicks on links to individual stories, in addition to returning the full text of the story, the database does the following within the user's record:
   - Automatically click the check box associated with the returned story's subcategory if it has not already been clicked.
   - Put the story's date into the date field associated with the story's subcategory.
   - Increment by one the field that tracks the number of times a story within the given subcategory was read by the user.
   - Calculate the percentage of stories the user has read within all subcategories by totaling the number of all stories read and dividing it by the number of stories read within the subcategory associated with each percentage field. (The first time a story is read, the percentage field for the subcategory related to that story will indicate 100%.)
5. The site will continue to update the user profile until the user leaves the Web site.
6. Each time the user comes back to the site, the cookie informs the database of the unique ID number, and the history of that user's interests can be recalled from the database. These interests will then be used to weight the types of stories that will be returned to the .swf, as well as the order from top to bottom in which they will be listed.
7. The subcategory with the highest percentage within the user profile will be used to help determine an initial banner ad to display. This example has nine banner ads, each of which is associated with one of the subcategories. When a link to a particular story is selected, a new banner ad that corresponds to the story's subcategory appears. This happens only if the story is of a different subcategory than the subcategory represented by the initial banner ad. This function satisfies the second feature of the revised site—more effective banner ad placement.

Examining the Impact on ActionScript

Sometimes a user wants to read stories from categories that the database hasn't returned. For this reason, buttons for the three top-level categories—News, Entertainment, and Sports—have been included. When a user clicks on one of the buttons, the database is queried for a list of all stories within that category. The list will, however, still be sorted from top to bottom based on the subcategories the user has shown the most interest in. Providing users with options is a key component of personalizing your Web site.

> **Note:** Please be aware that Macromedia Flash 5 is not an industry standard XML parser and does not "validate" data. The XML solution detailed in this project was designed to work specifically with Flash Player 5. We recommend that you consider other XML resources to determine the appropriate form to use outside of Macromedia Flash 5.

1 Open actionnews3.fla, save it to your hard drive, and look at the changes that have been made to the interface.

2 Click on the first frame of the Actions layer, open the Frame Actions panel, and read the ActionScript.

   Notice that most of the ActionScript used to generate the initial "top stories" list has not changed. As indicated earlier, all the intelligence has been built into the database. However, there are three exceptions.

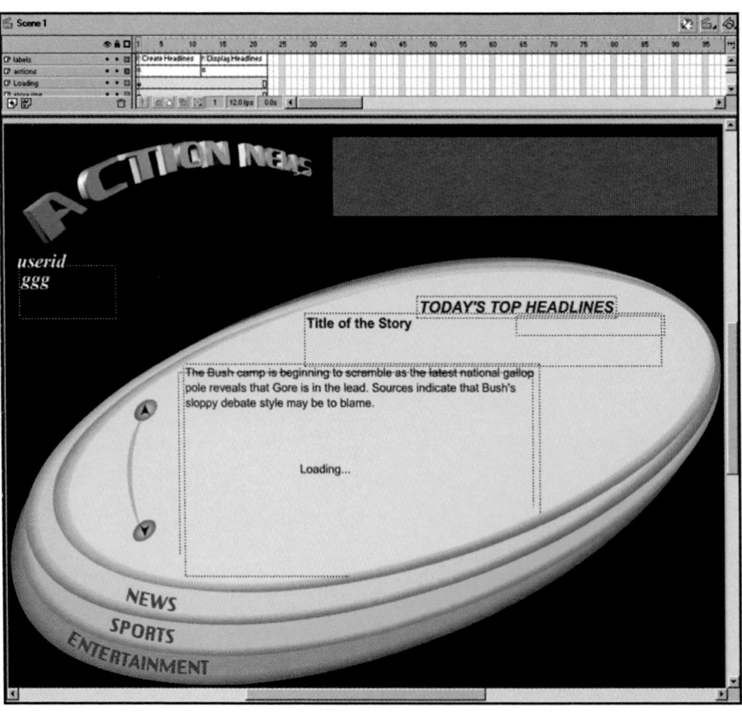

Notice that several things have changed between actionnews2.fla and actionnews3.fla.

First, in order to distinguish between the initial list returned upon entering the site and the one of the three lists that is returned when a category button is clicked, a filter has been added to the load script (the CategoryIDs act as a filter). This filter is "0." If you click on each individual button and open the Object Actions panel, you can see that the load script used to generate the category lists uses the filters "1," "2," and "3," respectively. All these filters do is tell the database which list is called for at any given time.

Second, the code used to load the banner ad onto level 10 has been modified. Instead of having a banner ad filename selected at random, it now waits for a variable to be returned from the database to tell it which banner ad to load. Here is the function that loads the banners:

```
function LoadBanner () {
    loadMovieNum ("banners/banner"+BannerID+".swf",
    ➥10);
}
```

(The ➥ symbol you see here is for editorial purposes only.)

This is a function called **LoadBanner**. When the XML has been returned to the .swf, Flash knows which banner to load. The ASP determines the name of the banner and returns it as the value of the variable ***BannerID***. If the value were **selected_banner"=1345**, for example, Flash would load banners/banner1345.swf.

Third, the XML is loaded differently. Previously, you loaded the XML from an XML file. Now you call an ASP page that builds the XML on-the-fly. You also

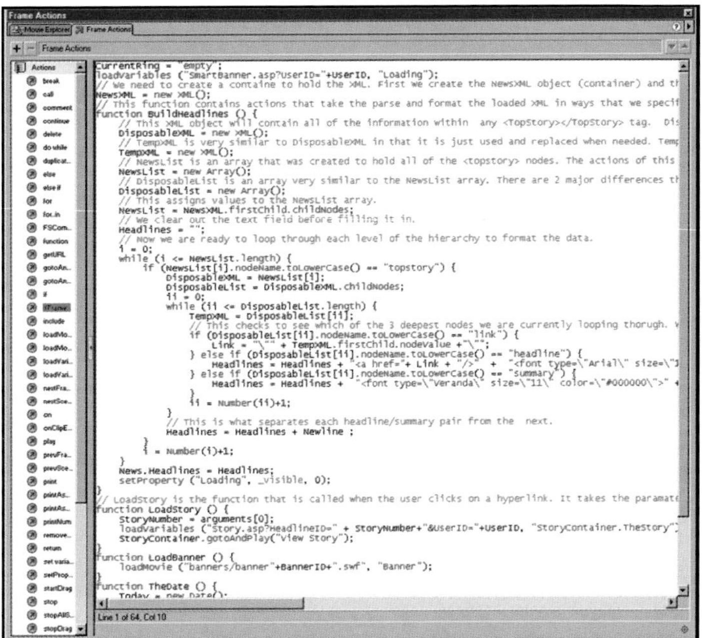

Inspect the code on the first frame of the Actions layer.

send the user ID of this user to the ASP page, which will help the back end determine what to send back. Flash knows this user ID because the ASP page in which it is embedded passed in that information when the .swf was loading. Here is the simple line that does so much:

```
NewsXML.load("actionnews.asp?ID="+id);
```

NewsXML is the name of the XML object in which the XML will load. You load information from the ASP page called actionnews.asp, and you pass it the variable called ***ID***. In the next steps, you'll look at these exceptions.

Developing Flash-Based Administration Tools

Content administration is a task that can be handled by anyone—including non-technical people. The idea is to develop an SWF-based tool that allows a user to put information into the database in the same way an SWF file gets information out of the database.

1 Open actionnews3admin.fla located in the folder on the companion CD and save it to your hard drive.

Notice the six keyframes. Each has a frame label and contains the interface for a specific content maintenance function:

- The frame labeled "Menu" is the first frame visited when the administration is loaded. It is the main menu of this administration section and contains buttons to the other sections of the administration.

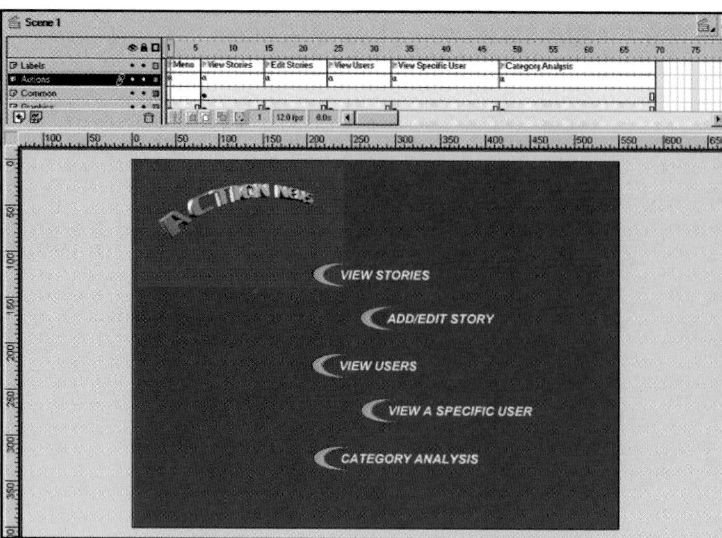

The first frame contains the menu that allows users to navigate to the various sections.

- The frame labeled "View Stories" dynamically generates a list of stories within one of the three top-level categories. You can view the stories individually, and there is an "edit" button that will send you to the edit page.

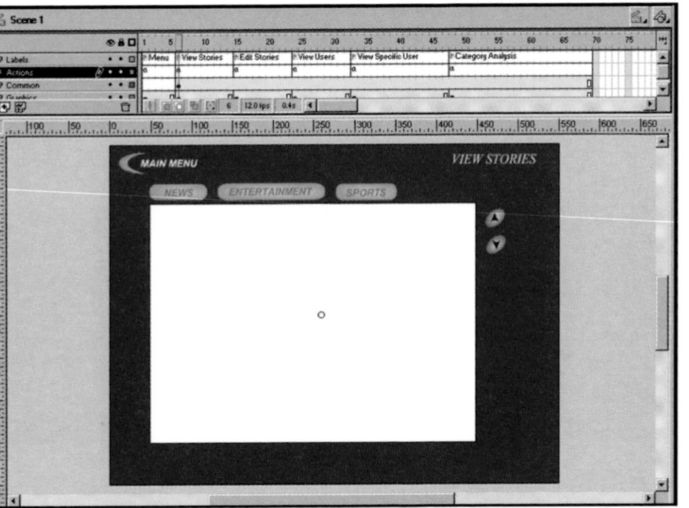

The user interface for viewing stories.

- The frame labeled "Edit Stories" provides the environment within which a story-record can either be created or modified. Here you can enter a story's ID to load that particular story.

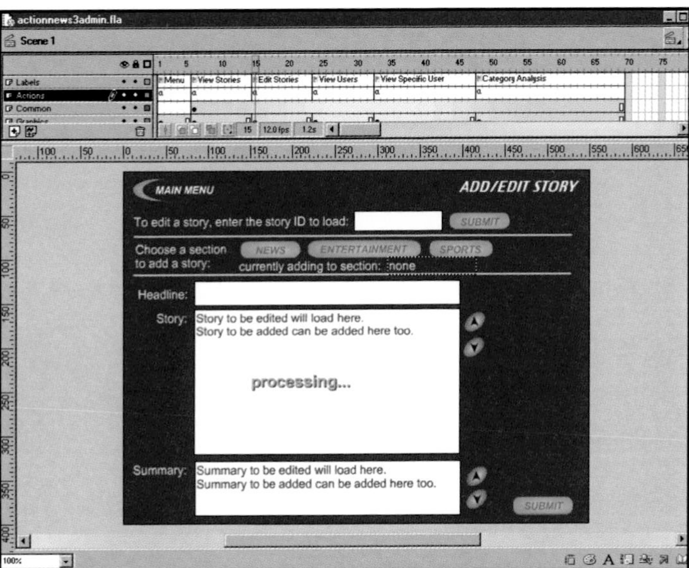

The user interface for editing stories.

- The frame labeled "View Users" dynamically generates a list of user ID numbers that are broken down by the months in which those user IDs were initially created. This is done so the list will not become excessively long. By entering the month of interest, you can load these user IDs.

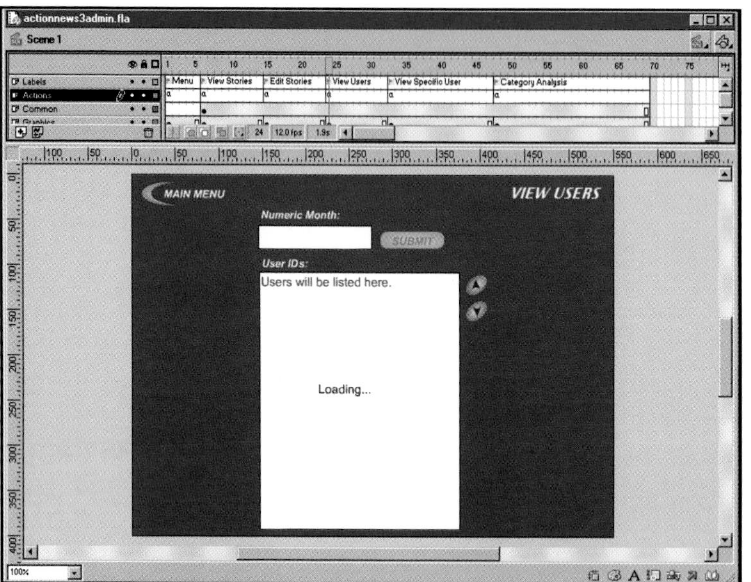

This allows administrators to see how many users there are.

- The frame labeled "View Specific User" provides the environment within which a user ID record can be reviewed. In this area, you can view a section's percentage of stories read by each user. The results are displayed as either a pie chart or a bar graph.

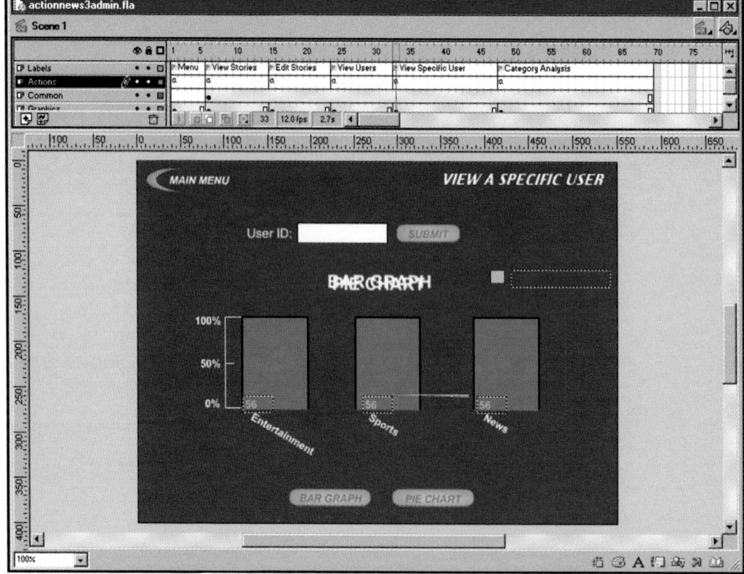

This allows you to see a user's viewing habits.

■ The frame labeled "Category Analysis" provides an example of a type of report that can be generated based on data that has been accumulated regarding site usage patterns. In this case it shows a bar graph or a pie chart for each of the three categories to indicate which section is read most often.

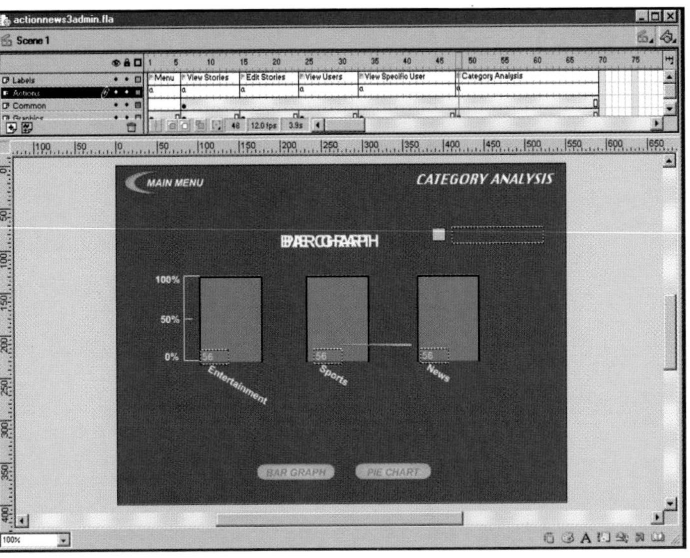

This allows you to see which categories are most popular or unpopular.

2 To see the list of stories by category, click the View Stories button on the main menu. Then click the category to load. If no category is selected, the default news listings will be loaded.

The ActionScript queries the database to have the dynamically generated list of the default category, News, returned to the SWF. (See Chapter 17 for more information about dynamically generated menus.)

Within this interface, the content administrator must select a category and then choose to either add a new story to the database or edit an existing story. Note that you must load a story by clicking it before you are able to edit it.

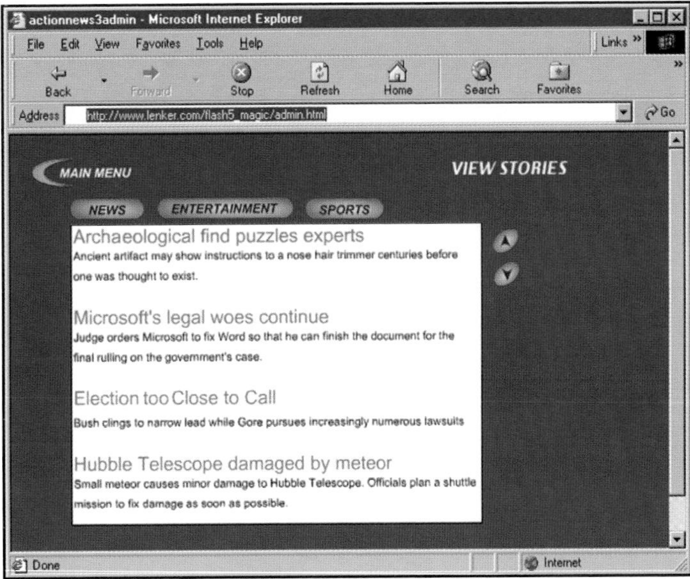

You can view stories in a specified category.

View Stories contains four buttons. One button sends you back to the main menu, and the three buttons labeled "news," "entertainment," and "sports" load their respective stories from the database. Each of these three buttons contains the same actions, except that it has its own identifier variable called ***categoryID***. Here are the actions attached to these buttons:

```
on (release) {
  _root.NewsXML = new XML();
  _root.NewsXML.load("Headlines.asp?CategoryID=4");
  _root.NewsXML.onLoad = _root.BuildHeadlines;
}
```

The first line creates a new XML object. The second line loads the correct headlines by the same method used in actionnews3.fla. When these headlines are finished loading, the familiar function **BuildHeadlines()** is executed. This is the same function used in all of the actionnews .fla files except for actionnews0.fla.

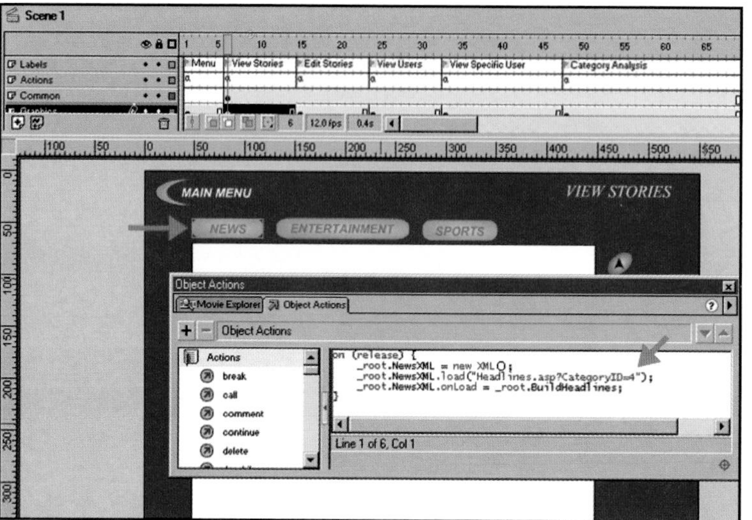

Each button has code assigned to it that contains an identifier called a **CategoryID**.

Also in this frame is a text field where the story list(s) will be displayed and the movie clip in which the story loads. This is the same movie clip that is in the actionnews2.fla. When a story is loaded, the movie clip moves to frame 2 to display the story. You will notice a new button in that window that is labeled "Edit Story." That button contains these actions:

```
on (release) {
  _root.headlineID = _root.StoryNumber;
  _root.edit = "yes";
  _root.gotoAndStop("Edit Stories");
  gotoAndStop (1);
}
```

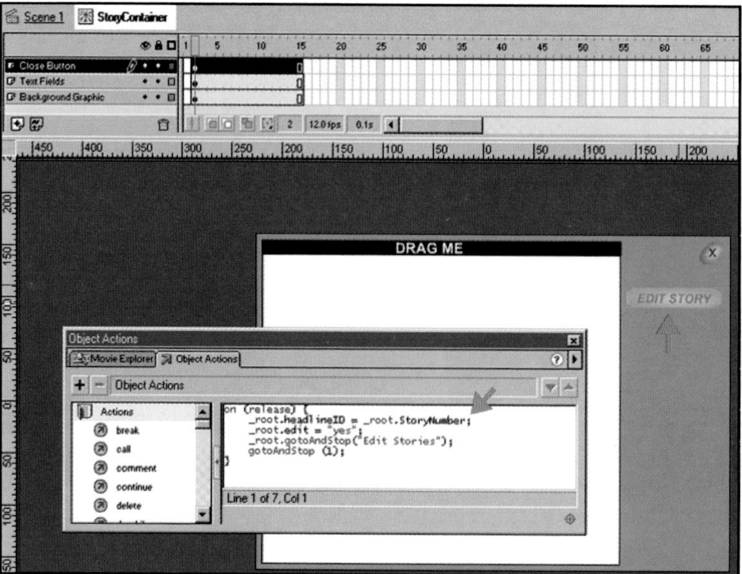

The edit button employs the story ID to determine which story to edit.

When the user clicks Edit Story, the main timeline goes to the edit frame, gives that frame the story ID, and sets the ***edit*** variable to **yes**. When the edit frame is visited, its first order of business is to see if ***edit*** is set to **yes**. If it is, a story is loaded based on the story ID.

3 Move to the frame labeled "Edit Stories." This frame has three sections. The top section allows the user to enter information to load a story, the middle section contains buttons the user can click to add a new story, and the bottom section allows the user to edit/add information.

The top section contains a text field where you can manually enter a story ID. You then press Submit to load the current information. This button contains these actions:

```
on (release) {
    EditStory();
}
```

When clicked, Submit calls the **EditStory()** function. Here are the actions within that function:

```
function EditStory () {
    loadVariablesNum
    ➥("story.asp?HeadlineID="+headlineID, 0);
    mode = "edit";
    section = "none";
}
```

(The ➥ symbol you see here is for editorial purposes only.)

First this function loads the story of interest based on the headlineID. Then it sets the ***mode*** variable to **edit**. The ***mode*** variable determines what should happen when the Submit button at the bottom of the page is clicked. The ***section*** variable is just for onscreen display, specifying which section you are adding a story to. In this case, it is set to "none" because you are not adding a story.

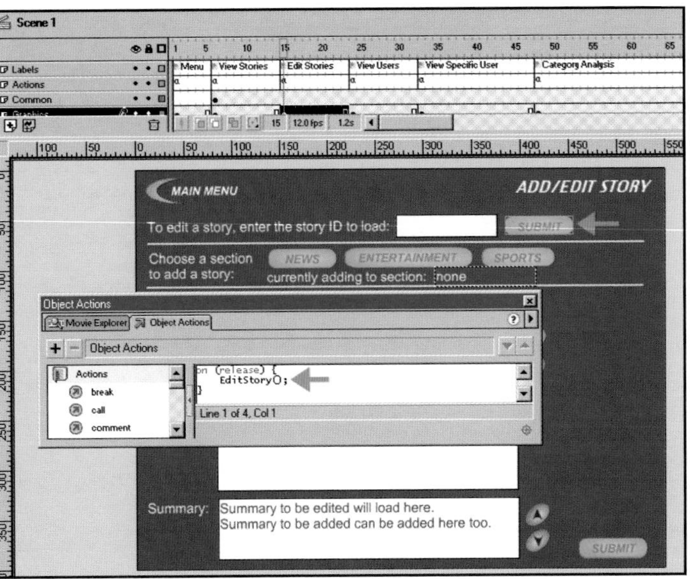

The top Submit button passed the contents of the text field to the **EditStory()** function.

The middle section contains three buttons—all of which have similar actions except for the filter ID that was mentioned earlier. When a button is clicked, it tells Flash you are going to add a story to that particular section. These buttons all contain similar actions. Here are the actions in the button labeled "news":

```
on (release) {
    Headline = "";
    Story = "";
    Summary = "";
    mode = "add";
    section = "news";
    CategoryID = 4;
}
```

The first three variables just clear the onscreen text fields. The ***mode*** variable is set to **add** so the Submit button knows what to do. The ***categoryID*** is set to the ID associated with News.

The bottom section contains three text fields: one for the headline, one for the story, and one for the summary. You will also see scroll buttons for the bottom two fields. If you are adding/editing information, it may be added/edited in these fields. When you finish, you can click Submit. The Submit button contains these actions:

```
on (release) {
    if (mode == "edit") {
        vl = 0;
        process = "yes";
        loadVariablesNum
        ➥("AddEditStory.asp?mode=edit&HeadlineID="+headlineID
        ➥+"&Headline="+escape(headline)+"&Summary="+
        ➥escape(summary)+"&Story="+ escape(story), 0);
        theurl =
        ➥"AddEditStory.asp?mode=edit&HeadlineID="+headlineID+
        ➥"&Headline="+escape(headline)+"&Summary="+escape
        ➥(summary)+"&Story="+ escape(story);
    } else if (mode == "add") {
        vl = 0;
        process = "yes";
        loadVariablesNum
        ("AddEditStory.asp?mode=add&CategoryID=
        ➥"+CategoryID+"&Headline="+escape(headline)+
        ➥"&Summary="+escape(summary)+"&Story="+
        ➥escape(story), 0);
        theurl = "AddEditStory.asp?mode=add&CategoryID=
        ➥"+CategoryID+"&Headline="+escape(headline)+
        ➥"&Summary="+escape(summary)+"&Story="+
        ➥escape(story);
    }
}
```

(The ➥ symbol you see here is for editorial purposes only.)

There is a movie clip on the Stage called "processing" with the instance name processing. It is programmed to display the word "processing" while the variable ***process*** is set to **yes**. This is so the user will actually see something happen when he clicks Submit. When Submit is clicked, the variable ***vl*** is set to **0**. The processing movie clip looks to see when ***vl*** = **1**. When ***vl*** = **1**, it sets ***process*** to **no** and displays a message that the information has been sent successfully. **vl = 1** is returned from the ASP pages that have been executed. So when ***vl*** = **1**, you know the process is complete.

There is also an **if** statement in that button action. It loads variables from an ASP page depending on the value of the ***mode*** variable. Notice that the **escape()** function is used around the strings. This ensures that the information is URL encoded before leaving Flash. If it is not URL encoded, it might not be sent or interpreted properly by the server.

4 Move to the frame labeled "View Users." This frame is very simple and contains just two text fields, two scroll buttons, and a Submit button. The short text field is intended to hold the numeric month number you are interested in loading. The large text field is used to display the list of users. The actions attached to Submit button are listed here:

```
on (release) {
    setProperty ("UserListLoader", _visible, 1);
    loadVariables ("Users.asp?MonthID="+monthID,
    ➥"UserListLoader");
}
```

(The ➥ symbol you see here is for editorial purposes only.)

The first action sets the **UserListLoader** visibility to **1** (makes it visible). This shows that the list is loading. The second action loads the information into that movie clip. **UserListLoader** contains an **onClipEvent** that is executed when the information is finished loading. That event formats the list so you can view it properly. These are the **onClipEvent** actions are:

```
onClipEvent (data) {
    List = new Array();
    List[0] = User;
    List = List[0].split(",");
    max = List.Length;
    _root.UserList = "";
    i = -1;
    while (++i<max) {
        _root.UserList = _root.UserList+List[i]+newline;
    }
    setProperty ("", _visible, 0);
}
```

This code takes the loaded information, sets it as the zeroth element in an array, and then uses the **split()** function to fill the rest of the array with the users. When that's finished, a loop takes the ***UserList*** variable and adds one user per line. What will appear in the text field is a list of users who have visited the Web site.

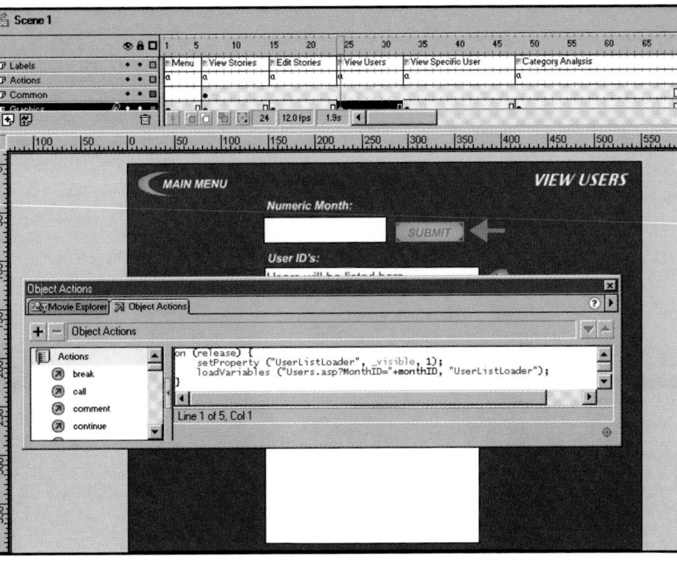

The code employs a monthID to specify which month's information to retrieve.

5 Move to the frame labeled "View Specific User." This frame contains a text field for the user's ID number. Click Submit to load that user's information. The only user information that's stored is the user's section visited percentage. That information is returned, and a bar graph is generated. Viewing the percentages as a pie chart is also an option. The ActionScript in the bar graph is mentioned in the next frame.

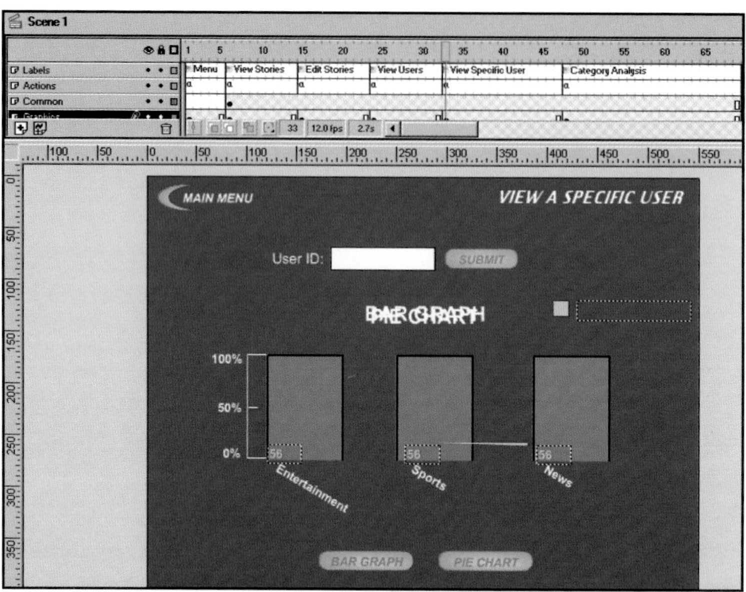

The Submit button passes the User ID text field contents to specify which user's data should be displayed in the charts.

6 Move to the frame labeled "Category Analysis." This frame contains one movie clip called "bar graph" and one called "piechart." The bargraph movie clip contains three bar movie clips. Each bar signifies one section of the Actionnews stories. Based on a percentage returned from the database, these bars will be scaled to display the accurate activity. The actions attached to this frame are listed here:

```
loadVariables ("Usage_asp", "Bargraph");
stop();
```

These actions are attached to the Bargraph movie clip:

```
onClipEvent(data){
    i = 1;
    while (++i<=4) {
        setProperty ("bar"+i, _yscale, this["percent"+i]);
        set ("percent"+i, this["percent"+i]+"%");
    }
```

The database will hand back three variables, ***percent1*** through ***percent3***. The values of these variables will be numbers between 0 and 100. The Yscale of the various bars, which are conveniently named bar1–bar9, is set exactly to the corresponding variable value. For example, if ***percent3*** = **36**, the Yscale of bar3 is set to 36.

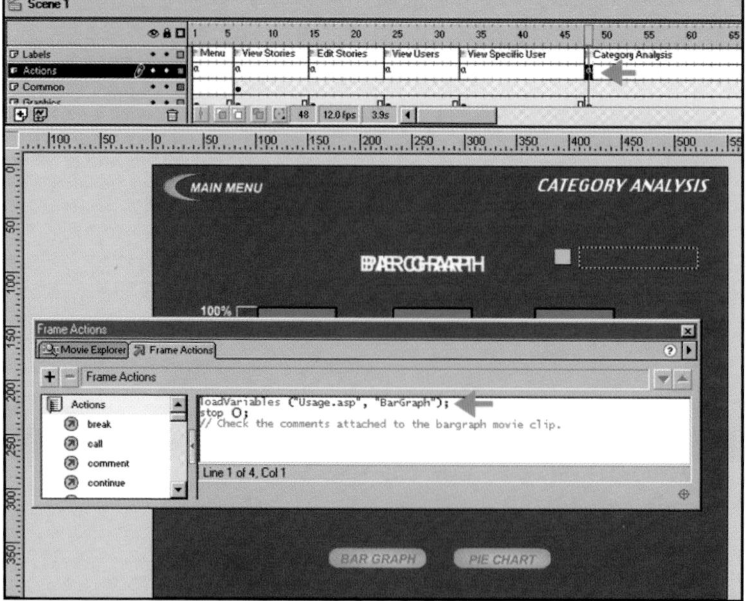

The code initiates the **Bargraph** function data when the frame loads.

There are literally thousands of variations on this site administration feature. Learning the basic mechanics allows anyone to develop administration tools that will add power, flexibility, and accessibility to any Flash-based Web solution.

Integrating with Existing Data Systems

In the real world of designing Flash-based Web sites, often the back-end database infrastructure is already in place and has been used with a standard HTML/JavaScript front end. In such situations, especially when dealing with large, big dollar situations, there is often resistance to SWF and very little flexibility on the part of the IT professionals responsible for developing the back-end system. This can present quite a problem. First, certain aspects of the server-side scripts need to be customized in order to work with .swf files. Second, the organization of the server-side scripts may represent a seriously flawed information architecture—one that the use of Flash is intended to remedy. In any case, be sensitive to the technical, political, and yes, even emotional issues that surround making the transition from a mainstream front-end, such as HTML/Java, to a more nouveau solution, such as SWF. Keep the following points in mind to make the notion of making such a change more digestible:

- Focus on the advantages of using Flash over HTML/JavaScript.
  - SWF plays more consistently in the major browsers and across operating systems. Often several versions of HTML/JavaScript-based sites must be maintained for compatibility with the various combinations of platform, operating system, and browser version. Because of the more diffused workflow of these traditional sites, modifications and bug fixing can take legions of developers, extend the timeframe needed to get to market, and become quite costly.
  - If used properly, the SWF format can offer much better download times.
  - Because the SWF interface downloads once, latency is reduced because only data has to be downloaded to the user's computer when the database is queried. With HTML/JavaScript, the code that describes the interface must be accessed, merged with the result of the database query, and downloaded to the user's computer again.
  - SWF allows principles of human interface design to be followed more closely. As an example, the principle of "visual persistence" is not violated by default with SWF. With HTML/JavaScript, every time new information must be incorporated into the interface, the entire screen goes blank in a disorienting flash (no pun intended) and regenerates with varying degrees of latency. This is known to subconsciously be very psychologically disturbing.
- Become familiar with the middleware that is being utilized. There is no fundamental difference between ASP, JSP, PHP, and ColdFusion. All function in the same manner. The reason they all exist is that they were developed to complement a specific software vendor's back-end solutions.
  - ASP is from Microsoft.
  - JSP is from Sun Microsystems.
  - PHP is from Open Source.
  - ColdFusion is from Allaire.
- Help the IT folks understand that what they give up in terms of having to make slight modifications to the back end can more than be made up for by the simplification that the Flash workflow brings to a solution.
- Focus on the strengths of the existing back-end solution.
  Often the majority of the investment in a Web site is in the back-end system. With SWF, the back end can almost always be carried forward with some modification. That can be great news to stakeholders who thought the "old site" was entirely a "sunk-investment."
- Capitalize on the fact that a lot of pride goes into a Web site. When the stakeholders in IT realize how much more fun, engaging, and successful an SWF solution can be, the sense of the site's overall value and impact are elevated, which makes everyone look good and feel good.

How It Works

The chapters in this section have touched on all major facets of integrating Flash-based front-end solutions with back-end database systems. The role of server-side scripts has been explored, and the power of personalization has been brought to bear on a sample project.

By practicing the techniques outlined here, you can develop Web-based solutions that bring the dynamics and charisma of the world's most innovative Web authoring tool, Flash 5.0, to bear on increasingly more sophisticated and complex Internet applications.

Two programs are designed to help developers create dynamic content in Flash: Macromedia Generator and Swift Generator. Swift Generator (http://www.swift-tools.com) offers a cost effective way to create dynamic content for Flash. You can find tutorials on Swift Generator in the directory devoted to these two chapters on the CD.

One parting note: The type of personalization that was incorporated into this solution was merely a token of what more complex and advanced customization filtering and rules-based solutions have to offer. It is not advisable to build a custom filtering solution from the ground up. Macromedia has developed some powerful tools that enhance both Flash-based and HTML/JavaScript solutions. Two Macromedia products stand out in particular: Aria and LikeMinds.

Macromedia Aria provides solutions for fast and accurate Web activity measurement and analysis. For a large percentage of online shoppers, difficult site navigation is the number-one reason for Web site failure. Unless a Web site is tuned to the needs of its audience, the audience will go elsewhere. After all, the competition is only a click away! It's easy to see why Web activity analysis is essential to any type of online business, including publishing, portal, and e-commerce sites.

LikeMinds is designed to encourage visitors to become repeat customers who return to a site for more. By helping Web sites interact with visitors individually and in real time, LikeMinds helps you achieve this goal. It quickly directs visitors to personally relevant content and products they are likely to purchase. One feature of particular importance is that LikeMinds enables Web sites to offer highly accurate product recommendations and targeted promotions for each individual Web visitor.

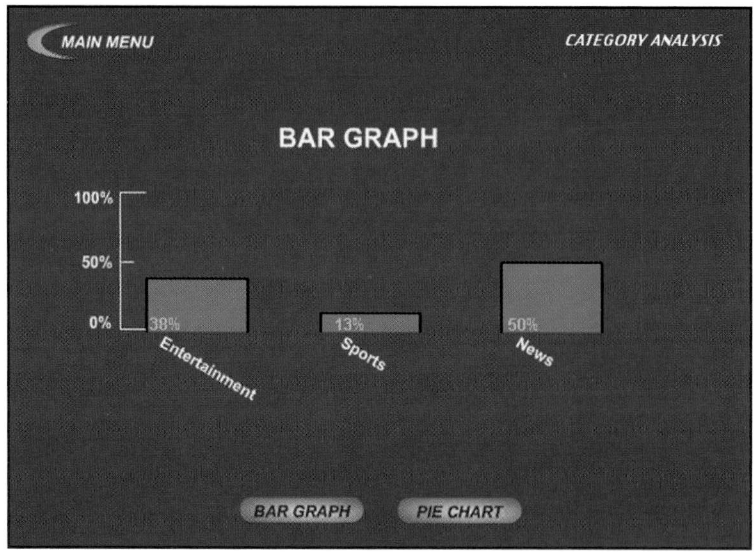

The Category Analysis section of the actionnews3admin.fla file displays user trends for each category.

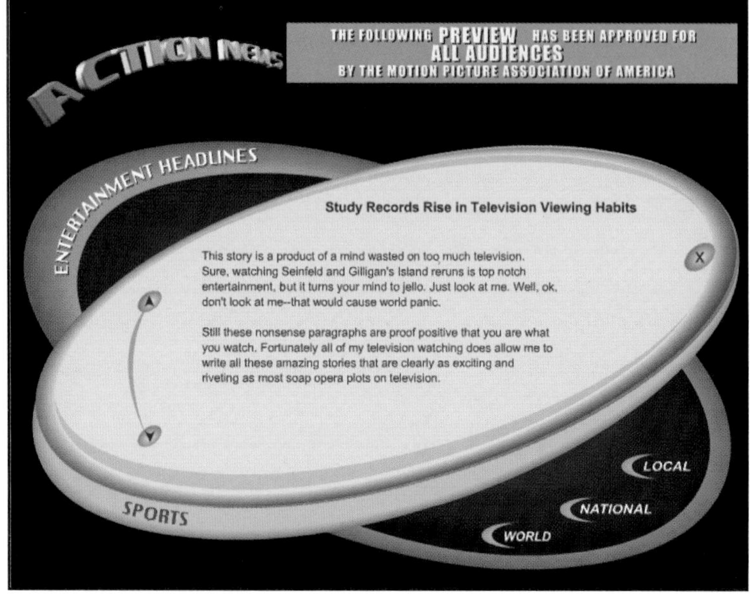

The database keeps track of every story that is viewed in each category.

To find out more about Aria and LikeMinds, visit the Macromedia Web site at www.macromedia.com/products.

Another firm, Net Perceptions, also offers customization-filtering software. Many firms stand by Net Perceptions's technology, which is a chief competitor for Macromedia LikeMinds. Information about Net Perceptions technology can be attained at www.netperceptions.com/products.

APPENDIXES

TROUBLESHOOTING TIPS

Even experienced programmers make mistakes. Computers don't. The curious thing about human beings is that we often assume we've done everything right, even though we have trouble remembering where we put our keys. Macromedia is hardly innocent of putting out bug-free software, particularly in the case of Flash. However, the truth is that when you find that something is not working with one of the techniques in this book or within your own projects, it's usually due to human error. Here are some tips and techniques for troubleshooting in Flash.

Save the Start and Final Files to Your Local Hard Drive

To use Test Movie, you will have to save the files from the book's CD to your local hard drive. Otherwise, Flash will attempt to save an .swf file to your CD drive, which won't work.

Compare Your Work-in-Progress to the Final File

If you are unsure about an instruction, or if your version of a project or technique is not working, check your version against the code in the final file. It's easy to fall prey to mistakes like typos, misplaced brackets, or mistaking an ***i*** for a ***1***. One easy way to make sure you're on the right track is to compare your code to the code in the final version.

Understand Comments

Throughout this book, you'll notice lines throughout the ActionScript code that appear to be in English rather than script. These comments, beginning with two forward slashes (**//**), are used by programmers to help document scripts. Comments are useful when you're sharing code with other people, debugging, or just trying to understand old programs when you need to revisit them. Code isn't always easy to read and follow, so comments are an important part of any good programming environment.

Check Your Instance Names and Variable Names

Some of the most common errors in Flash occur due to misspelled references to instances or variables. When you're coding in Flash, make sure your instance names match with any references to the instance names in your code. Similarly, make sure that variable names and subsequent references to those variable names match. You can't expect Flash to manipulate a variable if you reference the variable with the wrong name, and your ActionScript is not going to perform operations to an instance of a movie clip if you haven't referred to the movie clip using the correct instance name.

Watch Those Quotation Marks

If something is in quotation marks, it needs to stay in quotation marks. If a variable has been assigned a value with quotation marks around it (which means it's a string type), you need to make sure you keep it in quotation marks or it won't work.

Keep an Eye on the Timeline

If you have a line of code that refers to a movie clip, you need to make sure that you place it within a frame that contains the movie clip. For example, if you put the ActionScript in Frame 30 and your movie clip only goes out to frame 25, it won't work.

Don't Forget the Semi-Colon

Although it's not entirely essential, it is good practice to include the semi-colon at the end of each line, with the exception of loops (**while**, **do**, and **for**), conditional statements (**if**, **then**, **else**), and the **#include** directive. The semi-colon won't hurt at the end of a comment.

All Things Are Not Created Equal in Flash 5

In Flash 4, within an **if** statement, a single equals sign would test for equivalency; in Flash 5 you need to use a double equals sign (**==**). If you make a mistake and use a single equals sign, Flash won't give you an error message. If you have a single equals sign, Flash sets the left side variable to whatever is on the right side of the equals sign rather testing for equivalency.

Use the Check Syntax Command in Expert Mode

When the Actions panel is set to Expert Mode, the triangular menu button offers the option to Check Syntax. When you click Check Syntax, Flash attempts to compile the code in the Actions panel. If the script contains errors, a dialog box pops up, indicating that the errors found will be listed in the Output window.

Try the Toggle Trick to Test (Can You Say That Five Times Real Fast?)

Another way to test for syntax errors is to toggle into Normal Mode. Any syntax errors will produce a warning, and they will show up in your output window. This is also a quick way to format your code.

Toggling to Expert Mode is also useful if you want to employ a more time-tested approach to troubleshooting: Commenting out lines to see if they are causing problems. In other words, you can toggle to Expert Mode and then comment out lines of code to disable it for troubleshooting. For instance, suppose the following code is not working correctly:

```
while (i++<10) {
  Jobe = "cool";
  coolness( );
}
```

When this code is tested, you receive a **script is running poorly** message. At that point, you can switch to Expert Mode and make the following modification:

```
while (i++<10) {
      Jobe = "cool";
/*
coolness();
*/
}
```

The **/*** and the ***/** comment out the **coolness();** line, effectively disabling that line. So if the script works when you comment out the **coolness()**,you can know that by executing the function **coolness**, you were somehow causing a problem (in this case setting **i** to some number less than 10 on a continual basis). Note that you can always comment out more than one line of code. This technique can be very useful when you don't want to delete anything, you just want to disable it for the sake of troubleshooting.

To stay in Expert Mode, choose Edit > Preferences, click the General tab, and select Expert Mode as the default mode for the Action panel. Although the advanced sections of this book edit ActionScript in Expert Mode, you can always use the convenient pull-down menu and Action Explorer on the left-hand side of the Action panel to look up ActionScript keywords. If you can't remember the parameters for a particular function, you can switch to Normal Mode, select a command from the Action Explorer, fill in the parameters, and then change back to Expert Mode.

Get to the Root of the Problem

When using the **TellTarget** action to navigate to another movie, Flash offers a choice of several different methods for the syntax. In Flash 4, a forward slash (**/**) was placed before a movie. For instance, **../boo/fighter** would navigate a user up one level to a find a movie with the instance name boo and to the movie clip called fighter located within the boo movie clip.

Unfortunately, this does not work correctly in Flash 5. The only guaranteed way to find the desired movie is to use dot syntax (instead of the forward slash) and to avoid using **../**. Therefore the previous example would be written this way:

```
_root0.boo.fighter
```

Also note that Flash 5 should, in theory, use **_root0** and **_level0** in the same way. Both should control the main Timeline of the overall Flash movie. However, only the use of **_root0** will guarantee 100% success. This can be confusing to Flash 4 developers because **_level0** was always used.

Watch for Clues in the Colors

Pay attention to the color-coded text. If you type in a keyword or object method and the color doesn't turn blue or green, it probably means you've misspelled that word. To make sure color coding is turned on, open up an Action panel, open the pull-down menu in the upper-right corner of the panel, and make sure that Colored Syntax is checked. However, on very slow computers, the ActionScript editor might slow down when there's too much colored code in the editor. In such cases, you might want to turn off Colored Syntax to increase your typing speed.

Trace Your Steps

The **trace** function in ActionScript is very useful for debugging code, as you will see in the example below. At first it might seem as if this can be done just as easily with a temporary variable text field on the screen. But remember, this is just a simple example. With more advanced code, it is much easier to trace several variables simultaneously than it is to build 10, 15, or even 50 variable text fields.

Say, for example, you decide that you want to make a crosshairs movie clip follow the mouse. So you create a movie clip and attach these actions to it:

```
onClipEvent (mouseMove) {
   mouse_x = _root._xmouse;
   mouse_y = _root._xmouse;
   setProperty ("", _x, mouse_x);
```

```
    setProperty ("", _y, mouse_y);
    updateAfterEvent( );
}
```

Then you test the movie, and you see that you get erratic behavior. The code appears to be correct, but something must be wrong with it. At this point, you can add a few trace commands to help you identify where the problem might be. A likely approach to using the **trace** function in the code is shown below:

```
onClipEvent (mouseMove) {
    mouse_x = _root._xmouse;
    mouse_y = _root._xmouse;
    setProperty ("", _x, mouse_x);
    setProperty ("", _y, mouse_y);
    trace ("Mouse Xposition");
    trace (mouse_x);
    trace ("Mouse Yposition");
    trace (mouse_y);
    updateAfterEvent();
}
```

Four **trace** commands are now in the code. The first one and the third one are just words to help you identify what the number that will appear under it means. You are tracing the variables ***mouse_x*** and ***mouse_y***.

If you tested the movie right now, you would notice that every value of ***mouse_x*** is exactly the same as ***mouse_y***. That means the code is somehow setting both variables to the same value.

Unless there is more than one error, you can eliminate the possibility of the error coming after the first two lines because those are the two lines you traced. But now that you know the problem appears at least that early in the code, you know to look a little closer at the first two lines of code:

```
    mouse_x = _root._xmouse;
    mouse_y = _root._xmouse;
```

You immediately notice that both are set to **_root._xmouse**, although the second one should have been set to **_root._ymouse**. The problem is quickly solved, and the **trace** actions are deleted.

Of course, in this case it would have been easy enough to just visually find that error. But when you are developing very complicated code, or non-complicated but long code, this method will be useful for tracking down where you made an error.

More Information, Please!

Want to know what those Actions, Operators, Functions, Properties, or Objects do without having to search the help file or dig into the manual? Click to select the action line in the left pane of the Action window. Then click the (?) in the upper-right corner of the Action window. This opens the help manual right to the spot you need to find out what that new action does and how to use it.

Be Sensitive to the Context-Sensitive Action Window

The Action window is context-sensitive. This means you have to be careful to make sure you have the right symbol or frame selected when you're entering ActionScript. If you are not careful, you may assign code to the wrong symbol or frame.

Conclusion

Of course, all these techniques and tips pale by comparison to the universally recognized greatest tip of all:

Save backup files, and save often!

Find your favorite shortcut for saving and practice it until it becomes as natural as blinking. Programming is not for the light hearted. Flash 5's ActionScript has made a huge leap in overall capability relative to Flash 4, so get ready for a learning curve and potentially more numerous headaches in the troubleshooting department.

Unfortunately the adage "no pain, no gain" applies in the world of programming and Web development as much as it does anywhere else. Don't let that "pain" part scare you though. Coding in Flash 5 is relatively easy compared to similarly powerful programming languages such as Java and Javascript. If you employ the above tips, keep the ActionScript Reference Guide handy, and tap into a little good old-fashioned tenacity, you will do fine. Heck, you might even have fun.

B

COMMON PROGRAMMING TERMS

action

In past versions of Flash, actions were introduced to add interactivity and allow developers to go beyond simple linear animation. Actions were created to perform various tasks, such as controlling playback, storing variables, and so on. Over time, those actions have evolved into the full fledged scripting language of ActionScript.

algorithm

A set of steps to accomplish a specific task or to solve a particular problem.

argument

See *parameter*.

array

In ActionScript, an array is a special object designed to store a collection of data, with predefined methods for adding, removing, and altering the order of the array's elements. For example, a list of names could be stored in an array. The first element in an array is numbered 0, and the number of elements that can be accommodated is limited only by available memory.

associative array

An array that has additional information attached to each element. Associative arrays are created in ActionScript by assigning variables to each element, by populating the element with an object rather than a primitive data type, such as text or numbers.

boolean

A data type with only two states, true or false, that acts like an on/off switch.

class

A class is a template, or recipe, for instantiating an object. The parent of all ActionScript classes is Object, and that is used to create more complex classes by adding methods and properties. ActionScript provides a number of predefined classes such as Movie Clip, Math, Array, and so on. You can create your own custom classes by building on those predefined examples, or you can start from scratch with the Object class.

concatenate

To create a text string from two or more parts. The concatenate operator **add** can be used to combine text, numbers, variables, and the output of a function or object method. This example shows two text strings being concatenated with a variable:

```
Result = "Sally " + "Well" + " is great.";
```

Concatenating puts the two names together, and the variable ***Result*** contains "Sally Well is great."

```
Age = 12;
Result = "Sally is " + Age + " years old."
```

Now the variable ***Result*** contains "Sally is 12 years old."

counter

The informal name for a variable that is used in loops to count the iterations (the number of times through the loop) that have taken place.

declaration

To declare a variable or other object is to "create" it in memory without necessarily assigning it a value or populating it with data. In strict languages, such as C++, all variables must be declared at the beginning of a program. In ActionScript, however, variables can be declared as needed.

definition

Functions and classes can be defined. Definitions are unique because a function can be defined in a script regardless of whether it is ever invoked.

degrees

Unit of measurement for angles: 360 degrees equal one revolution around a circle. The formula to convert radians into degrees is:

```
degree = 360/(2π) * radians
```


function

A block of code separated for reusability or for clarity. Functions can also accept arguments and return values to the object that invoked them. Here is an example function definition:

```
function myFunction ( argument1, argument2 ) {
    // Statements
}
```

function definition

The code (ActionScript) that makes up the function. In other words, the code between the brackets (**{ }**).

hexadecimal

The decimal (base 10) number system with its ten single digits is just one way of expressing numeric data. Binary data, for example, can record any number as a sequence of 0s and 1s. Onscreen color is usually described with the help of the hexadecimal (base 16) number system, which includes the sixteen single digits 0, 1, 2, 3, 4, 5, 6, 7, 8, 9, A, B, C, D, E, and F. The advantage of hexadecimal numbering is that it can express numbers into the millions with only six digits.

index

The reference number used when storing or retrieving data to and/or from an array. For example, in the array

```
names[3] = "jennifer"
```

the index is 3.

initialization

An informal term used to describe the setting of a variable to a starting value. Initialization is also used to set the program to a specific starting point. For example, if you want a graphic to be on the Stage but invisible when the program starts, one of the first lines of code you would include would set the graphic to be invisible.

instance

An instance is an object of a particular class. For example, creating a new Array object is described as creating an instance of the Array class.

instantiate

To create an instance of an object.

iteration

The process of repeating a set of instructions a given number of times or until a specified condition is met.

library

Each Flash movie (fla) has its own library, a collection of symbols, sounds, fonts, and bitmap assets that can be used throughout the movie.

loop

A loop is a programming construct used to repeat a given set of instructions. Flash 5 has several loops: **for**, **while**, **do while**, and so on. These loops repeat the action within the loop until a specific condition is met. Additionally, **onClipEvent (enterFrame)** is a runtime loop that repeats the action within it until the program stops.

method

A function belonging to a class. For example, in **Array.length**, **length** is a method of the **Array** class.

object

An instance of a class, sometimes referred to simply as an instance. In this example

```
Sam = new Array();
```

Sam is an object of class type **Array**.

parameter

A placeholder variable that allows the user to pass values (arguments) to a function.

parsing

A technique used to break down something into its component parts. For example, you could parse a word into its individual letters, or you could parse a sentence into its individual words. Parsing could be used to search for all occurrences of a particular word in a document.

property

An associated state of an object. For example, a Movie Clip object has a number of properties, including **_xscale**, **_visible**, and **_rotation**.

radians

A unit of angular measurement. One radian is the arc of travel along the circle equal to the radius. To convert degrees into radians, use this formula:

```
radian = (2π)/360 * degrees
```

recursion

A function that calls itself, thus creating the possibility of calling itself to infinity.

statement

The term used to describe a piece of ActionScript, usually formatted as a single line of code ending in the evaluate operator (**;**).

symbol

For the purposes of optimizing and updating, Flash movies have extensive support for symbols, reusable chunks of data that can take the form of graphics, animation, sound, or bitmapped images. Symbols are stored once in the exported Flash Player file, but can be used several times.

variable

A place to store information of any type, designated by a word or letter. In the example

```
now = "march 3,2001";
```

the variable ***now*** equals the text string "**march 3, 2001**"

In the example

```
i = 22;
```

The variable ***i*** contains the number **22**.

C

WHAT'S ON THE CD-ROM

Warning: If you encounter problems with files not opening, please install the latest Internet browser of your choice (Internet Explorer and Communicator are included on the CD). If you continue to have problems with some of the .fla files or .swf files and you have not installed Flash 5, install the Flash 5 demo.

The accompanying CD-ROM is packed with all sorts of exercise files and products to help you work with this book and with Flash 5. The following sections contain detailed descriptions of the CD's contents.

For more information about the use of this CD, please review the ReadMe.txt file in the root directory. That file includes important disclaimer information, as well as information about installation, system requirements, troubleshooting, and technical support.

Technical Support Issues: If you have any difficulties with this CD, you can access our tech support Web site at http://www.mcp.com/press/CSupport_form.cfm. See also http://www.flash5magic.com for updates and more information.

System Requirements

This CD-ROM was configured for use on systems running Windows NT Workstation, Windows 95, Windows 98, or Windows 2000, and on Macintoshes. Your computer will need to meet the following system requirements in order for this CD to operate properly:

Memory (RAM): 24 MB

Monitor: VGA, 640x480 or higher with 256 color or higher

Storage Space: 10 MB Minimum (will vary depending on installation)

Other: Mouse or compatible pointing device

Optional: Internet connection and Web browser

LOADING THE CD FILES

To load the files from the CD, insert the disc into your CD-ROM drive. If Autoplay is enabled on your machine, the CD-ROM setup program starts automatically the first time you insert the disc. You can copy the files to your hard drive, or you can use them right off the disc, although you will not be able to save changes.

> **Note:** This CD-ROM uses long and mixed-case filenames, which requires the use of a protected mode CD-ROM driver.

EXERCISE FILES

This CD contains all the files you'll need to complete the exercises in *Flash 5 Magic*. These files can be found in the root directory's Examples folder.

EYELAND STUDIO RESOURCES

This CD also contains resources from Eyeland Studio from products sold at Eyewire (www.eyewire.com). These resources are subject to copyright restrictions that can be found at eyewire.com.

- **Flash-based interfaces from Eyeland Studio**

  These customizable interfaces from Eyeland Studio (www.eyeland.com) are sold at Eyewire (www.eyewire.com). These interfaces may not be given away or sold. See eyewire.com for copyright restrictions.

- **Flash-based animations from Eyeland Studio**

  These customizable animations, from Eyeland Studio (www.eyeland.com) are sold at Eyewire (www.eyewire.com). These interfaces may not be given away or sold. See eyewire.com for copyright restrictions.

- **Miscellaneous elements from Eyeland Studio**

  These files include a number of audio files and other resources that can be used with Flash from Eyeland Studio (www.eyeland.com). These interfaces may not be given away or sold.

MACROMEDIA DEMOS

Macromedia (www.macromedia.com) offers standalone products for creating awesome Web sites and graphics. Developers have discovered that they can rely on Macromedia's technologies.

- **Flash 5**

  Macromedia Flash 5, the professional standard used by artists and developers alike, enables you to create engaging graphics with the familiar Macromedia user interface and build advanced Web applications using scripting, forms, and server-side connectivity.

- **Fireworks**

  Macromedia Fireworks is a high-performance program for creating, editing, and animating Web graphics. It offers a complete set of bitmap and vector tools. You can launch and edit Fireworks images from inside Flash.

INDEX

Symbols

A

B

C

D

E

F

G

H

I

J-K

L

M

P

Q

R

S

T

U

V

W

X

Y

Z

THE NEW RIDERS PROFESSIONAL LIBRARY

Adobe Photoshop 5.5 Fundamentals with ImageReady 2
Gary Bouton
0-7357-0928-9

Bert Monroy: Photorealistic Techniques with Photoshop & Illustrator
Bert Monroy
0-7357-0969-6

CG 101: A Computer Graphics Industry Reference
Terrence Masson
0-7357-0046-X

<coloring web graphics.2>
Lynda Weinman and Bruce Heavin
1-56205-818-5

Creating Killer Web Sites, Second Edition
David Siegel
1-56830-433-1

<creative html design>
Lynda Weinman and William Weinman
1-56205-704-9

<designing web graphics.3>
Lynda Weinman
1-56205-949-1

Designing Web Usability
Jakob Nielsen
1-56205-810-X

E-Volve-or-Die.com
Mitchell Levy
0-7357-1028-7

Flash 4 Magic
David Emberton and J. Scott Hamlin
0-7357-0949-1

Flash Web Design
Hillman Curtis
0-7357-0896-7

HTML Artistry: More than Code
Ardith Ibañez and Natalie Zee
1-56830-454-4

HTML Web Magic
Raymond Pirouz
1-56830-475-7

Inside Adobe Photoshop 6
Gary David Bouton, et. al
0-7357-1038-4

Photoshop 5 & 5.5 Artistry
Barry Haynes and Wendy Crumpler
0-7457-0994-7

Photoshop 6 Effects Magic
Rhoda Grossman, et. al
0-7357-1035-X

Photoshop 6 Web Magic
Jeff Foster
0-7357-1036-8

Photoshop Channel Chops
David Biedny, Bert Monroy, and Nathan Moody
1-56205-723-5

Secrets of Successful Web Sites
David Siegel
1-56830-382-3

THE FLASH 5 MAGIC CD

The CD that accompanies this book contains valuable resources for anyone using Flash 5, not the least of which are:

- **Project files:** All the example files provided by the authors enable you to work through the step-by-step projects. You will find finished versions of the files within the same folder.
- **Software-related third-party software:** Demos of Flash 5 and Fireworks are included on the CD. Internet Explorer and Communicator are also included on the CD.

Eyeland Studio resources

This CD also contains resources from Eyeland Studio from products sold at Eyewire (www.eyewire.com). These resources are subject to copyright restrictions that can be found at eyewire.com.

- **Flash-based Interface from Eyeland Studio**

  These customizable interfaces, from Eyeland Studio (**www.eyeland.com**) are sold at Eyewire (**www.eyewire.com**). These interfaces may not be given away or sold. See eyewire.com for copyright restrictions.
- **Flash-based Animations from Eyeland Studio**

  These customizable animations, from Eyeland Studio (**www.eyeland.com**) are sold at Eyewire (**www.eyewire.com**). These interfaces may not be given away or sold. See eyewire.com for copyright restrictions.
- **Miscellaneous from Eyeland Studio**

  These files include a number of audio files and other resources that can be used with Flash from Eyeland Studio (**www.eyeland.com**). These interfaces may not be given away or sold.

Accessing the Project Files from the CD

The majority of projects in this book use pre-built software files that contain preset parameters, artwork, audio, or other important information you need to work through and build the final project.

All the project files are conveniently located in the CD's Examples directory. To access the project files for the Navy Bay project in Chapter 2, for example, locate the following directory on the accompanying CD: Examples\Chap02.

We recommend that you copy the project files to your hard drive.

> **Warning:** If you encounter problems with files not opening, please install the latest Internet browser of your choice (Internet Explorer and Communicator are included on the CD). If you continue to have problems with some of the .fla files or .swf files and you have not installed Flash 5, install the Flash 5 demo.

> For a complete list of the CD-ROM contents, please see Appendix C, "What's on the CD-ROM."

Colophon

Flash 5 Magic was laid out and produced with the help of Microsoft Word, Adobe Acrobat, Adobe Photoshop, Collage Complete, and QuarkXpress on a variety of systems, including a Macintosh G4. With the exception of pages that were printed out for proofreading, all files—text, images, and project files—were transferred via email or ftp and edited on-screen.

All body text was set in the Bergamo family. All headings, figure captions, and cover text were set in the Imago family. The Symbol and Sean's Symbol typefaces were used throughout for special symbols and bullets.

Flash 5 Magic was printed on 60# Mead Web Dull paper at GAC (Graphic Arts Center) in Indianapolis, IN. Prepress consisted of PostScript computer-to-plate technology (filmless process). The cover was printed on 12-pt. Carolina, coated on one side.